$15 m

THE ROAD TO EL DORADO

by

CRAIG J. CARROZZI

2925 Clement St, #1
San Francisco, CA 94121
E-mail: southtrails@yahoo.com

SOUTHERN TRAILS PUBLISHING

Cover art by Vladimir Ramirez-Carrozzi

Southern Trails Publishing
529 Brussels Street
San Francisco, CA 94134
(415) 467-7038

ISBN: 0-9620286-1-4
Library of Congress: 97-091717
Limited First Edition

Special thanks to my wife Priscilla, whose patience and belief kept me going; to my Dad, Angelo (Joe) Carrozzi, RIP; and to Len Appiano for his editorial assistance and encouragement.

THE ROAD TO EL DORADO

BOOK I

THE SITE VISIT

1

As the plane rose steeply and banked, Vachio shuttered his eyes against the glare of the early morning sun peeking over the ridge of the mountain. For a moment a red veil with black dots danced before his eyes and vertigo washed over his body. Vachio was tired, his nerves raw. He had spent a sleepless night, tossing and turning on his undersized, flea-infested bed, thinking about his assignment until the gray light of dawn filtered into the room. Now, airborne and headed to his job site, his restless thoughts were making his head ache.

Vachio reached into his pocket and pulled out a crumpled sheet of paper. He unfurled it and read the material as he had scores of times over the past months.

Job Profile
Colombia Group XX
Subgroup: Gamin Program

Job Title: Recreation Director/Counselor
Agency: SENA; *Casa de menores y escuela de trabajo* (Juvenile Detention Center and Trade School).
Site: Garrotero, Santander (Eastern Colombia).
Climate: Subtropical.

General Description: Garrotero is a town of approximately 30,000 inhabitants located 14 kilometers from the Santander department capital of Bucaramanga in the *cordillera oriental* of the Colombian Andes. Located in a fertile valley, the warm humid climate is ideal for the cultivation of sugar cane and tobacco, the major crops of the area and the base for the principal products, *panela* (bars of brown sugar) and cigars. The weather is generally comfortable, from the low '70s to the mid-'80s, with occasional hot spells in the '90s. Light clothing is adequate most of the time, although a sweater may come in handy occasionally, and bring suitable rain gear for periodic tropical downpours. The valley and the surrounding cooler mountain plateaus provide a rich variety of fruits, vegetables, grains, and livestock all year round. The cost of living is moderate by Colombian standards.

Job Description: Your main task is to create and coordinate an organized recreation program for the juvenile population. This should be a comprehensive program involving sports, arts and crafts, movies, etc. The majority of the students are street children, known in Colombia as *gamines* from the French word *gamin*, who range in age from 8 to 16. Most of these boys are runaways or were abandoned by their parents and had been living on the streets of Colombia's big cities before being picked up and institutionalized. Make no mistake, most of these boys are tough, undisciplined, distrustful, and cynical juvenile delinquents. The prison guards, with whom you must develop a cooperative relationship, are even tougher than the *gamines*, some of them bordering on brutal. Nevertheless, in cooperation with the professional administrators, you must win the confidence of the boys and guards to establish a self-sustaining recreation program that will continue on after you leave. The major goals of the program are to develop increased self-esteem in the boys, provide fun and enjoyment...and so on and so forth, thought Vachio, folding up the paper and stuffing it back in his hip pocket. In another half hour I'll finally get to see some of the people behind the words.

The plane banked sharply and began to level-off. Vachio felt a coolness on his cheek and turned to look out of the window. Save for some dark scattered clouds, trailers from a predawn downpour, the sky was crystalline blue. The jagged, green robed Andes reared over Bogotá, dwarfing the ant-like structures at its feet. Vachio craned his neck to look down at the city. Its great mass of masonry, brick, clapboard, tile, and corrugated steel buildings sprawled over the savannah and lapped onto the skirts of the mountains; soaring glass and steel towers issued from its Spanish colonial heart. Beyond the reaching fingers of the mushrooming suburbs and shantytowns lay miles of checkerboard farmlands and clusters of Spanish-tiled roofs forming islands in a sea of black-green earth.

Vachio sighed at the beauty of it. Way up in the air the filth and degradation was obscured. It looks like the Land of Oz, thought Vachio. With Bogotá the Emerald City. It must have been unbelievably pretty here before Bogotá grew out of control. Now I understand what that guy Gaitán was talking about.

A week before, an official from the ruling Liberal Party had come to the training center to give the volunteers a lecture on socio-political Colombia, 1978. Doctor Gaitán, with advanced degrees from Harvard and Oxford on his resume, was a handsome urbane gentleman in his early forties. A genuine *rolo*, a native of Bogotá, he came from a generation of *capitalinos* who prided themselves on their politeness, dignified reserve, and good grooming, based on an idealized concept of London gentlemen. Moreover, he was an articulate and witty speaker who achieved a record of sorts by holding the attention of the volunteers for a full two hours.

Doctor Gaitán talked about the political climate in Colombia: the administration of President Julio Cesar Turbay Ayala, known as the Turk, and his Liberal Party, and the policies of the opposition Conservative Party. Gaitán emphasized that Colombian democracy was at a crossroads. A majority of average citizens were growing cynical toward the political process in general and the established parties in particular. He quoted a popular saying on the streets, *"Liberal, Conservador, la misma mierda."* (Liberal, Conservative, the same shit). This cynicism was fueling a spectacular growth in insurrectionist groups such as M19 and la FARC, as well as contributing to the growing power and influence of narcotics traffickers.

Gaitán touched on some of Colombia's major social problems: an exploding population, mass migration from rural areas to urban centers, lack of transport infrastructure, uneven economic development, pollution, legions of unemployed and underemployed squatters and homeless people, and overloaded social services.

He cited historic reasons for Colombia's underdeveloped state: the pervasive and often pernicious influence of a landed oligarchy jealous of its privileged status, meddling from the United States and other great powers to promote and protect their commercial and political interests, and recurring periods of violence and political instability.

For most of the lecture Doctor Gaitán spoke in an even dispassionate tone, interspersed with moments of dead pan humor, but when he began to talk about Bogotá and the changes he had seen in his lifetime, his voice became charged with emotion and his eyes moistened. In response to a question from a volunteer about what should be done to improve the quality of life in the capital, Gaitán shrugged his shoulders and said, "What can you do for Bogotá? What can anyone do for Bogotá? You do what you can. The best you know how.... Doesn't my answer satisfy you?"

"No, not really," said the volunteer. "How about some concrete examples? How can I be of help?"

Gaitán smiled. "Well, let me put it this way. Bogotá is my city and I love her like I love my own sweet mother. She has her flaws, the bloom of youth is gone, but she is mine and I will love her until I die. But much as I want to believe differently, and perhaps it's a product of my own aging and faded idealism, I see Bogotá going from bad to worse. And Bogotá is a microcosm of what Colombia as a whole faces unless there are dramatic and rapid changes in the near future if not before."

Gaitán paused and surveyed the room with an air of kindly weariness. "I understand that most of you have been here for about a month now?... A few of you longer. Fine.... Well, I don't have to tell you about some of Bogotá's worst and most apparent problems. They are all too pervasive and evident. The air we inhale that tastes of diesel fumes. The piles of trash on the streets, often with poor children sleeping on them. The constant danger and insecurity of the streets and public transport from thieves and beggars. The heavily armed soldiers and police patrolling the streets, able to stop anyone without probable cause because of our decreed state of emergency. You have all certainly encountered these and other problems in your brief stay here. Right?"

Most of the volunteers nodded their heads.

"But of course, Bogotá still has much to offer in the way of culture and pleasant diversions. No? Have you sampled some of the good things as well?"

Again most of the volunteers nodded.

"Good. We still have much to take pride in. But I wish I had a time machine to take you all back and show you the Bogotá of my youth. No, not my long lost youth. I'm not ancient yet.... Just back to the early forties. Back to the Bogotá that I remember as a mostly clean, beautiful, and cultured city. A capital we were all proud of. A place of optimism and hope for a better future for our children. A place that...well, forget my fondly remembered youth. Even 15 years ago Bogotá was a decent place to live..."

"So what happened?" called someone from the back of the room. Titters and embarrassed looks passed among the volunteers.

"What happened?" Gaitán's face was impassive. "It's a complex equation. But, in a nutshell, as you North Americans say, too many people too fast. In my lifetime, Bogotá went from just under one million people to an estimated six million today. With no slow up in sight. An explosion detonated by a high birth rate, a massive influx of *campesinos* fleeing *la violencia* in the countryside, and economic refugees seeking jobs and services that only the cities provide. Bogotá is stressed and strained beyond capacity to handle this tidal wave of humanity. And worse, this growth is accelerating exponentially. We're like the proverbial man trying to plug the holes in the dike. For every leak he stops, two more break out until he runs out of fingers. All we can do is treat the most malignant symptoms of our problems without ever getting at the root causes .... So in a way, to sum up, it's fairly simple what we need to do. We need to achieve a balance between development and population growth. Because of cultural and religious beliefs birth control has been almost a taboo subject here. Happily, this is changing. But things need to change fast. Because unless we get a handle on these issues in this generation, we are doomed to fight a losing war and I look with horror on the world of our children and grandchildren."

In the hushed silence Doctor Gaitán smiled wistfully. "I know we can never return to the past, much as we'd sometimes like to...but it's ironic to think of what Bogotá and the surrounding savannah has become compared to what it was like before the conquest.... Would you like to hear?"

The volunteers assented.

"Good. Because that was part of the lecture anyway.... So, close your eyes for a moment and let's imagine we're back in the time of the first explorers/conquistadores of the interior, principally Señores

Quesada, Benalcazar, and Herr Federmann. These adventurers were lured to Colombia by the dream of El Dorado, that mythical kingdom of gold that spurred the Spaniards over most of the New World. Imagine the power of this idea. This emotion. The lust for gold. It attracted men of great vigor and daring, willing to endure incredible hardships and fear of the unknown. Gonzalo Jimenez de Quesada was such a man. And unlike the stereotype of many of the conquistadores, the ignorant illiterate swineherd types with nothing to lose, Quesada gave up a successful law career in Spain to take a lesser post in Santa Marta. He was a determined practical man who became infected with mad dreams of El Dorado. One day he set aside his law robes and led an expedition into the jungles of the Magdalena River Valley. Suffering brutal hardship and privation, he led his men out of the sweltering malarial lowlands to an Indian trail up a steep pass of the Andes to *la sabana*. Quesada's party, or at least the 166 of the original 800 who survived, came to this broad fertile plateau 9,000 feet above sea level. Imagine, after the privations of the lowlands, it must have seemed a veritable paradise. An enchanted green land with a bracing, healthful climate, mist shrouded mountains, and clear flowing water. Perhaps it was the real El Dorado. The El Dorado of the spirit. The El Dorado of a new Eden. But Quesada and his followers could only see gold.... There in the savannah, as they had for untold generations, lived the Chibcha Indians. They resided in peaceful villages surrounded by their cultivated fields, mined salt in the mountains, and, to their undoing, decorated their wooden huts with gold disks and themselves with emeralds. Confronted with this easy loot, the Spaniards quickly conquered and virtually enslaved the Chibchas. Quesada, whose mad dreams and restless energy is rumored to have inspired Cervantes' Don Quixote, settled down to enjoy the spoils. A few months later he was joined in the savannah by Benalcazar and Federmann. A huge conflict between the factions of conquistadores was avoided by Quesada, who persuaded all concerned to let the king divide the spoils, much to his advantage, of course. And the rest, as they say, is history. Modern day Bogotá, and by extension Colombia, was conceived from the legacy of El Dorado. A legacy of greed and lust for material possessions at whatever cost. A legacy that has brought freebooters and pirates from all over the world to our shores."

Doctor Gaitán smiled and shook his head. "Maybe after our little talk here today some of you will wish to return to your own country. But for those of you who choose to stay, we have much work to do to make Colombia healthy, and maybe as much to undo. The dream and the legacy of El Dorado still haunt us. But the promise of a different El Dorado also inspires us.... Any questions or comments?"

"Yeah," Vachio had blurted from the back of the room. "If I didn't know better, I could have sworn you were talking about California."

A long moment of silence had followed this remark and heads

turned to look at Vachio. Julie, a pretty blonde from Tiburon in Marin County, gave Vachio an outraged look. Vachio glanced around the room; only a handful of faces looked sympathetic.

"What exactly are you trying to get at?" asked Gaitán, a twinkle in his eye.

"The histories and events are similar," said Vachio. Then he stopped, unable to articulate what he felt, confused by the hostile and mocking looks of his Peace Corps compadres.

"Go on," said Gaitán.

"Well, the Gold Rush brought the first big flood of settlers into California, looking for their El Dorado. And too many people and too rapid development is deteriorating the quality of life and causing a whole lot of social problems and..."

"You can't compare the two," hissed Julie. "That's ridiculous. California is nothing like here." Julie's reply was taken up by most of the other volunteers and Vachio sputtered back at them.

"Wait a minute," said Gaitán. "He may have a good point. Though it might seem strange to compare a rich state like California in the wealthiest country in the world to a poor country like Colombia, the biggest difference may be in degree of problems. Is that what you mean?"

"Yes. I've seen plenty of the same problems you have here in Los Angeles and San Francisco."

"Very well. So what's your point?"

"Well, uh... I think we have more in common than a lot of people in this room think. And I think we better be damn careful about what we try to do here or we might make a bad situation even worse..."

Vachio was drowned out by a chorus of sarcastic remarks. Gaitán winked at him and moved on to another topic. Vachio had hunched down in his chair, glared at one of the more vocal of the volunteers, and clamped his mouth shut. From the corner of his eye he saw Julie smirking at him.

"What makes you so sure you know the right way for the world?" Vachio asked her under his breath.

Julie smiled and looked toward Gaitán. Vachio turned his face to stone and stared straight ahead. He wouldn't give her the satisfaction of showing her he was irritated by what she thought. Anyway, what did it matter? The future would take care of itself.

The plane hit a downdraft and Vachio felt the air rush into his lungs and tingles course up and down his spine. Gasps of fear issued from a few of the passengers as the 727 wobbled and bounced. Lightning flashed and rain pelted the windows. One of the stewardesses, her voice betraying anxiety, urged the passengers to buckle up and remain calm. The plane bucked erratically for a few minutes before the turbulence subsided and the dark clouds and lightning passed to their wake.

The pilot regained full control and smoothed their flight. It was just a quick Andean squall. Temperamental like the country, temperamental like Vachio.

Vachio took a deep breath and peered out of the window. They had left the green savannah far behind and were over a stretch of barren and eroded peaks fit only for condors. In the distance the sun glinted off a solitary snow-capped pinnacle. Vachio glanced at his watch. About another 10 minutes to Bucaramanga. His stomach churned in anticipation.

2

"We are about to land at the International Airport of Palo Negro in the City of Bucaramanga. Please fasten your seat belts, obey the no smoking sign, and put your seats in an upright position. Thank you."

Vachio peered out of the window and shook his head in puzzlement. Though the plane was descending at a steady pace and their velocity was lessening, they were still flying above eroded mountain peaks and among white cumulus clouds. About to land? Where? How? Then a narrow plateau, fringed with scrubby tropical growth, came into view. They were upon it in the next heartbeat and the plane touched down. The control tower and a long, low slung building shot past as the plane hurtled toward the end of the plateau. Gawd, this is like landing on an aircraft carrier, thought Vachio, unconsciously braking with his right foot.

Brakes hissing, the plane lurched to a stop, only a few yards from the wire fence at the end of the runway, a yawning chasm a few yards beyond that.

"Welcome to Bucaramanga," came the sweet voice over the intercom, "the City of Parks. We hope you enjoyed the flight."

The plane swung around and headed toward the control tower. Vachio reviewed the note his coordinator had given him. A group from the *Casa de Menores* is going to meet you at the airport. They should be easy to spot. It's a small terminal and all you have to do is look for the Director, Don Gustavo. He's red-haired, freckle-faced, and short. Looks a little like a leprechaun. He's a real character and a very nice person. He'll be looking for you, too, so you shouldn't have any trouble.

Vachio slipped off the plane with his shoulder bag in tow and walked across the hot tarmac to the terminal. Inside he immediately spotted a short, red-haired man wearing a pale yellow guayabera and tan slacks. The man noticed Vachio looking at him and took a hesitant step forward.

Vachio smiled and said, "Are you the man looking for a *gringo* to adopt?"

"Are you Señor Vachio?" asked the man, a startled look on his face.

"Yes. Are you my new boss?"

"Gustavo Prada Nieto, at your order," he said, shaking Vachio's hand firmly. "As Director of the *Casa de Menores* and *Escuela de Trabajo,* it's my honor and pleasure to welcome you here. We've heard many good things about you from Doña Fortuna."

"Then you have me at a disadvantage.... You must know a lot more about me than I know about you."

"Perhaps," said Gustavo, eyeing Vachio speculatively. "We weren't told you would speak Spanish so well."

"Really, I don't speak so well. I just practiced a few sentences for our meeting."

"No, you speak well. Very well for such a short time in Colombia."

"Well, I probably know more than my supervisor and Spanish teachers in Bogota suspect...but less than you're beginning to think."

"Señor Vachio, you speak plenty."

Vachio smiled. "Fine, but I don't always understand. You'll have to be patient with me sometimes."

"That's fine. We'll teach you to speak like a real *Santandereano*.... And now, I'd like to introduce you to my associate and right hand man, Francisco Morazon."

A swarthy man of medium build and height stepped forward. He was casually dressed, in his late 20s or early 30s, with a developing beer paunch and long sideburns framing a round cheerful face. "You can call me Pacho," he said, briskly shaking Vachio's hand. "And if you need anything, I'm here to respond."

"And this is La Señora Maria Elena de la Villa," said Gustavo. "Our very excellent social worker and the fair flower of the *Casa de Menores*."

"A pleasure to meet you,' said Maria Elena, limply shaking hands. She was an attractive woman in her mid-20s with a full, well-rounded figure, dark hair and eyes, and a flawless Mediterranean complexion. Her manner was reserved and gracious.

"Good. Now that we've all been introduced, let's get going. I have a big day planned for you," said Gustavo.

"Business or pleasure?" asked Vachio.

"A little business mixed with much diversion. Today we'll let you relax and get to know the town a little. Tomorrow we'll get serious."

"Sounds good to me."

"Do you have baggage to collect?" asked Gustavo.

"This is everything," said Vachio, pointing to his shoulder bag.

"That's all? Nothing more?"

"Yes. I'm only going to be here a week."

"You travel simply."

"I guess."

They walked through the terminal to the baggage claim area where DAS agents were checking passengers' identifications and randomly searching luggage. An armed guard was stationed at the terminal exit. All of the passengers from Vachio's flight were queuing up. Vachio automatically headed for the end of the line.

"Where are you going?" asked Gustavo.

"To go through the line."

Gustavo smiled. "Don't worry about that. You're with me. Let's go."

As they moved toward the exit, one of the agents looked up and called to Vachio to stop.

"Forget about this one. He is with me. I'll be responsible for him," said Gustavo with a big grin.

"Yes, Don Gustavo. I'm sorry. I didn't know."

"No problem. Keep up the good work."

Vachio felt vaguely uncomfortable. Some of the passengers stuck in line were giving them resentful looks. The guard at the door stepped aside with a grin and a nod and a polite greeting to Don Gustavo. Outside, they passed a line of taxi drivers, almost all of whom had a good word for Don Gustavo.

"You have a lot of pull here," commented Vachio.

"Not so much," said Gustavo carelessly.

Pacho gave a throaty chuckle. "Don Gustavo is being modest. He is well known throughout Santander. Even in Bogotá they know of him. Right, Don Gustavo?"

"Francisco likes to exaggerate. Pay him no mind."

"What?" Pacho guffawed. "Ay, Don Gustavo!"

"Here's my car," said Gustavo, opening the door to a late model, red Renault. "You sit in front, Señor Vachio. To see the view better."

They slid out of the parking lot and onto a winding, steeply descending road. Pacho launched into a long monologue concerning Colombia, Colombians, and what he knew about the United States and North Americans. Now confident that their guest understood Spanish well, Pacho spoke in a relaxed, slang embellished style that Vachio was hardpressed to follow. Vachio settled back in his seat, the warm humidity and the swaying motion of the car making him drowsy. As the others talked, Vachio nodded occasionally to show he was listening and let his mind drift into the passing scenery.

Sandy, red-tan earth, deeply eroded in places and supporting scrubby vegetation banked the well-maintained black top road. Green, mist shrouded mountain peaks marched to the northeast. At a bend in the road, Vachio caught a glimpse of a sprawling city on a broad plateau. He straightened up to get a better look but his view was blocked by a large road sign with the inscription: *El Que Pisa Tierra Santandereana Es Santandereano*. (He Who Treads On Santanderean Soil Is

Santanderean).

"Do you guys really believe that?" asked Vachio, pointing to the sign.

"Of course we do! Absolutely!" said Pacho, leaning forward to eyeball Vachio. "We Santandereans are frank and generous people. We welcome other good people from anywhere."

Gustavo, silent since they had entered the car, glanced back at Pacho and smiled. "It might be better to tell our young friend that we welcome and accept people who respect us and our ways. Wouldn't you agree with that, Maria Elena?"

"Yes. Well said, Gustavo."

"Yes! That's exactly the way it is here," said Pacho. "The way it should be. We're a proud people we Santandereans. And if we're provoked, we defend our honor with bravery and ferocity. All Colombia knows and recognizes us for that. But we're also straightforward, fair, and good. If you're a straight shooter, you'll get along well here. You'll be treated with esteem and affection."

"What do you think of what Pacho said, Señor Vachio?" asked Gustavo.

"If that's the way it is, it sounds fine to me. I believe in live and let live...up to a point. And please, don't call me Señor. That's too formal for me. My name is Gary."

"Gawdy," said Pacho.

"No, not like that. Gar-ee."

"Gaw-dy."

"No. Ah, that's fine."

"Would it offend you if we call you by your last name?" asked Gustavo. "Vachio has a nice ring to it and it's easy to pronounce for us."

"No, that's fine. Many people have called me by my last name. And my friends used to call me Vac."

"Vac. Like Vaca, eh," said Pacho with a laugh.

"Yeah. But I'm a Taurus the bull."

"Me, too," said Maria Elena. "Do you believe in astrology, Vachio?"

"Not really. But then again, I don't know much about it."

"Astrology is bullshit," offered Pacho.

Maria Elena gave Pacho a sharp look and said, "Vachio is an Italian name, right?"

"Yes."

"Do you speak Italian?" asked Maria Elena.

"Of course," said Vachio, putting on a clownish face. "Pasta, antipasto, ravioli, spaghetti, linguini.... You know, just like I speak French. Crepes, quiche, oui, non..."

"Eh, he's pulling our leg," said Pacho, laughing. "That's all right. He speaks Italian like I speak English. Eees right, Meester?"

"Not exactly. I did learn some Italian from my grandparents when

I was a kid. But I've forgotten most of it."

"Yes, but that would explain why you have a feel for Spanish," said Maria Elena."

"That helps. But I studied Spanish in school. And where I grew up, there were a lot of Mexicans and Central Americans so I picked up some of the language from them.... Unfortunately, most of my teachers in Bogotá don't seem to like the slang I learned from them and they've been giving me a hard time. But that's fine. I know I need to learn a lot more."

"No, you speak almost well. But you need to improve your accent," said Maria Elena.

"Are most of your teachers from Bogotá?" asked Pacho.

"Yes. And several from Medellín."

"Huh, careful what you learn or you'll end up sounding like one of those effete snobs from Bogotá," said Pacho.

Gustavo snickered. "He could do a lot worse, Pachito. They speak a very clear, liquid Castilian in Bogotá."

"Well, that's true, Don Gustavo. I just can't stand their mannerisms.... But as far as the language is concerned, there is no doubt that the best Spanish in Latin America is spoken in Colombia. Everyone knows that."

Vachio made a wry face and looked out at the scenery. They swung around a dizzying curve and an unobstructed view to the east presented itself.

"That's Bucaramanga," said Gustavo, indicating with outthrust lips to their left. Thousands of feet below them a forest of red-tile roofs covered a tilted plateau.

"Beautiful, right?" said Pacho, tapping Vachio on the shoulder.

"I don't know. I can't see that much from here. But it's much bigger than I expected."

"Big and getting bigger fast," said Gustavo. "It's the largest city and most important commercial center in Eastern Colombia. Although, it still has the feel of a large town."

"But it's nothing compared to *The Capital of the World*. Right, Don Gustavo?" said Pacho.

Gustavo laughed.

"*The Capital of the World*?" said Vachio.

"Garrotero. Our pueblo," said Gustavo.

Vachio covered his mouth to repress a snicker.

Gustavo noticed. "Garrotero may not seem like much to an outsider...but to us it is *The Capital of the World*. Although, in our bad times, and we've had our share during our history, we also have referred to it as, pardon my grossness Maria Elena, *The Asshole of the World*."

"What would you call it right now?" asked Vachio.

"Right now we're in a pretty good time. I'd call it *The Capital of the World.*"

"I'm glad to hear that," said Vachio. "But when was a bad time for you guys? And what was it like?"

"Well, good and bad are entwined throughout our history..."

"Garrotero is somewhat schizophrenic," said Maria Elena in a low sweet voice.

"Maria Elena! What are you telling him?" exclaimed Pacho.

"The truth."

Gustavo chuckled. "You'll have to excuse Maria Elena, Vachio. She's originally from Bucaramanga, not Garrotero. And to many people in Bucaramanga, we'll always be rustic bumpkins."

Gustavo raised his hand to silence Maria Elena's protest. "But in a way, she's right about our schizophrenia."

"Don Gustavo, what are you saying?" said Pacho.

"I'm about to explain, Francisco. Wait a moment.... You see, Vachio, Garrotero is known as the *Panela Capital of Colombia* because of our unsurpassed production of bars of *panela*. You know what *panela* is, right?"

Vachio nodded. "Brown sugar."

"Exactly. So, because of this, we think of ourselves as a center of sweetness and good flavor. And we believe it. This is one side of our personality."

"And the other?"

"It comes from our name—Garrotero."

"All right. And what exactly is a *garrotero*?" asked Vachio.

"A *garrote* is a kind of stick or cudgel. And at the turn of the century, during the Palo Negro Civil Conflict, which is known as The Thousand Days War in the rest of Colombia, our town became famous for killing our enemies by strangling them with *garrotes*, hence our name. And this tradition has continued during the worst of *La Violencia* and even to this day on rare occasions. You understand?"

"Yes, I think so. Garrotero means the *Town of the Stick Stranglers*."

"That's it."

"What a nice reputation." Vachio shook his head and smiled. "But you know something, there's a town in California not too far from where I come from and their name was Hangtown...for true and obvious reasons. But they changed their name to Placerville to avoid the stigma. Why don't you guys do the same?"

"Why should we?" broke in Pacho. "Like I said before, we have a well-deserved reputation for being fierce when others try to take advantage of us. Our ancestors killed with *garrotes* because it was the manly way. *Mano a mano*. A personal thing..."

"And because they often didn't have enough guns," added Gustavo.

"But why are you guys telling Vachio all this?" asked Maria Elena. "There are many people in Garrotero who hate the name and want to change it. Why are you trying to scare the poor guy?"

"Ah, Maria Elena, it's not like that. We don't mean to scare the poor *gringo*," said Pacho, giving Vachio a jovial pat on the shoulder. "We just want him to know of our history. Of our essence.... But Vachio, these are things from our past. We've learned from them. Garrotero is a good town. It's tranquil and wholesome. You won't find the dishonesty and drug use and loose women like you would in Bogotá or places like that. We have very few vices. Garrotero is a great place to live. A fine place to raise a family. You'll see."

"Yeah, yeah, I believe you," said Vachio, his head spinning. He turned from Pacho and looked out of the window, needing a break from the strain of understanding such a torrent of words. Fortunately, Pacho simmered down and Maria Elena and Gustavo fell into a discussion concerning the psychological profile of a newly arrived *gamin*.

As they descended the mountain, the air grew warmer and the vegetation more lush. Banana trees with elephant ear fronds, mango, avocado, papaya, and guava shaded rustic homes in niches carved from the mountain. Chickens, goats, mongrel dogs, and cattle roamed in small clearings and children lolled in the shade or played near front porches. The warm, increasingly humid weather, the bucolic landscape, and the swaying motion of the car lulled Vachio into an open-eyed slumber.

"Vachio! Vachio!" called Gustavo.

"Huh? What?" answered Vachio in English, shaking his head like a dog emerging from a pool of water.

"Are you bored with our company already?"

"No, of course not."

"Then?"

"Oh, it's just that I was so excited about coming here...you know, I didn't get much sleep last night."

"Ah, pardon me. I should have thought of that. And you must be tired from the flight."

"No. From getting up so early to get to the airport."

"Would you like to take a nap when we get to Garrotero?"

"No, no problem. Just give me some strong coffee and I'll be fine."

Gustavo laughed. "You can have as much as you want."

"And some *aguardiente* to go with it," said Pacho.

"Yeah, that'll wake me up."

They sledded down a final steep incline and the road came to a fork and leveled onto a highway running through a green valley. Gustavo swung left and they were soon speeding past restaurants, resort hotels, factories, small business shops, housing tracts, and numerous construction sites. It was a boom area, modern and exuberant. Only a smattering of rickety hovels on the hillsides and shabby temporary construction sheds gave it any real Third World flavor. Vachio was surprised but he kept it to himself.

"We're approaching Girón," announced Gustavo.

"What's a Girón?" asked Vachio.

"It's a beautiful, historic, colonial-style town. The River of Gold runs through it and the Spanish architecture is very well preserved.... We'll go there some day. It's worth it."

"And The Great Liberator Bolívar had a house there," added Pacho. "It's a museum now."

Gustavo chuckled. "Not to demean Girón's House of Bolívar, Vachio, but The Great Liberator is reputed to have houses in almost every town in Eastern Colombia and Western Venezuela. If you were to believe some accounts, he had almost as many houses as he did mistresses. I've been in countless towns that claim that honor."

Pacho guffawed. "Come on, Don Gustavo, it's a matter of verified historic fact that Bolívar had a home in Girón and in Bucaramanga. The Liberator loved Santander."

"And Gustavo, that's no way to speak of the dead," said Maria Elena. "With that edge of sarcasm. What will Vachio think?"

"Maria Elena, please don't misunderstand me," said Gustavo. "No one has more respect and admiration for The Great Liberator than I. He is not only our foremost national hero, but one of my own personal idols. I merely used that example to illustrate to Vachio how great his legend is here. In fact, let me humbly add, Bolívar graced Garrotero with his presence on several occasions in the late 1820s. He may even have stayed in the very house I live in."

"Oh, I didn't take it wrong," said Vachio. "You should hear how some historians in the United States make fun of the George Washington legend. To hear some of them tell it, he was a total clown who by pure luck, ambition, and circumstance came to be The Father of the Country."

"Really? In official history books?" asked Gustavo.

"In some, yes." Vachio shrugged. "No one is sacred there."

Gustavo nodded, a serious expression on his face. "It would seem you're right.... Especially considering what happened to the Kennedys, Martin Luther King, and Richard Nixon. But tell me, what do you personally think about this?"

"About what?"

"About the idea that no one is sacred. Don't you believe that certain people are worthy of special respect and admiration?"

Vachio felt all eyes upon him. He chose his response carefully. "Yes, I believe some people are worthy of special respect and admiration. But I also believe you probably never heard of most of them."

"That's an interesting thought," said Gustavo. "So I take it to mean that you don't think most of the great historical figures are worthy of respect."

"No. Well, it depends. What I'm saying is that no one should be made more than human. All these great historical figures had their faults. Some were really evil. So it's not like they should be blindly worshipped. At least not by me.... I don't know. I guess what I'm trying to say is that I don't have any heroes."

A dead silence reigned in the car. Vachio could feel Maria Elena and Pacho exchanging looks. Gustavo stared at the road, his face pensive. Vachio felt clammy sweat oozing from his pores. Damn! Why can't I keep my mouth shut sometimes, Vachio thought. Ah, what the hell. They're going to find out how I am sooner or later anyway. Just as well now.

"Are you Catholic, Vachio?" Maria Elena asked.

"Well, I was raised Catholic. But I don't practice it anymore."

"What religion do you practice?"

"Right now, none."

"Then, you're still Catholic."

Vachio shrugged noncommittally.

"Ah, I understand you," said Pacho in a jovial voice. "It's like many of us here. We're born and raised Catholic, we get married in the church, we baptize our children, and right before we die—we want a priest around to absolve us of our sins. But in between we want to have a good time. Right, Don Gustavo?"

"Speak for yourself, Pacho. Personally, I enjoy the ceremonies and rites of The Church. The grandeur and the mystery and the tradition. But, in reference to what Pacho said, we do have a saying here.... Church is for old people and children."

"*Eso*!" affirmed Pacho.

"When did you stop going to Mass?" Gustavo asked Vachio.

"When I was about 13. But I didn't stop completely. I used to go to Midnight Mass on Christmas and Easter with my friends to look over the girls and find out where the parties were."

Pacho laughed and slapped Vachio on the shoulder. "That's good. You say what other people only think. I like you already. You're a man after my own heart. Man, you almost seem like a Santanderean."

3

They came to another crossroads and Gustavo said, "We're on the outskirts of Bucaramanga. There to the left takes you downtown. We're going right on the highway to Bogotá."

"You mean the highway to Garrotero, Don Gustavo," said Pacho. "Our beloved Capital of the World. So our friend Vachio remembers."

"How could I forget?" mumbled Vachio.

The highway broadened to two lanes on each side and Gustavo gunned the car. They crossed a bridge over a brown water river and, down in the canyon, Vachio caught a glimpse of a shantytown of cardboard, wood, and scrap metal hovels, open sewer gutters carving channels in the dirt streets and flowing directly into the river. Then they were passing modern suburban tracts, hives of almost identical white stucco homes with red tile roofs and wrought iron gates. Prominent billboards trumpeted the progress and development of Santander.

"We're approaching the town of Floridablanca," said Gustavo.

"And?" asked Vachio.

"Nothing of special tourist interest," said Gustavo. "But it's a town with a long and distinguished history like that of Garrotero. But it's also a town in imminent danger of losing its identity."

"Why?"

"Because of the explosive growth in this area. Florida is currently a suburb of Bucaramanga. It will soon be swallowed up and become a neighborhood of Bucaramanga if things continue apace. It's a shame in a way. But progress can't be denied."

Gustavo suddenly pulled off the road and stopped beside a road stand offering fresh pineapple and assorted snacks. He jumped out of the car and beckoned to the others to join him.

"This is a strategic spot," said Gustavo, answering Vachio's unspoken question as to why they had stopped. "Across the road we have the gateway to Floridablanca and one of the most important industries in Santander...the liquor factory."

"What kind of liquors do they make?" asked Vachio.

"*Aguardiente*, of course. Gin, Rum, a fine coffee liqueur, and a few other things. You might want to take a tour of it someday. But for the moment, we can get you a coffee and a slice of fresh pineapple right here."

"Sounds good," said Vachio.

"Doña Floriza!" said Gustavo in a playful sing-song voice, addressing the middle-aged woman in the kiosk. "A *tinto*, some slices of pineapple, and a shot of *aguardiente* for our young friend from California."

"Right away, Don Gustavo. And for you?"

"Just a shot to toast the arrival of our guest."

"A shot?" exclaimed Vachio. "This early?"

Gustavo laughed. "Don't think this is a habit of ours. Let's just say this is your official drink of welcome to Santander. And it should wake you up. All right?"

"Well, yeah, all right."

"That's the spirit. Now Pachito, Maria Elena, join us for a toast."

"With pleasure, Don Gustavo," said Pacho. "But just a short one, eh. I have much to do today."

"I'll have a coke," said Maria Elena.

They took their glasses in hand, gathered around Gustavo, and stood for a moment in awkward silence.

"Would you do the honors, Señor Director?" asked Pacho.

Gustavo consented with a formal bow of his head, took a step forward, and raised his glass to Vachio. "We wish a warm welcome from our beloved land of Santander to our new friend and colleague...uh, Gady Vachio. May his stay be rewarding and full of good ventures, both in his personal life and in the performance of his duties. *Salud*!"

The men tipped their glasses and drained the fiery, anise-flavored cane liquor at a gulp. Gustavo and Pacho eyed Vachio to see how he handled the quick jolt. The liquor surged to Vachio's sleepy head and a hot current ran though him. He took a deep breath and washed the *aguardiente* down with a draught of strong, aromatic coffee.

"Man, that is an eye-opener," said Vachio.

The three Colombians laughed, more at the expression on Vachio's face than anything else.

"Delicious *aguardiente*, right?" Pacho asked Vachio.

"It's not bad. What kind is it?"

"*Aguardiente Superior*. From here in Santander."

"*Superior*, eh. You guys are sure modest here."

Maria Elena laughed but Pacho replied in all seriousness, "We call it what it deserves. It's the finest *aguardiente* in Colombia.... Don't you agree?"

"Well, uh, I've only tried a few different brands."

"Like which ones?"

"Usually *Cristal*. I liked that one best."

"*Cristal* is good," said Pacho grudgingly. "But *Superior* is better."

"This *Superior* tastes sweeter..." said Vachio.

Pacho and Gustavo exchanged a look.

"Would you like another shot?" asked Gustavo.

"Are you trying to get me drunk?" asked Vachio.

"If you like," said Pacho, grinning.

"No, that's all right. It's too early for me. But I will have some more of this coffee. It's delicious.... Another cup of this and I'm ready for anything."

"Good," said Gustavo. "You have a big day ahead of you. We're going to tour Garrotero and give you a taste of the surrounding countryside."

"What about the *Casa de Menores*? I'm anxious to see it."

"And I'm anxious for you to see it. But I planned a complete tour of the *Casa* and its facilities for tomorrow when you're more rested."

"Well, you're the boss," said Vachio, disappointed.

"We can take a quick look at it today if you truly want to."

"I would."

"Very well, then. Let's go."

They piled back into the car and proceeded. The highway soon narrowed to two winding lanes and they got stuck behind a slow-moving tanker truck with Che Guevara mud flaps. Gustavo tail-gated him for a while, honked a few times, swung in and out of the oncoming lane, and finally tried to pass on a blind curve. Vachio closed his eyes as they moved to pass, a tingle running down his spine. It was a crazy maneuver. Frantic honking from an oncoming car alerted Gustavo to cut back to his own lane and the squeal of air brakes from the tanker truck told Vachio the move had barely succeeded.

"Idiot!" muttered Gustavo, glancing at his rear view mirror and casually dismissing the incident.

The highway snaked through fields of rustling sugar cane and corn, the terrain gently rolling east to the foot of rugged purple mountains. Dark, menacing clouds hovered over the peaks, promising a cooling rain to the hot sun baking the valley. Vachio rolled down his window to catch the faint breeze. The close, humid air reeked of cattle dung, stagnant water, and rotting vegetation, a fecund heady odor after the cold, diesel stench of Bogotá.

After minutes of meandering talk, Gustavo rolled down his window, theatrically sucked in some air to catch the fragrant aroma of a passing rose farm, and with a broad smile said to Vachio, "Isn't this beautiful land?"

"Yes, very pretty," said Vachio in a distracted tone.

"Yes, it really is." Gustavo paused and glanced at Vachio to make sure he was listening to him. Then he cleared his throat, switched to a deep commanding tone of voice, and launched into a speech, employing the precision of elocution and dramatic flair of the trained orator. "You know, Señor Vachio, without meaning to sound like a cheap propagandist, we are truly blessed here in Santander. We have almost everything.... A mild agreeable climate, fertile soil, and ample rainfall and mountain streams to provide a rich and varied agricultural bounty. We have oil, uranium, and other natural minerals and resources to build a solid industrial base. Santandereans are known as predominately sober and industrious people. So, considering all these positive elements, Santander should be a paradise on earth..."

"Yes, but ..." said Vachio.

"But..." Gustavo laughed and said, "Pacho, how can I explain things to him without making it sound wrong?"

"You would know better than me, Don Gustavo."

"Should I tell him the story about God, the Archangel Michael, and Creation?"

"Yes, that's it! That's perfect, Don Gustavo.... That is, if he can understand it."

"Understand what?" asked Vachio, growing impatient.

"A story we Colombians tell about ourselves to explain why we don't have the paradise we should," said Gustavo.

"Yes, I already understood that. Why don't you just tell me the story."

"Very well. Here we go.... Way back when God was creating the earth, he paused on the sixth day as he was nearing the end of his task, and called the Archangel Michael to his side and said, 'Michael, I have created great oceans and continents, filled them with all manner of plants, animals, fish, and birds, and given over this wondrous paradise to man in my own image to pay me homage. But still I'm not content. I want to do something truly extraordinary. Create a land unsurpassed. My masterpiece among masterpieces. And I want you to help me.'"

"'Yes, Lord, whatever you desire,'" replied Michael. "'What do you wish of me?'"

"'I want you to tell me where to put this place.'"

"The Archangel Michael looked down at the earth and surveyed its seven continents. After considerable thought he said, 'There!' and pointed to the top of South America. 'That looks like a fine spot to me.'"

"'Very well,' said God. 'So be it.' And with a pass of his hand it was done. 'Now fly down there and behold my handiwork,' he ordered Michael!"

"Michael descended to earth and beheld a land that was lapped by not one, but two oceans—filled with fish and providing easy transport for travel and commerce. Then he found not one, not two, but three great mountain ranges—mountains to water the valleys, moderate the climate, enrich the soil, and give beautiful vistas to pleasure the eyes and soul. And there were rivers, forests, jungles, highland plateaus, plains, and even a touch of desert. Much of the land was blessed with boundless fertility, supporting an incredible variety of plants and animals. And for good measure, beneath the soil and in the mountains, the Lord placed a treasure trove of emeralds, gold, minerals, and oil."

"The Archangel Michael returned to heaven most impressed."

"'Well, Michael, what say you of my work?' asked the Lord."

"'You've truly outdone yourself this time, My Lord. The land you have created is fantastic, incredible, beyond my poor powers of expression. I bow before your almighty power and majesty.... But what will you call this wondrous land?'"

"'It will one day be called Colombia,' said the Lord. Then he burst into a fit of laughter, and laughed and laughed until tears came to his eyes."

"The Archangel Michael regarded God with consternation. 'Lord, what is it. Why do you laugh so?'"

"'Archangel Michael, just wait until you see the kind of people I put in Colombia to screw it up.'"

Vachio chuckled, Pacho laughed like a hyena, and even the serious Maria Elena giggled. Gustavo's delivery had been hilarious.

"No one in Santander can tell a story like Don Gustavo," said Pacho.

"What did you think of it, Vachio?" asked Gustavo.

"It was a good one."

"But what did you think of it? The idea?"

Vachio shrugged. "That story could apply to many places all over the world. Not just Colombia. Man, I've met lots of nice people since I've come here."

Gustavo smiled with pleasure and said, "I'm glad to hear that. And I hope you find us to be among the nice people as well. But I told you that story with two purposes in mind.... First, to show you that we can laugh at ourselves and at the incongruities of life. And second, that within the *Casa de Menores* there is a faction, mainly consisting of guards and a handful of administrators, who are thoroughly bad and selfish and are unworthy of your trust. You must beware of them. I warn you now because they will certainly try to ingratiate themselves with you for their own dubious purposes and to your detriment."

"What exactly do these people do that is so bad?" asked Vachio.

"They do everything possible to inhibit the smooth and humane functioning of a true reform school. The *Casa de Menores* is known as the Prison For Minors in Garrotero because of these people. And truthfully, it is a prison—much as it shames me to admit it—because these reactionary elements have their own interests in mind rather than the best interests of the boys. Isn't that right, Pacho?"

"Well, yes, Don Gustavo. We certainly have problems with some of the staff."

"To say the least," said Gustavo. Maria Elena maintained a discreet silence.

"Look, Gustavo," said Vachio, "I've been warned about this already. Of course, I don't know exactly what I'm getting into, and I appreciate any help you can give me, but don't I have to try to work with everybody in order to do my job?"

"Yes, of course. You must try. An idealist must always try to influence the bad and the ignorant. And I'm assuming you're an idealist. But don't waste your efforts on the cynical ones. Measure them carefully. Know well the people who will back your efforts."

"Well, I don't know anyone yet. And I'd like to go into this with an open mind."

"Of course, of course. I just want you to understand that you can rely on every person in this car."

Vachio stared at the road and thought, Can I rely on them? For what? And up to what point?

Gustavo gave Vachio a searching glance and read the doubt on his face. He took his right hand from the steering wheel, balled it into a fist, and thumped it against the windshield. "Listen, Señor Vachio, the reason you are coming here to work is because I requested you and made all the arrangements. Why did I do this? Because I am a progressive. An activist progressive willing to battle for what I believe in. Do you understand?"

"I'm not sure. What are you willing to battle for?"

"True progress."

"True progress?"

"Yes, true progress. I believe and demand that the *Casa de Menores* become a true reform school with the ability to educate, rehabilitate, give job training, guidance, discipline, and yes, even recreation, to a group of poor unfortunate children. Disdained children called *gamines*. Children who were born into this world with almost no chance at all. This is my vision. This is what I live and fight for. What do you say to that?"

"Well, that's certainly a worthy goal that I can support. But what's the *Casa de Menores* like right now?"

"Right now, under my direction, we have programs in place. We're progressing, moving in a positive direction. But as I mentioned earlier, most of the townspeople still refer to us as the Minors' Prison." Gustavo's voice rose and he raised his arm like an Old Testament prophet. The freckles on his face and arms seemed to flame. "But I have vowed to change this. And in order to effect this change, we must take these reactionary elements—who are so corrupt, so selfish, so depraved, so evil—and eliminate them."

Gustavo paused and glanced over to see Vachio fidgeting in his seat while staring straight ahead at the road.

"You see, Vachio," said Gustavo, switching to a calm voice, "I've been waging a campaign to have a number of the least qualified and corrupt guards removed. Some of them are guilty of gross brutality, having sexual relations with the boys, selling drugs and privileges and, worst of all, undermining my authority as Director. They have got to go."

"Can't you just fire them or something?" asked Vachio.

"Ay, if only it were so simple. If only I had the power to do it. The *Casa* would be a much happier place. But unfortunately, the guards have a very strong labor union, a regular mafia, and it's difficult to corroborate charges against them when they all stick together and the children are terrified to speak against them. And aside from this, it's difficult to move against them through official channels because of indifference. The government prefers to close its eyes to certain abuses if they were to occasion a public scandal. Better to keep it quiet and let things continue as they always have, especially if the victims are powerless *gamines*. Even my own political party wants me to back off. But I can't! I won't! My conscience won't allow it."

"So what are you planning to do?" asked Vachio.

Gustavo chuckled. "Oh, I have a few tricks up my sleeve. Sooner or later, hopefully sooner, they will slip up in a big way and my chance will come. In any case, there will be a final showdown. And either they go or I go."

"And meanwhile?" asked Vachio.

"Meanwhile, we plug along as best we can. That's why I have surrounded myself with young idealistic people such as yourself, such as Maria Elena, and such as Doctor Emilio Montoya, our staff psychologist, who you will soon meet. Youth and energy, professionalism and humanism, this is what we're looking for in the *Casa de Menores*. It inspires me and will have a positive influence on some of the staff members who aren't beyond redemption. So what do you say? Are you with me?"

"I promise to do the best I can," said Vachio.

"Good. I think you will be a tremendous help. We were positively impressed by your resume and by the report from your training supervisor. And now that I've met you, I'm impressed by your command of Spanish and by your confident presence. Qualities very important for what we need to do here. *Caray*! Give me your hand on it."

As they clasped hands, Vachio wondered if what Gustavo wanted him to do was what he wanted to do.

4

Gustavo pulled up in front of a long, whitewashed building with light brown trim and faded red, roof tiles. It reminded Vachio of several California Mission buildings he had seen.

"*Casa de Menores*," said Gustavo, intoning the words as though he were a train conductor. "Everybody out."

The curb was too high to open the door onto the narrow sidewalk so Vachio squeezed out from the driver's side onto the street. He stretched his cramped muscles and felt his body enveloped by heat. Then the clop of hooves against concrete turned his head and he saw a man approaching on a big tan horse.

"Man, Bonanaza," muttered Vachio, staring up at the rider.

He was a real cowboy, his dark leathery face hawk-like and alert, a broad-brimmed Panama hat pulled down low to his eyebrows. A machete in a silver studded scabbard was attached to his waist and his leather saddle was intricately embroidered. The horse was sleek and powerful and moved at ease under the light but firm hands on the reins. Horse and rider came abreast of Vachio, towering over him. The cowboy halted his mount and eyed Vachio, his look a mixture of curiosity and contempt. What's with this guy, thought Vachio, returning the stare but feeling apprehension.

"*Hola! Hola! Hola!*" called Gustavo from down the street.

"Don Gustavo," said the cowboy. "How goes it?" He gave Vachio a final sidelong look and nudged his horse over to the curb. Vachio, relieved, went to join Pacho.

The cowboy and Gustavo bantered back and forth while the horse took a dump on the street.

"Who is that guy?" Vachio asked Pacho.

"Capataz Prudencio. He's the overseer of a big sugar cane plantation and a good friend of Don Gustavo's."

"Oh, yeah? If they're such good friends, why did he call him Don Gustavo?"

"Oh, that's nothing. Just to show him public respect. In private he might call him son-of-a-bitch for all I know."

Gustavo motioned toward Vachio and the cowboy glanced back toward him, a slow thin smile creasing his taut features. Then he turned and cantered his horse up the street.

Vachio and Pacho joined Gustavo at the entrance to the *Casa de Menores* and were about to enter when they were hailed from down the street. A short, barrel-shaped man with straight black hair and a sweaty face hurried toward them, waddling like a duck and telling Gustavo he needed to speak to him at once.

"You better slow down, Dolfo," called Pacho, smiling maliciously. "Do you want to have a stroke and leave your wife a widow?"

"Very funny," gasped Dolfo. "I'll get back to you later. Right now I have more important things to do.... Don Gustavo, it's urgent that..."

Dolfo moved close to Gustavo and lowered his voice. After a quick explanation, Gustavo nodded and turned to Vachio.

"Pardon this inconvenience, Vachio. But something has come up that requires my immediate and personal attention. I need to change our plans."

"That's fine. No problem."

"I shouldn't be delayed more than an hour. Would you like to take a tour of the town while I resolve this matter?"

"Whatever you say."

"Good. Pacho! You and Dolfo take the truck and show Vachio the town. You know, a quick orientation."

"I understand, Don Gustavo. A little whirl around Garrotero City."

"Have him back here in about an hour.... Maria Elena, come with me. This concerns the new boy from Barranquilla."

Gustavo and Maria Elena disappeared inside, leaving Vachio impressed by Gustavo's quick decisive manner.

Pacho took Dolfo by his brawny arm and brought him over to Vachio. "Vachio, this is Dolfo Jimenez, the mad truck driver of the *Casa de Menores*."

As they shook hands, each mumbling "*Mucho gusto*," Dolfo eyed Vachio with frank curiosity. Then he turned to Pacho and said, "So this is the *gringo* we've been hearing about. Does he speak any Castilian or do we have to baby talk to him?"

"Ask him yourself."

Before Dolfo could ask, Vachio said, "You can speak to me as well as you can. It's up to you to make sense."

"Mother of God!" exclaimed Dolfo, taken aback. Pacho laughed uproariously.

"I'd say he speaks better than you, Dolfo. For sure he thinks better.... Not that that's any great feat."

"Don't be a fuck, Pacho," said Dolfo.

"You see how this guy is," said Pacho to Vachio, still laughing. "He's what we call a *mamagallista* here. He likes to talk trash. Just give it back to him like you did to keep him in his place."

"Sure. I like to talk trash, too," said Vachio.

"I noticed," said Dolfo.

They all laughed and piled into a metallic green, 1950s vintage Ford truck. "Where to?" asked Dolfo.

"Let's go to my house first. I want to tell my old lady I'll be late for lunch," said Pacho.

Dolfo grunted and slammed the truck into gear. They turned left off the main street leading to the center of town and followed a gentle incline toward the high mountains that bulked against the sky. The streets, almost empty in the late morning heat, were narrow, paved, and dusty, with a sharp pervasive odor of fresh leaf tobacco. Most of the houses were modest, one story jobs, compacted into tight blocks, with plaster fronts and heavy wooden doors and window shutters, whitewashed or painted in pastel colors that highlighted the red roof tiles and sprouting television antennas.

"Hurry up. I'm already late. Can't this junk go any faster," said Pacho to Dolfo.

"Relax, bro," said Dolfo, patting the dashboard. "The chuckholes are bad for my baby if I go too fast. Your old lady can wait another minute."

Pacho grunted an unintelligible reply.

"Hey, Pacho," said Vachio, winking at Dolfo. "Why does a macho man like you have to tell his wife he'll be late for lunch?"

"Because she wears the pants," brayed Dolfo.

"No, man, it's not like that," said Pacho, flushing. "It's that...you know, she's a good woman. She runs my house and is an excellent mother to my children. Of course I give her the respect she deserves."

"In other words, he's well-domesticated," said Dolfo.

Pacho snorted. "A *pingo* like Dolfo thinks because a man is a responsible husband and father he's been castrated. Huh! I take care of business, but I get out every once in a while.... Maybe some night we'll invite you along Vachio. We can go to La Quarta. There are some good girls there. What do you say?"

"We'll see."

"Don't listen to him, Vachio. Pacho's talking trash.. La Quarta is only a good place if you like ugly, toothless country girls. I know a much better place on the road to Bucaramanga. If you ever want to have a real good time, come talk to me. I know where to go."

"Yeah, but most of the time you don't even know where you're at," retorted Pacho.

"Yeah? Well, at least I don't have to tell my old lady what time I'm coming home."

"Yeah, and if you ever see Dolfo's woman, Vachio, you'll know why he never tells her anything. He's afraid to."

"Listen, you fuck..."

"Yeah, cool it," said Pacho. "We're here."

They pulled up in front of a tidy, whitewashed residence with dark green trim. To Vachio's eyes it was almost indistinguishable from the other homes on the block.

"This is my house," said Pacho with a sweeping flourish of his right arm. "At your order. Come in and meet my family, Vachio."

"I'll wait outside," said Dolfo.

They walked through the unlocked front door and into a cool dark foyer. Before they could get beyond the foyer, a little girl playing in the open air patio spotted Pacho and ran into his arms calling, "Papi! Papi!"

Pacho gathered her up and gave her a kiss. "This is one of my daughters, Vachio.... Claudia."

Claudia gazed at Vachio with wide trusting eyes. She was about four, plump, healthy, and vivacious.

"She's cute," said Vachio, smiling at her.

Claudia grinned and shyly buried her face in her father's shoulder.

"Francisco! Is that you?" An adult version of Claudia appeared in the patio and came toward them. She was plump and brunette, wearing an apron over a simple cotton pullover shift and cloth sandals. "What delayed you? The food is...Oh! You have a guest." She dropped her eyes in embarrassment.

"Love, I want you to meet Señor Vachio. He is the man from the United States who is going to be working with us at the prison."

"A pleasure," said Vachio, inclining his head slightly.

"The same." Then she turned on Francisco. "You should have told me before hand. The house is a mess."

"Don't worry about that. This was unexpected. Offer our guest a drink."

"Ah yes, of course. Would you like a lemonade, Señor?"

Vachio nodded.

"Wait here," said Pacho to Vachio, patting him on the shoulder. "I'll be right back. Have a seat and relax."

Pacho followed his wife out of the foyer and into the kitchen. Vachio was a little surprised and disappointed he hadn't been invited all the way inside. He was curious to see the rest of Pacho's house.

Vachio found a straight-back chair with a coarse cowhide seat and sat down. Just outside the door, he could hear Dolfo cursing softly, his head under the hood of the truck. Vachio glanced at the whitewashed plaster walls. They were smooth and freshly painted, with pictures of John F. Kennedy and Pope John XXIII prominently displayed. The shady foyer was cool and restful. Insects buzzed about the plants in the patio. Vachio began to feel relaxed.

Pacho's wife reappeared and handed Vachio a tall glass of pulpy lemonade accompanied by a slice of jellied guava. Vachio hesitated before drinking the lemonade, wondering if the water was safe. Then he shrugged and drank it. It tasted great. What the hell. Better to risk a few amoebas, he thought, than to insult his hosts.

Vachio had just sprawled his legs out and closed his eyes, feeling himself beginning to doze, when Pacho reappeared and said, "Hey, this is no time to take a siesta. We have places to see and things to do. Let's go."

They went out to the truck and Dolfo was nowhere in sight. "That *pingo*!" muttered Pacho. Then he yelled, "Dolfo!"

Dolfo poked his head out of the doorway of a store a short distance down the street. Slowly he tipped a bottle of soda to his lips, drained it, wiped his mouth with the back of his hand, set the bottle down inside, said goodbye to the storekeeper, and finally addressed Pacho, "It's about time, Doctor. I got tired of waiting for you in this damn heat."

"I didn't take that long."

"Long enough," said Dolfo, shambling toward them. "You ate some lunch, didn't you?"

"No, just a snack." Pacho grinned. "You know I get sick of that slop they serve at the prison."

"But it's good enough for someone like me, eh, Doctor?"

"That's your concern, old boy. Now let's get going. If we don't show Vachio something of the town before we get back, Don Gustavo won't be pleased."

"That's your concern, Doctor. I'm just following your Majesty's directives."

They returned to the truck and resumed the tour, Pacho and Dolfo bickering good-naturedly, old pals from way back, leaving Vachio to look, listen, and form his own opinions. Blocks of similar pastel houses and high narrow curbs sweep past. Within a few blocks they came to a zone of new houses and construction sites. Then they hit the edge of town, bordered by the highway to Bogotá, and turned south. Across the road, a field of sugar cane stalks, rustled by a moist breeze, swept to the base of the mountains. On the town side, a string of shack-like roadhouses were packed with grimy workmen taking cover from the blazing sun.

Pacho interrupted his running argument with Dolfo, pointed across the road to the sugar cane field, and said with enthusiasm, "That whole field is soon to come under construction. An entire new urbanization. Garrotero is growing and developing at an incredible rate."

Vachio nodded and made no comment.

In minutes they came to a large creek running alongside a resort and discotheque called *El Conquistador*. Dolfo turned right and they were headed on the decline back toward the center of town, passing through an older neighborhood, with somewhat more varied and distinctive houses.

Dolfo yawned and asked, “So, Vachio, are you married?”

“No. I’m too young for that.”

“How old are you?”

“23.”

“Too young?” scoffed Pacho. “I was married and a father before 20.”

“Well, that might be good for you. But I want to see a little of the world before I settle down.”

“Yes, that’s good thinking. Don’t be a *pingo* like Pacho and get tied down too young,” said Dolfo. “But I warn you, you better be careful around here or you’ll get hooked before you know what hit you.”

“Ah, I don’t think so.”

“You don’t think so, huh?” Pacho chuckled. “Man, the women of Santander are famous throughout Colombia for their beauty and good breeding. You couldn’t do better anywhere in the world.”

“Yes, that’s true. Much as I hate to agree with Pacho, he’s right.”

“Yeah, whatever you guys say,” said Vachio. “All I know, since I arrived in Colombia, most everybody talks about the women from Cali.”

“Yes, yes, the *Caleñas*, like the song says, they’re like flowers,” said Dolfo. “But the *Santandereanas* are the equal or better than them. And we have a song, too. *Campesina Santandereana*. That tells it all.”

“Sing it to him. But slow so he can understand it well,” said Pacho to Dolfo.

“Why don’t you, *pingo*?”

“No, man. You’re supposed to be the musician.”

“I can’t sing *bambucos* without my *tiple* in my hands.”

“You can’t sing anyway, *pingo*. Just hum it.”

“I can sing better than you.”

“Let’s see. Go for it.”

Dolfo pulled the truck over to the curb and turned off the engine. He cleared his throat, tapped a beat on the steering wheel with his fingers, and sang in a low raspy voice:

“Santanderean country girl...
You are rosemary liqueur.
I’m crazy for your love,
And if you don’t kiss me I’ll die.
Santanderean country girl...
Your lips are honied from my sugar cane fields
And taste like the fragrance of roses from my garden.
Santanderean country girl ...

Your breasts like volcanoes
To the rhythm of your waist.
Santanderean country girl ...
You taste of ripe fruit.

Vachio laughed. "Well, if that song is even partly true I may be in big trouble."

"Yes, but it's sweet trouble. The best kind of trouble," said Dolfo.

"I'll keep an open mind," said Vachio.

"Forget your mind. Keep your eyes open, man. Just look over there," said Dolfo, pointing down the street.

A young woman, pert and buxom, with shiny black hair cascading over her shoulders, was coming toward them. She saw the men in the truck giving her the once-over and her twinkling brown eyes played over them until she drew close. Then she smiled coyly and averted her face, letting the men focus on her swinging limbs, undulating lithely under a thin sheath of cotton cloth and taut brassiere.

"Hey, sweet cake," called Dolfo, ogling her, his face hanging out of the window. "Come here and talk to Papi."

The young woman turned her head, slowed her walk, and angled closer to the truck. She appraised Dolfo as though he were a cockroach, gave him a radiant smile, and said, "Not even in your dreams, old billy goat." Then she walked on without a backward glance.

Pacho and Vachio cracked up. After a moment of open-mouthed shock, Dolfo looked angry, then he lowered his head onto the steering wheel in mortification.

"Ay, Dolfo, even the little sardines put you in your place. What a *pingo* you are," said Pacho.

"Ah, she's stuck up. What do I care."

"Yeah, you're right. What do you care? You're used to that treatment anyway."

"Listen, you..."

"But what did you think of that girl, Vachio?" asked Pacho, cutting off Dolfo's retort. "She was nice, eh?"

"All right. If you like that type."

"That type? What do you mean by that?"

"Well, the best looking woman I've seen so far to my taste is Maria Elena."

"Maria Elena?" There was a long moment of chilly silence and Pacho and Dolfo exchanged looks.

"Vachio, Maria Elena is a married woman and her husband is a good friend of mine," said Pacho.

"Yeah, well, I didn't mean anything beyond what I said. Only that she's an attractive woman."

Pacho and Dolfo noticeably relaxed. "Yes, she certainly is. And a fine person as well," said Pacho.

"For sure, for sure..."

Dolfo suddenly hailed a man across the street. The man, after trying to ignore him at first, acknowledged the greeting when Dolfo climbed out of the truck. He motioned for Dolfo to join him and ducked into a small café.

"Pacho, let me take a few minutes and talk to that *pingo*. He owes me some money."

"I don't know, man," said Pacho, shaking his head. "It's about time to get Vachio back to the prison. I don't want any problems with Don Gustavo."

"Please, bro, I've been looking for this guy for a week."

"Yah, all right. But don't delay. Ten minutes, no more."

Dolfo lumbered off and Pacho got out of the truck and motioned to Vachio to follow.

"Now we'll have to walk to the plaza," said Pacho, a pained look on his face.

"Where is it?"

"Around the corner and down the street."

Vachio snickered. "You make it sound like it's miles away. For me it will be a pleasure to walk."

"In this heat?"

"I've been freezing my bones in Bogotá. This heat feels good."

Pacho grunted and started down the street. "We'll see how you like it."

Vachio grinned and followed him, just happy to leave the cramped stuffy truck cab. Pacho seemed bored by his tour guide job. Vachio was disappointed in the tour and his first impression of Garrotero. It was compact and easy to find your way around, the streets laid out in square blocks with numbered, intersecting *Calles* and *Carreras*, the town wedged between the highway to Bogota and some low hills to the west, but the architecture was functional and ordinary, almost nondescript. Some of the streets were littered with and smelled of steaming piles of horse and burro shit. Capital of the World? Vachio snorted. Compared to some of the towns he had already visited in Colombia, such as Villa de Leyva with its gorgeous colonial buildings and cobbled streets, or Zipaquirá and its Salt Cathedral in the green Savannah outside Bogotá, why, Garrotero was nothing more than a fair-sized factory town, without special distinction. No wonder Vachio was unable to find anything about it in his Santander tour guide except its spot on the map. He could understand why they had placed a prison here. Vachio mopped at the sweat oozing down his forehead. Pacho was right. It was damn hot.

They turned the corner and a broad plaza, encompassing two regular city blocks, spread before Vachio's delighted eyes. It was an oasis of manicured lawns and carved stone benches, festooned with shade trees, bushes, and riotous tropical flowers. Cobblestone paths entered from the corners and sides of the plaza and led to a burbling fountain at its center. Old-timers, straw hats pulled low over their foreheads, sat in the shade, shooting the breeze with friends or dozing with open eyes. Teenagers promenaded for each other and youngsters played under the watchful eyes of mothers or older sisters.

"This is the heart and soul of Garrotero. Where you can find almost anything you need," said Pacho.

"Yeah, it's nice," said Vachio, drinking in the sights and sounds. "I was beginning to think this place was dead."

"Dead? It's siesta time. Come here at night and you'll see plenty of life."

They strolled around the perimeter of the plaza. The streets flanking the long sides of the rectangle were lined with small shops and cafés, a movie theater, and a bank. At one end of the plaza was a bus stop and taxi stand. Vendors, some working out of small booths and others hustling on foot, offered their wares to the travelers waiting for the buses. A handful of ragged young beggars worked the strollers and loungers. At the other end of the plaza was the Town Hall and main church, far and away the most impressive edifice in Garrotero. It was fortress-like, a cut stone structure of colonial design with twin bell towers and a massive wood gate ribbed with steel braces.

"That's where all the government offices are located, for the mayor and the other functionaries," said Pacho, wiping at his brow and breathing heavily.

"Can we go in and look around?"

"We could. But we don't have enough time right now. Another day. Let's get back to the truck."

Dolfo was waiting for them in the truck, a grin splitting his chubby face, a gold tooth glinting in the sun.

"I got my money," he said.

"Good. You can buy us a drink," said Pacho.

Dolfo's smile faded.

"I'm just messing with you, *pingo*. Besides, if someone is going to treat it should be Vachio. He's a rich *gringo*. What do you say, Vachio?"

"I'm a guest. I wouldn't want to insult your hospitality."

Dolfo laughed. "This is a live one."

"Anyway, I was just kidding. We don't have time. Let's go. We'll drive through the old part of town," said Pacho.

They drove beyond the plaza, toward the low hills, and into the older and much poorer west side of town. Pacho pointed out the central market, a huge warehouse covering an entire block. As they approached the edge of town some of the streets were unpaved, others were in disrepair, and a few still had the remnants of cobblestones. It was a neighborhood of warehouses, cheap bars, faded and crumbling stucco homes, and a smattering of shanties with sheltering banana trees and lush weeds.

"This is La Quarta," said Dolfo. "The fine place Pacho wants to bring you to for the ladies."

They passed a medical clinic and Dolfo turned right, right again, and they were back in front of the *Casa de Menores* only two blocks from the central plaza.

"So, what do you think of Garrotero, Vachio?" asked Dolfo.

Vachio shrugged. "Well, it's a town."

5

Pacho ushered Vachio into the anteroom of the Director's office and introduced him to Julia, Gustavo's receptionist. Julia offered a sinewy, finely boned hand to shake and greeted Vachio in a warm husky voice. She was a slender woman of dark good looks, slightly past her prime, with brown, almond shaped eyes and long black hair that gave her an exotic, Eurasian appearance. Her manner was buoyant, unpretentious, and pleasantly flirtatious. Vachio surmised that she must have broken her share of hearts along the way.

"Gustavo told me to ask your forgiveness, Don Vachio. He is in conference right now with a man from Bucaramanga here on a special mission. Please take a seat and relax. He should be done in a short time," said Julia.

"Well, all right."

"Are you upset?"

"Yes. Because you called me Don. Just call me Vac."

"Very well. If you call me Julia."

"Done."

Vachio sat on the settee near the front door. It had intricately carved mahogany arm rests and plush red cushions, and was matched by an arm chair on the other side of the door. The rest of the room was occupied by Pacho's desk, littered with loose papers, Julia's smaller desk, augmented by a metal typing cart, and a bank of metal files filling one full side of the room. The white plaster walls were decorated with portraits of former directors of the *Casa de Menores* going back to the late 1800s. A noisy, overhead fan pushed the warm stagnant air around the room without offering much relief.

Pacho, in the middle of showing Vachio some of the personal effects on his desk, was distracted by a note passed to him by Julia. He got up and spent some time rummaging through the files, muttering imprecations, his scowl darkening as the needed document failed to appear. Julia finally stopped typing, went to Pacho's desk, and found the document inside a ledger book. Pacho grunted a thanks and sat down to some serious scribbling.

A parade of visitors passed in and out of the office. Most of them just said "Hello" and left. It was obvious they were there to get a look at the *gringo*. Vachio was introduced to a score of people and their names dissolved into a morass of Dons, Doñas, Señores, Señoras, Doctores, Professores, Maestros, and nicknames.

Sitting in the chair, his mind spinning from all the new names and faces, Vachio began to feel disoriented and restless. The "short time" promised by Julia had extended to 30 minutes. Vachio rose from his seat and paced the room. He craved movement and new sights. He felt uneasy, feeling that Gustavo was leaving him with baby-sitters.

Then Vachio became engrossed in one of the portraits. It pictured one of the directors from the 1800s, a man with muttonchop whiskers, an aquiline nose, a thin cruel mouth and sharp angular features. But what really struck Vachio were the slitted eyes and the uplifted chin. It was a portrait of pure arrogance, the face of a man who gloried in power and domination and could believe himself a god on earth. Vachio's skin crawled.

His study of the portrait was interrupted by the arrival of a fat guard with salt and pepper hair, excitedly demanding to speak to Don Gustavo. Julia, barely concealing her disdain for his request, referred him to Pacho. The two men became involved in a discussion concerning responsibility and fault for the actions of one of the prisoners. The talk grew heated and the two men left the office and continued it outside on the street.

"What was that all about?" Vachio asked Julia.

"The usual. Stupid little things."

"Stupid little things can become stupid big things if they aren't addressed. Right?"

"Of course. But I get several petty things a day like this from functionaries. My job is to determine what is important enough to bring to Don Gustavo's attention."

"That man seemed to think it was important."

Julia sighed and smiled. "Vachio, so you understand right now, everyone in the *Casa de Menores* thinks that what they do is the most important thing and they want attention for it. Unfortunately, if something goes wrong, they don't want to accept responsibility for it."

This answer made Vachio even more curious, but Julia refused to explain the details of the guard's complaint, fending off his follow-up questions with good-humored evasions. Then she stopped answering Vachio's questions all together and concentrated on her typing. Vachio's patience wore thin as the short time approached an hour and Gustavo failed to call him.

"Well, I'm going for a walk," Vachio announced abruptly.

"What?" said Julia, looking up.

"I'm wasting my time here. If I don't do something soon, I'm going to fall asleep."

Julia laughed. "Wait one moment. Don Gustavo should be about finished. Let me check with him."

Julia entered the inner sanctum and after a minute of banter, interspersed with laughs, she returned and said, "Go right in."

Vachio stepped into the office and stood just inside the doorway for a moment. Bright sunlight flooded the room from two huge barred windows. A man in a suit sitting before Gustavo's desk turned and smiled a welcome to Vachio.

"So, how was the tour of Garrotero?" asked Gustavo, his manner jovial, rising from behind his large desk at the back of the room and motioning for Vachio to come forward.

"It was an education."

Gustavo chuckled. "With those two, I can imagine."

Gustavo introduced Vachio to the man in the suit. He was a fiscal controller from the SENA office in Bucaramanga, just returned from a budget conference in Bogotá.

"So, Vachio, if I may have your indulgence again," said Gustavo. "We have just a little more business to finish up here and we'll be off.... Please, have a seat."

Vachio took a seat at the back of the room on a chair matching the ones in the outer office. As the two executives resumed their conversation, Vachio studied the room. Gustavo's office was twice as large as the outer one and contained four red plush chairs and, presumably for meetings with unwashed *gamines*, several bare wood ones. On the wall behind his massive desk hung two large maps, one of Colombia and the other of the Departamento of Santander, as well as a handful of neatly framed diplomas and awards for public service. In the left hand corner of the office, hanging limp from a wood pole, was the red, yellow and blue barred flag of Colombia. A handsome blonde wood bookcase filled with scholarly and legal tomes, some with leather binding, and a glass-fronted liquor cabinet with bottles and cut glass decanters sat within easy reach of the desk. The wall to Vachio's left and the one behind him were adorned with full-length paintings of the principal icons of South America's independence from Spain—Bolívar, San Martín, Sucre, and Santander. The white plaster walls, the hand carved wood ceiling beams, the lime green shutters, and the red-brown ceramic floor tiles gave the office a warm earthy ambiance. The ceiling fan and a more modern portable one atop the bookcase kept the room comfortable. Vachio liked the office. It was serious and loaded with history but not at all oppressive. It bespoke understated power and reflected the personality of a man who was simple in style but secure in his abilities and intelligence.

Gustavo stopped his conversation long enough to have *panela* tea and wedges of jellied guava with slices of cheese on top brought in for Vachio and for his visitor, Don German. While the men snacked, a series of polite questions were directed at Vachio. Then Gustavo and

Don German continued their enthusiastic insider's discussion, leaving Vachio to speculate on its import. Again and again Vachio heard the phrase, "*La Obra*" mentioned, uttered by Gustavo as though it were a benediction. Consumed by curiosity, Vachio was about to interrupt them and ask what they were talking about when Don German turned to him and asked, "Have you been out to see *La Obra* yet?"

Before Vachio could respond Gustavo said, "No, not yet. I plan to take him out to see it later today."

"What is it?" Vachio asked Gustavo.

"It's the new *Casa de Menores* we are constructing on the outskirts of Garrotero. Wait until you see it. It is incredible."

Vachio nodded and shifted in his chair. His supervisor had mentioned something about a new facility under construction. But at the moment, he was more interested in the current *Casa de Menores.*

Finally, after more discussion of *La Obra*, Gustavo rose from his chair and with his arm around German's shoulder escorted him to the door of the office.

"So, Gustavo, we're fine until the end of next month," said German. "But then, you know how it is...it's up to God and Bogotá."

"You worry too much, my friend. One has to have faith."

"I'm an accountant, Gustavo. I prefer a guaranteed budget."

"Well, I'll go to Bogotá in early December and see about a Christmas gift for us to take us through the New Year."

"I'll pray for your success," said German with a wry smile. "The best of luck."

German shook hands with Vachio and wished him well. Gustavo escorted him to his car and Vachio chatted with Julia while he waited. When Gustavo returned he was all smiles and bursting with energy.

"Now, Vachio, just let me go home and change my clothes and we'll embark on our little country expedition. I'll be only a moment. I live just across the street."

"That's fine. But I do have a couple of questions."

"Yes."

"What happened to my travel bag?"

"I had it taken to my house. Why? Would you like to change your clothes?"

"No. I just wanted to know where it was.... Uh, I also need a place to sleep for the night and for the rest of the week. Is there a hotel I can check in to before we get started?"

"Vachio, don't be ridiculous. You're my guest, of course. You'll be staying at my home tonight and for the entire week if you find the accommodations suitable."

"Well, thank you."

"Anything else?"

"Aren't we going to take a look around the *Casa de Menores* before we take off?"

Gustavo looked at Pacho, betraying just a trace of exasperation.

"This Vachio is determined to change the agenda you set up for him," said Pacho.

"No, we don't have to do it. But you said we could," said Vachio, looking directly at Gustavo.

"Very well. A lightning tour if you wish. Although, I've arranged a complete tour for tomorrow and I wanted you to see things from a fresh perspective.... But, as you please. Let's go."

Gustavo bustled out of the office, past a burly guard armed with a varnished wood billy club at the front street entrance, and led Vachio through a green foyer and into a sun drenched courtyard. Gustavo, with never a look at Vachio, strode to a fountain at the center of the courtyard and put his foot up on a narrow octagonal bench encompassing the base. The fountain featured a handsome two-tiered bird bath with a faded pink and white flamingo, its beak pointed to the sky.

"This is the nerve center of the *Casa de Menores*," said Gustavo in a staccato tone, sweeping his arm in a half-arc toward a line of pastel green doors set into cream-colored walls under an awning of faded brick roof tiles. "Here are the offices of the psychologist, the social worker, the head of discipline, the accountants, our school supply center, and a teachers' lounge. Through that iron gate is the entrance to the central patio where most of the student activities take place. And that door to our right leads to our chapel/meeting hall.... Got it?"

Vachio nodded, dazed and seething with questions, but aware that Gustavo had no desire to give this tour.

"Let's walk," said Gustavo."

Gustavo double-timed through a narrow corridor feeding off the courtyard, past a wide, barred door and an unused room with a caved-in ceiling and a pile of rubble in one corner, and into the kitchen and dining area. Vachio caught a glimpse of a half-dozen women with short stumpy bodies, massive arms, blue smocks, and flushed faces, their hair pulled back by bandannas. Then they were in a semi-open cafeteria with long tables and wood chairs aligned under open-sided *cabañas*.

"So," said Gustavo, "that's everything except for the outdoor patio, the dormitory, and the shops and classrooms. Satisfied?"

"But I haven't seen one boy yet."

"They're all in classes or shops right now. And I absolutely insist that you see them tomorrow. I've prepared an official speech of welcome for you and it's scheduled for tomorrow. You understand?"

"Oh, you didn't have to do all that. My style is informal. A simple introduction is enough for me."

"Vachio, I love to do things like that."

"All right."

"Now how about a coffee before we hit the road?"

"Sure."

They returned to the kitchen and Gustavo presented Vachio to the staff. The women paused for just a moment from their tasks of chopping, stirring, frying, and roasting to smile and bid Vachio welcome. Then at Gustavo's order, an ancient crone with dark, wrinkled parchment skin and strong Indian features shuffled forward and served Vachio a *tinto*, a demitasse of potent black coffee, and a buttered roll.

"Are you married, Don Vachio?" the old woman asked, a gust of wind from the open cafeteria sweeping her wispy, iron gray hair into her eyes.

"No, not yet."

"No? Well, you should be. You look like a healthy one." Then she gave a gummy smile, tapped under her right eye with her index finger, and shuffled back to her chair in a dark corner of the kitchen. The other women giggled, and a few made bawdy comments concerning Vachio's build and possibilities. Then the kitchen boss made a pointed remark to the youngest of the crew, a short sturdy girl with ruddy cheeks who was stirring a huge cauldron of soup, asking her what she thought of this eligible foreigner. Vachio felt his ears burn and he gulped down the coffee as though it were a shot of liquor. His ears began to buzz and nervous energy made him feel almost spastic. Gustavo grinned broadly at his discomfiture and exchanged jokes with the kitchen staff. Vachio was relieved when Gustavo took him in tow and lead him back into the courtyard.

"So, Vachio, I'll go change now. Do you want to come with me to the house or wait here?"

"I'll wait here."

Gustavo left and Vachio sat on the bench at the fountain and tilted his chin toward the sky. A pleasant breeze whirled around the courtyard, spinning a few leaves out of the rain gutters on the roof. An almost imperceptible drizzle fell out of the suddenly leaden sky. The cool breeze and the momentary solitude felt good to Vachio. Beyond the edge of the roof, he could see a thick phalanx of darker clouds advancing over the mountains toward the town.

"Vachio! What are you doing there?"

Vachio looked over his shoulder and saw Maria Elena standing in front of her office with a sheaf of files in her hand.

"Nothing much. Just thinking and waiting for Gustavo."

"In the rain?"

"I don't call this rain. But it feels good and cool."

Maria Elena smiled. "Well, don't have too much fun and catch a cold. I'll see you later."

"Listen," said Vachio on a sudden impulse. "Are you in a hurry?"

"Not really. I'm just going to bring these files over to Gustavo's office. Why?"

"I'd really like to meet a couple of the boys before I get rushed out of here for the day. Would that be possible?"

"Maybe. Most of them are in class or shop right now, but there might be a few around. Come with me and we'll see."

Maria Elena walked a few paces from her office to the iron gate Gustavo had pointed out to Vachio earlier. It was a fancy gate, more appropriate for a mansion's outer walls than for a correctional institution, with ornate, wrought iron circles and curly heart designs spaced at intervals down the length of the steel bars.

"Maestro Oliva," called Maria Elena.

A chunky man with curly, salt and pepper hair twisted his torso around and peered through the bars. He was middle-aged, his face grizzled and adorned with a bushy mustache and long sideburns with silvery streaks. When he saw Maria Elena and Vachio, he scrambled to his feet and came to slouching attention.

"Yes, Doctora, at your order."

"Are there any students about to meet Señor Vachio?"

"Yes, Doctora. There is little Abel, as always. And Geraldo, here from the farm with the milk delivery. And Horacio, too ill to attend class."

"Have them come here now if they are able, please."

"Right away, Doctora."

The guard walked halfway down the steps leading from the terrace to the patio and called for the boys. Vachio walked up to the gate and stared through the bars at the patio below. In contrast to the pretty courtyard, it was stark and bleak. A full cement basketball court was divided from a dirt soccer field by two long benches and a few scraggly trees. The building compound enclosing the open grounds were of aged masonry, painted white and institutional green, with a roof of rusting laminated metal and a few scattered old tiles hanging on for dear life. A line of trees with thin trunks and bushy foliage provided a dash of shade and relief.

Vachio's inspection was interrupted by the arrival of a very young boy. He bounded up the steps and threw his face against the gate. Grasping the bars in both hands, he smiled at Vachio, showing pearly, even teeth. The top of his head was shaved to the nubs and his dark eyes glittered with eagerness. Two dogs followed in his wake, wagging their tails and snuffling loudly, catching the scent of a stranger.

"Vachio, this is little Abel," said Maria Elena. "He's the pet of the *Casa de Menores*."

Vachio reached through the gate and shook his strong little hand. The boy was fleshed-out and healthy, his body straining against worn blue trousers and a faded yellow shirt.

Abel chirped out a greeting that Vachio failed to understand. Vachio responded with a simple, "*Hola*!"

"Are you the one who is going to bring us games and toys?" Abel asked Vachio.

"What?" Vachio looked questioningly at Maria Elena. "Where did I get this reputation from?"

"I couldn't tell you," she said, shrugging her shoulders. "But your arrival here is no secret to the boys."

"Obviously."

"Well, I have to deliver these files now. If I can be of further help, just let me know."

"Thanks."

Maria Elena walked off and little Abel tugged at the bars with both hands and repeated his question, "Are you going to bring us toys and games?"

Vachio hunkered down to the boy's eye level and said, "We'll see. After Christmas. We'll see."

"After Christmas? I want them now."

"Don't pester the Doctor," said the guard Oliva. "You heard what he said." Oliva eyed Vachio with a bemused smirk. Unlike his obsequious manner toward Maria Elena, his tone and posture were familiar and faintly mocking toward Vachio. "If he bothers you in the future, just let me know. I'll keep him in line for you."

"He's not bothering me now," said Vachio.

The scuffing of cloth sandals against the concrete steps caused Vachio to turn his attention from Oliva. Two teenagers were approaching; one was tall and wiry with a pleasant open face and the shadow of a mustache, the other had long curly brown hair, delicate features, and moved with an exaggerated feminine sway.

"Ah, meet two more of your students, Doctor," said Oliva. "This skinny one here is Geraldo. He's not a bad sort but he's a real yokel. Didn't even know how to use a toilet when he first came here."

Vachio reached through the bars and shook hands with Geraldo. The boy inclined his head, a grave expression on his face.

"And this beauty over here is Horacio," continued Oliva, gripping the boy by the arm and moving him up to the gate. "Better known as the Princess of the Patio."

"A very great pleasure, Profé," said Horacio in a simpering voice aggravated by a cold. He offered a long slender hand to shake but merely brushed his fingertips over Vachio's palm. "Electric!" he exclaimed, shaking his hand as though it had caught fire.

"Quit the clowning," said Oliva, laughing. "Señor Vachio is a new professor here. Respect him."

"Respect him? I'll do more than that. I want to be one of his pets."

"You're off to a bad start," said Vachio in an even voice.

"Why? Don't you like him?" asked Oliva, grabbing Horacio's thigh in a work gnarled hand. "He's juicy. Don't you think?"

The two boys broke into laughter.

"I guess I don't like him the way you do," said Vachio, looking straight at Oliva's hand on the boy's leg.

Oliva's face reddened and he let go of Horacio.

"I don't like him that way," interjected Horacio.

"Yeah, I can see why. He's way too old for you," said Vachio. Now the two boys were laughing at Oliva.

"I don't go that route," spluttered Oliva.

"Sure. Whatever you say."

"Hey, you have spark," said Oliva, his tone now friendly. "You seem like a regular guy. Just like the fat guy said."

"Which fat guy? I've already seen several here."

"Dolfo."

"Oh, yeah, Barrel Man."

"Barrel Man. That's good." Oliva laughed. "He does look like a walking barrel."

Oliva tried to continue the conversation but Vachio excused himself with an abruptness that startled all of them. Vachio didn't want the guard to get too familiar with him all at once; and although he had held his temper, he was irritated by the way Oliva had tested him.

Vachio turned and saw Maria Elena's office door ajar. He walked over and looked inside. She was at her desk, head bent over another file. "Maria Elena."

Her head snapped up. "Oh, it's you. You startled me."

"I'm sorry.... Uh, are you busy right now?"

"No, not too busy. Why?"

"I'd like to talk to you about those boys I just met."

"Have a seat."

Maria Elena's office was small and ill-lit, with only one barred window opening onto the interior patio. It was sparsely furnished and neat as a pin. Vachio sat down on one of the two metal folding chairs facing her desk.

"Would you like a coffee or something?" she asked.

"No, thanks. People have been offering me a coffee or something every 15 minutes."

Maria Elena laughed. "Get used to that. It's one of our customs."

"Tell me about it."

"So, what can I tell you about those boys?"

"Well, let's start with the little one."

"Abel."

"Yes, him. He sure looks young. How old is he?"

"Six."

"Six? But I thought you had to be at least eight to stay here?"

"Normally you do. But he's a special case. A very sad case." Maria Elena sighed. "Believe it or not, he's here because he killed a little girl when he was four."

"What?"

"It's a truly pathetic situation. The poor little guy has no consciousness of his act. And he's really a sweet natured kid. But the court decided to place him with us because his senile grandmother was taking care of him and she just wasn't capable of looking after him properly."

"Yeah, but a kid his age doesn't belong in a place like this. Couldn't they get someone else to take care of him?"

"They tried. But his only other known relative, an aunt, refused to take him because the people in her little town think he must have been possessed by the devil to kill someone at that age." Maria Elena shook her head. "Superstitions die hard in those kind of places."

"What about his parents?"

"Both dead. Killed in a bus accident when he was two." Maria Elena shrugged. "He was only supposed to be with us temporarily but, for lack of a better alternative, we've just kind of adopted him."

"But how did it happen? How did he kill the girl?"

"It was just one of those things. A senseless tragedy.... He was playing in front of his grandmother's house with a neighbor's little girl and he became angry when she took one of his toys. He hit her in the face with a rock and she fell back and hit her head against the point of the curb, fracturing her skull. She died of a brain hemorrhage before help could arrive."

"Man, what a thing."

"Terrible. But these things are the will of God."

"Huh.... Well, there was another boy. He acted very feminine."

"Horacio."

"Yes. Was he putting on an act to shock me?"

"Not by acting feminine. That's how he is. He was a professional street prostitute.... Originally from Cali, if I remember correctly."

"How old is he?"

"We think he's about 15. And we've had him here one year."

"And the last one?"

"Which? I don't remember. How is he?"

"Skinny. He was quiet and more respectful."

"Ah, yes. That would be Geraldo."

"Why is he here?"

"That's a good question. He really doesn't belong here."

"Then?"

"Well, it's a long story. Geraldo is here for his own protection. You see, he's a country boy from up in the mountains around San Vicente, and through a strange set of circumstances he became involved in an old blood feud..."

"Vachio!"

Vachio turned and saw Gustavo standing in the doorway.

"Let's go. It's time for a little diversion."

6

Gustavo had changed into a short-sleeved sport's shirt, cotton slacks, and loafers. Casual, but still better dressed than Vachio, who wore his customary T-shirt, jeans, and tennis shoes. A steady rain was falling as Gustavo summoned Geraldo from the patio.

"Are you going to give me a ride back?" the boy asked.

"Yes," said Gustavo. "I don't want you to get any sicker than you are in this weather."

"Many thanks, Don Gustavo."

Gustavo turned to Vachio and explained that Geraldo was a trustee who spent most of his time on a small farm belonging to the *Casa de Menores* just outside of town. He had come to the *Casa* to deliver the day's milk and have the nurse check him for a slight fever. The nurse had assured Gustavo that Geraldo had a mild flu that would soon run its course in the healthy air of the farm.

The three of them took off in Gustavo's car and drove to the west side of Garrotero, passing the crumbling walls of the town's soccer stadium, its field so worn by use that only bare patches of turf survived in isolated clumps. Vachio mentally debated whether to ask why Geraldo was detained in the *Casa de Menores*. "A blood feud," Maria Elena had said.

Geraldo sat quietly in the back seat, his eyes looking serenely at the passing scenery, occasionally wiping at his runny nose with the back of his sun bronzed hand. Finally, Vachio's curiosity proved stronger than his discretion. After a couple of preliminary questions that the taciturn boy answered with painful deliberation, he asked, "So how did you come to the *Casa de Menores*, Geraldo?"

"Señor?"

"How did you come to the prison?" Vachio asked, turning to look at the boy.

"Well, I...uh...uh..." Geraldo dropped his eyes and gazed at his lap.

"There's nothing to be ashamed of, boy," prompted Gustavo. "You can speak to Señor Vachio in confidence."

"Yes, Don Gustavo, I know.... But...it embarrasses me."

They passed a row of brand new homes and Gustavo turned onto a dirt road almost hidden by overgrown vegetation. The Renault bucked over water-filled chuck holes and ruts, bouncing Vachio up and down in his seat and rattling his teeth.

"If...if...he doesn't want to talk about it, that's fine," said Vachio. "No problem."

"No, there's no problem. It's all right. He's just shy." Gustavo chuckled. “Most of the other boys would fabricate some fantastic tale for you. But Geraldo’s not like that.... Really, all he did was steal a few goats.”

“Stole some goats? Did I hear you right?”

“Yes. He stole...how many was it, Geraldo?”

“Three, Don Gustavo. I took three.”

“But there were extenuating circumstances. You see...*Epa*!” Gustavo slithered the car around a sharp bend, mud spattering against the windows, and scattered a gang of turkey vultures feeding on the bloated carcass of a pig along the creek bank. They splashed over a sunken concrete bridge traversing a smaller feeder creek and Gustavo had to slow to a crawl to bypass a large boulder that had tumbled off the sodden slope fringing the right side of the road. Gustavo muttered to himself and concentrated on the muddy road ahead.

The rain slackened to an intermittent drizzle and bright sunshine poked through the forest canopy above them. Moisture glistened from ferns and luxuriant bushes lining the far bank of the stream as brightly tinted dragon flies skimmed the roiled water for prey. Vachio made a mental note to return to this spot and enjoy it at his leisure.

The road leveled and widened before them, the surface stabilized by a carpet of pebbles. Gustavo loosened his grip on the wheel and leaned back in his seat. “Now, as I was saying, I can’t blame young Geraldo for what he did. *Carajo*! I might have done the same thing in his place. Or worse,” said Gustavo, nodding at Vachio. “You see, it all began with young Geraldo here doing absolutely nothing wrong. A poor innocent caught up in the web of fate.... Geraldo was living peacefully with his uncle and family on a small farm in a mountain valley up near San Vicente. Doing what he was born to do, tilling the soil, caring for the livestock, minding his own business. But unfortunately, that mountain zone up there is *guerrillero* territory; although, to dignify them with the title of revolutionaries is more than they deserve. To me they’re nothing but glorified *bandidos* and they need to be stamped out.” Gustavo’s freckles darkened and a tight smile appeared. “But anyway, a group of these so-called heroes of the people paid a call on Geraldo’s uncle and offered him protection. That is, in exchange for a monthly allotment of food and drink, they would leave him in peace. You understand so far?”

Vachio nodded and Geraldo stared out of the window with a blank look on his face.

“Well, Geraldo’s uncle was very poor. All he had was a small plot of corn, some vegetables, a few fruit trees, and some pigs and goats. He barely produced enough for himself, his wife, Geraldo, and his seven children without contributing to the welfare of the shameless *bandidos*. So Geraldo’s uncle told the *bandido* leader that he couldn’t afford their tax and have enough left to feed his own family. They told him that was too bad and they decided to make an example of him so the other farmers would knuckle under. At gunpoint, they confiscated all his livestock and threatened to burn him out if he couldn't do better the next time they visited. So, as you can well imagine, Geraldo's uncle was frantic. He needed fresh milk for his little ones and he didn't have enough money to buy more goats. His wife was tearing her hair out, crying and carrying on, screaming at heaven for bringing this misfortune on them. The old man just couldn't take it. He cracked. Instead of doing something, he sat down with a bottle of *chicha* and drank himself into a stupor. But before he passed out, he told Geraldo to go to the other end of the valley and steal a milk goat from the Ortega Family. Like the dutiful nephew he is, Geraldo went and did what his uncle said. And being a poor innocent at that sort of thing, he was overtaken and captured before he got halfway home." Gustavo smacked his lips. "Well, the Ortegas wanted to kill him right there. There was a long history of bad blood between the families from *La Violencia* and it wouldn't be the first murder between them. But then, old man Ortega got a bright idea. He put a rope around Geraldo's neck and led him home as though he were the goat. After they sobered up Geraldo's uncle, they told him, 'Your price to spare this goat Geraldo his life is to sell this farm to me.' Of course, they wanted to pay only a small fraction of the true price. Geraldo's uncle agreed, as he had no future there with the threat of the *bandidos* anyway, and the Ortegas turned Geraldo over to the authorities instead of killing him. That's how Geraldo came to stay with us at the *Casa de Menores*.... Isn't that about what happened, Geraldo?"

"Yes, Don Gustavo," said Geraldo, his placid eyes now glittering with anger. "Exactly as you say."

"Any comment, Señor Vachio?" asked Gustavo.

"Man, that's fucked up. It sounds like Sicily."

"That's certain. But as things stand now, incidents like this occur over and over again. Strange things happen up in those mountains. Those hillbillies have their own code. We call it *La Ley del Monte*. Practically speaking, the sovereign law of this government barely exists up there.... But on the other hand, I also believe the Ortega's had a direct play in the entire matter. For my money, they were in league with the *bandidos* and the rural police. It stinks too much like a set-up. And it was well-known that the Ortega's coveted Geraldo's uncle's land.... But you know, for Geraldo's sake, this might be a good thing. He's away from that cycle of violence and he has opportunities here with us that he could only have dreamed of in that backwater."

"But what happened to your uncle and family?" Vachio asked Geraldo.

"They moved to Bogotá."

"Do you want to join them some day?"

"Of course, for a visit. But not to live. I like it here."

"Geraldo's a very good boy," said Gustavo. "A good steady worker.

He could go free today if he liked but we have work for him on our farm as number one assistant to the maestro. And that may well become permanent if he wishes. Would you like that, Geraldo?"

"I'm well content here for the moment, Don Gustavo. Well content."

"Yes," said Gustavo, winking at Vachio, "without mentioning that he's sweet on one of the daughters of the maestro. Right, Geraldo?"

"Please, Don Gustavo..." Geraldo blushed and ducked his head, a shy grin spreading across his angular face.

They emerged from the overhanging trees onto a stretch of road that was straight and well-maintained, a layer of crushed gravel providing secure traction. A cane field flanked the right side of the road and a narrow corn field the left. They soon came to a cow pasture and Gustavo swung through an open gate and up a moderate incline bordering the field. Three yapping, dun colored mutts raced up to the car and made feints at the tires. They were followed by two chubby little boys, wearing only bermuda shorts and baseball caps.

"*Hola! Hola! Hola!*" yodeled Gustavo, pulling off to the side of the road and parking under the heavily laden branches of an avocado tree. One of the boys turned and ran toward an open-sided, palm thatched *cabaña*, yelling, "*Papi! Papi!* Don Gustavo is here."

Vachio got out of the car and was soon surrounded by two curious boys and three suspicious, sniffing dogs. They were soon joined by a short, stocky man just approaching middle-age. He had curly black hair, a thin mustache, a sun-bronzed and seamed face, and wore old dusty work clothes. With mock solemnity, Gustavo presented Vachio to the whole group, including the dogs. Maestro Felipe, whose firm, callused grip and look-you-in-the-eye style made Vachio feel especially welcome, invited them up to the *cabaña* for a refreshment. Geraldo took this opportunity to slip away from them and join a skinny teenage girl who had beckoned to him from a corner of the ranch-style house adjacent to the *cabaña*.

As they walked leisurely up the path toward the *cabaña*, the air redolent of rain washed guava and lemon trees, Maestro Felipe explained to Vachio in a low gravely voice what the farm provided the *Casa de Menores*. "We have small plantings of pineapple and corn, which are principally for our consumption and for sale, and a good number and variety of fruit trees. But most of the land is pasture for our cattle. Milk production, and some cheese, is our main job here. And then we have some chickens for eggs, pigs, and a few ducks and geese." Maestro Felipe heaved a sigh and glanced toward Gustavo. "This is a very small spread. If we had more land I could do much more and save the *Casa* quite a bit of money."

"The farm also gives some of the boys a chance to live and work in a healthy environment," said Gustavo. "Where they can see the tangible product of their labor."

"Do they sleep here, too?" asked Vachio.

"Yes. The house has a dormitory just for the boys," said Gustavo.

"Do they try to escape?" asked Vachio.

"Not often. Only trustees are sent here," said Gustavo.

"In my eight years here we've only had three boys run," said Maestro Felipe.

"Huh, they must like it here, then," murmured Vachio, glancing around at the flowers and fruit trees and the low purple hills to the west. "I can see why. It seems pretty nice."

"Speaking of the boys, where are the rest of them," Gustavo asked Maestro Felipe.

"Down in the lower pasture cutting fodder."

"Too bad. We can't stay long and I wanted them to meet Vachio."

"They'll be back shortly. Wait a little while. Or I can send one of my sons for them."

"No. I made an arrangement with Capataz Prudencio for supper. And I want to take Vachio by *La Obra* beforehand."

"Ah, yes, *La Obra*," muttered Maestro Felipe, a shadow crossing his face.

The men sat at a rude wood table under the shade of the *cabaña*, surrounded by sweet smelling rose bushes. Chickens and broods of chicks scratched at the nearby hillside. Vachio stretched out his legs and took a deep breath. He liked it here. The peace and quiet, the cornstalks shimmering in the sun, the lazy pasture and its well-grazed grass.

"Have you ever tried *chicha*, Señor Vachio," asked Felipe.

"No.... But it's some kind of drink, right?"

"Yes. And I just happen to have some fresh home brew. Would you like to try a little?"

"Well... "

Felipe was already on his way to a nearby shed. He returned with a jug of milky white liquid. "Made from the sweetest corn," he said, popping the lid.

Vachio looked doubtfully at the jug. The liquid resembled curdled milk and had some weird fibrous stuff floating around in it.

"Try it. This is a day to experience new things," said Gustavo.

Felipe poured a generous serving into a chipped ceramic mug and passed it to Vachio. He poured another for Gustavo.

"No, thanks," said Gustavo, laughing. "It looks too rich for my intestines." Felipe nodded and kept the mug for himself.

"Health," said Felipe, raising his mug. Vachio took a sip. The *chicha* had the consistency of watery oatmeal and a sour taste. He looked over the rim of his mug and saw Felipe eyeing him expectantly. Vachio downed the rest of it, and almost gagged as the rough viscous liquid clogged in his throat. He choked it down, helped by a few swats on the back by Gustavo. Then he peered at Felipe through watery eyes.

"What are you trying to do to me?" asked Vachio.

Felipe smiled. "You can't drink it that way. This is unrefined *chicha*. You have to drink it slowly and savor it."

"Savor it? I don't think so."

Gustavo and Felipe cracked up, and after a good laugh at Vachio's expense, it was time to go.

"Well, I hope you'll be back for a visit soon. I'd like to show you around the entire farm," said Felipe to Vachio.

"I'd like that. This seems like good place to relax."

"It is that.... If you don't have to break your back working here," said Felipe, shooting a quick glance at Gustavo walking a few strides ahead of them.

Vachio grinned. "I'll come back alone later in the week. I'd like to hike around this whole area."

"That's fine. You're welcome anytime.... And the *chicha* should be better. It needs to age a little."

"It needs to age a lot before I'll drink anymore. I don't think it'll ever be my drink of choice."

Felipe chuckled. "Don't say that. You just need to develop a taste for it. You'll see."

Gustavo and Vachio drove off, chased down the incline by the yapping dogs and two of Felipe's young sons. Gustavo turned left on the gravel road and drove deeper into the countryside.

"It would seem that Maestro Felipe liked you, Vachio. He usually doesn't talk that much in an entire week."

"Well, I liked him, too. He seems like a straightforward, easy to get along with kind of guy."

"He can be..."

"But?"

Gustavo chuckled. "Maestro Felipe is a good man. He does a fine job with the boys we send him. But unfortunately, he sometimes forgets that the farm belongs to the *Casa de Menores* and not to him. And that it's my job as Director, in conjunction with our dietitian, to decide what should be produced for the overall good of the entire operation."

"Is that a problem?" asked Vachio, involuntarily shrugging. "I mean, does he just offer ideas and suggestions or does he do what he feels like?"

"He does what I tell him. But he has his own ideas and he can be a real burro.... He still thinks he's running his own farm in Venezuela."

"Oh, I understand. He's used to being his own boss."

"Exactly. And let me put it this way, his farm in Venezuela went out of business."

"Well, anyway, now that we have a moment, can we talk a little about my job?"

"What do you mean?"

"Uh, you know, what you expect of me. How much money is available for programs. Things like that."

"Vachio, not to sound evasive, but I'd really prefer to wait until tomorrow to discuss those things. Please, just relax and enjoy the rest of the afternoon and evening. Tomorrow I promise you my undivided attention and a complete rundown on all aspects of the *Casa de Menores* pertaining to you. Agreed?"

"All right. I won't mention it again.... Today."

"Good. And now, we're on our way to something very important to the future of the *Casa de Menores*. *La Obra*. My work. Something I've labored years to make a reality. Something that will be the crowning achievement of my life and career in public service. The new *Casa de Menores*."

"I'm looking forward to seeing it."

"You're going to love it. It's going to be incredible." Gustavo took a deep breath. "For recreation and sports, we'll have an Olympic swimming pool, one full length soccer field and four micro fields, two basketball courts, tennis courts, and a large game and recreation room. Additionally, we'll have an auditorium for films, concerts, and plays. You'll have your own office. We'll have modern classrooms, shops, and dormitories broken into small units. I could go on and on. But you'll see it. The new *Casa de Menores* is going to be a model for the future. A shining star of progress and enlightenment for all Colombia."

"It sounds fantastic," said Vachio, carried away by Gustavo's enthusiasm. "When will we be moving in?"

"Well, there are still battles to be fought with the bureaucrats in Bogotá before it's completely built and operational. But if all goes well, and I fully expect it will, we should be able to shift the majority of our operations there within six months.... A year at the latest."

Gustavo quieted down and concentrated on driving over another rough stretch of road. To their left, a procession of small farms rolled past, to their right, the immense sugar cane field continued. Gustavo slowed as they neared a crossroads and prepared to turn right. Suddenly a roan horse and rider galloped directly into their path. Gustavo slammed on the brakes and the car skidded on the gravel, fishtailing just around the horse and throwing up a cloud of dust. Gustavo regained control of the car and stopped. Vachio turned and looked through the swirling dust at a rearing horse and a young woman fighting to calm him down. She was dark and pretty, her face avid and unafraid as she brought the horse under control. Then she gave them an insolent look, as though the close call were their fault, and spurred the horse on, her long black hair streaming in the wind as horse and rider disappeared into a cornfield across the road.

"What an idiot!" exclaimed Vachio.

"An imbecile," agreed Gustavo, throwing the car into gear. "That was too close for my liking. There is no way I expected her on our side of the crossroads. One of the big cane hauling trucks would have nailed her for sure."

"Who was she?"

"I don't know. I've never seen her before. She's probably someone from Bucaramanga who came out here to ride."

Gustavo drove another mile, paralleling a chicken farm and the same cane field, and turned right again onto a dirt and loose gravel road. Now the low hot sun was in their eyes, the glare and the billowing dust obscuring even the high mountains. Insects splattered against the windshield and a fine powdery dust filtered into the car. Vachio rolled up his window and looked to the side of the road, watching the monotonous stalks of cane roll past. He was hot, sweaty, and anxious to get out of the rearing, plunging car. Then he spotted some cane cutters, their faces streaked with grime under their straw hats, machetes glinting in the sun as they hacked at the tough cane. Vachio wondered how they felt. Or maybe after a while at that kind of brutal work they mercifully felt nothing and grew completely numb.

"Are we almost there?" asked Vachio.

"Almost," said Gustavo, wrestling the steering wheel as the car slithered over a bare powdery patch of road.

"Man, this road is terrible," said Vachio.

"Yes, and for good reason. Heavy equipment from the construction site and the big trucks to haul the cane come through here regularly. They're later going to pave the road with tar and gravel. But they don't want to do it until we're finished with the construction."

"That makes sense."

"The construction is just around the bend here," said Gustavo, speeding up and taking the curve on two wheels. He stopped in front of a stone arch entranceway. "Here we are. Our future home."

Vachio was pleasantly surprised. A low stone wall spoked off the arch and bordered the road, containing a beautifully landscaped grassy knoll that leveled off above them to a line of cedar trees. Lush tropical bushes and flowers were set in beds, spotted adroitly amid the meticulously maintained lawn.

"Well, it seems like you are just about ready to move in," commented Vachio.

"Not quite," said Gustavo, smiling wryly. He put the car in gear and proceeded through the arch. They drove up a heavily graveled, tree-lined path and stopped under the spreading branches of a cacao tree. A small group of workmen were sitting in the shade on the stone wall beside a cement mixer.

When Gustavo emerged from the car he was greeted by a ragged chorus of, "Don Gustavo, how goes it? Don Gustavo, what's up?"

Gustavo acknowledged the greetings by saying, "Fine, fine. And you all? How goes *La Obra*?"

The men's expressions turned sullen when he mentioned *La Obra.*

One of them averted his face and spat over the stone wall. They were a grimy, hardbitten lot, dressed in a mishmash of worn crusty work clothes.

"Where is Maestro Vargas?" Gustavo asked the men.

"Here, Don Gustavo. I'm on my way," called a booming voice. A tall bulky man was approaching them from a footpath that led to the top of the knoll. He wore a gray, shapeless felt hat, the brim pulled down over his eyebrows, accentuating a wide smile splitting a cheerful moon face. He had massive arms and legs and a barrel chest, and wore good work boots, thick brown pants, and a beige, short-sleeved shirt splattered with specks of cement. He carried a long shovel slung over his shoulder as though it were a rifle.

"Ah, Maestro Vargas," said Gustavo, greeting him with a firm handshake. "How are you, my friend? How goes *La Obra*?"

"As well as can be expected, Don Gustavo.... Given the circumstances."

Vachio pricked up his ears and moved closer to get in on the conversation.

"Do you have any good news for us?" Vargas asked Gustavo in a low voice.

"Yes, Señor," said Gustavo in loud reply. "Our funding has been approved until the end of December. I received the word just today."

"Did you hear that, boys?" said Vargas, turning to the workmen. "We'll be able to celebrate Christmas after all."

They summoned up a few approving clucks and half-hearted smiles but they looked more like men who had been granted a stay of execution than anything else.

Gustavo took Vargas by the elbow, guided him up the path away from the men and asked, "What has been the mood of the men over the past week?"

"Not good. How could it be? They were all worried about *La Obra* coming to a stop. Some of them were already talking about pawning their tools to have enough money for the Christmas season."

"Huh, I can imagine. It must have been hard for them to concentrate on work with that uncertainty hanging over them."

"Yes, but they still produced. These are good men. I have full confidence in this crew. I just hope we can keep them. A few more late pay checks and I won't be able to hold some of them. After Christmas, it's going to be very difficult to keep them here even if the checks come on time. It's a powerful temptation for any working man to head for Venezuela right now. Those guys are fat and sassy with their oil money and they can't get enough construction workers right now. They pay a decent work man five times what they pay here. Hell, I'm tempted to go to Venezuela for a while."

"Tell me about it," said Gustavo. "Who would have ever thought those lazy bums of Venezuelans would be so lucky as to swim in oil.

There is no justice in this world."

Vachio, listening quietly, repressed a snicker.

"So, what are the prospects for funding at the same level for the New Year? Or even a little more. Building materials are slated to take a big jump in price," said Vargas.

"I can't promise you anything. But I'm going to Bogotá in a few weeks to see what money I can shake out of those *pingos*."

Vargas emitted a raucous laugh. "And I can only promise you that if God wills us the money the original plan called for, we'll finish on time and under budget."

"God has nothing to do with this. It all has to do with those self-important suits in the capital."

"It's just to say, Don Gustavo. You get us the money, we'll do the job."

"I know you will..."

Vargas cast a long curious look at Vachio, following a few steps behind.

"Ah, forgive me," said Gustavo, giving Vargas a sheepish look. "I want to present a new friend from the United States. For the moment he's here on a short visit. But, if all goes as expected, and I have no reason to think otherwise, he will be working with us for a long time."

Vachio stepped forward and his hand was enveloped by Vargas' massive, sandpaper rough hand. Vargas looked Vachio up and down. Then he half nodded, as though he had seen something he was looking for, and released Vachio's hand.

"My name is William Vargas. You can call me Willy."

"All right. You can call me Vac." The two men grinned self-consciously.

"Do you speak much Spanish? Or only a little?" Willy asked Vachio.

Gustavo chuckled and said, "He speaks well—maybe too well. I've already noticed that his tongue has a sharp point."

"Is that right? Well, good. He'll need it around here." Willy patted Vachio on the back. "Don't let anyone pull your leg without giving it back to them even harder. That's the Colombian way. If someone calls us a son-of-a-bitch, we call them a triple son-of-a-bitch."

"Right," said Gustavo dryly, "but make sure they're not armed first.... Now let's keep walking. I want Vachio to see *La Obra*."

They walked to the end of the path onto a broad, immaculately kept lawn, trimmed shrubbery bordering the fringes and brightly colored flower beds and saplings splashed amid the grass. The lawn fronted a sprawling, three story construction, the front with a finished stucco facade and fresh paint. They walked around to the side and it was all bare steel girders and a tangle of construction materials. *La Obra* was a great dummy front, like a Hollywood stage set. Vachio shook his head incredulously and thought, No way they finish in a year, let alone six months, unless they hire more men than those six guys taking a break outside.

They entered from the side and William explained the floor plan and the work in progress. Gustavo walked energetically from one unfinished room to another, his face beaming with pride. "This will be my office.... This will be for the social workers.... This will be the teacher's lounge.... This..."

Vachio and Willy, trailing behind him, exchanged more than one look, silently understanding each other's thoughts. Gustavo was intoxicated by his vision of *La Obra*, forgetting all decorum and behaving like a love sick teenager. But *La Obra* was a great skeleton. The bottom floor was tangled with loose electric cables, piles of bricks, steel girders, sacks of cement, and a host of other construction materials and implements.

Gustavo finally slowed down and turned to Vachio. "So, what do you think of *La Obra*, friend Vachio? It's absolutely magnificent, certain."

"Well, uh, it's truly impressive. The size, the scale, the concept.... But, I'm puzzled by one thing."

"What?"

"Why did you guys do the front landscaping before finishing most of the actual building construction?"

"Don't you like the landscaping?"

"Yes, very much. It's fine work. But now you'll have to waste men on maintaining it that could have been used for construction work. Not to mention the money. I mean, I always considered landscaping finishing work. It's usually done last, isn't it?"

Willy broke into his raucous laugh and shook his hand furiously. "Listen, I like the way this *gringo* thinks. Do the functional work first and the details last. And when I work for private companies like the Coffee Association, that's how we do things."

Gustavo turned red and his freckles darkened. "Very good, Señor Vachio. You're a quick guy. That was an excellent observation. Unfortunately, things aren't that simple."

"Why not?"

Gustavo smiled. "Vachio, do you believe that outward appearances are important?"

"I believe they're important to people who think they're important."

"But what do you think? Personally."

"I don't give it that much importance.... I feel like that saying you guys have in Spanish: Although you can dress the monkey in silk, he is still a monkey."

Again Willy broke into laughter and even Gustavo had to smile.

"Yes, well, that's fine and all so true. But let's just say, for the sake of this particular case, that appearances are very important—especially when you have to deal with unimaginative government bureaucrats and you need to impress them so that they will give more money for an underfunded project. Now do you understand?"

"Yes and no. I understand that you have to impress fools, but why waste money on landscaping before you have a functioning building when you could do the same thing with a model or an artist's rendition? In fact, why couldn't the very same boys from the *Casa de Menores*, with proper supervision, do the landscaping themselves and save you guys a ton of money?"

"Vachio, I congratulate you," said Gustavo, barely concealing his exasperation. "You have a truly practical mind. And if some of those *pingos* in Bogotá I have to deal with thought more like you, the construction might already be finished and we would be sitting in my new office sharing a drink. But that is only a beautiful dream. Now let me tell you how it really is here." Gustavo raised his arm in the air and said in a low intense voice, "In order for this project to have any chance at all to reach fruition, I've had to present and maintain a grand vision, a beautiful facade if you will. If not, government enthusiasm and financial support quickly wanes." Gustavo's voice started to rise. "You see, there are always certain reactionary, visionless imbeciles who say things like, Why build such a wonderful facility for a bunch of dirty *gamines*? And left unsaid is, They're little better than animals. This facility would serve us much better as a university extension..." Gustavo paused for breath, his eyes almost popping out of his head.

"So what you're telling me," said Vachio, breaking in excitedly, "is that this new *Casa de Menores* isn't a done deal even if you get all the money and finish the construction."

"No! It will be done! I swear it!"

"All right, all right," said Willy in a soothing voice, stepping between Gustavo and Vachio. "We believe you already."

Vachio stared pensively at the jumbled construction material on the floor. He believed the intent and purpose behind Gustavo's words, but he didn't want to count on promises that couldn't be kept.

"Well, I should be getting back to work," said Willy to Gustavo.

"Go, then," said Gustavo, already calm. "See you soon."

"Vachio, pleasure to meet you," said Willy. "Come by here anytime. We can have a beer or two. Maybe go to a *casa de cita* some day after work."

"All right, man. *Ciao*."

As Willy ambled away, Vachio turned to Gustavo and asked, "What's a *casa de cita?*"

"It's a whore house."

"Oh."

"Vachio, please come with me," said Gustavo in a subdued voice. "I want to show you one more thing."

Gustavo led Vachio from the interior of the construction to the gently sloping meadow behind it. A handful of humpbacked cattle grazed peacefully, slapping at black flies buzzing their flanks with the bristly tufts at the end of their tails. The meadow covered several acres, bordered by a cornfield at the back and barbed wire fences on its flanks.

"All this land belongs to the new *Casa de Menores*. The full regulation soccer field and the micro fields will be located there," said Gustavo, pointing to the scattered band of cattle. "The swimming pool is almost finished. There," he said, pointing down the slope to a long ditch half-filled with muddy water. Gustavo looked Vachio square in the eyes. "As you can see, much has been accomplished. This project is no dream."

"Yes, but..."

Before Vachio could finish, Gustavo turned from him, walked a few steps up the slope, and stooped down to grab a tuft of grass. Then, holding the grass in his clenched fist, Gustavo turned and faced the high mountains, a thoughtful expression on his face.

"You know, Vachio," he said in a soft voice, "I've spent three years on *La Obra* already. And more years than I care to remember planning and thinking about it.... Can you understand? I believe most men want to leave a monument to their life. Something positive to show that they stood for something during their lifetime. Well, this new *Casa de Menores* is my monument." Gustavo turned and looked at Vachio for the first time, his eyes moist. "I don't know if I could stand it if all my hopes and aspirations for *La Obra* went like this." Gustavo tossed the grass into the breeze and watched it scatter along the slope. "I want this more than anything I've ever wanted in my entire life."

7

Vachio, Gustavo, and Capataz Prudencio were seated under a beehive *cabaña*, a kingsize bottle of *aguardiente* before them, drinking shots out of the bottle cap and washing them down with tepid beer. *Vallenato* music blared from a portable tape player, the wailing singer, the dominant accordion sound, and the rasping accompaniment of a wash board reminding Vachio of Cajun country. A pleasant breeze ruffled Vachio's hair and the sun was sinking toward the high mountains, throwing a creeping shadow over the cane field just across the road.

Despite the softening afternoon and the endless supply of funny stories and jokes provided by Gustavo, Vachio felt tense and on-edge. Capataz Prudencio, sitting directly across from Vachio, tossed down his shots as though he were drinking water. His hard dark eyes swept back and forth across the cane field as though he expected trouble at any moment. His aquiline nose, wide drooping mustache, angular face, and graying barblike chin whiskers gave him the look of a human bird of prey. Occasionally, the dark intensity of his slitted eyes rested directly on Vachio, making him feel as though he were a mouse about to be pounced on. Prudencio let Gustavo do most of the talking, but at timely intervals, he would fix Vachio with those eyes and, though he couched his words in polite phrases, ask almost insulting questions about Vachio's background. It was clear Capataz Prudencio considered Vachio a tenderfoot—a citified *gringo* without a clue.

Vachio took one drink to Prudencio's two and fidgeted under his scrutiny. He had known more than one person like Capataz Prudencio—high-strung, always on edge, alert if not eager for trouble, and with a highly cultivated sense of machismo that had to be constantly reaffirmed—from his neighborhood. Vachio was quite certain that the machete strapped to Prudencio's side had been used for more than just cutting cane during his checkered career.

After a time, Capataz Prudencio called to his woman, who was hanging out wash next to their house, and told her to bring them food. The woman, as wiry-strong and tough-looking as her husband, appeared a few minutes later with a plate of greasy *empanadas*, crumbled *arepas*, and a *cilantro* flavored salsa.

Vachio selected an *empanada* and dipped it into the salsa.

"You better be careful, Don Vachio," said Prudencio. "That salsa will burn your tongue off if you're not used to it."

Vachio smiled at Prudencio. Gotcha, he thought. Vachio theatrically redipped the *empanada* in the salsa and took a huge bite. Prudencio stared at him, a mocking gleam in his eyes, waiting for Vachio to cry out and douse the fire with beer. Vachio chewed deliberately, a big grin on his face. The *empanada* was stuffed with rice and ground beef. The salsa was very mild to Vachio's taste. He poured more salsa onto the *empanada*, ate it, and smacked his lips.

"Very tasty," said Vachio. "But the salsa doesn't have any bite at all."

"What do you mean it doesn't have any bite at all? It has a bite," said Prudencio.

"Well, I suppose that depends on what you're used to, no? I mean, where I come from, California...we have many Mexicans. And I love Mexican food. I eat it all the time there. And I tell you, they have some salsas that make you feel like someone stuck a torch up your ass. Now this salsa..." Vachio dipped the *aguardiente* cap into the salsa and drank a straight shot. "...has an excellent flavor. My compliments to your wife. But no self-respecting Mexican would serve a salsa this mild to their baby."

Gustavo burst out laughing and Prudencio had a stunned look on his face. Vachio smiled benignly.

"Well, that's certain what you say about the Mexicans. They have that reputation. But you're not Mexican," said Prudencio.

Vachio shrugged. "You don't have to be Mexican to like pain."

Gustavo laughed again and slapped Vachio on the shoulder. "That was a good one, Vachio. I'll remember that one."

Prudencio now eyed Vachio in puzzlement, not sure how to take this *gringo*. A short time later Prudencio's wife came to the table, cradling a live chicken in her arms.

"Prudencio! How about this one for dinner? She's fat and ready."

"She looks good. Bring her here."

She brought the squirming chicken to the table and Prudencio rose to meet her. He took the chicken from her, cradled her in the crook of his left arm, wrapped his thick stubby fingers around her throat, and with a sudden twist of his wrist snapped her neck. The chicken gave a squawk that died in her throat and twitched spasmodically. Prudencio casually handed the chicken back to his wife and she left to pluck it, the dead animal jerking in her hand all the way back to the house. Vachio poured himself another drink, drained it, and stared vacantly at the high mountains.

"Do you like to hunt, Don Vachio?" asked Prudencio.

"Not really. How about you?"

"I'm enchanted by it."

"I imagined that. What do you hunt?"

"Now, mainly deer and wild boar. But when I was a young man, I used to go to the jungles of the Magdalena River Valley and hunt jaguars. That was real sport. Jaguars were very clever and dangerous."

"Were?"

"Yes. There are no more live jaguars close by here. All gone. It's a shame."

"Huh, I wonder why?" muttered Vachio.

"What?"

"Nothing."

"Do you have some kind of moral problem with hunting, Vachio?" asked Gustavo, closely watching his face.

"No. But I wouldn't do it for sport. I mean, if I had to hunt to eat, I would certainly do what is needed to survive. But as I told you earlier, I believe in live and let live. I don't go out of my way to bother creatures that aren't bothering me."

"You mean you like to keep your hands clean," said Prudencio, barely concealing his scorn, his jaw tightening like a steel trap and the cords bulging on his neck.

"It's pretty hard for anyone to keep their hands clean," said Vachio in a mild voice. "For example, you just killed that chicken. But I'm not going to have a problem helping you eat it. That makes me as responsible as you for its death."

This answer seemed to satisfy Prudencio and he relaxed, much to

Vachio's relief.

"Have you ever gone hunting?" Gustavo asked.

Vachio turned and eyed his questioner. Gustavo sat with his hands folded in front of him on the table, his eyes half closed, a vapid smile on his face. But Vachio was aware that this casual pose was simply that—a pose. Gustavo had played the clown and jokester, the crusading social worker, the subtle political animal, and now this—the psychologist. Behind the front of indolent and easygoing host was a subtle, calculating mind. Vachio's psyche was being probed and analyzed, and it was all premeditated and orchestrated by the Señor Director.

"Why do you ask?" countered Vachio, his tone sharp.

"Because I want to know if you make judgments based on pure theory or on actual experience. How do you know you wouldn't like to hunt if you've never experienced it before?"

"I have hunted. A few times. I used to catch frogs, tadpoles, and blue-belly lizards.... But I never killed them."

"That's not hunting. That's a child's play," said Prudencio.

"Now wait a minute. I also went on a rattlesnake hunt once," said Vachio, looking straight at Prudencio. "And we didn't use guns."

"Really? Rattlesnakes?"

"Really."

"But Vachio, I thought you came from San Francisco?" said Gustavo. "Why would you have snakes in a city like that?"

"We don't. But I used to work at a summer camp in the Sierra Nevada Mountains. We had plenty of snakes there. They nest in the rocks and come out to sunbathe when its warm."

"But why would you hunt something like that?" asked Prudencio, eyeing Vachio with a raised brow.

"To eat, man. They're good to eat."

"To eat?" Gustavo and Prudencio looked at each other in disbelief. "You're pulling our leg," said Gustavo, chuckling.

"No, it's true. It's no different than eating iguana. And I know you eat iguana here."

"You've tried iguana?" asked Prudencio, his tone almost respectful.

"Sure. And the eggs, too."

"Iguana is delicious," said Prudencio.

"But tell us about the hunt, Vachio," said Gustavo. "I want to hear about this."

Vachio grinned. He was on a roll now. He could feel himself alive to his audience, words leaping to mind and hands and features dancing to their music. Gustavo wasn't the only storyteller in this company.

"Well, like I said, I used to work at this summer camp.... And we had a baker there, a guy named Luther. An old black guy from Odessa, Texas. That's an oil town out in the plains. It's almost a desert really. And it's a place that rattlesnakes just love.... Anyway, old Luther was always telling us stories about how poor his family was and what it was like to grow up around Odessa during the *Great Depression*. He used to tell us that he was practically raised on rattlesnakes and jack-rabbits. But he was always telling stories and, like most Texans, he exaggerated like hell. You see, Texans are kind of like *paisas* here..."

"Like *paisas*. Yes, the *Antioqueños* exaggerate all the time," said Prudencio. "But they're fun."

"Well, anyway, I thought he was bullshitting. So one day I told him I would believe his story if he cooked me up some rattlesnake stew the next time someone killed one around the camp. Which happened pretty often near the swimming pool. Well, old Luther didn't like this idea. He was irritated with me because I didn't believe him. So he says to me, 'Boy, if I'm going to cook you some rattlesnake stew, you're going to have to come with me on a hunt to help me catch one. That's the only way you're ever going to taste some of my stew...'"

"That's the way it should be," interjected Prudencio.

"Yeah, so anyway, he gets me and another young guy who was teasing him to go out one morning to this rocky place near a big beautiful lake. And all we took for weapons were rocks and baseball bats. 'That's all I ever had to hunt snakes when I was half your age,'" said Vachio, imitating Luther's slow Texas drawl and cracking up Gustavo and Prudencio. "So for hours we were stumbling around on these huge, slippery granite boulders. It's getting hotter and hotter, and we can't find nothing except little baby rattlers that Luther says are too small. I'm about ready to say the hell with it and go back to the camp for a swim when all of a sudden we hear a shriek from the other young guy who was climbing a rock just above us. Well, I almost jumped out of my skin. But not Luther, he's cool and ready. He didn't even have to see what was up. He already knew because he heard the rattle from the snake. So he tells my friend to stay quiet and don't move a muscle unless he wants to get bit. Meanwhile, I was just off to the side and I could see the snake coiled up and within striking distance of my buddy. He was a big ugly one, too. Fangs out, ready for action. 'It's up to you, man,' Luther says to me. 'You got the angle.' Well, I had a rock in my hand about the size of my fist and..." Vachio stood up and pantomimed. "...I just leaned back and let it fly..." Vachio grinned and sat down.

"Well, what happened?" asked Gustavo.

"Huh, what do you think? I hit that snake right on the nose. Knocked one of its fangs right out of its mouth, too. The thing was thrashing around on the ground, almost dead, and old Luther went up to it and finished it off with his baseball bat. Then he takes out his skinning knife, cuts off the head, because they can bite from reflex even when their dead. Then he holds it up by the tail, and its length is almost as long as him, and he says, 'Boy, that was one hell of a shot! Now we got us some West Texas pheasant and you get the first taste.' So he cuts a chunk off the neck and gives it to me. 'Eat it raw, boy,' he says." Vachio stood up and grinned. "Any questions?"

Gustavo and Prudencio were laughing and toasting the story with *aguardiente*. Capataz Prudencio poured one for Vachio and smiled at him with real friendliness.

"I have just one question," said Gustavo.

"What?"

"Are you part Texan?"

"No. I'm 100 percent San Franciscan. A city boy all the way. And I've never gone hunting or eaten rattlesnake again."

"But, man, maybe someday we can go alligator hunting on the upper Magdalena," said Prudencio. "Just give me the word and I'll take care of all the arrangements."

"Uh, we'll see," said Vachio.

"As you say. But I offer you this in all sincerity."

Vachio inclined his head.

"And now," said Prudencio, "let's go to the house for a moment. I want to offer Don Vachio some *guarapo*."

"Let's go," said Gustavo, bouncing to his feet.

The house was a sprawling, one-story building made of cinder blocks and a corrugated metal roof. A jerry-rigged awning of cow hides, stretched over rough-cut wood poles, provided shade in the front of the house and formed a sort of porch. A cooler and a stack of crates filled with empty beer and soda bottles leaned to one side against the wall. Prudencio's wife was out front, preparing the chicken for barbecue on a crude wooden table as live coals whitened on a nearby grill. Loud music blared from a radio in the living room and squawking chickens pecked at corn in the dirt off to the side of the front door.

"Why all the empty bottles?" Vachio asked.

"Because there are no stores out here. Prudencio and his wife make a little extra money selling drinks and odds-and-ends to the cane cutters and whoever else happens by," said Gustavo.

Prudencio went to a nearby tool shed and returned with a large gourd filled to the brim with a clear liquid.

"What's it made of?" Vachio asked, eyeing the gourd with trepidation.

"Pure sugar cane juice and a little bit of beer to help it ferment faster," said Prudencio, handing the gourd to Vachio.

"Don't be shy. Drink up."

Vachio held the gourd to his lips and sipped. It had a slightly sour taste, but he liked it better than the *chicha*. He passed the gourd to Gustavo and it went around in a circle, ritual fashion, until the gourd was drained.

"Shall I get more?" asked Prudencio.

"No offense, Capataz, you're *guarapo* is excellent," said Gustavo. "But I'd prefer a beer. I'm not a *guarapo* man."

"Me, too," said Vachio.

Prudencio shrugged, popped open three beers with the flat edge of his machete, and passed them out. Soon a brisk *cumbia* came on over the radio and, to Vachio's surprise, the sullen Prudencio was transformed into a beaming, almost giddy adolescent. Prudencio went over to his wife and dragged her away from her work to dance.

"Come on, old lady! Shake it!" Prudencio urged her.

She looked embarrassed for only a moment before her face took on a faraway look and she merged into the rhythm of the music, moving her hips and upper body in a rapid shimmy. Prudencio held her by the waist with his right hand and by her hand with his left. He moved like a strutting rooster, his upper body rigid but his legs and feet moving at a quick pace.

"*Epa! Epa!*" shouted Gustavo. "Classic *cumbia*."

"This song reminds me of my Golden Era in Cartagena," said Prudencio, releasing his wife to execute a spin. "When I worked as a hunting guide for *gringos* and had money to burn. *Ay*, what parties we had then." Prudencio took a long swill of beer, wiped his mouth, and called, "Daughter! Come here! Come to dance."

"*Papi*?" A thin adolescent girl wearing a soiled apron appeared in the doorway and looked at her parents with a bemused smile. She had long stringy black hair and sharp features that accentuated her wide brown eyes. She reminded Vachio of a wary young deer going to the stream for a drink.

"Dance with our guest, Señor Vachio. Dance with him, daughter."

Vachio looked at her. She looked at him. Neither one made a move. Vachio didn't really feel like dancing and she looked embarrassed.

"Come on, Vachio," prodded Gustavo. "Don't you know how to dance to this music?"

"Sure, I know how. Whatever the music tells me to do."

"Then?"

Vachio sighed and extended his hand to the girl. She accepted it and they danced. They did a few self-conscious twirls on the hard-packed dirt, eliciting yelps of encouragement from Gustavo and a paternal smile from Prudencio. As soon as the song ended, the girl returned to her cooking in the kitchen and Vachio retreated to his beer.

"And now that we're warmed up," said Prudencio, rubbing his hands together, "let's go play *Palito* while we wait for the food."

"Good idea," seconded Gustavo.

Prudencio grabbed a case of beer from the cooler and led them around the house to a lot in back surrounded on three sides by a barbed wire fence. It was an up-sloping area of ragged weeds and rutted, tan earth. A huge papaya tree shaded the house side of the lot and the far end featured a few tall trees and a long low wood backstop.

Prudencio passed out three fresh beers and said, "The only way to play *Palito* correctly is with a case of beer on hand. Right, Gustavo?"

Gustavo laughed. He had drunk much less than either Prudencio or Vachio.

"What's *Palito*?" asked Vachio.

"You'll soon see," said Prudencio, handing him a softball-sized ball made of light steel. Then Prudencio ascended the slope and placed three sticks, resembling thin peg legs, one behind the other in front of the center of the backstop. Just then a dusty cane cutter showed up with a message for Prudencio and Gustavo handed him a beer.

"Listen, Lopez," said Prudencio, after listening to his message. "You don't have to go back to work and you can drink all the beer you want if you take care of the sticks for us."

Lopez grinned, showing a set of cane-rotted black teeth, and said, "With much pleasure, Capataz Prudencio. At your order." Prudencio grunted and Lopez ascended the slope and took up his post to one side of the backstop.

Prudencio took the ball from Vachio and hefted it in the palm of his hand. "This game is very simple. You just take this ball and try to knock the sticks over."

"Like bowling. Sounds easy enough," said Vachio.

Gustavo laughed. "Easy? This game takes much skill."

"Exactly," said Prudencio. "But the rules are simple. You can't pass this line on your run-up." Prudencio pointed to a line dug in the ground with a stick. "And each player gets one turn per round but three shots per turn. Whoever knocks down the most sticks in the agreed number of rounds wins. You understand?"

Vachio nodded and sipped his beer.

"Good. Now I'll go first so you can see the technique." Prudencio set himself, holding the ball lightly in his right hand, and focused his eyes up the slope to the sticks. After a moment of stillness, he took a short shuffle and rolled the ball toward the sticks. The ball dipped and swerved over the uneven ground but always seemed to right itself and continue on a course toward the lead stick. At the very last instant it struck a pebble and veered past the front stick. It thudded to a stop against the backboard.

"Shit!" exclaimed Prudencio.

"Almost, boss. Almost," shouted Lopez.

Prudencio grimaced and took two more shots. All of his throws were skillfully executed but he managed to down only one stick. With such an uneven surface, luck was a major element in this game. Gustavo took his three shots and had one near miss but a zero score. It was Vachio's turn. As he toed the mark, he felt the three men staring at him with special interest. The pressure of their attention and all the alcohol he had consumed had its effect. His shot was so far off the mark it missed the backstop entirely and rolled under the barbed wire fence, disturbing a family of hogs rooting in the weeds for tubers on the other side.

"Don Vachio," said Prudencio dryly, "the idea is to hit the sticks, not to slaughter one of my hogs." Then he and Gustavo burst into peals of laughter.

Vachio laughed with them but he felt ridiculous and nervous. He rolled another ball in the palm of his hand and stared at the sticks. "Ah, fuck it!" he muttered, and let it fly as though he were pitching a softball. The ball traveled in a low arc, the ground rushing up to meet it, and landed with a splash of dust about ten feet in front and a foot to the side of the sticks. Then it took a crazy sideways hop and struck the second stick which in turn knocked over the third.

"*Epa!* Good shot, man!" called Lopez.

Gustavo and Prudencio were shocked silent.

"That's how I hit the rattlesnake," said Vachio, grinning from ear-to-ear.

"You can't throw the ball that way," said Prudencio.

"Why not? I just did it."

"It's against the rules."

"What rules? All you said was don't cross the line and knock over the sticks. Period. You didn't say how." Vachio looked to Gustavo for support.

"It's just not done that way," muttered Gustavo. "That's not the correct form. And it can hurt your wrist."

"Well, it was a lucky shot," conceded Vachio. "But it's the results that count. Right?"

"That depends."

"Depends on what?"

"You can't do it that way. That's not how we play."

Vachio shrugged and took his next shot in the conventional manner, rolling the ball, and missed by a wide margin. Then he turned, looked directly at Gustavo, spread his palms, and said, "You see. You took away my initiative and instincts. Look at that result."

"Learn the correct form and you'll do better," said Gustavo.

"Correct form," muttered Vachio under his breath, retreating to a bench against the house. He had wanted to argue the point further but Gustavo's stolid convinced countenance had dissuaded him. It isn't worth the trouble, he thought. But if this is a sign of future inflexibility on the job...huh, problems.

They continued to drink beer and play *Palito* until the sun was a fiery red ball over the high mountains. Then in the soothing, brief twilight, a light breeze wafting the sweet and sour smell of the moist cane fields to their nostrils, they adjourned to the *cabaña.* Swatting at a horde of mosquitos, they ate a good dinner of barbecued chicken, fried *cassava,* rice, fried sweet bananas, and a light salad of grated onions and carrots drenched in vinegar. For dessert they had a plate of jellied guava and coffee with a jolt of *aguardiente* in it. This was followed by a shot of *aguardiente* for the road and after this, the tipsy Vachio barely remembered getting into the car and bumping over the pitch dark country road to Garrotero and Gustavo's house.

Gustavo ushered Vachio inside and without showing him around took him into the living room and asked him to wait a moment while he attended to something.

Vachio stood on wobbling legs in the middle of the room, the bright light making him blink like an owl, his surroundings an amorphous mass of shifting objects, the muted street sounds like distant surf. He looked down at the floor, a checkerboard design of black and white tiles, polished to a brilliant veneer, and after a moment it seemed to spin and tilt. A wave of nausea swept over Vachio and he almost lost his dinner. With an effort of will he fought down the nausea by closing his eyes and taking a series of deep and rapid breaths. Slowly he felt control of his functions returning to him. He became aware of the rasping swish of the overhead fan and the cool air descending from it.

Vachio opened his eyes and looked around the room. It was long and narrow. The diaphanous effect of the whitewashed walls dissipated and the furniture and other objects sorted themselves into distinct entities. The front of the room contained only an old cow hide chair, a reading lamp, and a low end table grouped together in a corner. At the back of the room, grouped before an old black and white television, was a handsome set of Neo-Colonial furniture. The set was made of hand-carved mahogany with red cushions, consisting of a couch, a settee, two arm chairs, and a coffee table. A small throw rug of tan cow hide lay under the coffee table and a number of magazines sat on top. One wall was dominated by two large rectangular windows with stout wood shutters that opened onto the street. In between the windows was a small framed portrait of a young Gustavo in military uniform, his hair cropped short, wearing an officer's insignia. On the far wall near the furniture was a large portrait of a dolorous Jesus Christ. On the long empty wall behind one of the armchairs were two crossed swords over a coat of arms. Vachio's eyes scanned along the wall and came to rest on a portrait of a gentleman with black hair, blue eyes, a brush mustache and a benevolent pose. Vachio stared at the portrait in disbelief. He blinked his eyes and moved over to stand directly in front of it. "It can't be," he murmured. Vachio stood there shaking his head. There was no doubt. It was Adolph Hitler.

"Damn! I know I ain't that drunk," he muttered. "This is no hallucination. This is a picture of Adolph Hitler.... What the fuck kind of boss do I have here?"

"Vachio!"

Vachio almost jumped out of his shoes, startled by Gustavo's voice. He turned to face him. Gustavo's face mirrored concern.

"You must be wondering why I have a portrait of Adolph Hitler."

"The thought crossed my mind."

"All right, it's like this, Vachio, and let me choose my words carefully.... It's not that I condone all that Hitler did and stood for—slaughtering the Jews and Gypsies and other such atrocities—it's not that at all. What I admire about Señor Hitler is the way he controlled his people and got them to work for the common national cause."

"You mean the way he brainwashed them."

"I wouldn't use those words. Control and persuasion are more appropriate terms. He appealed to legitimate national aspirations..."

"What? Like world conquest?"

"Vachio, please, hear me out.... If you haven't noticed already, Colombia is a disordered chaotic country. And has been since its inception. What we need here is more discipline and more control of the masses of people if we are to progress and become the powerful and respected country we should be. As a Colombian patriot, I believe Hitler had a model for some of what we need. Do you understand?"

"No. But right now I'm in no condition to understand much of anything."

Gustavo laughed, relieved. "We'll speak of this some other time. For now, I'll show you to your room and you can take a shower and refresh yourself for later tonight."

"Why? What's the program?"

"The mayor of Garrotero is coming over for dinner and to meet you later."

"Dinner? But we just ate dinner."

"No. That was a late lunch. It's still early."

Vachio rubbed his forehead. "You're going to kill me with hospitality."

"Come on, man. You're young," said Gustavo, laughing.

"Fine, at your order."

Vachio followed Gustavo out of the room, giving Hitler a mock salute on the way.

8

Gustavo led Vachio to the central patio, an open-air rectangle at the center of the home lit by a necklace of Japanese lanterns and embellished by a lush display of potted and hanging plants. A garden table and chairs sat at its exact center.

"Very nice," commented Vachio.

"Thank you," said Gustavo. "Except when it rains, this is where I socialize. The living room is too stuffy and noisy. This is my refuge and little oasis."

"Uh huh," murmured Vachio, looking up at a brilliant array of stars in the sky.

"Would you like to clean up now?" Gustavo asked.

"Please."

"Carmela!" called Gustavo in a loud voice.

"Señor?" responded a sonorous voice from an interior room at the other end of the patio.

"Come here and bring a bath towel with you, please."

"I'm coming."

Moments later a young woman emerged from the shadows and bustled toward them. She hit a pool of light cast by the lanterns and Vachio did a double-take. It was the same girl, wearing the same white pullover garment with red embroidery, he had seen near the plaza. The saucy one who had put Dolfo in his place.

"Don Gustavo?" she said, a towel draped over her arm.

"This is Señor Vachio, Carmela. The guest I told you about."

"Much pleasure," she said, smiling boldly at Vachio, then bowing her head slightly and giving him an unabashed once-over.

Vachio mumbled a greeting in return, responding to her interest by feeling hot and dizzy all over. His eyes strayed to her plunging, bare-shouldered neckline.

"Carmela, I want you to show Señor Vachio to his room and give him any assistance he needs. Understand?"

"Yes, Don Gustavo. At your order."

"Vachio, there is a bathroom adjacent to the bedroom. Take a shower and nap if you like. We have a couple of hours before the mayor arrives, and I have a few things to do. I'll talk to you later."

"All right, thanks."

Vachio followed Carmela through a narrow, curtained opening in the wall by the front door and they entered a small, pitch black room. Vachio stumbled against Carmela in the dark and she giggled and took his wrist to steady him as she fumbled for the light. Carmela flicked on the switch and the room was illuminated by a dim naked bulb hanging from a ceiling cord. A small brass bed was pushed against one wall and a four-drawer dresser toward the back of the room against the other, allowing barely enough room for an adult to squeeze past. A niche with shelves was carved into the back wall and a curtain covered an opening off to the side. The windowless room reeked of insecticide.

Vachio covered his mouth and sneezed.

"What's the matter?" asked Carmela.

"This room stinks."

"Because of this." She held up a large can of insecticide that was sitting on the dresser."

"Damn! You guys want to poison me?"

"No, not at all. Believe me, better this than the *zancudos* and mosquitoes. They can give you dengue fever." Carmela shivered at the thought.

"Yeah? Maybe I'd rather take my chances with the mosquitoes. That insect poison could turn me into a slobbering idiot."

Carmela laughed and her tone of voice was warm and intimate. "Hey, you really know how to speak Spanish. I didn't expect you to speak much at all."

"Surprise. But how did you know I was expected? Until today I didn't even know where I would stay."

"Because Don Gustavo told me.... This is my room, you know. He told me someone else would use it for a while."

"Oh, sorry to inconvenience you. Where will you be sleeping."

"With Don Gustavo's sister in a room at the other side of the house," said Carmela, making a face.

"What's the problem?"

"She snores. A lot!... I'd still prefer to sleep here," she said, moving closer to Vachio and smiling up at him. Vachio felt himself getting excited again.

"That's fine with me. We can arrange it."

Carmela backed away coquettishly and pulled the curtain aside at the back of the room. "The bathroom is through here."

A light clicked on and Vachio followed her through another narrow opening and into a small cramped bathroom.

"A shower, a toilet, a sink, and a mirror. Everything you need," she said.

"Not completely."

"What else?"

"A towel."

"Ah, of course. Here." Instead of handing Vachio the towel, Carmela nudged up against him and draped the towel over his shoulder, managing to brush her bare arm along his and crowding him with her hip. Vachio felt the blood rush to his head and as he reached up to secure the towel, he brushed one of Carmela's breasts with his hand. Carmela took a step back, smiling coyly, her eyes wide and a trace of red coloring her cinnamon colored skin.

"You better take your shower now," she said, slowly withdrawing from the room through another door that opened onto the patio.

"Yeah, a real cold one," muttered Vachio in English.

He closed the door and stripped off his grimy sweaty clothes. Then he examined himself in the small cracked mirror over the sink. His eyes were red-rimmed, the lids drooping, and his curly brown hair was disheveled and chalky with dust. He rubbed the tip of his itching crooked nose, broken several times in basketball games and beyond fixing. He combed down his mustache with the tip of his finger and rubbed dirt off his chin. Then he patted his flat stomach with the palm of his hand and surveyed the muscles of his arms and chest. Not bad, he thought. Considering he didn't get as much of the kind of exercise he liked since his arrival in Bogotá, he was still almost as solid and toned as he had been during his senior season of basketball in college. Vachio stretched his arms over his head and raised up on his toes, feeling the suppleness and well-being of healthy youth.

Then he stepped into the shower and turned the water on full blast. It started out lukewarm but quickly turned cold. Vachio was too tired, dirty, and numb to care. He let the water cascade over him, feeling himself melt down to a crouching posture. His head was buzzing from all the alcohol and hot sun but the nausea had completely disappeared. An hour or so of rest on the bed in the other room would give him his second wind. At least enough to face the mayor of Garrotero. Ah, the bed. Carmela came to mind and he felt a warm rush. She had really excited him. But why? As Vachio had told Pacho and Dolfo, voluptuous women like Carmela didn't attract him as much as slim petite women. But it was her boldness he had liked. The way she looked him over, blatantly sexual. No hiding behind a phony reticence, natural and direct. Even her coyness was only a tool to excite him more without seeming to tease. Vachio imagined her climbing into the sack with lusty abandon. The image made him smile.

He shivered and got out of the shower. The warm humid air, languorous and sensual, wrapped around him as he toweled off and went into the bedroom. Still naked, he threw the thin gray blanket off the bed and lay down under the sheet, leaving the dim light on, thinking merely to take a short rest. Vachio closed his eyes and covered them with his hands. His head and body started to spin as though he were on an amusement park ride. Kaleidoscopic images from the day flashed before him like a newsreel, beginning with the green savannah and ending with Carmela's inviting smile. Then the bed began to spin and Vachio felt it lifting into the air and flying through a cold dark tunnel. He was met at the end of the tunnel by a grinning, malevolent Hitler, urging Vachio to join his crusade.

"Vachio! Vachio!"

"Huh?" Vachio eased onto an elbow and twisted his body around to see Gustavo's red head poking through the curtain.

"It's time to get up. The mayor will be here in a short time."

"Yeah, sure. Was I asleep long?"

"Two hours."

"Damn! Well, fine. I'll be right out."

Gustavo's head withdrew and Vachio rolled off the bed. He was still buzzed, his head fuzzy. But worse, his eyes, throat, and nose were irritated and scratchy. "This damn insecticide," he muttered, wiping at his runny nose and rubbing his smarting eyes. "What were they thinking of spraying so much?"

Vachio threw on some clean clothes and evacuated the room. The patio was empty, but muffled music came from the kitchen. Vachio collapsed onto one of the garden chairs and pressed his nose against a broad, rubber plant leaf. He inhaled deeply, feeling groggy and cranky, cursing the insecticide. But a few minutes of fresh air dissipated most of his flu-like symptoms and cleared his head. Man, I don't know about sleeping in that room, he thought, running his hand through his hair. His hair. He needed to comb it. He went to the bathroom and struggled with his brittle, sun-dried hair, snagging his comb on knots and muffling cries of pain more than once. By the time Vachio emerged from the bathroom, he was mentally cursing this latest social obligation and his duty as would-be ambassador.

A few minutes later the mayor and Gustavo's sister arrived. The Mayor, Don Rafa, was a distinguished looking gentleman with silvery hair, a white mustache, and long sideburns. He had a hearty, florid face, an ample paunch bulging out his white *guayabera*, a thick gold chain on his wrist and a gold-plated watch, evidence that he was a man who enjoyed the good life. He gave Vachio a limp politician's hand to shake and regaled him with a grand welcome to Garrotero. Gustavo's sister, Doña Rosa, was a middle-aged, matronly spinster, dressed in black as though she were in mourning. She was fair-skinned with jet black hair and dark eyes. Both Rosa and Don Rafa looked slightly askance at Vachio, running their eyes over Vachio's worn jeans, tie-dyed green and white Michigan State T-shirt, and blue Converse tennis shoes. Vachio imagined their thoughts. What kind of Doctor is this? So young. So informal. So...

After the formal introductions, the men adjourned to the living room while Doña Rosa went to oversee the setting of the table in the patio. Gustavo mixed the guests a Scotch and soda, and after Don Rafa asked Vachio the usual round of questions about his impressions of Colombia and Colombians, the mayor slid into animated conversation concerning local politics and personalities. Vachio listened silently. Gustavo and the mayor were old cronies, and they spoke with an insider's knowledge and understanding that left Vachio totally out in the cold. Still, he followed along as best he could, and kept hearing the name *El Viejo* Miranda. From the context of the talk, Vachio figured him as a real *Honcho*. The mayor, on the other hand, he already had pegged as a glib front man—a flashy guy with a bloated ego who wasn't nearly as important as he tried to project.

Rosa called them into the patio for dinner and Vachio was dazzled by the snow-white tablecloth, silver utensils, antique plates and flickering candles. Dinner consisted of a thin noodle soup, bland white bread and a plate of thin-cut beefsteak, watery rice, boiled *cassava* with a red sauce, and a radish and onion salad. Compared to the afternoon barbecue, Vachio found this meal insipid.

Dinner conversation matched the meal. Except for Don Rafa, who delivered pompous spiels on the grandeur of Garrotero and Santander, everyone was cautious and restrained. Rosa was very much the proper *Doña*, and though she showed flashes of humor and probably had a different personality for other occasions, she kept the conversation on a polite superficial level. Gustavo followed the lead of his older sister, moderating his language and his customary flamboyant style. Vachio was bored to silence. After letting a cuss word slip out and being rebuked with a cold stare by Doña Rosa, he clammed up and only answered direct questions. Thoroughly undomesticated, Vachio loathed these polite dinner parties. But only a yawn or two betrayed his true feelings as his mind wandered off to more agreeable pursuits.

When Carmela came in with a tray of custards for dessert, Vachio rolled his eyes at her. She stifled a laugh and surreptitiously rubbed against him as she served, shaking Vachio out of his funk. After dessert, Gustavo brought out a bottle of coffee liqueur and Don Rafa fired up a fat long cigar, both local products. Vachio liked the liqueur, potent coffee candy, and leaned clear of the pungent cigar smoke spewed forth by the Mayor. Then, just as Vachio was beginning to feel mellow and expansive, it was all over. Don Rafa and Gustavo excused themselves, saying they had to go to a political meeting in another part of town, and Rosa went to the kitchen to clean up.

"You should get some sleep," Gustavo urged Vachio before leaving. "Tomorrow we get into the serious business."

"For sure. I feel dead," said Vachio.

After the men left, Vachio hung out in the patio for a while, hoping to see Carmela. But Rosa cleared the table and Carmela never ventured out of the kitchen. Vachio stayed out under the twinkling stars a while longer, his head drooping from weariness, but finally called it a night when the mosquitoes started getting to him.

He lay on the bed for what seemed hours with his eyes closed, listening to muffled sounds from the street, tossing restlessly. The bad effects of the insecticide returned. His throat became raw, his eyes itchy, and his nose runny. Then, to top it all off, he heard the unmistakable buzz of a circling mosquito. It was too much. Vachio jumped off the bed with a curse and turned on the light. As he searched the dark room he mumbled, "The damn bugs are already genetically immune to this poison.... But I ain't. Give me break."

He located the insect, looking fat and sassy on the wall near the bed, and rubbed it out. Vachio decided to leave the light on in case some of its sisters paid a call. Then he stretched out on his back and started counting to one thousand. Just as he started to doze, he heard the padding of sandaled feet on tiles and the light clicked on in the bathroom. Vachio's eyes shot open and a surge of energy made his heart beat faster. It had to be Carmela. There was another bathroom on the other side of the house for Gustavo and Rosa. Vachio yearned to get up and go to her in the bathroom, pretend he had to brush his teeth or whatever stupid excuse he could think up. But something held him paralyzed on the bed. He lay there quivering, all his senses alive.

A few seconds later Carmela pulled the curtain aside and tiptoed into the bedroom. Vachio watched her with his eyes half closed. She was wearing a short transparent, frilly white slip. She paused for a moment and eyed Vachio. Then a flicker of a smile crossed her lips and she went to the chest of drawers. She bent over and rummaged through one of the lower drawers, giving Vachio an eyefull of her powder blue panties and the bare smooth flesh of her upper thighs. Vachio felt himself trembling with desire. Suddenly Carmela banged the drawer shut and turned to face him.

"Are you having fun watching me?" she asked.

"Yes," said Vachio, raising up on an elbow and grinning at her.

"Why didn't you say something, then?"

"I thought I was dreaming at first. Now I know I'm not."

Carmela smiled and approached the bed, her breasts heaving, her eyes glittering like polished onyx. "So?... Do you like what you see?"

"Very much."

Carmela placed her hand on Vachio's bare upper chest and slowly traced her fingers down, drawing the sheet off a little at a time. "I like what I see, too.... So far."

Vachio gently caught her wrist and held her when she reached his belly button. Though hot flashes were running through him, he was troubled by one thing and he wanted to clear it up.

"Aren't you a little young for this?" he asked in a thick voice.

In answer, Carmela bent over Vachio and kissed him hard on the lips, her tongue probing into his mouth, her long glossy hair cascading over his shoulders and chest. Vachio, overwhelmed by her scent and the feel of her body, wrapped his arms around her and answered her kiss, all scruples obliterated. Carmela finally broke the embrace and, looking down at him, emitted an earthy laugh. "Does that answer your question?"

"What question?"

Playfully she grabbed the sheet and pulled it completely off Vachio. "Ah hah! I see that you do like me."

Without another word, Vachio slid over to the wall and patted the mattress. Carmela pulled the slip over her head and off, kicked free of her sandals, and flung herself into Vachio's arms. They rolled on the narrow bed in passionate embrace, covering each other with kisses, their hands grasping to pull off shorts and panties. When they came completely together it was as though they were on a raft on a stormy sea. Carmela bucked like a wild mare and dug her nails into Vachio's back. She came with a shuddering gasp, and just as Vachio was about to do the same, he pulled out of her and let it go on the sheets. Vachio lay on his side, breathing heavily, sweat rolling down his face.

"Why did you do that?" Carmela asked, prodding Vachio's back with the heel of her hand.

Vachio rolled over and looked her in the eye. She wasn't angry, just curious. "You don't want to get pregnant, do you?"

"If God wills it."

“Huh, I don’t know if God wants it,” said Vachio, shaking his head, “but right now I don’t.”

Carmela was momentarily taken aback by his vehement tone. Then she lay her hand on his cheek and said, “Not to worry, man. I’m as regular as a clock. And this is not my dangerous time.”

“Huh, famous last words.”

Carmela laughed and began tickling Vachio’s ribs. “You have a funny way with words. But you’re too serious in a funny way.”

“I can’t help it. That’s my nature,” said Vachio, pulling away from her and rolling over to look at the wall, a morose expression on his face. Carmela left him alone for only a minute before climbing on top of him and craning her neck to make a face at him. Vachio shrugged her off, her hair was tickling his nose.

“All right, what’s your problem?” she asked.

“No problem. I was just thinking about something.”

“Huh, maybe you think too much.”

Vachio rolled over and grinned at her. “Don’t say that. You can never think too much.”

“Then? Tell me what you were thinking about? Come on! Don’t be like that!”

“Well, it’s just that you bothered me when you said, ‘If God wills it.’ What does God have to do with this. This is our responsibility.”

“Oh, that’s just a saying we use. I didn’t really mean it. But why should that bother you so much?”

“It bothered me because I work with throwaway children. I’ve seen too many of them.... And I don’t want to be responsible for any...”

Carmela, leaning on her elbow, listened to him with an understanding look on her face. When he finished, she sighed and said, “You’re one of these halfway complicated ones...” As she spoke, she caressed his shoulder and ran her other hand along his flank. “...I understand what you’re saying, and it’s well thought. But put your mind at ease. You don’t have to worry about anything like that with me. I’m not a dumb cow. I assure you, everything is fine.”

Vachio studied her face. He believed her. Her demeanor was serious and bright lights shined in her eyes. He gave her a long lingering kiss and it soon led to a second round of more leisurely, gentle lovemaking.

Afterwards, Vachio fell into exhausted slumber and in the blue-black pre-dawn hours he awakened to find Carmela gone. He also found his throat and nose badly congested, and his eyes watery and itchy. “Enough of this shit,” he muttered. He put on his clothes, grabbed the top sheet and the gray blanket and went to the patio to finish his sleep on a hard wicker sofa.

9

Vachio was awakened by the crowing of roosters and a stab of bright sunlight slanting over the patio roof and into his eyes. He got off the wicker sofa, a bit stiff and sore, and put on his shoes. The house was cool and silent, even the insects were taking a break. Vachio decided to go out and explore the town on his own.

He went out the front door and a turn to the right and a short walk brought him to the main street heading toward the plaza. Almost immediately, Vachio had to hop off the street and onto the high narrow sidewalk, pressing his shoulder against a building, to avoid being struck by the driver side mirror of a passing blue bus. Then he received a blast of black diesel fuel. Hacking and coughing, he drew curious stares from a group of women, both young and old, dressed in light-blue cotton shifts. This group and a stream of others, coming from various side streets, were heading for a large building a block ahead. Vachio walked faster and joined one of the groups of women. The sharp acrid odor of fresh tobacco came to his nostrils. He followed the women through a massive doorway and into a warehouse crowded with bales of fresh tobacco leaves. Vachio stayed with the women, smiling at perplexed stares, and entered a huge cigar rolling room. Rows and rows of long tables were piled with stacks of leaves and before each table were men and women, predominately women, rolling the leaves into cigars and depositing them into boxes.

Vachio was so mesmerized by the skill and dexterity of the rollers that he failed to see a man walk out of a nearby glass walled office and approach him.

"At your order, Señor?" questioned a gravely voice.

Vachio turned and saw a man past middle-age, portly, with a curling white mustache, a Panama hat, a long unlit stogie clamped between his teeth, and a frilled *guayabera.* His voice and manner were commanding and autocratic.

"Oh, hello," said Vachio. "I'm just having a look at your operation."

"Are you interested in buying something?"

"Me? No, I don't even smoke."

The man grunted his disapproval and turned to issue orders to a subordinate who was coming over to check things out. Vachio turned on his heel and left before he was ordered out.

He went outside and continued up the street to the plaza, feeling the already hot sun beating down on his bare head. He entered a café across the street from the bus terminal and ordered a coffee with milk and a piece of pound cake. Then he took a seat at a small table at the rear of the café, sipped his coffee, and watched the people come and go, aware that a number of the café regulars were also watching him.

Overall, Vachio felt pretty comfortable. People in the café were neither hostile nor friendly. The regulars talked quietly among themselves and passing friends and acquaintances dropped in to say *Hola* and exchange town news. No one disrespected Vachio's privacy, and except for his clothes and being slightly taller than average, Vachio didn't particularly stand out physically from the crowd. The people coming in and out of the café represented a potpourri of the human race. Many of them were *mestizos*, of mixed Indian and European blood, but there were also people with strong African ancestry, and a good smattering of people with dirty blonde or brown hair and fair complexions. Vachio felt none of the overt racial tensions he had experienced in some other places, and with his Mediterranean skin and features, he realized he could blend in fairly well.

Vachio took his time, drinking in the leisurely, early morning pace of Garrotero. Then he paid his bill and returned directly to Gustavo's house. He walked through the unlocked door and found Gustavo sitting at the patio table with the morning newspaper spread before him, already finishing up breakfast.

"Where did you go so early?" asked Gustavo.

"Just out to the plaza to walk around and drink a coffee."

"Why did you go alone?"

"Why not?"

Gustavo smiled. "You're a little bit independent, aren't you?"

"No. I'm a lot independent. That's my style."

"I've already noticed. And that's good. But I hope it doesn't mean you won't take good advice."

"I'm always happy to take good advice. Bad advice I don't need."

"For sure.... Anyway, how did you sleep last night?"

"Truthfully, not very well. I think it would be better if you didn't spray anymore insecticide in the room. It really screwed me up."

"Really? How so?"

"Man, I had so many boogers coming out of my nose from all the insecticide that I could barely breathe. And I'm not exaggerating."

"Well, if you catch dengue fever you'll feel far worse than that."

"That's hard to believe."

"Believe it. We also call it bonebreaker fever. If you catch it, every bone and muscle in your body will ache. You run a fever and you have no appetite. It's terrible. All you can do is stew in your own juices and try to lie still until it runs its course. And it can last for a week or more."

"I'll take the risk."

"All right, as you wish.... Would you like some breakfast?"

"Sure."

Gustavo summoned Rosa and asked her to bring Vachio breakfast. Then he rose from his chair and handed Vachio the *Vanguardia*

Liberal newspaper.

"There is a story about San Francisco in the paper." Gustavo shook his head. "Vachio, you do come from a strange place."

"Why? What happened?"

"Read the story. It's on the front page." Gustavo's puckish tone turned brisk and businesslike. "I have to get to the office now and prepare things for your interview and tour of the *Casa de Menores*. Be there at nine sharp."

"That sounds very official."

"It is. Today is a day to be serious. You hear me?"

"At your order," said Vachio, bowing his head ever so slightly. "I'll be there at nine on the dot."

Gustavo left and Vachio cleared a space for himself at the table. He unfolded the paper and looked at the headlines. His eyes almost popped out of his head.

MAYOR OF SAN FRANCISCO AND CITY SUPERVISOR SLAIN BY DERANGED GUNMAN AT CITY HALL.

"What?" exclaimed Vachio. Shaking his head incredulously, he quickly read the wire service story. Apparently, former Supervisor Dan White had gone to City Hall to plead with Mayor George Moscone for the return of the position he had resigned. On being refused, the one-time hero fireman went berserk and shot the mayor dead in his own office with a gun he had smuggled into the building, then went down the hallway to kill the openly homosexual supervisor, Harvey Milk. There was speculation that the killings might be tied in some way to the mass suicide in Jonestown, Guyana, involving the formerly San Francisco-based People's Temple of Reverend Jim Jones...

"Here is your breakfast, young man," said Rosa, setting before him a plate of scrambled eggs mixed with diced onions and tomatoes, coffee with milk, a breakfast roll, and slices of fresh sliced pineapple and papaya. Vachio thanked her and stared sightlessly at the food for a good while.

What a month for San Francisco, he thought. First the thing with Jim Jones and now this. Looks like I got out of Dodge just in time. Wonder what the family thinks about all this crap.... Vachio had been shocked by the Jim Jones affair—the mass Kool Aid suicide-murder of more than 900 of his followers in the jungles of Guyana. But he was not surprised that the good Reverend had turned out to be such a psycho. Vachio remembered him well from his years in San Francisco, the omnipresent dark glasses hiding his eyes, the half-crazy sermons to his mesmerized congregations, his slick manipulation of the news media, and the way he had important politicians sucking up to him because he could deliver a large block of votes with a word to his obedient followers. Vachio had figured him as fairly harmless, a latter day Elmer Gantry or someone like that. But apparently Reverend Jim had begun to believe his own bullshit and gone completely off the deep end. Another in a long line of nut cases with messianic complexes who had come to California from the Great American Heartland to redefine themselves. And finding the Golden State more than a little tarnished, and with no where else to go but the Pacific Ocean, had walked the plank and taken a group of credulous innocents with him. Jim Jones, Charles Manson...sure. But Dan White? Vachio had gone to high school with guys like Dan White. He had even met Dan White the year before as he strolled around Vachio's old neighborhood canvassing voters before his long-shot election victory. Dan White, an All-American boy, native San Franciscan, good-looking, athletic, Irish Catholic, kind and polite to the elderly, children, and animals. How could it be? What screw had come loose in his head. The mayor and a supervisor dead? What a tragedy for the City. Vachio shook his head. Someday I'll find out what happened, he thought. But right now I have to focus on business here.

Vachio set the paper aside and ate his breakfast, wondering why Carmela hadn't served him. When Rosa returned to clear away the dishes, Vachio asked her in an overly casual voice, "Is this Carmela's day off?"

"Carmela?... Oh, you mean the girl?"

"Yes. You know, the one who served dinner last night."

"She left on an early morning bus for Socorro. Her mother is sick and she went to take care of her."

"I'm sorry to hear that. When do you think she'll return?"

"Who knows?" said Rosa, shrugging. "Maybe never. Her mother is very ill and there is no one else to look after her.... Would you like some more coffee?"

"No thanks," said Vachio, feeling both disappointed and suspicious. This had the fine subtle hand of Gustavo written all over it. The girl must have been a pro, Vachio thought. Socorro? She might just as well have gone to Bogotá or Cali. Man, what a start to this day.

Vachio walked into the living room and looked at the clock. It was time to go to the *Casa de Menores*.

10

Julia greeted Vachio with a big smile and a warm "*Buenos Dias*" and told him to go right into Gustavo's office. Gustavo looked up from some papers on his desk, greeted Vachio in a serious manner, and told him to have a seat. As soon as Vachio was settled, Gustavo folded his hands in front of him on the desk, leaned forward, and said, "So, what is your plan for the recreation program here in the *Casa de Menores*?"

Vachio was flabbergasted. Then he laughed. "You're joking?

Right?"

"Joking? No, sir. And I must say, I'm more than a little disillusioned by your response. Are you telling me you don't have a plan?"

"Well, sure, I'll be happy to give you a plan. But first I need to know what the budget for the program is, how many boys are here, what facilities are available, the hours when I work with them and who will be available to help me.... Among other things."

Gustavo smiled and pulled a manila folder out of his top drawer. Then he shuffled through the enclosed papers and selected a few sheets. "I've managed to secure a magnificent budget for fiscal 1979," he said, showing Vachio a dizzying list of items running into the hundreds of thousands of pesos. "For recreation and sports we have over 50,000 pesos available. Do you think you can manage with that?"

"Yes, that's plenty.... But I do have a question?"

"Yes."

"What access do I have to the money?"

"What do you mean? Access?"

"I mean, do I get to control my own account and use the money as I see fit?"

"Yes, of course. When you need things for the program, you just itemize them with the estimated cost and submit it to me. Then I can give you the money or a voucher at places where we have an account. Assuming the request is reasonable..."

Vachio nodded his agreement but that "assuming the request is reasonable" troubled him. It sounded like one gigantic loophole. Reasonable. Reasonable to who?

"How many boys are here right now?" Vachio asked.

"Approximately 60. As you can surmise, they come and go, but we generally have between 50 to 80."

"Do you ever have more?"

"Every once in a great while. We have had up to 120. That's our absolute capacity. But I don't anticipate anything approaching that in the near future."

"Do you have any programs already in place that I can build on?"

"Not in any organized way. The guards and our staff psychologist sometimes play soccer and basketball with them but they pretty much make do on their own. As you can imagine, the recreation period is a free-for-all. This condition must be remedied. And I'm looking to you for the organization. That's why you're here."

"How about movies?"

"Oh, yes. We have a projector and we used to show movies about once a week."

"Used to?"

"Unfortunately the projector broke down about four months ago and we haven't been able to get a part for it."

"Why?"

"Well, it was made in Czechoslovakia, a donation from their embassy, and we haven't found a repairman who has ever worked on this particular model. But it worked excellently and I believe the problem is minor." Gustavo rose from his chair and came around from behind the desk. "Come on. I'll show it to you. And then I want to present you to some of the other staff members who haven't met you yet."

They moved to the outer office and Gustavo ordered Pacho to get the movie projector. Pacho soon returned with a blue-gray, heavy metal machine that looked like something used during the heyday of Charlie Chaplin. Vachio forced down his laughter and examined the projector. A serial number and I.D. tag indicated the machine was made in Czechoslovakia in 1953. Gustavo plugged it in, put a film on, and hit the on switch. The wheel spun and the film passed through the lens but no picture or sound was forthcoming.

"We believe the projection bulb and the sound mechanism are damaged," said Gustavo.

"I have an idea," said Vachio.

"Yes."

"Let me take a photo of the machine and when I get back to Bogotá, I can go to the Czech Embassy and see if they can get parts for us."

"Excellent thought," said Gustavo, patting Vachio on the shoulder. "That's the kind of initiative we're looking for from you. Now follow me."

They went to the courtyard and over to the supply store. It was dark and gloomy, the windows blocked by rows of shelves containing art supplies, school books, snack foods, towels and items of clothing, and other sundries.

"You can requisition whatever supplies you need for the recreation program from here," said Gustavo.

Vachio peered at the items on the shelves, nodding his head in approval. "I see many things we can use."

"Don Gustavo." A dumpy, prematurely middle-aged woman came from the shadows behind her desk at the back of the room and approached them. She had a slightly sour expression on her face and small suspicious eyes.

"Ah, Doña Berta," said Gustavo. "I'd like to present you to Señor Vachio. Our newest addition here."

"Enchanted," she said, offering a limp hand.

"The same," said Vachio, studying her face.

"Oh, he speaks a little Castilian. How nice." Berta's tone was mildly sarcastic. She looked at Vachio through frosty eyes, a twisted smile on her lips. Vachio felt his hackles rise. For whatever reason, this woman seemed predisposed to dislike him.

"No, he speaks a lot of Spanish. Communication should not be a problem," said Gustavo.

"Really? How nice."

Vachio remained almost silent while Gustavo chit-chatted with Berta. He breathed a sigh of relief when they left the room.

The next stop was the Psychology Office where Vachio was presented to Doctor Emilio Montoya. He was a young man in his late 20s of dark good looks. Montoya got up from behind his desk and warmly shook Vachio's hand. His diction was clear and precise, his voice affable, and his opening words of greeting short and to the point.

"Well, now that you two have been introduced, I'll leave you to get to know each other while I go to attend to the assembly of the boys in Vachio's honor," said Gustavo.

Gustavo left and Montoya asked Vachio to take a seat. Montoya set his papers aside, gave Vachio a friendly smile, and asked, "So, what do you think of the *Casa de Menores* so far?"

"I'll have to let you know after I see more of it. Up until now it's been the Gustavo show."

Montoya laughed. "Yes, Gustavo can overwhelm a person at first. But he's an intelligent person and a very able administrator.... And if he likes you, a powerful ally."

"And if he doesn't?"

"Better that he likes you," said Montoya earnestly.

"I understand."

Montoya smiled. "I believe you do. You have an air of alertness about you."

"Walking around Bogotá will quickly do that for a person."

"Yes, for some persons. There are others who don't last long enough to acquire the necessary alertness. I myself attended the university in Bogotá. It took me awhile to adjust."

"Where are you from?"

"I'm originally from Popayán in western Colombia. But my family moved to Cali when I was about 10."

"Cali. Cali. Cali. I keep hearing about that place."

"Huh, no doubt as the pleasure capital of Colombia. The beautiful women, the sun, the salsa, the clubs, and the party atmosphere. Am I right?"

"Something like that."

"Yes, that's one side of it. And it's all true. But it has its other dark side.... Naturally, you should see Cali when you have the opportunity to travel. But I strongly recommend Popayán as well. It's a beautiful colonial city with friendly and cultured people. I think you would like it."

"When the opportunity arises," said Vachio.

"Good.... And now, on a more businesslike note, I'd like to know your general philosophy for working with troubled youths."

"Well, if it's anything like working with kids in the United States, and from what I've seen already in Bogotá there are certainly similarities in what a rough urban environment can do to children, well...I suppose my general philosophy is to try to convey to the children that there are choices and options beyond their direct experience on the streets."

"And do you think you can accomplish this through a recreation program?"

"No. I mean, recreation can be a valuable tool to win the children's confidence and open them up to what I'm saying but... I'm looking at myself as more of a counselor and friend than anything else. The recreation program itself I see as providing relief and a form of release from what I see as a very difficult way of life."

Montoya nodded approval. "I like what I hear. I believe you have a sound practical base. But I must caution you, you'll have to guard against a sense of frustration from conflict with others here who take a more authoritarian view of things."

Vachio shrugged. "You get that everywhere."

"Perhaps. But here it is something incredible. God knows, I've been so frustrated at times I've even doubted my own choice of profession." Montoya emitted a dry laugh. "I've even, on occasion, found myself longing for the life of an academic theorist, something I never would have imagined when I was a young activist at the university and certain I could change the world."

"Well, I'm still younger than you."

Montoya laughed. "True. But you can grow old very quickly in this work. Especially when you see some of your best efforts go for naught."

"How so?"

"Well, the truth is, and despite serious problems, we do some very good work here at the *Casa de Menores*. We take street boys, *gamines*, who have been abandoned, or run away from home, living on the streets in horrific conditions—stealing, begging, fighting, engaging in sexual activities at a frighteningly young age—and try to turn them into decent human beings with at least a fighting chance at life. We clean them up, give them a basic education, improve their nutrition so that their bodies and minds can develop in a normal way, and try to give them a sense of values and morality..."

Vachio nodded.

"Ah, yes, this all sounds very good and admirable. But here's the rub," said Montoya, scratching his arm. "Even in the instances of our most spectacular successes, where the boys come out of the *Casa de Menores* prepared to take their places in society as productive citizens, they are all too often shunned and treated as lepers on the outside. You see, Vachio, Colombia is a class riven society, and *gamines* are considered the lowest of the low. Something like the untouchables in India. They can rarely live down the unfortunate circumstances of the past in the eyes of some of our so-called decent citizens. So, as you can imagine, after a few months of this treatment, and in most cases with no family or conventional support group to fall back on, they usually return to an aimless life of crime and drug addiction on the streets. Just to survive. Or better said, just to endure life a while longer. The result: they end up dead, back here with us; or, if they survive long enough, they go to the adult prisons which are truly horrendous places; or, in the cases of the strongest, smartest, and most spirited, they take their place in organized crime. In some of the more benign cases we have boys who become smugglers and run in consumer goods from Venezuela and places like that with more affluent economies.... Are you beginning to understand our dilemma?"

Vachio nodded, a serious look on his face, and said matter-of-factly, "It's not so different from what I was dealing with in the United States as a counselor."

"Really? But one doesn't think of the United States as a class-oriented society."

"You'd be surprised."

"Perhaps I would be. But there has to be more social mobility there for the average person than there is here where family connections are almost everything."

"There is more money to go around, so there is more economic opportunity. But there is a class structure. And the delinquents I worked with in the States, especially blacks and Latinos, absolutely believe there is a class structure...with restricted opportunities."

Montoya was taken aback by this statement. "Yes, well, getting back to the problem I outlined.... I've been developing a pilot program to improve the situation. A bridge program that will see the student past the trauma of leaving here and enable him to continue his education or gain a productive job on the outside. Unfortunately, like many such excellent ideas here, money is a big problem."

"I can imagine. But what..."

"Vachio!"

"Yo!" said Vachio, turning to find Gustavo in the doorway.

"Sorry to break up your session here. But we're just about ready for you."

Vachio rose and shook Montoya's hand. "It's been a pleasure to talk with you."

"The same. And welcome to the *Casa de Menores*. Truly."

Vachio followed Gustavo out of the office and to the gate to the patio. There, a solidly built man in his mid-to-late 30s with curly black hair, a dark complexion, vivid green eyes, and wearing a collared dress shirt and green slacks waited to greet them. He surveyed Vachio with an air of cool appraisal, a sardonic smile on his thick lips.

"Vachio, I'd like you to meet Professor Alfonso Cabrera," said Gustavo. "Our chief of discipline and the man with whom you must most closely work to implement your program."

"Pleasure," said Vachio, nodding formally, feeling the tension emanating from Cabrera.

"Well, I'll leave you gentlemen for the moment to give you a chance to get acquainted," said Gustavo. Then he opened the gate and said, "Oliva. Sound the bell." The loud and incessant clanging of a hand-held brass bell resounded in the lower patio. Then the sounds of sandal-shod feet scuttling over concrete and murmured voices rose to the upper patio. All the while Vachio and Cabrera faced each other wordlessly, sizing each other up.

"So what's your plan for the recreation program here?" Cabrera asked abruptly.

"I don't know yet," said Vachio.

"You don't know? How is that possible?"

"I have to see the facilities and equipment. Know the schedule and all that."

Cabrera gave an audible snort. "Equipment is a waste here. Things like that are too good for some of the animals we have in here. They just destroy everything anyway."

Vachio stared at Cabrera, taken aback, but feeling cold anger welling inside him.

"My advice to you," continued Cabrera, "is that the best recreation program for the *Casa de Menores* would be military-style daily calisthenics. Hard physical exertion and discipline. That's what these boys need."

"What's the point of that?"

"To keep them under control. I'd like them as tired as possible so that they keep out of mischief at night. Or hasn't Don Gustavo told you about some of the filth that goes on here among the boys?"

"He hasn't told me much."

"Well, the filth and depravity is disgusting. It's my job to minimize it. And I expect you to cooperate with me in this mission."

"Cooperate? Of course. But if all you want from me is a program of calisthenics, then you don't even need me here. That's not what I've been trained to do, and that's not what I'm going to do." Vachio's face was flushed and his voice had risen.

Cabrera looked toward the gate to see if Gustavo was within earshot and said in a low voice, "Well then, Señor, maybe we don't need you here." Then he turned on his heel and walked away.

Damn, thought Vachio, staring at his retreating back. His name shouldn't be Cabrera—it should be *Cabrón*.

"Listen, Vachio!" called Oliva. "Don Gustavo says all is ready. Come in."

In a daze, still shaken from his encounter with Cabrera, Vachio passed through the gate and stepped out onto the terrace. There, holding onto the railing with one freckled hand and speaking through a hand-held microphone stood Gustavo, addressing a throng of boys aligned in military formation according to height in the glaring heat of the patio basketball court. Gustavo motioned for Vachio to stand beside him. Then he ran the boys through a series of military commands and salutes. The boys obeyed with alacrity and Gustavo looked to Vachio for approval. Vachio stared straight ahead, unimpressed, thinking this was one weird show. Finally, Gustavo ordered the boys to stand at ease, and introduced Vachio to them with great and flowery formality.

As Gustavo spoke in his measured orator's voice, Vachio surveyed the lines of boys in the patio. Most of them had shaved heads, came in all sizes and colors from darkest black to milky white, and wore a ragged mishmash of clothes. The boys gazed up at Vachio with smiling and speculative faces. Vachio grinned at them and winked uncomfortably as Gustavo went on and on, extolling the virtues of their new recreation director. It took all Vachio's willpower to keep from bursting into laughter as Gustavo slowed his pace to give emphasis to each single word and brought his introduction to a dramatic crescendo:

"...And it is truly this way, my children. In the last two days, I've had the opportunity to come to know and appreciate Señor Vachio. I find him a simple man of good virtues and sentiments. And though he is a genuine Doctor, graduated from his illustrious university with honors, in his simplicity he does not require that you address him as Doctor. But simply as Ga..., uh, Vachio. Because he has come to be your friend. Isn't that right, Señor Vachio?" said Gustavo, turning to Vachio with a broad smile.

Vachio grinned and nodded his head, though he had no recollection of telling Gustavo what he wanted the boys to call him, and he felt something of a subtle putdown in Gustavo's emphasis on his simplicity.

"...Students, Señor Vachio has come here to bring you only good things. Sports, games, movies, arts, drama, and whatever other activities his fertile brain can devise for your diversion and edification. Moreover, Vachio has come here to be your friend and counselor, your confidante and priest confessor. With all the advanced techniques and resources of his country, the great United States of America, at his fingertips and available to you through him, never hesitate to go to him for help. Imagine, my children, he has come all these thousands of miles from the great city of San Francisco de California to share his life with you and give you the benefit of his experience, intelligence, and good heart..."

Vachio felt a wave of dizzyness wash over him. Why was Gustavo laying the bullshit on so thick? Why was he awakening all these ridiculous expectations in the boys? In their place, Vachio knew he would be skeptical of this blatant propaganda. Some of the younger boys were staring up at him, their eyes alight with visions of recreation nirvana. Vachio shook his head in disgust. Gustavo's talk was only setting him up for a great big fall.

"...So, without further ado, I present to you the newest member of the family of the *Casa de Menores*...El Señor Gawdy Vachioooooo..."

The boys broke into raucous and sustained applause, waving and yelling up to Vachio on the terrace. Despite his best efforts to maintain a cool demeanor, Vachio felt chills run down his spine and his body flush with a warm glow. Gustavo pumped his hand and gave him a ceremonial hug.

"Vachio!" said Gustavo, proffering him the microphone. "Would you like to direct a few words to the students?"

"Actually, no," said Vachio without hesitation. "I'll just go down into the patio and meet them."

"As you wish," said Gustavo, the smile fading from his face, appalled by Vachio's lack of style.

"You told them I was simple," said Vachio, and started down the steep concrete steps. Before Vachio reached the patio floor, most of the boys broke ranks and rushed him, eager to be the first to speak to him and shake his hand. The boys mobbed around Vachio, led by the youngest and smallest of the students. Most of the older boys hung back in a group on the fringe, watching Vachio with guarded, vaguely mocking expressions on their hard cynical faces. The younger boys slapped Vachio's back, pulled at his arms and legs, and shouted out their names to him for recognition, offering instant friendship and already asking him for favors. Vachio shook as many hands as he could and tried to learn a few of the names and nicknames hurled at him. The boys jabbered at Vachio in slang-spiced street Spanish, almost a *gamin* dialect, and laughed uproariously when he misinterpreted them. Vachio deliberately answered back in California-Mexican-Vato speak, and was pleased to see the looks of delight and consternation on their faces.

"Maybe we better start speaking to each other in normal Spanish," said Vachio, raising his hand to quiet them. "And all you guys trying to pickpocket me might as well give it up right now. What do you think? That I'm stupid enough to bring anything valuable here among you guys?"

The boys howled with laughter and snapped their hands in appreciation. The older boys exchanged sober looks and moved forward to meet Vachio, the younger ones parting to let them pass. Three of them, the oldest, biggest, and strongest, Rolo, Amarocho, and Pedro Caballero, were a defacto delegation within this group and peppered Vachio with questions and wisecracks. Then, after a few minutes, satisfied with what they had learned, they drifted away and Vachio was again besieged by the clamoring younger boys. Vachio's head began to ache. The young boys shouted each other down, and made so little sense that Vachio could only shrug his shoulders, shake his head, and urge them to calm down and take turns. Finally a few of them began pushing and shoving each other and Gustavo intervened and put an end to the interview.

"All right, boys. It's time for you to get back to your classes," shouted Gustavo. "You'll have plenty of other opportunities to speak to Vachio."

The boys grumbled but quickly settled down and straggled off.

"When will you come back to play ball with us?" asked Leal, one of the older boys.

Vachio looked at Gustavo. "How about later today?"

"No, not today. We have a full schedule. But tomorrow should be all right. You can play at their mid-morning break if you like. At 10:30."

"Fine, then. I'll be here at 10:30," said Vachio to Leal.

Leal snickered. "You better be ready, man."

11

They returned to the courtyard and Gustavo presented Vachio to another new face. "Vachio, this is Fredy. He's our other truck driver and all-around handyman here at the Casa."

The two men shook hands and grinned at each other. Fredy was a short wiry man with wavy dark hair and an infectious smile.

"Fredy, I want you to take Vachio with you when you go to deliver the furniture on the other side of town. Take your time. Show him a few sights if you like. But have him back here in time for lunch. You hear me?"

"Yes, Don Gustavo. I understand."

Gustavo left and Fredy told Vachio to relax and have a seat in the shade under the potted rubber tree. "We still have a few minutes," said Fredy. "They're still loading the truck." Vachio sat and Fredy talked. He had a quick energetic manner and a cheerful voice. He plied Vachio with ingenuous questions concerning the United States and Bogotá. Vachio answered as best he could, even exaggerating a tad when he noticed Fredy's wide-eyed delight.

Finally Fredy let out a wistful sigh. "Can you imagine, Vachio, here I am, almost 30 years old, and I've only been to Bogotá once. In truth, I've hardly ever gone out of Santander.... And look at you. You're much younger than me and you've already seen a lot of the world."

"Not so much. Not nearly as much as I want to see. I mean, one of the goals of my life is to see a lot of things. But so what? Some people never go anywhere and they're perfectly content where they're at."

"That's certain. And personally, I am pretty happy in Garrotero..."

"The Capital of the World, right?"

"Right," said Fredy, flashing his infectious smile. "That's true for me. It's to say, I have a good wife and three fine children and a job I like. I was born in Garrotero and I'll probably die in Garrotero. And that's probably the way it should be. But...I meet someone like you, and I can't help feeling a touch of envy."

Vachio shrugged. "No doubt there are many people who would envy what you have."

"Perhaps. But it's bad to feel this way. Envy is a terrible thing."

"Tell me about it."

"Well, they should have the truck loaded by now. Shall we go?"

Just as they reached the outer doors, a tall lanky man with long sideburns and bowed legs intercepted them and introduced himself to Vachio as Miguel Cardenas, Chief Financial Controller for the *Casa de Menores*. Vigorously shaking Vachio's hand, Cardenas invited him to step into his office and meet his staff. Before Vachio could answer, and ignoring Fredy's protest, Miguel set his strong wiry hand against the small of Vachio's back and swept him into a broad sunny office with three desks and the clatter of busy typewriters. Miguel paused at the first desk and introduced Vachio to Arminda. She was a young woman, angular and willowy, with large expressive eyes and attractive brunette looks. She smiled at Vachio and held onto his hand for just an instant longer than would be considered polite. Vachio gently extricated his hand. He noticed that Arminda had an abundance of curly black hair on her slender pale arms. Miguel chuckled and retired to his desk at the back of the room.

"So," said Arminda, "how is that other *gringo*, Forrest?"

Vachio shook his head, a blank look on his face.

"You know, Forrest. He's even taller than you and very cute. From the Peace Corps, too. He came here once on a visit. But he only knew a few words of Spanish."

"I'm sorry, but I don't know him."

Arminda was unsettled. "But he's a *gringo*, too. One of your *paisanos*."

"Hey, what can I tell you? Not all *gringos* know each other."

"Oh, that's too bad."

"Why?"

"Because I wanted you to tell him that he's an ingrate for not coming back to visit us."

Vachio laughed. "Well, if I meet him, I'll be sure to tell him. And ingrate isn't the right word—he must be a fool not to come back and visit someone like you."

Arminda smiled but her face was wary. "Ah, you already know how to throw flowers. I think one has to be careful with you."

"Maybe."

"Vachio, come on back here," called Miguel. "I want to show you something."

Vachio excused himself and strolled toward the rear of the room. On the way he stopped to shake hands with Jessie, a bespectacled young man fresh out of business college, wearing a white shirt and tie.

He peered at Vachio through his wire rimmed glasses, his thick black hair slicked back with oil, his pencil-thin mustache glued in place. He reeked of cologne and his manner of speaking was just a touch evereager and diffident. After introductions, Jessie immediately launched into a description of the revolutionary accounting system he was bringing to the *Casa de Menores*. Vachio listened politely, unable to follow the technical explanation.

"Hey, young Jessie!" said Miguel. "Leave the poor guy alone and get back to work."

Jessie assumed the look of a scolded puppy and mumbled under his breath, "We'll talk later. I know we have a lot in common."

Vachio made it to Miguel's desk and again had his arm almost dislodged from his shoulder socket by a vigorous shake. Miguel, the boss of the department, was dressed in jeans, a cotton pullover shirt, and cowboy boots. His bare arms were as lean and leathery as beef jerky and his breath smelled of an early shot of liquor. He pulled a photo from one of the desk drawers, got up, and led Vachio over to the sunlight streaming in through the open window. Then he draped his arm over Vachio's shoulder, handed him the photo, and said, "That's me in my younger days with one of the biggest catfish ever taken from the Rio Magdalena. You better believe we made one hell of a *sancocho* with it."

"That is a big one. But what's a *sancocho*?" asked Vachio.

"What? You haven't had *sancocho* yet? Man, you're missing one of the great pleasures in life. It's almost as good as..." Miguel grinned and made an obscene gesture. "It's a soup we make with fish or chicken, or fish and chicken. It's delicious." Miguel touched the tips of his fingers to his lips.

"I have to try it."

"Well, sure, of course! Do you like to fish?"

"Ah, once in a while."

"Great! I knew you were a sportsman. One can tell just by looking at you..."

"Oh, yeah?"

"Yes, one can see this. And anyway, logic dictates that a man who leaves a nice easy life such as one has in the United States, well...that man must have an adventurous soul."

"Huh..."

"So it's settled. We'll arrange a fishing trip to the Magdalena. Down near Barranca. And afterwards, I'll prepare us a *sancocho* with what we catch that you'll never forget."

"That sounds good to me. But we'll have to do it when I come back to work here in January."

"Whenever. It's done. The important thing is that we have the intention."

Fredy stuck his head in the doorway and said in a loud voice, "Don

Miguel, we have to leave now. The truck is ready."

"Ya, Fredy, fine. There's no problem. Relax." Miguel shook Vachio's hand one final time. "It's good to have you here. I expect we'll be seeing a lot of each other."

As Vachio headed for the door, with Fredy waiting impatiently, arms folded and a bored look on his face, Arminda stopped him and said, "Come by and say hello to us once in a while. Don't be an ingrate like your *paisano*."

"Well, I am going to be working here. I suppose we'll see each other.... Often."

"Come on, man," said Fredy, tugging at his arm. "We've got things to do."

They went outside and Fredy gave Vachio a quizzical look and asked, "Did you like her?"

"Who?"

"The girl. That Arminda."

Vachio shrugged. "I don't know.... She was friendly.... And cute."

Fredy grinned wryly and shook his head.

"What's the problem?" Vachio asked him.

"No problem. Just that she's old, brother."

"Old? She looked very young to me."

"Not so young. She's at least 22."

Vachio cracked-up. "You call that old? You're crazy."

"To be interested in her as a real girlfriend, that is old," said Fredy, his tone and manner serious. "For example, I married my wife when she was 16. And we became *novios* when she was 14. That's a good age for a woman you're seriously interested in."

"Huh! Where I come from, you can get thrown in jail for messing around with a girl that young."

"Really?" Fredy eyed Vachio in amazement.

"Really!"

"That's barbaric! What a thing."

"Whatever you say," said Vachio, laughing.

Still shaking his head, Fredy brought Vachio to a large flatbed truck and pointed to the load, mostly chairs with rough cowhide seats and varnished end tables. "The boys make these in woodshop," said Fredy. "They're pretty good, eh?"

"Yes. They look fine. Good work."

Vachio and Fredy climbed into the truck and just as they were about to take off, Dolfo came over to pay his respects.

"So, you have the *gringo* for the day," said Dolfo to Fredy, grinning. "Take good care of him. We wouldn't want our new pet to get lost and get into trouble."

Fredy laughed and said, "Come on, Dolfo, leave the poor guy alone. Let him get used to things."

"Don't worry about it," said Vachio to Fredy. Then he turned to

Dolfo. "Hey, Dolfo, you must get lost all the time."

"What do you mean, son?" he answered, still grinning.

"With that stomach you have...you must like every cantina you find. No wonder they call you Barrel Man."

Fredy cracked up and started the truck. Dolfo spluttered out a weak retort, no longer grinning.

"See you later, Barrel Man," said Fredy, throwing the truck into gear and chugging away from the curb. "Barrel Man. That's a good one," said Fredy to Vachio. "But we don't call him that. Where did you hear that?"

"I made it up."

They drove in silence for about a block, Fredy liberally using the horn to scatter children and dogs until they reached quieter streets.

"How do you like Garrotero so far?" Fredy asked.

"So far...fine."

"And how do you like living in Bogotá?"

"Bogotá? Well...Bogotá is Bogotá."

"Huh. It's ugly, certain? Too many people and cars and thiefs. It's not easy and tranquil like here."

"Well, it has many nice things, too."

"Like what?"

"Um, museums, restaurants, night clubs.... Lots of cultural events and activities from all over. And..."

"What about the women?" asked Fredy, cutting Vachio off.

"What about them?"

"How are they compared to the women here?"

"Damn, I don't know. I've only been here two days."

"Yes, but you must have an impression."

Vachio sighed. "Well, in Bogotá there are many women of all types. It's more cosmopolitan and they dress more elegantly than here."

"Ah, yes?" Fredy grimaced. "Do you have a girlfriend?"

"Uh, yeah. I guess you could call her that."

"Is she Colombian or a *gringa*?"

"She's Colombian."

"Ah, yes!" said Freddy, pleased. "Have you gone to bed with her yet?"

"What?"

"Have you slept with her yet?"

"I don't think I should answer that question. That's between me and her."

"Ah, come on. I don't even know her. You can tell me. I promise not to tell anyone else.... Come on, man. Between men."

Vachio could see that Fredy would never leave him in peace until he gave him something. "Yeah, all right, then. Yes, we have slept together."

"Vachio, no!" said Fredy, a genuine look of horror on his face.

"How could you?"

"What? What's the problem?"

"Vachio, you can't have sex with your real girlfriend. Not with the *novia*. That's what prostitutes are for. You have to respect your *novia*."

"But Fredy," said Vachio, shrugging his shoulders, "we did it with much respect."

Fredy burst into laughter and slapped the steering wheel. "You did it with much respect?"

"No. We did it with much respect. I didn't have to force her into anything. She's an independent woman."

"Ay, Vachio. That's funny."

"If you say so. But I don't get you."

"Well, I guess you don't understand what a real *novia* is..."

"No? Maybe not. What would you call someone like my friend."

"I would call her a lover, not a *novia*. Now that you've had sex with her, you wouldn't consider marrying her. Right?"

"Yes, I would. Why not?"

"Why? Because that's not the way things are done. How could you ever trust a woman like that in a marriage?"

"The same way I'd trust a woman I didn't go to bed with before marriage. I don't see what one has to do with the other."

"Ah well, I guess you guys are different from us."

"Different? How so?"

"You know, you North Americans have looser morals."

Vachio chuckled. "Yeah? That's strange. I know North Americans who think just like you, and Colombians who think like me. Maybe this is just how you think."

Fredy looked uncomfortable. "No, well...ah, let's forget about it." A few moments later Fredy's smile returned and they pulled up in front of a long, low slung concrete shed. Fredy was hailed by a florid-faced man with a huge beer gut. The man summoned two stocky workmen and they began unloading the truck.

"I'll settle up with Don Gustavo later," said the man.

"Ya, that's fine," said Fredy. "We'll be back in a few minutes for the truck."

Fredy grabbed Vachio by the bicep and said, "My house is just a short distance from here. Would you like to see it?"

"Sure."

Fredy led Vachio to the corner and down the street. They came to an older, two story building with a cracked stucco front and faded paint. The front door was open and soft romantic music played on a radio inside. They entered and Vachio was met by the pungent aroma of raw tobacco leaf. Sitting at a low table in one corner of the living room, carefully rolling cigars and laying them in boxes, was a woman in her mid-20s and a girl of about six. They were so intent on their task that neither one noticed the entrance of the two men.

"Love," said Fredy. "Wake up."

"Ay, you scared me," she said, placing her right hand against her bosom and rising to her feet.

Fredy introduced Vachio to his wife and his daughter. Fredy's wife bowed her head slightly, averting her eyes, and mumbled a greeting. She was petite, work-toughened, and still plump from her latest pregnancy.

"Can I get you something to drink? A beer or a soda?" she offered.

Vachio was about to say yes to a beer when Fredy consulted his watch and said, "Um, maybe we better not. We have to get back to the prison right away. Lunch is almost ready and you're the guest of honor. Don Gustavo would throw a fit if we're late."

"Whatever you think," said Vachio.

"Another time, then," said Fredy's wife, grinning shyly. "Someday you have to come over to dinner so that you can try a real Santanderean specialty."

"I'd like that. Just tell me when."

"Soon. Very soon," said Fredy. "Now we must go."

As they walked to the truck, Vachio asked how much money they made rolling cigars.

"Just a few pesos per cigar," said Fredy. "But every little bit helps. Between my wife, my daughter, and my oldest son we pull in some fair extra money. Many families in Garrotero make ends meet this way."

"Aren't your children kind of young to be working?"

"No. They don't do it all the time. Just between school and play. And the little ones are good at it. They have very nimble fingers. Much better than mine which are twisted and clumsy from heavy work."

The truck was swept clean and waiting for them. Fredy drove double-time to the *Casa de Menores*. He pulled the truck around to the back entranceway and into a combination truck port and storage facility. Another metal gate led directly through to the dining area. While Fredy collected the ropes used to keep the furniture secure on the truck, Vachio peered through the gate. A group of guards was seated at a long table facing the already assembled boys under the pavilion. Two other guards, *garrotes* in hand, strolled among the lines of boys, alert to punish any breach of discipline. Gustavo and the other administrators were no where in sight. Vachio watched, quiet and unnoticed.

Then one of the boys spotted him and Vachio, found out, stepped through the gate and onto the tiled stage. He was greeted by whistles, shouted greetings, questions, and lewd jokes. Vachio smiled in embarrassment. The din increased. Suddenly one of the guards cracked his stick down on the nearest table and shouted for silence. The noise petered out almost at once and looks of fear rippled among the ranks of the boys. Vachio, startled by the sharp report of the stick, felt a rush of adrenalin and his face went hard as he looked at the guard, a short burly man with long curly sideburns and a pink scar running along the line of his jaw.

"That's how we handle these savages," said the guard, grinning at Vachio. "You better learn, too."

Vachio shook his head in disgust.

The guard laughed and slapped his *garrote* against his palm.

"Vachio! Hola, Don Vachio!"

Vachio turned his attention from the mass of cowed boys to one of the guards at the table.

"Yes."

"Come sit with us," said the guard. His smile, broad and ingratiating, beamed from a dark handsome face. "You're going to be one of us now. We need to get acquainted."

Fredy came to Vachio's side and put a protective hand on his shoulder. "Vachio is going to sit with the administrators. Don Gustavo made that very clear."

"That's fine," said the guard. "But he can sit with us until they get here. We just want to get to know him a little. And tell him how we do things around here."

Fredy looked doubtfully at Vachio.

"It's all right, Fredy. I need to work with these guys, too."

"Absolutely correct. One can see how intelligent you are," said the guard, his voice syrupy and assured. "Come on, sit with us.... You too, Fredy. Don't put on airs because we have a special guest."

The guard made room for them, ordering two of his companions to an adjacent smaller table, and Vachio and Fredy sat down.

"My name is Jaime Galindo," said the guard, flashing a white-toothed smile, a gold eye-tooth glinting in the sun. "I'm captain of my shift and chief officer of our guard's union. Anything to do with the guards, I'm the man to see."

"Glad to meet you,"mumbled Vachio, instantly wary of Galindo's oily manner.

An awkward silence followed. Then Galindo introduced Vachio to the other guards at the table. One of them, sitting directly across from Vachio, was a thickset man with a square head and close-cropped hair named Torres. He took Vachio's hand in a bonecrushing grip as they shook, and with a knowing leer said, "Dolfo says you're a regular guy. That's certain, right?"

"I don't know what you mean by that," said Vachio, withdrawing his hand.

"What do you mean, you don't understand? You know, a regular guy. Uh uh..." Torres' beetling brows furrowed in thought, his blue-gray eyes showed puzzlement verging on anger.

"What he means by a regular guy," said Galindo smoothly, "is that you have good sensibilities. That you aren't a stuffed shirt Doctor like a lot of these *pingos* here. Dolfo told us you seem to have an understanding of reality. A sense of the practical way to do things.... Is that right?"

Vachio stared into Galindo's grinning face and shrugged. "Only time will tell that. And I suppose it all depends on whether we have the same concept of what's practical."

For a moment Galindo's smile faded and a hint of anger welled in his tawny eyes. Then he laughed and slapped Vachio on the back. "Very well said. I like that answer." Galindo turned and called to the young woman serving soup to the boys. "Blanca! Bring something to drink for Don Vachio."

The girl emptied her tray and came to the guard's table. She was the same one the older women had teased the day before when they learned Vachio was single. Remembering, she blushed slightly, and asked, "What can I get you? A *panela*? A lemonade?"

"A coffee," said Vachio.

"In this heat?" she asked.

"You heard him, girl," said Galindo. "Get him what he wants. Whatever he wants."

"Yes, Profé," she answered, lowering her eyes, her chubby cheeks glowing red. "Right away."

As she returned to the kitchen, her stout peasant body jiggling, Galindo followed her with his eyes and murmured, "What a good girl. A real good one." He turned to Vachio and said in a low voice, "What do you think of her? You like her? She's sexy, eh?"

"Ah, she's not really my type," said Vachio.

"No? But why not?" Galindo grinned and looked at the other guards. "She's almost as juicy as some of the boys in here."

"What did you say?" asked Vachio.

Several of the nearby guards snickered.

"You heard me. And no offense. We're just trying to find out what exactly you like."

"It's none of your business," said Vachio, keeping his tone even. "But I can tell you this, I try not to mix my pleasures with my job. It can get very complicated."

"Yeah, we'll see. We'll see," said Galindo, cackling.

"So what do you like?" Vachio asked him. "Dogs, cats, sheep, everything?"

Instead of taking offense, Galindo cracked up, as did several of the other guards.

"Vachio!"

Vachio turned and saw Gustavo and most of the other administrators preparing to sit at two tables on a raised concrete platform closer to the kitchen. Gustavo's face was flaming red and he clenched and unclenched his fists. "Vachio, you are the guest of honor today. Your place is here at this table with us."

"Yes, of course. I was just talking with the guys here," said Vachio, rising and starting for the other table.

"We'll talk some more later," said Galindo in a low voice.

Vachio joined Gustavo, Maria Elena, Emilio Montoya, Pacho, Don Miguel, and Cabrera at the table of honor. Vachio sat next to Gustavo, puzzled by his anger. Gustavo stared straight ahead, his jaw clenched. The others looked embarrassed and subdued.

"All right, what did I do?" asked Vachio.

Gustavo turned and looked at him, his voice low and tight. "Precisely this, I come in here and find you laughing and joking with the worst and most corrupt of all the guards. That Jaime Galindo. Public enemy number one. What was he telling you?"

"Ah, nothing important. He was just talking trash to see how I would react."

Miguel laughed at Vachio's choice of words; the others maintained a discreet silence.

"Well, watch out for him," said Gustavo, casting a brooding glance toward the guard's table. "He is pure trouble."

"Don't worry, Gustavo. I don't think we're going to be friends."

"I expect that you won't."

With this tense beginning, what should have been a festive lunch turned into a somber affair at Vachio's table. Gustavo kept glancing over at the guard's table, open hostility on his face. Jaime Galindo was aware of this and played it for all it was worth. He held court, talking and cracking jokes in a loud voice, demonstrating his power over some of the boys by giving them pieces of bread as rewards for implied services rendered. Vachio watched this byplay soberly, now suspecting just what he was really up against. Meanwhile, the conversation at Gustavo's table centered around Vachio, mostly polite questions concerning his early impressions of the *Casa de Menores* and Garrotero. As a group, except for Don Miguel who was irrepressibly himself, there was almost none of the frankness Vachio had experienced from them individually. Alfonso Cabrera, in Gustavo's presence, outdid everyone else in making Vachio feel welcome. Vachio regarded him with raised eyebrows, diplomatically answered his questions, and wondered.

It was a good and special lunch prepared in Vachio's honor. Generous portions of thick, barbecued steak for all, accompanied by fried cassava, rice, a light salad, small potatoes, barley soup, and cake for dessert. Several of the boys looked over at Vachio during the meal, smiled, and gave him the thumbs up sign, knowing they were getting this feast because of his presence. Vachio could only smile and shrug in return.

12

After lunch, Gustavo took Vachio on a tour of the workshops and classrooms. They had a metal shop, a woodworking shop, and a shoe shop to produce the standard cloth sandals used at the *Casa de Menores*. Vachio, chastened by his experience at lunch, was relatively quiet and watchful. The Maestros were friendly and the boys, in the presence of Don Gustavo, on their best and most respectful behavior. Vachio felt an affinity for the position of the Maestros. At the formal lunch they had sat apart from the intelligentsia of the *Casa de Menores*. They were not accorded the social status of a true Doctor or professional, yet they were distinguished from the guards as teachers rather than pure enforcers. As a consequence, they seemed to enjoy a more relaxed relationship with the boys than either the Doctores or the guards. What Vachio wondered was where the Maestros stood in the power dynamics between the administrators and the guards.

After the shops, Gustavo took Vachio to the boy's dormitory. The atmosphere was close and fetid, reeking of insecticide, with two long parallel rows of cots on a highly polished tile floor. Two boys, lying in adjacent cots, were sick.

"This is Sergio," said Gustavo, indicating a young boy with a cool compress on his head. "He has dengue fever."

Vachio extended his hand but as the boy reached to shake he moaned in pain and fell back on his pillow.

"That's all right, Sergio. Lie still," said Gustavo.

"Sorry," said Vachio, hastily withdrawing his hand. The boy was pale and wan. To cover his embarrassment, Vachio asked Gustavo, "How do you treat this dengue?"

"You don't. You just try to keep as still and quiet as possible until it runs it's course.... I know you suspect I was trying to poison you, but that's why I sprayed your room so heavily with insecticide. And why it smells of insecticide in here."

"But this boy caught it anyway."

Gustavo shrugged. "You can only do so much. Then it's a matter of pure chance."

The other boy Vachio already knew. It was Horacio, still running a slight fever from an infected cut on his leg, or, more likely, malingering to cut classes and shop. In front of Gustavo, Horacio was deferential and polite, with none of the simpering flirtation of the day before. Vachio shook his head, gave Horacio an ironic smile, and said, "You're a pure macho man today, eh."

"I don't understand what you are talking about, Señor," said Horacio.

Gustavo chuckled as they left the dormitory and said to Vachio, "So, you already know about Horacio."

"I met him yesterday under different circumstances."

"But you know he's a homosexual?"

"I figured it out."

"How do you feel about working with boys like him?"

Vachio shrugged. "I've worked with boys like him before. And for that matter, on other jobs, with men like him, too. I'll take him as an individual.... What's your feeling?"

"Well, I don't worry about Horacio because he's a truly feminine boy. I assume he was born the way he is. But in general, we try to discourage homosexual activity here. Much of it comes from the fact that the boys have no access to women."

"Uh huh." Vachio wasn't convinced it was as cut-and-dried as Gustavo put it, but he wasn't going to argue the point. Suddenly Vachio emitted a tremendous yawn. He felt sluggish and dim-witted from lack of sleep, the heavy lunch, and the stifling heat. "Sorry, I'm not bored, Gustavo."

"No need to say you're sorry. If you feel like taking a siesta, go right on over to my house and do it. You look tired. We can save the rest of the tour for tomorrow. Believe me, I have plenty of other business that requires my attention."

"Well, all right, then. I can barely keep my eyes open."

Vachio went to Gustavo's house feeling on the verge of collapse. But after a soothing shower, and a mere hour or so of rest in the shadowy coolness of the windowless room, he felt revived and ready to explore on his own. Enough of the *Casa de Menores* and being led around by Don Gustavo, he thought. No one says what they really think when he's around. Besides, I'm tired of all the attention I'm getting there. It's time to get away and digest things for awhile.... Ah, I know. I'll go see Maestro Felipe at that *Casa de Menores* farm.

Vachio passed through the dusty streets to the edge of town, almost deserted in the afternoon heat, and at the end of the paved street found the road to the farm. As he strolled along the rutted dirt path, sheltered from the intense sun by the spreading fronds of the ferns and trees along the banks of the stream, the real and imagined problems facing him at the *Casa de Menores* receded from his consciousness. With a start, Vachio realized he was alone with nature for the first time in months. Feeling the gravel crunch under his feet, inhaling the fragrant aroma of wildflowers and damp grass, listening to the buzz of insects and the gentle lapping of the water over the rocks, Vachio grew mellow and relaxed. He walked, feeling the sheer joy of it, losing all sense of time and place.

Thirty minutes of easy walking brought Vachio to the gates of the farm. He was met halfway up the driveway by the pack of yapping mongrel dogs and by a stunted boy with his scalp shaved to the nubs.

The boy calmed the dogs and peered at Vachio from beneath a floppy blue baseball cap. His face was streaked with dirt and his hand was wet and sticky from the ripe mango he was sucking on.

"Hi," said Vachio.

"Hi," said the boy. "Hey, are you that *gringo* guy Geraldo was talking about?"

"I could be. Who are you?"

"Ambrosio. But you can call me Medellín. Everyone else does."

"I can understand why."

Medellín looked perplexed. "Why?"

"Because you come from Medellín?"

"Right." The boy's gray-blue eyes suddenly grew dull, like a placid pond on a cloudy day. He launched into a stacatto monologue, his disjointed sentences sounding as though his mouth were stuffed with marbles. Vachio looked at Medellín askance, unable to understand him. Finally he shook his head and continued toward the house. Medellín, still talking, tugged at Vachio's arm all the way up the driveway.

Near the house, Geraldo appeared, chewing on an *arepa*. He waved to Vachio and came forward to meet him. "Don Vachio, how are you? Maestro Felipe is down in the lower pasture cutting fodder. I'll take you to him or we can wait for him here.... As you like."

"Let's go to him. I came to see the rest of the farm."

"I'm going with you guys, too," chimed in Medellín, jumping up and down.

"No," said Geraldo. "Stay here and finish your lunch. Don Vachio doesn't want to hear your nonsense."

"It's all right. He can come," said Vachio.

"Yeah, that's right. Listen to Vachio, Geraldo. You dumb country yokel. You mishatched piece of dog turd."

"What," said Geraldo, balling up his fist and stepping toward Medellín.

Medellín fled down the driveway, laughing hysterically, the dogs yapping at his heels.

"Little idiot," muttered Geraldo. "One of these days I'm going to forget myself and really let him have it."

Medellín stood before a stick and wire fence near the bottom of the driveway, making faces and capering like a chimp, the dogs dancing around him.

Vachio and Geraldo couldn't help laughing. Suddenly Medellín stopped clowning and gave them a smile.

"What's with that guy?" Vachio asked in a low voice. "Is he a little crazy?"

"More than a little, Don Vachio."

"Geraldo, don't call me Don."

"Yes, Don.... Yes, Vachio."

"Why is he like that? Was he born that way?"

"Well, I don't know how the poor guy was at birth. But I know that he was one of those *gamines* who liked to take the caps off of the fuel tanks of buses and inhale the diesel fumes to get high. And I'm pretty sure he used to sniff glue, also."

"Oh, that's why. He's got fried brain cells. I wondered why I was having trouble understanding him before you came."

"We all have trouble understanding him sometimes. He just doesn't make any sense."

"He did when he insulted you."

"Yes. He's good at that. That part of his brain works."

"Huh. Can he work?"

"Truthfully, not very well. Maestro Felipe doesn't want him here."

"Then why is he here?"

"Because Don Gustavo wants him here. His filthy mouth is always getting him into problems in the patio and he gets beat up a lot. So, Don Gustavo is right. Medellín does better here because we've learned to ignore him when necessary. But he drives Maestro Felipe crazy."

"How old is he?"

"I don't know exactly. Ten or 11, maybe."

"Man, he could pass for seven or eight with that body of his. But his face looks like some one much older."

"That's the way it is. He's a real *gamin*."

Medellín opened the gate and went through to a pasture bordered by tall leafy trees and a burbling stream along the lower perimeter. Vachio and Geraldo followed behind him. Before they had gone very far they spotted Maestro Felipe coming toward them. He was pushing a wheelbarrow overflowing with fresh cut, long coarse grass. Right behind him came another boy with another full wheelbarrow and behind him came a line of cows and calves herded by two yipping boys wielding green saplings. Medellín raced forward to help herd the cattle, yipping and slapping his thigh as though he were riding a horse. Two of the cows lowered their horns and backed protectively against their calves, snorting and lashing their tails.

"Hey, be still!" yelled Maestro Felipe, stopping to turn and fix Medellín with a furious look. "You're spooking the cows, you little fool."

Medellín stopped his antics at once, and fell in beside one of the boys at the rear of the line while keeping a wary eye on Maestro Felipe. Vachio approached Felipe and said, "How goes it, Maestro?"

Without replying, Maestro Felipe pulled out a green handkerchief and dabbed at the sweat running down his bristly chin. His face was brooding and hard set.

"If this is a bad time, I can come back on another occasion," offered Vachio, feeling distinctly uncomfortable.

Maestro Felipe scowled, thrust the handkerchief into the rear pocket of his soiled pants, and said, "No, it has nothing to do with your visit. It has to do with those fucking bureaucrats at the *Casa de Menores*....

Please, pardon my bad mood."

"Hey, no problem. But what happened?"

Maestro Felipe gave Vachio a quick suspicious look. "Ah, it has no importance," he mumbled.

"Whatever you say. But if you tell me, it stays between you and me. I need to find out what it's going to be like to work at the *Casa de Menores*. For me. That's why I'm on this visit."

"Well, I'm sure they won't treat you like they do me—with such little consideration.... So yes, I'm going to tell you. Because I don't care if those *pingos* know what I think of them or not."

"They won't hear anything from me."

Maestro Felipe hefted the wheelbarrow, waved the rest of the procession forward, and began walking and pushing at a fast pace. Vachio fell in beside him. "It's like this, Vachio, the damn bureaucrats at the *Casa de Menores* do what they want. They're totally unreliable. They failed to order a new shipment of cattle feed on time and I get stuck cutting grass all day to feed them when I should be working in the cornfield. They completely throw off my work schedule. But they don't give a damn. They just give me lame excuses or say that I didn't put in the requisition on time. Sure, it's my fault. I'm not allowed excuses if something goes wrong and the *Casa de Menores* doesn't get its full ration of milk. But for them...Shit! The life of a working man is hell. If they would just let me order the things directly, this wouldn't happen. I tell you..."

As Maestro Felipe continued his tirade, Vachio stared at the ground, almost sorry he had got him started. Felipe stopped for breath and Vachio said, "That's really shitty."

"Ah, but what is one to do? That's how life is when you're in my position."

Maestro Felipe pushed his load to the concrete floored feed and milking station, part of it covered by a corrugated metal pavilion, and banged the steel wheel barrow skids onto the ground. "You better stand clear," he said to Vachio. "The cows don't know you and they get nervous with their calves around."

Vachio stood back as Maestro Felipe helped the boys coax the cattle into their feeding stalls with slaps on their rumps from his callused hand. The cows eyed Vachio with suspicion as they moved past him, keeping their big bodies between him and the calves. Maestro Felipe grabbed a pitch fork and dug it into a pile of dried hay next to the trough. One of the boys started feeding the fresh grass into a steel grinder. Vachio stood with his hands in his pockets and watched them work, Felipe's complaints running through his mind. Will things be this way for me, too? Or maybe this Felipe is just an old whiner, bitter about losing his own farm and having to work for someone else.

Maestro Felipe ordered half the boys to go to the upper pasture and collect grass there. Then he turned to Vachio and said, "Sorry,

Vachio, but I don't have time to show you around the farm today. And I can't spare Geraldo because I need him to supervise the younger boys in the upper pasture. But you're welcome to look around for yourself. Sample some fruit. Whatever you want. I just have too much to do before nightfall."

"Hey, no problem," said Vachio. "I understand. I just came out here to relax and get away from things anyway. Some time alone will do me some good."

"That's good. Because I already have more than enough of my own to handle. And except for Geraldo, Don Gustavo sends me boys who don't know the meaning of real farm work."

"Are they so bad?"

"Ah, no. They try. But most of them are from cities and it takes them a while to get the hang of things and build up their strength. Then when they're finally capable, they get rotated back to the prison or sent home, and I have to start all over again with new ones. What do you think of that?"

"Well, I suppose Gustavo wants as many of them as he can to get an opportunity to learn something useful."

Maestro Felipe grunted and resumed forking hay. Vachio said goodbye and wandered back toward the now empty lower pasture. He stopped to pick a couple of oranges from a tree bursting with the fruit and immediately peeled one and ate it. He strolled along the bank of the stream, most of it hidden by dense undergrowth, thinking about the *Casa de Menores*. From what he had already seen and heard, Vachio knew the *Casa de Menores* was a house divided—even worse than his terse job description had implied. This isn't a challenge, it's more like Mission Impossible. But it shouldn't be dull.

Vachio found a break in the bushes, near the back end of the pasture, where the ground was bare and trampled from the cattle going to drink from the stream. He sat on a big flat rock in diffused sunlight under a willowy tree. He sucked on his second orange and stared at the shallow trickling stream, watching dragon flies and mosquito hawks dive bomb for prey. He thought about everything he had heard and seen over the last few days. The bombast of Gustavo and Pacho. The quiet reasoning of Maria Elena and Emilio Montoya. The not so subtle overtures from the guards. And the boys. Especially the boys. For the most part, their situations were so pathetic it made Vachio's head ache just to think about it.

After a while of quiet contemplation, Vachio grew drowsy. He got off the rock and, careful to avoid hidden cow pies, spread his shirt on the ground and lay flat on his back, interlacing his fingers over his eyes, savoring the pregnant aroma of the plants and the soft breeze rustling through the tree tops. He felt himself gradually drifting away with the breeze.

"Vachio! Hey, Vachio!"

Vachio shot upright, startled from his sleep. It was Medellín standing before him, an impish look on his face.

"You were sleeping, eh?" said Medellín.

"Yes. Why did you wake me up that way? You want to give me a heart attack?"

Medellín laughed. "You looked funny."

"Funny, eh?" Vachio jumped up and tackled Medellín, tossing him softly onto the spongy ground.

"Now you look funny," said Vachio, looking down at the giggling boy. "Now what do you want?"

"Maestro Felipe wants you to come up to the house for a drink. He's all finished for the day."

Vachio looked at the sun; it was dropping quickly. He had been out for a few hours at least. He felt refreshed and energetic. He stretched out his hand and helped Medellín to his feet. Medellín grabbed Vachio in a bear hug and held on. Vachio picked him up and carried him like a sack of potatoes, Medellín laughing and burbling nonsense.

"Come on, boy," said Vachio. "Get on your feet and walk now. I don't know where I'm going. You have to show me the way."

For a moment Medellín looked at Vachio in astonishment. Then he raced ahead, yipping like a cowboy, slapping his hand against his thigh.

13

Vachio returned to Gustavo's house at dusk. Rosa opened the door for him and said reproachfully, "Where have been? Gustavo has been looking for you?"

"Oh, here and there. Why was he looking for me?"

"To tell you that you'll be eating dinner tonight at the *Casa de Menores*."

"That's fine."

A moment of awkward silence followed. "He's over there right now waiting for you," said Rosa.

"All right. I'll just wash up and go."

Rosa gave Vachio a funny look and went to the kitchen. "What's with her?" Vachio mumbled. "I'm not Gustavo's pet dog."

Vachio found Gustavo in his office, bent over some papers. He was in good humor and jokingly asked Vachio, "What happened? Did you get lost in our great metropolis of Garrotero?"

"No, I got lost in the country near the farm."

"Oh? Well, good. I hope you worked up an appetite because you're right on time for dinner. Let's go already."

Dinner was a far cry from lunch. The only administrator eating with them was Don Miguel, a bachelor, and the food was sparse and bland. Rice, boiled cassava, plantain, lettuce and onion, a fried egg, a dinner roll, and a thin potato soup.

"Is this a typical meal here?" Vachio asked Gustavo.

"Yes. What do you think?"

"It's sufficient. But it could use more fresh vegetables instead of so many starches."

"We've tried that. But the boys just don't like it."

"And vegetables are considerably more expensive than the staples like cassava, rice, and potatoes," added Don Miguel.

"Why?" asked Vachio. "Are they scarce here?"

"No. We have everything here," said Gustavo. "Though this is a subtropical zone, we grow cold weather vegetables and crops on the Mesa de los Santos. We have carrots, radishes, spinach...we even have apples and pears, though of poor quality."

"Then why are they so expensive?" asked Vachio.

"Because most people here are accustomed to their starches. It's the tradition. And most of the typical dishes are cooked with them. Even wealthy people with the money to buy what they want tend to eat starchy meals."

"So where do the vegetables go?"

"We ship most of our cold weather produce to Bogotá," said Don Miguel.

"But whenever you want vegetables for yourself, Vachio, just go to the main market here and you can get whatever you want. The prices probably won't seem too high to you," said Don Miguel.

"Yeah, maybe."

During dessert, Gustavo called two of his favorite *gamines* over for a chat. One was Rolo, about 15, and the other was Fabio, about eight. Despite the differences in their ages, they recited almost identical lines, as though they had rehearsed. They told Vachio how much they appreciated the *Casa de Menores* and what a wonderful opportunity Don Gustavo was giving them to get their lives together and prepare for the future. Vachio took their testimony with a grain of salt. He remembered how differently Horacio had behaved in Gustavo's presence. But he did note a genuine respect and affection toward Gustavo from these boys.

Gustavo went to his office for a few minutes and Miguel took the opportunity to introduce Vachio to two of the night shift guards. One of them, Ramon, was a Che Guevara look-a-like with a brown beret and a scraggly beard. The other, Garcia, was a graying man, short and rotund, with a ready smile and a hearty laugh. Both of the men were friendly, and expressed enthusiasm for an organized program of recreation. Then they excused themselves and supervised the return of the boys to the patio.

When Gustavo returned he took Vachio through the corridor to the heavy metal doors of the guard's quarters. The room was cavelike, humid as a sauna, with low ceilings, sweating walls, and the musty smell of dirty socks and stale urine from an open toilet stall. Three off-duty guards, wearing tank tops and shorts, puffing away on cigarettes and cigars, looked up only briefly from their game of cards to acknowledge their guests. The card table was illuminated by a hanging naked bulb. Four cots were ranged along the back of the room and the peeling blue walls were plastered with beer posters and pictures of seminude models.

Gustavo led him to an unoccupied corner of the room and asked, "What do you think of the guard's dormitory?"

Vachio grimaced. "I think I like the boy's dormitory better."

"Really?" Gustavo looked crestfallen.

"Yes. Why?"

"Well, it's that, I was thinking about where you might live when you come back to work here in January.... And if you want, we could set up a place for you in here. There is plenty of room."

"I don't think so," said Vachio, wrinkling his nose. "But thanks anyway."

"But why not?"

Vachio didn't know where to begin. The room was horrible. But he could see Gustavo was in earnest and he didn't want to hurt his feelings. "Well, you know, I like to read a lot. And the light in here is bad.... And there's no privacy."

"Oh, is that all." Gustavo switched to his best sale's pitch voice. "That's no problem. We can set up partitions so that you have your own area. And get you a good reading lamp..." Vachio was shaking his head."...It would be ideal in many respects. You can stay here free of charge, with all your meals provided and your work at your fingertips.... You could save plenty of money for traveling..."

"I appreciate the offer. But I'd rather find a place in town." Vachio's tone was definite and firm.

"Very well," said Gustavo, obviously disappointed. "But I would do it if I were in your place."

"But you're not. And I need my privacy sometimes. I know that I need it."

"As you say." Gustavo rubbed his temple. "I might have another suggestion for you by tomorrow."

"I'll be listening."

Gustavo brought Vachio back to the kitchen and they had a drink and passed the time with the kitchen staff for a while. Then Gustavo asked Vachio to follow him and they went straight to the patio. The turnkey was surprised to see them and fumbled around with the keys before letting them onto the terrace. This gave one of the duty guards, Ramon, time to come over and meet Gustavo, his eyes shifting nervously from his visitors to the patio below.

"Don Gustavo, at your order?" said Ramon. The other guard, lounging in a chair at the end of the terrace, leaped to his feet and went to the railing.

"It's nothing, Maestro. I'm just here to show Vachio what the boys do here at night. Go back to your station."

Gustavo and Vachio moved up to the railing and peered down into the patio. Vachio squinted his eyes to better see the shadowy figures moving about under the murky yard lights. His attention was immediately drawn to a group of boys playing basketball. They were using a ball so old and worn the black rubber inside was bulging through the leather. Vachio chuckled, watching the erratic bounces the ball took, remembering how he had often played with a ball just like that.

"Why are you laughing?" Gustavo asked him.

"The recreation program can definitely use a new basketball. That's my first order of business."

"Of course. We'll get you two new ones if you want. That's more than provided for in the budget."

The two of them reverted to silence and Vachio scanned the entire patio floor. Another large group of boys was playing micro soccer. The rest were broken up into scattered knots, talking, spinning tops, playing table games under the roof awnings and, more than a few, lying on benches with their arms wrapped around each other.

"As you can see," said Gustavo, breaking the silence, "it's total chaos here at night."

"Chaos? I don't agree. I see a very definite order to what they're doing, and most of them seem to be having a pretty good time."

"You think so?" said Gustavo, raising an eyebrow.

Vachio shrugged. "That's what I see?"

"Well, I see too many boys standing around doing nothing."

"Doing nothing? There is all kinds of activity going on down there."

"Ah, there we do agree. But much of it is the wrong kind of activity.... Don't you see those boys lying around in each other's arms?"

"Yes, I noticed."

"That kind of filth has to end. I want every single boy in the patio, unless they're ill or incapacitated, involved in a wholesome activity. I want them so occupied they won't have the time or energy to think of sex. You understand?"

Vachio looked at Gustavo in bemusement. "Can I speak frankly?"

Gustavo chuckled, breaking the tension. "Do you know any other way? Please, speak your mind."

"These are young boys with plenty of energy and raging hormones. If they're determined to have sex with each other, they will always find a way. And I don't see how you, me, or anyone else can control that short of keeping them tied up and isolated from each other."

"That goes without saying, Vachio. Don't think I'm either naive or unrealistic. From their street experiences, these boys are certainly not sexually innocent. But without getting into the moral implications of homosexuality, it is our role here to minimize their sexual activities, as it should be for any children of their age and emotional development. And your recreation program can be a valuable tool for achieving this goal. This time of night can be very important for your program. The regular recreation period is only one hour, between four and five, on normal school days. But after dinner, and until clean-up and lights out, the boys have three hours of unorganized time. Now tell me, what are your ideas for filling this time?"

"Well, uh, the movie program for one thing, followed by discussions..." Vachio was at a loss for words, he debated whether to tell Gustavo what he really wanted to do.

"Yes..."

"To tell you the truth, I would look on this time as a good opportunity for me to really get to know and talk to the boys on a personal level. You know, do some real counseling. That's where I think I can be of the most value."

"Of course, Vachio. Of course. I expect that from you. But I also expect to see a formal structure and organization. A regular schedule of events and activities."

"Yes, but...Look, Gustavo, when I was a boy, my friends and I knew how to organize ourselves. All we wanted from the recreation director was equipment, an arbiter to settle disputes, and someone to sponsor us for organized leagues for our teams. We knew how to entertain ourselves, and it taught us how to think for ourselves. The recreation director was a facilitator, not a dictator. And that's what we wanted."

"Vachio, remember, you're still a very young man with much to learn.... Especially here in a completely different country and culture from your own."

"But it isn't so different concerning these boys."

Gustavo held up his hand. "Vachio, just listen to me. Take advantage of my experience and knowledge. Structure and organization. That will facilitate everything you want to do."

"Yeah, well, we'll see what we can do."

"Yes, Vachio, we'll see. And I want you to think long and hard about what I've been telling you."

"Jawol," muttered Vachio, staring bleakly at the yard, realizing they were at a philosophical dead-end.

"Well, let's go," said Gustavo. "I guess you've seen enough for now. I don't want to put too much on you at once."

They left the prison and Gustavo said, "It's still early. Would you like to go to the plaza for a while."

"Sure," said Vachio absently, lost in thought.

They walked the three blocks to the plaza in silence, the night air warm and still, hoards of moths flitting around the dim street lamps.

They reached the plaza and strolled toward the town hall, running a gauntlet of passersby and loungers, all with a word for Gustavo, and Gustavo, like the master of ceremonies at a banquet, had quips and greetings for each individual. Vachio was presented to a dozen new acquaintances, and it took them a good 20 minutes to walk the one block to the steps of the town hall.

They sat on the steps overlooking the plaza and Gustavo immediately struck up a conversation with a small group of men seated nearby. Vachio sat in virtual silence, watching the parade of teenagers promenading around the plaza, thinking of what Cabrera and Gustavo had told him about keeping the boys occupied and out of trouble. An organized program of recreation. Organization. Structure.... Sure. Of course, thought Vachio. But these guys make it sound like they want a ringmaster to direct teams of animals in a circus tent. This is not what I had in mind. If every other part of their time is regimented, as appears to be the case, than they also need a break and a chance to be creative. Vachio shook his head. This is definitely going to be a problem.

"Why are you so quiet, Vachio?" asked Gustavo, breaking off his conversation with the other men.

Vachio yawned. "Oh, I'm a little tired. Still getting used to the heat, I suppose... And I was just thinking."

"About what?"

"Oh, nothing important." Vachio decided to change the subject. "I was wondering, what was the time of The Violence like around here?"

Gustavo gave Vachio a sharp look. "You know something of our history?"

"Yes, something. What you read in books. But you lived here in that time. What was it like here in Santander?"

"It was terrible. A period of utter madness. What started out as a political conflict degenerated into a series of revenge killings and senseless atrocities. It's a time that all Colombians are ashamed of and we pray that we never see the like again."

"Was it really that bad?"

"Bad? No! It was brutal and horrible. For example, if you can imagine, it was so bad in certain isolated mountain zones that soldiers of certain notorious brigades threw babies up in the air and speared them on their bayonets while shouting the slogan, 'Not even the seed will survive.'"

"What was it like here in Garrotero?"

"In Garrotero?" A faraway look came into Gustavo's eyes and he stared out over the plaza and spoke in a dead monotone. "I was a young boy then and my parents did their best to protect me from the worst of it. But I realized how terrible it was. These very steps we are sitting on ran red with blood..."

"And? What do you remember?" prompted Vachio.

Gustavo shrugged. "What happened here was a microcosm of

what happened throughout much of Colombia. Inflamed passions broke free of all restraint.... The night of the day Jorge Gaitán was assassinated in Bogotá in 1948, the trouble began here between Liberals and Conservatives. I can still hear the shouts of visceral rage and the tolling of the church bells. There were shots, clubbings, stranglings with the *garrotes*. It was utter chaos and madness. Friends against friends, even family against family. It was a period of infamy that went on in spurts for years afterwards.... Truthfully, Vachio, I don't even like to think about it or talk about it. I lost family members during that time."

"All right," said Vachio, staring at his shoes. Again they lapsed into silence.

Minutes later an older man with unruly gray hair and a pronounced limp from a club foot approached them and said, "*Hola*, Don Gustavito. How are you this little night? And who is your little friend?"

The man had a demented air and every other word out of his mouth was used in the diminutive form, but he smiled genially and seemed harmless enough. Gustavo tolerated him and his questions, answering in a patient manner, but from his demeanor it was obvious he wished the man would go away.

"And where do you come from?" the man asked, abruptly turning to Vachio.

"I'm from San Francisco in the United States."

"Oh, San Francisco. I hear that's a beautiful city.... And what are you doing here? Visiting?"

"No. I'm going to work here in the *Casa de Menores*."

"Work here?" The man's genial smile disappeared and his face distorted with anger. "What are you doing here taking jobs away from Colombians?"

"I'm not taking a job away from a Colombian," said Vachio, making an effort to keep his tone cool and reasonable. "I don't even get paid by Colombians. I get paid by the United States government."

"Oh, I understand," said the man, his voice harsh and accusatory. "You're a spy, then. Working for the C.I.A."

Vachio began to boil.

"Ignore him," said Gustavo, laying a hand on Vachio's arm. "He's a *bobo*. A fool."

"A fool, am I?" exclaimed the man. "Not such a fool that I can't recognize a *gringo* spy."

"I'm no spy. I'm here to work as a recreation director in the prison."

"A recreation director? For what? A Colombian can't do that?"

"I'm sure one could. But up until now the job hasn't existed.... Ask Gustavo."

"Don't even listen or talk to him. Just ignore the *bobo*," said Gustavo. "He wants to feel important."

Vachio stared toward the plaza, trying to follow Gustavo's advice. But the lame man loomed over him and said in a loud voice, attracting the attention of other men nearby, "He shouldn't be here. Why is the United States sending people here to work? Why are they always sticking their noses in our business?"

"What the hell do you know about me?" burst out Vachio, starting to rise. "You don't have a reason for fucking with me."

Gustavo tightened his grip on Vachio's arm and said, "Calm down. Just ignore him. He is a fool."

Seething, Vachio glanced toward the nearby men. Their faces looked anything but sympathetic. Vachio pursed his lips, wrapped his arms around his midriff, and hunched over, his eyes on the ground.

"What do you have to say?" said the man, almost touching Vachio's shoulder.

"He has nothing to say to you, *bobito*," said Gustavo. "Go! Now!"

The man gave Vachio a final angry look and limped off into the shadows beyond the church.

"It's a good thing he was an old man," said Vachio, shaking with suppressed anger.

"Don't worry about that fool," said Gustavo in a soothing voice. "No one in town really likes him. He's a crank. The way he talks in that squeaky ugly voice, using all those diminutives as though he were an infant. We just tolerate him because we know he's not all there in the head."

"Well, that's fine," said Vachio, feeling calmer, his voice turning melancholy and reflective. "But I wonder how many people here feel like him. I've already had to deal with that kind of talk more than once in Bogotá.... You get tired of it, you know. I can't take responsibility for all the real and imagined things the United States has done to Colombia."

"I understand and sympathize with you, man. But you will find ignorant people anywhere and everywhere. It's just something you're going to have to endure. All you can do is act as an individual and people will respect you for yourself. Remember that and you'll be fine."

"What you say makes all the sense in the world, Gustavo. But when I feel blind hostility, it's not always easy to stay reasonable."

"Don't worry about it. It will be fine. Everything will be fine."

"I hope so."

14

The next morning, Vachio was out at the crack of dawn and ate breakfast at one of the café's near the plaza. After breakfast, he asked the owner about renting rooms in town and was assured that he would have no problem, considering he had a steady job at the *Casa de Menores* and an iron clad reference in Don Gustavo. Vachio filed this information for the moment and talked to the man about Garrotero. Before he knew it, an hour had elapsed, and by the time Vachio returned to the house Gustavo was gone. Vachio accepted a coffee from Rosa and chatted with her for a while. The sun was already hot and bright in the patio. Vachio sighed and stretched lazily. He felt himself falling into the slow-paced rhythm of the town.

Eventually Vachio wandered over to the *Casa de Menores*. Julia allowed him into Gustavo's office and he waited with his arms folded as Gustavo, busy and distracted, muttered over some papers on his desk. Vachio had the distinct impression Gustavo was making him wait. Finally, without looking up from his desk, Gustavo said, "Vachio, good morning."

"Good morning," answered Vachio.

Gustavo looked up at him. "You went out early again and missed breakfast."

"No. I went out early and had breakfast at the plaza."

Gustavo smiled wryly and shook his head. "You are determined not to let me be a good host."

"No, it's not that. You are an excellent host."

"Then?"

"In hot weather I like to get out early. And besides, I wanted to make some inquiries about housing here."

"I told you I was going to help you with that."

"I know. But I can't get used to having everything done for me."

"Fine. I understand. But will you accept a recommendation from me?"

"Of course."

"I have an invitation for you from a German couple who live here in town. They want you to come over for dinner tonight. But aside from that, if you guys hit it off well, I believe they are interested in having you live with them. They have an extra room for rent."

"I'll be happy to see them and look over the situation."

"They are good friends of mine and excellent people. Also, they are the only foreigners living in Garrotero. I think it would be good for you to get their perspective on life here."

"That could be."

"All right, then. Now would be a good time to confirm the invitation. They're just across the street and a few buildings down from here.... They run a plastic factory. You can't miss it. Just listen for the noise of the machinery."

"Aren't you going with me?"

"No, Vachio, I have a very busy schedule today. Just go and present yourself. They're expecting you. Ask for Don Raimundo or Doña Renata." Gustavo looked down at his papers.

"All right. But do you have any plans for me later?"

"No, Vachio. You are on your own. What are your plans?"

"I'm going to play basketball with the boys later today. And then I suppose I'll just hang around and get to know some people here."

"Ah, yes. That's good. Very good," said Gustavo. "Until later, then."

Vachio left the *Casa de Menores*, crossed the street and walked down the block. He knocked at the first door and felt like an idiot when he found he was at the wrong place. He was directed to the next block. There, the muted clang and hum of heavy machinery in front of a massive green door told him to stop. He pushed in the door and entered, catching surprised looks from men attending large machines. Vachio stood in the entrance, the clatter of the machines resounding in his ears, the stench of chemicals, machine oil, and melted plastic almost nauseating him. "What can I do for you?" one of the men asked him.

"I need to talk to Don Raimundo," yelled Vachio.

"He's not here. But Doña Renata is. Go through this door," he shouted, patting the one next to the entrance.

Vachio entered and saw a woman with auburn hair sitting at a desk with a telephone pressed to her ear. She failed to hear him. The noise from the machinery, though less than outside, reverberated in the office. Finally she looked up and said something. Vachio couldn't understand a word. She hung up the telephone and motioned him forward.

"You must be Vachio," she said, shaking his hand. "I'm Renata.... Sorry, but that's all the English I know."

"That's fine. Talk to me in Spanish."

"You speak enough?"

"Enough."

"Well, my husband Raimundo isn't here right now. But we want you to come for dinner tonight. Ya?"

"Yes. What time?"

"Around six. If it's convenient for you."

"Sure."

"I'm going to make fried chicken and potato pancakes.... Do you like German food?"

"Yeah, I like potato pancakes a lot.... Do you know how to make sauerbraten?"

"Yes, but that takes a long time." She smiled and wrote her address on a slip of paper. "We live very close to here. Sorry I can't chat longer, but we're very busy today with a rush order."

"No problem. We'll have time tonight."

Renata showed him out the door and onto the street. "We live around the corner and about three blocks up," she said, pointing. "Don't get lost."

"Yeah, I'll try not to."

"O.K., see you later. I have to work now."

Now she was very cordial, thought Vachio. Wonder what her husband is like. Vachio returned to Gustavo's house and changed into shorts and a T-shirt. He still had time before the mid-morning break. He decided to stroll down to the soccer field to pass the time. For a while he watched a cow chomp at the stunted grass along the edges of the field. Then a group of youngsters noticed him and came over to stare and talk.

"*How chu today, meester*," said the boldest of the group.

"Fine," said Vachio in Spanish. He bantered with them for a few minutes, quickly running through their limited repertoire of English. Then he warmed up for his basketball game by kicking the soccer ball around with them. Vachio worked up a good sweat and headed for the *Casa de Menores*, the youngsters accompanying him part of the way, one or two of them asking him for money. Vachio laughed this off and they soon melted away.

Vachio entered the *Casa de Menores*, sweat rolling down his face, and met the disapproving look of Alfonso Cabrera, stationed by the fountain as though in wait for him. Vachio nodded to him, mumbled a greeting, and started to walk past.

"Vachio! Where are you going in such a hurry?" Cabrera asked.

Vachio stopped and forced a smile. "I'm going to play basketball and soccer with the boys on their break."

"Dressed like that?"

Vachio's smile disappeared, a look of puzzlement replacing it.

"Didn't you understand me? Dressed like that?"

"Well, yes, I understood your words. I just don't understand what you mean. How else am I supposed to dress to play ball?"

Cabrera smiled and spoke in an almost fatherly tone. "Vachio, my young friend, you have to remember your position here. The boys need to respect you. By dressing like that, you are coming down to their level. That is no way to begin."

"Really? So how do you suggest I dress?"

"Like me. Slacks and a *guayabera*. The proper dress for a Doctor or Maestro."

Vachio repressed a snicker. "Señor Cabrera, this may not be the proper dress for a Doctor, but it certainly is the practical and proper way to dress to play basketball and soccer. And on this subject, I'm an expert. My clothes are appropriate for what I'm going to do.... Now, if you'll excuse me."

Cabrera glared at Vachio as he walked past him to the gate. "You shouldn't even play with them. You should just referee. That's your job."

Vachio turned and looked at Cabrera. "Even if I was just going to referee, I'd wear these clothes. Don't soccer referees wear shorts?"

Cabrera turned almost purple, shook his head, and headed straight for Gustavo's office. Vachio asked Oliva to let him through the gate.

Vachio stood on the terrace for a moment, struggling to control his anger.

"You answered him well," said Oliva. "He was trying to play with your mind."

"Can I get the basketball?" Vachio asked Oliva.

"Of course, Vachio. Whatever you want."

Oliva sent Little Abel, who was free and just hanging around with the two shaggy patio dogs, to get the ball. Vachio joined him on the court and instructed him to recover the shots that bounced away. Little Abel smiled brightly, eager to please. "And will I get a tip from you later?" he asked.

"We'll see about that," said Vachio, throwing up his first shot, the basketball feeling good in his hands.

Vachio shot and rebounded, shot and rebounded, the sun beating down on him, still upset from his exchange with Cabrera. "Sure, play ball in a nice shirt," he muttered, slapping the lopsided ball against his palm. "Why not in slacks and wing tips, too? Real intelligent. *Pingo*!"

Vachio's first shots were far off the mark. But as he worked up a lather, and got a feel for the lopsided ball, his shots began to fall. Abel cheered him on and Vachio nodded in satisfaction. He was anxious to impress the boys, and he knew that one way to do this was by showing them what he could do on a basketball court.

The bell rang and the boys boiled out of the workshops and classrooms. As they rushed toward Vachio, shouting his name, he nailed two long shots. Shouts of admiration and cries of "lucky" were elicited. Vachio grinned and held the ball in his hands. Then he faced the fast assembling boys and said, "So, some of you guys think my shots are lucky, eh? Well, bring out your players and let's see what you guys have to show."

"Right here. I'm one of the best," said Leal.

Vachio was besieged by a clamoring mass of boys, all claiming to be among the best.

"Don't tell me about it," Vachio said, turning to throw up a shot. "You pick among yourselves. I've never seen any of you play before. Nine guys to start."

After minutes of furious discussion, cursing, and some pushing and shoving, three of the patio bosses, Amarocho, Rolo Espinal, and Alfiler Rivera emerged and selected six other boys: Gaby, Leal, Mico Ortiz, Mocho, and Pedro Caballero. Vachio was astounded by the choice of Mocho. His hands were shriveled stumps with tiny knobby fingers at the ends. But he could play—well. Sides were chosen and Vachio made the do-or-die shot for first outs.

Rolo flipped Vachio the ball and said, "Too bad I have to embarrass you now in front of the whole patio."

Vachio laughed.

"What's so funny?"

"You talking trash to me. Are you actually going to try to guard me?"

"No. I'm going to stuff you."

"Yeah, we'll see," said Vachio, flipping the ball to Bambuco. He was immediately pressed by two players and he lobbed the ball back to Vachio. Rolo lunged for the ball and Vachio dribbled between his legs to avoid him, leaving him flailing at the air. Vachio maintained his dribble, swept past Alfiler at midcourt, and went all the way down the court and scored a lay-up. The boys watching along the sidelines were astonished.

Vachio held the ball under the basket and waited for Rolo. "First lesson, man, never talk trash unless you know who you're dealing with. And don't lunge at the ball like a blind bull. You have to play defense with your feet."

"Man, just give me the ball," said Rolo, hearing the jeers of some of the boys lining the court. "You got lucky."

Rolo took the ball out and it was quickly returned to him. He tried to drive past Vachio but had it stripped loose. Vachio recovered the loose ball and tossed it to Mocho under the basket for an easy score.

"See how I moved my feet," said Vachio to Rolo. "But you should have passed the ball anyway. You had two guys open."

"Worry about your own team," barked Rolo, his face crimson.

"You want to improve your game?"

"Just play."

Having made his point, Vachio fell back on defense. As the game proceeded, Vachio was content to pass the ball, take a few outside shots, and watch. The boys played a helter skelter style of ball, more interested in scoring baskets and looking good than playing as a team. Though they could dribble and shoot, the overall skill level was low, and the fundamentals of team play were poor. Vachio tried to coach them as they played but his advice and suggestions were badly received. With Vachio's team winning easily, the boys on the opposing team spent more energy arguing and assigning blame than playing, while the boys on Vachio's team gloated shamelessly. Vachio could only shake his head and smile ruefully. He knew he had a tough job ahead of him. But the game had served its purpose. He had identified most of the leaders in the patio.

At the end of the game, Leal ran up to Vachio and said, "So you can play basketball. That's fine. But that's a *gringo* game anyway. Why don't you play soccer with us and see how you do. I'll make you look foolish."

"Anytime, little brother. If you play soccer like you do basketball, I'm not too worried."

The young boys surrounding Leal broke into peals of laughter.

"Yeah, we'll see," shouted Leal, walking away. Then he laughed and boasted to a group of younger boys of what he would do to the new recreation director on a soccer field.

The bell rang to end the break and the boys dispersed. As Vachio headed for the terrace, he felt his arm grabbed from behind. He spun around and found Rolo.

"What's up?" Vachio asked him.

"Man, you know how to play basketball. I should have kept my big mouth shut. You made me look foolish."

"Ah, don't worry about it. You have talent. Learn the fundamentals and no one will embarrass you."

"You really think so?"

"Yes. But it depends on you. If you really want to learn."

Vachio waited. Rolo was looking at the ground and shuffling his feet. "Do you want to say something else? Say it?"

"You're going back to Bogotá, right?"

"Yes. On Saturday morning. Why?"

"Do you think you could deliver a letter to my mother for me? She hasn't heard anything from me for a while."

"Where does she live?"

"In south Bogotá. Out near the airport."

Vachio hesitated. Rolo's face was imploring him.

"Well, yes. Why not."

Rolo's face lit-up. "That's great. When can I give you the letter?"

"Right now."

"Uh, I haven't written it yet."

"Well, it has to be some time before Saturday. But tomorrow would be the best day. I don't know what's going on Friday."

"All right. I'll have it by tomorrow."

"One more thing."

"Yes."

"Don't tell anyone else about this. I don't want to be regarded as a messenger service. Understand?"

"Yes, of course. Just between you and me.... I have to go now or I'll get in trouble."

"Later."

Vachio walked up the steps and was met on the terrace by Emilio Montoya.

"Mister Vachio, I was watching you out there. That was quite an exhibition. You really know how to play basket."

"Well, compared to them," said Vachio, wiping at his dripping face with the front of his T-shirt.

"Not only compared to them. You looked good out there."

"Ah, I played a little ball in college. But believe me, you should see some of the things a real top player can do. They make me look like I make them look."

"You're being modest."

Vachio chuckled. "I'm not so modest. I can play. But there is no way I could ever make a living at it.... Man, I'm burning up."

"Let's get something to drink in the kitchen," suggested Emilio. "An ice guava juice or something like that."

"Good idea."

They emerged from the patio into the courtyard and Vachio saw Cabrera, standing by the fountain, eyeing his sweating body with disgust. Montoya nodded to Cabrera in passing and said, "Cabrera, how goes it?"

"Well," said Cabrera, smiling. "Very well, Doctor."

Vachio and Montoya passed into the corridor and out of earshot of Cabrera.

"What do you think of sports?" Vachio asked Montoya.

"The practice of sports is a fine thing. Like the saying goes, a strong body and a strong mind."

"Yes. And a good way to blow off steam, too. To clear your mind of unpleasant things. Like now, for example..."

"Oh? Is something troubling you?"

Vachio and Montoya found seats at the empty administrator's table and sat down. Vachio lowered his voice so the kitchen workers couldn't hear him and said, "Cabrera thought it was inappropriate for me to play basketball with the boys. Especially the way I'm dressed."

"Did he? Perhaps you misunderstood him."

"No. He said so in clear certain terms."

"How strange. I myself often play soccer with the boys. And of course, I wear shorts and a light shirt. I find it's a good way to break down some of the barriers between us and gain their confidence."

"There you go. That's how I feel, also." Vachio shook his head. "I don't know where Cabrera is coming from."

"Well, I suppose he feels he needs to maintain a certain distance from the boys to perform his job as disciplinarian."

"That's a diplomatic way to put it. But what does that have to do with how I choose to relate to the boys?"

"I really couldn't say," said Montoya, and changed the subject by calling for two guava juices. One of the women brought Vachio a towel, and clucked at him about catching a cold in the light breeze. Vachio decided to forget about Cabrera. The guava juice was delicious.

"So, you're a soccer player," Vachio said to Montoya.

"Not really. I just play to keep fit. But, as you can see, I haven't played as much lately as I should." Montoya patted his stomach. "How about you?"

"I can play enough to fake it. But I'm sure those boys will get some revenge on me tomorrow for what happened today."

"You're going to play soccer tomorrow?"

"I think so. At the regular recreation time. Would you like to join us?"

"With pleasure. If my duties permit."

"Good. I can use your help. Those guys gang up on me verbally and half the time I don't know what they're saying. I could use an interpreter."

Montoya chuckled. "Don't feel bad, we don't always understand them, either. Those boys have their own dialect. And they will put you to the test. But you'll learn."

"I better learn to speak some of that slang fast."

"No, you don't need to learn to speak it."

"No?.... Well, I need to understand it."

"Yes, of course. By the way, what were you talking to Octavio about?"

"Octavio? Who is that?"

"The tall boy with the curly black hair. The one you were talking to before you came up the steps."

"Oh, Rolo."

"Yes, Rolo is his nickname because he's from Bogotá.... But tell me, what were you talking to him about? He looked serious."

"Nothing much. He just asked me to deliver a letter for him to his mother when I return to Bogotá."

"Interesting," said Montoya, rubbing his chin. "In fact, that's wonderful."

"Why?"

"Because he already feels as though he can trust you."

Vachio shrugged. "Maybe he just wants to use me."

"Well, of course, up to a point. But delivering a letter to his mother is a very personal thing. He has never asked me to do anything like that."

"But why doesn't he just mail it?"

"His mother lives in one of those shantytowns in south Bogotá. Addresses are hard to find and the mail doesn't always arrive."

"Oh, that makes sense."

"This is a fine opportunity for you, Vachio. Octavio is one of the most respected boys in the patio. Many of the younger boys look up to him. If you can develop a good rapport with him, it will certainly facilitate your program. Many of the other boys will fall right into line."

"That would be good.... But tell me more about Ro...uh, Octavio. How long has he been here?"

"Almost three years. And he has made tremendous progress in that time. In truth, I'd say he is one of the few boys in here who has a legitimate chance to make it on the outside. He just needs someone to give him an opportunity. He is an intelligent and charismatic young man."

"Why was he brought here?"

"Octavio was a prototype *gamin*. He ran away from home when he was about eight, and through cunning and strength he made a place for himself on the streets of Bogotá. He eventually became *El Vale*, the main leader of a gang of *gamines*. He was picked up while traveling with his gang in Bucaramanga during a police sweep and sent here."

"Why did he run away from home?"

"He claims he was abused by one of his mother's lovers."

"Do you believe him?"

"Yes. That's not uncommon. And besides, he maintains a relationship with his mother. Even when he was a *gamin*, he used to give her money. And she comes here to visit once in a while. We would like to send him home in another year."

"Do you think he's ready?"

"I think he's ready now. But I don't know about his situation at home. Maybe you can shed some light on that for me when you deliver the letter."

"I'll be happy to do what I can."

"Excellent. I truly appreciate it."

"It's my pleasure. It gives me a chance to be a real sociologist and not just a glorified babysitter."

"You have a funny way with words," said Montoya, laughing.

Vachio finished his juice, feeling pulpy fibers jamming between his teeth, and asked, "What can you tell me about that boy with the big mouth? That Leal?"

"Leal..." Montoya shook his head. "That boy is definitely not one of my favorites. He is pure trouble. Of the type that becomes so thoroughly institutionalized, he can't live on the outside. We've released him five times just to be rid of him, but he always manages to come back to us. Unfortunately, the *Casa de Menores* is the only place where he feels comfortable."

"Does he have a family?"

"Yes, a broken one. His mother is Venezuelan and lives just across the border in San Antonio. She has tried to keep him but he always runs away after a few weeks. Leal likes to stay with his natural father in Bucaramanga. But he is too old and tired to handle him well. So, Leal runs wild and always does something to end up back here with us. I hate to say this, because one doesn't like to give up on anyone, but I put Leal in the almost hopeless category. And it's a shame, because he is an intelligent kid."

"What is there about him that bothers you so much?"

"Where do I start? He is a pathological liar and instigator. He likes to stir up trouble just to bring attention to himself. He is a bully, has a cruel streak, and is generally disliked by most of the boys in the patio for being a known *sapo*."

"What's a *sapo*?"

"A *sapo* is an informer."

"Yeah, that would make him unpopular."

“Not only that, but some of the information he gives is pure fabrication to get back at patio rivals. I believe that the only thing that has saved him from a brutal beating is that he has a relationship with one of the guards.”

“I see.”

“Watch out for Leal, Vachio. He may try to ingratiate himself with you, but you can’t trust him. He can cause many problems for you.” Montoya rose to leave. “Well, I have to get back to the office.”

Vachio impulsively shook his hand. “Thanks for the information.”

“You’re welcome. Whatever I can do to help.”

15

Vachio walked outside the *Casa de Menores* into the bright sunlight, intent on returning to Gustavo’s to take a shower and a siesta. But he was detoured on the front steps by a reception committee composed of Pacho, Dolfo, Fredy, and Don Miguel. They were grinning like hyenas and repressing snickers. From the sly glances they were exchanging, Vachio knew they had been talking about him.

“Well? Get on with it. What’s up?” asked Vachio.

“Sit down, Vachio,” said Miguel in a solicitous voice. “We want to congratulate you.”

“Congratulate me?” muttered Vachio, sitting on the stoop. “Why?”

“Because thanks to you, we will be enjoying a holiday at the *Casa de Menores* in your honor.”

“What?”

“That’s correct, Vachio,” said Pacho. “Don Gustavo has declared this Friday the *Day of the Gringo*. No offense, eh. And, ay, do we have plans for you.”

The four of them burst into raucous laughter.

“What kind of plans?” asked Vachio.

“Only the best,” said Miguel. “You are going to be officially blooded here...”

“Yes, just like a young bullfighter,” brayed Dolfo.

“What?”

The men burst into laughter at the expression on Vachio’s face. Don Miguel patted Vachio’s shoulder. “It’s nothing bad, my friend. We plan to take you to a special place in Santander. A place close to all of our hearts. A place where you can drink, make merry, eat the food of the gods, and perhaps...”

“Be introduced to a nice *viejita*,” said Dolfo, on cue.

“A *viejita*? What do you mean by an old woman?”

Again the men burst into laughter.

"A *viejita* is a woman of pleasure, Vachio," said Miguel. "You understand?"

"Oh, you mean a prostitute."

"That's right," said Pacho.

"But he makes it sound so vulgar," said Fredy.

"Well..."

The men roared with laughter. The hot sun and the noise began to make Vachio's ears ring. For effect, he buried his head in his hands. Pacho and Dolfo made a few more choice comments, eliciting more guffaws. Then a window shutter banged open just to Vachio's right and a raspy voice said, "Enough already! What's all the commotion about? How do you expect a person to get any work done?"

The men fell silent, their gleeful expressions turning sour. They lowered their heads and shifted their weight from one foot to the other. Vachio glanced toward the window, shielding his eyes from the sun. A woman with short black hair, sharp features, and dark glittering eyes was leaning out of the window, regarding the men in frowning disapproval. Then she caught Vachio's eye and smiled. "Can't you see this poor guy is sick?" she said, her tone softer. "You should all be ashamed of yourselves. You guys are like incorrigible children."

"Ah, relax, Opala," said Fredy. "He's not sick. He's just tired from playing ball in this heat."

"Yeah. We're just having a little fun with the guy. It's our way of making him feel welcome here," said Pacho.

"He doesn't look like he feels so welcome," said Opala. "The poor guy."

Vachio straightened up at this. "I feel welcome. Don't think I can't answer for myself."

"Ah, yes?" said Opala, her eyes flickering. "Then, maybe you deserve what these guys are giving you."

"Maybe. And maybe it's none of your business, either."

"What?"

The men roared with laughter.

"You better watch it with this *gringo*, Opala. He has spark," said Pacho.

"Huh. He's probably C.I.A. trained," said Opala, staring at Vachio with her hands on her hips.

"No. Just street trained," said Vachio.

Miguel stepped over to the window and said, "Vachio, let me formally introduce you to Opala Hortensia Prada de Miguez. She works in accounts, also. And is one of the intellectuals of the *Casa de Menores*."

Vachio looked at Miguel. He had put a slight edge on his pronunciation of the word intellectual, but his face was goodnatured and impassive.

"Doña Opala...Señor Vachio, our new friend."

Vachio lurched to his feet and went to the window to shake Opala's hand.

"Thank you, Don Miguel," said Opala, squeezing Vachio's hand. "It's nice that at least one of you men still has proper manners."

Pacho and Dolfo exchanged grimaces and excused themselves. Miguel soon followed, as Opala dominated Vachio's attention and the general conversation. Fredy caught Vachio's eye and nodded toward Opala with an ironic expression on his face. Vachio smiled and continued his conversation with Opala. Fredy shook his head, smiling bemusedly, and winked at Opala as he sauntered down the street in Miguel's wake.

"It looks like you scared all those guys away," said Vachio, glancing at Fredy's receding back. "What happened?"

"Nothing. They don't like to fool with me. I've put them in their places more times than they like to remember. Especially Pacho and that vulgar Dolfo. Two of a kind."

"Ah, they don't seem so bad. They just like to joke around."

"No, they're not so bad. They just totally lack culture. You see, I'm a liberated woman and a Communist. I don't think they're funny, and I don't put up with their sexist stereotypes. You hear me?"

Vachio nodded, looking at Opala hanging out of the window. She was a tall woman, big-boned, with ample shoulders, hips, and breasts, just starting to run to fat around the belly and legs. Her fair skin and dark eyes and hair made her the spitting image of a Spanish peasant woman. She spoke with great earnestness, occasionally spraying her listener with a fine mist, and gestured dramatically. In the course of their conversation, Vachio had stepped away from her, and Opala had leaned farther and farther out of the window to keep him in range.

"So what do you think of all that?" Opala asked.

"All what?"

"About my being a liberated woman?" she said, leaning even farther out of the window and jiggling her ample bosom a few inches from Vachio's nose.

"That's fine. Whatever works for you," answered Vachio, his eyes wandering to a drop of perspiration sliding down her neck toward her cleavage.

"Really? You're not intimidated by that? You believe that men and women are equal?"

"Well, sure. Why not?"

"Comrade!" Opala gripped Vachio by the bicep and squeezed his skin with enough force to leave a welt. "I think I like you. But..." Opala struck a coquettish pose. "...maybe you're just trying to flatter me because you really are a spy from the C.I.A. and you want to find out about the revolutionary activities here."

"That's true. And maybe you're doing the same thing to me because you think I'm a spy and you want to uncover me."

"Well, are you?"

Vachio laughed. "Yeah, like I would tell you if I were. Please.... O.K., you got me. I'm here to spy on the secrets of your sugar cane and tobacco fields."

Opala looked nonplused, then her eyes narrowed.

"I was just pulling your leg," said Vachio. Then he raised his hand in the air. "I swear to you I don't work for the C.I.A.... Hell, I don't know if I could even get into the C.I.A. You have to be pretty smart to qualify."

"Oh, you are smart. And you have a sense of humor," said Opala. "That I like. You don't seem like most of the Cro-Magnons in this town. Maybe we are going to be good friends. And I don't make friends easily."

Vachio rolled his eyes. She certainly has a high opinion of herself, he thought.

"We should get together and do something together outside of work," said Opala.

"Well, yeah, we could..." The silence lengthened as Vachio left it at that.

"How about hiking? Do you like hiking?" Opala asked.

"Yeah, sure."

"Then? When?"

"As soon as I get back from Bogotá in January. That is... if I'm accepted."

"Oh, you'll be accepted. But maybe we could get together sooner..."

Before Vachio could reply, Gustavo appeared, a huge grin on his face, and said, "Hey, Opala! What are you doing to poor Vachio? At least let him get used to Garrotero before you try to convert him to your cause."

Opala laughed. "I'll convert you first, Gustavo."

"I'm afraid you'll have to give up on me," said Gustavo, putting his hand on Vachio's shoulder. "You know I'm a dyed in-the-wool monarchist. Long live Emperor Bolívar!"

"Ay, Gustavo, you're too intelligent for that. Be serious. I know that some day you will see the light."

"Perhaps you're right, Comrade Opala. But for the moment, more mundane matters require my attention.... Vachio, it's time for lunch. My sister has prepared something special for us at my house."

"Let's go," said Vachio.

"We'll talk more later," said Opala to Vachio.

"For sure."

Gustavo chuckled softly as they walked up the street, and instead of going to his house, he ushered Vachio into a small store-café. He ordered two *tintos* and sat facing Vachio, an amused grin on his face.

"What's so funny?" asked Vachio.

"I was just wondering what you think of our house Communist?"

"Who? Opala? Or the Che Guevara look-alike guard?"

Gustavo laughed. "Opala, of course. Our guard Che is no Communist. He just likes the look.... Now tell me, what do you think of Opala?"

Vachio shrugged. "I don't know yet. But she reminds me of some Jehovah's Witnesses I've met."

Gustavo laughed. "No, she's not that bad."

"No? Well, she sure doesn't seem very popular with Pacho and the other guys."

"That's an understatement."

"But why so much?"

"Well, she has a sharp tongue."

Now Vachio laughed. "A sharp tongue? Like one out of every three people I've met here so far."

"She goes beyond sharp, Vachio. She can be downright venomous at times. And she has a tendency to get...shall we say, a bit too dogmatic for some people's taste."

"Yeah, I saw that side of her. But what do you think about her?"

"Me?... Well, I'm her boss. So she is much more respectful with me. But truthfully, I don't think she's so bad. I don't take her Marxist tape recordings as seriously as some other people in this town. And we enjoy teasing each other about politics and human relations."

"She's definitely not afraid to voice her opinions."

Gustavo smiled. "Did she tell you that she's married and has a little daughter?"

"No. She didn't mention that to me."

"Interesting."

"Why?"

"Let's put it this way, Vachio.... Her husband has been away studying in Moscow for the last four years."

"Has he been home to visit during that time?"

"No. And only God knows if he'll ever be back."

"I see."

Gustavo chuckled. "Watch yourself, Vachio. Opala is a tigress. And I think she has her eye on you."

"Oh, my God! I'm scared," said Vachio sarcastically.

"Well, I'd never want to interfere in your private life, Vachio, but..."

"I understand what you're saying. Thanks," said Vachio, cutting further conversation.

"Very well, then."

16

"Vachio! What are you doing here already?" asked Renata.

"It's six. Like you said."

"Nobody comes on time here," she said, smiling.

"Who says I'm nobody?"

"Well, I didn't mean that. Don't take things so literally."

"I don't. I was just kidding you. But I am one of these compulsive on time people. Especially when I don't have anything better to do."

"I see. Well, I'm in the middle of preparing dinner and Raimundo hasn't arrived from work yet. What do we do?"

"No problem. I can come back later if you want."

"No, no. Don't be ridiculous. Come in and have a seat."

Renata closed the door and went out back to the kitchen. Vachio found a seat on a couch with red print cushions and looked over his surroundings. The living room and adjoining dining area were small and modestly furnished. The sofa and a flanking love seat were made from old packing cases and homemade cushions. An old stereo system with huge speakers and scores of records lined one wall. A lounge chair of striped canvas with a guitar resting in it, along with a battered coffee table and a black and white television set on a metal stand, faced the sofa and divided the living room from the dining area. A painting of a skinny black man carrying a huge blue bail against a bright yellow backdrop was featured on the wall opposite the stereo. A garden set with a glass-topped table and metal chairs and a small end table formed the dining room. The set-up had a Bohemian, haphazard look, with books and magazines lying around, and various watercolors of dubious quality adorning the side walls.

"Here is something cold to warm up with," said Renata, handing Vachio a beer.

"Thanks. But how did you know I like beer?"

Renata swept her long russet bangs away from her eyes and took a sip of her own beer before answering. She was in her late 20s, a solidly built woman with strong features and a sprinkling of freckles. "Gustavo told us."

"Gustavo, eh." Vachio took a sip of beer. "What else did he tell you about me?"

"Oh, not too much.... He said you weren't dangerous."

"Come on, he must have told you more than that. Tell me."

"Why? Are you looking for compliments?"

"No. I'd just like to know what kind of impression I'm leaving so far."

"Well, all right. I suppose I can tell you. Gustavo told us you're intelligent and open. And seem like a nice person.... All right?"

"And? What about negative comments?"

Renata shifted uncomfortable from one foot to another. "Ay, nothing. Nothing much..."

"Nothing much?" Vachio smiled and said in a wheedling voice, "Please, tell me. I won't be offended. It will help me to know."

"Well, you asked. He said you're a little stubborn and temperamental. And maybe just a bit cocky for being as young and naive as you are."

Vachio guffawed. "Gustavo's a sharp man."

"That's for certain. Now, you'll have to excuse me, I need to check on the chicken and do some other things. You can watch T.V. or play the stereo if you like."

"Thanks. I'll amuse myself."

Renata retreated to the kitchen and Vachio chuckled as he took another sip of his beer. Naive, eh, thought Vachio. Good. Let Gustavo think that.

Soon Vachio was down on his knees, shuffling through the record collection. He found albums by the Kinks, the Beatles, the Stones, Crosby, Stills, Nash and Young, Wilson Pickett, James Brown, and a host of others. It was a 60s time warp collection. Vachio was pleased. He hadn't seen some of these albums in years.

Minutes later, while perusing the lyrics to Jethro Tull's *Aqualung*, thinking nostalgically of wild parties in his first year of college, Vachio heard the front door thrust open. He jumped up and saw a big broad man in greasy coveralls framed in the murky entrance light.

"Well, well, well, what do we have here? A genuine American Man," he said in German accented English, his voice bluff.

"Und you must be a genuine German Man," said Vachio, exaggerating the German's accent. "I'm Gary. You must be the famous, never present Raimundo."

"Oh ho! So this *gringo* has spark. As advertised," said Raimundo, switching to Spanish and heartily shaking Vachio's hand. "That's good. You'll need it here."

"For who? For the Colombians or for you?"

"For both, my son. I just hope you have a good sense of humor and don't take everything personally."

"I hope the same for you."

"That's what I like to hear." Raimundo laughed delightedly and patted Vachio on the back, peering at him through thick, wide-rim glasses that gave his nose a long pinched appearance. He had long dark hair, bushy sideburns, and a walrus mustache. "I can see we'll have a lot to talk about," said Raimundo. "But you'll have to excuse me for a moment while I change out of my work clothes. The smell of machine oil nauseates me away from work."

"Not only you, man. Phew! Nasty!"

Raimundo smiled and pointed at Vachio. "We already started without even a preliminary treaty. Very good. I'll be back at you."

Raimundo went to the bedroom to change his clothes and Vachio settled back on the sofa, grinning happily. He liked Raimundo's informality and good humor. The rough word play had created a quick and acceptable intimacy for Vachio.

After holding a brief session with his wife in German, Raimundo returned to the living room and handed Vachio a fresh beer. Now he was dressed in shorts, a tank top, and sandals. Curly black body hair sprouted from under the fabric of his clothes and from his bare skin. Raimundo picked up the guitar, sat on the beach chair, and took a long drink of beer. Then he strummed a Beatles tune, humming as he played, watching Vachio all the while. Vachio stared at the wall and waited. Abruptly Raimundo stopped playing and rested the guitar on his lap.

"So, Gary, do you play a musical instrument?"

"No."

"Why not?"

"I guess I had other interests. But I like music."

"Too bad. I was hoping we could play together.... But you can sing at least, can't you?"

Vachio laughed. "Not very well."

"Ah, it's not important that you do it well. For my purposes, I only require that you do it with spirit. To accompany me."

"Well, maybe if I drink enough."

"Then drink up," laughed Raimundo. "It's not every day that I find someone here who can sing in English."

"Why would I want to sing in English? I want to improve my Spanish."

"Because I like to sing songs in English."

"Good for you," said Vachio, shrugging.

"All right, let's make a deal. I'll only speak to you in Spanish if you sing with me in English every once in a while. What do you say?"

"Done."

"Great! Now let's sing," bellowed Raimundo, taking up the guitar and playing a few chords.

"Nah, I don't feel like singing right now. Let's talk."

"Ay, man! What do you want to talk about that can't wait?"

"Whatever. For example, why do you like to sing in English so much?"

"Because I love good music, man. Rock and roll, soul, and all that kind of jazz, man." Raimundo bounced out of his chair and switched on the stereo. He selected the Beatles' *Rubber Soul* album and put it on. "You see, man, I used to play lead guitar in a band in Germany. We often played for the American G.I.s in Frankfurt and those were some crazy times. I mean, wild and fun times." Raimundo paced back across the room and grabbed his guitar, his eyes gleaming, his movements forceful, his body exuding energy. "You know that most Germans don't like the American G.I.s. They are a constant reminder that we're an occupied country still."

Vachio shrugged and grinned wickedly. "As it should be. Who in their right mind would ever trust Germany again?"

"Uh, well, we're not talking about why they're there. You know, most Germans don't like the G.I.s because they're prototypical macho men who don't know how to behave in a civilized country. You know, most of them are ignorant, rowdy, show no interest in German culture or language. You know, like most common soldiers..."

"No, I don't know. But if they were so damn bad why did you play music for them?"

Raimundo guffawed. "I didn't say me—I said most Germans. For me the G.I.s were great. You know, man, because my band really sucked. We were just hackers having a good time. Sometimes German crowds would even throw things at us. But when we'd go to the military base to play for the American G.I.s, we'd get treated as though we were super stars. We would give them what they wanted — the Stones, Elvis, Wilson Picket, James Brown, the Beatles.... Man, after an hour or so of hard drinking, those guys would be up and dancing on the tables and singing along with us. It was *cheverisimo*!"

Raimundo's eyes glowed and he strummed the guitar and sang along with the record. Vachio was holding his sides from laughter. The song ended and Raimundo set the guitar down.

"So, what brought you to Colombia?" Raimundo asked.

"The Peace Corps. You heard of it?"

"Of course. I knew a few Peace Corpse volunteers when I lived in Bogotá. But why did you join?"

Before Vachio could answer, Raimundo grinned and said, "You know, man, it's well known in Europe that Peace Corpse is just a way for the United States to keep its unemployment down. Is that why you joined?"

Vachio laughed. "That's a new one on me. Since I arrived in Colombia, I've heard that we're a front for the C.I.A., the unwitting stooges of American imperialism, or a Christian religious group like the Mormons."

"Well, which one is it?"

"That I know of...none of those. And from what I've experienced, we're just a bunch of altruistic people who like to have a good time, help people, and not get paid very much."

"Help people?" Raimundo's voice was scornful. "Most of the Peace Corpse people I met would be lucky to help themselves. They were kids with no experience. How can they do any serious work?"

"Maybe they were spies."

"Bah! They weren't competent enough to be spies."

"Careful, man, so many good things to say about my group. Is this how you normally go about trying to rent someone a room?"

"Nothing personal, Gary. But like I said, Peace Corpse is just a way to lower unemployment and let some kids make their mistakes in someone else's country."

Vachio was beginning to feel irritated by Raimundo's relentless barrage. "Well, I don't know about all that other stuff you said, that's your opinion, but the total amount of people employed by Peace Corps all over the world would hardly put a dent in U.S. unemployment. So, that reason is obviously bogus. And besides, don't you like Peace Corps volunteers overseas better than U.S. troops? Like in some countries I could mention."

Raimundo burst into laughter. "You really do like to argue. Good. Me, too."

Now Vachio felt relentless. "I like to debate, man. Not argue. Especially as long as it isn't anything so stupid as what we were talking about."

"Ah, don't be so sensitive. *Salud*!" said Raimundo, raising his bottle. "To Peace Corpse. Some of you guys are good partyers anyway."

Vachio chuckled."Hey, you know what the Spanish teachers in Bogotá call us?... *Cuerpo de Paseo*. The Vacation Corps."

"They could call you worse things," said Raimundo.

"Yeah, truthfully, we don't get that much respect. Not even from other Americans here.... Like last week, I went to the U.S. embassy to cash some dollars because they give us a better rate than the banks. So while I'm there, I go to the cafeteria to check out their American food. And while I was there, I tried to strike up a conversation with some of the foreign service workers, and man, I'm not exaggerating, once they found out I was in Peace Corps they treated me like I had leprosy..."

"Ah hah! I know what you mean. We had a friend named Sandra in Bogotá, from Boston. She was a foreign service worker. Man, she used to make us laugh. At parties, whenever she met someone new, she would always ask, 'And where did you to school?' And if she didn't like the answer, she wouldn't talk to them anymore."

"Yeah, that's the attitude I'm talking about. The same shit. But I didn't trip. Listening to some of the conversations in that cafeteria, most of which revolved around how afraid they were in the streets; and complaining about the lack of certain foods and amenities in Colombia, well...I figured being slighted by some of these guys was nothing to get worked up over. In fact, it was a compliment in a way."

Raimundo roared with laughter. "What happened? You didn't go to the right school?"

"I don't know. I went to the School of Common Sense."

Raimundo rose, still chuckling, and went to the kitchen to check on the food, his booming voice saying in English, "And where did you go to school, Chef Renata?"

Vachio laughed. Raimundo returned and handed Vachio a fresh beer. "Reina says the food is almost ready."

"Good. I'm hungry."

Raimundo took a seat facing Vachio and said, "So, Gary, let's forget all the crap. Why did you really join Peace Corpse and come to Colombia?"

"All right, no crap." Vachio chuckled, they had already fallen into speaking in a Spanish base with English slang tossed in when it felt right. "I principally joined up for the adventure. You see, I planned on coming to South America anyway; it's something I always wanted to do. And Peace Corps seemed a good way to do it."

"What? That's all? You mean you didn't join because you want to save the poor benighted world like some other Peace Corpse people have told me?"

Vachio snorted. "Come on, man, you have to be either a fool or a terminal ego freak to think like that. I mean, I feel I have something to offer. But I'll be doing the same kind of work I was doing in the United States, and there was plenty of work for me there in the field of juvenile delinquency."

"That's for sure. But I'm surprised to hear you admit it."

"Why wouldn't I? I was trained to be a social worker. If there were no problems, they wouldn't need people who do work like mine."

"So you have experience working with delinquents?"

"Yes, I do. Plenty. In fact, I was a borderline delinquent myself at one time."

"All right, but do you have experience working in a prison?"

"Not exactly. This will be a little different."

"A lot different," laughed Raimundo. "I wish you luck. You are going to need it."

"Salud," said Vachio, tipping his bottle and drinking. "Now why don't we forget about the prison for a while."

"Perfect! Let's have a good time." Raimundo picked up his guitar. "Let's sing."

"No, not yet."

"Why not?"

"Man, you are overbearing."

"No, brother, just enthusiastic. What's wrong with a little wine, women, and song? Or are you one of these puritanical sort of Americans?"

"No. But as far as I can see, we have no wine, you're the only one here with a woman, and I don't feel like fucking singing yet. So get off my case, *pingo*!"

Raimundo chortled. "Fine, mister. Then would you object to some Crosby, Stills, Nash, and Young? You know, man, Woodstock?"

"Yeah, I can go for that."

Raimundo put the album on and Vachio slid his beer under the sofa. He wanted to pace himself.

"How did you end up here?" Vachio asked Raimundo.

"In Garrotero? Or Colombia?"

"Both."

"I first came to Colombia in 1970 with a program something like a West German Peace Corpse. But, unlike you guys, we had to be experts in our fields and we received professional wages."

Vachio mock bowed to Raimundo and chanted, "You are a god. You are my hero. Can I please kiss your hand?"

"Hey, screw you. I'm just telling you how it was..."

"Yeah, fine. So in what field were you an expert?"

"I came as an electrical engineer with a specialty in machine technology and plastic fabrication."

"What did you do?"

"I worked as a technical advisor and trainer in factories in Bogotá and Medellín. More in Medellín. That's why my accent is more like a *paisa* than like a *rolo*."

"Yeah, you sound like one of my Spanish teachers from Medellín. But I don't get it, you sure have a German accent when you speak English."

Raimundo grimaced. "Because I don't care about ze fucking English."

"Obviously.... But anyway, you've been here eight years now?"

"That's correct. Eight years."

"Why?"

Raimundo rose and paced over to the stereo to change the record. "Because, man, this is my home now. I love Colombia. I have no plans to leave."

"Oh yeah?"

"Yeah." Raimundo stood in front of Vachio, his eyes intense. "I don't know if you can understand this. Very few of my fellow Germans do. But it's like this.... In West Germany, sure, I can make a very nice living as a technician. You know the routine, get a new car every other year, buy a nice house, even have a fucking television in the toilet if I want..."

Vachio snickered, interrupting Raimundo. "Huh, I bet a bunch of people here wouldn't mind living like that."

"Relax, son, I'm getting there. Be patient.... So fine, I'm a friggin' respectable technician. But what significance does that have in Germany among all the rest of the technicians and the other good Burghers? To me—nothing! I'd be just another nameless cipher. A Herr Nobody. But here, I'm Don Raimundo. Boss of the plastic factory. A man of substance and respect. Do you understand?"

"Of course. You want to be a big fish in a small pond."

"No, man, you don't understand. I want my identity and individuality respected."

"Yeah, yeah. I was just giving you a hard time.... Kind of."

"Ay, man, you are a case," said Raimundo, sitting down. "We're going to have a great time together. I can see that right now."

Vachio giggled. "Uh huh, if we don't kill each other first.... But tell me, why Colombia? Why not somewhere else like a tropical island?"

"Because Colombia offered me just the right combination of industrial development and social disorder. This is a place where you can maneuver once you understand the culture. There are ways around everything and you can really get things done if you know what you want to do."

"You want to be more specific."

"Look, man, it's hard to explain. You have to be here for a while and immerse yourself in the way of life."

"You could say that about anywhere."

Raimundo snorted. "Anywhere? Don't believe that. Hell, in West Germany, it's so controlled, so efficient, you need a permit from the government to wipe your ass."

"But ze trains run on time."

"Yes, Mein Herr. Because if they're even 30 seconds late, my anal retentive compatriots are staring at their watches and muttering about intolerable inefficiency. After living here for a while, I realized how absurd that attitude really is."

"But don't you think inefficiency and disorder make it harder to get things done?"

"Not necessarily. Not when you understand the culture."

"How about an example?"

"All right, for example.... For me to run a plastic factory in West Germany, I would have to be a megamillionaire just to get started and deal with all the government regulations. That would be impossible for someone like me. But here, I found three Colombian partners, none of whom are real rich, and all the bureaucratic obstacles disappeared like this." Raimundo snapped his finger.

"And how are things going?"

"It's going well. I mean, it's a struggle to get things off the ground but at least we have a chance. In Germany, if you could even get a little venture going, it would soon be swallowed up by the big fish. But we're going to make it for sure."

"Why did you pick this town for your venture?"

"Process of elimination. My partners and I considered a number of sites all over Colombia. We selected Garrotero because of reasonable start-up costs, good workers, and a place where Renata and I wanted to live."

"All things considered, what do you find so special about Garrotero? It seems like an ordinary town to me."

"Ordinary? Man, you don't know! This Garrotero is incredible. It is absolutely folkloric."

"Folkloric? How do you mean that?"

"You know, folkloric in English?... No, it's not exactly the same. Huh, have you ever read *Quiet Days in Clichy* by Henry Miller?"

Vachio shook his head.

"Well, did you know that the people of Garrotero call their pueblo The Capital of the World?"

"Yeah, Pacho from the *Casa de Menores* told me that a few dozen times. What a joke."

"No, man, it's no joke. In a certain way, they are right. This dumpy little town has everything in the way of human emotion and tragicomedy. All the greed, lust, jealousy, blood feuds, romance, beauty, farce...you name it. It's all here. The whole fucking human circus. And it provides me endless diversion..."

A knock on the door halted Raimundo in mid-sentence.

"If you're a friend, come in," shouted Raimundo.

The door swung open and Gustavo stepped into the living room. "Forgive me. I hope I'm not interrupting."

"Ay, don't talk nonsense," boomed Raimundo. "The Great Don Gustavo, First Citizen of The Capital of the World, is always welcome in my house."

"If only some of my enemies felt that way," said Gustavo, smiling broadly. "How are you doing?"

After the usual round of salutations, with Gustavo sticking close to the door, Raimundo said, "Don't just stand there. Come in and join the party. You're staying for dinner, of course."

"No, thanks for the kind invitation, Raimundo. But I really must be going. I have a prior engagement."

"Well, stay for a beer anyway. A few minutes can't hurt."

"Fine, then," said Gustavo, sitting next to Vachio on the sofa. "Just one beer."

"Famous last words," said Vachio.

"No, not for Don Gustavo," said Raimundo, laughing. "He is a well-disciplined man. It's a shame."

Raimundo entered the kitchen and returned a moment later with a beer for Gustavo. Renata was right behind him.

"Doña Renata, a very good evening to you," said Gustavo, rising from his seat.

"The same to you, Gustavo. And what about this nonsense that you are not staying for dinner?"

"It's true, Doña Renata. Unfortunately, I have a previous engagement."

"Oh, a romantic rendezvous?" asked Renata, smiling.

"No, nothing so pleasant. More like a political thing."

"Well, too bad. Dinner will be served in about five minutes. If you change your mind, you are always welcome to stay."

Renata returned to the kitchen and Gustavo got to the real point of his visit.

"So, how are you two getting along?" Gustavo asked, looking at Raimundo.

"Very well. This *gringo* is providing me with a lot of diversion."

"This kraut is easy to entertain," piped up Vachio.

Gustavo laughed. "I'm pleased that things are going so well. Is everything settled between you?"

"Settled? Like what?" asked Vachio.

"Why, about boarding here when you come back to work in January."

"Uh, we haven't talked about that yet," said Raimundo. "I never discuss business on an empty stomach. And besides, the business is Renata's job."

"Well, the important thing is that you guys are getting along well and developing a friendship. Everything else will take care of itself," said Gustavo smoothly.

"I haven't even seen a room or heard a price mentioned," said Vachio.

"*Salud*! Here's to the monkey business," boomed Raimundo.

The three men clicked bottles and took long drinks. Then Gustavo cleared his throat and asked Raimundo, "How are the two new boys working out at the factory?"

Raimundo turned serious. "One is excellent. But the other one, that Enrique, is slow. If I don't see any improvement tomorrow, he'll have to go back to the *Casa*."

"What are you guys talking about?" Vachio asked.

"We have several boys from the *Casa de Menores* working part-time at Raimundo's factory," said Gustavo. "It's a wonderful program. They acquire valuable work experience and make some pesos for themselves."

"What do they do?" asked Vachio.

"Mostly piece work. They cut excess plastic when the containers come out of the molds and things like that," explained Raimundo.

Gustavo looked at his watch and got up to leave. "I really must go now. But continue the party." Gustavo reached into his pocket and handed Vachio a key. "This is for the front door. I'll leave the inner door unlatched for you. So, you are free to come back at whatever time you desire.... And now, I must disgracefully close this session."

17

As soon as the door closed behind Gustavo, Raimundo burst into gleeful laughter.

"What's so funny?" asked Vachio.

"Gustavo. The most folkloric of all the folklorics.... *Gustavo Prada Nieto*, alias *El Chorizo*."

"*Chorizo*!" exclaimed Vachio, laughing. "Yeah, that's good. He looks like a sausage with that pasty, freckled complexion."

"Yeah, but don't you call him that. That's what his enemies call him. And then it's like one of those cheap westerns—you better smile when you say that, partner."

"Or what?"

Raimundo's lips tightened. "Gustavo's pulled guns on more than one occasion."

"Why? Does he have many enemies?"

"He has many enemies. Almost as many enemies as friends."

"What's the problem?"

"Garrotero, man. The Town of the Stick Stranglers. There are vendettas and stupidities that go back generations here. And aside from that, Gustavo is a political figure in the Liberal Party and is directly related to the most powerful man in town. In fact, one of the most powerful men in all of Santander."

"Who's that?"

"El Viejo Miranda."

"Miranda. Yeah, I heard Gustavo and the mayor talking about him the first night I was in town.... *Viejo*, eh. How old is the guy?"

"He's not that old. But he is wise. Believe me, the guy misses nothing that goes on around here. He is another of the very folkloric characters I've been talking about. Very folkloric."

"Why? What's his, uh...thing?"

"He's just an incredible personage. For one thing, he owns half of Garrotero—property, sugar cane, tobacco, you name it. He has fingers into everything. For another thing, he dresses like a complete slob, as though he didn't have a dime to his name, and he speaks in a low guttural voice that makes him sound drunk all the time and uses the gross vocabulary of the commonest campesino. Yet, he writes beautiful poetry, and contributes regularly to the Vanguardia Liberal newspaper.... Yes, sir, Miranda is a real Don. He is so important he doesn't have to put on any airs. And he's a shrewd and intelligent player. Nothing of any importance goes on around Garrotero without *El Viejo* having something to say about it."

"And Gustavo does things for this guy?"

"Of course, son. They're family."

"Uh huh.... So what about you and Gustavo? Are you two good friends?"

"Yes, we're friends. We became friends shortly after I moved here."

"Really? What was the attraction?"

Raimundo laughed. "Well, Gustavo has been around much more than the average person in this town.... I think he likes to talk to me because I'm a foreigner and I have a different view of the world than most of the people who grew up in this place and have never been anywhere else."

"What about you?"

"Gustavo's a good guy."

"Is he really?"

"What do you mean?"

"What about that picture of Hitler in his living room?"

"Oh, you already saw that? Well, that's nothing. It's a joke."

"A joke? I didn't get that impression."

"No, man, it's nothing. Nothing. Don't worry about it."

"Don't worry about it. I have a boss who has a picture of Adolph Hitler on his living room wall facing Jesus Christ and you say I shouldn't worry about it."

"All right, calm down. Listen to me. Like many men here, Gustavo has something of the *caudillo* complex, but he is basically a very decent human being. Folkloric, yes! But decent. He's been a good friend to us. And as director of the *Casa de Menores*, he has done progressive things with the boys that were never considered in the past. His heart is in the right place."

"What are some of the things he has done?"

"Well, he's responsible for bringing you here," chortled Raimundo. "Up until now the recreation program has consisted of one of the staff throwing a ball into the patio and telling the boys to entertain themselves."

"Yeah, what else?"

"Many things. He's the one who initiated the outside job program for the boys. And he has maintained it against tremendous opposition from his political enemies in town."

"Why would they oppose a program like that?"

"If for nothing else, it's a good opportunity to attack their enemy—*El Chorizo*."

"But how do they justify it?"

"By saying that juvenile delinquents—most of them outsiders at that—are getting paid money to work while fathers of families go unemployed."

"Well, that's a good point."

"A good point?" Raimundo's voice dripped scorn. "Man, these aren't regular jobs that can support a family. In the case of my factory, it's strictly piece work. We hire a few kids when we have big orders on a temporary basis. They make a few pesos, gain some work experience, and maybe some self-respect. That's all. Most of our regular employees, machine operators and such, are men from Garrotero and get full union benefits. But for the piece work, cutting, sorting, and boxing, we hire mostly women and younger men. They generally have more nimble fingers and can make more money than a man who has always been a laborer.... But of course, there never lacks some idiot who wants to make a political issue out of it. That's the way it is here."

"What do you mean?"

"Man, you'll see soon enough. Anything can become a political issue here. For example, they raise the bus fare 20 centavos because the price of gasoline goes up and all hell breaks loose. A great clamor goes up from the leftists and the poorest of the poor, a few buses get torched, some poor fools get pounded on by the police, the students demonstrate, a curfew is enforced, and a week later, it's business as usual with the new fare in place. Pure folklore."

"Pure folklore? That sounds dangerous to me. How do you know the lid won't blow off completely one of these times? Like it has in the past here."

For a moment Raimundo looked uncertain. "Nah, it's not as bad as it seems," he said gruffly, almost as though he were trying to convince himself. "You just have to know how to mind your own business and keep your head down at certain times. It's not a problem."

"Yeah, if you say so. But I'm not so sure. You know, there is a Peace Corps volunteer who was kidnaped here and is still being held."

"Yes, I heard of that. And I also heard he is a real jerk that no one where he worked wanted to protect.... Listen, man, for you, if you're smart, things are like this. On Market Day here, Sunday, the *campesinos* come in from the sticks to sell their goods. Some of them start drinking early in the morning and are drunk by noon. Then, before you know it, two guys who were drinking together and talking like best friends are calling each other triple son-of-a-bitches and are pulling out their machetes and going after each other. Then you have a big show and a fight. But usually, the guys are so wasted no one gets seriously injured."

"But what the hell are they fighting about?"

"Who knows? Some stupidity from the past. Maybe a rivalry over some loose woman. Whatever idiocy. I saw one guy get a piece of his ear slashed off and a week later he was back drinking with the guy who fucked him up as though nothing had happened.... But my point is, these are personal matters between them. If you are not involved, you have nothing to worry about."

"Yeah, well, in Bogotá, they told me the Santandereans can get seriously violent."

"Yes, that's their reputation from past civil wars. But right now it's pretty calm here. And anyway, you're from the United States—one of the most violent places on earth."

"Good point," said Vachio, laughing. "The pot shouldn't call the kettle black."

"Exactly. And some of the violence here is exaggerated. For example..." Raimundo got up and rubbed his hands together, a gleeful look on his face. "Take Gustavo. My nickname for him is The Avenger of the Wild West because of something that happened a few months ago." Raimundo paused for a moment. "Like I've been saying, some things seem worse than they really are. I'm not sure you'll understand this."

"Try me."

"Well, all right... You see, I have this old Opel that almost never runs. It's a good car. But I can't get replacement parts for it here so the mechanics have to try to improvise and it's usually in preventive maintenance..."

Vachio laughed.

"Anyway, this one night, I had it parked on the side street next to the factory. The battery cables were defective and it had been sitting there for about a week. I was working late at the shop, and I had just stepped out of the front door to go home when I hear shots. Pow! Pow! Pow! Next I see this old bum in tattered clothes running past me and down the street as though he were being chased by the devil himself. Then Gustavo comes around the corner and approaches me, a smoking gun in his hand and a big smile on his face. So I say, 'Gustavo, what the hell happened?' And he tells me, his manner calm as can be, 'A thief was trying to steal your car, Raimundo. But relax, everything is under control. I scared him away.' So I tell him, 'Thief? You mean that old bum who ran past here?' And he says, 'That was no bum. That was a desperate criminal. And he was about to get away with your car.' So I start laughing and I say, 'Gustavo, many thanks for protecting my interests. But it would be pretty difficult for anyone to steal my car without the battery cables in place. I think it was just some poor old guy looking for a place to sleep.' Gustavo looks at me, shakes his head, and says in a very serious tone of voice, 'Raimundo, never underestimate the capabilities of a Colombian thief.'"

Vachio laughed until his sides ached.

"Ah hah! You do understand," said Raimundo. "Good. Good. There may be hope for you, son.... And isn't that Gustavo a case?"

"Yeah, a regular Clint Eastwood."

Raimundo guffawed. "But don't get the idea Gustavo is a clown. He is a true *folklórico*. And a genuine personage. On Easter Sunday, or at big political events, he gives speeches at the plaza in front of thousands of people. And he is a fabulous speaker. Man, I've seen him hold a crowd entranced for an hour. When he gets rolling, even his enemies listen up."

"All right," interrupted Renata. "You can continue this at the table. The food is ready. Come before it gets cold."

Still chuckling, the two men followed Renata to the table and sat down. Vachio's mouth watered as he looked over a steaming plate of potato pancakes, crispy fried chicken, rice, and a tossed garden salad. Raimundo piled additional food onto his plate and invited Vachio to do the same. Vachio was pleased to comply, heaping sour cream and applesauce onto the potato pancakes. While Raimundo told another folkloric Gustavo story, Vachio listened and savored his food, pausing between chews only long enough to help himself to more chicken.

Finally Vachio paused for air and with a contented sigh said, "Renata, this is a great meal. The only thing missing is a little red sauerkraut."

Renata looked up in surprise. "Red Sauerkraut? You know about that, too?"

"Sure. I've had German food many times."

"Why? Is your family part German?"

"Ay, Reina," boomed Raimundo. "How could he be part German with a name like Vachio and that mafioso face?"

"Fortunately, I'm not part German," said Vachio, giving Raimundo a sharp look. "I'm Italian on my father's side and Basque on my mother's side."

"Basque. Ay, yai, yai!" exploded Raimundo. "Italian and Basque. What a combination. Terrorism and anarchy run in this man's blood. Don't let him near any gasoline or..."

"Raimundo! Hush!" said Renata. "I want to know why Vachio is so familiar with German food.... Have you been to Germany?"

Vachio stifled a chuckle at the chastened look on Raimundo's face and said, "No, I've never been to Europe. But I used to work at a restaurant in San Francisco that served Continental Cuisine. And the head chef was German. So I got to try my share of German food."

"Did you like working there?" asked Renata.

Vachio shrugged. "I didn't particularly like or dislike the work. It was just a way to make money for school. But the place was interesting because of all the different types and nationalities of people working there."

"Huh, I can imagine," said Renata, a dreamy look in her eyes. "San Francisco is a very cosmopolitan city, isn't it?"

"Cosmopolitan is an understatement. Like in the restaurant, it was almost a Tower of Babel. I mean, we had Chinese, Koreans, Filipinos, Jamaicans, Mexicans, Salvadorans, Nicaraguans, Costa Ricans, French, German, Dutch, Austrians, Peruvians, Hondurans, Arabs, and a few more I can't remember right now." Vachio chuckled. "Hell, we even had a handful of native born Americans.... But no joke, you could walk into that kitchen at almost any time and hear conversations in six or seven different languages."

"How did everyone communicate?" asked Renata.

"English.... But with some it was Pidgen English."

"Did that bother you?"

"No, it was an education. It taught me how to communicate with all different types of people. Kind of like working at a poor man's United Nations.... And I enjoyed learning about all the different foods and customs."

"It sounds exotic," said Renata.

"It was that."

"I studied in Paris one summer and it was something like that. Open and cosmopolitan. I loved it," said Renata.

"And now? How do you like it here?"

There was a long moment of silence. Raimundo and Renata exchanged glances. Then Renata said, "It's peaceful and sane here. After living in the craziness of Bogotá and Medellín for five years, it's a nice change.... Not that this is completely new for me. I grew up in a small town near Munich."

"Yeah, but this still must be quite an adjustment..."

Raimundo looked increasingly uncomfortable as their conversation unfolded. "Hey, Vachio!" he interrupted. "Can I tell you anything about the people in the *Casa de Menores*?"

Vachio was going to ignore Raimundo and continue his conversation with Renata, but he took a good look at his face and noticed anxiety behind the bluster. "Sure, tell me what you know. How about that Cabrera? You know him?"

"Yes, of course. What about him?"

"He's been trying to give me a hard time."

"Cabrera? Really? He's usually not a bad guy."

"Yeah, well, he's got some bug up his ass. I mean, he's telling me to run the kids through hard calisthenics every day so that they're too tired for homosexual activities at night. And then he got on my case about wearing shorts to play basketball with the kids. What kind of attitude is that?"

"He really did that?" exclaimed Renata. "How curious."

Raimundo chuckled. "Don't worry about it. Cabrera has his ideas, but he's basically a decent guy. It's just that he has a little bit of the religious fanatic in him. He joined one of those Evangelical churches and since then has become a bit heavy on the moral stances.... But he is up front. He won't be devious with you."

"I don't know," said Vachio, shaking his head. "I'm getting very negative feelings from this guy. On a personal level."

"Huh, could be he feels threatened by you."

"I don't know why. I just want to do my thing with the kids. I'm not looking to impose anything on anyone."

"Yeah, but you see, Cabrera doesn't have a college degree like you and the other administrators. Yet he fancies himself a real Doctor. So he feels insecure sometimes. But don't worry about it. As long as Gustavo is on your side, he'll come around. Or at least he won't hinder you."

"A real Doctor, huh." Vachio grimaced. "Funny, but Gustavo made a point of telling the kids not to call me Doctor."

Raimundo laughed. "That's good. The truth is, they call almost any half-ass idiot here a Doctor. Be thankful that they don't call you one, because more than likely they would be making fun of you."

"Well, yeah, I understand that. And I don't want them to call me Doctor. But I found it strange that Gustavo made an issue of it. You know, like he was putting me in my place instead of letting me establish my own."

"Nah, don't worry about it. You're thinking too much. It's nothing,... So anyway, we know who you don't like. Now who do you like?"

"The Social Worker. Maria Elena."

Both Renata and Raimundo laughed.

"Yes, she's easy to like," said Raimundo.

"And nice to look at, too. No?" said Renata.

"Yes, but I don't mean it like that," said Vachio.

"Maria Elena is an excellent person," said Raimundo. "And in her work, considering the limitations placed on her, she is very competent. Very professional."

"Yeah, that's my impression of her."

"Who else?" asked Raimundo.

"I like the psychologist. Uh, what's his name?... Emilio."

"Ah, yes, Emilio Montoya. He's the best. In fact, he's too good for the *Casa de Menores*."

"What do you mean?"

"He won't be with us much longer. He's been offered a position at a university in Quito, Ecuador. And even though Gustavo has done his best to talk him out of it, he has accepted."

"He didn't tell me anything about that. When is he leaving?"

"In about six months—something like that. It's too bad, he'll be missed."

Vachio poked at the remaining crumbs of food on his plate, feeling sharp disappointment. Of all the people he had met at the *Casa de Menores*, Montoya was the one with whom he had felt the most affinity—an affinity of temperament and general outlook on life.

After coffee and dessert, Raimundo and Vachio returned to the living room. Raimundo turned on the television and chortled as The Streets of San Francisco appeared on the fuzzy black and white screen. "Just to make you feel at home, Buddy Boy," Raimundo said to Vachio.

"I don't think it will."

"Well, at least distract yourself for a while. I need to do something." Raimundo went into the kitchen and had an animated conversation with Renata in German. Then he returned with a large basket filled with empty bottles and said, "We're out of beer. Take these bottles and exchange them for ones with infusion. Here's some money."

Vachio's temper flared at Raimundo's peremptory tone and manner. "What's up? Are you too lazy to go with me?"

"No. I want you to have the cultural experience to yourself. The store up the street is very folkloric."

"Fine. Then let's go together."

"No, man. I need to do something here."

"All right, then. But let me buy the beer." Vachio realized Raimundo wanted to talk things over with Renata. "Where's the store?"

"Out the door to the right. Straight up the street about a block and a half. Got it?"

"Yeah."

"And get some toilet paper, too."

"*Jawhol, Mein Sheiskopf.*"

Raimundo stared at Vachio in surprise. "Where did you learn to say shit head in German?"

"At the restaurant. I learned to cuss in about seven different languages. It came in handy when people tried to order me around when they shouldn't. You dig, man?"

"Yeah, man, I dig?" said Raimundo with a laugh. "Your German is like my Oxford English. So let me rephrase.... Please buy some paper for the shit can. Is that better?"

"Much better," said Vachio, passing through the doorway and into the night. Vachio strolled up the quiet, empty street, aiming at a Coca-Cola sign illuminated by a single bright bulb on the next block. The night was clear and comfortable, stars twinkled and comets flashed across the equatorial sky. Crickets chirped and toads croaked from a lush gully on the other side of an adjacent, graffiti-laced wall. Vachio paused and inhaled deeply. A sense of well-being flooded through him. "I might just get to like this place," he muttered.

Then he reached the store and swung into the entrance, his smile fading in the dimly lit interior, choked off by the thick cigar smoke, a sudden silence, and three pairs of suspicious eyes. Vachio pretended to scan the goods stacked on shelves behind the counter. Two men, slouched on rickety chairs before a square wood table covered with empty beer bottles, watched Vachio from a corner behind him. A solidly built man with long graying sideburns and piercing eyes stood behind the counter. No one smiled. No one spoke. Vachio suddenly felt very jittery. He nodded to the men at the table, stepped forward, and swung his basket of bottles onto the counter. The two men answered his greeting with blank faces.

"At your order," prompted the man behind the counter.

"I need beer. The same number as in this basket. And..." Vachio couldn't remember the proper word for toilet paper. "And..."

"Yes, what else?"

"Paper for the bathroom."

"What?"

"You know, paper for the bathroom..."

The man behind the counter looked at his friends, a sarcastic smile creasing his face. "It sure is difficult to understand these *gringos*."

Vachio felt a rush of anger as the men chuckled at him and snapped out, "Let's try another way.... I need paper to clean my ass. Understand that?"

For a moment the man behind the counter stood with his mouth agape, a beer bottle poised in his hand over the basket. Then one of the men at the table burst into raucous laughter.

"That's the way to communicate," said the other man at the table, tipping his bottle toward Vachio.

The counterman grinned at Vachio, the tension seeping out of the room. Then he reached behind him, grabbed a roll of toilet paper, and said, "The correct name for this is hygienic paper."

As the counterman filled up the basket with cold beers and rolls of toilet paper, he asked Vachio questions. Then his voice turned insinuating and he said, "So you're having a little party, eh?"

"No. Just dinner and some beers with Raimundo and his wife."

"Raimundo the German?"

"Yes."

"Raimundo is one of my best customers.... Is he a friend of yours?"

"Yes. A very good friend," said Vachio, exaggerating to measure the man's reaction.

"Don Raimundo is a good man. He's done a lot for Garrotero." The counterman's voice had turned almost obsequious. He reached under the counter and brought out a bottle of *aguardiente* and two shot glasses. He filled the glasses and passed one to Vachio. "Sorry about our little misunderstanding earlier," he said, raising his glass. "Welcome to Garrotero."

"*Salud*!" said Vachio, tossing down his shot. Then he lapsed into silence. The counterman's sudden show of friendliness struck him as insincere. "Well, I better get going," said Vachio. "They're waiting for the beer."

Vachio hoisted his basket and beat it back to Raimundo's house, mulling the encounter over in his mind. Things had turned out all right, but it could easily have gone in another direction.

"What took you so long?" asked Raimundo, looking up from the television set as Vachio came through the door. Then he noticed Vachio's pensive face and asked, "What happened?"

"Ah, some jerk at the store tried to give me a hard time." Vachio plopped onto the sofa and folded his arms across his chest.

"So tell me what happened?"

Vachio told him the whole story, including the sense of alarm he had felt on entering the store. At the end, Raimundo shrugged, popped open two beers, handed one to Vachio, and said, "Forget about that, it's no big deal. They were just having a little fun with you."

"No, man, it wasn't fun at first. And it wasn't what they said to me...it was the tone of their voices and their looks."

Raimundo had turned his attention back to the television set after a commercial break. "Ah, don't be so sensitive. Forget about it. It was nothing.... Watch this Streets of San Francisco episode. It's a good one."

"I already saw it. It's weak," said Vachio, angered that Raimundo was dismissing his concerns so casually.

"Well, I like it. It's cool.... Say, do you recognize any of the scenery?"

Vachio glanced at the television screen, then looked in earnest as he recognized the interior of an old, gilt-edged Catholic church. "Yeah, I do know that church. That's Saint James. One of the oldest in the city..."

"Wait a minute," said Raimundo, holding up his hand, his face glued to the tube. "Let me watch the rest of this scene."

Vachio sighed and watched along with him. A fair-skinned Hispanic cop, his face tense and full of hate, was pointing a gun at a dark-skinned, Cholo-looking hood with bushy hair. The hood had taunted him earlier, accusing him of being a sell-out to his race. As the cop's finger itched on the trigger, Karl Malden stood in the background, urging the cop not to fire, telling him to do his job as he should, invoking the name of the cop's old, dignified mother in Salinas. Finally the Hispanic cop's face relaxed, Malden's words had hit home, and he lowered the point of his gun and sagged on his feet. The terrified hood stood trembling in place; Michael Douglas rushed in from the back and arrested the hood. Karl Malden comforted the other cop, assuring him that he had done the right thing. They faded to a commercial.

"That was great!" said Raimundo. "But what did they mean when the hood called the cop a *Tio Taco*?"

"Oh, that's like when one Latino says another is brown outside and white inside."

"Yeah, so? The guy was white. He was a white Latino."

"Right. But that's not referring so much to skin color as to culture."

Raimundo shook his head. "That's absurd. What do color and culture have to do with each other? Culture is something you learn, it's not genetic."

Vachio shrugged. "Don't ask me to explain it. It's a big complex in the United States. I mean, talk about absurd, I grew up around a lot of Latinos and they used to call me a White Boy. But here in Colombia, when people find out I have an Italian last name, they say I'm Latino because Italian is Latin ancestry."

Raimundo laughed. "And what do you think of that?"

"I think it's absurd. I identify myself more as an individual. I don't want to carry a bunch of cultural baggage around with me. I think my person goes deeper than race or culture. And that's universal. It can go anywhere."

Raimundo looked at Vachio in surprise. Then he changed the subject. "What were you saying about that church before?"

"I was saying that it's only about five blocks from where I grew up. I've been there many times."

"Really? It didn't look like a very nice neighborhood."

Vachio shrugged. "It wasn't the best, but it wasn't the worst, either. I don't have any regrets about growing up there."

"Do a lot of Latinos really live there?"

"It's mostly Latino in that section."

"Ah hah! That explains some things about you."

"You think so?"

The Epilogue came on and Raimundo returned his attention to the screen. The Hispanic cop, Martin, changed from Martinez, took a leave of absence to get back in touch with his identity. Malden and Douglas speculated that he was on his way to becoming a complete human being and a good cop.

"Just that easy. Way to go, Buddy Boy," muttered Vachio.

Raimundo got up, switched off the television, and said, "Follow me. It's time to do the monkey business."

He led Vachio through the kitchen and into a small patio at the rear of the house. Raimundo leaned up against a concrete wash basin in the middle of the patio and said, "Well, son, Renata and I have decided that we like you enough to give it a try..."

"That's good. Now I have to decide if I like you guys."

Raimundo flinched and his grin tightened.

"Just kidding," said Vachio. "I like you guys well enough to give it a try, also. But make me a formal offer. And where am I supposed to sleep?"

"Right over here," said Raimundo, stepping toward a room that flanked the patio. Raimundo switched on the light and ushered Vachio inside. The room had a double bed with boxes and crates piled all around it, leaving scant space to move around. A small bookcase sat against one of the windows near the foot of the bed.

"What do you think?" asked Raimundo.

"It looks like a warehouse in here. What's with all the boxes?"

"Oh, that's nothing. We'll clean it out for you. We brought too much stuff from Bogotá with us for a house this size."

"This place is big enough for what I need," said Vachio, flopping onto the bed and bouncing up and down on it. "Good. It's nice and firm. The way I like it. This will do. How much?"

"One moment," said Raimundo, stepping out of the room and going to get Renata. Vachio rolled off the bed and looked through the books on the shelves. There were titles in English, Spanish, and German. Raimundo had a collection of Henry Miller books, as well as a smattering of Hemmingway, Fitzgerald, and Mann. "All the expatriate stuff," muttered Vachio. He turned away from the books just as Raimundo and Renata entered the room.

"So, Vachio, are the accommodations to your liking?" asked Renata.

"I think so. But tell me the price."

The price was to Vachio's satisfaction, about 25 percent of his salary, and after a brief haggle as to whether Vachio would also eat on a regular basis with them, the deal was closed and they shook hands all the way around.

"So you're definitely agreed to boarding with us when you come to work here in January?" asked Renata.

"Definitely. It's a done deal. My word."

"Very well, then," said Renata. "I'll leave you two now. I'm very tired."

Renata retired to the master bedroom and Raimundo followed her. Vachio went to the living room and opened up another beer, happy the business was settled. Raimundo soon joined him, picked up his guitar, and sat down directly opposite Vachio.

"Are we ready to sing now?" he asked, strumming a few bars.

"Why do you have so many Henry Miller books?" countered Vachio. "Is he your hero or something?"

Raimundo laughed and plucked a tune on his guitar while singing, "Little Colette she had no sense, serving the breakfast without her pants. Spoiling the coffee, burning the eggs, all of her brains are between her legs. Oh, quiet days in Garrotero..." Raimundo broke up, unable to finish.

"What the hell is that?" asked Vachio.

"It's from the movie about Henry Miller. Quiet Days in Clichy. Music by Country Joe and The Fish.... Haven't you seen it?"

Vachio shook his head.

"Well, you are culturally deprived. You have to see it. Or at least read the book. It's a Bohemian classic."

"Says who?"

"Says I. Don Raimundo. It's funny as hell."

"Whatever you say, man. But tell me, why do you think Miller is so good?"

Raimundo set the guitar across his knees and, looking straight at Vachio, said in English, "Because he was able to do what he wanted without playing the fucking game. Not many can boast of that. He is one of the few American writers I respect."

Vachio shrugged. "Well, maybe I'll read him and see what gets you so excited."

Raimundo grunted and took up his guitar. He began singing a Beatles tune. Before he knew it, Vachio had joined in and they worked through a medley of songs in both Spanish and English. They sat there for hours, singing, drinking beer, talking, and listening to records. By the time Renata got up and informed them in no uncertain terms that it was time to end the party, it was well past midnight.

Raimundo accompanied Vachio on the walk to Gustavo's house, laughing and talking all the way, his voice ringing in the dead silence of the pueblo. At the door they shook hands and exchanged a spontaneous embrace. This surprised Vachio. It was certainly something that men commonly do in Latin America, but not something he did lightly.

"All right, brother, sleep well," said Raimundo.

"Yeah, brother. The same."

18

Friday morning Vachio awoke to the rooster's crowing feeling great. Thursday had passed like a fuzzy dream. He had started out with a mild hangover and accompanied Gustavo to a regional meeting of SENA bigwigs in Bucaramanga. There, he sat bored through a fiscal meeting, awakening only long enough to deliver a brief address on why he had come to Colombia to work and what he planned to accomplish. Vachio's impromptu presentation was well-received by these predominately upper class functionaries, and after the meeting, Gustavo congratulated him and evinced surprise.

"You spoke very well. I'm impressed. Sincerely."

Vachio shrugged. "Hey, I went to a Jesuit school for a while. I know how to lay on educated rhetoric—if I have to."

Gustavo took Vachio on a quick tour of Bucaramanga, then back to Garrotero for an afternoon session of soccer with the boys at the *Casa de Menores*. After the game, Vachio drank *tinto* and chatted with some of the *profesores* in the cafeteria, ate dinner at the home of one of Gustavo's sisters, and spent the rest of the evening reading after taking a walk around the plaza. All in all, it had been a quiet, uneventful day, probably more typical of what Vachio could expect when he returned in January to work and settled into his routine.

Vachio got out of bed and stretched in the diffused soft light of the patio, his eyes bright, his batteries completely recharged. He ate the breakfast laid out for him on the patio table, read the paper, prepared his bag for departure early the next morning, and generally puttered around. Gustavo had told him not to go to the *Casa de Menores* until about ten. Vachio was more than a little impatient. Today was the day of his *fiesta*. "The hell with it," muttered Vachio, glancing at the clock and seeing that it was only nine. "I'm going now."

Vachio ran into Miguel in front of the *Casa de Menores*. He was wearing sunglasses and already smelled of liquor. Miguel stuck out his sinewy hand and gave Vachio a brisk handshake.

"Hey, Vachio. How are you?"

"I'm fine, Miguel. And you? It seems to me you're off to an early start."

Miguel laughed. "Just priming up for the big day for you, brother. I hope you're ready for it. Because this is a holiday for us and we're ready for a good time."

"Sure, I'm ready. All I have to do is be here, right?"

"That's the spirit," said Miguel, slapping Vachio on the shoulder. "Now if you'll excuse me, I have to go to the office and tie up a few loose ends before we leave."

Vachio slapped the side of his neck. What Miguel had said about tying up loose ends reminded him that he needed to find Rolo and get the letter to his mother from him.

Vachio followed Miguel inside and went to the gate. Oliva was on duty. The turnkey greeted Vachio warmly and let him in without being asked.

"Is Rolo about?" Vachio asked.

Oliva pointed toward the gate leading from the patio into the dining area. "He's down there. Passing through the head count."

"Will he delay long?"

"Long enough. Why? Are you in a hurry?"

"Well..."

Oliva stuck his hand inside his shirt and pulled out an envelope. He held it up so Vachio could read the names. "Is this what you came for?"

The letter was addressed to Elvira Ramirez, from Octavio.

"Yes."

Oliva handed Vachio the letter. "He asked me to give this to you if he didn't have the opportunity himself."

"That's fine."

"This is a good thing you're doing for the boy. His mother will be pleased to have news of him."

"It's no big deal."

"I've been watching you," said Oliva, sticking out his hand. "I like your style. Count on me if you ever need some help here."

"Thanks. After some of the things I've been hearing around here from some of the other guards, you don't know how happy what you said makes me feel."

"I can imagine," said Oliva, giving Vachio a wry look. "It's not easy to know your friends in this place."

Vachio folded the letter, stuck it in his pocket, and walked out into the courtyard. To pass the time, he went to the kitchen for a coffee.

Pacho found him there a few minutes later.

"Where have you been?" asked Pacho.

"Around. Why?"

Pacho grinned. "I've been looking for you. Gustavo is outside waiting for us."

"Already? Early?"

"Ay, man, don't complain. This is like a holiday. The earlier the better."

"I'm not complaining. I'm just shocked."

"Let's go."

Gustavo and Miguel were waiting for them in the car. Pacho and Vachio slipped into the back seat and they were off. Gustavo, Pacho, and Miguel were in high spirits, laughing and joking as they drove through the heart of town and toward the road to Bogotá. Vachio sat quietly, thinking over what Oliva had said to him at the last, "It's not easy to know your friends in this place."

Gustavo noticed Vachio's serious face in the rear view mirror. "Is something troubling you, Vachio?"

"No," said Vachio, shaking his head. "I was just thinking about something. Nothing important."

"Ay, well, cheer up, man," said Pacho. "This is a joyful day. You have to be more like we Santandereans—happy, vital, alive."

"Man, spare me the stereotypes."

Miguel cracked-up. "Ay, this Vachio. He'll never be a politician."

"That is definitely not certain. You should have heard him yesterday under other circumstances," said Gustavo.

They drove outside of town, turned onto a dirt road, and penetrated a large sugar cane plantation. Gustavo turned onto a tree-lined dirt road and up to a large, ranch-style house, shaded by palms and bougainvillea, with a wide veranda and a handsome red-tiled roof. A slim, distinguished looking gentleman with silvery hair and a Panama hat sat in a wicker chair awaiting their arrival. Surveying the scene from the back seat, Vachio felt as though he had been transported back to the 18th century.

They got out of the car and Gustavo presented Vachio to Don Villalobos, lord and master of the plantation. Then a lengthy explanation, complete with biographical details, was given for Vachio's visit. Don Villalobos listened politely, his ear cocked to one side as though he were hard of hearing, nodding at appropriate times and injecting good-humored comments. His carriage and speech were impressive. He was a born and bred aristocrat.

After Gustavo finished, Villalobos yanked on an old fashioned bell cord to summon a servant from inside the house. An attractive young woman, full-bodied and clean-limbed, with tawny skin and flowing black hair, wearing a simple shift and sandals, appeared before them.

"Señor?" she said, waiting for Villalobo's command with her head slightly inclined and her dark eyes hooded by long lashes.

"Luz del Alba, please bring our guests hot *panela*."

She went inside the house and returned shortly with a tray loaded with coffee mugs full of steaming *panela* tea. As she distributed the refreshments, Vachio was struck by her looks and carriage. Her movements were as lithe and graceful as a young lioness. Then it hit him. He had seen her before. She was the woman on the horse they had almost run over on Vachio's first day on the road near the construction site. Luz del Alba flicked her eyes as she served Vachio, but her impassive face gave no sign of recognition or any particular interest. Then she was gone.

"This is the principal product of my ranch," said Villalobos to Vachio. "Here we specialize in *panela*. It makes a fine, invigorating drink. Don't you think, Señor Vachio?"

Vachio nodded. It tasted like all the rest of the *panela* he had drunk during the week. He preferred coffee.

"I drink at least a quart of *panela* a day," continued Villalobos. "I believe it keeps me healthy and vigorous, even at my advanced age."

The men finished their *panela* and Gustavo said, "With your permission, Don Villalobos, we'd like to show Vachio the *trapiche*. It would be a novelty for him."

"Of course. At your pleasure. But you'll excuse me if I don't accompany you. These old bones take a while to warm up in the cool mornings.... I believe you know the way."

Gustavo nodded and led the group to a dirt path leading away from the house. Vachio lagged behind and Miguel dropped back to talk.

"Takes his old bones a while to warm up in the cool mornings," scoffed Miguel. "More like he wants that sweet young thing to warm them up for him. The old buzzard isn't even discreet anymore since his wife passed away.... It must be nice to be rich."

They came in sight of a long, open-sided shed. Quantities of flies buzzed in and around it and the air was redolent of caramel.

"You know, Vachio, when I was a young man, I worked in a sugar mill like this one."

"So, how was it?"

"Hard work. Very hard work. It makes me appreciate the kind of job I have now."

Gustavo and Pacho were gabbing with the foreman. With a slight gesture, Gustavo indicated to Miguel to show Vachio around. Miguel grinned and ushered Vachio from one work station to another, explaining the different functions and duties of the men and women workers. Vachio saw mounds of cut cane, the steel grinding machines to extract the juice, bubbling vats of liquid sugar, finished blocks of *panela* piled on long tables, and workers packing the blocks in wax paper. At the end of the tour, Miguel called over a sweating shirtless worker who was bringing up raw cane in a wheel barrow.

"Would you like a taste of one of the more important by-products?" Miguel asked Vachio.

"What's that?"

"*Guarapo*. Have you tried it yet?"

"Yes. I didn't like it that much."

Miguel laughed. "This should be better quality."

"We make some of the best," said the worker. "We call it medicine for the head."

"Bring it," said Miguel.

The worker went to a nearby shed and brought back an unlabeled bottle. Vachio submitted to the ritual without comment. This *guarapo* is better than what I drank with Prudencio, he thought. But it ain't ever going to be my favorite drink.

"How is it?" the worker asked Vachio."

"It's fine."

Miguel took a long swallow. Then he wiped his mouth and said, "Vachio, today you're going to try some of the best and more typical things Santander has to offer. Simple things. But good things. We hope you find them to your satisfaction."

"Well, if I don't, I'll surely tell you."

Miguel chuckled and patted Vachio on the back. "I'm beginning to think you really would."

A short time later the men returned to the car and proceeded due south on the highway to Bogotá. Cane fields and small plantations swept past, flowing back from the road in uneven waves to gullies and crevices at the foot of the lush eastern mountains, the properties separated by walls of piled stones. To the west they were shadowed by a burbling stream, the thick tropical vegetation along its bank giving way to scruffy eroded hills and a broad mist-shrouded plateau in the distance. Miguel pointed out landmarks and maintained a running commentary.

Then, at a bottleneck where the eastern mountains jutted close to the road and the stream converged from the other side, they halted at a combination toll booth and inspection station. Uniformed guards carrying automatic weapons looked them over carefully.

"The boys look a little nervous today," said Miguel.

"Well they should be," said Gustavo. "Two soldiers were murdered up near San Vicente just the other day by some miserable terrorists."

"Don Gustavo! How are you today?" asked the toll collector.

"Fine. Fine." Gustavo handed him some money, exchanged some small talk, and off they went. Vachio was beginning to wonder if there was anyone in Santander Gustavo didn't know.

Minutes later, Gustavo pulled off the road into a large dusty truck stop. Several gleaming big rigs, complete with Che Guevara mud flaps and colorful macrame cab window trim, reposed in the warm sun. The

Casa de Menores pick-up truck was parked alongside.

"Good. Some of them are already here," said Pacho.

Beyond the parking lot lay a rambling, ramshackle building with pitted stucco and a corrugated steel roof. Long wooden tables and cow-hide chairs were aligned in front of the building under a low metal awning. A large stone barbecue grill smoked at one end, thin strips of meat hanging from wooden poles alongside. A *cabaña*-style refreshment stand stood just beyond the grill, shaded by luxuriant banana and mango trees. A group of men from the *Casa de Menores* was already seated at one of the tables, drinking beer and *guarapo*. When they saw Gustavo's group, they let out whoops of welcome. Fredy was there, along with Dolfo, Jessie, the guard Ramon, and some other guards Vachio didn't know.

"Don't be fooled by the appearance of this place," Gustavo said to Vachio. "It's rustic, but they have some of the best typical Santanderean food around."

"Yeah? It looks like a truck stop to me. But in the United States, we say they have the best food at truck stops."

"Is it true?"

"Not necessarily."

"Well, this place is special," said Miguel, grinning. "Not only for the food. This is a full service truck stop."

Pacho guffawed.

"What's that mean?" asked Vachio.

"Maybe you'll find out later," said Pacho, winking at Miguel.

They joined the others at the table. Vachio sat next to Miguel and Ramon. Gustavo went inside to speak to the owner. Miguel called for beers and a dark buxom woman with a bare midriff and a short tight skirt came over to serve them. Miguel regaled her with suggestive compliments as she set down the beers. The woman merely smiled, showing a number of gold teeth, and tossed her long black hair away from her eyes.

"Hey, sweetness, are you going to pay attention to me today?" asked Miguel, tapping her elbow.

"No."

"Why?"

"Because I'm in charge of the bar today," she said in a matter-of-fact tone. "You know what that means."

"Ay, that's a disappointment."

"Why? You can come back another day."

"It's not for me. We have a special guest here today that I want you to know. A *gringo*."

"Who? This one?" she said, nodding toward Vachio.

"Exactly. What do you think of him?"

The woman looked Vachio up and down. "He doesn't look bad. But can he talk?"

"Yes, of course. But your great charms seem to have struck him deaf and mute."

The men roared with laughter and snapped their hands. Vachio blushed, his mind snapped awake.

"Actually, I can talk like a parrot," Vachio said to her.

"You said that too clearly to be a *gringo*," said the woman.

"As I said, I talk like a parrot."

"No. These guys are pulling my leg. You're not really a *gringo*."

Vachio shrugged, looked around the table for effect, and held up his right hand. "I swear to you that I'm an authentic *gringo*."

"Check his passport," interjected Pacho.

"I don't believe you guys," said the woman.

"What's so hard to believe," said Vachio. "We're not an endangered species."

The woman still looked dubious.

"No, he really is a *gringo*," said Miguel. "I'll vouch for him."

Suddenly the woman extended her hand to Vachio. "Pleased to meet you. My name is Mila. Do you like me?"

"Sure."

"Good. Then come back another day when I'm not on bar duty. I've never had a *gringo* before."

The whole table burst into laughter, along with a group of truck drivers at a table at the other end of the building. Vachio felt inspired to play the clown.

"Another day?" said Vachio in a mournful voice. "That's cruel. You've got me too excited to wait."

"Well, it's early. But I could go get one of the other girls for you."

"No, that won't due. Anyone else would be spoiled for me after seeing you."

Mila gave Vachio a slow smile and patted his hand. "Now I know I was right. You're no *gringo*. You're too much of a bullshitter. You must be related to Miguel here."

Then with a toss of her long mane of hair, she returned to the bar. The other men laughed and laughed, and teased Vachio about falling in love.

"Ay, Vachio," said Miguel, patting his back. "We're going to have fun with you. Before you leave here today you will be thoroughly blooded."

"Now do you understand what we meant by a full service truck stop?" asked Pacho.

Vachio smiled and sucked down his beer. The men were nodding to him in approval. He was a hit. One of the boys.... But am I really? he thought. And where is Montoya?

"Say, where's Emilio Montoya? Is he going to come?" Vachio asked Pacho.

"Uh, no, Vachio. Doctor Montoya sends his regrets. He had a

previous commitment he was unable to change."

Vachio heard a low snort from Miguel. Vachio looked at him. His face was flushed, his eyes mirthful. He was already well buzzed. He leaned close to Vachio and said in an undertone, "Montoya is good people. But this isn't his kind of entertainment.... The good Doctor has more refined tastes."

"What? And you don't think I do?"

"No. You're a poor fuck like us," said Miguel in a tone of great approval.

"Thanks. Glad I'm giving you the right image."

Gustavo emerged from the interior of the café accompanied by a squat balding man wearing shorts, sandals, and a soiled, pale green *guayabera*. They stood near the door for a moment in serious conversation. Then Gustavo announced, "Vachio! I'm pleased to tell you that Chef Parra here has a veritable smorgasbord of Santanderean delicacies for your pleasure."

"I'm ready," said Vachio, reminding himself not to ask about the precise ingredients if something looked too weird.

"Hey, Parra!" called Miguel.

"Sir, at your order."

"Do you have any *Hormigas Culonas* for our guest to sample?"

Parra grinned. "Of course. But they're not too fresh."

"Doesn't matter. Bring them on."

Vachio wondered if he had heard right. *Hormigas Culonas*? Big-Ass Ants? Must be a nickname for something. Like Rocky Mountain Oysters...Like Rocky Mountain Oysters? Uh oh.

"Hey, cool it, Miguel," said Gustavo with a chuckle. "Do you want to scare the poor guy before he even gets to the main dishes?"

"Ay, Gustavo, don't underestimate our guest. We would be very poor hosts indeed if we didn't offer him the most singular delicacy Santander has to offer."

"Well said. Well said," added Fredy. The other men took up the chorus.

"Fine, then," said Gustavo, following the smirking Parra into the kitchen. Vachio was dying of curiosity.

"Now tell me, what are these Big-Ass Ants?" he asked Miguel.

"Exactly that—Big-Ass Ants."

"You mean the insect kind?"

"Yes. But these aren't ordinary ants. These are giant, winged-ants."

"Really? I haven't seen any since I've been here."

"Correct. Because they only come out of their underground burrows twice a year. Usually after being disturbed by especially heavy rains..."

"Now not even twice a year all the time," said Fredy. "Too many people have been eating them."

"Anyway," continued Miguel, "the females come out of their dens and take wing to lay their eggs somewhere else. We only eat the females. Their rears are filled with the succulent eggs that give them such a wonderful flavor. I'm not lying, they are truly delicious."

The other men nodded in approbation.

"And what's more," said Jessie, the young accountant, looking nervous and self-conscious before the older men, "we attribute certain qualities to the consumption of these ants. For example, they are a potent aphrodisiac."

"Now what would you know about that?" asked Dolfo. "Do they give added strength to your hand?"

The men brayed with laughter, burying poor Jessie in a tide of ridicule. He dropped his head and wrung his hands.

"But young Jessie is right, even if he lacks the experience to back it up. We Santandereans are rightly proud of our Big-Ass Ants. Just look over there," said Pacho, pointing to the cab door of one of the big rigs. "A symbol of our pride."

Vachio saw a decal of a large winged insect. He had noticed it before and thought it a wasp.

"There it is. Our Big-Ass Ant. Symbol of fertility and abundance. Symbol of a hard-working people," said Pacho.

Miguel guffawed and drained the rest of his beer. "Hey, Mila!" he called. "Bring us another round of beers. And a bottle of *aguardiente*. A big one."

As Mila brought the loaded tray over, her hips undulating under the tight skirt, Miguel stared at her. Then he smiled and said to Vachio, "There is another quality we attribute to eating the Big-Ass Ants.... Throughout Colombia, the women of Santander are known for their wasp-like figures. This is a direct result of eating the Big-Ass Ants. And here's the proof—the fair Mila, raised on Big-Ass Ants."

Mila laughed. "Except that I was raised in the Department of Cesar, *pingo*. In Aguachica.... But the ants are delicious," she added, patting Vachio on the shoulder. "Try them."

Parra brought out a bowl filled with crispy black truncated ants. They had been fried in butter and heavily salted, the wings, legs, and head removed. All eyes were on Vachio as he took one of the ants, examined it, and popped it into his mouth. Gingerly he chewed and swallowed. It reminded him of soggy popcorn.

"So?" asked Pacho.

"It's not bad. But I mostly taste salt and butter. It reminds me of when I used to eat snails; all I could taste was the garlic and butter."

"Snails?" Except for Miguel, the men recoiled in disgust.

Vachio popped another ant into his mouth and washed it down with beer without chewing it. Satisfied, the other men dipped into the bowl and broke up into individual conversations.

Vachio caught Miguel eyeing him, a speculative expression on his face.

"Something bothering you?" Vachio asked him.

"You never did say what you really thought about the ants," Miguel answered in a quiet voice.

"Between you and me, it won't be my favorite food."

"Well, these aren't fresh. He had to drown them in salt and butter. But eat a few more. It's an acquired taste."

"Too late, man," said Vachio, indicating the already empty bowl. "What a shame. Maybe another time."

Miguel chuckled, poured a shot of *aguardiente* for Vachio and himself, and said, "I see that you're not always what you seem to be."

"Who is? Are you?"

"To your health," said Miguel with a wink, raising his glass and draining it.

Another truck load of *profesores* from the *Casa de Menores* joined the party. Once they were settled, Gustavo came over to propose a toast. "To this reunion and the good fellowship of all the best elements of the *Casa de Menores*."

The men let out a chorus of "*Bravo! Bravo!*" and slammed down the *aguardiente*.

Then lunch was served. First came *Mute*, a thick corn soup, almost a stew, with generous chunks of beef, pork, potato, and tripe, accompanied by hot *arepas* fresh from the griddle and mild salsa. This was followed by heaping platters of barbecued, thin-cut beef and highly seasoned, boiled, and barbecued goat, the specialty of the house. On the side were plates of rice, boiled and fried cassava, and vinegar drenched slices of raw onion and radish. Beer, *guarapo*, and soft drinks were served on demand.

Vachio ate heartily, though sparingly of the goat which he found too tough and greasy for his taste, and drank in moderation. Most of the other men were now bombed, and Vachio had to constantly reassure them of how much he liked the food, their company, and Santander. After a while he became vaguely irritated, answering the same questions over and over, obligated to be the center of attention, obligated to submit and conform to the scrutiny of the men. A strange mood came over him. He felt claustrophobic and pressured, as though he were a herded animal. Vachio grew silent and picked at the crumbs on his plate. He suddenly itched to get off by himself for a while.

As the meal wound down and dessert, coffee, and *panela* were served, Gustavo quieted the boisterous atmosphere to formally introduce Vachio to the guards and shop teachers he hadn't already met. He assured Vachio that only those of the highest moral character and competency had been invited to this welcoming feast, and that Vachio could rely on any one of them to assist him in the *Casa de Menores*. This sentiment was echoed and effusively guaranteed by every man at the table, as well as by one of the drunk big rig drivers who had come over to share the company and grab a free drink.

After the dishes were cleared, another bottle of *aguardiente* was ordered and a series of maudlin toasts were proposed. Vachio needed a break.

"Where can I find a bathroom?" he asked Miguel.

"Go through the restaurant and out the back door directly to your left. But watch out that *las viejas* don't grab you," said Miguel.

The other men laughed and proposed a toast to *las viejas*.

Vachio shook his head and passed into the cool interior of the restaurant. He paused for a moment under the breeze of an overhead fan. It was a simple place. A single large room with an adjoining kitchen, a rust-colored stone tile floor, a half dozen rough tables, a line of chairs against one wall, and a hand painted mural with a tropical motif on the back wall. He crossed the room to the open back door, feeling the floor tilt slightly, and stopped on the threshold. He shaded his eyes against the glare of the mid-afternoon sun and looked around. Just to his right, two hammocks, a snoring big rig driver occupying one of them, hung in the shade of the back porch. A crude table loaded with knives, an ax, and a hand mallet sat just beyond. A butchering block, darkly stained from blood, scattered chicken feathers wafting about its legs, and a large pile of fire wood was located next to a lean-to shed attached to the kitchen. Beyond the shed, shaded by a large tree, was a chicken wire pen with a couple of tethered goats, some piglets, and squawking chickens and geese. At the back of the property was a barracks-like cinder block building with multiple doors. Two young women, garbed in white slips and leather sandals, were hand washing sheets at a stone basin. They looked up from their work and gave Vachio curious looks. Then one of them, a big-busted woman with tinted blonde hair smiled and motioned for Vachio to join them. Vachio waved and went into the bathroom. When he came out, Miguel was waiting for him on the porch.

"So, Vachio, what do you think of these *viejas here*?" asked Miguel, indicating the young women washing clothes.

"They're all right."

"Glad you think so. Because the boys and I were talking, and if one of them provokes your interest, we're willing to treat you."

"Well, uh..."

"It's nothing. Just consider it a gift of welcome. A token of our esteem."

"No, thanks. I'll pass this time."

"But why?" Miguel looked genuinely offended.

Vachio chose his words carefully. He realized this was a gesture on their part to solidify their camraderie and he didn't want to offend them. "Well, I've drunk a lttle too much. I'm a little groggy.... It would be a waste. For me and of your money."

"Ah, I understand. In that case, let's get back to the party."

Vachio hesitated for a moment before following Miguel. He looked beyond the back building to the swiftly flowing stream, a rustic suspension bridge beckoning him to cross and explore the wooded shore beyond. How he wanted to just take off and get lost for a while. Then he sighed and returned to the whooping and hollering men.

The party had reached the "I esteem you" phase. First one man, then another, would propose a toast to Vachio and his future at the *Casa de Menores*, and the brotherhood of *aguardiente* was consecrated with promises of eternal friendship and undying esteem. Gustavo, who had drunk sparingly, was settling the bill with Chef Parra. Vachio took it all in and tried to keep a smile on his face, the claustrophobic sensation hitting him with redoubled force.

"You better enjoy this, Vachio," said Miguel. "This is your honeymoon."

BOOK II

BOGOTA

1

The door swung open and Vachio was greeted by the imperturbable mestizo face of Blanca, the maid and indispensable keeper of the house. She regarded him silently for a moment, her lusterless dark eyes and her pale face with high cheekbones, graven, patient, and long-suffering.

"Did you have a good trip?" she asked.

"Yes. An exciting one."

"You're tanned. The weather was nice, eh?"

"Nice and hot. Delicious."

"Not like here, eh?" she said with an involuntary shudder.

"No, not like here."

"Are you hungry?"

"I could eat something."

"Put your bag away and come to the dining room. Everything is ready," she said, turning away as she spoke.

Vachio shut the door and stood in the entryway for a moment, inhaling the musty, mildewed air that no amount of germicide could dispel. Blanca wasn't to blame for the odor, she kept a spotless house. The problem was a lack of ventilation and the dank, cool climate of Bogotá. It bred mould, mildew, and moss. Spores suffused the air, penetrated the walls, attacked clothing, and when the icy winds swirled off the high peaks of the Andes, the damp cold reached to the very marrow of your bones.

Vachio hefted his bag and climbed the steps to his room on the second floor. His room, what a joke. It was a bizarre, three-sided, steel-ribbed, glass cage wedged between the wall and the stairway balcony in the middle of the hallway. Located next to the bathroom, it was literally a fish bowl. The other residents passed by Vachio's room constantly. And in the mornings, Vachio had to put on his clothes in a rush so as not to scandalize the other residents with his naked body as they waited their turn at the bathroom.

Vachio tossed his bag on the foot-too-short bed, noted a pile of still unwashed clothes in the corner, and went downstairs to the dining room. Osvaldo Rivas, a Chilean, and like Vachio a boarder at the house, and Juan Pablo Macias, an Argentine married to Pilarcita, the daughter of Doña Pilar, were already finishing up breakfast. They paused for only a moment to greet Vachio before resuming another of their adversarial conversations.

Vachio sat down to his breakfast of one fried egg in an individual mini-frying pan, bread, butter, marmalade, and a mug of hot chocolate.

As he ate, he tried to pick up the thread of the conversation between Osvaldo and Juan Pablo. It concerned a dispute between Chile and Argentina. Vachio buttered a roll, and then looked up in surprise as Osvaldo's voice cracked across the table at Juan Pablo:

"...General Pinochet may be my mortal enemy and a dirty dog," said Osvaldo, his face livid, "but he is still man enough to wipe up the floor with any overrated army of back-stabbing, conceited Argentines if this dispute comes to actual war."

"Are you finished?" asked Juan Pablo, his voice and manner calm. "Can I have my say?"

"Say it!" said Osvaldo, his knuckles whitening as his right hand closed on his napkin.

"Comrade, you know as well as I that it's one thing to knock the shit out of your own unarmed people, but quite another to fight a professional military force with advanced weaponry. I don't think our brave General Pinochet and the Chilean army would have such an easy time with real soldiers as they did with poor slum dwellers and café intellectuals.... Wouldn't you agree, Professor?"

Osvaldo's face blanched and his lips clamped tight. He rose, let fall his napkin in a gesture of disdain, and stalked out of the room. Juan Pablo looked after him, amusement on his face.

Vachio was stunned by Osvaldo's reaction. Normally he was calm and rational, possessed of a smooth urbane style and a rapier wit. But Juan Pablo had shattered his cool.

"What was that all about?" Vachio asked Juan Pablo.

"You heard."

"Only the end of it."

Juan Pablo shrugged and straightened his tie. "Really, it was nothing, che. Just a minor difference of opinion."

"Come on, man, nothing? I've never seen Osvaldo angry like that."

"Bro, it's a total stupidity. You see, Argentina and Chile are having a dispute over some islands and their territorial waters in the Straits of Magellan. Not that this is anything new. But this time it's a more serious matter because a geologic survey indicated that the surrounding waters probably contain oil."

"Oh.... And?"

"It's been reported that some shooting has occurred and that a military build-up is taking place as we speak. Here. You can read about it yourself, che," he said, passing Vachio the morning El Tiempo.

"But what's your argument with Osvaldo?" asked Vachio, accepting the paper and setting it aside for later.

"Well, Osvaldo agrees with the claims of the Chilean government, or people as he likes to put it, against the Argentine government. He says that those islands have always belonged to Chile.... This is debatable."

"You feel that they belong to Argentina."

"No. My position is that both governments should keep their bloody hands the hell out of there and leave those freezing, wind-swept islands to the penguins and birds as the creator intended."

"Osvaldo wouldn't anger because you said that? What else?"

Juan Pablo grinned. "He became angry when I pointed out that Chile is a long, anorexic, poor excuse for a country with less than half the population of Argentina and no where near the resources. I told him that if it came to actual war instead of saber-rattling, Argentina would give them a kick in the ass and send them back to Santiago.... That's when he became offended and started babbling about Chile's German and Israeli trained army and British trained navy and such. And you heard the rest, che. Stupid, no? But he'll get over it."

"I don't know, man. You know how proud he is of being Chilean."

Juan Pablo emitted a short, bitter laugh. "Sure, che, national honor and all that shit. I know. I used to believe in all that crap, too. But imagine, two refugees like ourselves arguing over these stupidities. It's absurd. Deep down we both know that this whole incident is a charade fabricated by two inept military governments who need to distract their populations from their own misery. A misery caused by the brutal, bungling mismanagement of the countries by these same governments.... But, when we talked of war, I'm *Argentino* and he's *Chileno* and we have to defend our countries macho. It's like they say, bro, the best patriots are expatriates.... Anyway, che, how was your trip?"

Before Vachio could answer, he was cut short by a wailing male voice from one of the upstairs bedrooms. "Blanquita! Ay, Blanquita!"

"Señor?" answered Blanca, passing through the dining room to the foot of the stairway.

"Bring me my breakfast, please. I don't feel well."

"Right away, Alfredito. *Ya voy!*"

"Huh," muttered Vachio in English so Blanca couldn't understand. "Comrade Alfredo, defender of the oppressed masses, can't get up and wants breakfast in bed again."

Juan Pablo guffawed. He had picked up some fractured, slang-spiced English working on the docks of Port Arthur, Texas for a year. "Don't be so hard on boy. He young. Impressionable.... He not bad kid when you know `im. He just...just...*Como se dice, innocente?*"

"Naive?"

"*Eso!*"

"Maybe so. But I have a problem with someone that claims to be an egalitarian Socialist but makes his maid wipe his ass for him. It's too much..."

"You shouldn't speak English," said Blanca, giving Vachio a reproving look as she passed through the dining room on her way to serve Alfredo.

Juan Pablo chuckled and said in a low voice, "She suspects we were talking about her boy. Blanca is an astute one.... And you have to understand, che, she is as much a mother to Alfredo as his real mother."

"Whatever. I think he's a spoiled brat."

"No, bro, he's not so bad. Just young. He needs help and guidance. That's all. I don't want him to make the same mistakes I did. I wouldn't wish that on anyone."

"Well, that's fine," said Vachio, shrugging. "You're his brother-in-law. And he thinks you're a revolutionary hero."

"Yes. That's his problem. He thinks revolutions are romantic and full of glory. He thinks when the revolution occurs he'll be a great leader. Another Castro.... The poor innocent. Him and thousands of others."

"Well, like you said, that's his problem. But he gets on my nerves. Especially when he calls for Blanca in that whiny tone of his. It's like when someone runs their fingernails over a chalkboard. Uh..."

Juan Pablo laughed and raised his mug of chocolate. "Salud to your safe return." Juan Pablo finished off his chocolate and carefully wiped his mustache with his napkin. "And now I better get going or I'll be late for my gig."

"Where are you going?"

"Downtown. Near the Plaza de Toros."

"I'll go with you. I want to do some Christmas shopping."

"All right. But I'm leaving in five minutes. Be ready. I can't wait."

Juan Pablo went upstairs and Vachio sipped his chocolate. Be ready? I'm ready now, thought Vachio. I'll have to wait for him. He'll delay at least 10 minutes, fussing with his hair. Then he'll have to listen to his wife lecture him about staying out too late and wasting his money on drinks with no good friends.... That's at least 15 minutes. Vachio smiled and shook his head, thinking about Juan Pablo. He was a strange character. Though he claimed to be an unreformed "Heepie," he was quite conventional in most aspects of his life. Away from work he was careless of dress and appearance, but once Juan Pablo put on the suit, he was fastidious to a fault; every hair on his head had to fall perfectly into place and his flowing mustache was meticulously groomed and waxed at the tips. Juan Pablo was employed as a school photographer, and though he claimed to hate the work, Vachio had seen him in action and was impressed. Juan Pablo had a knack for persuading difficult children to cooperate and was equally good at charming their mothers. As a consequence, despite his professed lack of enthusiasm, his business was growing. "What the hell, bro, we have to eat," said Juan Pablo after Vachio complemented him on his work. "But this is just until something better comes along."

All in all, though Juan Pablo was subject to pendulum mood swings ranging from morose to quietly exalted, Vachio liked him. He had an acerbic humor and an alert street sense that Vachio appreciated. Moreover, he was the only person in the house other than the maid who had truly gone out of his way to make Vachio feel welcome.

Vachio set down his mug and glanced around the gloomy dining room. All of a sudden he felt depressed. He wished training was over and he could begin his job. He didn't like this house and felt no warmth from his host family. Six more weeks, he thought. Six more weeks.... Vachio slipped into reverie, thinking over his first days in Bogotá and in this house in El Barrio Chapinero.

2

It was a raw drizzly afternoon, three days after Vachio's Peace Corps group had arrived in Bogotá. They had spent the first days in the shopworn Hotel Tundama, smack in a red light district complete with 10 peso whores, near the Plaza Bolívar in the heart of the Old City. Vachio had ridden uptown to Chapinero in a cab with another volunteer and the Peace Corps family coordinator and been deposited in front of a drab, two-story brick house in a cul-de-sac just off the Avenida Caracas. After speaking briefly to the maid, Blanca, the family coordinator left Vachio at the front door and told him to call her if there were any problems. Then, trunk in hand, butterflies fluttering in his stomach, Vachio was escorted into the house and up the stairs to a closed bedroom at the front end of the hall. Seconds later, with Blanca preceding him, he was bade to enter the room and approach a large four post bed, the throne and office of Doña Pilar, a bedridden arthritic woman with a wealth of iron gray hair, sagging jowls, and bright avaricious eyes. Her back propped against two pillows, a pot of tea and assorted pastries on the bedstand, a soap opera playing on the only television in the house, she extended a flabby white hand to Vachio and said, "Welcome, my son. Please come closer, I don't hear as well as I used to." The soft but firm pressure of her hand guided Vachio to a kneeling position next to the bed, their faces level. "You are going to be very happy here, my son..."

As she continued in a soft caressing voice, Vachio was surprised by her use of the more formal *usted*, for you, while addressing him as *mijo*, my son, in the same sentence. It struck him as a contradiction in language and intent to use *mijo* without using the familiar for you, *tu*. It bespoke intimacy and distance at the same time. Doña Pilar reached the end of her welcoming talk and casually mentioned that Vachio would need to give her $250 *pesos* every two weeks for laundry services. This was news to Vachio. The family coordinator had told him that all services were included in the monthly stipend to the family. He stared at Doña Pilar's outstretched hand.

"I'm a little short of cash right now," he told her. "I'll get back to you later."

"At your convenience, my son. But don't forget. I know how youthful minds can wander."

"Don't worry, I certainly won't forget," said Vachio, planning to speak to the family coordinator about this as soon as possible.

"Very well. I can see you're a boy of integrity. And if you need anything, or just want to talk, I'm at your order. Please consider me as your mother in the absence of your own."

Right after his interview with Doña Pilar, Alfredo had approached Vachio in the hallway. He was a short, chunky boy of 20, with his mother's eyes and cherub cheeks, dressed in slacks and a fine tan sweater. He seemed a trifle nervous and high-strung as he introduced himself, his eyes moving restlessly from Vachio to his trunk. Vachio was pleased to meet someone close to his own age, though Alfredo's fidgety manner put him off. "We should have a talk," said Alfredo. "I'll have Blanca bring us some coffee and rolls. Join me as soon as you're ready."

Vachio agreed and they were soon seated in straight-backed chairs in an alcove at the other end of the hallway, gray light filtering through a lead glass, beveled window, bread and coffee on a round table at their elbows. After a few polite inquiries concerning Vachio's background, Alfredo recited a list of grievances Colombia had against the United States, mentioning abuses by the United Fruit Company, the loss of Panama, and the shameful exploitation of Colombia's raw natural resources by multinational corporations based in the United States. Then Alfredo grilled Vachio as to why he had come to work in Colombia and what he was going to do. Was he CIA? Did he know Alfredo was a convinced Marxist-Leninist? A Fidelista? The leader of his university Communist cell?

Though taken aback, Vachio tried to answer Alfredo's questions with tact. But as the questioning continued, Alfredo grew more and more peremptory, more full of himself. His face turned red and swollen and his manner bullying.

Suddenly Vachio's eyes narrowed and he stared straight at Alfredo. "Listen, man, for the last time.... I don't work for the CIA. And I don't know or care anything about your political activities. You understand? You can have a revolution for all I care."

Alfredo sank back in his chair, his mouth hanging open, the air going out of him like a punctured balloon.

Vachio would have laughed if he hadn't felt so irritated. The kid had gone too far.

Alfredo quickly recovered from his surprise. He leaned forward in his chair, grinned, and said in a warm voice, "You seem all right. Sincere. I think we'll be friends.... By the way, could you lend me $100 pesos until next week?"

Vachio told Alfredo exactly what he had told his mother. Alfredo got up without shaking hands and left him alone.

Still upset from his meeting with Alfredo, Vachio went to his room to stow his gear. There was no closet in the tiny room and no drawers, only a small bed and night stand, and a few hooks on the wall. Vachio shook his head in disgust. I'll have to live out of my trunk, he thought. And this room is like an icebox. I need to get out of here for a while and think.

Vachio threw on an extra sweater, locked his room, and started down the stairway. There he ran into a short wiry guy with long flowing black hair and a well-groomed mustache. He was dressed in patched jeans and an old shirt.

"Hi. How are you doing?" said Vachio, feeling awkward as hell. No one had shown him around the house or introduced him to the other residents.

"Ah, you're the new American."

"Yes."

"You speak Spanish? A little?"

"Enough."

He grinned. "That's good. We've had others here that didn't speak any.... My name is Juan Pablo Macias."

Vachio introduced himself and they shook hands.

"So...what is..."

"I'm married to Pilarcita," said Juan Pablo, quickly divining Vachio's question. "She's Doña Pilar's daughter. We have the bedroom across the hall from you."

"Oh. I haven't met her yet."

"No, she's involved in her usual occupation—looking for a job. She won't be back until this evening."

"What kind of job is she seeking?"

"She's a lawyer. Six months out of law school."

"Oh. Is it difficult to find work here for a lawyer?"

Juan Pablo gave Vachio his first trademark bitter laugh. "The trouble with being a lawyer in Bogotá, che, is that there are almost as many lawyers as there are criminals. And between you and me, it's hard to distinguish the difference between them most of the time.... Apologies to my wife."

Vachio stared at Juan Pablo in surprise.

"I'm not from Colombia, che. I'm from Argentina. You'll have to excuse my directness."

Vachio took a close look at Juan Pablo's eyes; they were red-rimmed, the pupils concentrated, the lids drooping. Juan Pablo's speech was slow and mellow. This guy is stoned, Vachio thought.

"So what are you doing now? What's your program for today?" asked Juan Pablo.

"Nothing. I was just going to walk around the neighborhood to familiarize myself with things. We were downtown the first three days.

I don't know anything around here."

"Then I'll go with you—if you like. I know my way around. And I'm not working today."

"Well, sure. Let's go."

Juan Pablo first took Vachio on a walking tour of the neighborhood. El Barrio Chapinero was a formerly chic district, in a state of slow decay, of somber brick row houses and small green parks. La Avenida Caracas, one of Bogotá's principal thoroughfares, bisected the neighborhood and gave it miles of shops, stores, and commercial offices. As they walked, Juan Pablo showed Vachio the key bus and buseta routes, and pointed out among the teeming crowds a few of the pickpockets and confidence men who infested Bogotá's streets. He warned Vachio of their tricks and told him how to avoid them.

After a few hours of walking, they climbed onto a bus and headed for the more upscale Chicó District. They went to the glittering new UniCentro Shopping Mall, and after that, in the late afternoon, Juan Pablo invited Vachio to drink dark beer at a North End pizzeria. After one pitcher of beer, Juan Pablo loosened up and gave Vachio the outsider's insider view of the family of Pilar Nuñez Restrepo:

"The thing about this family, che, is that about five years before I met Pilarcita, they were living much better than they do now. The old man owned a pretty large cattle ranch outside of Villavicencio. He had a dozen peons, thousands of cattle...the works. They derived a nice income from the place. Here in Bogotá, they had the house and several maids. The family was living in good style, che, on the fringes of Bogotá's better society—with ambitions of moving higher. The two eldest daughters married into good families and Pilarcita was doing well in the university. Doña Pilar was riding high, bro. I can only imagine how pretentious she must have been then, knowing how pretentious she is now with next to nothing." Juan Pablo paused and took a long sip of beer.

"So what happened to them?" asked Vachio.

"It all fell apart, che, like a house of cards. I don't know why exactly, it's something they rarely mention, but for some reason, old man Restrepo started to drink and gamble heavily.... Rumor is he had a long love affair out on the ranch with some young woman and fell apart when she dumped him.... But, who knows, che. He's a pretty simple guy really. My guess is that the way Doña Pilar wanted him to live and act finally got to him. Even Pilarcita can't explain it to me and she was always Daddy's little girl. The family just says he went crazy and tries to forget his existence. He ended up losing most of the ranch and its assets to cover his gambling debts. Now all they have left is the house in Bogotá and a small piece of land in the *Llanos* with a few cows and pigs. Doña Pilar told everyone that they lost their money because of a disease that wiped out their cattle.... But her society friends dumped her. And after that, she took to her bed and has never really gotten out of it. She claims it's her arthritis and varicose veins, che, but I figure it's psychosomatic. A classic case."

"What happened to the father? Is he dead?"

"No, che, he's alive. But he might as well be dead. He's a broken shell. Disgraced. He stays out at the ranch most of the time and rarely comes to the city. His authority and respect with the family are gone. The old lady calls the shots. It was her idea to take in boarders to get Pilarcita and Alfredo through the university. And she'll do whatever she can to get extra spending money for Alfredo so that he can maintain appearances at the university.... Have you met Alfredo?"

"Yes. Not pleasantly."

"What happened?"

Vachio told Juan Pablo about his session with Alfredo. At the end, Juan Pablo laughed, raised his glass to Vachio, and said, "Alfredito didn't waste any time seeing what he could get out of you, che. He's always trying to scrounge money. But you handled things right. You put him in his place. He won't keep bothering you.... And he's not a bad kid. Not really."

"Yeah, maybe. But he gave me a bad first impression."

"Forget it, che. It's not all his fault. He's Mami Pilar's little boy and he follows her example. He's her favorite child and only son. And the baby of the family to boot.... The one thing that keeps the old lady going is to maintain appearances for her boy. He is the center of her universe. It drives my wife nuts."

Vachio chuckled. "Come on, she can't be that bad."

"She has an obsession with appearances. She'll make us eat badly to buy a new sweater for Alfredito. It's craziness. Like a disease. The old lady is a complete hypocrite."

Vachio eyed Juan Pablo thoughtfully. "I guess you don't like your mother-in-law very much."

"It's hard for me to live at her house, che. I don't agree with her style of life. So we have our problems.... But I've said enough about her. Hopefully things will be better for you."

"I don't know, man. I already have a problem with her."

"How's that?"

Vachio told Juan Pablo about the extra money she had demanded for the laundry.

"I don't know anything about that. Before you, there were two other Peace Corps guys. And I think they paid money for laundry. But it wouldn't surprise me if she's been scamming them. She'll get what she can."

"Oh yeah?"

"Yes. And one of them, Ronald, he's engaged to marry one of Pilar's nieces. You'll probably meet him soon. He works in Medellín but he comes to Bogotá as often as he can to see his *novia.* And when he does, he stays at Doña Pilar's house."

"Huh..." Vachio looked at the empty pitcher of beer. "Do you want another pitcher? My treat."

"All right, if you like."

"And how about a pizza? I'm hungry."

"What for? We can go home and eat dinner pretty soon."

"That's all right. I haven't eaten since early this morning. I'll buy."

"Then I'll buy beer, che. I don't want you to think I'm after your money like Alfredo and the old lady."

Vachio laughed. "They'll soon learn I don't have any money to get after.... Just what I get from Peace Corps."

They ordered a medium pizza and another pitcher of beer. After their glasses were filled, Juan Pablo proposed a toast: "For the pleasure of having someone else I can talk to at the house of Doña Pilar."

Vachio laughed. "So how did you end up with this family?"

"Che, I'm not sure myself. In life, things just happen sometimes. And Pilarcita and I just happened..."

"That's all right. If you don't want to talk about it."

"No, che, nothing like that. I just don't understand what happened myself." Juan Pablo took a sip of beer and continued, "We met about two years ago. I had been in Bogotá about three months, unemployed, my money almost gone. Anyway, I met her at this café where I used to hang out to get out of the cold and talk to other would-be artists and intellectuals. I had seen her around before. She was a slim attractive girl. Very attractive. And I knew she was a student and had a serious temperament from observing her. Then one day she sat at my table and we became acquainted. Che, we hit it off almost immediately. I tell you, bro, in those days, I was lonely and beat and broke. And she was interesting and sympathetic to me and...well, one thing led to another and we ended up in bed soon enough. And you know, I thought I could control this affair and keep it at a certain level. I never even thought of marrying her, che. It was just another adventure to me. I swear it.... But one day, we were in my pensión room, and it was raining and storming and we stayed in and made love all day and...Shit! We let down our precautions and she got pregnant." Juan Pablo took a long sip of beer and Vachio joined him. "Anyway, I tried to talk her into having an abortion but she absolutely refused. Prior to this, she had come off as a modern, liberated woman. Now, all of a sudden, she started laying all these Catholic guilt trips on me...."

"So you got married?"

"Not at first, che. I was confused, but I was pretty sure I didn't want to get married. I tried to avoid Pilarcita; but she was relentless. She may be a small woman but she has a strong will and a mean temper when she's angry. She kept showing up at my hang-outs, brow beat me in public, and denounced me to my friends. It was a nightmare, che. She just wore me down.... Finally, one afternoon, after we made love, she cried and cried. I couldn't take it. I promised to think over marrying her and agreed to give her a decision the next day.... Che, I thought of running to the coast. I don't even like Bogotá that much. But then, as I sat in that musty cold room, her smell in the bed and all around me, I thought, why not? I'm sick and tired of running from place to place. Why not settle down and get my life in order. Pilarcita is intelligent and good in bed. Living in her mother's house would certainly be better than the drafty pensión room that kept me with a permanent cold. I was really fond of her if not exactly in love. She had social connections that were advantageous to business opportunities. I always liked children and have a good way with them. One of my own would be nice. It might even help me forget some of my hate and anger.... Che, the more I thought about it, the more the idea began to appeal to me. Marriage? Why not? It's another adventure. And if things don't work out—I can always disappear and resume my wandering.... The next day I told Pilarcita, yes."

Juan Pablo stopped talking and picked up a slice of pizza. Vachio told the waiter to bring another pitcher of beer. By now it was dusk. A cheery fire crackled in the stone fireplace at the center of the pizzeria. Candles in red holders flickered on the tables. The booths were filled with animated young people wearing designer jeans and Italian shoes.

"So? Are you sorry you got married?"

"It's a mixed bag, che. I have a beautiful daughter who I dearly love. But I can't honestly say that I'm happy with my wife. Or, to be just, she with me. Our relationship is lukewarm. And we're both frustrated by our work situation and having to still live with her mother. The situation is rotting me, che. And she is frustrated and beginning to take out her frustration on me.... I tell you, bro, I'm getting restless. That's why, if you don't mind, I'd like to practice my English with you once in a while to stay sharp. If things don't improve for the better soon, I'm thinking of heading up North."

Vachio shrugged. "What makes you think it will be any better for you there?"

"I don't necessarily, che. Don't forget, I worked in Port Arthur, Texas, for almost a year. And I had to work like a dog to barely pay the bills. It wasn't the Golden Land I expected. I lived better in Argentina when I was a boy."

"What a surprise, eh?"

"Not a pleasant one, che. I mean, I even slept under a bridge and on park benches with American white men when I first arrived at Port Arthur. That's not the image I had of your country growing up in Argentina."

"Don't ever believe the United States is an easy place to get established in unless you come with money."

"I learned that, che," said Juan Pablo, looking thoughtful. "But I still think the United States is a better place to make money in than anywhere else if you're motivated and willing to work at whatever is at hand. But if I go back, I'd like to try my luck somewhere else. Maybe in California.... What do you think of that, che?"

Vachio shrugged. "Many people make a go of it in California. That's why we have such a large population.... But many don't. You pay your money and take your chance."

It was Juan Pablo's turn to shrug. "That's fine. Like anywhere. A person has to be able."

"Just so you know."

Juan Pablo raised his beer mug and toasted. "I like you, bro. You don't bullshit. You talk plain and straight."

They finished off the pizza and worked on the pitcher of beer. Then, as they waited for the waiter to bring their change, Vachio said to Juan Pablo, "One thing puzzles me about you."

"What?"

"Why did you come to Colombia in the first place? You haven't said a good thing about this country in all the time we've been talking."

Juan Pablo laughed. "No, che, don't misunderstand. Colombia has many wonderful things. For example, it is a country of unsurpassed natural beauty. And the people in general are fine. It's a place I wanted to visit even as a boy. Unfortunately, my first visit to Colombia was as a piece of driftwood washed up on the beach."

"What?"

"It's the story of my life, che. I don't think you really want to hear it."

"Why not? We're having a good time. Go ahead."

Juan Pablo took a long drink of beer. "It's the story of a fool, che. I have no excuses except perhaps for my misplaced idealism. That, and the fact that there are many others like me in South America right now and I was always well-accompanied in my folly."

"What folly?" Vachio was growing exasperated.

"I first came to Colombia after getting out of prison."

"Prison? Why the hell were you in prison?"

"I was a Montonero, che. Have you heard of them?"

"Yeah, some kind of left-wing group in Argentina. Didn't a bunch of you guys get disappeared."

"Correct. And I was one of those. But I came back from the dead, che.... Although not exactly whole."

"How did you get involved with the Montoneros?"

"It was at the National University in Buenos Aires, che. What can I say? I was young and naive.... Like Alfredo."

"But how?"

Juan Pablo sighed. "I was involved with a woman. The first real relationship I ever had. She was a Montonero. From a poor family. And she educated me to the injustices in our society.... But it's not as simple as all that, che. It had to do with the times as well. I was at the university during the worst period of chaos and instability of the Isabel

Peron regime. Buenos Aires was a zoo. Demonstrations all the time, police beating up students, murders, disappearances. I got caught up in the excitement and emotion and I became radicalized. I grew a beard and long hair, was expelled from the university, and cut my ties with my bourgeois parents. With my girlfriend, I joined a Montonero activist cell and lived underground for several years. I participated in burglaries and vandalized property. But I swear to you, che, I never hurt anyone. That is not in my nature."

"How did you end up in prison?"

"One of the members of our cell was captured by the secret police. Under torture, she betrayed the rest of us. I was taken and sent to a very notorious prison near the Paraguayan border. And that's where I received a taste of hell, che."

'You were tortured?"

"I was burned with cigarettes, tickled with cattle prods, spit on, beaten, and doused with icy water."

"Shit!"

"But that wasn't the worst of it. The worst of it was the mental isolation and uncertainty. The lack of any human affection or comfort. I was in total despair, che. I started to go mad.... Finally, I tried to hang myself. I knew death had to be better than life. But I was saved by one of the guards..."

Vachio looked at Juan Pablo and drank his beer, wondering if this were all true.

"That was the turning point for me, che. The guard saving my life made him seem like a friend. Suddenly all my hate became focused on my former comrades from the Montoneros for betraying me to the authorities and for leading me astray.... I know this is irrational, che. But in my depressed mental state, that's what occurred. I renounced all politics, concluding it was a fool's game manipulated by a select few who either coopted or corrupted their followers into betrayal of ideals—regardless of their ideology or good intentions. After all, my friends had turned me in to save their own skins. Why should I be any different? Who did I think I was? A hero? No. I had a new ideology, formed by pain and disillusionment. Look out for Juan Pablo." Juan Pablo sighed. "My captors were delighted by this change in me. Within a year, I was judged politically rehabilitated and set free. I tried to return to my parents' home in Mendoza but my father disowned me and told me to leave. That's when I started drifting, like a ship without an anchor. I worked, doing whatever I could get, and hustled my way through Brazil, Venezuela, Colombia, Panama, Costs Rica, Mexico, and the United States. After that year in Port Arthur, I accepted a berth on a cargo ship and came back south to Santa Marta, Colombia. Then I came to Bogotá and decided to stay for a while.... And you know the rest, che. Now I'm a married man with a little daughter."

Vachio whistled in a soft voice. "You've had a hard time of it, man.

Maybe it is time to rest."

Juan Pablo laughed. "It wasn't all bad, che. I had many wonderful adventures and saw some incredible things in the course of my exile. And I had a pretty happy childhood as well. I mean, che, I was an unlikely revolutionary. Where I was raised, Mendoza, it's a beautiful place at the foot of the Andes. And though my family wasn't particularly well off, we were comfortable. My father was a skilled leather worker and my mother a school teacher. As a child I roamed the foothills and fields. I loved animals, che. And I was a good student. I went to the National University on a scholarship to study to be a veterinarian. And then...well, that's the way it goes."

3

Vachio and Juan Pablo left the pizzeria and caught a buseta going to Chapinero. As soon as they were settled in their seats, Juan Pablo asked, "So what about you, che? Up until now, I've done most of the talking. Why did you come to Colombia?"

"Because I signed up for the Peace Corps and this is where they sent me."

"You didn't ask to come here?"

"No, not at first. I asked for Brazil. But the recruiter told me that the program is ending there. So he tried to convince me to go to Zaire in Africa. I said I would accept that, but that I preferred to go to South America. So we looked through the job descriptions and found this one for a recreation director in a prison in Colombia."

"And that was it?"

"No, not exactly. He gave me a problem. He kept telling me to consider Zaire. But after making me sweat for about four months, I finally got this assignment.... The guy was too much. It was like he wanted me to beg or something."

Juan Pablo cracked up. "Beg to work in a prison in Colombia? Give me a break."

"Yeah, man, it was crazy. He was set on having me build latrines in Zaire. He kept telling me there were other applicants ahead of me for the assignment in Colombia. Then when I arrived here and talked to my supervisor, she said she never saw any other application except mine and she liked it from the beginning. He was just playing head games with me.... But here I am."

"Why did you want to come to South America in particular?"

"Well, for one, I have a brother-in-law from Ecuador. So from all the stories I heard from him, I wanted to check things out for myself.... What else? I already knew Spanish pretty well. And really, since I was a little boy and read about South America, I always planned to come here." Vachio's face lit up. "Yeah, man, before I leave, I expect to see the Amazon Rainforest, Rio, Inca ruins, and all sorts of other things I've seen through books and television.... This is definitely the sort of adventure I want in my life."

"But why didn't you just come here on your own? Why did you come with this Peace Corps?"

"Because it seemed like the best way to do it. I mean, to actually live and work in a place rather than just tour around in it has to give you much more depth and experience in the culture.... But if Peace Corps didn't accept me, I would have looked for another way."

"So what about it, che, what do you think of Colombia so far?"

"Man, I don't know. But I'll say this, I was nervous all four days in Miami during our orientation, but as soon as we arrived in Bogotá this feeling came over me like...this is the place, Colombia. This is exactly where I want to be at this time in my life. This is the place for adventure and adventurers.... And I'm ready for my share."

Juan Pablo laughed. "Well said, bro. Well said. Let's just hope most of your adventures are good ones. There is no doubt Colombia is an unusual country. It's strange, you know. It repels many people...but for others, it gets under their skin and grabs hold. And right now, it offers unusual opportunities..."

"Such as."

"Well, in many respects, Colombia is a poor and underdeveloped country. But there are also unbelievable quantities of money circulating here, che."

"Sure. From the drugs."

"Yes, che, from the drugs. But you don't have to be a drug dealer to get some of this money." Juan Pablo paused and fingered the tip of his mustache. "The airport here is well-named. El Dorado. The conquistadores never found El Dorado because it didn't exist then. But now it does. The money going in and out of that airport on any given day is staggering, che. Much more than even the greediest Spaniard could have imagined. I tell you, it's maddening to think about this, che. One can do very well in Colombia depending on what you're willing to do."

"Yeah? And what are you willing to do?"

"I'm still not sure, che. And maybe I better shut-up because I think the beer is talking now."

The buseta pulled up at a stop next to a small park. A *gamin* boarded and conversed with the driver in a low voice. Vachio watched him with interest. The boy was short and sturdy, with curly black hair glistening from a light drizzle, a soot-stained face, and baggy ragged clothes. The boy shook his head and grinned as he talked, his voice wheedling, pleading with the driver for something Vachio couldn't quite hear. The driver finally nodded, mumbled something into the boy's ear, and lowered the *sabanera* music playing on his radio. The boy turned to face the passengers, many of whom were already squirming in their seats, embarrassment and irritation commingled on their faces.

"Ladies and Gentlemen, may I please have your attention for a moment," said the *gamin*. "In this, the International Year of the Child, when we all must be especially aware of the plight of the poor and abandoned children of the world, I would like to dedicate a song to this worthy cause. This song, of my own invention, is called *Los Desamparados*."

The driver pulled away from the curb and into the manic traffic, horns tooting on all sides, drowning out a few mumbled curses and groans from the passengers. The boy began singing in a high reedy voice. Some of the passengers stared out of the windows at the rain-slicked streets; others eyed the boy as though he were a stone. As the *gamin* continued singing, he pulled a crumpled blue beret from out of his front pocket, unfurled it, and strolled down the aisle to collect donations. Juan Pablo and Vachio, sitting near the front, gave him some loose change that came to a few *pesos*; some people shook their heads and gave him nothing; others dumped worn bills into the hat. By the time he finished his routine, he had a decent haul. The driver pulled over to pick up a passenger and the *gamin* returned to the front of the buseta and surreptitiously slipped him a bill. Then the boy exited the vehicle and Vachio watched him cross the street and join up with a gang of similarly dressed companions.

"Nice little game they run," Vachio commented to Juan Pablo. "He made some nice change for a few minutes of effort."

"More or less. Nothing special, che."

"He made enough to get a good meal."

"Sure, if the money were only for him. But it isn't. He has to split it with the rest of the gang and give the lion's share of it to the leader, *El Vale*. Usually some older guy who exploits these poor kids." Juan Pablo snorted and gave Vachio a wry look. "You see, che, even at this pathetic level, the rich get richer. *El Vale* works his own games and keeps all his own money if he wishes. The others all have to cut him a percentage of their take and accept his leavings." Juan Pablo emitted his bitter laugh. "Just like any other good capitalist operation. Che, it's a hell of a world we live in."

"How do you know so much about the operations of *gamines*?" asked Vachio.

"When I first came to Bogotá, I used to buy grass off a gang that hung out near the lift to Monserrat. And I'd get high with them once in awhile.... You know, che, people tell you a few things when they're loaded. And you observe some other things."

"Yeah. I've been making some observations of my own since I arrived."

"That's good, che. You have much to learn if you want to work effectively with these *gamines*. Much."

Vachio shot Juan Pablo a quick look. "Maybe not quite as much as you think."

Juan Pablo chuckled. "Don't get cocky, son. This isn't the United States."

"No, that's true. But you don't know how and where I grew up, either."

"All right. Tell me."

"I'll tell you, but first off, I'm not trying to say my condition was the same as these *gamines*. Not at all. I came from a strong family. I mean, we had our problems, but we stuck together when things got tough...and things did get tough for us. Without exaggerating the thing, my neighborhood was a nasty place if you didn't know how to handle yourself..."

"That could be, che. But don't even try to tell me it's as bad as here."

"As bad? I don't say that. But just as bad in a different way."

"This is a Third World country, che. You can't make a comparison."

"I'm not making a comparison, man. I'm just going to tell you about my experience growing up where I did. Nothing more. And straight up, it was no picnic. It was violent, there were strong racial tensions, and we were flooded with cheap street drugs. There was even terrorism. In San Francisco at that time we had the Zebra Killers, the Zodiac, riots at San Francisco State University over Vietnam and other stuff...all kinds of shit, man. It was a confusing time. You had to keep your head on straight to avoid a hard fall. And it wasn't easy. You could just blunder into problems. I was sitting in the back of a bus one day going to baseball practice and I got a knife put to my throat.... I mean, it could have gone very wrong for me. I was no angel as a kid. And I ran with guys that got in trouble. You could buy drugs on every other street corner and the pressure was always there to go along.... Yeah, I could have taken a hard fall. In some ways I was lucky. Two of my best friends growing up died before they were 18..."

Juan Pablo was now regarding Vachio with a sober look on his face.

"It's just to say, man, without making this sound like some ghetto sob story, I've been around plenty of people living on-the-edge and from day-to-day. And I'm no stranger to the streets. I've spent my share of time on them.... I know the mentality."

"All right, che, I believe you. But it's not the same here."

"No, not the same. But there are always similarities. Big cities always have things in common."

"Well, this is so. My experiences underground in Buenos Aires have certainly helped me here."

They jumped off the buseta in Chapinero and returned to the house of Doña Pilar. As soon as they entered the hallway, quick feet descended the stairway and they were confronted by a slim young woman with handsome features. Her dark eyes flashed at Juan Pablo, the pale skin of her cheeks shot through with red streaks. For a moment she looked at Vachio, surprised, then she turned her full attention on Juan Pablo.

"You've been out drinking again," she said.

"Don't start on me now, Pilar. We have a guest," said Juan Pablo. "This is Gary Vachio. The new boarder here.... Vachio, this is my wife."

Pilar made an effort to control her anger and extended her right hand. "A pleasure to meet you," she mumbled.

"The same," said Vachio, feeling extremely uncomfortable. Pilar was staring at him now, her eyes penetrating and accusatory. Vachio imagined what was going through her mind. Here we have another no-good drinking buddy for my wastrel husband. Vachio knew this routine.

"Well, if you guys will excuse me, I need to put my things away," said Vachio. "I'll talk to you later."

"Yes, che. Later," said Juan Pablo. Vachio retreated to his room and lay on the bed. A few minutes later he heard the door across the hall slam shut and the sounds of a muffled argument. Vachio rolled over on his side and let out a sigh. He had entered a house full of problems.

Vachio grabbed the only book he had brought with him from the States, *The Idiot* by Dostoyevsky, and tried to get comfortable. It wasn't easy. The room was like an ice box. He put on a heavy sweater over his long sleeve flannel shirt and curled up on the bed. He was still cold. A short while later Juan Pablo walked past on his way to the bathroom.

"Hey, Juan Pablo!" Vachio called. Juan Pablo stopped. "Why is it so damn cold? Don't they have heat here?"

"Yes, che, there is heat.... In the old lady's room. And there is the fireplace downstairs. But that is for special occasions only." Juan Pablo emitted his laugh. "That's the way it is here, che. You have to endure it."

Vachio grunted and rolled over onto his stomach. He read his book and, as time passed, felt the cold seeping into his bones. Then, just as he was about to get under the wool blankets, Blanca came and informed him that dinner was served. Vachio sprang off the bed and followed Blanca downstairs, excited by the prospect of his first meal with the Restrepo family.

The dining room was small, chill, and gloomy. The only light was provided by a frosted overhead lamp with a low voltage bulb. A long table, eight straight-backed wood chairs, and two mahogany sideboards were squeezed into the room. A silver punch bowl and a set of goblets decorated one of the sideboards, and some old text books and a manual typewriter were piled haphazardly on the other. A large painting of The Last Supper hung on one wall. Three places were set for dinner. Blanca struck a match and lit two candles in silver holders. Vachio stood quietly, watching his shadow play against the yellowing white wall.

"Sit here," said Blanca, pointing to a seat at the head of the table. Vachio obeyed and immediately felt a pleasant draft of warm air against his back from the open kitchen door.

"Am I eating alone?" Vachio asked Blanca.

"No. The others will be along shortly."

Blanca brought Vachio a thin barley soup with a couple of pieces of fatty meat floating on top.

"Should I wait for the others?" Vachio asked her.

"No. Eat."

Vachio tasted the soup. It was insipid. He added a pinch of salt and a load of pepper. While Vachio was slurping up the last of the soup, Juan Pablo and another man entered.

"This is Osvaldo Rivas," said Juan Pablo, introducing him to Vachio. "He is Chilean."

Vachio stood up and shook hands with him. Osvaldo was a short gaunt man with a pencil thin mustache and a Clark Gable hairstyle and look. He wore a threadbare suit but was immaculately groomed. At Juan Pablo's urging, Osvaldo told Vachio a little about himself while he ate his soup.

"Like our Argentine friend here," said Osvaldo, "I'm a refugee in Bogotá.... Are you familiar with Salvador Allende and what happened in Chile in 1973?"

"Yes," said Vachio.

"Well, I was a supporter of Allende from the very beginning. Before he actually became president of Chile. And as a university professor, I used my position to advance our cause." Osvaldo paused and delicately wiped his lips with his napkin. "As one can well imagine, when Pinochet took power after the coup of '73, I was a marked man. I went into hiding. Suffered from privation and the fear of discovery. And was finally smuggled out of Chile and to Colombia in late 1974. Since then I've lived a hand-to-mouth refugee's existence. My face..." Osvaldo tapped a hollow cheek with his ring finger. "...was once considered quite handsome by women. Now it is prematurely careworn and aged.... I'm only 35."

Vachio looked at him and clucked sympathetically; Osvaldo looked like he was in his mid-40s.

"Are you sure that wasn't from dissipation?" asked Juan Pablo, grinning maliciously. "Didn't you tell me that before the coup you were a great playboy?"

Osvaldo gave him a quick look. "I did indeed live the high life for most of my youth. Those were heady times for Chile and for me in particular. But most of the damage was done by the trials and tribulations of these last fugitive years. Still, I'm not bitter. I still cry for what happened to my country, but over these last few years I've acquired a fatalistic perspective on the devastating turn my own life took. The truth is, I'm one of the lucky ones. I'm still alive and relatively intact. Many of my friends and associates are dead, insane, or gone without a trace."

"But how do you feel about the United States? And about Americans like our friend Vachio here?" asked Juan Pablo.

"Man, you are a shit disturber," Vachio said to Juan Pablo in English.

"Che, we're all refugees of sorts here. There is no reason to hide our feelings." Juan Pablo laughed. "Tell us what you think about the C.I.A. and their role in the coup, Osvaldo."

Osvaldo chuckled. "Juan Pablo likes to try to provoke me, Vachio. It's a sort of game for him. What he doesn't understand is that I am a true intellectual. I enjoy taking both sides in an argument...just to put myself in the shoes of the other guy to try to understand his viewpoints and motives. So I will answer his question—without bitterness. Now, believe it or not, I can understand why the C.I.A. helped Pinochet and the military overthrow the democratically elected regime of Salvador Allende. From their geopolitical perspective it was a correct—though morally heinous—reaction. Obviously, as a confirmed Socialist, I am in utter disagreement with the economic system and foreign policy of the United States. But I bear no ill will toward Americans in general. I understand the difference between people and the political expediency of governments and their insiders."

Osvaldo finished with a suave smile and started in on his soup. Juan Pablo gave Vachio a wry look and picked up his own spoon. Seconds later Blanca brought Vachio his main course. It consisted of four sardines fresh from the can, glistening with oil, their dead eyes staring, laid over a bed of soggy white rice, flanked by wilted vinegary lettuce, long cut slices of plantain, and a tall glass of Coke. Vachio stared at his food for a good minute without touching it.

"Is there something the matter?" Osvaldo asked Vachio.

"Is this a typical Bogotá dish?" Vachio asked,

"Well, no, not exactly. Though they do flavor plain food here."

"This is typical Doña Pilar food, che. At least for us. She eats something different in her room," said Juan Pablo.

"I don't like sardines," said Vachio.

"Doña Pilar probably thinks she's doing you a favor, che. She believes *gringos* only eat canned food." Both Juan Pablo and Osvaldo broke into laughter.

"Yeah, well, not in my family. We mostly ate fresh food.... This sucks!"

"Better get used to it, che. The old lady is going to squeeze every peso out of the deal with you that she can."

"Then it's a good thing we ate that pizza earlier."

Juan Pablo nodded and Vachio put his head down and began to eat. Vachio hid his thoughts from Juan Pablo and Osvaldo but he was disgusted. His first meal at the Restrepo house was like prison fare and not one member of the family even bothered to eat with them. Some Colombian family I have, Vachio thought, forcing a forkful of sardine down his throat. Damn...

Over dinner, Juan Pablo and Osvaldo argued the merits of Argentine and Chilean wines, each extolling the virtues of the grape from their respective countries. Vachio listened with interest and Osvaldo asked him, "Do you like wine?"

"Yes."

"What kind do you like best? Red or white?"

"I like dry red wines. Strong wines with body and strong personality."

Juan Pablo laughed. "You mean good country wine, che. Good peasant wine."

"I suppose you could say that. One of my grandfathers used to make his own wine. It was that kind."

"Well, we have plenty of that in Argentina. Especially from Mendoza where I come from.... We always had our good red wine to accompany a thick juicy steak and fresh-baked crusty bread. Ay, che, that was heaven. What else do you need?"

"I personally would prefer something more sophisticated," said Osvaldo. "In Chile we have wine-making down to much more of an art than in Argentina. That is why you can find excellent Chilean wine all over the world."

"You're crazy, che."

"Crazy? Go to any good wine shop here in Bogotá and let's see how much more Chilean wine there is than Argentine."

"Only because you guys have a more developed marketing and distribution system—not because your wine is superior."

Vachio interrupted his laughter and said, "Each of you give me the name of a good, relatively inexpensive dry red wine and I'll tell you what I think."

"Well, che, I could give you the names of good Argentine wines but you probably wouldn't be able to buy them outside of fancy hotels and restaurants. Most of what they sell from Argentina here in the wine shops is the worst."

Vachio looked at Osvaldo.

"Santa Carolina, my friend. It's a dry red Cabernet available at almost any wine shop here. It's a decent Chilean wine that fits what you like. And the price is reasonable.... Don't forget, Santa Carolina."

Over strong black coffee and a dish of custard, they talked about books. Osvaldo was a professor of Latin American Literature at Los Andes University. His eyes lit up when Vachio told him he was reading *The Idiot*.

"Is Dostoyevsky a favorite author of yours?" Osvaldo asked.

"Not particularly. I'm reading *The Idiot* because it was a going away present from a friend.... He said I must be an idiot to go live in Colombia and this book should be my Bible."

Juan Pablo laughed but Osvaldo remained serious and said, "Dostoyevsky is my all-time favorite writer."

"Why?" asked Vachio.

"Well, aside from the fact that my maternal grandmother was Russian, which I believe gives me an appreciation of the Slavic mind, I've always found Dostoyevsky's complex characters and labyrinthine plots congenial to the Chilean history and temperament..." Osvaldo ignored Juan Pablo's loud snort. "...His writing has always hit me in the gut. He was a genius."

"What do you think of Garcia Marquez?" Vachio asked him.

"A fine writer. *100 Years of Solitude* is a classic."

"I read that one," said Vachio. "Peace Corps recommended that to us to give us insights into Colombia."

"And what did you think of it?"

"Well..."

Sitting alone at the dining room table the day after his site visit, Vachio well-remembered how that first meal at Doña Pilar's was saved by the company. The food was insipid but the conversation was spicy. And it was only because of Juan Pablo and Osvaldo that he hadn't left Doña Pilar's for the home of some other Colombian family. It would have been easy enough. The Colombian Family Cordinator, a native of Bogotá, was furious when she found out about Doña Pilar's laundry scam, and also about the kind and quantity of food Vachio was receiving.

"I can have you moved to another family by tomorrow. It's outrageous what this woman is doing. The stipend we pay her is more than generous," said the coordinator.

"Well..." Vachio shifted uncomfortably in his chair. He had waited three weeks before reporting the situation to give Doña Pilar a chance to back down. But instead of backing down, she had ordered Blanca not to wash Vachio's clothes until he paid her. "Maybe you could just talk to her. I mean, the location of the house is great. I can walk to the Training Center. And I like some of the people living there..."

"Yes, Gary, but it's obvious you're not having a good experience with this family. We want you to have the best situation possible here. And I take it as a personal insult, as a Colombian, that this Doña Pilar is not showing you proper hospitality. And I can certainly get you a family that will."

"Yeah, well, I certainly don't take this as a reflection on all Colombians. It's just that...at this point, it seems like more of a hassle to move and get used to some other family than to just stay. They don't bother me and I pretty much do my own thing. I can live with them. I just don't want them ripping me off."

"Very well. I'll talk to her." The coordinator had called Doña Pilar on the phone and laid into her for not honoring the terms of the agreement. From then on, there was no more mention of extra laundry money and the food improved in quantity if not in quality. That was good enough for Vachio. But he couldn't help feeling a twinge of envy when he saw what warm relationships some of the other volunteers had with their Colombian families.

Just the luck of the draw, thought Vachio, stirring the dregs of his chocolate. But I won't be here much longer.

Vachio rose and went to the foot of the stairs to wait for Juan Pablo. It was exactly 15 minutes since he had gone upstairs to comb his hair. Seconds later Juan Pablo came bounding down the stairs.

"Are you ready to leave here now, che?" he asked.

"I was ready a long time ago, man."

4

Juan Pablo handed Vachio his camera tripod and said, "I was going to take a taxi, but with you to help me with the equipment I can take a bus and save some money for beer."

"Thanks. Glad to be your burro.... Just remember me when you buy your beer."

They stepped outside into glaring cool sunlight and walked up the street to 59th and Caracas. They stood on the corner for a moment, breathing diesel fumes, watching the flowing potpourri of cars, buses, busetas, vans, motor bikes, and even one horse drawn wagon clopping along on the far right hand side of the street. It was loaded with produce and old bottles, and manned by a solitary, grizzled *campesino*, his straw hat pulled low over his forehead, a bandana over his nose and mouth to filter some of the fumes and grit of the road. The motor vehicles buzzed in and out like angry bees, horns tooting, respecting no lane markings, acknowledging no pedestrians, obeying the laws of aggressive occupation of space and self-preservation in a controlled game of chicken.

Vachio raised his hand to flag down a buseta, *Plaza de Toros* emblazoned on its windshield.

"No," said Juan Pablo, waving the buseta off. "Let's get a chicken bus. It's better with all this equipment, che."

He gestured to a decrepit bus in the far lane. The driver swerved across two lanes of traffic, belching black smoke, and jolted to a halt in the middle of the intersection. They piled in and headed for the back of the bus, grabbing onto the hand rails as the bus lurched forward, stepping around and over baskets of produce and bales lying in the aisle next to mostly coppery skinned owners wearing wool *ruanas* and broad-brimmed black hats. They found seats and stowed the equipment, drawing curious stares from the more obvious country folk. The interior was rank from the odor of unwashed bodies and wet wool.

The bus wheezed and coughed along La Caracas, receiving and depositing passengers like an old dog trying to shake off an infestation of fleas.

"So, I forgot to ask you," said Juan Pablo. "How was your visit to Santander?"

"It went fine."

"It went fine? Nothing else?"

"Well, I'm still digesting it. But...it was...*folclórico*."

"*Folclórico*? When did you start using that word in that context?"

"I learned it in Garrotero."

"All right, why is it *folclórico*?"

"Because, according to them, it's the Capital of the World and the *Pueblo de los Garroteros*."

Juan Pablo broke into such loud laughter several passengers turned to stare at them. "If they told you that, they must think it's *folclórico*. Now you tell me about it."

Vachio gave him a rundown on some of the things he had experienced and the observations he had made. One of the highland Indians in the back of the bus eavesdropped on his account and, at pauses, would turn around and give Vachio a gold-toothed smile of encouragement. By the time they arrived at their destination, the man had pulled a bottle of *aguardiente* out of his *mochila* and offered Vachio a hit.

"Too early for me, boss," said Vachio, following Juan Pablo to the door. "And we have to go now. But thanks."

"Thanks to you, young man, for making this trip agreeable."

As they walked up the street toward the high school, Juan Pablo, who had remained quiet during the account, said, "This Garrotero doesn't sound all that *folclórico* to me. But at least it sounds as though they like you.... At least."

"At least?"

"Listen, that's something. I've been in towns where they'd just as soon spit on you as invite you for a drink. This Garrotero sounds like the kind of place where a guy could get in serious trouble if he were an idiot or a jerk."

"So you're saying I'm not an idiot or a jerk?... At least?"

"At least."

"Thanks for the vote of confidence."

"Hey, you're the one who wants to be a social worker. It's a fool's game, che." Juan Pablo laughed to take the sting out of his words.

"Man, you know why I like talking to you so much?"

"Why?"

"Because after talking to you with your way of thinking, life seems easy with my way of thinking."

"At your service, bro." Juan Pablo stopped in front of the entrance to the high school and took the tripod from Vachio. "Have a nice day," he said in English, a dopey grin on his face.

"Yeah, you too."

Vachio started down the hill away from the Plaza de Toros, surprised to feel sweat on his brow. It was a pleasant sunny morning, though fingers of mist were already penetrating gaps in the high peaks. Vachio removed his jacket and wished he had brought a hat. This cool, high altitude equatorial sunlight was trickier than the hot tropics. It burned you inside out, before you were even aware of the danger, like overexposure to a heat lamp.

Vachio pointed his nose toward the downtown skyscrapers and walked, watching the throngs of passersby who had come out to enjoy this rare morning. He had no particular plan or place to go—just walk and absorb the street action. He felt alert and hyper from his early morning plane trip from Santander and from the cool bracing highland air. Vachio shook his head and chuckled, recalling an incident from his visit to Garrotero, startling a woman walking her baby in a stroller. He smiled and walked swiftly away from her. Ah, big city paranoia, he thought. But it still feels good to wander free in the streets after being led around by the nose for a week in Garrotero.

A buzz of voices, the smell of roasting meat, and brilliant flashes of color led Vachio to a street fair at a large tree lined plaza on La Avenida Septima. Normally Vachio avoided crowds but, feeling playful, he plunged into the festive throng. He reached the central fountain and spied naked *gamines* splashing around in the brown water and spraying unwary strollers. Vachio flipped a two peso coin into the fountain and watched the melee as the *gamines* scrambled after it like squalling sea gulls. Then, chuckling, he bought a roasted ear of corn from a vendor to have something to munch on. Before leaving the circle near the fountain, he was approached by two phony emerald merchants. Vachio laughed them off and joined the milling knots of people circulating along the shrub and flower lined paths.

A *Sabanera* quartet strolled the perimeters of the square, accordions and guitars in hand, serenading likely prospects with traditional favorites. Young lovers and elderly couples walked hand-in-hand while children scampered about shaking balloons on sticks. Solitary old gentlemen in shabby suits sat on stone benches, watching the activity with clouded nostalgic eyes while ragged beggars with imploring eyes stretched sinewy hands toward the well-to-do. Flagstone paths radiating from the central square were crowded with booths selling food and beverages. Mobile vendors with pushcarts sold giant corn-on-the-cob, barbecue meat on skewers, popsicles, ice cream, sweets, and snacks. Hustling young men offered cartons of Marlboros. Skinny, white-helmeted police wearing olive drab walked in pairs, their rifles slung within easy reach. There were artisans' booths, tables laden with used books, darting-eyed gentlemen offering flawed and glass emeralds and fake Rolexes to tourists and bumpkins, and even a contingent of Otavaleño Indians from Ecuador, resplendent in white, twin braids dangling down their backs, flashing gold-toothed grins as they displayed their colorful blankets, sweaters, and shawls. Long-haired Colombian hippies dominated the length of a stone retaining wall, working in pairs, one stretched out on the grass, the other hawking hand-crafted knickknacks and embroidered leather products laid out on *ruanas* on the ground.

Vachio gravitated to the used book tables and was pleased to find a copy of *Chronicle of a Death Foretold* by Garcia Marquez. After a brief haggle, he paid for it and squirreled the cheap paperback edition in his back pocket. Then he wandered over to the hippie section and idly surveyed the collection of belts, bracelets, beads, tooth necklaces, rings, lucky charms, astrological pendants, hand painted scarves, and sundries. He paused before a display of paintings depicting Andean scenery and highland Indians at work and during festivals. Vachio liked the paintings, but he was more impressed by an assortment of nativity scenes with Indian characters done in water colors spread on a blanket on the ground. Vachio stooped down for a closer look. They were Christmas cards. This was something he could use.

"Can I help you?"

Vachio looked up. A slim attractive young woman with flowing black tresses, long eyelashes, and an infant in a multicolored sling on her back gazed hopefully down at him from her perch on the stone wall.

"I'm just looking for now. But I like the paintings. Did you do them?"

"No. But I did the cards."

"They're nice, too."

"Thank you."

Vachio took his time and selected five cards he liked best. Then he stood up and addressed the woman. "I'll take these. How much for the five?"

"Forty pesos. They're normally 10 each but I'll give you a deal on five."

Vachio figured he could argue her down but the price struck him as fair for original work. "Fine. I'll take them." He reached into his wallet and passed her a 200 peso note.

"I don't have change for this. Maybe you'd like to buy something more."

"No." Vachio reached for his money.

"Wait..." The woman studied Vachio's face. "If you'll stay here for a moment and watch my things, I'll go and get change."

"That's fine with me. But what if a customer comes?"

"Sell the cards for the price I told you. If they want a painting, tell them to wait for me."

"Well..." Vachio was doubtful.

"I'll be right back."

The woman left before Vachio could reply. Shrugging, he leaned against the wall and waited. Two French tourists came and wanted to buy a couple of postcards. Vachio told them they cost 15 pesos each but allowed them to bargain him down to 10. They walked away well-satisfied with the deal. Vachio chuckled to himself and stuffed the 20 peso bill in his pocket. Maybe I'm in the wrong profession, he thought.

Then a young man approached, walking as though he were stalking a dangerous beast and eyeing Vachio with suspicion. He was tall, with dark Carib Indian features but piercing blue eyes, his rust-colored hair tied in a pony tail in back, a black and blue headband restricting his long bangs. He wore a shark's tooth necklace, painted leather thongs around his wrists, thin white cotton pants, sturdy sandals, and a beautiful sky blue *ruana* with black and blue borders.

"Who are you?" he asked Vachio in a soft but firm voice.

"A customer. Who are you?"

"I'm the artist who did these paintings. Where is Marina?"

"Marina is the woman who does the cards?"

"Yes."

"She went to get change for me over there somewhere," said Vachio, motioning to the other end of the plaza. "She asked me to watch her things until she gets back."

The man relaxed noticeably and leaned up against the wall beside Vachio. "Sorry for the suspicion. But one has to be careful here."

"No problem. I didn't take it personally."

"You see, Marina and I are together. So if she trusted you enough to leave you alone with our things, I'll assume you're all right."

Vachio chuckled. "The question is, can I trust you guys? She went off with 200 pesos of mine."

"That's nothing. One painting of mine is worth 10 times that."

"I like that. That's how an artist has to think. Now you just have to find customers who agree with you. Right?"

"Correct. And they're not always easy to find," said the man with a rueful laugh. Suddenly he stuck out his hand. "My name is Jairo."

They shook hands. Then Jairo pulled a half smoked joint out of his pocket and asked Vachio, "Do you smoke?"

"Yes. But I don't like to when I'm walking around the city."

"Why?"

"It makes me paranoid."

"You mean, it makes you more alert and aware," said Jairo with a laugh.

"No. I'm usually alert. It pushes me over the edge to paranoia. I start imagining dangers that aren't really there."

"It does that to me once in a while." Jairo looked around for the police and struck a match. "Do you mind?"

"No. Spark it up. I'll take one hit to be sociable."

"This is kick-ass Colombian Gold," said Jairo, switching to clear English. Then he lit the joint, took a deep drag, and passed it. Vachio took a good long toke and held it, his cheeks bulging, smoke seeping out between his compressed lips. Jairo laughed appreciatively.

"You're Americano, right?" Jairo asked.

Vachio nodded, holding the smoke. Jairo took another hit and offered the joint again but Vachio, already feeling buzzed, refused. Jairo was right. It was kick-ass stuff. A warm fuzzy feeling settled over Vachio.

"Where did you learn English?" he asked Jairo.

"In Santa Marta on the Caribbean Coast. That's where I come from originally."

"But how? You speak well."

"In school and hanging out with tourists and some American and English friends."

"You've never been to an English speaking country?"

Jairo shook his head.

"You must have good ears. Your pronunciation is good and clear."

"Thanks. Glad to know I haven't gotten too rusty. Now how did you learn Spanish?"

"More or less like you learned English."

"How long have you been in Colombia?"

"About six weeks."

"What part of the United States are you from?"

"San Francisco."

"Really?" Jairo's monotone voice warmed and his eyes brightened. "San Francisco. City of cool gray love. Flowers, hippies, free concerts, and cool people."

Vachio laughed. "Man, who have you been talking to?"

"A friend of mine from your city. He owns a *gringo* bar in Santa Marta. Maybe you know him. Chuck is his name."

"No, I don't think I know him. But Chuckie sounds like he's been quoting Herb Caen columns from more than a few years ago."

"Who's Herb Caen?"

"A newspaper gossip columnist in San Francisco."

"Then, what my friend Chuck says about San Francisco isn't true?"

Vachio shrugged. "Yeah, it's true for some people. Especially for people who come from somewhere else with that idea in their head.... But let me put it this way, if your buddy feels that way about San Francisco, why did he move to Santa Marta to open a bar?"

"Well, I don't know. But Santa Marta is a real hip place,

too...beautiful beaches...tropical pleasures...a snow capped mountain in the near distance. I love it. There is no comparison to this *Cachacolandia* here."

"*Cachacolandia*?"

Jairo laughed. "Yes. That's what we coast people call high-landers. You know, the cold gets into their blood or something. They're not as live or fun-loving as us. Nor as loose and friendly. It costs me dearly to live in the Andes. I miss the sea air and the tropical breezes."

"So why don't you go back?"

"Because my woman is a *Cachaca* from Manizales. And though I hate to admit it, I agree with her that there is more of a market for our work in the big inland cities. Andean motifs are in fashion right now."

Vachio cracked-up. "So you don't like highlanders, but you married one. And now you paint them."

"What can I say?" said Jairo, smiling broadly and fingering his shark tooth necklace. "Love is blind and business is business. Besides, Marina has the good bourgeois business sense that I lack. I have the talent and the inspiration. She has the calm intellect. We make a great combination..."

Comparing Marina's Christmas cards to Jairo's paintings, Vachio wasn't convinced who had the edge in talent.

"...By the way, speaking of business, I have some remedies for the head and perception enhancers at a good price." Jairo held up his rainbow-striped *mochila* and patted it.

"Say what?"

"Ten dollars American for a gram of high grade *periquito*, cocaine. You can't beat it. What do you say?"

"I'll pass."

"Why? Don't tell me it's too expensive. I know what it costs in the United States. About $140 for shit this good."

"Nothing to do with price. I'm not into coke. It doesn't do it for me."

"You've probably never had anything as good as this."

"I probably have. But no thanks," said Vachio, finishing with an edge of finality to his voice.

"All right, all right. It's cool." Jairo set his *mochila* on the ground and stared at one of his paintings. Vachio folded his arms and thought, Where the hell had that Marina gone? To the bank?

"Hey, man, if you ever get to Santa Marta be sure to look up my friend Chuck," said Jairo. "He'll treat you right. Whatever you want."

"We're not supposed to go to Santa Marta. It's red-lined."

"Red-lined? What's that mean?"

"It's means we're not supposed to go there because it's too dangerous from guerrilla activities or drug smuggling. I think Santa Marta is because of drug smuggling. You tell me. How is it there?"

Jairo was momentarily taken aback. "Well, uh, it has been getting more dangerous there. Too many of those crazy *Guajiros* have been coming in and working for big coke distributors from Medellín and Cali." Jairo shook his head. "They're fucking things up for guys like me."

"Guys like you?"

"Yeah, man, you know, I'm not a real dealer," said Jairo in English. "I sell just enough to provide my own recreation and to make enough money to tide us over through the bad times. That's all. I'm not about murdering people and all that. I'm just trying to get by and practice my art."

"Yeah? I've heard that story before. My best friend used to tell me something like that. He ended up getting hooked on heroin and driving his car off the freeway one rainy night."

"Hey, man, don't lay no trips on me. This isn't the fucking rich United States here. The male unemployment rate is something like 30 percent and it isn't because people are lazy. There just aren't that many opportunities for young people.... You do what is necessary to survive. And if the United States likes to consume drugs, then there will always be a country like Colombia ready to sell it to them." Jairo grinned. "Nothing personal, man, I like Americans. But you guys definitely have a drug problem."

"And Colombia doesn't?"

"Bro, for the most part Colombia sells drugs to the U.S. and Europe. The average Colombian doesn't consume them."

"Not yet. But you can't deal with something like cocaine and not have it come back on you someday.... It's the old saying, man, what goes around comes around. And anyway, I was talking about you personally. Not your country."

"I can handle it," said Jairo, drawing up and sticking out his chest. "It's no problem for me, bro."

"Whatever you say."

"Man, what are you doing in Colombia?"

Before Vachio could answer, he spotted Marina approaching and said, "Here comes your partner. Finally."

Marina walked straight up to Jairo and kissed him lightly on the lips. "Why did you delay so long, love?"

"I'll tell you later," said Jairo.

Marina turned and gave Vachio his change. Vachio pulled the twenty out of his pocket and handed it to Marina.

"What's this for?" she asked.

"You had a customer. They bought two more."

"Hey, why didn't you give me the money?" Jairo protested.

"Sorry for the suspicion. But one has to be careful here."

"You are a *jodido*," said Jairo.

Marina smiled and stuffed the money in her pocket. Then she asked Jairo to take the baby off her back so she could feed him. Time to go, thought Vachio.

"Well, it was a pleasure to meet you two," said Vachio. "I'll be leaving now."

"Why don't you stick around for a while. I don't talk to Americans like you very often," said Jairo.

"Nah. I'm suddenly very hungry."

Jairo snickered and reached into his *mochila*. "Here. Take one for the road," he said, slipping Vachio a joint. "For the business and for watching our stuff."

"Thanks. The best of luck to you two."

5

Shortly after leaving the plaza, Vachio put on his jacket and plunged into the teeming crowds of the downtown district. Dark clouds had scudded over the mountain rim and a billowing gray mist was enveloping the city, coating the streets with a damp sheen. A chill wind whipped papers into the air and dust and grit into the eyes. Some walkers took cover in cafés and fruit juice emporiums, but most people plowed forward and bucked the elements, wrapping their overcoats and *ruanas* tight to their bodies and covering their heads with umbrellas and newspapers.

Vachio lowered his head and walked with fast purposeful strides. Though he wasn't exactly sure where he was going, it was important to look as though he had an idea to avoid unwanted encounters with watchful hustlers. He was searching for a restaurant called El Refugio Alpino. One of his Spanish teachers had taken him there after a drinking session on a Friday night a few weeks before. He remembered it as a quality restaurant but he was fuzzy as to its exact location. Vachio was determined to find it. The per diem money he had saved on his site visit was burning a hole in his pocket and he couldn't think of a better way to spend it than on a good meal in a dark quiet place where he could think.

He reached Caracas and turned to retrace his steps along 23rd on the opposite side of the street. The drizzle was turning into a steady sopping rain. He was on the point of stopping someone to ask directions when he spotted it across the street: El Refugio Alpino in script lettering over a mural of the Swiss Alps painted onto a false glass front. Vachio crossed the street and nodded to an old beggar woman shivering in the dubious cover of the entryway. He opened the door and stepped inside.

As soon as the door closed, Vachio was embraced by toasty warmth from a crackling fire and the melodic strains of a Viennese waltz. El

Refugio Alpino. The Alpine Refuge. The restaurant was aptly named. Vachio's city jarred nerves were soothed by the warmth, the music, the dim, candle-lit interior, the mahogany wood paneling, the thick burgundy carpet, the black-suited waiters, the posters of Swiss Chalets on the snow-blanketed Alps, and the tinkle of silver cutlery and soft conversation. An unctuous waiter noted Vachio's casual dress and led him to a corner table for two that was out of view of most of the other diners. Vachio chuckled to himself, appreciating the waiter's professionalism.

"Would you like a cocktail before lunch, sir?" he asked.

"A glass of red wine. Santa Carolina."

"Which year, sir?"

Vachio shrugged. "At your discretion, but medium price. That way I can blame you if I don't like it but not feel too bad."

The waiter raised his bushy gray flecked eyebrows. "Sir?"

"It's my way of thanking you for this very, but very private table."

"Ah, very good, sir," said the waiter with a slow smile. "But I trust you'll like what I bring you."

"Probably. I'm not that hard to please."

The waiter handed Vachio a red leather, bound menu and retired, his spit-shined shoes padding over the carpet. Vachio opened the menu, thinking he could never casually afford a restaurant like this in San Francisco on a Peace Corps income. He chuckled to himself. Friends and family back in the States think I'm leading a life of self-sacrificing deprivation, he thought. Well, I am. At Doña Pilar's house.... Vachio's eyes scanned the list: Filet Mignon in Bernaise Sauce, Steak Tartar, Swordfish cooked in lemon butter, Beef Stroganoff, Stop! The Beef Stroganoff sounded right. Something simple and hearty to go with red wine and a cold afternoon. Vachio set the menu aside.

The waiter brought his wine, a basket filled with an assortment of hot breads, and a silver demitasse of sweet butter. At the waiter's request, Vachio sampled the wine. It was excellent. A full-bodied dry Cabernet.

"How do you like the wine, sir?"

"I like it. But it doesn't taste medium price."

"It isn't. It's free. Compliments of the house.... To allay your solitude."

"Thank you. I like it even better."

The waiter grinned and took his order. Vachio leaned back in his chair and sipped the wine. He was beginning to feel the charm of this secluded table. He ate dark bread and drank more wine. He began to feel delightfully languorous and relaxed, his tensions and concerns slipping away. Vachio closed his eyes and daydreamed.

The waiter brought him a plate of chilled crisp lettuce and a tray loaded with sliced carrots, onions, radishes, green tomatoes, olives, salami, Italian peppers, and a ranch dip. Vachio ate it all, including the sprigs of parsley. Then came a tureen of steaming cream of asparagus soup. Vachio spooned it down to the last drop and polished off the bread. Then came the main dish, a generous serving of Stroganoff, the tender juicy sirloin tips swimming in a sauce loaded with mushrooms and sour cream. His ravenous appetite was equal to this, and he sopped up the sauce with another helping of bread. Vachio topped things off with a cup of strong aromatic coffee and a thick slice of German chocolate cake.

Then he flopped back in his chair, his belly bulging, totally sated. Over a second cup of coffee, Vachio surmised that he had regained in one sitting the five pounds he had lost since coming to Colombia. Dinner won't be necessary tonight. Hell, maybe even breakfast tomorrow, he thought.

Vachio looked over the bill and shook his head incredulously. With extra tip money included, it came to just over 10 dollars. A meal of this quantity and quality would easily have cost Vachio more than 50 dollars at the restaurant where he had worked. Fifty dollars was 25 percent of his Peace Corps salary. Some things in life were very strange—especially economics. When the waiter came to collect the bill, Vachio asked him the time. It was after two. Vachio had been in the restaurant more than two hours.

Outside the door, the old beggar woman was still squatted over her pad of cardboard. Vachio handed her a crumpled five peso note. She squinted at it with cataract-clouded eyes and felt it with rough gnarled fingers. Then she looked up, gave Vachio a gummy smile, and made the sign-of-the-cross. "God will pay you back, sir," she croaked.

The rain had stopped but the fog had thickened, creating a damp ethereal world of bulky phantasmagorical figures. Vachio plodded out of the business district, the food gurgling in his stomach, and headed for a quieter drag that fronted a freeway and a street lined with small factory shops. Vachio walked with his head down, feeling drowsy and leaden. He was ready for a *siesta*, but he wondered if he should walk off some of the meal before catching a bus. He decided to walk. The swirling fog reminded him of San Francisco, and Vachio had always appreciated an occasional walk in thick fog. It lent an air of mystery and intrigue to the most mundane things and people. It could transport his mind to another dimension, making him believe he was in touch with extraordinary forces.

Vachio smiled, remembering the woman he had met only months before at the Marina in San Francisco. She had emerged from the swirling mist along the bay's rocky edge and they had fixed their eyes on each other. It was instant mutual recognition. She was tall and slim and wore a black leather jacket, long chestnut hair swirling in the breeze. They had approached each other and begun talking as though they had known each other for years. She was from Copenhagen, Denmark...Ursula ...Vachio remembered her fondly. Their one week affair made up in heat what it lacked in duration. Vachio could still see her avid China blue eyes and her delicately boned face, her soft hair cascading over the pillow, her limbs twining around him like vines. Even though she returned to Europe never to be heard from again, she had left Vachio a lasting legacy. He now associated fog with pale beauty and cool fire.

Vachio's reverie was shattered by a cry for help from the grassy embankment bordering the freeway. He went to the edge and peered through the mist. A ragged *gamin* was waving to him midway down the knoll.

"Water. Please, we need water," he called.

Vachio stood transfixed and mute, a shiver running down his spine. Beyond the boy near the foot of the slope at the edge of the concrete retaining wall, their forms hazy and shifting, cars and trucks blasting by them, was a gang of boys huddled around one of their members who lay prone and unconscious on a bed of newspapers. Two of the boys were bent over him, fanning his face with pieces of cardboard while the others gesticulated and called support to his deaf ears.

"Water. We need water.... Señor!"

Vachio shook himself. "What happened to him?" he asked, his voice sounding hollow in his own ears.

"We don't know. He just passed out. Like that." The boy snapped his fingers. "Fainted. Like dead. Please, bring us some water. We need water."

"But where?"

"Over there! Anywhere!" said the boy, gesturing toward the immense city and the brooding Andean peaks, his voice cracking from anxiety. His face was ashen, highlighting the dirty smudges on his cheeks, his coal black curly hair, and his round brown eyes. "Please, water. Something!"

"I'll go see."

Vachio returned to the sidewalk and scanned the area. Except for a handful of passersby it was almost deserted, and most of the shops across the way were closed for the *siesta.*

"Shit!" Then he spied a man pushing a cart loaded with fruit. Vachio ran toward him, waving his arms and calling out, "Hey! Hey!"

The man stopped in his tracks and raised a long knife in the air, thinking Vachio was a street maniac.

"No! No! No problem!" said Vachio, showing his hands palms out as he drew closer. "I just need some water. Or maybe some juice. There's a boy over there. He's bad. He needs some kind of liquid."

The man lowered the knife but he continued to eye Vachio suspiciously. He was short, chunky, and middle-aged with a hard boiled appearance. His thinning, graying hair was combed straight back. His chin was stubbly, a jagged scar traversed his lower jaw, and he boasted a fierce mustache. He wore a frayed, red wool sweater and his toes were poking through his shoes.

"They're over there," said Vachio, pointing toward the mist-curtained slope.

"I don't see anything," said the man, squinting. Vachio realized he was nearsighted. The man showed his knife again. "You better not be playing with me, my young man."

"No, man, I'm not playing. You can't see for the fog. Come with me a ways and you'll see."

Something in Vachio's urgency convinced the man and he slowly wheeled his cart forward. When they reached close range and the man distinguished the boys, he stopped his cart abruptly and spat out, "Those *gamines*! You can't do nothing for them."

"Just some water. Just in case."

"I don't have water."

Vachio glanced over the fruit in his cart. He had mangos, pineapples, grapes, and oranges.

"Give me a couple of oranges, then."

"You're wasting your time. What do you think..."

"Just give them to me! Here!" Vachio shoved a 10 peso note at him.

The man ignored the money and handed Vachio two oranges. "Go. Just take them. For all the good it'll do."

Vachio ran back to the spot where the boy, obviously the leader of the gang, stood waiting. He rolled the oranges down the slope and followed on their trail. The boy snatched them up, flung a thanks over his shoulder, and raced to his companions. He cut open one of the oranges and forced the juice between the fallen boy's compressed lips. Nothing. He remained inert and unresponsive.

Vachio came up to the group and the boy's parted and let him through. He knelt down and looked at the unconscious child. He couldn't have been more than eight, though he had the wizened weathered features of a much older person. He looked very bad. His face was sallow and his breathing wheezy and intermittent.

"Can you do something for him?" the curly-haired leader asked Vachio.

"I'm not a doctor. I don't know what to do for him. Can't you call an ambulance?"

The boy's eyes glazed over and he redoubled his efforts to revive his friend. Nothing. A couple of the younger boys began to sob. They were held and comforted by their older companions. After a few minutes of this, the leader looked up and for an instant his eyes met Vachio's. Then he shook his head and resumed his futile efforts to revive his friend.

Vachio rose and trudged up the knoll. The look of total desolation and helplessness in the eyes of the leader had struck him like a physical blow and turned his stomach. He had seen that very same look before—in his own mirror—the day he heard that his friend Ricky had died.

Vachio came abreast of the fruit vendor.

"Well?" asked the man.

Vachio bowed his head.

"I told you," he said, not unkindly.

"He's dying like a dog," said Vachio.

"No, not like a dog. Like a fly. They die like flies." The man's face twisted in anger. "You're a foreigner, aren't you?"

"Yes."

"Well, these things are a shame. Terrible. But if you stay long enough, you'll get used to it."

"I don't want to get used to it."

"Believe me, better that you do. Or you'll end up crazy—or worse."

"But why can't they call an ambulance or something? What the fuck!"

The man gave a sardonic laugh. "Ambulances are for rich people, friend. Not for people like them or me."

"Is that how it is? Just so?"

"That's how it is!" said the man, his voice rising in anger. "Just so! And it makes me want to do this to the shit people responsible for it." The man raised his arm and drove his knife into a fat mango with such force it splattered juice onto Vachio's arm.

Vachio nodded and walked on into the comforting anonymity of the fog, his swirling thoughts lost in the indifference of the great city.

6

Over a solitary mid-morning Sunday breakfast, Vachio fingered the sealed letter from Rolo to his mother. Having nothing else on his agenda, Vachio decided to deliver the letter and fulfill his promise.

"Good morning," said Juan Pablo, rubbing his bleary eyes and flopping onto a chair.

"Damn, man!" said Vachio. "You look half dead."

Juan Pablo yawned and lay his head on the table in response.

Vachio chuckled. "Why don't you go back to bed?"

"I can't," said Juan Pablo, his voice muffled by his crossed arms. "I have a little job today.... Besides, the old lady is on my case for staying out late last night, so I can't get any sleep anyway."

"Maybe if you didn't stay out so much she wouldn't be on your case all the time."

Blanca glided into the room and served Juan Pablo coffee. Juan Pablo raised himself to a slouching position and thanked her.

"Would you like breakfast? Or maybe a couple of aspirins?" asked Blanca.

"Breakfast, Blanquita. Just breakfast. I'm not hungover. Just feeling sleepy and lazy as hell."

Vachio waited until Juan Pablo had a few sips of coffee before he slid the letter over to him and asked, "Do you know exactly where this address is? All I know is that it's somewhere out near the airport."

Juan Pablo squinted at the address and at some rough, scrawled directions on the back of the envelope. "Yes, I more or less know where this is at.... I did a job out there not too long ago." Then he gave Vachio a sharp look. "But why do you want to go out there? That is a very dangerous neighborhood, bro."

"To deliver this letter. I promised one of the kids at the prison."

Juan Pablo grunted. "Maybe you should forget your promise. That place is like a no man's land. Especially for someone like you."

"For someone like me? I grew up in a bad neighborhood."

"Whatever, che. Just warning you, nothing more."

"Thanks. I'll watch my step. Now, how do I get there?"

"The best way to get out there is by taking the airport bus and by getting off at this main street marked on the envelope. Then you'll have to look around for yourself and ask directions from people. This is one of those squatter neighborhoods without good street signs or exact addresses."

"Then maybe I should take a cab instead of the bus?"

"No! You'll spend a fortune if you go in a cab. And you might not find the address anyway."

"All right. I'll try my luck."

"Be careful, che. Keep a watchful eye."

Vachio caught a rattling old bus and settled down for a long haul. By bus it would take over an hour to get out by the airport. It was another leaden gray day. Vachio stared out of the window and watched the city sweep past. He felt vaguely depressed and lethargic. He had dreamed about his old friend Ricky the night before—something he hadn't done for years. In the dream they had been playing football. For some reason, Ricky was on the opposing team and Vachio had tackled him after he caught a pass and laid him out flat on his back on the grass. Vachio had extended his hand to help Ricky to his feet. Ricky had remained motionless, his eyes staring blankly. "C'mon, man, quit playin' around," Vachio had said. Ricky remained inert and without any sign of life, his face transformed into that of the dying *gamin* Vachio had seen that afternoon. Vachio screamed, "No, not you! Not you!" Then he awoke, trembling, cold sweat on his brow.

The bus left the bustling core of the city and advanced along a wide boulevard lined with factories, blocky apartment complexes, and shops. Beyond the front line of the shops and factories lay teeming, concentrated neighborhoods, the houses and apartments interspersed with occasional garbage strewn open lots. Vachio watched and wondered. Only decades before these outlying districts had been quaint, cobble-stone pueblos surrounded by verdant farmland. Now they were dusty and dirty barrios, one indistinguishable from the other, with antennas and thin steel girders scratching the sky. It was a solid urban clutter of graffiti-splashed concrete, glass, and steel, laid out in neat gridiron streets; their old identities swallowed up and masticated by the progress of Bogotá. "Is this progress?" muttered Vachio.

As they drew closer to the airport, scattered fields of green, garbage dumps, sprawling junkyards, and ramshackle settlements replaced the solid flow of concrete edifices. Vachio spotted his street and banged his hand against the wall to signal for the bus to stop. He got off and stood for a moment on a street running right into the heart of a huge auto junkyard. This was the street he was supposed to take. Vachio shook his head and hesitantly entered the junkyard, his street becoming a corridor of rusting, squashed hulks of cars and piles of rubber tires. As he stood indecisively at a junction in the line of wrecks, a man emerged from behind a pile of cannibalized engines and hailed him.

"What can I help you with?" the man asked, his round face streaked with grease, looking askance at Vachio.

"I'm looking for this place," said Vachio, showing the man his directions.

The man glanced at the directions, grunted, and said, "Keep going straight ahead until you get past the wire fence and you'll find it somewhere not too far beyond there."

"But..."

The man turned on his heel and went back to his pile of engines.

Vachio walked through the junkyard, past the fence encircling the property, and entered a squatters' town. On the side of a brick storage shed adjacent to the junkyard someone had painted in bold white lettering, *Barrio El Dorado*. A rueful laugh escaped Vachio. The guy who did that must be a comic, an absurdist, or incredibly optimistic, thought Vachio, surveying the fantastic collection of habitations within the sweep of his vision. Except for a handful of squat, solidly built cement brick structures, most of the homes were little better than hovels, constructed of salvaged boards, pieces of sheet metal and plastic, spare bricks and concrete, corrugated roofing material, thin plastic sheeting, bailing wire and rope, and whatever other bric-a-brac and refuse was deemed serviceable. The houses reminded Vachio on a large scale of the nesting material used by birds in big cities. The streets were unpaved and muddy, raw sewage ran in ditches along the fronts of the houses, and mounds of garbage smoldered in empty lots. Bands of mangy dogs scavenged the streets and chickens clucked and pecked at the earth behind wire enclosures between the houses. Potbellied little children with runny noses, smudged faces and dull eyes, bundled up in patchwork clothes, played in the streets. Slatternly, prematurely-aged women washed clothes and tended cooking fires in improvised backyard kitchens. Shabbily dressed young men with sullen eyes huddled around fires burning in steel drums and passed bottles of *aguardiente* back and forth. The odors of putrid garbage, wood smoke, burnt rubber and plastic, sour liquor, and human waste wafted through the crisp damp air. At regular intervals, the drone and roar of airplane engines blasted the ears.

Vachio searched through the narrow, maze-like streets for his address. Street signs were improvised and haphazard, and few of the habitations had posted numbers. Vachio was aware of curious, suspicious, and predatory eyes following his course. But no one made a move to molest him or even ask him his business. Finally, giving up on finding the house himself, and spurred by the beginning of a cold drizzle, Vachio approached a young man wearing a red sweater.

"Good morning," said Vachio.

"Good morning," said the young man, his eyes curious and sympathetic. He had been watching Vachio for the last few minutes.

"Can you tell me where to find the house of the Señora Elvira Ramirez?" asked Vachio.

"Why do you want to see her?"

"I have a letter for her from her son in the *Casa de Menores* in Garrotero."

"And what's he to you?"

"I work there. And since I was coming to Bogotá, I told him I'd deliver a letter for him.... That's all."

The man nodded his head and smiled. "Well, you almost found the house yourself. It's right there across the street.... That brick one. Come on."

The man walked across the street with Vachio and rapped on the metal door. Vachio was surprised. Though the brick work was rough and amateurish, the house was one of the better ones he had seen in this shantytown. It even had a small cement porch and a door mat to keep the muck out of the house.

"Doña Elvira!" called the man. "There is someone here to see you with a message from your son."

"I'm coming," answered a faint voice from the interior.

"You'll be fine now," said the man, shaking Vachio's hand and taking his leave.

Vachio was admitted to the house by a very surprised woman. With almost girlish embarrassment, she asked him to take a seat on her worn couch. From the adjoining room, Vachio spotted a brood of children peering at him from around the door frame. For a long moment they sat in silence, neither knowing what to say to break the ice.

"Here is the letter from your son," said Vachio.

The woman accepted it with thanks and turned it over and over, her hands almost fondling the thin paper of the envelope.

"And how is my Octavio? Is he well? Is he eating well?" she asked.

"Considering where he's at, he's doing very well.... And that's not only my opinion...but also that of the psychologist and social worker."

"Thanks be to God.... He truly is a good boy, you know. You see how he remembers his mother. Even when he was living on the streets, he always found time to visit and give us what food or money he could.... You understand? He did what he had to do because of our circumstances. Things weren't good for him here."

Vachio nodded. Doña Elvira fell silent and stared at the letter. In many ways she reminded Vachio of Rolo. She was raw-boned and sturdy, possessing the kind of body that could extract all the sustenance from the least morsel of food or drink. And though she was at least in her early 40s, her hair was jet black and her angular, high-cheeked face was almost seamless in its stoic serenity. She was a woman built for the long-haul, to endure and suffer as needed and take her pleasures in snatches along the way.

"Can I offer you something to drink?" she asked Vachio. "A soda or something..."

"All right. Something hot. For the cold." Vachio knew she was dying to read the letter.

"Coffee? Chocolate?..."

"Whatever you have is fine with me."

She excused herself and went into the adjoining room. Vachio settled into the cushions, a spring poking at the small of his back, and surveyed the room. The cement floor, half covered by a threadbare throw rug, was very clean. The couch, an arm chair, and several wood folding chairs were crowded into an approximately 8-by-10 space. The distinguishing characteristic of the room was a corner niche dedicated to the Virgin Mary. It consisted of a two-foot-tall plaster statue surrounded by candles in red-tinted glass holders standing on an end table, and a handmade rosary wound around the base of the statue, the beads made of dried coffee beans.

A girl of about 11, thin and reedy, with long stringy hair and dolorous eyes, brought Vachio a mug of steaming hot cocoa and a bread roll. Vachio sipped his cocoa and encountered a slice of melting goat cheese in it. Doña Elvira was offering him the best she had in the house. Vachio looked up and saw the girl staring at him. Beyond her near the entrance to the adjoining room, six other small children were gaping at him. Vachio suddenly burst into laughter. The children retreated in giggling confusion.

Doña Elvira soon rejoined Vachio and they had a halting chat. In his letter, Rolo had enclosed some money, and he asked his mother to come to Garrotero for a visit soon. Then to make conversation, Vachio asked her how many children she had.

"Twelve," said Doña Elvira.

“Twelve,” murmured Vachio, his face growing pensive. He couldn’t imaging how Doña Elvira coped, let alone maintain the dignity and strength she manifested. She was a testament to the resiliency and adaptability of the human species. It set the wheels spinning in Vachio’s head.

A short while later, Vachio, still pensive, found himself on the bus for the long ride back downtown, the dreary urban landscape rewinding before his eyes. His experiences of the past few days had caused him to understand something on a visceral level that prior to this time had been understood only on a theoretical level. It had been one thing for him to read books by thinkers like Aldous Huxley and Paul Ehrlich concerning the imminent perils of world overpopulation, but to actually see a young boy die of privation in the street and a Doña Elvira trying to raise 12 children in the warren of Barrio El Dorado really slammed home the point. That Colombia’s population growth was outstripping its resources and development was all too evident in the explosive and cancerous growth of shantytowns around its major cities, bursting like mushrooms and fungus from dead discarded material. Looking at things dispassionately, Vachio saw small hope of a decent life for a young person growing up in a place like Barrio El Dorado. Shantytowns like these, and the misery and despair they engendered, offered a limitless supply of recruits for the drug mafias and guerrillero groups, not to mention the less organized bands of street kids and individual criminals who preyed on society. Even scarier, there were countries far worse off than Colombia. And scarier still, it was almost impossible to get any authoritative leader to even admit that overpopulation was a legitimate problem. Yes, some would admit that it was a potential problem in some distant future, but brisk economic growth and development and science would set things to right. Vachio shook his head. He had heard these assurances so many times. What did these assurances mean against the steady growth of a Barrio El Dorado or the deterioration of a place like the South Bronx in New York or the rantings of an Adolph Hitler and his ilk for more living space? How could boom and bust economics that squandered natural resources like a drunken sailor on a binge ever keep up with the relentless advance of the human species? This was a biological problem, and Vachio felt that most of his generation was living through it right now, and even the more privileged people were suffering from it on a subconscious level. True quality of life was in decline. The public denial was almost total. The human race was running like a herd of lemmings to the edge of the cliff.... Vachio shook his head and tried to think of something else. The gray city rolled on and on and on.

7

After returning to Doña Pilar's house, Vachio took a siesta and woke up in the early evening feeling much better, his doom and gloom apocalyptic thoughts dispelled for a time by the yearnings of optimistic youth. Vachio decided to give his once-in-a-while girlfriend Claudia Calimberti a call.

Vachio dialed the number and Claudia's clear, well-modulated voice answered on the third ring.

"Well, I'm a little surprised you're at home," said Vachio. "What's wrong? Are you ill?"

"No, not at all. I just came back from seeing my parents off at the airport....They've gone to San Andres island on holiday."

"Nice. Why didn't you go with them?"

"Because I have way too much work to get done. I'm preparing for a show next week."

"Ah, I see. Well, are you way too busy tonight to get together?"

"No. I only plan to work another hour or so..." Then, before Vachio could suggest something, Caludia asked, "Why don't you come over to my place around 9:00. I need to talk to you about something."

"Oh?" This last sounded vaguely ominous to Vachio. "What do you want to talk about?"

"Nothing I'll discuss on the telephone. We'll talk later."

"All right. Fine."

"*Ciao.*"

Vachio hung up the phone and went to his bedroom to lay down for a while. He stared up at the ceiling, pensive, his brow wrinkled. The last time Vachio had seen Claudia was at a Peace Corps party on the Saturday before he took off for his site visit. Claudia had given him the silent treatment on the taxi ride back to her place after they left the party. Vachio knew why. He had paid scant attention to her during the party, leaving her to mingle on her own in the midst of wild revelry. She resented that, Vachio thought. And I guess I don't blame her. But she knows I don't want to get too serious. I even introduced her to everybody as my friend. I'm not playing games with her. What does she expect?... Ah, hell! She must have done a lot of thinking while I was away...

Vachio closed his eyes and remembeed how he had met Claudia Calinbert. About a week after his arrival in Bogotá, Vachio had been invited to a small dinner party by a Colombian acquaintance he had made while playing basketball at a university gym. At the party, during the pre-dinner cocktail time, his eyes were drawn to her at once. She was a slender petite blond with sculptured facial features, a high intelligent brow, and lively green eyes. He made eye contact with Claudia and before he was consciously aware of what had happened, they were in deep conversation, their foreheads almost touching, the rest of the people at the party fading into the background. They raced through the preliminaries. Claudia was 24, a year older than Vachio, and a native of Bogotá. Her father was an Italian immigrant from Florence and worked in the import-export trade. Her mother was from a respectable old Bogotá family fallen on indifferent economic times. Claudia had graduated from Los Andes University in Bogotá with a degree in marketing and had then gone on to Florence, Italy, for two years to study fashion design. In association with her father, she ran a boutique in the Chicó District and on the side created an exclusive line of women's clothing. Claudia was smart, cosmopolitan, and ambitious. She was the quintessential modern, Europeanized Colombian woman. Vachio understood and surmised all this from their conversation and his perception of her—a perception somewhat distorted by the subtle perfume she wore and by the fresh scent of her shiny hair.

After dinner, as they danced close, he became aware of the feline grace of her body and the way she molded herself against him. It wasn't too long before they slipped away from the party to take a walk in the crisp night air. Then they were standing under a tree in a small park, locked together, sharing kisses and caresses. They would have made love right there and then if Vachio had a place to take her or money for a room. But since he didn't, they returned to the party and agreed to meet again. The unspoken promise they had made the night of the party was consummated two nights later in a pensión room after they had watched an early evening movie Vachio couldn't even remember. From that point on their relationship settled into a series of sporadic and often hurried meetings. Both Vachio and Claudia had very busy schedules and very different interests. They usually only managed to see each other about two times a week. They both also dated other people. And Claudia had a much more serious suitor than Vachio in the person of Arnulfo Botero. Vachio had met him. Arnulfo was about 30, a mature professional man from a good Bogotá family, and a nice guy to boot. He was also handsome, had a comfortable income, and was serious about settling down and starting a family. Botero was far and away the favorite in Claudia's mother's eyes. Vachio knew this. Claudia had made a point of telling him. Claudia's mother. Vachio grimaced at the thought of her.

Vachio sighed, rolled off the bed, and stood up. Maybe things will seem less complicated after a good meal, Vachio thought. But I sure didn't like the tone of her voice tonight.

"Dinner is prepared and waiting for you downstairs," said Blanca, talking to Vachio through the glass partition.

"Good. What's on the menu?"

"Sardines."

"Sardines..." Not again, thought Vachio. It was the third time in a week. "Well, uh, I'm really sorry, Blanca. I forgot to tell you. I had a big late lunch and I'm going to meet a friend later tonight. So instead of dinner, I'll probably just eat a snack later."

"Then, you don't want your dinner here?"

"No, not tonight. Sorry I didn't tell you sooner."

Blanca's face betrayed nothing—not even the slightest trace of irritation or judgement. "Don't worry, Vachio. It won't go to waste."

"Thanks, Blanca. You're my true friend here."

On the way out the door, Vachio decided to grab a sausage sandwich at the Club Bavaria or go to a chicken joint after a beer or two. It was just after six, twilight was descending over Bogotá, urged on by the dark clouds sweeping over the savannah. The vehicle traffic, even on a Sunday afternoon, was manic normal; on a work day it was manic intense. Vachio dodged across the six lanes of the Avenida Caracas and headed north. Three blocks later he came to a stairwell, marked by an unobtrusive sign, that led down below street level to the Club Bavaria. Vachio took a seat at a small corner table and ordered a stein of dark beer.

After his first sip, Vachio tipped his chair back against the wall and scanned the long cavernous main room to see if any of his fellow Peace Corps trainees or volunteers were hanging around. The Club Bavaria, because of its excellent dark beer at reasonable pitcher prices and its proximity to the training center, was a gathering place for the trainees and Bogotá-based volunteers. But not tonight. Vachio didn't see one familiar face. Just the usual collection of Bogotá business-type guys putting away pitchers of foamy dark beer to start off their evening. Too bad, thought Vachio. He would have liked to talk to one of his acquaintances about his site visit experiences.

After finishing about half of his stein of beer, Vachio began to feel restless. Though the Club Bavaria was a Chapinero District institution, it was by no means Vachio's favorite place. The atmosphere was usually too close, loud, and crowded for his taste. The bar was dark and very smoky, with wood-paneled walls, beamed ceilings, replica heraldic emblems of the Teutonic Knights, and one of the longest bars Vachio had ever seen in his life. The Club Bavaria definitely had character. But the charm of the place was lost on Vachio. He polished off his beer and left without eating anything.

Vachio hit the street and started up Caracas again. He weaved his way through a throng of eager Christmas shoppers, his eyes dazzled by the neon brilliance of upper Caracas. The bars, cafés, and restaurants were jammed. Vachio inhaled the savory aromas of spit-roasted meats and chicken. His appetite flared powerfully. He paused in front of a Hofbrau style restaurant to stare at a roast pig displayed in the window. The *lechona* stared back at Vachio through dead eyes, an apple sticking out of its mouth, a huge chunk of flesh torn out of its side. He shook his head and moved on. Just up the street he came to a spiffy new chicken place and, after giving it a quick inspection, decided to eat there. He had half a chicken, with potatoes and cole slaw on the side, and walked out feeling well-fortified for his meeting with Claudia.

Since it was still a little early, Vachio decided to walk the two miles to Claudia's place instead of hopping onto a buseta. Moving briskly in the chilly air, Vachio came to the corner of Caracas and 72nd and waved in passing to a line of flamboyantly garbed transvestites shopping their wares to passing johns. As Vachio often passed this corner, the regulars had come to recognize him and one of them shouted after him, "Hey, *Papacito*! Are you ready to have a good time with me yet?"

"Sorry, man," said Vachio, half turning, "but I already have a date with a real woman."

Most of the other transvestites whistled and kidded the man who had addressed Vachio. But he only smiled and replied, "*Papacito*, there is no woman more woman than I. You understand? You don't know what you're missing, *pobrecito*."

Vachio laughed and continued on his way. He entered the Chicó District and left the main commercial drag, La 15, to walk the shadowy residential streets. In no hurry, he took a zigzag course, pausing to look at some of the more interesting houses in the soft moonlight. Finally he turned a corner and came to Claudia's place, a steel and glass, nine story tower of futuristic design, shining like a lighthouse among the more somber, wall encircled homes on the block. Vachio approached and waved to Manuel, the security guard, seated at a wide desk before the thick glass doors in the brilliantly lit lobby. Manuel buzzed him in and smiled a greeting.

"Here to see the Señorita Claudia?" Manuel grinned in a conspiratorial manner.

Vachio nodded.

Manuel was a hulking young man, impeccably turned out in a blue suit, his thick black hair greased and combed straight back. He was also well-spoken and had good manners. Vachio thought of him as the cheerful thug. Aside from his formidable physique, Vachio knew Manuel carried a snub-nosed revolver and had an Uzi stashed under the desk.

Manuel called Claudia's suite and she told him to let Vachio pass.

"Have a good time," he called, still grinning, his voice insinuating, as Vachio waited for the elevator. "Her parents have gone to San Andres for a week."

"Yeah, I know."

Vachio entered the elevator and pressed the button to the penthouse apartment. He was whisked to the ninth floor and deposited in a narrow foyer before a highly varnished, solid wood door. Before he could knock, the door was swept open and Claudia stood before him, looking very pretty, her hair loose and cascading over her shoulders, her body sheathed in a white jumpsuit. She smiled gravely and kissed Vachio on both cheeks. But when Vachio tried to pull her to him and give her a real kiss she stepped back, a flustered look on her face, and motioned toward the living room. Her brother, Marco Antonio, was rattling around in there and had a clear view of them.

"So?" muttered Vachio, shrugging. Normally he wouldn't have cared one way or another; he wasn't much for public demonstrations of affection, but he wanted to gauge Claudia's mood.

"Wait for me in the living room one moment," said Claudia. "I just need to put my sketches away and I'll be right with you."

Vachio nodded and went into the living room. Marco Antonio, his brow furrowed in thought, was pacing in front of the huge glass windows, the curtains thrown open to the brilliant night lights of Bogotá. When Marco Antonio saw Vachio he stopped pacing and greeted him cordially. He was a slim, darkly handsome youth with an excitable temperament, and fancied himself a real lady's man.

"Sit down and relax," said Marco Antonio. Then he resumed his pacing as though Vachio weren't there.

Vachio flopped onto a plush, tan leather sofa and draped an arm over one of the glittering stainless steel supports. He chuckled as his tennis shoes almost sank from sight in the snow white shag rug. A bottle of Moet-Chandon rested in a silver ice bucket on the onyx table at his feet. Soft classical music played in the background. Vachio caught himself staring at the bottle of champagne.

"Ah, forgive me," said Marco Antonio. "Would you like a glass of champagne?"

"All right, thank you."

Marco Antonio went to get a glass for Vachio from their well-stocked bar in a niche at the corner of the room.

"What's the occasion?" Vachio asked. "This is good champagne."

"No special occasion," he said, filling Vachio's glass. "We just drank a toast with our parents for their trip." Marco Antonio served himself a half glass of champagne and raised it in the air. "Salud. For the pleasure of your company."

"While the cat's away the mice will play," said Vachio in English, raising his glass toward Marco Antonio.

"What did you say?" asked Marco Antonio, wrinkling his brow. Marco Antonio had gone to high school for two years in Cherry Hill, New Jersey, and though he had an accent like the Wild and Crazy Guys from Saturday Night Live, he spoke passable if incomplete English. Vachio explained the expression to him and Marco Antonio burst into gleeful laughter.

"Yes, I fully expect to play.... In fact, I have a...eh, how do you say? Ah, yeah! A hot date tonight."

"That's good," said Vachio, overjoyed he was going out and leaving him alone with Claudia. "What time are you going?"

"Oh, I'm a little bit late already," he said, winking. "But I'll let her wait a while longer. The anticipation will do her good."

"Uh huh."

Marco Antonio yawned and stretched for effect. The 20 year old man of the world, thought Vachio.

"Well, I suppose I should be getting ready now.... Help yourself to the champagne if you want more. *Ciao! Ciao!*"

With Marco Antonio out of the way, Vachio kicked back and sipped his chilled Moet-Chandon. It was delicious. As was the warmth generated by a modern central heating system. Idly Vachio surveyed the collection of Impressionist Art arrayed along the living room walls. This sure ain't Doña Pilar's house, he thought.

"Ah, you found the champagne," said Claudia, striding briskly into the room and sitting at the far end of the sofa away from Vachio.

"Thanks to your brother. He gave it to me."

"Was he drinking with you?"

"Only a sip or two," said Vachio, indicating the glass Marco Antonio had left almost untouched on the onyx table. "He's got his mind on other things."

"All right, that's fine. He gets stupid when he drinks.... Especially when he drinks champagne."

"That's cute, big sister looking out for her poor irresponsible little brother. He must love that."

Claudia grimaced and tossed her mane of hair with a twist of her neck. Vachio knew it bugged her when he teased her about Marco Antonio. In her mind, she was the one who kept him from becoming a total wastrel. She had told Vachio that their mother let him get away with whatever he wanted, always taken in by his charm and looks and his soulfully repentant, "I'm sorry. Forgive me, *mamacita,*" after one of his debauches; as for their father, he was often away on business and couldn't exert his discipline.

"So anyway, how have you been?" Vachio asked. "Have you been very busy?"

Claudia frowned and folded her arms across her breasts, as though to form a barrier between them, before answering, "Yes, I've been busy. Very busy. But you could have called me sooner."

"I went to Santander for a week on my site visit.... Remember? I told you about that at the party."

"Oh, right." Claudia dropped her arms to her side and her face relaxed.

"How did your site visit go?"

"It went fine." Vachio chuckled. "In fact, they treated me like a movie star or something. It was quite an ego rush."

"What exactly do you mean by that?"

"Well, just that people were very very hospitable and made a fuss over me. You know, it's kind of funny, they would ask me things that only the president of the United States should answer for."

"Oh? And did this hospitality include by chance any *campesina* girls with bad teeth from chewing on raw sugar cane all day?"

"Believe me, they don't all have bad teeth," said Vachio. Claudia tightened her lips and Vachio hastily added, "So what have you been doing?"

"The same things. Work, study, design..." She let her voice trail off. Seeing Arnulfo Botero was left unsaid. "Gary, I need to tell you something..."

"All right, sis, I'm taking off now," called Marco Antonio, his right hand already turning the door knob. "Don't wait up for me."

"Marco Antonio!" Claudia shot to her feet. "You get back here at a decent hour. I don't want you dragging in here at daybreak like you did the last time Papá was away."

"Yes, my Colonel," said Marco Antonio, saluting Claudia. Then he walked out the door, a derisive laugh trailing behind him.

For a moment Vachio thought Claudia was going to follow Marco Antonio out the door and say something else to him. But she subsided onto the sofa with a big sigh and sank into the cushions, a pouting look on her smooth face, her arms folded over her belly. Vachio gave a silent chuckle and reached over to massage her closest shoulder with his left hand. She looked very appealing to him at this moment. It wasn't often he saw her lose her businesslike poise and show a chink in her armor. He steadily kneaded her shoulder and neck and felt her soften under his hand.

"Why don't you leave the kid in peace," suggested Vachio in a quiet voice. "You'll save yourself some frustration."

"Someone has to get after him. Marco Antonio is headed for big trouble if he doesn't slow down. I don't like the crowd he hangs around with—they're too fast."

"Ah, I don't know. He seems a little wild, but he doesn't strike me as stupid. He should be all right."

"You don't know him like I do," said Claudia, staring straight ahead. "He's reckless and takes foolish risks to impress his imbecile friends."

"All right," said Vachio, laughing. "But when you were his age, weren't you away in Florence studying?"

"Yes. So what?"

"So what were you doing when you were away from home with no one to control your life?"

A small grin split Claudia's lips. "I was having the time of my life. But I was never foolish and reckless like Marco Antonio."

Vachio laughed and slid over next to Claudia. He wrapped his arm around her and she snuggled up against his chest. Vachio didn't want to talk about Marco Antonio anymore. With his free hand he toyed with the zipper at the top of Claudia's jump suit.

"If I pull this zipper down will your suit peel off like a banana skin?" Vachio asked, tugging it down far enough to expose the top of her breasts. She was wearing a bra underneath.

Claudia caught hold of Vachio's wrist and looked him straight in the face. Her cheeks were taking on a nice pink glow. "You are incorrigible," she said.

"Just the way you like me," he answered, disengaging his hand and going back to work on the zipper. Claudia extended her lips for a kiss but as they started to gather steam she abruptly broke off and looked at Vachio again.

"Why am I doing this?" she asked

"Because you like it.... I hope."

Claudia held him at arm's length and said, "But what is there between us? What are we?"

"We're friends. No, we're more than friends."

"We're not! We're lovers--nothing more!"

"So what's wrong with that?" sighed Vachio, moving away from her and sinking back into the cushions. "You make lover sound like a bad word."

"No, it's just that...we have no future. Right?"

"We have the present. The future will take care of itself.... Anyway, you know how I feel about things. Why are you bringing this up again?"

"Because things aren't good enough for me this way anymore. Gary, I was going to tell you.... Arnie has made a formal proposal to me."

"Uh huh. Well, what can I say? This isn't exactly unexpected, is it?"

"No, but I thought you should know.... To give you the opportunity to make a decision."

"Me? I think you're the one who needs to make a decision. You already know where I stand." Vachio turned his head and stared straight ahead at the lights of downtown Bogotá.

Claudia looked at Vachio in silence for a moment, her face grave and pensive. "Maybe you're right," she said, her voice a murmur. "Excuse me for a moment."

Vachio looked after Claudia as she left the room. He was thoughtful, apprehensive. He knew she had arrived at some sort of decision concerning them. Vachio sighed and poured himself another glass of champagne. Might as well, he thought. It will soon go flat anyway. Be a shame to waste such good stuff.

Vachio leaned back and sipped his champagne. If it is all over between us, he thought, Claudia's mother will certainly be happy. He thought back to the first time he had met her. Doña Nicoleta Calimberti was a tall slim woman in her mid-40s, still elegant and attractive, dressed in a black gown with small silvery sequins, all set to go out for dinner at an exclusive club. Claudia presented Vachio to her and she surveyed his long hair and casual dress with a raised eyebrow. Still, she kept her voice neutral and her words buttery, and was most gracious in her short introductory chat with him.

The second time Vachio met her was a different story. Now that Claudia had brought Vachio around twice, Doña Nicoleta knew there was serious interest. That afternoon, while Claudia was tied up on the telephone, straightening out some problems with one of the employees at the boutique, Doña Nicoleta served Vachio a tall glass of fine red wine and with soft elegant words gave him a thorough grilling.

"Now what did you say you had a degree in?" Doña Nicoleta asked Vachio, her voice syrupy.

"Recreation." Usually Vachio told Colombians he had a degree in Sociology, because most of them had never heard of a degree in Recreation and he was a juvenile counselor, but in this case he decided to be literal.

"Recreation? I never realized that was a serious academic endeavor. Whatever do you do in this field?"

"Well, the field is unlimited. It's basically directing people in how to best use their leisure time. For example, what Claudia does, directing fashion shows, that's a form of recreation for wealthy people. Or, what we're doing right now, drinking wine and having a chat—that's recreation. Some people would even pay money for the pleasure of doing this.... Especially if the other person were a celebrity."

"Well, uh, that's very interesting. But I can't imagine what sort of people would need someone to tell them what to do with their free time."

"That's a good point Nicoleta. May I call you Nicoleta?"

Doña Nicoleta nodded assent.

"Anyway, I really can't tell you why so many people need someone to organize their free time. I guess they just have too much free time on their hands. But fortunately for people like me, there is such a need."

Doña Nicoleta eyed Vachio suspiciously, suspecting she was being put-on, but her voice remained sweet. "And what exactly is your specialty in this, uh, field?"

"I work with juvenile delinquents and potential delinquents. Here in Colombia, I'll be working with *gamines*."

"*Gamines*?"

This time Vachio clearly heard the disgust in Doña Nicoleta's voice.

"Excuse me." Doña Nicoleta abruptly terminated the interview and had a long conversation with her daughter in private. Later that night, in the privacy of a dark booth at Doña Bárbara's Jazz Club, Vachio told Claudia about his short conversation with her mother.

Claudia sighed and looked unhappy. "Yes, Gary, I know my mother can be a ridiculous snob at times. But that doesn't excuse the way you baited her, either. She told me what happened."

"Really? What did she say?"

Claudia hesitated only momentarily. "She said you remind her of one of those café dilettantes who dream utopian children's fantasies."

Vachio laughed. "That's not too bad. One of the women in my training group told someone I was a slob and a know-it-all.... I must be improving my image."

"That's not funny. You have an absurdist attitude toward life.... I'm not sure I like that about you. It wouldn't hurt you to take a more serious attitude toward certain things."

"Like what?" said Vachio, his voice suddenly cool and sober. "You mean like the way I dress? The way I cut my hair? The way I ignore certain little social niceties? The way I think? Is that what you mean?"

"Well, yes, since you mention it. You're entirely too inflexible about..."

"Inflexible? That makes two of us. It sounds to me like you're trying to mold me into something that I don't want to be. Why? I'm not telling you how to dress or act. I like you just the way you are. I'm only asking for the same consideration."

Claudia smiled. "But you could make things so much easier on yourself. If you would just..."

"Look, Claudia, no offense, but I don't want your world of fashion cachet and *regio regio avant garde du mode*. I was around all that when I worked in that fancy restaurant in San Francisco. It holds no allure for me. I'm a down-to-earth person.... You understand?"

Claudia had stared at him helplessly after that little speech. It kind of summed up their relationship outside of bed.

Ah, yes, thought Vachio, downing the rest of his champagne. He stood up and paced restlessly about the room. What is she doing?

Suddenly the music changed from light classical to Jazz by John Coltrane. Vachio smiled and paced in time to the music. This was something else they enjoyed in common. Claudia had picked up an appreciation of American Jazz from her father. Her father. Except for a brief hello and handshake on the way out the door one evening, Vachio had never even talked to him. Too bad. From what Claudia had told him, he sounded like a good guy. Oh well...

"Will you pour me some of that champagne?" asked Claudia.

Vachio stared at her. She had a bright and wild look in her eyes that he had never seen before.

"Didn't you hear me?"

"Yes. I'm just surprised. Didn't you already have a glass with your parents? You're going over your limit."

"Are you going to pour me a glass or do I have to pour my own?"

"Hey, no problem. Coming right up." He poured her a tall glass, emptying the bottle to the last drop. "It's your lucky night. You get to kill the bottle."

"Lucky? We'll see how lucky," she said, taking the glass and drinking it down. Her eyes brightened even more and took on an almost dangerous glint. "Let's dance."

"To this music?"

"Why not? I feel like dancing."

Vachio didn't need to hear anymore. He took her in his arms and they swayed to the languorous music before the twinkling night lights. Claudia had put on a musky perfume and had left the top of the jump suit unzipped. Vachio soon discovered she had removed her bra as well. Before too long, Vachio had the jump suit unzipped to the waist, there was nothing on underneath, and was starting to peel it off her when Claudia grabbed his hand and said, "Wait. Not here. Let's go in the bedroom."

Vachio was reluctant to let her go. She had him all heated up. "But why? It's so nice here with all these pretty lights."

"No!"

Vachio shrugged. "Whatever you like."

Claudia disengaged herself and walked quickly to her bedroom at the end of a long hallway. Vachio followed at a more leisurely pace. By the time he stepped through the door, Claudia had already discarded the jump suit and was lying naked on the bed. Vachio stood and looked at her for a long moment. She had a nice taut body with medium-sized, firm breasts and that wealth of golden hair falling over her shoulders. Her honey-colored skin glowed alluringly against the white sheets.

"Take off your clothes," she said huskily, her eyes almost feverish.

Vachio quickly stripped off his clothes and started to dive onto the bed.

"Wait!" said Claudia, holding up her hand. "Turn sideways a second. I want to look at you in profile."

"What?"

"Turn sideways."

Vachio, feeling slightly self-conscious, did as she asked. "How's this?"

Claudia smiled, running her eyes over Vachio. "You have a body like one of those Greek statues."

"It's like I say, clothes aren't that important."

"Huh, they are important. But there's no doubt—you look better with your clothes off."

"Yeah? Then why don't you hire me as a model?"

"You don't have the look. I need men who look good with their clothes on."

"All right, if that's how you feel...the show's over."

Without another word, Vachio climbed onto the bed, pressed his lips onto Claudia's, and ran his hands over every curve and crevice on her body. She responded with a passion and enthusiasm Vachio had never felt from her before. They went at it for a sweet long time. When they finally slid apart, they were slick with perspiration and tingling all over.

"Man! What's happening with you tonight?" Vachio exclaimed, breathing rapidly. "You've never been so wild."

"I don't know," she said, biting Vachio on the shoulder. "I just feel free."

"Free from what? Up until now I've always felt that you've been holding back with me."

"Well, perhaps I have. A woman has to protect herself from someone like you."

"Someone like me? How's that?"

"Someone who holds back emotionally."

Vachio sighed and remained silent.

"Well, it doesn't matter anymore," said Claudia softly, as though talking to herself. "I realize now exactly where we stand."

Vachio pillowed his head between his arms and stared at the stark white ceiling. He knew where they stood, too, and he wasn't happy about it. But she was right. He had always held back from her and now their time was up. With things decided between them, they relaxed and talked over some of the good times they had shared together. Then they made love again, but this time it was mechanical, going through the motions, and barely worth the effort.

Around 2:30 a.m., Claudia looked at her watch and said, "I think you better go now. I don't want my brother to find you here."

Vachio, who had almost drowsed off to sleep, awoke with a start. "What? You're going to throw me out on the streets at this hour?"

"You can get a cab."

"They're not so easy to get at this hour. And I'll have to walk to a main street to find one. Why don't you just let me stay until early in the morning? Your brother won't see me leave here.... Unless he comes in while I'm leaving."

"No. I can't take the chance. My brother has a big mouth and I don't want my parents to know about us."

"Like they don't suspect."

"It doesn't matter. They might suspect, but they don't know."

"Ay, you and your social conventions." Vachio got off the bed, still mumbling complaints, and put on his clothes. This was the time of night when it was very easy to encounter problems on the streets. As Vachio thought about it, he grew more and more irritated. This was a stupid thing to do.

"You know, I wouldn't do this to a dog.... Let alone a friend," said Vachio. "Just let me sleep on the floor. I won't touch you."

"No! Don't make things ugly." Claudia rose and put on her night gown. "You really must leave."

"All right, all right. I'm going."

Despite his irritation, Vachio gave Claudia a big hug and a kiss. He thought of saying something cliche and stupid, like they could still be friends, but he decided against this. They could never be just friends. There was still too much physical attraction between them. It was just over. Period. And good luck. Vachio sighed as he slipped from her arms and walked out the door.

"Good luck," said Claudia.

"Yeah," said Vachio, turning to look at her one last time. "I'll need it. Especially right now."

"Don't be so dramatic."

Vachio hit the dark silent streets and headed toward Caracas. It was almost three. He hit La 15 and stopped to look around for taxis. Three, already full, whizzed by without slowing up. The street, except for a few loud drunks, was deserted. Everything was closed. "Ah, the hell with it," muttered Vachio, and started to walk at a brisk pace with his hands shoved in his pockets to protect them against the chill.

He had gone about five blocks without mishap when he spotted a pair of soldiers, rifles slung over their shoulders, coming directly toward him. Not now, thought Vachio. He approached them without breaking stride, trying to look confident and nodding in greeting to them. One of the soldiers nodded back and looked ready to walk on but his partner stopped, blocking Vachio's path, and said, "Papers."

"Fuck!" muttered Vachio, digging his wallet out of his pocket. While Vachio fished around for his I.D., the soldier, just a kid, asked him what he was doing out on the streets so late.

"I had a date," said Vachio, handing him his identification card. "You'll notice this card is signed by the Office of DAS, eh."

The soldier looked at it briefly and handed it back to Vachio. "That's fine. You can go."

"*Gracias*," said Vachio in an exaggerated tone, and walked on before they could think of some other reason to bother him. Since arriving in Bogotá, he had been stopped by the police or soldiers almost a dozen times. At first, he had reacted nervously to these orders for identification and occasional searches. But now he was just sick of it. He had learned to treat these events as routine. Though with a nervous shaky kid, as many of the soldiers were, it was best to take nothing for granted. This was the price of living under a state of emergency, and the police and military personnel had a right to feel nervous. Exploding bombs, gun fire, and acts of terrorism were everyday events in some section of the sprawling city. But what Vachio couldn't understand was why he was stopped so often. Many of the other trainees had never been stopped and searched; and Mark Hill had told Vachio, "I've only been stopped here twice. Both times when I was with you." Vachio had complained about this in class one day and Clarita, one of the Spanish teachers, had told him, "Well, of course, man, *tu tienes la pinta de sospechoso* (You look suspicious). Maybe I do, Vachio thought. It's hard not to feel resentment when they have that kind of power over you—to stop you and harass you and mess with you anyway they want. Even to haul you into jail for a while. I guess my resentment shows. Huh. But I wonder how the average Colombian feels. They've been living with this shit for more than a generation.

As Vachio neared Caracas, he noticed a man in a long overcoat slinking along behind him, maintaining a distance of about fifty feet. Vachio speeded up his walk and the man kept pace. Vachio crossed the street. The man waited a few moments and then crossed after him. Vachio turned the corner and increased his pace even more. He reached the corner of Caracas and 70th and the man was still on his tail. Three transvestites were still hanging out at the corner. Vachio went right up to them.

"Hey," he said, without looking behind him. "Is there a guy coming after me?"

One of the transvestites, with orange frizzy hair and silvery dancing tights said, "Yes. And he looks like a guy with bad intent."

"All right." Vachio turned and glared directly at the man, his face fully revealed in the glow of a street lamp. The transvestites stood shoulder-to-shoulder with him and did the same. The man stopped and looked at them.

"Hey, *Papi*, you want some business with us?" said orange hair.

The man gave them a baleful look. Then he crossed Caracas and headed in the opposite direction.

"Thanks," said Vachio. "He followed me for three blocks."

"For nothing, brother," said orange hair. "It gets rough out here at times. Be careful."

"Yes, thanks again. But I'm almost home now."

The man tapped his forefinger under his eye. "Don't be too confident. Keep your eyes open."

Caracas was brightly-lit and a few cafés and cantinas were still open. Vachio covered the ten blocks or so to 61st and turned down the dark cul-de-sac toward his house. The same homeless man who showed up every night some time after eleven lay sleeping under a pile of rags next to the neighbor's house. Vachio stopped and looked at him for a moment. He was a roundish hump on the sidewalk. Vachio had never actually seen his face. Vachio shook his head and moved along. He was too tired and irritated to think about this man right now.

He came to Doña Pilar's house and rang the bell three or four times. Nothing. Vachio fidgeted from one foot to the other. He was cold and he had to take a piss real bad. Come on, he thought. Let me in. He had a key but that was useless after six at night. There were two dead bolts and a sturdy wooden beam barricading the door from the inside. Blanca's room was way in the back of the house. On two other occasions he had come home almost this late and Pilarcita and

Juan Pablo had let him in. Vachio rang the bell again. Nothing. Damn! Doña Pilar had told him he could come home whenever he wanted on weekends.

Vachio reached into his pockets and pulled out some loose change. He threw the coins at Juan Pablo's and Pilarcita's bedroom window on the second floor. Nothing. He threw the coins harder, making them ping off the window and rebound all the way to street. Suddenly the window flew open and Pilarcita stuck her head and torso into the cold air and screamed, "You triple son-of-a-bitch! What the hell are you doing coming here at this hour?"

For a second Vachio was too shocked to speak. Pilarcita was wearing only a filmy nightie, her boobs bursting through the fabric, her eyes popping out of her head.

"Hey, I'm sorry," Vachio finally managed. "But can you let me in? I'm freezing my ass out here."

"You can go to hell if you're cold.... You triple son-of a-bitch!"

That did it. All of Vachio's pent-up frustration and anger boiled out. "Well, fuck you! You stupid bitch!"

Pilarcita had seen many movies in English. She understood this. The window banged shut, rattling the glass, and Vachio knew he was out in the street until Blanca woke up at around six. "Shit!" First Claudia and now Pilarcita. Juan Pablo must have stayed away all night again. Pilarcita is taking it out on me. "This is not my night with women," muttered Vachio.

All at once Vachio felt like a deflated balloon. The adrenalin that had carried him from one encounter to another was gone. He shivered in the cold. He needed to find a warm place. He walked over to the homeless man and said in English, "Looks like we're in the same boat now, buddy." The pile of rags moved ever so slightly but there was no response. "Well, I guess we're not in the same boat." Vachio pulled a twenty peso note out of his wallet and slid it under a corner of the rag pile. "Better luck to both of us," murmured Vachio, and headed up the street toward Caracas.

He found a dingy café-bakery a few blocks away and settled into a corner table. The smell of fresh baked bread for the morning rush was nice, but the bleary-eyed clients, most of them drunks and just off-duty night workers, depressed Vachio. It was the electric blues time of morning. Vachio felt a buzzing in his head and fatigue had him limp and washed out. I'm in the twilight zone, he thought.

He ordered coffee and a sweet roll from a frowzy yawning waitress in a light blue smock and then went to the back of the place to find the toilet. It was even worse than Vachio imagined. The bowl was stopped up and reeked of human waste, the floor was slippery with urine and dirty water, and littered with filthy toilet paper and scraps of newspaper. Vachio shook his head in disgust and held his breath. Then he took aim from the doorway and emptied his bladder, disturbing a big rat that was hiding behind the toilet bowl. "Damn!" yelped Vachio, slamming the door shut. "I've really gone from the penthouse to the outhouse tonight."

Vachio stuffed his wallet down his pants and into his shorts. Then he returned to his table, drank his coffee and ate his roll, and fell asleep with his head between his arms resting on the hard table top.

8

Blanca let Vachio into the house at six and he went straight to bed to catch a few hours of shut-eye. Vachio would have liked to sleep until noon but he had a meeting, or debriefing as he thought of it, with his supervisor concerning his trip to Garrotero.

The alarm roused him at 8:30 and Vachio, feeling and moving like a zombie, got out of bed and scooped up the clean clothes he had laid-out the night before. He headed for the shower and encountered Pilarcita coming out with only a towel wrapped around her otherwise nude body. Both of them stopped in their tracks for a moment and glared at each other like two junkyard dogs. Then Pilarcita clutched her wet towel tighter to her bosom and retreated to her room.

"Bitch!" muttered Vachio, stepping under the shower head and turning on the tap. The icy water dribbled over him and Vachio, shivering and grinding his teeth, allowed just enough water to moisten his body before shutting off the tap. The shower possessed an electrical device attached to the head to warm the water, but Vachio had given up on the benefits of this technology after receiving a couple of healthy jolts of current during his first showers. Now, like the Spartans of antiquity, he gritted his teeth and endured the frigid mountain water. Vachio vigorously rubbed soap all over his body, trying to get his circulation going as well as to clean his skin, and quickly rinsed off. Then he toweled his body until it was red and glowing. One thing is certain, he thought, this cold shower has cleared my head considerably.

Vachio skipped breakfast and hit the streets. Though it was a good three miles to the Peace Corps office in the Chicó, Vachio preferred walking to wedging himself onto one of the moving sardine cans of the morning rush. He threaded his way through the ant hill throngs going to work along the Avenida Caracas, covering the pavement in zig-zag strides. As he walked, reflecting on the occurrences of the night before, Vachio began to chuckle to himself. What a night. Dumped by my girlfriend, stopped by the police, followed by a freak with bad intent, barred from my house, slept in a ratty café... Damn! Things can only get better. Claudia is right. I am an absurdist. How else should I take all that bullshit? Cry?... Nah!

A strange giddy feeling came over Vachio. It was a beautiful sparkling morning, the sun beaming through scattered white clouds, the sky a sharp blue. Vachio's eyes became pleasantly aware of the pretty brunette women in their high heels and stylish outfits passing him poker-faced on their way to work and school. His nose filtered out the stench of the diesel fumes and drank in the savory aromas of fresh brewed coffee and oven hot bread emanating from the bakeries and cafés thickly lining his route. Even the insane screech and rattle of the traffic sounded cheerful to his ears.

Vachio reached the broad confluence of Caracas and five or six other streets merging into its flow. A circular grassy island in the middle, featuring a mammoth sculpture of the Liberator Bolívar astride his horse in commanding pose, as though he were a colonial traffic cop, shunted the honking vehicles in a whirling circle and spun them with centrifugal force to all points of the compass. Vachio paused at the corner and chuckled at this sight. It reminded him of the turgid meeting of spring melt swollen streams and rivers in the mountains, the cars and buses like spawning salmon leaping and jostling to get up the rivers and tributaries.

Vachio waited for an opening to appear in the flow of traffic and raced into the street, his head swiveling from side to side, cars braying at his heels, his heart pounding in his chest. He reached the other side of the street, adrenalin pumping through him, and exclaimed to a man standing at the corner who had witnessed his mad dash, "This must be like the running of the bulls at Pamplona."

"No, señor. This is much more dangerous," answered the man, looking at Vachio as though he were crazy.

"Could be..."

Vachio penetrated the Chicó District and walked up La 15. Here there were fancy boutiques, expensive restaurants, jewelry stores, mini-malls, and travel agencies. Now feeling hungry, Vachio turned off onto a side street and went to a German bakery wedged between two apartment complexes. Vachio ordered a double *café con leche* and a hunk of cherry strudel. Still early for his appointment, Vachio killed some time by chatting with the immigrant baker, a Bavarian by birth, comparing impressions of the city with him. Then, fortified, he resumed his trek.

Though it was a quicker and more direct route, Vachio stayed off the commercial drag and walked along the tree-lined residential streets. The Chicó was an affluent barrio of large houses, fancy modern apartments and condos, a smattering of mansions, and a sprinkling of small parks. Massive stone walls, topped by broken bottles embedded in mortar, bristling razor wire, or stylish wrought-iron spikes, surrounded most of the big homes. Additional security was provided by armed guards and elaborate alarm systems. Many children were dispatched to school in the morning accompanied by bodyguards to discourage kidnappers. Vachio would shake his head in wonder every time he saw these things. The wealthy Colombians and foreigners of Bogotá lived a siege-like existence, beautiful birds of paradise living in gilded cages, hostages to the great mass of poor citizens and professional criminals they rightfully feared. This ain't no way to live, Vachio thought. I wouldn't if I could.

Vachio reached Peace Corps headquarters and rang the bell. The offices were located in an attractive old Victorian house, complete with conical spires and gingerbread frills. It was unmarked and a security guard scrutinized all visitors before allowing them inside, precautions taken in the wake of threats from various revolutionary groups who considered Peace Corps a C.I.A. front. At that moment, a Peace Corps volunteer named Richard Starr was being held for ransom somewhere in the remote fastness of La Huila Department by a band of *La FARC guerrilleros*. Another such occurrence was likely to terminate Peace Corps Colombia once and for all, and according to what Vachio had heard from some administrators, more than one Washington bureaucrat was itching to pull the trigger. Peace Corps Colombia was on borrowed time and it was no secret. On arrival in Miami for orientation, Vachio's group was issued this warning:

"Be very careful and maintain a low profile at all times. And don't be surprised if you end up being transferred to another country before you finish your service. Colombia is a politically volatile place."

There was certainly good reason to take this warning seriously. Vachio's training group included six transfers from Peace Corps Nicaragua, refugees from the Sandinista-led revolt against the long reign of the Somoza Family. Much of Latin America was seething or under military repression, and Colombia was feeling and generating its share of heat. Still, despite the uncertainty facing the program, the atmosphere around Peace Corps headquarters was pretty relaxed and friendly. Gallow's humor and fatalistic attitudes were de riguer, along with the sentiment that we might as well enjoy ourselves here while it lasts.

Vachio was admitted by the security guard and he took a seat on the long black leather sofa in the central lounge area and watched the usual hum of activity. Supervisors and office staff, most of them casually dressed, walked up and down the creaking staircase between floors, stopping to pause and chat at frequent intervals. The staff was almost equally split between North Americans and Colombians, and Spanish and English were used in easy interchangeability. A steady trickle of volunteers and trainees, or *Aspirantes* as they were called by the more formal Colombians, arrived for medical checks, meetings, to request for materials, or just to look up friends and catch up on the latest gossip and social activities. There were also a regular handful of volunteers, based in Bogotá and with too much time on their hands, who frequently showed up to curry favor with the administrators in the hope that an office job would open up. An administrative position paid Stateside wages, a princely sum in Colombia, and was often a stepping stone for aspiring young bureaucrats with their eyes on Washington D.C.

Vachio was only there a few minutes when his supervisor, Doña Fortuna, as she was respectfully called by the Colombians, appeared at the top of the staircase and greeted him in her usual cheerful upbeat manner.

"Are you ready for me now?" Vachio asked her.

"Sorry. But I'm running a little late today.... Sean and Nancy are with me right now. They ran into a few problems on their site visit that we need to work out."

"That's cool. We're on Colombian time anyway, right?"

"Right." Doña Fortuna smiled. "We'll be only a few minutes longer."

Vachio settled back into the sagging cushions and thought, Sean and Nancy had some problems on their site visit, eh. I wonder what kind. Vachio chuckled. Knowing Sean, even if everything went as smooth as silk he'd be worrying because things seemed too good.... Sean and Nancy were a young married couple and two of Vachio's closest associates in the *Gamin* Sub-group. They made an odd couple. Even Sean said their relationship was like the Woody Allen movie, Annie Hall. Sean was a Woody Allen character himself, a fairly conventional career-minded worrier, complete with overblown neuroses and a dry subtle wit. Nancy, a few years older than Sean, was an eternal seeker with a strong feminist bent. Before hooking up with Sean at the University of Wisconsin, she had entered and left a nunnery, lived on a commune, and worked as a nurse in a free clinic on the South Side of Chicago.

"Hey, Vachio, how are you?"

Vachio looked up and saw Luz Marina, the young Colombian nurse, poking her head out of her office door.

"I'm fine. How about you?"

"Pretty good.... Why don't you come into the office for a quick check?"

"Why? I told you I feel fine."

"It's always a good idea to get a check-up after a site visit."

"Ah. I know when I have a problem."

Luz Marina took Vachio by the arm and gently pulled him into the medical office.

"So where were you on your site visit?" she asked, unslinging her stethoscope.

"In Santander."

"Bucaramanga?"

"No. A town called Garrotero. Have you heard of it?"

"Of course. I'm originally from Bucaramanga."

"Oh, I didn't know."

"Breathe deep," said Luz, putting the cold metal on his chest. "Ah hah, very good. Your heartbeat is slow and strong." Luz pulled out another instrument and started to examine Vachio's ears. "How did you like Santander?"

"It was fine. Most of the people I met were friendly and hospitable."

Luz Marina grinned. "Yes. In general, we Santandereans are warm people. Not like the people..." She glanced toward the door to see if anyone was within hearing range. "...not like many of the people here in Bogotá."

Vachio laughed. "Come on, Luz, don't tell me an educated cosmopolitan person like yourself buys into those stereotypes. They just have a different style here."

"Well, you're right, it is a stereotype. But generally speaking, there is some truth to all stereotypes. Believe me, I have an idea. I've lived half my life in Santander and the other half here in Bogotá."

"Yeah, well, you are living here. It can't be so bad."

"My family is here now. My job is here now. But my heart remains in Santander."

"Beautiful. Sounds like the makings of a song."

Luz Marina gave Vachio a sharp look. "Anyway, how did you find the weather at your job site? Maybe a little hot, eh?"

"It was tolerable."

"It will get hotter in a few months." Luz Marina smiled. "But not too much hotter."

"Is that it?" Vachio asked, standing up. "I have a meeting with Fortuna."

"Yes, that's it. You seem fine.... That is, unless you have some specific complaint. Intestinal problems or something of that nature."

"No."

"Fine, then there is no need for tests. Where you're at is a healthy place. Your main problems would come from amoebas, which you could just as easily get here, or from dengue fever."

"Dengue fever. I keep hearing about that. What can I do to prevent catching it?"

"Buy a good mosquito net and pray for luck."

"That's all?"

"I wouldn't worry too much. It's not usually fatal to a strong healthy person." Luz Marina patted Vachio's arm and smiled cheerfully. "It's just extremely uncomfortable and debilitating."

"Sheesh! Thanks for the great medical advice."

"At your order. Can I help you with anything else?"

"Yes, come to think of it." Vachio walked over to a large box on a wall shelf and grabbed a fistful of condoms. Then he turned to Luz Marina with a grin and said, "Santander taught me to stay prepared."

For a second Luz Marina's cheeks reddened but she quickly recovered and said, "You need so few? I guess you don't need to be that prepared.... What a shame."

Vachio laughed and left the office, pleased by her quick wit and sharp comebacks. He had never seen that side of Luz Marina before. She was usually very serious.

Vachio resumed his seat on the soft couch and scanned the books on the shelves behind him. He turned away after a brief search. Nothing new. Just the same old, mostly outdated, texts written by foreign service types concerning Latin American history, culture, and economics, relieved by a few copies of *The Ugly American* and some trash novels. Vachio sighed and put his feet up on the battered coffee table, just noticing that the soles of his feet were sore from pounding the pavement over the last few days.

A few minutes later a man with long curly hair and a dark scraggly beard entered the office and sat on a couch a short distance from Vachio. He wore a faded gray and white *ruana*, patched jeans, and dusty hiking boots. He surveyed Vachio in deadpan silence for a few moments before grinning and saying, "Never seen you around here before, partner. My name is Dennis Rabin. Who are you?"

Vachio introduced himself and the two men talked. Dennis was originally from Newark, New Jersey, and spoke with a fast clipped East Coast accent. He was tall and burly and had played some football at Rutgers. He told Vachio he was terminating his Peace Corps career after a three year stint in a fisheries program in a small village near Cartagena on the Caribbean Coast.

"So how was it for you here, man? Did you have a good experience?" Vachio asked.

Dennis laughed. "Yeah, man, it was great. You know, except for the malaria, the man-eating alligators, and the cannibal Indians."

"Yeah, all right. Whatever you say."

"You don't believe me?"

"I've heard that line a few dozen times. You veterans need some new material."

"I ain't bullshitting you, man. They have stuff like that where I worked."

"Could be. But I think I'd be more scared going to your hometown for a visit. Why don't you tell me about Newark."

Dennis laughed. "You're a wiseass."

"When I have to be."

"Yeah, so what are you supposed to do here?"

"I'm supposed to work in a prison."

"Oh, yeah?" Dennis looked impressed. But before they could continue the conversation, Luz Marina stuck her head out of the medical office and told Dennis to come in for his physical.

"You're not going to stick another needle up my ass, are you?" Dennis asked her, looking genuinely nervous.

"I'm not sure," said Luz Marina, grinning amiably. "I'll have to look at your chart. But I suspect you're due for at least one.... Now come on."

"Aw right, aw right. Don't rush me." Dennis looked at Vachio. "That woman is a sadist. She enjoys sticking needles into us. Especially into me."

"Nothing like enjoying your work.... Good luck."

Dennis entered the medical office and Vachio looked up and saw Nancy and Sean at the top of the staircase. They were discussing something in low heated voices, and Nancy looked nervous and upset.

"Hey, you guys," Vachio called up to them, rising from his seat and going to meet them. "How was Cali?"

The two of them stopped arguing and started descending the stairs. "Cali was fine," said Sean.

"It was nice. Very nice," said Nancy.

"How did the site visit go?" asked Vachio, facing them halfway up the stairs.

Nancy frowned. "Well, there are some problems to be worked out," said Sean ruefully. "How did yours go?"

"Pretty good, all things considered. I found a place to live already and..."

"We have to go right now," said Sean, cutting Vachio off. "We'll talk about this later today."

"Yeah, what's up?"

"Fortuna is waiting for you. You better go see her."

"Yeah, all right. Later." Vachio looked after them as they left the building, wondering what had happened to them on their visit.

Vachio shook his head and finished his climb up the stairs. He turned onto a narrow corridor and entered the open door into Doña Fortuna's office. It was small, and packed to the gills with a desk, chairs, cardboard boxes, and wall-to-wall shelves overflowing with books and How-to manuals.

Doña Fortuna looked up and greeted Vachio with a cheerful smile and a chirpy, "It's so good to see you. You're looking very well." She was dressed in her usual serious office style; a long pepper and salt skirt, a dark mohair sweater, and dark low-heeled shoes. Her dark brown hair was cut short and sober and she wore almost no makeup. Doña Fortuna was in her early 30s, but she was making an effort to look older.

Vachio returned her greeting, stepped around a pile of loose papers, and found a chair.

"Sorry about the mess," said Fortuna. "But I'm in the process of moving. They're finally going to give me a larger space."

"Looks like you can use one."

Fortuna smiled, leaned across her desk toward Vachio, and was all attention. "So, tell me, how did your site visit in Santander go?"

Vachio gave her a quick run down on his experiences and impressions, emphasizing the hospitality of the people, the stated willingness to cooperate of most of the administrators, and his success in finding a place to live. He mentioned his misgivings concerning some of the guards and their relationship with the boys but left out most of the details.

Up to this point, Fortuna had mostly listened, occasionally injecting a "That's wonderful" and "Gary! I'm so glad!" You had a good experience." But now she turned serious and said, "Gary, I have to tell you. Not everyone here is happy about sending a volunteer to work in a correctional institution. I want you to tell me honestly—do you think the job is potentially dangerous?"

Vachio shrugged. "I don't think it's any more dangerous than working with juvenile delinquents in the United States. And it can't be any more dangerous than working on the streets here like Arlo and Randy do.... I don't know. But I don't feel danger is my first concern about this job."

"Well, I just want you to know...if at any time you feel that things are getting too hairy there, let me know. It won't be any trouble to fix you up somewhere else."

"Thanks. I appreciate that. But I most definitely want to give it a try at the *Casa de Menores*."

Fortuna gave Vachio a smile of approbation and turned to other matters. Soon they were interrupted by another staff member and Fortuna excused herself and left the room for a private consultation.

Vachio leaned back in his chair and smiled. Fortuna was the kind of person people sought out for therapeutic talks. Almost from the moment they had met at orientation in Miami, they had established a good rapport. Fortuna was Vachio's idea of an almost ideal supervisor. She was enthusiastic, concerned, supportive, and on-the-ball, yet willing to give the volunteers the space and freedom they needed to develop on their own. Fortuna was almost too good to be true. And there were a few administrators in Peace Corps Colombia—cynical, political types—who sneeringly referred to her as Mary Poppins behind her back. Vachio could understand why some people would look at her this way. She was one of these relentlessly optimistic and idealistic persons who can get on the nerves of more self-serving individuals. "That act has to be a phony," was one of the comments Vachio had overheard concerning Fortuna. But Vachio, as skeptical and suspicious as he was in most instances, detected no phoniness in Fortuna's manner. She was a genuinely concerned person who had dedicated her life to social service—along the lines of a secular nun. She had served four years as a regular volunteer in an ugly shantytown on the outskirts of Cartagena, winning tremendous respect and affection from barrio inhabitants, and taking on the responsibility for the education and support of two blind twins with her own income. Now, for the last year, she had served as a group coordinator, overseeing and nurturing the pilot *Gamin* Program.

Vachio chuckled. Mary Poppins? He had seen another side to Fortuna's personality on excursions to institutions for troubled boys and girls. If crossed, she had a tough, stubborn streak and was more than willing to speak her mind and assert her authority when the situation called for it. When the Colombians called her Doña, and most of them did, it was a title spoken with respect.

Fortuna returned to the office and apologized for interrupting the interview. Then she sat down and said, "You know, it just struck me, I almost forgot to ask you. What do you think of your future boss? The Director, Don Gustavo?"

Vachio hesitated for a long moment before answering. "Uh, well, he treated me great. He was my host and I stayed at his house during the visit."

"He is a nice person. And quite a character as well, no?"

"He is most definitely quite a character."

"And charming."

"Yes, very charming. He knows everyone in town. But...aw, forget it. That's all right."

"Forget it?" Fortuna raised an eyebrow. "Tell me, Gary."

"Well, I can't put my finger on anything specific so this might sound ridiculous but...I don't know, he's almost too charming. You know what I mean?"

"No, Gary, not exactly."

"I don't know. Maybe it's my problem. But I've never trusted people who are that smooth and charming.... It makes me think they might be peddling snake oil."

"Gary! Really?"

Vachio laughed. "Maybe it's my big city upbringing, but there were times during my visit that I felt like I was listening to a street corner hustler with good diction.... You know what I'm talking about. You went to college in Berkeley and dealt with people like that on Telegraph Avenue, didn't you?"

Fortuna laughed. "Well, I don't think I'd describe the Señor Director that way, Gary. But I think I do know what you mean. Let's just hope your suspicions are unfounded.... Now, the most important question is—do you think you can work with him?"

"Yes. And the reason I say that is because he himself said he was the main reason that I'm going to work there. He has a stake in me. I trust that."

"Good." Fortuna flipped through a stack of papers on her desk and handed Vachio a print-out. "Here is your schedule for this week. You don't have Spanish classes this afternoon. Only a group session with Lothar to talk over the psychological impact of your site visit."

"Oh boy. Fun."

"Do you have any other questions or concerns?"

"Yes. Do you have any way to help me understand some of these *gamines* better? I tell you, at times during my visit, I didn't have a clue of what they were saying. They talk a whole different brand of smack than what I'm used to."

Fortuna laughed. Then she fished around in her pile of papers again and came up with another print-out. "Here. This may help you a little. It's a mini-dictionary of some common *gamin* slang and phrases."

"Thanks." Vachio glanced quickly over the material and started to rise.

"And Gary..."

"Yes."

"I wouldn't worry too much about not having a clue. Because I most definitely think you do."

9

After his meeting with Fortuna, Vachio had plenty of time on his hands until his afternoon group session. He hung around the office a few minutes to see if anyone he knew would turn up, then decided to go to the training center for a light cheap lunch and to catch up on news about his Peace Corps training group.

Thinking about his group and their weeks in Colombia together, Vachio chuckled to himself. The first Peace Corps Volunteers in the early 60s were known as *The Children of Kennedy*; Vachio thought of his particular Peace Corps group as *The Children of Saturday Night Live*. It was loaded with characters worthy of John Belushi, Chevy Chase, Gilda Radner, Jane Curtin, Bill Murray, and Dan Akyroyd. Vachio's group was an eclectic mix that came from all points of the United States and, though most of them were in their early 20s and fresh out of college, ranged in age from 21 to 64. As a group, they were irreverent, friendly, studied hard and played hard, had a strong esprit de corps, and professed a strong desire to use their talents for the benefit of their host country. Politically, they ran the gamut from right-wing conservatives to closet anarchists. For religious faiths, they offered Christian Scientists, Born Again Christians, Lost Again Christians, Jews, Catholics, Atheists, Agnostics, Psuedo-Buddhists, Back to Naturists, and even a Moonie. Some of their motives for joining Peace Corps, aside from the universal urge to serve others, were to save the world for Mom, Apple Pie, and Chevrolet, to end bad relationships gracefully, to delay or evade payments of college loans, to start a new life and adventure at an advanced age, and, in the case of one hedononistic couple from California, because they had read in Stewart

Brand's Whole Earth Catalogue the description of Peace Corps as the best paid vacation the United States government offered.

Absorbed in his thoughts, Vachio reached the training center seemingly in no time, forgetting all about his sore feet. The main training center building, a converted and at one time elegant residence, was a rambling two-story wood and brick house. It featured a front lawn and shrubbery and a back lawn and shrubbery, plus a number of small hutches at the back end of the property that served as language labs and study cubicles.

Vachio went to the lounge at the front of the house, the original living room, and spotted Cowboy Bob curled up like an old cat in the overstuffed arm chair by the fireplace.

"Hey, man, wake up," said Vachio, taking a seat on the large sofa in front of the fireplace. "You should be doing something productive like studying your Spanish."

Cowboy Bob slowly turned his head, his gray eyes peeking from drooping lids and baggy crinkled skin, and drawled, "Go to hell."

Vachio laughed. "Man, I'm surprised you're still around, Bob.... Glad to see you, though."

"Yeah, thanks. I appreciate that.... But gimme a couple a minutes to get myself together and then we'll talk.... All right." The Cowboy's voice was slurred and he rubbed at bleary eyes.

"Sure, man. Take your time. Sorry to disturb your nap."

"Uh, yeah..."

Vachio sank back into the cushions and waited, chuckling to himself. Cowboy Bob was showing his age. He was in his mid-50s, but he could pass for a man of at least 10 years older. He was thin and wiry, an old desert rat, with wrinkled leathery skin and thinning gray hair. A few weeks before, Vachio had shared a cab ride with him and the cowboy had said, "Look at me, man. Can you believe it? I've been stoned every day of my life for the last 17 years." Vachio had looked at him and answered, "Yeah, I can believe it. In fact, if you had told me 20, I'd believe that."

Cowboy Bob was the first volunteer in his group Vachio had met. They had come on the same plane from San Francisco seated across the aisle from each other on their way to orientation in Miami. They soon fell into conversation, Cowboy Bob treating Vachio to drinks, and discovered they were partners in the same adventure. During the long flight, Cowboy Bob, a fabulous raconteur, told Vachio the story of his life. Cowboy Bob was a retired Rexall Drug executive. He had lived in San Francisco for more than 30 years, settling there after serving in World War II. According to the Cowboy, he had lived a dual existence for years. By day, a straight and competent corporate man, by night and weekends, an enthusiastic Bohemian and man-about-town. He had tipped drinks in North Beach watering holes with Kerouac and Ginsberg in the heyday of the Beatniks. He had imbibed LSD in the

Haight-Ashbury during the first free and easy days of Timothy Leary and his Merry Pranksters, and listened to impromptu jam sessions with the Grateful Dead. Now, at an age when many men would look for an easy chair in the sun, Cowboy Bob was seeking new adventures in Peace Corps. He had already served a short stint in northern Brazil, vaccinating cattle, and had somehow, "For reasons of health," as he put it, wrangled a transfer to Colombia. He was rejoining Peace Corps after spending a month in California to rehabilitate his health and visit his daughter.

He became known as Cowboy Bob in Vachio's group for two very different reasons. One, he had grown up on a ranch outside of Ely, Nevada. Two, he always wore an expensive pair of cowboy boots and kept a stash of cocaine secreted in one of them. Vachio enjoyed talking to Cowboy Bob but he was wary of hanging around with him in public. On just their fourth night in-country, Vachio, Cowboy Bob, and a half dozen other *aspirantes* met at the Club Bavaria after classes and put away many pitchers of dark beer. Then, the night still young, they decided to walk to Doña Barbara's Jazz Club in the Chicó. As they walked along the dark residential streets, Vachio kept mumbling in a low voice, "This ain't cool. This just ain't cool." Here they were, eight *gringos*, cocky and reckless from drink and other substances, some with bottles in hand, roaring in a disheveled group through a ritzy neighborhood with security types lurking all around. Then to make matters worse, someone fired up a joint and passed it around. "I don't like this, you guys. This is begging for trouble," Vachio said. His warning was drowned out in the group euphoria. A minute or so later it happened. They had paused under a tree in a small park to catch their bearings when they were hailed by two plainclothes men and a young soldier. Before the men were upon them, the stub of the joint was ground underfoot, but the smell of Colombian Gold lingered strongly in the crisp air. Sniffing like bloodhounds, the two plainclothes men directed the soldier to point his M16 at them. Then they produced identification. They were agents of DAS, Colombia's equivalent of the F.B.I. Vachio cursed to himself. He knew Cowboy Bob had a vial of cocaine somewhere on his person. Cowboy Bob was told to empty his pockets. He produced keys, matchbooks, and money. Vachio breathed a sigh of relief. The remains of the joint were buried in the grass and mud. No one else had anything worth worrying about; open containers weren't a big deal in Bogotá. Still, the agents knew something was going on. They were persistent and threatened to haul the trainees in for a more thorough session. Fortunately, Janie, a nurse who had spent her share of time in emergency rooms and was one of the transfers from Nicaragua, stayed calm and collected, and in her excellent Spanish did a great job of distracting the agent's suspicions. Still, all of them were frisked, and one of the agents while searching Audry, who had a round firm butt and was wearing skin tight jeans, got his jollies by feeling her up and making lewd comments to his buddies. Then, content to have humiliated the *gringos* for their stupidity, the agents disappeared into the night, leaving an outraged but chastened group of trainees. While some of the others tried to calm the hysterically angry Audry, Vachio sidled over to Cowboy Bob and asked, "Where the hell did you stash the coke?"

Cowboy Bob smiled and patted his left pocket. "It was in the bottom of my pocket wedged up against my crotch. What did you think, that I was going to pull it out for them? For something like that they're gonna have to reach themselves."

"Jesus, man! That could've been our butts. We got lucky."

"Nah, you worry too much. Most of these young macho men here don't want to touch an old man's pecker. And if all else fails..." Cowboy Bob pulled out a wad of pesos and grinned.

Vachio snorted. "Yeah, well, not all of us have that option. I ain't exactly rich."

"Too bad, boy. I feel sorry for you."

"Why?"

"Because I'd sure hate to be here on a Peace Corps salary."

Remembering that night, Vachio tingled nervously all over again. It had been a very close call. Vachio's career had almost ended before it started. The Peace Corps Director had made drug policy clear on his first address to the new trainees. He had said, "Obviously, cocaine and other drugs are cheap and readily available in Colombia. And I'm not naive enough to think that a certain number of you don't use them.... All I have to say on the matter is this. Don't do anything to embarrass us. If you get caught with drugs and I find out—you're gone. You get the Braniff Airlines award."

After that night, Vachio made it a point never to walk around the streets with more than three Americans at a time. They were too conspicuous, and in some cases, too innocent or reckless to be trusted.

"So how did your site visit go?" asked Cowboy Bob, finally stirring from his semi-coma.

"It went all right. How've things been around here?"

"Ah, it's getting downright oppressive around here," he groused.

Vachio laughed. "Now how is that? They been getting on your case?"

"Yep. Not that I give a flyin' frig. But they've banned our entire group from havin' any more parties at the training center."

"Well, big surprise. They could have booted some people over that last party if they really wanted to be hardass."

"Ah! That party was nothin' compared to some that I've seen in my time. Nothin'."

"No. It was somethin', man. It was somethin'."

Vachio would never forget that party. He had come early to help set-up and a hard core group of trainees were already loading up and itching to party. There was an air of abandon about them, an almost frantic urge to madness. The party was being held to celebrate their group reaching the midway point of training without losing a single member and as a farewell bash for a handful of volunteers deemed advanced enough to begin their job assignments early. Everyone had been primed for a big blowout, including some of the more temperate trainees. After six weeks in Bogotá, nerves were frayed and tensions were running high. While they moved tables and chairs out of the way to make space for dancing, Vachio wondered at the large number of trainees, Colombian Spanish teachers, and friends who had already showed up. By the time Vachio left to go pick up Claudia, people were already walking up and down the staircase to the rooms on the second floor and disappearing into the bushes in the backyard. Things were jumping and it was barely eight o'clock.

Vachio returned to the training center about 9:30, holding Claudia in one hand and a bottle of red wine in the other. The party was going full blast. Driving Cumbia music blasted from oversized speakers and vibrated the wood-paneled walls. Dancers crowded and bumped in two connecting rooms, spinning and whooping in the shadowy darkness. A full long table was laden with snacks, soda, wine, and hard liquor. An ice chest was filled with beer. Cowboy Bob sat in the hallway at the foot of the stairway, guru-like, his chair tilted back, dispensing hedonistic wisdom and pharmaceutical potions to a cadre of disciples. The old security guard was already fully crocked and nodding off in a chair, his floppy hat pulled over his eyes. People stood in loose knots and yelled at each other to be heard over the music.

"*Que locura*!" said Claudia, after Vachio led her on a quick circuit of the training center.

"No. It's not that crazy yet," said Vachio, serving her a glass of white wine at the long table. "But it soon will be."

Bobby McCullough roared up, his eyes ablaze, ogling Claudia. "Come on, you guys. Let's get with it. Drink till you drop and then do drugs. This is all night. All night." Then he gathered up one of the Spanish teachers and took her for a wild spin around the dance floor.

Claudia stared after him as though he were insane. Vachio laughed and took a big gulp of red wine. The look on Claudia's face was priceless. This was his meat. Bubbling truthful conversations, all pretence and inhibition gone, could be heard on all sides.

In a short while, Vachio and Claudia were caught up in the ebb and flow of the party, separated and rejoined at ever lengthening intervals as they pursued different inclinations. Claudia danced stylishly, drank moderately, and participated in cool respectable conversations. Vachio danced, drank a lot, smoked a joint or two in the coolness of the garden, and participated in ecstatic stream of consciousness outbursts.

He hooked up with Sean Miller, who after a good toke of weed would let loose his Woody Allen neurotic humor, and Percy Fong, a budding Zen spiritualist from a hard-scrabble Arizona copper mining town. At key points in their discourse, Percy would stroke his wisp of goatee and exclaim with a joyous laugh, "That's right, Señor. That's right!"

After a long session with these two, Vachio went inside to get a drink and check on Claudia. Now the music was throbbing Disco-Funkytown. Claudia was dancing with Bobby McCullough and looked like she was having a good time. Vachio went to the refreshment stand and found Burly Bob Bennet badgering Michelle, a cute girl and staunch Christian Scientist, into trying the first alcoholic drink of her life. Vachio interrupted Big Bill and Michelle slipped away to another part of the room.

"Why are you bugging her so much?" Vachio asked.

Burly Bob cackled, he was good and looped, and said, "Man, she has to try at least one drink. She doesn't know what she's missing in life."

Vachio shook his head. "Why? So she can act as goofy as you?"

Burly Bob's smile tightened. "It's my mission tonight to convince her to drink at least one. She's a virgin, you know."

"Yeah, well, if she doesn't want to drink, why should she?"

Burly Bob gave Vachio a brief stare, then he set off in pursuit of Michelle. But he didn't get very far. Janie, Big Bob's wife, had him in her sights and was about to put a rope around him. Vachio chuckled. Marital bliss with the boss nurse, he thought.

Jock "Tex" Wilson sidled up to Vachio, Jack Daniels on the rocks in hand, and said, "Boy, I don't know 'bout you, but I think the shit is gonna hit the fan after this is all said and done. These kids are outta control."

"Man, you're not exactly what I'd call moderate," laughed Vachio. Jock was a down-to-earth, 50 year old retired airline pilot who had seen it all and done most of it in his time.

"Yeah, but I can hold mah liquor and keep mah fun at a reasonable level.... But goddamit! Ya'll got to expect this from a bunch of wet behind the ears kids who think they invented good times and clever talk. If we get into trouble over this, I gotta blame that goddam Jim Berger from the Peace Corps office who's supposed to be chaperonin' this party."

"What happened to him?"

"That ol' boy took off about an hour ago with one of those young Spanish teachers. Not that I blame `em now. She's a real honey. But goddamit! The shit's gonna hit the fan. Mark mah words."

"Why? What's so different about this party."

"People are just gettin' too goddam blatant. They need to be more discreet about things. We got too goddam many of these In-crowd kind of folks..."

As Jock talked on, Vachio saw Julie Christiansen step onto the dance floor and launch into a wild solo dance. She was dressed in a tight black dress, black nylons, and calf high black boots; her long blonde hair sparkled like pale gold and swirled about her face; her long shapely limbs gyrated, her white skin contrasting to the dark silken material of her outfit. She was sensual, beautiful, and appealingly dangerous. A black widow spider spinning a web. Vachio was bowled over. Julie was, at least in public, one of the most self-contained and serious of all the trainees, and usually wore jeans and boutique peasant blouses.

"Damn!" murmured Vachio. Most of the other dancers stopped and gave her room. On an impulse, Vachio went out to dance with her. Julie danced on indifferently, her china blue eyes barely flickering over Vachio. He might as well have been a shadow on the wall. Vachio slowed his motion and looked into her eyes. They were frozen glass, the pupils wide black holes, transfixed on some private nightmare. Vachio felt a chill on the nape of his neck and tried to take her hands and draw her back to consciousness. She absently flung him away and spun to the other side of the room. "All right. All right," murmured Vachio, getting away from her. "It's your trip." At the end of the song she stood limp, her face ashen and her eyes vacant. A girlfriend took her gently by the arm and led her away. Vachio poured another drink and felt himself shiver. "That is one gone, messed-up girl right now," he muttered to himself. "Totally."

Vachio went back outside and found Percy Fong helping Mark Hill over to the bushes to puke. Mark was a farmboy from Missouri and had gone overboard without his steady girl around to keep him in check. Dan Joyce and Patty Kleinhoff were glued together in a dark corner. Soon they snuck off to one of the language hutches, Dan winking over his shoulder to make sure everyone knew what was up as they left. Percy came over to Vachio, after leaving Mark propped against the fence, and spluttered, "This is getting crazy, Señor! Crazy!" He laughed gleefully, his bony Oriental face alight.

Soon Mark Hill caught his second wind, pulled himself together, and joined Vachio and Percy. "It was the altitude that got me," he said in his laconic style. "I'm a sea level drinker."

After another 20 minutes or so, Vachio began to feel restless. The party continued at full blast, but it had reached that stage of excess where people were engaged in an endurance contest and stream of consciousness thought becomes babble. Vachio figured it could only go downhill and get sloppy from here on out. When Claudia found him in the garden, she had no problem convincing him to leave. To his surprise, it was almost two a.m.

The next morning, Vachio returned to the training center for a barbecue and a hungover Mark Hill filled him in on the gory details. Supervisor Jim Berger had returned to the party about three a.m. A quick inspection revealed drunken trainees strewed across the back lawn, burnt out roaches scattered near the bushes, and to top it off, he walked in on Dan and Patty going at it hot and heavy on a table in one of the hutches. He had bawled out some of the trainees sober enough to care and stormed out after directing them to clean up the place. "I passed out on the lawn myself and never made it home," said Mark with a sheepish proud smile. "And I had my share of company." Fortunately for the trainees, Jim Berger had screwed up by leaving them unsupervised. He kept the worst of the details quiet. But he passed the word at the barbecue that future parties at the center were probably history and someone was likely to be sent home as an example to the others. Cowboy Bob was the most eligible candidate. In recent weeks he had grown surly and uncooperative, missing Spanish classes and seminars without bothering to give an excuse. And when he did attend class, it would have been better if he had stayed away. He either nodded off or was a pain-in-the-ass to the teachers. It had all begun to unravel for Cowboy Bob after he suffered a kidney infection and spent a week in the hospital. He seemed to realize his body was beginning to fail him and his life of hedonistic adventure was on borrowed time. Prior to the hospitalization, he had at least pretended to go along with the program, and despite his lifestyle, he was a capable man. Now he didn't care at all. He did his drugs, partied, and waited for the ax to fall. This is why Vachio was surprised to see him still around.

"Now why the hell do you think someone was going to get booted over that party?" asked Cowboy Bob. "Because they were havin' a good time? Hell, no one got hurt. No one's the worse for wear."

"No, man. Because of the drugs. People were being too obvious.... Stupid."

"Hell! Drugs, you say. America runs on drugs of one kind or another. And who the hell would know better than a guy like me? I pushed them for a legal living. Drugs to wake up on, drugs to go to bed on. Drugs to give you an appetite, drugs to take it away. Hell!"

Vachio laughed. The restaurant he had worked at had certainly run that way.

"Bunch of bullshit hypocrisy," continued the Cowboy. "And I'm good and sick of it. As long as a person can function and keep his act together they got no right to tell 'im what to do.... Damn fascists."

"Yeah, well, a lot of people can't handle it. Believe me, I know from personal experience."

"Sure. You're right," said Cowboy Bob, his voice low and raspy. "I won't argue with you there. But a lot of people can't handle life. So let's prohibit life. Why not?"

"So what happened? Did they say something to you?"

"Yeah. They called me in for a chickenshit meeting and told me I needed an attitude adjustment. And if I didn't think so, it might be best for all concerned if I terminated.... Terminated! Nice word, eh."

"And?"

"Nothin'. I don't intend to change a thing. They can damn well boot me out of here if they want to. Or they can send me out to my job right now. Hell! I don't need this juvenile training. I already went through the same damn thing in Brazil. All I'm gonna to do is stick needles in cow's bungs. I've had mucho practice with that. And I don't need but 50 words of vocabulary to get my point across with the locals. Hell!"

"Hey, Cowboy Man! *Que pasa*?"

Vachio turned around and saw Bobby McCullough approaching them. His handsome face was lit up with a big grin and his step was bouncy.

"Bobby me boy. How the hell are you?" said Cowboy Bob.

"Fine. Fine. But a toot would do me excellent,"said Bobby, looking around and lowering his voice. "Got any?"

"That can be arranged. Wait a while."

Vachio and Bobby exchanged more subdued greetings. They didn't have anything against each other, but they weren't exactly friends, either. Vachio thought Bobby a likable guy, bright, witty, full of life, with a quick Philadelphia urban style, but he didn't like the way he tended to dominate his circle of friends and acquaintances. Vachio didn't blame him for it. Bobby had natural charisma and exuberance, attracting both men and women like a magnet, but Vachio was too much the lone wolf to feel his pull.

After a few minutes of shop talk Cowboy Bob, creaking and teetering on stiff ligaments, came to his feet and said, "All right, fellas. Let's go find a quiet corner somewhere."

"Cowboy, my man," said Bobby. "Roota-a-toot-toot. *Vamos muchachos*."

"I'll pass," said Vachio.

"It's on the house," said Cowboy Bob.

"That's cool. I had a long week. I want to dry out."

Cowboy Bob shrugged in acquiescence but Bobby said in a scornful tone of voice, "Yeah, sure."

"What's up? You need me to hold your hand?" snapped Vachio.

Bobby turned red and started to splutter. "No...you... it's just that you think you have some kind of moral superiority or something."

"Nice try. Don't mistake indifference for anything else.... Anyway, you're a big boy. And I'm no narc. Do your thing."

Cowboy Bob chuckled and patted Bobby on the shoulder. Bobby started to say something else but then he thought better of it and followed Cowboy Bob out of the room.

10

Vachio went to the cafeteria-study hall to see who was around. There were only a handful of trainees, their heads bent in concentration, writing letters home or studying their Spanish. Most of the others were on site visits, had gone out to eat lunch, or were just screwing around somewhere else. Then Vachio spotted Sean Miller and Nancy Wysocki in a far corner of the room and went over to join them.

"Hey, you guys. How's it going?" said Vachio, taking a seat next to Sean, facing Nancy across the table.

"Things have been better," said Sean.

Nancy folded her arms and said nothing, a set stubborn look on her face.

Vachio realized they were still hassling over whatever went wrong on their site visit. In the awkward silence that followed, he wondered if he should excuse himself and go elsewhere. But before he could make a move, Sean rose from his chair and announced, "I need some air. I'm going to the bakery to get a *mil hojas*.... Do you want anything?"

Nancy shook her head.

"Do you want to go with me?" Sean asked Vachio.

"Well, uh...all right. Why not."

"Are you sure you don't want anything, honey?" Sean asked Nancy again.

"No.... Thank you." Nancy was tight-lipped, almost trembling.

The two men left the building and headed for Caracas.

"Phew! What's with Nancy?" Vachio asked Sean.

"Oh, she had a bad time on our site visit. The head of the *gamin* center where they want us to work is a middle-aged Spanish priest, and he has some very definite ideas about women."

"What kind of ideas?"

"Traditional ideas. Some of which I can understand. But you know what a feminist Nancy is." Sean shook his head. "This is a big problem. We love Cali as a city and as a place to live. I like the job and the *gamin* center, and I think I can get along with this priest and work something out for the two of us but...gee, I don't know. Nancy was pissed. And she'd rather look at another job site right now."

"What did Fortuna say?"

"She told us to think about it and get back to her later.... Good ole Fortuna. You know how she is. She told us she'd back us no matter what decision we arrived at." Sean let out a sigh.

Vachio watched for a gap in the traffic so they could cross the street. "Come on, man. Let's go for it."

The two of them raced across the street and made it to a quieter section a few blocks from the bakery.

"You know, Gary," said Sean, breathing faster, "this whole episode is a metaphor for our relationship. We just can't quite mesh."

"Ah, come on. I've seen you two agree on a lot of things."

"Maybe. But not the real important things.... For instance, she's five years older than I am..."

"So."

"You say, so. But I think that is important. And what about these things: She was raised Catholic and I was raised Protestant. She refused to give up her own name after we married. She keeps her own money. She's Polish descent and I'm German descent..."

Vachio couldn't help himself. He started giggling.

"That's not funny," said Sean. "I think her folks still hate Germans because of World War II."

"I'm sorry, man. I'm not laughing at you. It's just that I don't know what to say.... I mean, I like both of you guys. And some of the differences you're mentioning shouldn't be so important but...I don't know."

They came to the bakery and Sean forgot his problems for the moment. His eyes lit up like Christmas bulbs as he surveyed the display of rich pastries.

"One thing I like about Bogotá, they have great bakeries," said Sean.

"Yep. They have a good variety."

Sean ordered his favorite, a *mil hojas*, a multi-layered crusty delight topped with chocolate and bursting with Bavarian cream filling. Vachio grabbed a coffee and they took seats.

"So, anyway, aside from the problems, was Cali everything we've heard that it is?" Vachio asked.

"Cali is great. The weather, the amenities...and the women are as beautiful as advertised." Kevin laughed and shook his head. "That was another problem I had with Nancy. You can't help but look."

"Yeah?"

"Yes."

"I need to see this place for myself."

Sean finished his *mil hojas,* licking the last bit of cream from his lips, and abruptly rose and said, "I think I'll go for a walk now. I need to get off by myself for a while and think."

"Sure, man, I'll see you back at the training center."

Vachio returned to the training center and grabbed a light lunch of a sandwich, a yogurt, and another coffee. He chatted for a few minutes with the amiable Colombian couple that ran the concession and then returned to the cafeteria. Nancy was still seated at the same seat in the corner of the room.

"Where's Sean?" she asked as Vachio took a seat.

"He went for a walk. Said he needed to be alone to think."

"What did he tell you?"

"Not much. Just that you had problems with some Spanish priest."

"Problems? More like A Problem—the sexist old priest who runs the place."

"Yeah, well, my future boss has a picture of Adolph Hitler on his living room wall."

Nancy blanched. "Are you going to make fun of me or do you want to listen?"

"Actually, I was being serious. But I'm sorry. Go ahead."

Nancy launched into her account and Vachio listened. Nancy and Sean had visited a private institution for *gamines* and other troubled boys on the outskirts of Cali. According to their job descriptions, Nancy was to work as a nurse and help organize their health clinic; Sean was to work as a general administrator and pitch in with the recreation program. Both of them had been impressed by the institution. The facilities were modern, with room to expand, ably run, and boasted better accommodations for health, education, and recreation than most government entities. Both of them were well received by the boys and by the majority of the staff. They both liked Cali as a place to live. But then there was Father Peña, the Director and *jefe maximo* of the institution. He was traditional, autocratic, and a great admirer of the Generalissimo Francisco Franco.

"The man is a retrograde troglodyte when it comes to women. He showed me no respect as a person or as a professional," said Nancy, her midwest twang becoming more and more pronounced. "Sometimes he didn't even acknowledge me and only spoke to Sean, like I'm his shadow or his subordinate. And...he's against my living at the school. He said it wouldn't be right to tempt the boys with a woman around at all hours. Can you believe that?"

Vachio shrugged. Nancy was a woman well able to tempt men. She was a cute brunette, with an attractive petite figure and a warm, spirited personality. "Well, I don't know the guy. But from what you tell me, it sounds more like you made him uncomfortable. He's probably afraid of tempting himself, not the boys."

"Hey, you might be right. I didn't even think of it that way."

"Well, you know, I went to Catholic school. I've seen more than one randy priest."

Normally Nancy would have laughed at this, but this time she dropped her eyes and stared at the table. She was really depressed and upset. Vachio wasn't used to seeing her this way.

Nancy quieted down and Vachio concentrated on his food. A few minutes later, Audry showed up and sat down next to Nancy. Audry was Vachio's buddy, too. A cowgirl from Colorado, she was usually upbeat and ready for adventure, but she also had a sour look on her face and a tale to share of macho culture disrespect from her site visit. Nancy and Audry commiserated, in harsh and acerbic language, and

Vachio listened with his head down. He felt as though, in that moment, they regarded him as their enemy.

Vachio picked up his tray and took it back to the snack bar. He found Mark Hill there, ordering coffee, and greeted him warmly. Mark and Percy Fong were his two closest confidantes in the entire Peace Corps group.

"So how did your site visit go?" Mark asked.

"What? Do you really want to know? So far I can't tell anyone because they want to tell me about theirs."

"Well, yeah, I'd be like that, too. But you know I don't have a real job description so I don't have a site visit."

Vachio laughed. Mark was slated to work in the central Coffee Association of Colombia office in Bogotá. Instead of a week-long site visit, he was given staggered one-day excursions to coffee farms and district offices outside of the city.

"So how did it go? Almost everyone I've talked to so far has been bitching about theirs," Mark said.

"Got a couple of hours."

"No. But I can spare one.... If you don't bore me."

"All right. Let's grab a seat."

Mark paid for his coffee and they headed back to the cafeteria.

"But before I get into my thing, anything exciting happen to you last week?" Vachio asked.

"Nah, not really. They sent me out to this place called Fusagasaga."

"Fusawasawasa?"

"Fusa-gasa-ga."

"Huh. Was it as weird as its name?"

"Nah. Pretty ordinary. But it was down the slope a ways so at least it was warmer than here.... Oh yeah, but there was one thing we did last week. They took us to a poultry factory." Mark shook his head, still incredulous. "They had all these thousands of chickens strung up by their feet and this guy just went around all day cutting their throats with a butcher knife."

"Nice job. Sounds like collecting tolls on a bridge."

"Yeah. Mass murder production. It was kind of interesting."

They sat down and Vachio told Mark all about his site visit. After about 15 minutes, Vachio noticed Mark's interest start to flag. One thing about Peace Corps volunteers, almost all of them thought their own experiences and insights were the most interesting. Vachio shrugged and pulled out his list of *gamin* slang and showed it to Mark. This was something he would appreciate. During Mark's first week with his Colombian family, the De Anza's, he met a young and attractive dental student niece and, while he denied it was love at first sight, they immediately became a steady item. Mark was quickly drafted into the extended family and ushered about town by a group of young relatives in their *chevere* Chevy. As a consequence, though Mark's standard Spanish needed considerable improvement, he was advanced in trendy slang and relished using it. As for Vachio, he enjoyed speaking Spanish and wanted to master it completely. He loved the fluidity and agility of the language and the way it lent itself to creative word combinations. Slang was part of the living language, a mirror of the country's culture. While Vachio and Mark perused the list, laughing and joking as they tossed words and phrases across the table at each other, the room steadily filled as trainees came in for their scheduled classes or seminars.

Lothar Moeller, clipboard in hand, came up to Vachio a few minutes before two and said, "Hi, Gary. I just wanted to tell you that you have a group session with me in Room B3 in a few minutes."

"Yeah, thanks, Lothar. Fortuna told me already."

"All right. Just checking to make sure."

Lothar moved on to tell some of the other trainees and Mark, looking after him, shook his head and said, "Boy, I sure wish I had his job."

"Yeah, whatever exactly it is that he does," said Vachio. Lothar Moeller, a former Peace Corps Volunteer from the late 60s who never left Colombia, wore a number of hats. He was the financial controller of the training center, resident pop psychologist, and had some other vague position as a training consultant. Lothar was in his early 30s, kept a neatly trimmed Van Dyke beard to go with a mop of curly brown hair, was a snappy dresser who favored Ivy League preppie, occasionally smoked a pipe, and was a well-known man about town. Vachio called him the King of the Chicó. Three or four times on the way to the Peace Corps office, Vachio had spotted Lothar in earnest conversation with various elegant *Bogotanas* at his favorite café on the Calle 15. He also dated several women from Vachio's training group. Vachio occasionally wondered about the guy. Lothar was smooth and had a veneer of sophistication, but every now and again his small-town Indiana upbringing surfaced and he came off as an earnest poseur. Well, whatever works for the guy, Vachio thought, as Mark Hill commented sarcastically on the way Lothar smoked his pipe.

At two, Vachio went to Room B3 for his group session. For a few minutes he and Lothar were alone. The others straggled in singly and in pairs until by about 2:10 their group was almost complete. Vachio looked around the room and exchanged a surprised look with Jerry Espy, another guy from his *Gamin* Group. There were 12 women in this group session and only two men.

At 2:15 Lothar called the group in session. The theme of the day was, "Now that you've been to your job site, what do you feel will be your greatest cross-cultural challenge to overcome? Julie Christiansen was first up. She had just returned from a site visit to a small farming community in Cundinamarca where she was supposed to work as a women's health advisor; one of these vague general assistance programs where you organize town meetings and try to counsel *campesina* women to boil their drinking water and to stop using baby formula and such. Vachio had to chuckle to himself when he heard Julie's job description. Not that he minimalized the importance of this work, just that it was hard for him to imagine Julie of all people in this role. From previous group sessions together, Vachio knew Julie's background and general outlook on life. She had grown up in Tiburon in Marin County, one of the most affluent towns in one of the richest counties in the United States. She was a doted-on only child. Her father was a molecular biologist and her mother a pediatrician. Intellectually, Julie was weaned on Ansel Adams, John Muir, the Sierra Club, and the Audobon Society. At an early age she was taken on hikes and camping trips to the Grand Canyon, Yellowstone Park, Yosemite, Yucatan, and assorted other national and international preserves and ruins. Her parents belonged to a circle of friends that believed in a coming Ectopia—a buzzword for the marriage of human and natural resources in partnership with applied sciences to create a sustainable and idyllic future society—and passed this belief on to their daughter. In their first group session together in Bogotá, Julie had described her particular corner of the San Francisco Bay Area, Tiburon, implying that it represented a typical California lifestyle. She had laid it on thick, conjuring up many of the stereotypes about California as a haven for affluent, enlightened, sensitive people who participated in touchy-feely hot tub sessions and experience-it-to-the-max encounters. A place where true communion with nature was compatible with high technology and a fast modern life. "There's just something special about Marin County," Julie had concluded that day. "It seems to promote a special awareness about life. Probably because of its marvelous setting and unique lifestyle." Vachio had been unable to repress a snort at the conclusion of Julie's talk. Lothar, who had almost dozed off, straightened up and addressed Vachio. "Gary, do you have a joke to share with the group?"

"No. We already heard it."

"Would you like to elaborate?"

Julie had stared at Vachio in tight-lipped anger.

"Well, what Julie said about California promoting a special awareness about life in people." Vachio shook his head and grimaced. "That's the joke."

"Why?"

"Because I come from California, too. About 15 miles from where she grew up, and I sure don't see where living there gave anyone any special insight into life. You either develop it or you don't.... Wherever you grow up."

"You sure don't have it," snapped Julie, her face flushed.

"You know...ah, forget it. She'll just make everything personal."

Lothar was alert and rubbing his hands together with relish. Up to this point, the session had been dull and tedious, most of the trainees speaking abut themselves in self-conscious superficial terms while the rest politely listened. But now a maverick had appeared.

"No, Gary, I think it important that you vent your feelings on this matter. Please continue."

Vachio took a deep breath. "All right, it's like this.... Since I got together with this group and they found out I was from California, I've had to listen to all this crap about how freaky it must have been to grow up taking a hot tub in guacamole sauce..."

Except for Julie and Lothar the group burst into laughter.

"Anyway, where I grew up, it sure wasn't like that. And neither is most of the rest of California. I would say far more people are just struggling to get by and pay the bills than live like what she was describing. Including where she grew up.... That's my special awareness of things."

"Julie. A response?" said Lothar.

"Because he doesn't understand, he's just being negative. Where I come from an awareness about life is cultivated and nurtured."

All eyes turned to Vachio. Julie had delivered her response in a smooth, assured manner. Her attitude struck Vachio as smug and complacent. Vachio had glanced around the room before answering. Except for Edgar, a Colombian-American trainee from Jackson Heights in Queens, New York, he was receiving very hostile vibes. Vachio felt that the others wanted to believe, though in a less exaggerated manner, in the world Julie was describing, with Marin as a metaphor for the United States as a whole. When he thought about it later, he realized they almost had to believe in the hubris of her position to justify their own presence in Colombia. They had to believe the United States was the bright shining beacon for the rest of the world to follow to reach a better future. Vachio wanted to believe all this as well. He just wasn't so sure and was willing to openly explore his doubts. But now wasn't the time. "No, I guess I've said enough," said Vachio, and Lothar had closed that first group session on that note.

Julie was clearing her voice to speak to this group session about her site visit. Vachio was alert. There was an air of tension in the room.

"I have to admit, I had a difficult time on my site visit," said Julie. She paused for effect. Julie was a poised and fluent speaker. "And I feel very stressed about my situation here right now." The group leaned forward and listened sympathetically. "The biggest problem I believe I will have here is that, I , as an American woman, am going to have trouble getting respect as a professional person in this macho culture..."

A chorus of approval and yeahs of affirmation went up from the female volunteers. As Julie continued speaking, the group session took on the character of a revival meeting. The women leaned forward in their seats, eyes bright, listening avidly as Julie pursued her theme and gave concrete examples of obnoxious and demeaning behavior from Colombian males toward her. Julie was a tall willowy attractive blond. She would have attracted plenty of sexual interest from both men and women in the United States. In Colombia, her long shiny blond hair attracted the attention of men like moths to a flame.

Julie finished and the next trainee, Rachel, pursued essentially the same theme. "Most of these Colombian men are sleaze buckets. They are totally obnoxious to women out on the streets. I don't know how many times I've been harassed just walking to the training center..."

"Yeah, sister, that's right," said Monica Overstreet, a self-declared feminist. "We sure do know what you're talking about."

Vachio and Jerry Espy exchanged looks. Rachel was short and rather plain. Neither Vachio nor Espy had seen her attract much attention from Colombian or American men.

"And the women here," Rachel continued, "it's hard to make friends and have a good conversation with them because they are so geared to doing everything to please men. They dress up for them and primp and defer to them.... Like a, like a bunch of little airhead Barbie Dolls..."

Boy, she's sure been dealing with a different breed of Colombian women than I have, thought Vachio. Where are these women she's talking about? Vachio looked at Lothar to see if the moderator was going to inject some balance into this session. Lothar was kicked back in his chair, his legs crossed, a benign half-smile on his face. Every now and then he'd send a yearning sympathetic glance toward Julie Christiansen. Ah, the sensitive American male playboy, thought Vachio, disgusted. Without thinking things through, Vachio raised his hand.

"Gary. Do you have a comment?" said Lothar.

"Yes, thank you.... Rachel, I walked with you to the training center about a little over a week ago. You remember?"

"Yeah, I remember."

"Well, I remember you getting upset about some of the looks you received walking along Caracas that day. But I don't remember you getting any more strange looks than I did. So maybe the problem here is that you're just not used to getting this much attention.... And maybe you better enjoy it while it lasts."

A gasp went up from most of the female trainees and Monica spit, "Why you chauvinist pig. That's a terrible thing to say."

Rachel, who usually had a sharp quick tongue, had a shocked look on her face. As the hubbub continued, Jerry Espy caught Vachio's attention and silently mouthed, "I can't believe you said that." Then he winked.

"Hold on now, hold on now," said Lothar, repressing a grin. Slowly the noise receded. "Now, Gary may not have expressed himself in the most tactful manner, but he brings up a good point. We all must remember that we are in a different culture. And in Colombia, it's perfectly acceptable for a man to do what they call, *echando flores*, or throwing flowers to a woman. Which is a form of compliment here. And shouldn't be taken in a bad way.... Is that what you wanted to express, Gary?"

"Well no, Lothar, not exactly. I mean, I certainly understand the difference between innocent compliments and sleazy come-ons. And I can understand why somebody would be upset about getting them.... But the point I'm trying to make is that in my experience here so far, I've found the Colombian women pretty aggressive, too. I mean, this is an aggressive culture. And we all better start adjusting to it.... Women and men. And as for gaining respect as a professional, the woman social worker at my job site had plenty of respect from her colleagues. She..."

Except for Rachel, who was still looking at him goggle-eyed, and Jerry, the rest of the group shouted Vachio down.

11

After Vachio's series of intense adventures and misadventures, he decided to take it easy and maintain a low profile for a while. For the most part, he worked diligently and kept to a routine, studying his Spanish, going on day trips with his *Gamin* Group to assorted homes for runaway boys and girls, hanging out with his friends and stopping after a few beers, and going to bed at a reasonable hour. Vachio avoided drugs, controversy, and compromising relationships with women.

His situation at the house of Doña Pilar remained status quo. For a week after being locked out of the house, Vachio and Pilarcita glared at each other on the few occasions their paths crossed. No one apologized and no one specifically mentioned the incident. Except for the bad feelings, it was as though the blow-up had never occurred. Then Vachio woke up one morning and decided it wasn't even worth thinking about. What was the point of carrying a grudge? His days in Bogotá and with this family were numbered. Besides, it was almost Christmas, and in less than two weeks after that he would be on his own again. Vachio could hardly wait. He knew he was past ready. He felt like a young, well-conditioned baseball player enduring six weeks of spring training when three would have been sufficient. It's time to get it on for real, he thought, as he chafed and fidgeted through another class of boring verb conjugations and the use of subjunctive clauses. Let me loose.

The Saturday before Christmas, Vachio toured various spots around Bogotá and picked up a basket, assorted cheeses, boxes of crackers, candies, dry meats, and a good bottle of red wine. He assembled these items into a Christmas basket and presented it to Doña Pilar.

"Ay, my son, this is a beautiful Christmas basket," she said, her eyes lighting up. "Thank you a thousand times."

Doña Pilar was genuinely delighted. In the next few days, she passed the word and Vachio was treated more cordially by the family. Pilarcita even sought him out one evening while he was sitting at the dining room table and asked him how things were going. Pilarcita was in better humor these days. Christmas had come early for her. She had received a job offer from a law firm and was going to begin work in February. One morning, Vachio caught her humming a happy tune as she waited in the hallway for her brother to get out of the shower.

Christmas Eve, Vachio came back from the training center and found the house of Doña Pilar in cheery anticipation. The plastic was off the furniture, a crackling fire warmed the living room, a large tree sat in a corner of the room, and red and silver tinsel fluttered from the walls. Doña Pilar was dressed in a green silk gown with white trim and was propped in an easy chair, looking matriarchal and benevolent as her family grouped around her. Pilarcita was there, Juan Pablo, Alfredo, Pilar's sister, Trudy, and two young nieces. Even Osvaldo made a cameo appearance and drank a glass of brandy with the family before leaving for a university party with a beautiful young literature student.

Vachio was handed a large glass of some red rum punch concoction and stood awkwardly in the center of the room as everyone wished him a "*Feliz Navidad*." Vachio returned the greetings and settled into the love seat. He tried to look interested as family matters were discussed and played dumb at the cow's eyes cast in his direction by one of the nieces. Then Alfredo, of all people, came over to talk. After a few minutes of conversation, Vachio told him he needed to go out and buy a bottle of wine for the Christmas party at the training center later that night.

"Let's go," said Alfredo. "I'm tired of this old woman's talk."

They hit Caracas, crowded with people making last minute purchases, and headed for Vachio's favorite wine shop.

"Why haven't you ever introduced me to any of your *gringa* friends?" Alfredo asked out-of-the-blue.

"I didn't think you'd be interested in any capitalist sows."

"Ay brother, that's no problem. I could convert them to the cause."

"Who's cause? Your cause?"

"The cause has room for people of varied interests and backgrounds."

"I see.... Well, anyway, if you want to meet a few, you're welcome to come to our party tonight. But once you get there, you're on your own."

"Ay, bro, I can't tonight. We have our traditional dinner at my aunt's and after that I'm going to party with some friends from the university."

Vachio shrugged.

Before entering the liquor store, Alfredo stopped Vachio and said, "Now listen. After you pick out the wine you want, give it to me and let me negotiate the price."

"Why?"

"You know. Because they'll try to cheat you because you're a *gringo*."

"You think so? I come here all the time and they have good prices."

"Just let me do the talking."

"Whatever," said Vachio, irritated.

They entered the store and Vachio quickly selected a bottle of Santa Carolina. He placed it on the counter and the proprietor smiled at him and prepared to wrap it up.

"Just one moment, maestro," said Alfredo, scowling. "How much are you going to charge us for that?"

The man tapped the price tag on the bottle and answered, "200 pesos."

"That much?"

"You can try the store down the street. He charges 250 for this."

"But the store over there charges 150," said Alfredo.

"Really?" The man's voice was scornful. "You don't want it. No problem."

"We'll take it," said Vachio, paying the man and putting the bottle under his arm.

Alfredo caught up to him outside and tugged at his arm. "Why did you buy it? That man is a thief."

"If you know a store with better prices, let me know. I don't. And I've been to most of them around here."

Alfredo muttered about the exploitative proprietor all the way to the house. But he simmered down when supper was served. It was the best meal Vachio had ever seen at Doña Pilar's house—Roast chicken with herbs cooked in white wine, scalloped potatoes, peas and rice, fresh baguettes, and for dessert, chocolate cake and coffee.

"That was delicious," said Vachio, rubbing his stomach.

"It gives me such pleasure to see you content, my son," said Doña Pilar, smiling on Vachio. "Consider yourself among family."

Vachio leaned over and whispered to Juan Pablo, "It's just too bad I've never seen food like this any other time. Or eaten with the whole family."

"And you never will again here. *Feliz Navidad*, che. Enjoy it."

About an hour later, the family piled into two cars and headed for Doña Pilar's sister's home on the North Side of Bogotá. The real Christmas feast would be served at around midnight. Despite Vachio's improved relations with the family, he was not invited. Left alone, he drank a second cup of coffee and talked to Blanca for a while. Then he washed up, changed his clothes, and left for the Christmas party at the training center.

Vachio left Caracas after a few blocks and took a route along residential back streets. It was crazy. Car horns tooted. Fireworks of tremendous power—Roman Candles, M-80's, Cherry Bombs, flares, and blazing pinwheels—roared and sputtered on all sides. *Globos*, small balloon devices powered by the hot air of blazing candles, floated up between the buildings and into the dark sky, casting beacons of incandescent light and keeping the fire department hopping, their sirens piercing the general din, from one end of the city to the other. Children, waving sparklers and throwing firecrackers, ran laughing along the streets. The normally paranoid and reserved citizens of Bogotá were in an ebullient mood. Family groups lounged outside their houses in front of ornate Nativity scenes, conversing and drinking in the cool, sulfurous air. Dozens of total strangers called "*Feliz Navidad*" to Vachio and he stopped to drink a couple of shots of *aguardiente* offered to him along the way. By the time he reached the training center, he was rosy-cheeked, half-deaf, and with a slight buzz-on.

He entered the house and was met near the door by Janie. She smiled at Vachio and said in a good-natured, wheedling voice, "Now Gary, you are going to be cool tonight. Right?"

"What?" Vachio stared at Janie in disbelief. This was Janie—big, good-looking Viking woman, boss nurse, recreation director of their group, and Number One party animal. "You're telling me to be cool?"

Janie frowned and her voice turned hard. "Hey, you know what happened at the last party."

"Not really. I left early that night.... Remember?"

"Well, they're only letting us have this party here because we promised to keep things under control. Remember that."

"When have you ever seen me out of control?"

Janie laughed. "I haven't. But I know your type. You're a shit disturber. You instigate things and then you stand back and laugh at the mess."

"Me?" Vachio chuckled. "I'm as innocent as they come. What have I ever done to deserve this reputation?"

Big Bob sidled over to get in on the conversation. "Oh yeah, you're real innocent."

"All right, then, for what it's worth." Vachio raised his right hand. "I do solemnly swear to be cool at tonight's party.... There. Happy?"

Janie laughed. "See what I mean about you. You're always saying stuff to agitate people."

"Hey, I'm the one who should be agitated. Getting accused of all this stuff. Give me a break."

"Are we still going to be friends when we get back to the States?" asked Janie, smiling.

"Hey, hey! What's this?" rumbled Big Bob.

"Who knows if we're going to be friends when we get back," said Vachio. "I guess we will if we want to be."

Janie gave Vachio a strange look. Then she turned away to greet some new arrivals and give them the official warning from headquarters.

Vachio went over to the refreshment table, deposited his bottle of wine, and mixed himself a hot rum punch. He sipped his drink and looked around. There were fewer people than usual and the atmosphere was much more subdued. A number of trainees with good relationships with their Colombian families were sharing Christmas with them. And some of their main party people, knowing in advance this gig was going to be carefully watched and under wraps, were celebrating Christmas in less restricted places. Vachio considered all this and shrugged his shoulders. He really didn't care one way or another how this party turned out. For the first time since arriving in South America, he felt a touch of nostalgia and homesickness. This wasn't the first Christmas he had spent away from his family, but it was the first one in which he had no contact with them at all.

"Hey, Señor!" Percy Fong came up to Vachio, grinning genially. "*Feliz Navidad*."

"Yeah, Merry Christmas and all that.... Man, I'm surprised to see you here. I thought you get along good with your Colombian family."

"I do. I just wanted to say Merry Christmas to all my partners here. I'll be joining my family a little later. They don't really get their thing going until after midnight."

Vachio nodded. He was acquainted with Percy's Colombian family. They were gracious people. He had eaten at their home several times and had even stayed overnight once at their invitation.

"Sounds like a plan," said Vachio.

"What about you?"

"Nothing. I'll just hang around here until they boot me out or I get bored."

"Nothing going on with your family?"

"Yeah. But they all went over to one of the relative's house and I wasn't invited.... They did give me a good dinner for a change, though."

Percy laughed. "Are you going to be able to get into the house?"

"Oh, yeah. For sure tonight. They have to get back in later. So they'll have the maid sleeping on the couch until they get there."

"When does she get to see her family?"

"Tomorrow. But she only has a sister or something around Bogotá."

"Well, *Feliz Navidad*, Señor," said Percy, raising his glass.

They toasted and drank and Vachio asked, "So, do you know for sure where you'll be working now?"

"Yeah, I'm gonna be in Ibagué in Tolima. Working with the Coffee Association."

"Think you'll like it there?"

"Yes, I think so. It has a nice climate and beautiful countryside just outside the city. And there's a few volunteers there to show me the ropes."

"Are you going there right after graduation?"

"Yeah. I have to find a place to stay and get settled in. How about you?"

"I'm not sure. But I think I'll take a quick trip to Cali."

"Really?"

"Yeah, why not? I already have a place to stay. And my boss over there told me they don't get geared up after Christmas until about the 15th anyway. So...I'll take that settling in allowance lump sum and take me a little *paseo*."

"You're lucky, Señor. Very lucky. I wish I could go with you."

"It's all skill, man. All skill." Vachio laughed to show he knew he was lucky in this case. Things had fallen into place for him. Many of the trainees in his group were still without firm job sites— let alone set living accommodations.

Percy left a short while later and Vachio immediately began to feel alone and depressed. For some reason, Vachio couldn't get into this party. He felt removed and distant, as though he had already left to start his new life in Garrotero. He nursed his rum punch and drifted on the fringes of the action, his mind cool and observant. A handful of the trainees were dancing and drinking with an almost desperate intensity, as though they were trying to avoid bursting into tears, while others, who were normally festive partyers, were unusually laid-back and subdued.

"Come on, man, what's with you tonight?" asked Rachel, grabbing Vachio and pulling him out onto the dance floor. "Don't you want to party?" Rachel was garbed in a tight blouse with a plunging neckline, a black mini skirt with little tassels, and was barefoot for dancing.

"Oh, yeah. *Feliz* fucking *Navidad*," said Vachio, going passively.

As soon as they hit the floor, Rachel began to dance in a bold and suggestive manner and commented on how hot the room felt. Vachio looked at her and was unmoved. It was funny. Ever since he had made that remark to her during the group session, she had been after him. Vachio had carefully steered clear of her. He liked her well enough, but he wasn't interested in getting involved with her. But then again, a night like tonight was a good time for a casual fling. People were feeling lonely and sentimental over the holiday and the end of training together. Why not? thought Vachio. It's the perfect time to hit on her. And I know she's thinking the same thing about me. But... Vachio looked at her. Rachel smiled back incitingly. Nah. I don't feel nothin'. Not even raw lust. What's the point. Let her hook up with someone more interested.

A dance later, Rachel drifted away, flinging a frustrated glance at Vachio over her shoulder. Vachio didn't care. He just wanted to float along, pass the time, and watch everything with the crystal clear clarity of the detached mind and disengaged emotions.

Shortly after midnight, Bobby McCullough, Julie Christiansen, Erica McNamara, Crazy Steve, Red-haired Dolly, and some volunteers Vachio barely knew showed up. It was the loose clique within their group, derisively referred to as the "in-crowd" by Jock Wilson. They arrived in high spirits and pretty well buzzed from the looks of them. But after circulating around the party for only a few minutes, they looked ready to bolt the premises.

"Man, this party is dead," said Bobby to Vachio. "We were better off at the party we left."

"Where were you?"

"Over at Randy's pad. It was live." Bobby shook his head. "I've never seen one of our parties this weak. What's going on?"

"The word is out about us. Janie told me we need to keep it cool so they don't give us any trouble over our graduation party."

"Yeah, she mentioned something like that to me the other day. That's why I went to the other party first.... But this still surprises me." Bobby looked around and shook his head in disappointment. "Hell, I guess I'll go back to the other party. It's better than this."

"Yeah, this is pretty weak. But it's all right if you just want to kick back and talk."

"Hell with that! It's Christmas. I want to roar."

Vachio laughed.

"You want to come with us, buddy?" Bobby asked.

"Nah, I ain't in the mood for that kind of thing tonight. I feel like just mellowing out."

Bobby gave Vachio a funny look. "All right, man. *Feliz* fucking *Navidad*."

Bobby went around to say hello to a few more friends and then went to gather up his friends for the return trip to the other party. Vachio stuck around for another hour. Then he quietly said goodnight and went home and kept Blanca company for a while before going to bed.

12

New Year's Eve, Vachio met a group of trainees at Doña Bárbara's Jazz Club to start the evening. The purpose of this get-together was two-fold, to ring in the New Year with a few drinks among friends, and to finalize plans for the big graduation bash on the fourth. Because of the close proximity of their graduation to the New Year, the trainees had decided to concentrate their energies and remaining money on the graduation party and leave the New Year's Eve celebrations to volunteers stationed in Bogotá.

Sitting at a private booth in the back of the club, Janie and Big Bob, Audry, Vachio, Bobby McCullough, and Erica talked it over. All of them were anxious to arrive at some sort of accord and get on to celebrations scattered around town. But there was a strong disagreement as to where to hold the party. Some of the trainees wanted to hold it in a public restaurant with a folkloric dance show, at a cost of $500 pesos a head, while others wanted to have it at the training center in the usual pot luck style. The real issue was money. A segment of the trainees had brought quite a bit of money from home or received stipends from savings there, while others had only the money they received from their Peace Corps living allowance. For those receiving money from home, $500 pesos was no big deal, for those on the stipend, it was a hefty one shot expenditure. All during the final week of training the argument had gone back and forth—the training center or El Chibcha Restaurant? Time was growing short. An immediate decision was needed to make the necessary arrangements. The discussion, fueled by beer and wine, grew heated.

"I'm telling you," said Bobby McCullough, his face avid, his voice earnest, "El Chibcha is a class place. For the money, we get dinner, pitchers of Sangria, a folkloric dance show, and a nice setting. Plus we don't have to do any work in preparation. Everything is set up for us. After the reception at the Ambassador's House, we just go over there and party hearty.... $500 pesos for that is damn reasonable."

"Yeah but, you're forgetting something," said Audry. "What about the liquor? Most people don't only want to drink Sangria. Drinks will cost a fortune in a place like that. And not all of us have the money."

"Ah, you just sneak a bottle in your bag or back pack," said Bobby. "What's the big deal?"

"Maybe I don't feel like sneaking around. In the training center we won't have to. We just bring our stuff and party."

"Ah! I'm tired of the training center. And our graduation party should have a little more class than a place like that."

"What do you think?" Janie asked Vachio. Vachio took a sip of beer before answering. He had stayed quiet up until then. Truthfully, he didn't care one way or another. He had a monetary windfall coming to him when he received his settling in allowance, but he was sympathetic to Audry's argument. A number of volunteers had already told him privately that they wouldn't attend a graduation party at a public place because of the cost and hassle. El Chibcha was way downtown and far from most of their residences.

"Well, I'm leaning more toward having it at the training center. It would be less expensive that way and we'd be more in control of our own party.... And besides that, I went to El Chibcha for a snack one day when we had a couple of meetings over by there and...to tell you the truth, I wasn't that impressed."

"What was wrong with it?" snapped Bobby.

"I'm not saying it was bad. But I had a coffee and an *empananda*, and for the high price, it wasn't anything special."

"Well, my Colombian family recommends it highly," said Bobby. "And they're people of good taste. You remember that they let us stay that weekend at their *finca* in Melgar."

"Yeah, I remember," said Vachio. "But that's got nothing to do with this. I mean, I'm sure they mean well, but it's like me telling a visitor to San Francisco to visit Fisherman's Wharf and eat. It might be good and fun for them, but I wouldn't do it myself because I know everything is overpriced."

"So why don't you recommend a better place?" said Bobby.

"I did. I vote with Audry. The training center."

"What exactly is your objection to El Chibcha?" asked Erica. "I went there with Bobby to look it over and I liked it."

"It's fine, I guess. But I just got the feeling it's one of those artsy fartsy tourist clip joints.... You know what I mean?"

"No, not really?"

"Well, one thing I know for sure," said Janie, "if we have the party at the training center, I'll end up doing most of the work.... And this time I'd like to just relax and have a good time."

"That's right," said Big Bob. "She does too much at these functions."

Vachio knew this was true. But he also knew Janie was the type of person who took charge of these events and brought the work on herself.

"So what do you say?" Bobby asked Vachio.

Vachio looked at Audry and shrugged his shoulders. "Whatever. I gave you my opinion. But it looks like you already have your minds made up about El Chibcha.... So do what you're gonna do. I'll go. But I know some other people who won't."

"I don't know if I'll go," said Audry.

"That's up to you," said Bobby. "We can't please everyone. But it would be crazy if you don't make it."

The group left the booth to have a final drink out in the main room. Canned Jazz played over the speakers. It was about ten o'clock. The live band scheduled to play was already about an hour late. Vachio found an empty spot at the bar and sat down. Doña Barbara's was jammed with stylishly dressed young Colombians and foreigners, ready to ring in the New Year with a flourish. Vachio looked around at the scene. This was a big cocaine bar. There were plenty of the type of people, gold chains and little silver coke spoons dangling from their necks, that made regular trips between Colombia and Miami. There were probably more than a few of them snorting up in the bathrooms and in the private booths at that very moment. It reminded Vachio of some of the clubs he had gone to in the Marina District in San Francisco. The same kind of fast lane hip environment patronized by young urban professionals and the hustlers who catered to their recreational needs. And here I am, thought Vachio. Almost 1979 in the land of El Dorado of white powder gold.

Audry came up to the bar and stood next to Vachio. She was still upset, her round ruddy cheeks taut and her eyes focused to dark points.

"Do you want something to drink?" Vachio yelled over the noise.

"No. I'm getting out of here. This place is too expensive for me."

"Yeah, it is expensive.... But hey, I'll treat you to one. Happy New Year's and all that."

"No, that's all right. I'm not in the mood. But thanks."

"Ah, come on. Forget about the graduation party. That's for another day."

"I don't want to forget about it. I'm pissed off at the way they manipulated the whole thing. Not everyone has money to blow that way."

"Yeah, you're right. I can only do it this time because I know I can afford to spend my settling in allowance on other things. Otherwise, I'm in the same boat you are."

"Well, I can't risk spending mine. I need it."

"So what are you going to do now?"

"I'm heading back downtown near where I live. I heard there's a party at one of the volunteer's places near the Plaza de Toros."

"Oh yeah. The one at Yvette LeFlore's place."

"Is she the black woman from the group before us?"

"Yeah. That's her."

"Are you going?"

"Yeah, I was thinking about it. I don't want to hang out here tonight. I mean, look, the live band was supposed to start up over an hour ago and we still have nothing but taped music. This sucks."

"Yeah, this place is a rip-off.... *Vamos*?"

"All right, I'm with you. Just let me finish this drink." Vachio drained what was left of his screwdriver, rose from the high bar stool, and went over to a table where the others had congregated.

"Well, we're out of here," said Vachio. "Happy New Year's."

"Where are you going?" Janie asked.

"To that party at Yvette LeFlore's. How 'bout you guys?"

"We're going to a party in Los Andes later with Bobby's Colombian family."

"Have a good one."

Vachio and Audry hit the street. It was cold and drizzly, but the air smelled of fireworks and burnt rubber. Vachio quickly flagged down a packed buseta.

"Wait a minute," said Audry. "This one will leave us a good ten blocks from where we want to go."

"That's cool. We can walk."

"But it's crazy out there tonight."

"Exactly."

Audry still looked dubious but she followed Vachio onto the buseta. They wedged there way to the middle of the lurching vehicle and held tightly to the steel bars. Vachio hovered over Audry as though she were his girl. These tight-packed busetas were notorious for wandering hands and surreptitious pinches.

The buseta roared from the Chicó and into Chapinero, blasting cumbia music over the speakers and shedding and receiving bright-eyed and tipsy celebrants. The firework's displays on the streets were awesome, probably double the quantity and volume Vachio had seen on Christmas Eve, and people were making bonfires of old automobile tires and clothes, casting a pall of black smoke and a horrible stench over the city.

They exited the buseta in Lower Chapinero and Vachio followed Audry through residential streets toward Yvette's place. Too late Vachio realized Audry was right about how crazy things were on the streets of Lower Chapinero. The atmosphere was festive but with a hard edge that was absent on Christmas. Gangs of youths wandered the streets carrying water balloons, eggs, and corn flour to throw at those unlucky enough to meet them. The tire bonfires were lined up two or three to a street and Roman Candles and myriad other explosive devices whistled through the air. Shouts of glee, the howls and yelps of dogs, tooting horns and squealing tires, and curses of pain and anger mingled with and pierced the constant blasts of the fireworks. Vachio's eyes watered from the acrid smoke and his ears hurt from the explosive blasts of cherry bombs, M-80's, and other even more powerful explosives he couldn't identify.

"Man, this is wild. Too wild," said Vachio, shouting to Audry. "I should have listened to you. This is like walking through a war zone."

"Well, it's too late now."

"Let's move fast."

They stuck to the shadows along the houses and avoided knots of people. Then about a block from their destination, a kid ran past them and tossed a fiery pinwheel in their path. It jumped and sizzled only a few feet from them, throwing off multitudes of hot sparks.

"Yeow!" screamed Audry, holding her arm. She had jumped right into a wave of sparks as she tried to sidestep the pin wheel and it perversely jumped after her. Then the pinwheel bounded back to the middle of the street and burned itself out.

"Damn punk kid!" said Vachio. "Let's see your arm." Vachio examined her arm as best he could. "It doesn't look too bad."

"Yeah, that's easy for you to say. It hurts."

"Well, let's go. They should have something for you to put on it at the house."

"I told you we should have waited for a different buseta. I told you."

"Yeah, yeah, I'm sorry. If it makes your arm feel any better—you were right."

They made it to Yvette's place without further mishap and were greeted by a rude shock. There were only a handful of people there. "L.A. Girl!" exclaimed Vachio to Yvette. "Where in the hell is the party?"

"I'm afraid this party broke up early, Mr. Cat from San Francisco. You all should've come earlier. You missed out on the barbecue I made. But hey, if you just want to hang out for a while, I've plenty of cold beer left over and some dynamite herb."

"Man, we almost got killed coming over here. Look at her arm."

Audry showed Yvette a circular red burn mark on her bicep.

"Uuh uuh! What happened?"

"Fireworks attack."

"Well, it's not so bad. We'll fix it right up. I've got some stuff in the bathroom. Come on with me, girl," said Yvette to Audry. Then she turned to Vachio. "Just make yourself at home. Meet my friends."

Vachio stood awkwardly in the center of an almost bare room and looked at six strangers. Two were Colombian women dressed in the best Bohemian-Hippie-Bogotá style, with patched jeans, cotton mens' shirts, bright long scarves hanging from their necks, an assortment of colorful cloth and leather bands wrapped around their wrists, and thick woolen socks covered by leather sandals. There were two young men, tall and lean, bookends, with *ruanas* draped over their shoulders and thick dark beards. Vachio sized them up as Peace Corps volunteers just in from some cold Andean job site. Then there was a young black woman, presumably one of Yvette's roommates, and another woman with bushy frizzy hair, glasses, and a black leather coat. Vachio was aware that this last woman was checking him out.

"Help yourself to a cold beer," said the black woman, indicating a tin wash basin in one corner of the room filled with ice, water, and bottles of beer and soda.

Vachio was quick to take her up on her offer. He grabbed a beer and fiddled around with it in the far corner of the room, stalling for time until Yvette returned. He didn't feel particularly welcome. It seemed that he and Audry had arrived just as they were all about to leave for somewhere else. The others resumed interrupted conversations and Vachio sipped his beer and checked them out in silence.

Yvette returned to the room with Audry in tow and introduced Vachio to her friends. The Americans were all from her Peace Corps group. The two guys were visiting from Manizales. The Colombian women were their friends. The woman with the frizzy hair, Dana, was visiting from Cúcuta. The black woman was named Sandy and was Yvette's roommates. Vachio and Audry shook hands all the way around and then fell silent. They exchanged glances and nodded at each other in wordless agreement. Nothing going on here. They felt like intruders.

"Well, we're gonna get going now," said Toby, one of the guys from Manizales. "How about you?"

"I'll be along in a while," said Yvette. "Let me take care of my friends here first."

"Anyone else want to go with us?" he asked, looking only at Dana and Sandy.

"No, I'm going with Yvette," said Sandy.

"I might not even go," said Dana. "I'm pretty burned out."

Toby grunted, adjusted his gray *ruana*, and told his friends it was time to move out.

"Better be careful out there," Vachio said as the group reached the door. "It is most definitely crazy."

"Thanks, guy, we're not exactly TRAINEES," said Toby.

"That doesn't really matter tonight. I don't think the street punks are checking credentials."

Toby looked as though he were going to say something else but he settled for giving Vachio a dirty look and turned to leave. As soon as the four of them left the tension seeped out of the room.

"What was that dude's problem?" Vachio asked Yvette.

"Oh, nothing. Toby's all right. He just takes himself a little seriously sometimes."

"You have another party to go to, I take it."

"Yes. At the pad of some friend of Toby's girlfriend.... Hey, I'd love to invite you guys, but I don't really know those people myself.... I don't know if it would be cool."

"That's all right," said Vachio.

"Yeah, anyway, we'll hang out here for a while," said Sandy.

"Sounds good to me."

Yvette sat cross-legged on a cushion on the floor and busied herself rolling a joint. Dana, Audry, and Sandy were sitting in a semi-circle talking. Vachio sat in a straight-backed chair and relaxed, listening to the intensifying sound of fireworks outside and watching the flashes of Roman Candles whizzing past the second story window.

Yvette fired up the joint and started passing it around. After two good tokes, Vachio realized this wasn't ordinary grass. It hit him fast and hard. He felt a vague uncomfortable tingling throughout his body and the women's voices sounded as though they were coming from underwater. When he spoke, his own normally deep steady voice sounded tinny and hesitant. After one more good hit he felt as though he were glued to the chair and paranoid thoughts started to enter his brain.

"Man!" exclaimed Vachio. "What is this stuff?"

"This is genuine grade A Colombian Gold," said Yvette, laughing. "Do you like it?"

"I don't know yet. It's blowing me somewhere I'm not sure I want to go." Vachio refused any more grass and concentrated on his bottle of beer, the cold glass in his hand the only thing breaking through the numbness suffusing his body. After a time he lost the thread of conversation going on around him and was only aware of the explosions and sirens emanating from the streets. He had never heard anything like it. He could actually feel the building shiver from the explosions. He imagined that they were under attack and he trembled ever so slightly and involuntarily. Then, as though waking from a nightmare, his eyes were drawn to Dana and he gave a low chuckle. With her bush of kinky hair, the black leather, tight jeans, and black boots, she reminded him of some of the girls from the Mission District parties in his teenage years. She had that hard punky front. Looking at her, Vachio flashed back to some of those parties—the dim lights and black posters, the smell of chewing gum, hair spray, and cheap perfume, the smoke from Mexican rag weed and cigarettes, the slangy urban talk with a sprinkling of Spanish, the music of Santana, War, and Tower of Power, and the full-bosomed feel of the Latina girls as they slow-danced into the early morning hours. Through his stoned haze, Vachio saw Dana smiling back at him. He imagined himself dancing with her, her come-on smile drawing them tight together.

A flurry of blasts, pops, and shouts reverberated outside. Suddenly everyone in the dark room was on their feet and exchanging hugs and kisses. "Happy New Year. Happy New Year."

Moving like thick molasses, Vachio felt himself envelop Dana in his arms. She smelled of musk and leather and her thick rough hair tickled his cheeks. He felt a responsive pressure and then they released and made the rounds of the others. After this activity, Vachio sat down heavily in the chair. He felt deliciously languorous.

"Well, people," announced Yvette, "it's time for us to be heading on to that party." Her eyes turned question marks on Vachio and Audry.

"Which way are you going?" asked Audry.

"Toward the Bullring."

"I'll go with you. It's on my way home."

"No problem, sister. What about you, Cat?"

"Man, I don't know," said Vachio. "I feel good just sitting in this chair.... That was some kick-ass weed."

Yvette guffawed. "Well, you're welcome to just kick back here as long as you feel like it. There's plenty of beer leftover and..." Yvette opened the closet and tossed a sleeping bag on the bare floor near Vachio. "If you want to crash here, you're welcome."

"Thanks, I may take you up on that. I sometimes have trouble getting into my house after a certain hour."

"*Mi casa es tu casa*," said Yvette.

"I'm going to hang out here, too," said Dana. "I've had enough partying for the night. And I need to get to the airport early."

Yvette gave a chesire cat smile and glanced toward Vachio. Then Dana went over to her and they held a whispered conversation. All

Vachio could make-out was Dana asking if he could be trusted without anyone around and Yvette answering, "The Cat is cool. Don't worry about nothing."

Then the other three women were gone and Vachio and Dana were alone in the room. While Dana fiddled with her backpack and unrolled her sleeping bag and a blanket, Vachio opened up another beer. Vachio was still pretty stoned but he felt himself coming down a little. Watching Dana ignore him as she fussed over her things, he wondered if maybe he had misread her signals. Well, whatever, he thought. This is as good a place to hang out as any. He had no desire to fight his way over the wild streets back to Upper Chapinero.

"How do you know Yvette?" Dana suddenly asked.

"I met her at a Halloween party at Randy's house....You know Randy?"

"The guy from New York City? The one who works with the *gamines*?"

"Yeah, him."

"Sure. He was in my group. Same as Yvette.... Hey! Why do they call you the Cat from San Francisco?"

"They don't. Only Yvette calls me that. You see, at the Halloween party, I showed up without a costume. So she painted cat whiskers on me and told everyone I was The Cat from San Francisco."

"Yvette's cool. I like her."

"Yeah, me too. We had a long talk at the Halloween party. She lived in South Central L.A. so we were unwitting neighbors for a year when I went to school down there.... It was the year they had that big shoot-out with the Symbionese Liberation Army.... Remember that?"

"Was that the thing with Patty Hearst?"

"Yeah, exactly. I was living about 20 blocks away from where it happened. But I tell you, I know that they knew Patty Hearst wasn't in that house with Commandant Sinque and the others. No way they would have wasted that place like they did if they knew she was in there."

"Probably not."

"For sure. The next day I was in this coffee shop on Figueroa Street where a lot of cops hang out and they were laughing and joking about it.... Calling it the South Central Barbecue."

"That's cold."

"Yep. They got some mean cops in L.A. I know from experience..."

Dana gave Vachio a quick look but she didn't say anything.

"So where are you from in the States?" Vachio asked her.

"New Haven, Connecticut," she said, sitting on her sleeping bag and leaning against the wall.

"That's where Yale is, right?"

"Right. You been there?"

"No. I just know Yale is there.... Did you go there?"
"No way. I went to Stoneybrook College."
"You have an interesting face. What's your ethnic background?"
"My father was Italian and my mother was Puerto Rican."
"Good combination."
"It's an explosive combination," said Dana, laughing. "But it seems to work for them."
Vachio could see that Dana was relaxed now. She began to talk without prompting questions. She worked as a special education instructor at a school in Cúcuta, on the border with Venezuela. "School is out until the 15th of January so I'm taking a little unofficial vacation," Dana admitted.
"*Cuerpo de paseo*," said Vachio, laughing. "Just like the Spanish teachers say."
"Toughest job you'll ever love," added Dana.
"Where are you going?"
"To Ecuador. I'm flying out tomorrow to Cali and then I'm going by bus to the border."
"Oh yeah? I'm headed for Cali myself."
"When?"
"Two days after we swear in. On the sixth. I'm like you, I don't have to work until the fifteenth."
"Oh, I'll be in Quito by then. But I'm going to stop in Popayán and Pasto first. I know volunteers in both those places and they say it's absolutely beautiful."
"Sounds good.... Say, how do you like Cúcuta? That's not too far from where I'll be working. Maybe I can pay you a visit and check it out."
"Cúcuta?... Well, it's a border town. And it's hot, dry heat. But...I guess it has a few good things. I'm getting used to it and making some friends. But I still miss Nicaragua."
"Oh, you're one of those volunteers that transferred in from there. We have some in my group, too. How long have you been in Colombia?"
"Three months."
"Which country do you like best?"
"I liked Nicaragua better."
"Really? Why?"
"I liked the people better. They were simpler. More sincere."
"What do you mean?"
"Well, maybe it's not a fair comparison since I work in a border town now. And border towns are always weird. But Nicaragua is a lot less developed than Colombia and most of the people were less sophisticated.... But in a good way. They weren't spoiled yet. And, well," Dana emitted a long sigh. "I had a boyfriend there. I was really in love with that guy. And I think I still am a little."

"Oh.... Hey, were you in a combat zone?"

"I sure was. I was in Estelí. I saw several fire fights before they pulled me out of there.... It got pretty scary. And my boyfriend, Mauricio, he was a real Sandinista. I was even more scared for him."

Vachio pulled himself off the chair and lay down on the sleeping bag Yvette had given him. He felt completely relaxed and mellow now, all the nervousness and paranoia from the weed gone. "So tell me about this Sandinista of yours," Vachio said, his eyes shut, but aware Dana was looking him over from close range.

"Oh, he was a great guy. He had revolutionary ideals and fire.... And he was a poet, too."

Vachio broke out in a low chuckle.

"What's so funny?" Dana snapped.

"No offense, eh. But every other Nica I've ever met claims to be a poet."

"Well, Mauricio was. He used to write me beautiful love poems.... No other guy ever did that for me."

"All right, all right. I'm sorry. It's just that I've known quite a few Nicaraguenses."

"Why? Were you there or something?"

"No, I've never been to Nicaragua. But San Francisco has a pretty fair-sized colony of Nicas. I went to school with a bunch of them."

"Really?"

"Oh yeah. In fact, after the earthquake in Managua, when was it, in '74?"

"'73 or '74."

"Anyway, one of my friends offered to pay me a couple of thousand bucks to have a paper wedding with a relative so they could come to the States."

"Did you?"

"Nah. I could have used the money, but I didn't want the complications. Those sort of things can always turn into more than paper weddings if you're not careful."

"I might have done it," said Dana. "You know that Somoza ended up stealing most of the relief money sent to rebuild Managua and left the city center in ruins and the people destitute?"

"So I've heard."

"Yes, he did. And some people still wonder why the Nicaraguan people want to get rid of him. His family has run that country like their own personal *finca* for years.... With the help of the United States government I'm ashamed to say."

"Now, now," said Vachio in a mock tone. "We Peace Corps volunteers aren't supposed to get political."

"Oh yeah, right. Like our being here isn't a political act. I just pray the Sandinistas overthrow that pig and the people finally get some justice."

Vachio laughed. "Your Sandinista boyfriend did a good job on you."

"No, he didn't. My eyes and ears showed me what I know.... And what's your deal anyway? Are you some kind of right wing reactionary or something?"

"Hardly," laughed Vachio. "I'm just messing with you. Seeing how deep your convictions run."

"After what I've seen, no one can question my convictions. Somoza is a pig. He feeds fresh steaks to his guard dogs and lets his people die of malnutrition. What do you call someone like that?"

"Well, Eisenhower said, no wait, or maybe it was John Foster Dulles his Secretary of State, talking about the first Somoza - 'He's a son-of-a-bitch. But he's our son-of-a-bitch.' I guess I can second that opinion without blowing my apolitical cover."

Dana laughed. "Did he really say that?"

"Yep. It's a matter of record. And I really treasure those moments when a politician slips up and says something candid like that. It's like what Teddy Roosevelt said when he was negotiating with the Colombian government for the Panama Canal rights..."

"What did he say?" asked Dana, sitting up on her sleeping bag, her eyes bright.

"He said trying to do business with the Colombian government is like trying to do business with Calabrian pirates. So he went ahead and helped foment the uprising that separated Panama from Colombia.... Of course, now, Teddy was nothing like politicians nowadays. He often said things on the record like that and went ahead and did them."

"How do you know this stuff?"

"Reading is one of my hobbies. And I have a good head for trivia." Vachio laughed. "Big deal. That and five pesos will get me a *café con leche* here."

"Yeah, but it's interesting stuff to know."

"Well, as long as you think so, I'm happy."

Vachio noticed the conversation was turning both their voices warm and fuzzy. He edged his sleeping bag closer to hers.

Then a loud boom sounded above the gradually diminishing fireworks outside and the room and the street were plunged into total darkness.

"What was that?" hissed Dana.

Vachio got up and took a quick look out of the window. A swath of Chapinero and part of downtown was without power. Dana rose from her spot and stood next to Vachio. He could feel the warmth of her breath and the leathery smell from her jacket. He started to feel excited.

"What do you think happened?" asked Dana, leaning ever so slightly against Vachio, her eyes staring uptown.

"My guess is that M19 or La Farc is leaving a New Year's day calling card.... They must have blown up one of the electric substations."

"Huh. I wonder if Colombia is going to get as bad as Nicaragua."

"Who knows. But they've had *guerrillera* movements here for decades. It comes and goes. It's almost a tradition."

Vachio turned and slipped his arms around Dana's waist. Her face grew serious and she extended her lips for a kiss.

"What time did you say you were leaving for Cali tomorrow?" Vachio asked.

Dana hugged him tight and rubbed her cheek against his chest. "I didn't say. But I'm leaving at six in the morning for the airport."

"Uh oh. We don't have much time, then."

13

At around three o'clock on graduation day, a group of regular *aspirantes* assembled at Tres Corazones Bar just across Caracas from the training center for a final toast. Tres Corazones was a dank smelly dump, a long dark warehouse with low ceilings, metal folding chairs, and battered throwaway tables. It was mostly patronized by uniformed Bogotá garbage men. But it was also a Peace Corps training group tradition. Tres Corazones sold standard Colombian beer at a peso less than anywhere else the trainees knew about, two pesos less per bottle at case price, and the owner had the other patrons trained to leave the Peace Corps trainees, especially the women, in peace.

Bobby McCullough, Audry, Vachio, Janie and Big Bob, Percy Fong, Erica, and Mark Hill drank Bavaria's, Aguila's, and Club Colombia's and reminisced about training. Talking it over, it seemed to them that they had already packed a lifetime of experiences into their three months of training. And there was also a feeling of self-congratulations for a job well-done. Of their entire training group, they had lost only two people to early termination. Cowboy Bob, who had run out of rope and been given the Branif award, and a 64 year old woman, Dalia, who had ostensibly failed to achieve a minimum passing grade on her Spanish exam. The inside scoop was that the higher-ups feared that her health was too fragile. It was too bad. She had badly wanted to stay.

"Here's to Dalia," said Erica. "She was a neat lady."

They all raised their bottles in salute. "At least she had three months of *Cuerpo de Paseo*," seconded Bobby.

They all laughed. "And at least she lasted longer than a bunch of people from the last training group," said Big Bob.

Again they laughed. The training group before them was infamous in the annals of Peace Corps Colombia. They were known as *Los Terribles*, The Terrible Ones by the Spanish teachers. For whatever reason, their group had been incredibly rowdy and uncooperative. They actually lost four trainees at orientation in Miami because of a brawl at a get-to-know-you party at the hotel pool, and they finished training in Bogotá with almost 40 percent of their group terminating. In comparison to *Los Terribles*, their group had been a model of decorum and cooperation.

Bobby McCullough drank his beer and talked incessantly. He was so stoked sparks seemed to shoot off him as he spoke. He had done very well on his Spanish test, scoring a 3, and he brought the conversation around to that subject.

"How did you do?" he asked Vachio.

"Not so good. I only got a 2."

"What? You got a 2?" exclaimed Janie. "What happened? Were you loaded when you took the test?"

"Nah, nothin' like that. It was like something personal between me and the examiner."

"What do you mean?"

"Ah, she was one of these snooty *Bogotanas*. You know, very prim and proper..."

"Man, that shouldn't be a problem," interjected Bobby. "We all know you speak well. You just need to play along with their prejudices."

"Yeah, maybe. But I got off on the wrong foot by addressing her in the familiar, using Tu and all that."

"Uh oh," said Janie. "That was definitely a mistake."

"Hey, they told us to take it just like a friendly little conversation. So I did. But you're right. Madame wasn't too happy about it. I got the impression she thought I was vulgar..."

"Now why would she think that?" laughed Big Bob.

"...And aside from that, and she was right, I didn't go out of my way to use the subjunctive and all that other grammatical crap that lots of ordinary Colombians don't even use. But that's cool. I don't care. Once we get out on our job sites the test score don't mean nothin'. It's all about communication.... I mean, hell, Sean Miller got a 2+ on his test. So how can you take it seriously?"

"Sean Miller got a 2+ on his test?" exclaimed Erica. "I only got a 2+." She shook her head. "That's a farce. Sean can't even order food at a restaurant without stumbling all over himself."

"Yeah, but he knows how to use the subjunctive on a test," said Vachio.

A short time later the group broke up to go home and change clothes for the graduation ceremony at the residence of the American Ambassador to Colombia. Vachio, instead of going home, went with Mark Hill to wait at his house. Mark lived in the Chicó within walking distance of the Ambassador's house and Vachio didn't feel any need to change his clothes. They sat in Mark's small bed room and talked about trips they might make together on vacation.

"Yeah, man, I definitely want to go to the Amazon," said Vachio. "That's something I've dreamed of doing since I was a little kid. And I'm going to do it—for sure."

"Well, if you do, let me know. I think I'd like to go, too."

"I'll let you know." They shook on it.

"Are you going to the party at El Chibcha tonight?" Vachio asked.

"I don't think so. It's too damn expensive for two people. And Monica's family has a celebration planned for me anyway."

Vachio laughed. "You're dead meat, man. You're already married."

"No, I'm not." Mark's face colored.

"All right, man, whatever you say. But I say you're just as good as married."

"I don't think so. We have some big differences to work out." Mark sounded irritated. "And I'm getting tired of everybody talking like we're already married."

"Hey, relax, I'm not saying it's a bad thing for you. Monica seems like a great woman. Who knows? Could be the best thing that ever happened to you. She's smart, pretty, and going to be a dentist to boot. From where I sit, you got it made in the shade." Vachio laughed, rubbing it in.

"I don't want to talk about it anymore."

"All right. All right."

"So do you want to get going now?" Mark asked, looking at his watch.

"Isn't it still kind of early?"

"It's not too early. And they'll probably have good food and champagne. Maybe even an open bar."

"Good point," said Vachio, jumping off his chair. "*Vamos*!"

They walked the short distance to the Ambassador's house and waited as heavily-armed security guards checked their papers at the front gate. The Ambassador's residence was magnificent, a huge white house with columns and fancy shutters. It looked almost like an old southern plantation mansion. Vachio and Mark were let through and they entered a large circular foyer. Much of the marble floor was covered by a huge rug featuring the eagle of the United States, and portraits of former ambassadors adorned the beautifully painted and trimmed out walls. A buffet table loaded with fruit and vegetable salads stood to their right, and maids with black and white-trimmed uniforms served appetizers and drinks. Only a few trainees had arrived, and a short trim distinguished looking gentleman was holding court in the center of the foyer with these. For the moment, Vachio and Mark stayed on the periphery.

"Not bad, eh?" Vachio commented to Mark, and flagged down one of the maids carrying a tray of champagne. Another maid spotted them and came over with crackers loaded up with smoked salmon and white fish. Vachio took two of these and smacked his lips. "Kind of reminds me of the restaurant I used to work at," he said. "But this time they're waiting on me."

"Hey, Gary, look who's here," said Mark, making a face.

Vachio followed his eyes and saw Kendra. She was a volunteer in Bogotá, one of the ones always hanging around the Peace Corps office looking for something to do. She was a notorious gossip and a possible snitch. She came to almost every party and social event held in Bogotá by volunteers or trainees.

"Who invited her?" asked Mark. "She's not in our group."

"Ah, she gets invited to everything by someone in the office. They'll probably give her a job there one of these days."

"Huh! They should have asked us if we wanted to invite her. This is our graduation."

"Ah, who cares. Why worry about stuff like that with all the good eats and drinks, man." Vachio grabbed a couple of finger sandwiches to go with his champagne. Then he went over to the buffet table and loaded up a plate with carrot salad. Mark shook his head in disgust and went to talk to Percy.

Vachio took his salad and wandered over to the knot of people surrounding the Ambassador. Vachio stood in silence for a while, munching on his salad and sipping champagne, listening to the respectful questions lobbed at the ambassador.

"In the diplomatic corps, Colombia is considered a second level country," said the ambassador. "It has certain amenities not available in other places. But of course it isn't comparable to working in Paris or Geneva or..."

"Yeah, but do you get danger pay here?" Vachio broke in.

For a second there was dead silence. Then Erica tittered. The Ambassador grinned and said, "No, I don't. But that's a good idea. I might bring it up with President Carter the next time I see him."

"I would," said Vachio.

This started a discussion of the Richard Starr situation, the volunteer kidnapped by La Farc and held hostage in the mountains of La Huila. The Ambassador was handling these negotiations personally and was expecting a breakthrough any time. Vachio stuck around and talked to the Ambassador. Vachio liked him. The Ambassador, a Hispanic guy from Texas, or *Tejano* as he preferred, had a good sense of humor. But after about 10 minutes, the crush of trainees surrounding the Ambassador grew too much for Vachio and he drifted away to get another glass of champagne before the graduation ceremony began.

As soon as he removed himself from the circle of trainees surrounding the ambassador, Vachio was approached by Kendra.

"Y'all should be ashamed of yourself coming here dressed like you are," she said in her thin, barely southern Texas twang.

"What are you talkin' about? I'm wearing my Sunday best," said Vachio, sipping his champagne. He was dressed in his almost new jeans, his best pair of blue suede Puma tennis shoes, and was actually wearing a shirt with a collar, the only one he possessed.

"Oh, you! Don't you have any sense of etiquette? Don't you have any respect for the Ambassador?"

"Are you serious? I've been talking to the guy for 10 minutes and he wasn't tripping on my clothes. What's your problem?"

"What's my problem? You're the one with the problem."

"Well, then, if that's the case, I have only one thing to say to you. I'll take care of my problems. And you run along and take care of your own. *Capiche*?"

Kendra turned red as a beet and retreated in disarray.

The reception area was now buzzing like a bee hive as trainees, supervisors, functionaries, and other assorted hangers-on from the American community looking for a party circulated around the foyer. Vachio picked steadily at the food and was pretty well filled by the time the trainees were called to assemble in a long gallery room. They sat on wood folding chairs and listened to the usual spiel about representing the United States with dignity, honor, and distinction from the Peace Corps Colombia Director and the Ambassador. At the end of his address, the Ambassador opened up the floor to questions. Bobby McCullough's hand shot up into the air and he looked ready to jump from his seat. The Ambassador acknowledged him.

"Yes, Mr. Ambassador," said Bobby in an unctuous tone Vachio barely recognized from him. "We would like to know why our privilege of using the diplomatic pouch to bring books here for us has been rescinded?"

"Well, unfortunately, that was a determination made in Washington," said the Ambassador smoothly. "Believe me, if I had my druthers, you Peace Corps people would still have access to that service. All right?"

"Well, no! When we joined, we were told we could use the diplomatic pouch. And personally, I have quite a few engineering books I want to bring here. Big thick books that would cost a lot of money coming through the regular mail. And I'm not even sure we can trust the regular mail..."

Vachio turned and looked at Bobby. He was really feeling his oats, almost scolding the Ambassador. Vachio could see a number of women giving him admiring looks, and Bobby was well aware of this. As he continued talking, he seemed to bloat up in his seat and his voice soared with confidence.

"So what exactly do you want to know?" the Ambassador asked, looking at Bobby as though he were a little yapping dog pissing on his leg.

"WE want to know just exactly why this privilege was rescinded."

"Because Washington felt there was too much abuse going on with the service. As a policy consideration, they've decided to limit access. You guys aren't the only ones this is affecting. Some of the embassy staff people have also been included in this prohibition." The Ambassador gave a wide no mea culpa smile. "It's nothing personal against you Peace Corps people. I can assure you of that."

"Yeah, too much abuse," Vachio whispered to Mark Hill. "Like bringing in porno magazines and all kinds of other contraband stuff. But now they want to limit the goodies to only the usual top diplomatic immunity suspects."

Mark covered his mouth and giggled. Bobby reluctantly gave up the stage and the graduation ceremony continued. Soon enough, they were standing with their hands raised in the air, pledging to protect and defend the constitution of the United States and so forth and so on. Then it was over. The new volunteers swirled around in the foyer for a few minutes, hugging and congratulating each other, and getting a final taste of champagne. Vachio, checking around, was surprised at some of the people who weren't going to the graduation party at El Chibcha. They were only going to get about forty of the more than sixty volunteers, barely enough to cover the minimum deal Bobby and Janie had worked out with the place.

Vachio got in a cab with Percy Fong, Audry, and Candy and they settled in for the long ride downtown.

"Wasn't that cool how Bobby talked right up to the Ambassador about the diplomatic pouch?" exclaimed Candy, her eyes glowing with admiration. Vachio looked at her and chuckled to himself. Candy had a big-time crush on Bobby.

"Well, he spoke well," said Vachio. "But he didn't accomplish anything except to hassle the Ambassador a little.... And so what? He ain't gonna lose any sleep over it and we're not gonna get to use the diplomatic pouch for books."

"Yeah, who cares? How many people are going to use that pouch anyway?" said Audry.

Percy had his hands folded on his lap, looking serene and zen-like in the back seat seated between the two women.

"Well, I thought it was real cool!" said Candy, her freckle speckled face reddening. "At least he had the nerve to speak up and say something about it."

"Yeah, he did that," said Vachio.

The new volunteers told the driver to let them out of the cab at a liquor store a few blocks from El Chibcha. They each bought a bottle of their favorite beverage and hid them in book bags and oversized purses. Then it was on to El Chibcha.

The front of the restaurant, a fairly recent addition to the establishment, was ultra modern with white walls and track lighting, adorned with imitation mystic symbols and religious icons of Los Chibchas, the long-time and now vanished former rulers of *La Sabana de Bogotá.* Mixed in between the Chibcha artifacts were modern art paintings, for sale, done by some artistic acquaintance of the owners. Long tables, arranged in parallel rows, were set up all the way to the division between the new front of the restaurant and the dark cavernous back room. Janie sat near the front door, collecting money from those who hadn't already paid. Vachio looked at her and shook his head.

"Don't tell me they have us seated here in the front of the restaurant," Vachio said.

"Yes, they do. What's wrong with that?"

"Ah, man, the back is the room with all the character. And that's where the band is. How are we gonna hear anything?"

"The owner says we can hear fine from here. And there wasn't enough room for all of us in the back."

"How's that? The back room has more space than the front."

"Yes, Gary, but this is a popular place. People make reservations way in advance."

"Meaning, we don't get any priority even with a group this large. Right?"

"Come on, man, don't give me all these negative waves. It's gonna be great. You'll see. You just need to get into it with a positive frame of mind."

"Yeah, all right."

Janie turned to collect money from Candy and Vachio walked away already feeling suspicious about the place. Bobby had told him their group was to be seated in the old room near the live band. This was not a good start. Vachio settled into a seat as close to the old room as he could and looked around. False pillars dividing the two rooms obstructed the view of the bandstand and the cleared area where the folkloric dance troupe was to perform.

"I don't like this," Vachio said to Audry, who had taken a seat just to his left. "We're not gonna be able to see anything from here."

"These pillars do get in the way, don't they?"

"Well, I just hope the food is good."

The food was mediocre. It was typical food, a thin barley soup, yucca, fried bananas, potatoes in a mild sauce, Spanish-style rice, and a small salad. For his main course, Vachio had *Sobrebarriga*, a cut of beef popular in Colombia, very tender, taken from the stomach area. The *Sobrebarriga* was the best part of the meal. The rest of the food was available at any dive restaurant for a fraction of the cost and about the same quality. Still, compared to the Sangria, the food was top-notch. The Sangria was served in beautifully decorated ceramic pitchers, Spanish colonial design, with convincing antique nicks and chips. But what came in it was some kind of watery punch with no kick or flavor. All the volunteers seated at Vachio's table complained about it.

After drinking the first pitcher, Vachio called the waiter over and said, "Now, *mano*, do you think on the second round we can get some wine put in this Sangria."

"Sir?"

"Speaking frankly, this Sangria tastes like Kool-Aid."

"That can't be, Señor. We have some of the best Sangria in Bogotá."

"Then Bogotá is hurting for Sangria. Believe me, I've drunk my share of Sangria. I used to work in a restaurant that served it. And one of our bartenders was a Spaniard. Here," Vachio proffered his cup to the waiter. "Try it for yourself."

A small grin tugged at the waiter's lips and he said, "I'll see what I can do about it."

The next pitcher was marginally better. At least Vachio could taste some wine this time. But it was still weak. He reached under the table and surreptitiously opened up the bottle of red wine he had brought in. It wasn't the right kind of wine for Sangria, but it would have to do. He poured half a cup of wine into his ceramic mug and mixed in the Sangria. Then he returned the bottle of wine to the book bag under the table.

"*Salud*!" he said to Audry. She had seen what he had done and quickly followed suit. Vachio turned around and looked at the volunteers behind him. Several had bottles they were pouring into their cups under the table. Others were making trips to the bathroom and going for walks around the block. The atmosphere soon became boisterous. Vachio chuckled to himself. Peace Corps volunteers have a good time even when they're getting ripped off, he thought.

Only about 15 minutes late, the band and *baile de folklore* began performing. As Vachio feared, the columns and people seated in front of them in the other room prevented the volunteers from seeing much more than an occasional flash of women wearing white voluminous dresses with red piping and men with cotton shirts open almost to the waist and blue and red kerchiefs around their necks. As for the music, the low sound of poorly amplified bambucos that could be heard was almost completely drowned out by the noise generated by the raucous volunteers. Some of the Colombians seated in the other room turned around to give them dirty looks and the waiters cautioned them to keep it down. Most of them were in no mind to cooperate. They had been promised better seats than this.

Bobby got up and tried to quiet people down a little. Vachio noticed he looked very loaded. Everyone nodded at his admonitions and then ignored him. Bobby and a few other volunteers took up stations at the junction between the two rooms to get a better view for themselves, blocking what little line of sight had been open to the others. At this point hardly anyone cared. They all realized they had been taken. Muttered complaints and sarcastic conversations rippled along the tables.

Bottles were brought out and consumed with reckless abandon. The show went on, the music tinkling in the background.

"I knew we should have had this party at the training center," said Audry. "This is a total rip-off." She was drinking rapidly now, and she had that deer-in-the-headlights look.

"Well, it's too late now," said Vachio. "Might as well make the best of things." He poured more wine into his glass and passed the bottle over to Audry.

"*Vivá El Chibcha*!" said Vachio.

"*Carajo*!" said Audry, echoing the epitaph many Colombians responded when the name of El Presidente Turbay was mentioned after a *Vivá*! Audry poured some more wine and, in an act of defiance, left the bottle on the table. Vachio looked at the bottle for a while, realizing it was probably a bad idea to leave it there in plain sight. But then again, he felt this haze settling over his brain and he really didn't care anymore. What the hell!

A short time later, Vachio got up and went to the front door to get a breath of fresh air. He noticed other bottles, some of them hard liquor, that had been smuggled in and left openly on the tables. Many of the volunteers were glaze-eyed and oblivious, laughing and chatting, some even crying as they began to feel maudlin about their last night together as a group. Vachio found himself hugged and kissed and slapped on the back by a few people he had barely spoken to during training. He suddenly burst into laughter. The whole crazy scene tickled his sense of the absurd.

The open bottles of smuggled-in liquor weren't mentioned until it was time to tote up the bill. Suddenly the waiter from Vachio's table appeared in front of him with one bottle of wine and another of Scotch.

"These bottles will have to be paid for. There is a corking fee."

"How much?" asked Vachio.

"800 pesos for the wine and 1600 for the Scotch."

Vachio almost choked on the water he was sipping. They didn't want a corking fee, they wanted what the restaurant charged on their list for the same liquor. Vachio shrugged and pointed toward the table near the door where Janie and Bobby sat. "Go talk to them. They're handling the money."

The waiter scurried off and Vachio laughed and said to Audry, "Maybe if we just ignore this it will go away."

Audry was too wasted to know what he was talking about. She turned from Vachio and hugged Candy. Vachio turned and saw a commotion at Bobby and Janie's table. Two waiters were there, and between them they had four smuggled bottles of booze they had confiscated from the volunteers. Janie, her face beet red, was talking and gesticulating for all she was worth. Bobby looked ashen. The two waiters listened and calmly pointed to the liquor menu. Vachio whistled. Now this was going to be a problem. Vachio drank more water and made a strong effort to clear his head.

The next thing he knew Bobby had come up alongside him and was demanding to know what he had done.

"What do you mean? What have I done?" said Vachio.

"You brought booze into the restaurant," said Bobby, almost spluttering. "And left it right on the table. Now they want to charge us thousands of pesos more."

"Hey, man, stop yelling at me. Lots of people smuggled booze in. And I saw about a half dozen bottles left right on tables. Don't try to scapegoat me. I wasn't even the one who left a bottle on the table."

"Yeah, but they found one of your bottles. Someone has to take responsibility for this."

"Yeah? Well, it ain't gonna be me."

"Who should it be, then?"

"How about you? You're the one who wanted to come to this rip-off place."

"Rip-off! This is a class place, man. That's why we have to pay this corking fee. They're right. We fucked up."

"Yeah? Well, they fucked up, too. They didn't give us our money's worth. Not even close."

"So what do you propose we do?"

"I say we pay them what we agreed and nothing more. Then we walk right out of here. What the hell do you think they're gonna do? Call the cops?"

Bobby was almost apoplectic. "We can't do that, man. This is a class place."

"Man, what have you been smoking? This is a clip joint. I say we tell them to go to hell."

Bobby's eyes rolled in his head and his lips clamped together, then he turned and stalked off to consult with Janie. Janie soon came over to talk to Vachio.

"I can't get anywhere with these guys," she told Vachio. "They insist on charging us the menu price of the liquor."

"Like I told Bobby, we can just walk out of here. I'm sure they won't do anything about it if we just pay the 20,000 pesos we agreed on—and throw in an extra tip."

"No. Most of these people are too chicken to do that. And I already asked the waiters if we could add on to the tip."

"Ask again."

Janie threw up her hands. "No, I'm sick and tired of this. You ask." Janie gave Vachio an angry look and returned to her table.

Vachio began to boil. These guys really are looking to put the blame on me for this, he thought. He turned and saw a good number of drunk and stoned volunteers eyeballing him. "Son-of-a-bitch," he muttered. "What happened to this Peace Corps solidarity I was hearing about a few minutes ago?" Vachio was tempted to get up and leave the restaurant. But he didn't.

Within minutes his waiter was back. "The Señora said I should talk to you about this most grave situation."

Despite his irritation, Vachio laughed at the waiter's choice of words. Before answering the waiter, Vachio swiveled in his chair and turned to Sean Miller. "Hey, Sean, we have a grave situation here. I think we need someone with a 2+ in Spanish to handle it. You want to help me out here?"

Sean laughed and made as though he were washing his hands of the problem. "You're on your own. But good luck."

Vachio turned back to the waiter, struck by a sudden inspiration. "I just want you to know," said Vachio, "I think you and the other waiters did a fine job tonight. You guys are very professional."

The waiter smiled. "Thank you."

"No, for nothing. Remember, I used to work in a restaurant, too. I only say something like that when I mean it. Now...excuse me, what's your name?"

"Antonio."

"Antonio. I'm Vachio. A pleasure." They shook hands and the waiter looked at Vachio with raised eyebrows. "Now, Antonio, first off, I admit to you that we were wrong to bring in the liquor. But you have to admit, the prices here are very high. Too high for most of us to afford a bottle here."

"I'm sorry, Señor Vachio. That may be so. But someone still has to pay for this liquor."

"Yes, yes. As I said, we messed up bringing it in here. It was a mistake. But..." Vachio paused for effect. "Just between two old restaurant workers like ourselves, it hurts me to tell you, the food we ate was very ordinary, we couldn't see or hear the show, and the Sangria was like water. I mean, we have some legitimate complaints here ourselves..."

The waiter nodded impassively.

"...Truthfully," continued Vachio, "the only thing good about this place tonight was your service. So maybe we can resolve this little situation some other way..."

"Like how?"

"Well, what's your tip on the total bill?"

"Eight percent."

"Eight percent! See, that's terrible. You guys are the most professional group here and you only get eight percent? That is management abuse. Why, in the United States, you'd get at least 15 percent in a place like this. Standard. Maybe more..."

The waiter was all ears.

"Anyway, we're all *gringos* here and we appreciate good service. I can speak for all of us when I say that we were going to sweeten the tip for you guys. You've earned it. But now... with this little situation we have. Well, after paying for these bottles, I don't think anyone is going to feel much like giving you guys anything extra.... So what happens? You do your job. And the owner and manager eat this free money and have a good time with it. And what do you guys get? Your standard eight percent. That's a shame. As usual, the rich get richer, eh..."

Antonio was silent. Vachio knew he had him hooked.

"Or...you guys can forget you ever saw these bottles and you can expect double your normal tip.... What do you say?"

"I think you are making very excellent sense, Señor Vachio. I'm going to speak to my companions about this right now."

Antonio talked to the other two waiters, pointing once or twice toward Vachio. After a minute or so, Antonio smiled and gave Vachio the thumbs up sign. Vachio grabbed his book bag, rose from his chair, and went over to talk to Janie.

"It's all set," he told her.

"What's all set?"

"The problem with the bottles. All we have to do is double their tip and get rid of these damn things before the manager sees them. Then we get out of here before they change their minds."

"Are you sure?"

"I said it's all set." Vachio pulled a 50 peso note out of his wallet. "I figure each person should throw in about 25 pesos more—but here's 50 from me because I know some of these people aren't gonna want to pay anything."

"Are you leaving now?"

"Yes. I need some air. See you around."

"Bye." Janie gave him a quick hug and peck on the cheek.

Vachio stomped outside and headed down the street. He was still upset by the way some of the volunteers had turned on him. Especially Bobby. About halfway down the block, Vachio heard a loud, "Hey, Señor!" He turned around and saw Percy Fong coming after him. Vachio stopped and waited for him.

"What's up? The party over?" Vachio asked him.

"Yeah. Janie gave us the word to get the hell out of there."

"But everything's cool? They took the extra tip money?"

"Yeah. But we figured it wasn't a good idea to hang around and let them change their minds.... What did you tell the waiter anyway?"

Vachio gave Percy a quick synopsis.

"That was smooth, Señor. Real smooth. But what gave you the idea?"

"I don't know. It just came to me.... I was thinking about this dinner I had with two ex-Peace Corps guys from one of the first groups in Colombia in the early 60s.... Anyway, these guys told me that when they first arrived in Bogotá most of the Colombians they met were accusing them of being C.I.A. and treating them rude. Then one day, a group of them went to see a bullfight and they got into an argument with some rich bitch who was blocking their view with her sun umbrella. So anyway, she calls security, and they get into a brawl with some cops...and according to them, were kicking some butt until they were overwhelmed by superior numbers. They got hauled off to the city jail and spent a night locked up before Peace Corps got them out. The next day, it was front page news in El Tiempo. And later that afternoon, one of the guys involved in the fight took a taxi and the driver started talking to him. When he found out this Peace Corps guy was one of the ones who had messed up some of the police, he shut the meter down and said, 'You don't pay in my taxi.' And then that night, this same guy goes to eat at a restaurant and he told the waiter he was one of the guys from the fight at the bullring. So this waiter says, 'This meal is on me. You don't pay at my table.' So thinking about that, I figured Colombian society hasn't changed that much in 15 years. And it was worth a try."

Percy nodded his head. Then he said, "But why did you take off? We were thinking of going somewhere else to party."

"Not me, man. Some of these people get too loaded and they blow it. I've had enough of this scene.... And I'm pissed about how some of the guys were blaming me for the bottles. That was chickenshit."

"Come on. man, don't be pissed. It's not worth the energy. And you've had too many good times with these guys for that.... Don't let this be the last thing you remember."

Vachio stopped and looked at Percy. "You're right, man. You're absolutely right. But I gotta get away right now and cool down. It's just time to move on."

BOOK III

QUIET DAYS IN GARROTERO

1

The cab pulled up to the front door and Vachio got out and pulled his seaman's chest and one leather bag out of the trunk. He paid the driver and knocked on the door, feeling the steamy heat of mid-morning, smelling the horse dung in the still air. Vachio had returned unannounced to Garrotero, two days ahead of schedule. The door swung open and Vachio was greeted by a young woman. She was short, stout, and very dark-skinned, with long straight glossy black hair tied up in a bun in the back.

"Who are you?" Vachio asked.

"I'm Marta. I work for Don Raimundo and Doña Renata.... Who are you?" Marta was missing one front molar, making her speech come out in a whistling lisp.

"I'm Vachio. Didn't Raimundo tell you I was coming?"

"Oh! You're the *gringo*... I mean, the American who is going to live with us."

"With us?"

"Yes. I live here now, also."

"Oh?" Vachio hefted his trunk and bag and stepped into the doorway. Marta slowly stepped out of the way. Suddenly a baby bawled out from somewhere in the rear of the house. Vachio set down his gear in the middle of the living room and looked at Marta. "Is that your baby?"

"My baby?" Marta giggled. "No. That's Don Raimundo's and Doña Renata's baby."

"What? That can't be. She wasn't even pregnant when I was here seven weeks ago."

Marta shrugged. "It's their baby. And I help take care of her."

Vachio shook his head. He had no idea he was joining a growing family when he agreed to stay with this couple. He needed to have a talk with them. Vachio picked up the chest and the bag and walked to the rear of the house to put them in his bedroom. Marta followed on his heels. Vachio opened the door to the bedroom and stopped in his tracks. The bed was covered with women's clothes and the room was still crowded with unpacked cases. There was nowhere to set his things and unpack.

"What the hell is this?" Vachio exclaimed in English.

"What did you say?"

"Are these your clothes?"

"Yes."

"Would you mind getting them off my bed?"

"Your bed? I sleep in here."

Vachio emitted a dry laugh. But he didn't find the situation humorous. "You mean we're sleeping in here together?"

"Certainly not," said Marta. "Don Raimundo said I could sleep in here on the nights I stay over. I have no idea where you're supposed to sleep."

"We'll see about this. Where are Raimundo and Renata right now?"

"Don Raimundo is in Medellín. Doña Renata is at the factory."

Vachio piled his chest and bag at the foot of the bed and stepped past Marta. "We'll see who's sleeping where," he called over his shoulder as he went out the front door. Marta stared after him, a stolid look on her round face, a hint of a smile tugging at her thick lips.

Vachio almost trotted over to the plastic factory, working up a quick sweat in the heat. He entered the open steel door, the sounds of clanging machinery and burnt plastic hitting him, and unceremoniously opened the office door and stepped inside.

"Vachio! What are you doing here?" Renata asked.

"I don't know. I thought I was supposed to live here."

"But we didn't expect you yet."

"Well, I like to surprise people.... But I find I'm the one who's surprised."

"What do you mean?"

Vachio told her the gist of his conversation with Marta.

"Relax, Vachio. Marta was just teasing you. She's going back to Barichara tonight. She's not going to live with us full time until we move into our bigger house."

"We're moving into a bigger house?"

"Yes. Next week. It's a wonderful old house—with two floors and a big interior patio. You'll even have your own toilet."

"Where is it?"

"Right across the street from Gustavo's house. Just a block from the *Casa de Menores*. It's perfect for you."

Vachio nodded his head, somewhat mollified. Then he remembered the baby he had heard crying. "Why didn't you guys tell me you had a baby?"

Renata smiled. "Because when you were here, we didn't. The adoption papers went through six months faster than we expected.... Thanks to Gustavo's help."

"Well, I'm happy for you. But I didn't exactly count on living with a little baby."

"What's the problem? Do you have something against babies?"

"No. But..."

"If you're concerned about the noise—don't be. Where we're going to live it won't matter. The place is huge. It was even used as a hotel at one time."

"All right." Vachio decided to keep the rest of his doubts to himself for the time being, but he wondered what else these Germans had failed to mention to him. "Where is Raimundo?"

"He's been in Medellín on business for the last three days. But he should be home early this evening." Renata shuffled through some folders in front of her. "Now, Vachio, I don't mean to be rude. But I have work to do." As if to punctuate her remark, the phone rang and Vachio found himself ignored.

Vachio got up and slipped out of the factory. He had plenty to talk over with Raimundo, that was for sure. Vachio decided to pay a visit to the *Casa de Menores* and see what was going on there.

No one was stationed at the front door of the *Casa de Menores* and the place was very quiet. He entered the outer office and saw Julia, alone, pecking away at her typewriter.

"Hello, Julia! How are you?"

Julia looked up and gave Vachio a warm smile of welcome. "I'm fine. And you?"

After the usual series of salutations, Vachio asked, "Is Gustavo around?"

"No, he's in Bucaramanga today. He won't come into the office until Monday. In fact, none of the functionaries are here. They all start working on the fifteenth."

"So who's taking care of the boys?"

"The guards and the kitchen staff work their regular shifts. And I keep track of the office. But that's about it. Everyone else is off for the Christmas break." Julia smiled. "It would be better if you returned on Monday."

"Yeah, maybe so."

"Would you like a coffee?"

"All right."

"I'll get it." Julia rose from her chair. "I'll be right back."

"No. Don't bother. I thought you had it here."

"It's no bother. I can use a break. Wait a moment."

While Julia was away, Vachio went to the barred gate and looked down into the patio. Most of the boys were lounging under the awnings, staying out of the hot sun as they waited for the bell for lunch. Vachio scanned the faces and noticed a number of new boys. A large number. Huh. Vachio twisted to see through the metal grillwork and saw that Oliva was the duty guard.

"Hey! Maestro Oliva! How goes it?"

"Vachio! You're back." Oliva rose from his stool.

"No, man, that's all right. I'm not coming in. I just want to ask you something."

"Say it," said Oliva, resuming his seat.

"How many boys are there here now? It seems to me there are more than when I was here before."

Oliva laughed. "There are more. We have 120 students."

"One hundred twenty! That's double the number.... What happened?"

"What else? The President of the Republic made a visit to Bucaramanga so they cleaned up the streets for him. They rounded up all the *gamines* they could catch and dumped them on us. The *pingos*!"

"Shit!" Vachio felt dizzy thinking about it. One hundred twenty boys, bursting with energy, hormones, and repressed frustrations. How was he going to handle this? Sixty would have been tough enough to start. Nothing but surprises so far. Most of them unpleasant. The honeymoon is definitely over, Vachio thought.

Vachio excused himself before he was spotted by one of the boys and returned to the office. He drank his *tinto* and talked to Julia. As on his site visit, she was pleasant and vague, the perfect secretary for Don Gustavo. Vachio soon left her to her work and returned to the house to set his things in some kind of order within the cluttered bedroom.

Marta had removed her clothes from the bed and Vachio laid his stuff out. He shifted a number of boxes to a far corner of the room and piled them one on top of the other. Sweat started to pour down his face. It was an exceptionally hot sultry day, the air stifling in the room. Vachio turned on the overhead fan, put on a pair of jogging shorts, and took off his shirt. Then he mopped his face with a towel dipped in cold water.

"Ah, the hell with this now," he muttered. "It's too hot." He pushed his clothes to one side of the double bed and flopped down onto the firm mattress. Marta entered the adjacent patio, wearing only a white slip, and set to work on a pile of clothes on the wash basin. She turned on a portable radio and hummed along to the *Cumbia* and *Vallenato* music as her thick arms methodically worked the clothes over an old-fashioned washboard. Her humming was slightly off key but somehow pleasant. Vachio watched her through the cracked louver blinds and fell into the rhythm of her pumping arms. He was deliciously tired. Four days of running around with Sean and Nancy in the heat of Cali, and another four days of running around and dealing with problems in Bogotá. Vachio didn't even want to think about that place for a while. It had ended badly for Vachio at Doña Pilar's house. Someone, probably one of Alfredo's college friends, had stolen a ring from Vachio's room. And Doña Pilar had charged him regular room and board while he was away in Cali just for leaving his luggage in her house. He had argued with her, then paid her off and taken his luggage and himself to a pensión for the remainder of his stay in Bogotá. The old lady will never get another penny from me. Yeah, what goes around comes around, he thought, feeling the noon heat embrace him like a warm soft blanket. Marta's humming was fading into his subconscious. Most people take *siestas* at this time in Garrotero, Vachio thought. It's time for me to do the same.... Yeah, I really like this custom...

Late in the afternoon, Raimundo returned from his trip to Medellín loaded down with an armload of packages and bags full of goodies.

"Hey, how's it going, man?" Vachio said, quickly getting off the couch to help him with the packages.

"*Hola!*... You came early."

Vachio was taken aback by Raimundo's less than enthusiastic greeting and by his appearance. Though he was dressed in a suit, he looked disheveled and preoccupied.

"How was your trip?" Vachio asked.

"Fine, fine. Medellín is always nice..." Raimundo dumped the packages in the kitchen and went into the bedroom to change his clothes.

"When you're done in there, can we talk about some things?" Vachio called into him.

"It's not a good time right now. I need to get right over to the factory and see how things are going."

"Yeah, but...this will only take a minute."

Raimundo ignored him. Then he charged out of the bedroom, dressed in his coveralls and a work shirt, and headed for the door. "We'll talk tonight," said Raimundo. "Marta!"

Marta came out of the back and Raimundo spent several minutes talking to her. Vachio looked on from the back of the room in hurt surprise. Then he shook his head, beginning to feel angry, and retreated to the bedroom. He opened up a book, but he couldn't concentrate and the sentences blurred. "What the hell is going on here?" he muttered.

Vachio stayed holed-up in the bedroom, feeling too sluggish to leave the house, until Renata returned in the early evening. Vachio burst out of the bedroom and cut her off in the living room. He was determined to have his questions answered concerning his living situation.

"Can we talk for a few minutes?" he asked her.

"In a little while, Vachio. I need to look after the baby right now and change my clothes."

"But..."

Renata stepped past him and went into her bedroom. A few minutes later Renata, accompanied by Marta bearing a white swathed bundle, came into the patio. They stood in a sun-lit patch and with inclined heads cooed and gibbered nonsense talk to a softly whimpering baby. Marta handed the bundle over to Renata and she stepped toward Vachio and said, "Come and see the baby."

Vachio sighed and came over. He wasn't one to get gooey and drool over infants. He liked children, but he preferred them at a more developed stage.

"Isn't she beautiful?" said Renata, turning to show Vachio the baby, her eyes glowing with a warm soft light.

Vachio had to admit, after taking a close look, the baby was pretty.

She had sparkling brown eyes, a smooth creamy complexion, and regular features. "Yes, she is beautiful," said Vachio, rubbing her downy cheek with his index finger. "What's her name?"

"Sylvia.... Sylvia Marie."

"That's a pretty name." Vachio now had Renata's attention. "Now, I wonder if..."

Sylvia let out a gurgling fart, cutting Vachio off in mid sentence, and the women laughed and exchanged looks.

"Let me take her, Doña Renata," said Marta. "She's gone *popo*."

"Ay, my little *Stink Hund*," said Renata in Spanish-German. "Now we have to clean you up."

Vachio stood back in frustration as the women took the baby into the bedroom to change her diaper and examine her *popo*. Then they would spend some more time warming up a bottle to feed the little "*Stink Hund*" some more ammunition.

"Ah, the hell with it!" muttered Vachio. He flipped on the stereo and played Aqualung at medium volume. A few minutes later Renata came out of the bedroom and admonished him to lower the sound. Vachio shook his head and complied. Little by little his questions were being answered. It was already plain that day to day living was going to be much different than what Vachio had been led to believe at the dinner during his site visit. This was not what I bargained for, he thought. What the hell kind of freewheeling Bohemian lifestyle is this?

Vachio sat tense and stiff in the corner lounge chair waiting for Raimundo to come home from work. As the time passed, he grew hungry. He hadn't eaten since early morning, scrambled eggs and coffee at the airport. He went into the kitchen to look for a snack.

"Wait until Raimundo comes home," Renata said. "Then we'll eat the gourmet food he brought from Medellín."

"And what time will that be?"

"He called a little while ago and said soon. Very soon."

"Soon?"

"Yes, soon."

"Huh. Maybe I'll go out and get something. I'm very hungry."

"Aye, Vachio. Don't be so impatient. Here." Renata handed Vachio a tasteless white bread roll and told him to help himself to the orange maramalade.

Vachio inhaled the roll in two gulps, it only whetted his appetite, and resumed his seat on the lounge chair. Now his thoughts turned resentful and paranoid. So, I have to wait for the Lord and Master of the house to arrive before I can eat, eh. Well, maybe tonight. But not in the future. There is no way I'm going to put up with another situation like I had at Doña Pilar's. And no reason I have to now that I'm drawing my salary.

By the time Raimundo came home, greasy from working on the machines, it was almost 8:00 and Vachio was entertaining thoughts of staying with these Germans only long enough to find his own place. After a long chat with Renata and a change into shorts and a T-shirt, Raimundo came into the living room and handed Vachio a beer.

"What's the matter with you?" Raimundo asked Vachio in a bluff tone. "You look like your best friend died or something."

"No, nothing like that. But I do expect my friends to tell me what's going on.... Especially when I'm going to live with them."

"What do you mean by that?"

"What I mean is—why didn't you guys tell me you were going to adopt a baby and have a live-in maid?"

"Oh, is that all." Raimundo snorted. "It's no problem. We're going to move into a bigger place."

"Yeah, that's another thing. Why didn't you tell me you guys are going to move? You had my address and number in Bogotá. All it would have taken was one card or one phone call. Nothing more."

"Ah, what's the big deal? Things got hectic around here. None of that is important, you're going to love the new house."

"Yeah? If I decide to move in with you."

"What idiocies are you saying?" said Raimundo, his eyes widening. "What about us? We couldn't even be sure you were going to come back here."

"I would have told you if I wasn't. That's how I am."

"Ay, man, forget all that nonsense. You're here and everything is going to be fine.... *Salud!*" Raimundo reached out to click his bottle with Vachio. Grudgingly Vachio did the same. They both took a long drink of beer.

Then Vachio wiped his lips and said, "I just want to make one thing clear. I'm not a demanding person. But if you guys are going to do things that affect me, I want to know about it beforehand. If not, I'd just as soon find my own place and live on my own. All right?"

"Sure, sure. Don't worry about it."

"I don't mean to sound hard, and I'm not saying that you guys are like them, but I don't want any more shit like I had with that family in Bogotá I told you about.... If things are going to be like that, I'd rather live alone."

"Yeah, yeah man, you already said that. Calm yourself. Don't be paranoid."

"I'm not paranoid. I'm just letting you know how I feel right now. I'm not going to be played with again."

Raimundo, looking irritated, put on a record and blasted the sound. Vachio watched him with narrowed eyes, knowing Raimundo still didn't get the point.

Renata called them and they sat down to eat. A picnic style repast was spread out on the table. Thick black slices of pumpernickel bread, cream cheese, sweet butter, pickled herring, thin slices of Danish ham and Cotto salami, Spanish pimiento olives, a fresh tossed green salad, and a cold crisp bottle of Rhine wine. As they picked at the food and sipped the wine, Raimundo grew jovial and Vachio shoved his concerns aside. Raimundo told earthy jokes, raucous laughter erupted in waves, and after eating, Renata brought out Sylvia Marie to feed and share in the conviviality.

"Man, you know, there is nothing I like better than sharing good food and drink with friends," said Raimundo, popping an olive into his mouth, his walrus mustache tips drooping to his lips. "This is the life. *Salud!*" He drained his glass of wine and poured out some more.

"Maybe you guys should have opened up a restaurant," said Vachio.

Renata and Raimundo turned sharp eyes on him.

"What? What did I say?"

"We had a restaurant," said Renata. "In Bogotá."

"Oh yeah? What happened?"

"It was a good restaurant. In the Chicó," said Raimundo. "We had continental cuisine and a nice wine list. But it failed..."

"Why?"

"Our biggest mistake was hiring too many friends," said Renata. "They took advantage of us. Some of them started taking quantities of food home and feeding their friends for free.... You can't have a successful business that way."

"No. That's for sure," said Vachio.

"But anyway, we learned our lesson," said Raimundo. "From now on we get other people to share the risks with us and we keep our friendships separate from business."

Renata and Raimundo were both looking at Vachio.

"That makes sense," he said. And now we're even, he thought.

"Speaking of which," said Renata. "If you have the money with you, we would like the rent."

"Oh, sure." Vachio took out his wallet and peeled off ten 200 peso notes. "2000, right?"

"Right," said Renata, scooping up the bills. "And how about another $1000 a month for meals?"

"I don't know..."

Raimundo took a sip of wine and noisily cleared his throat. "What do you mean, you don't know? Believe me, there is no where else in this town you can find food like this."

"Yeah, but how often do you go to Bogotá and Medellín to get it?"

"About twice a month."

"Twice a month. See! You only brought back enough food this time for a few meals.... And I don't care if I eat food like this anyway. The regular food here is good."

"You'll get plenty tired of fried yucca, potatoes, and rice after a while," sneered Raimundo.

"Come on, man, I didn't just get off the boat. I've been here almost three months. I know what's available to eat. And besides, I don't keep a regular schedule. I eat when I'm hungry."

"So do we," broke in Renata. "Because of the factory."

"Yeah, that's my point. Maybe we won't want to eat at the same times.... Like tonight."

"Look, Vachio, why don't we try it for a month and see how things go?" suggested Renata.

"Well..." Vachio looked at them. Maybe they were pressed for money. "All right. For one month."

They drank more wine and Raimundo broke out another bottle. Then came a knock on the door. It was Gustavo.

"Don Gustavo," boomed Raimundo. "Join us and sample some of this, ugh, fine German wine."

Gustavo came to the table and warmly shook Vachio's hand. "Julia informed me that you were in town already. Welcome back to The Capital of the World."

"Thank you."

"I only have one question for you."

"Yes."

"Are you ready to begin work?"

"I'm ready."

"Good."

Gustavo sat down and Raimundo started to fill a tall glass of wine for him.

"No, no, Raimundo. Not so much. Just a taste for me."

"Aye, Don Gustavo. Relax. Don't tell me you have something against German grapes."

"Is it sweet?" Gustavo asked.

"A little. Try it."

Gustavo took a sip and then agreed to accept half a glass. After a few more sips he and Raimundo were in earnest conversation.

"I tell you, Raimundo, I'm about ready to launch my campaign against those degenerates in the *Casa de Menores*. Their time has come."

"What are you planning to do?" Raimundo asked him.

"I can't reveal exactly what I plan. But believe me, this time those degenerates are in for a big surprise. Bogotá will have to pay attention to the situation," Gustavo chortled. "Something will be happening in a couple of weeks. A month at the latest. You can count on it."

Gustavo drained his glass. When Raimundo tried to refill it, Gustavo laughed and moved it to the other side of the table.

"I have some other things to do tonight," said Gustavo, rising from the table. "We'll talk more soon."

"As you say," said Raimundo, looking disappointed.

Gustavo turned to Vachio. "You begin work on Monday. Come by the *Casa de Menores* around 10. I'll be in my office catching up on some paper work. We can take some time and I'll show you what equipment we have and the room I had in mind for your office."

"That's fine with me," said Vachio.

"Good. Until Monday, then." Gustavo turned to Raimundo. "Don Raimundo, I now adjourn this session."

Raimundo made a mock bow. "Don Gustavo, I'm always at your disposition to talk over any plot."

After Gustavo left, Vachio drummed pensively on the glass table top. "What the hell is he up to?" he asked Raimundo.

Raimundo laughed. "His great plan to get rid of the guards he doesn't want."

"How many guards does he want to get rid of?"

"He'd like to get rid of around half of them. But he'll be happy if he can dump the worst 25 percent."

"Oh, that's just great."

"What do you care? It doesn't affect you."

"It doesn't affect me?" Vachio snorted. "I'm supposed to work closer with the guards than with anyone else. How am I supposed to gain their cooperation in the middle of a civil war?"

"Ah, it doesn't concern you. You're just here for a while. Don't forget that."

"Yeah, just a while. Just two years."

"Forget about it, man. Your main concern is to entertain the kids. Remember that and everything else will be fine."

Vachio sipped the dregs of his wine and stared off into space. Sure, it's no problem for Raimundo, he thought. He can sit back and laugh at whatever happens. Garrotero *folclórico*. But I'll be right in the middle of it.

Raimundo corked the bottle of wine and went to put it in the refrigerator. When he returned he emitted a big yawn and said, "Well, I'm all done in from my trip and from that repair job I had to do this evening."

"Really? I'm full of energy after that nice long *siesta* I took this afternoon. I'm ready to stay up all night and sing Beatles' songs with you."

"No, not tonight. But you can watch television and listen to the stereo if you like."

"Sounds exciting. Henry Miller would be proud of you."

Raimundo gave Vachio a dirty look and said, "When I have to work, I have to work."

"Are you working tomorrow as well."

"Yes. We have a rush order to get out and one of our machines was idled while I was away. We need to catch up."

"You need to catch up."

"Good night," said Raimundo.

"Yeah, good night."

"Are you going to watch television?"

"I might. I don't know yet."

"Well, if you do, keep the sound low. Renata needs her sleep. She's pregnant."

"What?"

Raimundo turned and shuffled off to his bedroom.

2

Vachio arrived at Gustavo's office in the *Casa de Menores* at 10 sharp on Monday. Gustavo looked up at him with a bright smile and said, "Well, you are very prompt. That's definitely a good habit you North Americans have. Something we Colombians need to improve."

Vachio shrugged. "Many North Americans are not prompt. I'm sure there are quite a few Colombians who are."

Gustavo laughed. "Well, there are a few. Unfortunately, I must confess, I'm not always one of them..."

Vachio waited.

"I'm afraid I've called you over here for 10 o'clock and I can't give you my full attention as yet. I'm waiting for a very important phone call from Bogotá. Forgive me. If you'd like to come back in an hour or so, I should then be at your total disposition."

"That's all right. I'll just go to the patio until you're ready. That's where we need to do our business anyway.... Right?"

"Right. That will be fine."

"Oh, but I did want to tell you one thing," said Vachio.

"Say it."

"When I went to the Czech Embassy in Bogotá and showed them the picture of your projector here..."

"Yes."

"The guy laughed and said it would be easier to request a new one than to find spare parts for the old one. Then he told me it might be worth our while to sell it to a museum to raise the money for the new one."

To Vachio's surprise, Gustavo failed to laugh at this anecdote. "Did he say that? Well, he was probably just pulling your leg because you're from the United States and he's a Communist from the East Block."

"I didn't get that impression. I think it was good advice."

"Now Vachio, don't give up so easily. I'm sure, with patience, we can find a technician to fix our machine. We Colombians are very good at cannibalizing replacement parts."

"All right. But how do I get a movie program going in the meantime?"

"Well, you could go to the Colombo-Americano language school in Bucaramanga and see what they can do for you. They lend us movies once in a while. And since they're your *paisanos*, maybe they can offer you something."

"Yeah, maybe. That's a good idea."

"Fine. Meanwhile, I'll look into getting our machine fixed. ... It was an excellent projector. It gave us years of good service."

Vachio nodded and left Gustavo's office for the interior patio. Jaime Galindo, Boss of the Guard's Union, was the first man to greet him and let him through the gate.

"Well, well, Meester Vachio is back with us," he said, shaking Vachio's hand. "What's the word from the capital?"

"Bogotá is still Bogotá," said Vachio.

A shout went out from one of the boys sitting on the terrace and the inmates started assembling from all points of the patio. Vachio felt his blood tingle and quick nervousness course through his body as his name was called and a mob of boys surged to the foot of the steps.

"Stay below," barked the guard Torres, thumping his *garrote* against his thigh. Galindo, smiling easily, his gold eye tooth glinting, plied Vachio with questions. Vachio distractedly answered, looking past him to the mob of eager faces waiting for him below.

Torres turned from the boys and shook Vachio's hand with calculated strength. "So, Don Vachio, did you bring us those pornographic magazines? The Swedish ones?"

Vachio looked at him blankly.

"Don't you remember, Vachio?" prompted Galindo. "We asked you to pick up a few Swedish stripper magazines in Bogotá for us. The kind we can't buy here."

"Oh, yeah," said Vachio. Now he remembered. Galindo and Torres had asked him to buy some magazines for them on the last day of his site visit. Vachio had promised them nothing, and never seriously intended to buy them. "Well, I'm afraid I don't have any."

"Why not?" demanded Torres.

"I never saw any."

"They aren't that hard to find," said Galindo. "If you look."

"Bogotá is a big place. Maybe I wasn't in the right part of town."

Galindo and Torres exchanged looks. Vachio excused himself and eased past them to go down into the patio. He was greeted halfway down the stairs by Rolo, Leal, Amarocho, and Caballero. They hurled questions at him, echoed by a chorus of piping voices behind them: "Did you bring us new recreation equipment? Did you bring us movies about *pistoleros* and killers? What have you brought us?"

Vachio held up his arms. "Right now I don't have anything for you. Man, I just got here. Give me a chance to..."

"You should have got some stuff in Bogotá," said a tall skinny kid Vachio didn't know. "They have more of everything there and you can buy things cheaper."

"Yeah, that's certain! That's certain!" came the chorus.

Vachio whistled under his breath and grinned. He couldn't argue with this logic. They were right. But how was he supposed to explain to them about budgets and chain of command when he had been promoted to them as some sort of *gringo* Santa Claus? Vachio glanced behind him. Galindo and Torres were watching with amused smiles.

"Look, guys, I can't do anything about new equipment right now. But very soon..." Whistles and shouts of derision came from most of the boys and a few of them even threw up their arms and walked away. "Very soon We, and I emphasize We, should have some things for you. Now, for the moment, what exactly do we need here?"

The boys laughed. "Better you ask us what we have. That'll be faster than asking us what we need," said Leal.

"Well?"

The same old basketball from his site visit, the black bladder bulging farther out of the torn orange rubber, and one battered micro-soccer ball were tossed up to Vachio.

"Wasn't there another soccer ball?" Vachio asked.

"There was," said Rolo. "But they don't last very long when you use them constantly."

"All right," said Vachio. That was simple enough, he thought. My inventory of the recreation equipment is finished.

Vachio came down the steps and into the midst of the boys. Little Abel tugged at his arm and screamed, "Make me fly! Make me fly!" Other smaller boys took up the refrain.

Vachio, surrounded by sweating shouting boys, touching him, yammering for his attention, began to feel dazed and claustrophobic. "All right, all right! Step back!" he yelled. The boys stumbled back, startled by his booming voice. Vachio reached down, grasped Little Abel under the arm pits, and picked him up. Vachio shifted all his weight to his legs and thrust skyward, shooting Little Abel a good six or seven feet into the air. He caught him coming down and set him on his feet.

Little Abel jumped up and down, wide-eyed, exhilarated. "Do it again! Do it again! Make me fly." Other small boys called to Vachio to do it to them. Vachio laughed. This is something I don't need equipment for, he thought.

"You're pretty strong, Profé Vachio," said the tall skinny kid. "But we have a boy here who is stronger than you."

Vachio looked at the kid's young con man's face. "So? No one said I was the strongest man on earth. Least of all me.... And who are you?"

"They call me Barranca. And I say you're not even the strongest in the patio."

"Good for you. What do you want? A medal? A kiss?"

Some of the boys laughed and snapped their hands. Barranca was flustered for a moment but he regained his composure. He turned to one of the younger boys and said, "Go get Coco."

A few seconds later a tall, thick-chested black kid emerged from the rear of the pack and was ushered toward Vachio. He ducked his head shyly and mumbled a greeting, obviously uncomfortable as the center of attention. Vachio shook his hand. It was rough and callused from wielding a machete.

"I didn't meet you the first time I was here," said Vachio. "When did you arrive?"

"A few weeks ago," he mumbled.

"Why are you called Coco?"

"Because I used to climb trees and cut down coconuts. I'm from a town near Barranquilla. On the coast."

"All right, all right," said Barranca, stepping between Vachio and Coco. "Now let's see which of you is stronger. I say Coco..." Barranca eyed some of the other older boys. Their eyes and fingers communicated wagers without words.

Vachio waited, amused, realizing these kids thought he had no clue.

"Now you guys grasp hands and squeeze until one of you gives up," said Barranca.

Vachio snorted. "You don't give orders to me, kid. Who do you think you are?"

Barranca had a crew of younger boys. At a sign from him, his little puppets whistled and chirped, "Vachio's afraid of Coco." Barranca stood with his arms folded. Then he motioned the boys to silence and said in a loud voice, "Are you afraid, Profé Vachio?"

"Go ahead, Vachio," said Rolo. "You can win. Coco is big but he's soft."

"You want to see how soft I am," said Coco, lazily raising a broad scratched fist and waving it in front of Rolo's face.

Rolo sneered at him.

"If Vachio is afraid, you guys can have a go at it," said Barranca.

Vachio laughed. "All right, guys. This one time we'll do something stupid like this."

Vachio stuck out his hand. Coco no longer looked shy. He was alert and intent. Vachio quickly grasped his hand by the knuckles and the end of the fingers and gave a short sharp squeeze. Coco yelped in pain and withdrew his hand. The contest was over in a couple of seconds.

"That wasn't fair," said Barranca. "You guys have to do it again."

Three boys who had won bets from him quickly disagreed and warned him of what would happen if he didn't pay up. Coco, still shaking his hand, didn't look eager for a rematch anyway. Vachio patted him on the shoulder and said, "Coco, there's only one thing to be learned from this. Don't listen to fool people who try to manipulate you into doing things for them."

Coco nodded and turned an ugly look on Barranca.

"What are you looking at, Coconut Head," snapped Barranca. "You cost me money you stupid fool."

With a grunt Coco started for him. Barranca turned tail and ran, his long skinny arms flapping, cursing over his shoulder as he went. Coco soon gave up the chase and lay down on one of the benches under the awnings.

"That Barranca is a *pingo*," said Rolo to Vachio. "Coco is very weak right now from an attack of amoebas. He never should have set up the match."

Vachio shook his head. Dealing with these kids is going to be like handling nitroglycerin, he thought.

A few minutes later, Gustavo descended the steps and watched in surprise as Vachio, surrounded by a group of laughing younger boys, hurled a screeching Little Abel high into the air.

Vachio set him down and breathing hard from his exertions, turned to Gustavo and asked, "Well, are you ready for me now?"

"Yes. But what exactly were you doing here?"

"Recreating with the kids. Establishing rapport."

"I see. You have some interesting methods."

"Yes. The latest in North American technology."

Some of the nearby kids snickered.

Gustavo reddened and serious eyes swept over the boys. They quieted down at once.

"I was just kidding," said Vachio, wiping at his face with his shirt.

"Of course," said Gustavo. Then he rattled a ring with dozens of keys looped around it. "Let me show you your office."

Vachio and a line of curious boys followed Gustavo to a broad high door on the right side of the patio yard. As Gustavo fumbled with the keys, trying to find the right one for the lock, Barranca came up alongside Vachio and said in a low confidential tone, "I just want to let you know, Profé Vachio, count on me to help you in any way you need. I aspire to be your number one assistant.... All right, meester," he finished in proud English.

"All right. I'll keep you in mind."

"Please. You don't know how bad some of these other kids are in here. But I can be trusted."

"Trusted to help yourself, no doubt."

"Ay, Profé Vachio. Do I seem that way?"

"No. You don't seem that way—you already showed me."

"Ay, man..." Barranca patted Vachio on the back.

Gustavo got the door unlocked and it creaked open on dry neglected hinges. Gustavo turned on the light and they entered a room about 15-by-15, with a high ceiling, open on the top sides and back at the junction of the metal roof to admit air, with two stout creosote soaked beams running across the top to help support the exterior awning. A tangled pile of old, mostly damaged school desks, chairs, plywood partitions, cardboard posters, and boxes of old school books and papers crowded the floor.

Almost upon stepping into the room, Vachio's eyes started to water and he sneezed. The concrete floor and the junk was covered by a film of dust, wood shavings, and pellet-like excrement. Vachio looked up and saw a half dozen little bats folded up in their wings hanging from the beam in the darkest corner of the ceiling.

"So what do you think of this space for your office and supply room?" Gustavo asked him.

"I think it will be fine.... Once we get all this trash out of here and clean it up." Vachio sneezed and rubbed at his watering eyes. He wondered why this hadn't already been done.

"We also have a ping pong table in here," said Gustavo, moving some posters out of the way and raising a small dust cloud. "See?"

Vachio came closer and looked it over. It was scarred but serviceable. "I see. But why isn't it being used already?"

"No interest by staff," said Gustavo matter-of-factly.

"And no ping pong balls," added Barranca. "But we do have two paddles."

"Where?" asked Gustavo.

"In the carpentry work shop, Don Gustavo."

They moved back outside and Vachio sneezed violently and spat out dusty saliva.

"Are you all right?" Gustavo asked him.

"Yes. But I think I'm allergic to bat shit."

The nearby boys tittered.

"We'll need to do something about those bats," continued Vachio.

Gustavo shrugged. "Most of them will leave once you get activity going in that room. But you'll always have one or two coming and going."

"All right. I suppose I can live with them if they can live with me. But when can we have that room cleaned out?"

"This week. I just need to speak to Maestro Ordoñez concerning where to store what we have in there. Some of the things, especially some of those desks, will be repaired and used in the future."

Vachio nodded.

"Any other questions about the room?"

"Not for the moment."

"Good."

"But I do have a few questions about other things."

Gustavo consulted his watch. "Very well. I have some time before I need to go to Bucaramanga. Let's go to the cafeteria and get something to drink."

The bell clanged to call the boys back to classes and shops. As Vachio followed Gustavo toward the terrace, a few of the boys ignored the bell and frisked along beside them, calling to Vachio to come back later and play. Gustavo shooed them away and gave Vachio a quick look.

On the terrace, Galindo smiled at Vachio and said, "Why don't you come back for the recreation period today. I'm off duty then. We can play a little soccer together."

"Yeah. Maybe."

"Good. Until later, then."

Vachio noticed Gustavo's jaw tighten after this exchange. He and Galindo had studiously ignored each other.

"So what do you want to know about?" Gustavo asked Vachio as they sipped guava juice under the cooling air of an overhead fan in the cafeteria.

"First, what can you tell me about that tall skinny kid called Barranca? He wasn't here on my site visit."

"No, he was away in Barrancabermeja living with his mother on a trial basis. It didn't work out. So he's back with us again."

"Again?"

"Yes, Barranca has been with us off and on for years. He's another of those thoroughly institutionalized boys."

"What kind of kid is he?"

"He's not a bad kid. At least not malicious like some of the others. He's bright and full of life. But he has his moody and temperamental moments." Gustavo was thoughtful for a moment. "His mother is a prostitute in Barranca and leads a chaotic life. He had a rough insecure childhood. At least here he has a routine and a program for himself."

"Can he be trusted?"

Gustavo chuckled. "Sure. Up to the point that it's to his advantage. He has good business instincts."

"Not today he didn't," muttered Vachio.

"What?"

"Nothing..."

"What else is on your mind?" asked Gustavo.

"Well, I have to admit, I'm a little concerned by how many boys are here now...120, right?" Vachio whistled through his teeth.

"Believe me, Vachio, you're no more concerned than I am. This number of boys crowds the classes and the shops. It also forces me to detail extra guards for certain events and strains the budget. It's difficult for all of us. You'll just have to do the best you can until I can make other arrangements.... Like we all will."

"What are you going to do?"

"Accelerate home releases. Shift some of the boys to other institutions where appropriate. The usual."

"How long will this take?"

"I've already begun. For me, the optimum level of students at this facility is 60. Up to 80 is manageable. At 120, which is the number we do have now, we're a warehouse. But I accepted the challenge because it was the holidays, classes were out, and I'm only a humble servant of the Colombian people and our distinguished president."

Vachio laughed.

"Just do your best, Señor Vachio. I don't expect miracles. At least not right away."

"All right, fair enough. But when can I get some recreation equipment? I did my inventory. We're down to almost nothing."

Gustavo finished his juice and stood up before answering, "Come to my office tomorrow morning.... No! Make that Wednesday morning and we'll see about getting you some equipment. Meanwhile, you should have plenty to do getting yourself and the boys organized. And now, you'll excuse me, I have an appointment."

3

Vachio's first week on the job at the *Casa de Menores* was an exercise in frustration. True, almost everyone on the staff wanted to welcome him, drink a *tinto* with him, ask his impressions of Colombia and the United States, talk politics, even tell him of business schemes they had in mind, but almost none of them could find the time to help him get his recreation program off the ground.

It started on Tuesday with Maestro Ordoñez, the man in charge of maintenance and facilities. Gustavo introduced Vachio to him by saying, "Here is the man who will get your office in order for you." Ordoñez warmly shook Vachio's hand and said, "At your order, Profé." But before Vachio could get him to the room to figure out where to store the old desks and the other junk, they were interrupted by a teacher who had a "small thing" for Ordoñez to fix. Ordoñez followed the teacher and didn't appear again until the afternoon. By the time Vachio cornered him, just before his recreation period was to start, Ordoñez slipped away on another errand and Vachio didn't see him for the rest of the day. This game of hide-and-seek went on for the rest of the week and by Friday, Vachio was no closer to getting the junk cleaned out of his office than he was on Monday. The only thing Vachio managed to accomplish was to pull the ping pong table out of the room and have it dispatched to one of the work shops for a fresh coat of green paint and to have a metal brace put on one of its legs. Raimundo bought some balls on a trip to Bucaramanga and the boys were able to play ping pong with their taped and patched paddles along with the version of paddle ball they were playing all along.

Then there was Doña Berta, the guardian of the supply shop. On Wednesday, Vachio went to her to requisition poster board and magic markers to make signs designating the groups, leaders, and scheduling of fields for the recreation period. Vachio picked up what he needed from the shelves and set it on her desk. Doña Berta passed him a requisition form and told him to fill it out. Vachio complied. Doña Berta picked up the form, studied it, looked at what he had put on her desk, and said, "Everything looks in order. But before I can release any supplies, I'll need this signed by Don Cabrera and countersigned by Don Gustavo."

"You're kidding me. Right?" Vachio asked.

"Not at all."

Vachio felt hostile vibes coming from her. This wasn't just a case of bureaucratic red tape. It was personal. His voice took on a hard edge. "Why are you giving me problems? Gustavo said I could get what I need—within reason. And the forms would go to him for signature later."

"No, Señor! That's not how it works. You must have misunderstood him."

"No. I don't believe so."

"Vachio, don't take this wrong, but your Spanish can stand some improvement."

"That's true. But I think WE understand each other very well. For some reason, and I don't know why, you don't like me. And you want to give me a problem."

"Not at all. This is standard procedure. For everyone."

"Really? Then how come Don Miguel just came through here and picked up some typing paper without even filling out a requisition?"

Doña Berta's face colored. "His requisition was filed previously."

"Really? Why don't we call him in here and ask."

"Are you questioning my word?" she flared.

"No. Only your memory."

Doña Berta thrust the paper toward Vachio. "Get out of my office. And don't come back until you have those signatures. Until then you get nothing."

"You know, you're not hurting me. You're only hurting the boys. The things are for them."

"Get out!" She followed Vachio to the door and slammed it after him.

Don Miguel popped out of the adjacent office and asked, "What was that all about?"

"I don't know. That woman has some problem with me."

"But why?"

"I don't know. She's got a bug up her ass."

"Ah, she's all right. It must be a misunderstanding."

Vachio was still boiling. His voice was low and jagged. "Miguel! When you picked up your paper, did you have to get your requisition signed and countersigned."

"No, of course not. But I'm head of my department."

"Well, so am I. Or at least I'm supposed to be."

"Correct. You're head of recreation."

"And I certainly didn't ask for anything unreasonable."

Miguel shrugged, smiled, and returned to his office. Vachio decided to play it Berta's way for the moment. He went to look for Cabrera to get his signature. Maria Elena informed Vachio that Cabrera had gone to visit relatives in another town and was out until the following Monday. Gustavo laughed about Berta's officiousness and signed the requisition. Then he left for a meeting in Bucaramanga. Vachio took the signed requisition back to Berta but she still refused to issue the supplies without Cabrera's signature.

"But Cabrera is gone until Monday," said Vachio. "And I have a couple of the boys ready to help me make the posters."

"That's not my problem. And we're short on some of the things you want." She sniffed. "I think educational concerns take precedence over a recreation program."

Vachio, now feeling only helpless disgust, turned on his heel and left the room. I'll have to talk with Gustavo about this later, he thought. Right now I can't get bogged down in her unprofessional bullshit.

But of all Vachio's problems that first week, his greatest was with Don Gustavo himself. Tuesday morning, bright and chipper, he went to Gustavo's office to see about the new recreation equipment. Julia greeted him with a bright smile, sat him on a comfortable chair, had a *tinto* brought to him, and said, "Don Gustavo is in a meeting right now. But he should be with you shortly."

Vachio drank his *tinto* and talked to Pacho and Julia. The morning sun rose and flooded the office. The time passed and Vachio began to fidget. After an hour he got out of his seat and paced the office. Julia looked at him with increasing irritation as he disturbed her work. "I suppose the meeting is taking longer than he expected." Julia tossed Vachio a sympathetic smile. "Why don't you come back in a while."

"No. He told me to come this morning. I'm here."

Julia shook her head and rose from her chair. "All right. Wait one moment." She went into Gustavo's office and held a brief conversation with him. Then she emerged from the office and said, "Don Gustavo begs your pardon. But he can't get away right now. He says to come back tomorrow afternoon. *Mañana por la tarde*."

For a moment Vachio was angry. "Why didn't he just tell me that when I got here instead of wasting my time?"

A pouting look came over Julia's face. "Is talking to us a waste of your time?"

"No. Well...ah, I didn't mean it that way."

"That's all right. I understand. But you have to understand, Don Gustavo is a very busy man. Many people want his attention."

"I do understand. But he told me to come this morning."

"Unexpected things happen around here all the time."

"No doubt.... Well, anyway, can you give him this requisition for the recreation equipment for me."

"Of course, Vachio. With the greatest pleasure. At your order always."

The next day, early afternoon, Vachio was back in the outer office. Julia greeted him with a bright smile and said, "Hi, Vachio. How goes it?"

"Everything is fine. How about you?"

"Fine."

"And Gustavo?"

"Gustavo? Oh, he's away in Bucaramanga for the rest of the day."

"Without me?"

Julia shrugged. "He has a SENA meeting today. He does every month."

"Then why did you guys tell me to come here this afternoon?"

"Well, I don't know why HE said that. The meeting must have slipped his mind. I recommend that you try again tomorrow afternoon. *Mañana por la tarde*."

"Yeah, *mañana por la tarde*," muttered Vachio, leaving the office. Slipped his mind. Yeah, right, thought Vachio. I doubt anything he's interested in slips his mind.

That night, after three or four beers, Raimundo confirmed Vachio's suspicions. "*Mañana por la tarde*!" Raimundo guffawed. He was in a good mood, relaxed and happy after getting out his rush order. "*Mañana por la tarde* is a polite way of telling you to—let me put this delicately in my Oxford English—to fuck off."

"Yeah, that's what I figured, too. But why? What's the point?"

"Well, recreation isn't exactly a high priority program. Remember, they've been getting along for more than a hundred years without an official recreation program."

"That's not what I mean. What I mean is, why is he bullshitting me? Why not just tell me to my face that he isn't going to give me the equipment right now?"

"Because my son, that would be the height of bureaucratic bad form. You're supposed to figure out these buzz phrases for yourself and understand which way the wind is blowing."

"That's bullshit! Like an adult talking to a child. I don't need that garbage. Tell me directly and let me know where I stand. Then I can look around to make my own arrangements."

"Well, that's an admirable attitude, Gary. But things just don't work that way here. Be patient. Don't rush it.... And besides, you never know about Gustavo, he could get a bug up his ass and decide that your recreation equipment is a priority. Then you'll be set."

"In other words, at his whim."

"Righto, mate. He is the skipper."

"Yeah, fine. But that's not what he told me on my site visit. He told me that there was 50,000 pesos in the recreation budget and that I would have access to it. Immediately."

"Gustavo has to say a lot of things to a lot of people to get done what he does."

"Great. Meanwhile, I have absolutely no credibility with the kids because of what he said to them about me. They're already beginning to think I'm a joke because I haven't delivered any equipment. And I never promised anything—Gustavo did."

"Ah, he's always making promises to those kids. He has to. But they don't take them that seriously."

"That's fine for him. But that's not my style. I don't make promises I can't deliver. And promises have been made in my name, without my permission, that make me dependent on other people to fulfill. That sucks, man. For real."

"Ay, man, don't take yourself so seriously. Nothing is going to rise or fall because of your individual efforts. They're never going to build a statue of you here in Garrotero."

"That's not the point. This isn't about me. This is about doing my job the best I can with these kids. And if I'm not allowed to, I can damn well look in other directions. And they can find themselves another clown." Vachio stared at the living room tiles, a set hard look on his face.

Raimundo guffawed, clapped Vachio on the shoulder, and poured out two shots of *aguardiente*. "This calls for stronger stuff," he announced, handing Vachio the glass. "*Salud*."

They downed their shots and Raimundo sat directly across from Vachio and looked right into his eyes. "Now listen, and this is between you and me. Gustavo trusts me and he has probably told me more about the *Casa de Menores* than even his sidekick Pacho knows." Raimundo paused for effect. Vachio doubted that Raimundo knew as much about the *Casa de Menores* as Pacho but he decided to keep quiet and listen. "The thing about the official budget he showed you on your visit, well, more than anything, it's an elaborate work of fiction. It's concocted in Bogotá by accountants with the best of intentions—that's certain. But along the way money gets diverted to other places, and some just mysteriously disappears into the pockets of God knows who. So, by the time money starts arriving at the *Casa de Menores*, the sum is not nearly what it was supposed to be. You dig?"

Vachio nodded.

"So Gustavo has priorities. Food, clothing, shelter, staff, health, education..." Raimundo shook his head. "I'm afraid recreation is well down the list. As it should be. And right now, he's especially upset, because the money for La Obra has been cut off. And that is his baby."

"Fine. I understand that. But you still don't get my point."

Raimundo threw up his hands. "What's your point?"

"That he tell me what to expect. I can work with no equipment at all, and do the best I can. But I can't work with the expectation of things and services that will never be provided. Do you dig?"

"Yeah, man, I dig. And that's why I've told you all this. Now you know."

"That's fine. But I don't work for you. I work for him. And if this is a pattern, well..." Vachio let his voice trail off. Then he said in English, "You said I have to see which way the wind is blowing. Well, I think I do. And I see it blowing smoke right up my ass."

Raimundo grabbed his guitar, strummed it, and sang, "Little Colette she has no sense, serving the breakfast without her pants.... Oh, quiet days in Garrotero."

As frustrating as things were that first week on the material side of getting the program up and running, it was almost equally frustrating on the human relations side. Vachio's efforts to enlist the guards as his helpers came to nothing.

That first week, much to Gustavo's and some of the other administrators disgust, Vachio made a point of eating lunch at the guard's table three of the five days. Monday through Thursday, he went to the *Casa de Menores* and hung out at the patio for a couple of hours each night, hoping to get to know the guards and the boys better without all the programs and distractions of the day. At the end of the week, Vachio had drawn some conclusions. As a group, the guards were taking a wait and see attitude with him. They were friendly enough, at least superficially, but wary and suspicious. Vachio couldn't blame them. He was well aware of Gustavo's determination to get rid of some of them. And for all the guards knew, Vachio was Gustavo's boy, sent to spy on them. When Vachio directly asked on-duty guards to come down into the patio and help him get the boys in order, he was politely informed that they had duties, such as covering key possible escape points, that precluded their help. Jaime Galindo was more blunt. "Vachio, you want our help. And yet, you couldn't even do us the favor of picking up a few Swedish magazines for us in Bogotá." Jaime finished by shaking his head and mournfully clicking his tongue. A few of the younger guards offered to help Vachio on their off-duty time, but this meant that they wanted to play soccer or basketball with him, not get involved in organizing and supervising the mass of boys for group activities.

On Thursday afternoon at the recreation period, Torres, the burly crew-cut sidekick of Galindo, decided to play basketball. Torres and Vachio were on opposing sides. Torres, much shorter than Vachio, tried to compensate by playing extra physically, bodying up on Vachio and throwing his weight around. It didn't help him much. He wasn't a very good player. Vachio had his way with him and all the boys saw this. Torres grew frustrated. Finally, Torres put up a shot and Vachio blocked it right back into his face. Some of the boys laughed openly.

Torres, furious, his face beet red, threw a deliberate elbow at Vachio as they went for a rebound under the basket.

"Hey, man! Watch that!" Vachio snapped at him.

Torres mumbled something about Vachio being a sissy. Then as Vachio dribbled the ball up the court, Torres followed on his heels, deliberately trying to trip him up and shoving him with his arm and elbow. Vachio passed the ball ahead and said to Torres in a low voice, "All right, man. You want to play this way. So can I. I warn you."

Torres, his face contorted in anger, said nothing. The ball came back to Vachio and he started to dribble toward the basket. Torres resumed his shoving and tripping defense. Vachio abruptly pulled up and did a spin dribble, his free arm swinging around and catching Torres dead on the chest. Torres flopped back and landed right on his ass. For a moment he was stunned. Then before he could think about what had occurred, Vachio offered him his hand and said, "Sorry about that. That's my foul. Here's the ball."

Torres ignored his hand. Vachio shrugged, dropped the ball next to him, and trotted to the other end of the court. Vachio had made his point. Torres knew what had happened was no accident. He stopped playing dirty and from then on, he treated Vachio with grudging respect. And Vachio knew the word would get to the other guards—don't try to physically intimidate the new recreation director. Not that this was necessary. They had much better ways to get to Vachio.

The second night Vachio went to the patio, he witnessed one of the guards beating three boys on the soles of their feet with his *garrote*. The guard, Ramon, the Che Guevara look-alike, was considered one of the more humanitarian guards in the *Casa de Menores* by Gustavo.

Vachio sidled over to the other guard, who was casually watching, and asked, "What did those boys do to deserve this?"

"They got caught molesting one of the younger boys."

Each boy received five whacks with the *garrote*. Then they were made to prop their feet onto a bench and hold their bodies up with their extended arms. Two of them were crying, the other bit his lip until it bled.

"Is this normal punishment?" Vachio asked.

"No. For what they did, they're getting off pretty easy." The guard laughed. "But we certainly have lighter punishments than this. It depends on the infraction."

Sobered, Vachio left the terrace and went down into the patio. The boys said nothing about the punishment to Vachio. They were stoic. It was just the way things were and completely routine. Vachio was experienced enough in juvenile work to know that such things, and worse, went on in most correctional institutions. And for that matter, Vachio had seen his share of corporal and mental punishments dished out in Catholic schools as a boy. This foot whacking was the worst thing Vachio witnessed in his first week at the *Casa de Menores*, but judging from the cuts and bruises he saw on some of the boys, it was pretty evident there were crueler things going on.

Still, all things considered, Vachio wasn't too disappointed by the attitude of the guards toward him. He hadn't expected much, and they were living up to his expectations. As long as they didn't actively try to hinder his work, Vachio felt he could live with them and do his job. Of more concern were certain administrators who had promised him help but had no intention of delivering on those promises.

Vachio's dealings with the boys were the most complex of all. For the first few days his entrance into the patio was hailed by many of the boys as though he were the second coming of the savior. This was heady stuff and massaged Vachio's ego, but the excitement generated also made it difficult for Vachio to get the boys to settle down and listen to his plans for an organized program. The idea was to divide them into units, each with its own leader responsible for organizing the day's activities, and to rotate them among the limited athletic courts, dividing what equipment and games were available. Vachio would then oversee the whole operation.

On paper the plan was excellent. In practice it was chaos. The boys, after joking and jiving with Vachio for a while, would then run amok. Vachio could always capture a core of kids to participate in a sport that he directly supervised, but that was about it. Vachio was working against nature. The recreation period was at the end of the day, right before dinner, and after going through lines and checks, classes and shops, regimentation from dawn to near dusk, most of the boys were in a mood to bust loose and go crazy. Some of the younger boys spent the whole hour racing from one end of the patio to the other, laughing and shouting, playing with the dogs, roughhousing with each other. Vachio could sympathize with this. The boys were blowing off steam and having a good time in their own way. To Vachio, that was the definition of Re-Creation. And besides, there wasn't enough equipment or facilities to keep all the boys occupied in an organized sport, game, or craft even if Vachio thought this desirable. But the administration, especially Señor Cabrera, didn't see things this way. He wanted the boys to remain automatons for the entire day, like soldiers practicing without weapons.

Another major problem with the master plan was in gaining the cooperation of the older boys. After a few days, and Vachio's failure to produce the promised new equipment, he saw the disillusionment in some of their eyes. On the third day, Amarocho, one of the most influential boys in the patio, threw his hands in the air and walked away in disdain as Vachio talked. Vachio knew what he and some of the others were thinking. Promises, promises, promises. He's no better than any of the other adults we've had in our lives. You can't trust him. Or anyone else.

This attitude generated another obstacle for Vachio. How to convince the boys to aid and abet the program for the sake of helping themselves. The patronage system was alive and thriving in the *Casa de Menores*. Very little was accomplished without applying the law of enlightened self-interest. Barranca put it succinctly to Vachio on his second day of work, "I'm ready to break my back for you, Profé. But couldn't you see fit to bring me a few cigarettes or candies for my efforts. Some of the guards know how to take care of us. How about you?"

"I'm not one of the guards, man. I have a different function here. I'm not your patron. This program is for you guys."

Barranca raised a skeptical eye at this. "Yeah, but it will make you look good if it works. Right?"

"Right. But why should I bribe you to make it work?"

"Because that's the way it is," said Barranca, shaking his head in disgust and walking away. Vachio shook his head as well. He knew Barranca's words echoed the feelings of most of the boys. Vachio quickly understood—identifying the natural leaders among the boys was easy, gaining their willing cooperation without sanctions or bribes was another matter.

Still, despite the ups and downs and the ingrained corruption, Vachio enjoyed working with the boys. At night, when all the functionaries were away, and if no mass punishments were in progress, such as making all the boys stand in military formation for an hour at a time, Vachio could go down into the patio in a relaxed frame of mind and just talk to the boys. He felt very gratified when Rolo came up to him and put his arm around his shoulder and said, "Vachio, I want to thank you for delivering that letter to my mother. She came here over Christmas and visited me. She said you're a good person and that I should listen to you."

"Will you do it?"

"Do what?" Rolo wrinkled his brow.

"Listen to me. And get some of the others to listen to me."

"Oh, I listen to you. But I can't make anyone else listen."

"Why not?"

"Why?" Rolo laughed. "Because most of them are *gamines*. They don't listen to anybody."

"They seem to listen to Cabrera, Don Gustavo, and the guards."

Rolo looked serious for a moment. "Well, we obey those guys. We have to you, you know. If not..." Rolo rolled his eyes. "But we don't always listen to them. You know what I mean?"

"Yeah, I know what you mean."

4

By Friday afternoon, Vachio had a new home in Garrotero. The two story residence, an old white stucco and adobe building, more than 150 years old, was located a block up the street from the *Casa de Menores* and directly across the street from Don Gustavo's home. Vachio got his first look at the place right after lunch. The entrance way was protected by massive, solid wood, green doors, designed in another era to withstand hostile entry, secured at night with a two by four anchored on solid steel bits that opened onto a hallway with another massive door at the end. Beyond the second door Vachio found a large inner patio, cemented over, with three bedrooms and a dining area spoking off the patio. Behind the dining area, through a narrow opening carved into the chalky walls was a large kitchen. Behind the kitchen was a smaller back patio with a tool shed, a sink and basin to wash clothes, and a fruit bearing mango tree. The floor space abutting the central courtyard and under the roof awnings, where most of a person's time was spent to take advantage of the open air and any stray breeze, was covered by worn and faded yellow and blue tiles. The second story had a small bedroom, three large rooms, and a small bathroom.

Overall, though the wood staircase and plank flooring creaked and moaned under his feet, Vachio liked his new home. It had rustic character, loads of space, and a great location near the main town plaza. It also looked like a great party house with ample room for overnight guests.

"So, what do you think?" Raimundo demanded after showing Vachio around the place. "It's fabulous, eh."

"Ah, I don't know. I was getting used to my small room at the other place. It was nice and quiet and off the beaten track."

"What? Are you crazy? This place has everything. And you are now residing among the elite of Garrotero City. What else can you ask for?"

"How about that bedroom over there," said Vachio, pointing to the one next to the bathroom on the ground floor.

"Sorry, my friend. That is the master bedroom. Reserved for the Masters of the house. But, as our loyal retainer, you may have any room on the second floor."

"All right, Don Pingo. I'll take the room next to the bathroom upstairs."

"At your order, sir. I'll have your bed put there." All the moving was being handled by workers from the plastic factory.

"Tonight we'll toast this house properly," said Raimundo. "But for the moment I have work to do. *Ciao*, mon."

"Yeah, *ciao, ciao*."

After stashing his things, Vachio returned to the *Casa de Menores*. As was becoming the norm already, he loitered in the shade of the outer patio, chatted with Hernando, the somewhat feeble minded but puppy-dog friendly janitor, and with any other maestros, guards, or functionaries who happened by. Then every hour or so, Vachio would go into the kitchen with one of them and have a *tinto* or an *Agua de panela* and talk some more. There was little for Vachio to do until the recreation period at four. But Gustavo had told him it was important to *mostrar cara,* show your face, to let everyone know he was dedicated and on the ball. Vachio felt it was a tremendous waste of his time, but that he might as well go along until he had an office and materials so he could work on something more productive.

At about three o'clock, Cabrera, day overseer of the patio, approached Vachio and said, "I have to inform you of something, Vachio."

"All right. Inform me."

"Our distinguished psychologist, Doctor Montoya, is going to address the boys today down in the patio at the recreation hour."

"All right. For how long?"

"Oh, probably about 15 minutes. Then you carry on as normal when he's finished." Vachio seemed to detect a sardonic tone in Cabrera's last sentence.

"Thank you, *Maestro*. *Muy amable*."

"At your order."

A few minutes later Montoya popped out of his office and greeted Vachio. "Ah, Vachio, how goes it?"

"Fine, fine. And you?"

"As well as can be expected." Montoya paused for a moment. "I'm sorry to disrupt your program today. But at our administrative meeting yesterday, we decided it was very important that we start out the new year by reaffirming some of the things the students need to work on. For example, hygiene. We need to impress on them the need to be more careful about their cleanliness. There has been an outbreak of hair lice..."

Vachio listened impassively to Montoya, wondering why he hadn't been invited to attend the administrative meeting. Was he or wasn't he an administrator? Apparently not. He hadn't even been told about the meeting.

"I shouldn't take very long," finished Montoya. "Fifteen minutes. Maybe 20 at the most."

"That's all right, Emilio. Whatever. I'll probably be here tonight for a few hours anyway." Vachio hesitated for a moment. He wanted to get Montoya alone and talk to him about some of the things that had been happening to him; to find out if he was just being a paranoid *gringo* or if he had legitimate reason for concern. "Do you have some time for a *tinto*? I'd really like to talk some things over with you."

Montoya hesitated. "Well, I...I really need to look over my notes for my address to the boys. But we'll do it soon."

"Yeah, all right." Vachio followed him with his eyes back to his office. A minute later Don Miguel entered Montoya's office and Vachio heard laughing conversation. Now he knew. Montoya was avoiding serious conversation with him. He was polite, attentive, even cordial, but he was maintaining his distance. Vachio shook his head in disappointment. He had believed they would become friends after the warmth Montoya had showed him on his site visit. But Montoya was acting differently now, as though he had already left the *Casa de Menores* behind and didn't want to get involved in any controversies. Vachio had felt this change his first day back. This last incident confirmed it. Suddenly Vachio felt extremely lonely.

At four o'clock the boys were assembled in the patio, lined up in military formation, and made to wait in the broiling sun for ten minutes until Montoya appeared and spoke to them from the terrace. Vachio stood on the terrace, his back propped up against the wall, and listened. Montoya spoke of hygiene; he spoke of duty to self, the *Casa de Menores*, country, and Don Gustavo. Then he spoke of the great sacrifice Vachio was making to leave the United States and come to work with them. Doctor Montoya was eloquent and inspired. His talk lasted 40 minutes. But why he had wanted a special assembly to make it was beyond Vachio. Nothing he said to the boys hadn't been said before, and the message would have been better received in the cool confines of the classrooms. All during the speech, the boys stewed in the heat, shuffled their feet, and tried to shield their eyes from the glare of the sun. It struck Vachio as more of a punishment than anything else. The recreation period was shot.

When Montoya was finished, the boys broke ranks and raced around like mad wind-up toys for the ten minutes remaining to them. Vachio stood on the terrace and watched.

"How did you like my little speech?" Montoya asked him, his face still avid.

"It was...very distinctive."

Montoya beamed and walked away. Even he, as intelligent and competent as he seems, isn't immune to this little power thing, Vachio thought. But what's it accomplish?

"Why aren't you down in the patio?" Cabrera asked, suddenly coming up from behind Vachio.

"What for? There's only five minutes left."

"One should never waste time."

"That's true, Maestro Cabrera. One should never waste time." Vachio made a move to walk past him and leave the terrace but Cabrera wasn't through speaking.

"What did you think of Doctor Montoya's speech?" he asked.

"It was fine. But I think it could have been given at a better time."

Cabrera smiled slightly. "Did you notice how Doctor Montoya commanded the respect of the boys? You could learn something from his manner."

Vachio sighed. "Look, what works for Doctor Montoya may not work for me. I'm down in the patio with these guys. He's up there in his office most of his time."

"It would be the same if he were down here like you."

"Maybe. But I'll need to find for myself what works best.... Have a good weekend."

Vachio left, leaving Cabrera staring after him. So that whole damn farce was for my benefit, thought Vachio. What a joke. Preempting the recreation period for that nonsense. Vachio's resentment grew the more he thought about it. By the time he reached the kitchen to get a coffee, he was mumbling to himself.

The kitchen workers gave him a steaming cup of fresh coffee and a hot roll. Vachio stood at the counter, sipping his coffee and chatting with the women as they bustled about putting the finishing touches on dinner. Then out of the corner of his eye he spotted Opala waving to him from the edge of the boy's *cabaña*. For a moment Vachio pretended he didn't see her. Since returning to Garrotero he had only seen her once, and though he wasn't avoiding her, he hadn't gone out of his way to see her. Vachio glanced over at her again and she was looking directly at him. She waved again. Vachio picked up his cup and went over to say hello.

On approaching, Vachio swung around a pillar that had obstructed his view of the table and he saw Doña Berta seated with Opala. This was the last person Vachio wanted to deal with at that moment. He hesitated. Doña Berta encouraged him with a sour look.

"Sit down. Join us," said Opala.

"I wouldn't want to interrupt your conversation," said Vachio.

"You're not interrupting anything. We were just talking," said Opala. Doña Berta studiously sipped her cup of *panela*.

"Talking? You mean gossiping," said Vachio, laughing to show he was joking.

"I don't gossip," said Opala. "That's for idle people. When you're a true revolutionary, you have no time to be idle."

Doña Berta rose from her chair, snuffling as though hit by a sudden allergy attack. She glanced distastefully at Vachio. "Pardon me, Vachio. But I need to get back to work." She looked at Opala. "Are you going to stay here?"

"For a little while longer. It would be rude to leave Vachio alone after inviting him to sit. Don't you think?"

"Whatever you say," said Doña Berta, giving her a wry look. "Until later, Vachio."

"That woman just doesn't like me very much," murmured Vachio, as Berta left the dining area.

"No! She just doesn't know you yet."

"Exactly. So wait until she gets to know me, then she'll have a legitimate reason not to like me."

Opala laughed. "Well, I don't know what the problem is between you two, but Berta is good people. She's my best friend in this place."

"Yes, that may be, but since I arrived here..."

"No, Vachio, please don't tell me. I like both of you."

"All right. I won't tell you."

"But I will tell you something, Vachio. Poor Berta has had much tragedy in her life. She's a victim of sexist oppression. Her no-good boyfriend, the love of her life, ran off with some floozy right before they were to marry and left her alone to take care of her ailing mother. She..."

Vachio mentally shrugged as Opala rattled on in her high excited voice about her friend's traumas. Vachio didn't understand why Berta's traumas should penalize the boys by refusing to give Vachio professional treatment. Maybe he reminded her of her no-good boyfriend or something.

Opala finally paused for breath and regarded Vachio with shining eyes. "Say, you really are different than most of the men here."

"What makes you think that?"

"Because you've been listening to what I have to say without giving me any of the usual male reactionary defenses. You've demonstrated fine sensitivity."

Vachio restrained a laugh. Opala was confusing indifference with sensitivity. "Well, don't give me too much credit."

"But you deserve it."

Vachio did laugh this time. "You really don't know me, Opala. Usually I would argue with you just to do it."

"That can be stimulating."

"Yeah, but the way I am, if you say something is white, I'll say it's black. Then if you agree with me and say it's black, I'll turn around and say it's white."

Opala's expression turned serious. "Well, it sounds to me like you're a person without firm convictions. That's bad."

"Why?"

"Because there is a black and a white. When you deny that, you are engaging in an exercise in intellectual sterility."

Vachio chuckled. "You make it sound like a terminal disease."

"It is. You can become a creature consumed by selfish nihilism. In short, a waste of a human being."

"Oh, my God! Well, anyway, I'm not that far gone. I do have a conviction..."

"What is it?"

"I believe in the color gray. And in every shade in between."

Opala shook her head. "Too indecisive. You need some instruction. Why don't you come to a meeting with me? It will really open up your eyes."

"A Communist meeting?"

"Yes. Though we prefer the word Socialist."

"Yeah, maybe. We can talk about that later."

Opala grinned. "That's fine. I can wait. The true revolutionary is patient. The triumph of Communism is a historical certainty."

"Uh, yeah."

Opala leaned forward and looked at Vachio's face. "Why were you so red when you came over here?"

"Was I?"

"Yes."

"I guess I was upset about something."

"About what?"

"Certain differences of philosophy with certain administrators."

Like what? With who?"

Vachio was silent for a moment, wondering if he should tell her. Then he thought, why not? No one else wants to listen. Vachio gave her a quick rundown of his differences with Cabrera and on some of the things he experienced down in the patio. As he talked, Opala leaned forward and listened intently, her lips slightly parted, her dark eyes playing over Vachio's features.

When Vachio finished, Opala patted the back of his right hand and said, "You are learning very quickly the true nature of things here. This place is a dark pit. The inevitable result of this unjust exploitative society.... But you see, you can't blame the boys—or a man like Cabrera—for the things they do. They are victims."

"Oh, I'm not blaming anybody. I'm just trying to find the best way to deal with the situation on a practical level."

"No! You can't deal with the situation. It's a lost cause. Only a revolution to completely remake this society can do that. Vachio, even if you can help a few of these boys, you must realize that it's only a band-aid. It's no solution. There are thousands more to take their places in *Casa de Menores* all over Colombia. It's..."

Vachio's eyes started to glaze over. He stood up. "I better get going. I have a lot to do at my new house."

"Yes. I should get going, too. I still have a few things to finish up in the office. You know, I can't afford to slack off. They're waiting for any excuse to fire me..... You know, because of my politics..."

"I can imagine."

There was a long pause. Opala was waiting for Vachio to make some sort of suggestion.

"Shall we go," he said.

Opala shook her head and stepped past Vachio to walk ahead.

Vachio purposely lagged behind. The kitchen workers watched them, giggling and making comments. Vachio stopped to say good night to them. Opala disappeared through the door. Vachio followed a few seconds later and he found Opala waiting for him near the spare room in the dark corridor.

"Why haven't you come to see me?" she asked playfully, stepping directly in front of Vachio.

"I don't know. I've been pretty busy getting started here."

Opala laughed. "Are you busy tomorrow?"

"If I want to be. Why?"

"When are we going to take that hike we talked about before?"

"Soon," mumbled Vachio.

"How about tomorrow?"

"Well... Sure, why not?"

"Good. Tomorrow for sure." Opala moved closer and took Vachio's right hand. "Your hand is warm." Her voice was soft and purring.

Vachio shifted his weight from one foot to another. He wasn't sure he wanted any part of where this was heading.

Opala leaned forward and pecked Vachio on the lips.

"Why did you do that?" he asked.

"I don't know. I had the urge.... Did you like it?"

"Let's try it again. You surprised me that time."

Opala smiled and engulfed Vachio in her arms. This time Vachio returned her kiss and held her tight. Opala pulled back after a lingering second kiss and said, "Pass by my office on your way out and I'll give you my address. I don't want the gossips here to see us.... Tomorrow we'll go early in the morning. I know a fantastic place for a picnic. No one around for miles."

Vachio laughed. Opala kissed him again, hard. Vachio started to respond. Then she pulled loose with a slight giggle and whispered, "I'll be looking forward to our hike. Come by my office in a few minutes."

Opala brushed past Vachio and left him alone in the corridor. "I don't know about this," he murmured, shaking his head. "I just don't know."

5

Vachio left his house before sunrise Saturday morning. He walked the deserted streets, only a few yapping dogs attesting to life, the sky blue-black over the eastern mountains, and found Opala's house a half dozen blocks above the central plaza. He rapped on the door and received no answer. He rapped harder and the door was answered by a woman past middle age, dressed in a thin nightgown, rubbing sleep from her eyes.

"Excuse me," said Vachio. "Sorry if I woke you. Is this Opala's house?"

"Opala? Yes, this is her house. I'm her mother. Who are you?"

"I'm a friend. We're supposed to go on an outing..."

"Oh, yes, yes. She told me last night. I'm sorry. Come in, please."

Vachio stepped into the dark interior of a modest home. It smelled strongly of dirty diapers and humid masonry.

"Opala's not awake yet."

"I'm sorry to disturb you so early. But she told me 5:30. That's what time it is."

"It's no problem. I'll wake her."

Vachio shook his head. It really doesn't pay to show up on time here, he thought. The mother left Vachio in a small living room and went to get Opala. Vachio looked around. The whole house was narrow and cramped. Vachio heard the mother calling softly to Opala. A few seconds later there was a general stirring around and a young boy began to wail. Moments later Opala came into the living room dressed in a nightgown.

"Early riser," she slurred, her voice thick with sleep. "You're prompt."

"Yes, unfortunately. You want me to come back later?"

"No, no. I'll be ready in a moment. Relax. I'll be right back."

Opala left the room and lights came on as Opala's mother returned. She shoved a cup of warm *panela* into Vachio's hand and apologized for the appearance of the house. Then she retreated to the kitchen to get Vachio a piece of bread. A minute later another young woman came into the living room carrying a baby girl in her arms. She was dressed in a transparent nightie that came down to mid-thigh and didn't appear embarrassed in the least to see a strange man standing in the living room.

"Hi, I'm Gertrude," she said, cradling the baby in her left arm and extending her hand to shake. "I'm Opala's younger sister."

"Glad to meet you," said Vachio. He looked her over; she was better looking than Opala. "Is that your baby?"

"Yes. My pride and joy." She moved closer to show Vachio the baby's face and brushed against him in the process. Her voice grew soft and flirtatious as she told Vachio her daughter's name and other little details.

"Gertrude!" The two of them looked up. Opala was standing in the doorway, dressed, her arms crossed. "Mama needs you in the kitchen."

"Well, it was nice meeting you," Gertrude said to Vachio. "Will I be seeing you again?"

"Probably."

Gertrude turned to leave and Opala stared her out of the room.

"Come with me," Opala said to Vachio. "I want you to meet my son."

Opala showed Vachio down the hall to a tiny bedroom, crowded with a large antique brass bed and a chest of drawers. A young boy with curly hair and a chubby face sat on the bed, bawling like an abandoned calf. Tears ran down his cheeks, smudging his face. As soon as he saw his mother, he commenced a plaintive, sobbing wail, "Don't go, mama. Don't go.... Aah! Don't go."

Opala fussed over him and tried to get the boy to say hello to Vachio who stood in the doorway, embarrassed, shuffling from one foot to the other. When the boy refused to cooperate, crying louder and eyeing Vachio with distrust, Opala began to speak sternly to him.

"Leave him be," said Vachio. "It's no problem."

"It is a problem. He needs to learn manners."

Vachio shrugged and returned to the living room. I didn't count on this, he thought.

Opala finally calmed the boy down and left him in her mother's care. Once the door closed behind them, she let out a sigh and said, "That boy drives me crazy sometimes. Can you understand? I need to get away now and then."

"I suppose so."

The two of them walked briskly through the now awakening town. Roosters crowed on all sides and early risers were headed for the market. Opala assumed a cheerful chatty demeanor and led Vachio through a twisting warren of streets on the south side of town below the market. There was a stale sour smell of urine, cheap alcohol, and bad plumbing. Roosters, goats, and dogs wandered the dirt paths between the shacks and crumbling houses. A few hungover inhabitants watched the hikers pass in bleary-eyed wonder.

"I don't recommend walking around here at night," said Opala. "But it's all right early in the morning."

"Oh, I've seen more dangerous places in my time."

"In Colombia?"

"Yes. And the United States, too."

Opala glanced sideways at Vachio but she made no comment. They soon hit a narrow dirt path running through overgrown brush beyond the last shacks, crossed a narrow plank over a trickling, plant choked stream, and began to ascend a series of gently rising rock strewn hills. As the sun rose above the mountain rim, illuminating the terrain in stark relief, they reached a narrow plateau. Vachio was surprised by its bareness. It was a desert of chalky washed-out soil, scrub plants, and widely-spaced spindly trees.

"Why is the terrain so dry in such a warm moist climate?" Vachio asked Opala.

"Because the ground was exhausted hundreds of years ago by too much farming and abandoned. Since then, heavy rains and strong winds have done their work, leaching and eroding the soil until you see this moonscape that we have now. Erosion is a big problem throughout Santander."

"Who did it? The Spaniards?"

"No. At least not in this valley. Indians farmed corn here for many generations. Corn is hard on the soil unless you take care of it properly."

Vachio nodded. "Yeah, some archaeologists think that might be what happened to the great Mayan civilizations. Their numbers grew too great and they exhausted the soil in the Yucatan peninsula. Then they disintegrated into smaller groups."

Opala smiled. "You like natural history?"

"Oh yeah. Reading about natural history is one of my hobbies."

"I read a lot, too. My father was a teacher. He got me into the habit. Now it's my one vice."

Vachio laughed. "Well, if you're going to have a vice, that's not a bad one to have."

"True." Opala smiled at Vachio and walked ahead. Vachio took a sip of water and followed her. He was beginning to enjoy this outing. The air was fresh and cool and it felt good to get out and tramp. Vachio felt all the bad feelings and apprehensions from the job melting away from him. And Opala was a decent hiking companion. She walked like a trooper, carried on a good conversation, when Vachio could steer her away from ideological monologues, and was informative concerning the local terrain and history.

They reached the end of the plateau and began to ascend a steep rocky hill. Now the sun blazed down on them and the wind whipped dust into their eyes and mouths. About halfway up they stopped to rest behind a rocky outcropping and brought out the water bottle.

"This is the worst part of the hike," said Opala. "After we get to the top it gets much easier."

"It's not so bad. Though I'm not in shape for this like I used to be when I worked in the mountains."

"I do this as often as I can to stay in shape. I'm preparing for the day that...well, someday the revolution may take me to the hills."

"Are you serious?"

"I'm very serious," said Opala, and her eyes were cool and unwavering.

Looking at her eyes, Vachio almost believed her.

Before they resumed the hike, Opala unbuttoned her shirt and tied it up around her midriff. She wore no bra underneath. Then she took Vachio by the hand and said, "Forward, Comrade. We're going on to a beautiful place."

They finished the ascent of the peak, steering a zigzag course on a narrow footpath, and Opala clambered atop a mound of boulders at the summit. The wind whipped her hair about her eyes and she looked over the plateau and the blue-green mountain buttresses with evident delight.

"I feel like the queen of the world up here," she called down to Vachio. "Come up and see my kingdom."

Vachio scrambled up the rocks and joined her.

"Look! Not a single person to be seen," she said.

Vachio looked. It was a desolate kingdom she aspired to rule—scrub plants, chalky dirt, stunted trees, and barren mountain peaks.

"Isn't it beautiful?" she said, her eyes glowing.

"It's impressive," murmured Vachio. Suddenly Opala turned her head and offered her lips to Vachio. He kissed her, without real enthusiasm, and Opala pressed her body against his. When they separated, her cheeks were rosy and she was breathing deeply. "Let's go! Forward," she urged.

Looks like it's going to be tough to just be friends with this woman, thought Vachio.

On the other side of the peak they entered a world of overgrown vegetation, willowy trees, and buzzing insects. A shadowy world of diffused sunlight, gurgling water from little streams, soft black earth, and spiny flowers. Vachio was astounded and delighted by the metamorphose. They descended a steep narrow path, the air humid and still, their shoes sinking into loamy gunk where rivulets crossed the trail. Vachio began to sweat profusely and batted insects away from his eyes.

After an hour or so they descended a final steep declivity, half sliding, snatching at branches and vines, scratching their arms and hands, and reached level ground in a sun-splashed grotto. They looked around in wonder. A small waterfall cascaded down a rocky moss-crusted cliff at one end of the grotto and into a pool that overflowed into a lazy, shallow, meandering stream that ran along the floor of the basin and disappeared into a wall of vegetation at the other end. Huge, gnarled old trees, their branches laced with Spanish moss, loomed over the creek, shading the hikers from the hot midday sun, and dappling the sparkling water. Dragonflies skimmed over the water and black and orange butterflies fluttered from rock to rock. It was a fairyland.

Vachio and Opala found a large flat rock at the edge of the stream and sat down to eat their lunch of bread, cheese, and fruit. Vachio took off his shirt and basked in the diffused sunlight. He noticed Opala casting looks at him as they ate.

"Man, I could use a nap after that hike," said Vachio, placing his shirt on the rock and laying on it. "But it was worth the effort. This place is great."

"Yes, I love it here. It's such a magical spot..."

Vachio peeked at her through half-closed eyes. He felt nervous and uncertain. He just didn't feel attracted to her.

"I'm hot and dirty," she said after a long silence. "I think I'll go for a dip."

"Good idea. Did you bring a bathing suit?"
"A bathing suit?" Opala laughed. "For what?"
"To swim."
"I don't need a bathing suit here. Who is here to see me?"
"Me."

Opala smiled and stripped off her bell bottom jeans. Then she undid the knot around her midriff and took off her shirt. She left them in a pile next to Vachio and stood looking at him, wearing only white panties. "Are you coming?" she asked.

"In a few minutes," said Vachio, shading his eyes to get a better look at her. I should be trembling with desire, he thought. But I'm not. There's no chemistry.

Opala gave him a final impatient look and headed for the pool at the foot of the waterfall. She plunged in and splashed around like a water buffalo. The water came up to her waist. She saw Vachio watching her and smiled at him. "Come in. The water feels fine." She moved under the cascade of water and took a shower, wringing out her curly black hair and rubbing herself with vigor. It looked so inviting. Vachio stripped to his shorts and waded out into the water to meet her under the falls.

As soon as Vachio came within reach, Opala reached out and gathered him up to her bosom. They embraced and kissed, the water cascading over them, and Vachio felt one of Opala's hands slipping into his shorts. Almost in spite of himself, he began to feel excited. Naked slippery bodies in a firm embrace, an experienced probing hand on his cock, an almost idyllic setting, Vachio felt his mind and emotions spinning out of control. He sensed danger. Opala was someone he could not quite trust. But he was beginning not to care.

Before he realized how it had happened, Vachio found himself on the flat rock lying atop Opala. She grasped his waist in a vise-like grip with her arms and locked her legs around his thighs. Just as Vachio was starting to get to it, urged on by Opala's somewhat theatrical moans and sobs, he happened to look up beyond the trees and spotted something moving in the bush. Vachio blinked and focused on the spot. A figure emerged from the shadows. It was an old *campesino*, wearing a straw hat and carrying a machete in his right hand. He was getting his jollies watching them down in the grotto. Vachio laughed. Then his peepee shriveled up like a punctured balloon.

"What's wrong?" asked Opala, loosening her death grip on Vachio's torso.

Vachio rolled onto his side. "Look up beyond those trees there. See that man? He's been watching us for I don't know how long."

Opala spotted him and hurriedly got up and put on her clothes. "The old pervert," she said in a low voice. "We better leave."

"Why?" asked Vachio, looking toward the bush. The man had already melted away out of sight.

"This is private property and that man is probably the watchdog of the old oligarch who owns this place."

"Now you tell me," said Vachio, catching some of Opala's urgency and putting on his clothes. "But do we have to go now?"

"We better. This old man has been known to fire shots at trespassers." She shook her head and hefted her pack. "What a world, eh?"

"Yeah, what a world," said Vachio, taking a last look at the grotto.

6

Vachio came home late Saturday afternoon to a party. Raimundo had rounded up a quartet of veteran musicians and convinced them to jam at the house. There was a guitarist, a tiple player, a cornet and sax man, and a bongo player. Raimundo kept them well-oiled with beer and *aguardiente* and the men enthusiastically performed their repertoire of Sunday at the plaza marches and traditional folk music. Some of the instruments were off-key, the old musicians occasionally forgot what number they were performing in the middle of a tune and would stop for a fresh drink, but nothing could dim Raimundo's admiration and enthusiasm for these *Musicos viejos*.

"Is this *chevere* or what? I've got a band jamming in my own house!" he exclaimed to Vachio. "Yeah!"

Raimundo sat gazing at the musicians, guitar in lap, and listened intently to a new tune, something that sounded similar to a German beer hall number. Raimundo tickled the strings on his guitar and joined in, though what he played had no relation to what the they were playing.

"What the hell are you doing?" Vachio asked him in English when they stopped for a break.

"Well, you know, man, I'm just playing that good old American jazz music. Improv in Garrotero City." Then he broke into raucous laughter and had to translate for the musicians. Raimundo was on a roll and, as the evening wore on, he kept it going. Snacks were served, several trips were made to the store, just two doors away, for fresh firewater and beer, and different people wandered into and out of the house. It turned into an impromptu housewarming party. The musicians staggered home early but the party continued until the early morning.

Vachio met a group of young students, several of them architects, who had an office and a side door that actually opened into Raimundo's entryway. At first they were very polite and respectful, but as the evening wore on, and the liquor took hold, they began to hit Vachio with the usual, "Why is the United States always exploiting us and holding us back from becoming a great country questions?"

One in particular, Tomás Barboso, the son of a prosperous tobacco merchant, grew particularly obnoxious toward Vachio. Tomás was the oldest of the group, light-skinned, very Spanish-looking, with dark hair and eyes. He had studied in Bogotá and traveled around much of Colombia. The others deferred to him and he talked and carried himself as *El Verraco*, the leader of the gang.

After talking to Vachio for a while, he went into their office and returned with a copy of Sputnik, a magazine produced in the Soviet Union.

"This would be my model for Colombia. Not the *Yanqui* way. I'm a Marxist. And a fan of the Soviet Union," he declared.

"Good for you," said Vachio, accepting the magazine and flipping through the pages.

"But I do drink Coca Cola with my rum," said Tomás, drawing a laugh from his sidekicks. "That's a *gringo* formula I like."

"Yeah? Well, I don't drink Coca Cola. So maybe you're more of a *gringo* than I am. Or at least more of what you seem to think a *gringo* is about."

Tomás turned red and his friends looked to him for a come back. At this point Raimundo intervened, strumming furiously on his guitar and belting out *Guantanamera*. Everyone else joined in and sang along with him. At the end of the song, Tomás looked at Vachio and said, "That's a Cuban song. The land of Fidel. *Vivá la revolución*!"

"*Que Vivá*!" shouted his comrades and Raimundo.

"So, Meester Vachio, what do you think about that?" Tomas demanded.

"About what?"

"About Cuba? And Fidel?"

"Well, believe it not, there were some Cubans in my grammar school class..." Vachio could see that they didn't believe him. "And they left after Fidel took over because they had their property taken away..."

"Then they must have been worms. Traitors to the revolution. Supporters of the reactionary Batista and his mafia crew."

"Possibly. But anyway, I couldn't get all emotional about Cuba like they did. I had no personal stake in it. And if Castro could improve the lot of the average Cuban, well, that was fine with me. But now when I look at Cuba, it seems as though Castro is as big a stooge of the Soviet Union as Batista was for the United States. So what's the difference? It's just like the novel Animal Farm. If you're on the low end of the scale—you get screwed. Capitalist or Communist."

An uproar arose from the students and they drowned each other out as they bombarded Vachio with retorts. "What you say is well-thought," said Arnulfo, once the noise simmered down, "but I'm sure the average American doesn't think like you do about these things."

Vachio laughed. "Normally I wouldn't speak for the average American but this time I think I can safely say, the average American could give a damn about Cuba. Whether it's Communist or Capitalist or whatever other *ist* it is or may become. But there are a bunch of Cuban refugees in Florida who care and they won't forgive Castro. That's a big problem. Especially for your average American. The average American who is mainly interested in going to Cuba to sit on its beautiful beaches and drink rum."

Tomás muttered something under his breath. Then he said, "Do you know that before Castro took over, Cuba was a big whorehouse for the *Yanquis* and the Mafia."

"Right. Just like Las Vegas now. But what's your point? Is there any place in the world where there is no prostitution?"

"Cuba!"

"Huh, I would like to see that."

Before Tomás could say anything more, Raimundo played *Cielito Lindo*. The others joined in. Then a young woman poked her head into the doorway. Arnulfo pointed her out and Tomás went outside to talk to her. Vachio breathed a sigh of relief. The guy was getting on his nerves.

Raimundo took a break after playing three songs in succession and people broke up into individual conversations. Vachio drifted off to lay down in the hammock Raimundo had already strung between two support pillars. He had a headache from all the shouting. Arnulfo followed him over and sat on the couch. Arnulfo had a dark complexion, a ready smile, and was mestizo in appearance. His manner was quiet and thoughtful. Like all the other students Vachio met that night, Arnulfo's politics leaned to the left and he was resentful about American imperialism and corporate meddling in Latin America, but he asked questions without all the bombast and shouting of some of the others and listened carefully to Vachio's replies.

"So what's your opinion about the Panama Canal situation?" Arnulfo asked.

"What can I tell you, man? President Carter doesn't call me up and ask my opinion before he makes a foreign policy decision. I would like to think I'm that important, but I'm not."

Arnulfo chuckled. "Yes, but doesn't the American president have to take into account the wishes of the American people?"

"Yes, that's how it's supposed to work. But we have a representative democracy. I can cite many incidents in American history when the people weren't consulted one way or another. Honestly, I think I have about as much influence over my government as you do over yours."

"But the United States is a superpower. You guys have so much influence and power over us smaller countries. Especially over Latin America because of our historic relationship and proximity."

"That's true, Arnulfo. But speaking as an individual, I'd say that most North Americans are about like most Colombians. They're trying to live their lives and get by as well as they can. They don't really have time to concern themselves with the whole world. They're trying to survive in their own. Living day-to-day. Just like most of the rest of the world."

"Then what are you doing in Colombia?"

"Me? Well, I wanted to try life in another country. And I plan to see a few more. That's my definition of living day-to-day. I can do it here, there, or anywhere else. In the end it's all the same to me."

"You really feel that way? You don't miss your friends and family?"

Before Vachio could answer, Raimundo regained his voice and belted out a few more songs, drowning out everyone within the confines of the courtyard. Then Gustavo arrived, bringing a bottle of Spanish champagne.

Raimundo jumped up to get glasses. Then he gathered everyone around one of the pillars near the front entrance, poured the champagne into the glasses, sprinkled the few remaining drops onto the pillar, and toasted the new home.

After everyone drank, Raimundo laughed and said, "To the good ship Clichy," and shattered the empty bottle against the post. All the men laughed and toasted the christening. Renata was not amused. She ran up with a broom and dust pan, scolded Raimundo in German, and made it plain he was to clean up the mess. "*Mach Schnell*!"

The Colombian students decided this was a good time to say good night and one-by-one they filed out the front door and retired to their office next door. Renata led Gustavo over to the table to serve him a late snack. Vachio went to join them and Raimundo followed after sweeping up the glass on the floor.

While munching on paté and crackers, Gustavo out-of-the-blue launched into a diatribe against the faithless bureaucrats in Bogotá. "*La Obra* is paralyzed. They have definitely halted funding for the foreseeable future and we had to lay off the workers yesterday. It's an absolute disgrace. A scandal. A farce. They just don't understand how important a new and modern *Casa de Menores* is to the country." Gustavo halted to flick some crumbs off his lips. Then he went on in the same vein for a good five minutes, Raimundo egging him on with timely rejoinders.

Vachio grew bored. He was tired from the hike, sleepy, and half drunk. Besides, while Gustavo was denouncing bureaucrats in faraway Bogotá, Vachio was having the same problems with bureaucrats right in the *Casa de Menores*. Gustavo included. He was beginning to think it was all bullshit and ego posturing. Why did everyone make these grandiose promises anyway? For what? For who? All Vachio wanted was some recreation equipment and minimal cooperation in getting set up. When Gustavo had come in his hopes had risen. He had figured to talk to him about some of the problems. But now, in the mood Gustavo was in, ranting and raving about his damn *La Obra*...

Gustavo tapped Vachio on the shoulder and said, "And the person this work stoppage really affects is our friend Vachio here. I fully expected to have him in the new *Casa de Menores*, with all its wonderful fields and recreational facilities, within six months. But now...it may take as much as a year."

"I'm really not concerned about all that," said Vachio.

"What?" asked Gustavo.

Raimundo filled Gustavo's glass with white wine and said, "Now is as good a time as any, Gary. Why don't you tell Gustavo what you told me. Everything is permissible tonight."

"What do you want to tell me?" Gustavo asked Vachio. "As you know, I'm at your disposition."

Vachio took a deep breath. "I want to know why I can't get any money for the recreation equipment I need. I want to know why I can't get even minimal cooperation from the people who are supposed to help me get set up."

Gustavo gave Vachio a suave smile and a reassuring pat on the back. "Vachio, be patient. You've only been here a week. And you knew the guards would be a problem."

"I'm not really talking about the guards. I'm talking about Doña Berta and Maestro Ordoñez and some of the other good administrators who are supposed to be on my side. Man, I don't even need their special help. I just need them to do their jobs so that I can do mine."

Gustavo drank his wine and listened, unperturbed. "Human relations are always tricky, Vachio. A week is so little time. They'll come around. If you're still having a problem with them next week, tell me and I'll speak to them."

"All right, I will. But they're not my biggest problem. My biggest problem is getting the money for the recreation equipment. The kids are giving me hell because I can't make good on a promise I never made."

Gustavo sat up straighter in his chair but his face remained calm. "I can understand your frustration, Vachio. On a small level you are dealing with what I deal with on a large scale. On a small scale you are dealing with a malady that is endemic in Colombia and retards our progress..."

Vachio exhaled heavily and shook his head.

"Say what's on your mind," said Gustavo.

"Gustavo, I don't want to hear about what's endemic in Colombia. You made promises to me, not the country of Colombia. If no one else in this whole town cooperates with me, at least I thought I could count on you."

Gustavo smiled. "And you can, Vachio, you can. I fully expect to keep every promise I made to you on your site visit. But, at this time, because of the bunglers and thieves in Bogotá, we are in the midst of a financial crisis. A serious one. So serious, I was hard-pressed to cover the costs of essential food items this week."

"Then why didn't you just tell me this?"

"I didn't want to burden you. And on a practical level, it makes no sense to tell everyone at the *Casa de Menores* what is going on. It would only sow panic and discord among the staff. Do you understand?"

"Yes, I can understand that. But..."

Gustavo's suave smile was back. He was on firm ground now. "Vachio, I'm a busy man. You're not the only person in the *Casa de Menores* that comes to me with problems. Everyone does. And they all think that their problem is the most important and demands an immediate solution from me..."

"Yeah, but..."

"For example, right after you complained to me about Doña Berta, she came to my office and complained to me about you."

"What did she have to complain about? All I did was ask her to issue me some materials for the program. Isn't that her job?"

"Yes, Vachio, of course it is. But she complained that you have no manner. That you are rude and impatient. And that, my friend, is no way to get things done here."

Vachio broke into laughter.

"Why are you laughing? I believe she has a legitimate complaint against you."

"I'm laughing because I got as far with her being rude and impatient as I did with everyone else being polite and patient. I got no where! Absolutely nowhere!"

"Well, you're just a real Nowhere Man," brayed Raimundo, and started strumming this Beatles tune on his guitar.

Gustavo threw up his hands. "Look, Vachio, let's put an end to this conversation for the moment. I apologize if I've been unable to meet your expectations. But as I explained, there are extenuating circumstances. Grave problems. And I see no solution for a few months or so."

"So what do you want me to do for a recreation program? Cabrera wants to know when it's going to start."

"Vachio, don't worry about Cabrera or anyone else at the *Casa de Menores*. The only opinion you truly have to concern yourself with is mine. As long as I'm satisfied with what you're doing, there is absolutely no problem for you. Now listen, this is all I expect from you for now. Put your program in place."

"How?"

Both Gustavo and Raimundo cracked up. Vachio clenched his hands under the table and bit his lip.

"Vachio, it's your job to figure out how to make the program work. That's why I brought you here," said Gustavo.

"Fantastic. Do you want to tell me how to make it work without any equipment?"

For just a moment Gustavo's face tightened from exasperation. Then he gained control and said, "Vachio, my only advice to you is this. Be creative. Be assertive. The same way you showed by going to the Czech Embassy in Bogotá to check on getting the projector fixed. You are starting a program from scratch. Be assertive, I repeat."

Renata put an end to the conversation by bringing little Sylvia into the room and offering her to Gustavo. "Now you sit with Uncle Gustavo while I get some food for you, *Schotzie*."

"No, Renata, please," said Gustavo, folding his arms. "I'm absolutely terrified to hold babies. Why do you think I'm a confirmed bachelor?"

While Renata and Gustavo bantered, Vachio stared at the table, depressed. Nothing's been resolved here, he thought. And if what's going on here is a trend rather than an initiation—then I have no future here.

7

"Be Assertive." Vachio woke up Monday morning muttering this to himself. "All right. I'll show them just how assertive I can be."

Vachio went to the *Casa de Menores* at 8:30 a.m. and badgered Pacho until he agreed to get an extra key made for the recreation room in the patio. Then he dogged Pacho's footsteps until he summoned Fredy and issued him the order to go get the key made.

"Thank you, Pacho," said Vachio.

Pacho muttered an "*a la orden*" under his breath and walked off with a sour look on his face.

Vachio smiled and turned to Fredy. "I'll go with you to get the key made."

"Sure. The place is just by the plaza."

"Let's go."

They walked out of the *Casa de Menores* and into bright sunlight. They came abreast of Vachio's new home and he pointed it out to Fredy.

"That's where I'm living now. *Chevere*, eh?"

Fredy's ready smile disappeared and a frown spread across his face. "You're living there? Right there?"

"Yeah, there, " said Vachio, pointing out the massive green door.

"Ay, man. *No me diga*. Don't tell me." Fredy crossed himself.

"What? What about it?"

"Man, don't you know? That place is haunted. It's full of spooks and ghosts and probably even has a curse on it."

Vachio burst into laughter. "Ay, Fredy! Don't scare me, man."

"No, man, I'm not kidding. Why do you think the owner had so much trouble renting that place?"

"Because it was a dump until he fixed it up. That's what Raimundo told me."

"No, that's what he told Don Raimundo. He needed to tell him something. No one in Garrotero wanted anything to do with that place. It's full of spooks and evil spirits." Fredy shook his head and crossed himself again.

"That's crazy. Why do you say that?"

"Because it's true, man. During the Palo Negro War, 22 men and 11 horses were slaughtered in cold blood in that place and their spirits still inhabit the house."

"Yeah, well, I've been there three nights and I still haven't seen any."

"But you must have heard them. Many people have heard them walking around at night."

"Well, I have heard the floors creak. But that's because the wood is so old."

"No, man, those are the spirits of the dead men and horses." Fredy shook his head. "I wouldn't live there for anything."

"Yeah, well, I'm not too worried about dead people. Shit, I didn't do anything to them. Why should they bother me?"

"Because some of them are evil."

"Well, evil or good, I'm a lot more worried about live people than I am about dead ones."

Fredy shook his head and dropped the subject. They arrived at the locksmith's and had the key made. Vachio took it and said, "All right, man, thanks. I'll see you later."

"Where are you going?"

"To Bucaramanga to see about a movie projector."

"But what do I tell Pacho?"

"About what?"

"About the key. I was supposed to give it to him."

"Tell him I have it. Tell him Don Gustavo said to give it to me." Fredy looked doubtful. "You have the receipt. That's all you need to give to Pacho. The key is for me."

"I don't know, Vachio..."

"*Ciao.*" Vachio turned and walked to the waiting bus. Forget giving the key to Pacho, he thought. It might take an executive order to get it away from him once he has it. Be assertive. Vachio chuckled. He liked this.

Vachio settled into his seat for the bumpy, swaying, 45-minute ride among the cane fields and small farms. He was accompanied by a collection of students and poorly dressed country people going to

Bucaramanga for higher education, to sell or buy wares at the big market, and to jobs as domestics and laborers.

After an uneventful trip the bus left Vachio just down the street from the Centro Colombo-Americano in Bucaramanga. Vachio stepped up to the plain clothes watchman at the front door and asked to see the Director.

The watchman smiled cordially and said, "The Señor Director isn't here right now. Can I be of service?"

"Well..." Vachio explained his mission. The watchman was a very engaging person. Five minutes later, Vachio was still standing at the front door, giving Manny a rundown on his background and history. Manny smiled a lot, complimented Vachio on his Spanish, and more than once suggested that the Colombo-Americano was always on the lookout for native English speakers to work as teachers. Manny finally invited Vachio inside and told him to wait by the front door while he went to get the Assistant Director. Vachio stood just inside the doorway and watched the students enter and leave the building as one shift of classes finished and another was to begin. There was a large proportion of young men and women, many of them well-dressed, well-groomed, and sporting expensive jewelry. The Colombo-Americano obviously catered to the middle and upper middle-class population of Bucaramanga.

Manny returned, accompanied by a short slim Latina woman wearing jeans, sandals, and a man's shirt. She stuck out her hand and gave Vachio firm shake.

"Hi. I'm the Assistant Director, Mercedes Borrego. How can I help you?" she said in Spanish.

Vachio introduced himself in Spanish and started to explain his mission in the same language when Mercedes chuckled and said, "All right, that's enough. I just wanted to see how much Spanish you knew. Heck, I'm from Denver, Colorado. We can speak English."

"Sure, whatever," said Vachio, wondering why she had done that. Then he explained about the *Casa de Menores* and the projector.

"I believe we can help you with that," said Mercedes. "We've lent movies to the *Casa de Menores* before."

"How about lending us a projector?"

"Sure. If you bring it back."

"You don't have to ask the Director about it first?"

"No, I have the authority. Between you and me, he's essentially the director of social functions and I'm the director of practical functions. *Comprendes*, Mendez?"

"Yeah, I think so."

"O.K. Follow me and we'll see what we can dig up."

Mercedes moved away, quick and energetic in her movements, Vachio following on her heels.

"So are you Mexican-American?" Vachio asked her.

"I'm a *Chicana,*" she said, her voice a trifle sharp.

"Isn't that the same thing?"

"Yes. I'm just surprised you know."

"Why wouldn't I? I'm from California. I went to grammar school with more Latinos than any other group of people."

"Oh?"

They entered a utility room and Mercedes showed Vachio a couple of projectors and a wall shelf with movies. "Most of our movies are pretty bad," she said. "Propaganda stuff about American industrial might and democracy. Hand-me-downs from the U.S. Embassy."

Vachio went through them and found a film about animal life in the United States. "This should work for now. Maybe I'll find some other sources around town."

"The kids should like that movie," she said. "It's pretty good actually."

"How about the projector?"

"You can take it now. Or, if you're not in a rush, it's time for my break and we can go have a coffee."

"Sure, I have time. I don't really start work until four in the afternoon."

"Aren't you working now?"

Vachio smiled. "Yeah. I guess I am."

They went to Mercedes office to drop off the equipment and were soon on their way. Mercedes took Vachio to a large café next door to the Colombo-Americano. It was jammed with students. She stopped in front of the entrance and said, "If we go in here we won't be able to talk. How about we go to this other place I know a few blocks from here. It's much quieter. We can talk in peace there."

"Whatever you say."

They walked to a hole-in-the-wall place a few blocks away. It consisted of a few metal tables on a patch of sidewalk enclosed by a low cinder block wall facing the street.

"A nice young couple runs this place," said Mercedes. "I think you might like them."

"Is the coffee good?"

"Of course."

"I'm home."

They took seats and were waited on by Alfonso and his very pregnant wife, Luisa. The couple was very cordial and Vachio was soon chatting familiarly with them.

"If you don't mind, I'd really like to practice English with you sometimes," said Alfonso. "It's a big ambition of mine to learn to speak it well but we can't afford classes so I have to pick it up however I can."

"Sure. When I come here, feel free to speak to me in English."

Alfonso grinned and went to get their coffee.

"You were right," Vachio said to Mercedes. "They seem like nice people."

"They are. But their business is struggling. I hope they can keep this place going until they get established."

"Well, I'll be back."

Mercedes brought the conversation around to the Colombo Americano and, as the watchman Manny had mentioned, said that the Colombo was always on the lookout for native English speakers to teach a class or two.

"Some of our Colombian teachers have poor accents," said Mercedes. "And we don't always get the most qualified Americans, either."

"Uh huh..."

"Do you have much of a background in English?"

"Yes. I'm only a few classes short of an English degree."

"And you said that your recreation program is from four to five in the afternoon and at night. Right?"

"Yes."

"Do you think you might be interested in teaching a morning class when a new session starts. It's a good way to pick up some extra money for traveling or whatever."

Vachio grinned. "We Peace Corps volunteers aren't supposed to do side jobs for money."

Mercedes laughed. "No! Well, we have two Peace Corps volunteers teaching part-time right now. Maybe you know them. Forest and Hugh?"

"I've met them.... Briefly."

"You haven't been in touch with them since you came here?" Mercedes' voice registered surprise.

"No, not yet. I've been pretty busy in Garrotero trying to get settled in."

"Oh, well...we're having a get together this Sunday at Forest and Hugh's place. Why don't you come? It will give you a chance to meet the *gringo* colony of Bucaramanga."

"Sunday? Sure, I'm not doing anything Sunday. At least not that I know of."

"Good. I'll give you their address."

"I already have it. My Peace Corps supervisor gave it to me. What time?"

"Oh, from about noon on. It's just a little pot luck kind of thing."

Mercedes finished off her soda and started to rise. "I need to get back to work now."

Vachio started to gulp his coffee. He also had a hot *empananda* uneaten before him.

"No, no, take your time. When you're finished, just come to my office and pick up the projector and film. It's already signed out to you and Manny knows."

"All right, thanks. When do you need the projector back?"

"Don't worry about the projector. We have three. I'll let you know when we need it back."

"And the film?"

"Bring it back some time next week and get more if you like. I'll try to order some new ones."

"Thanks."

"My pleasure. I've had some dealings with the *Casa de Menores*. Anything you can do for those poor kids will be something worthwhile." Mercedes shook her head. "Recreation director in a juvenile prison. That sure is a strange Peace Corps job."

"Yeah, I've been told that more than once."

Mercedes stuck out her hand. "You have all my best wishes on that job."

"Thanks."

"And think over what I said about teaching English. We start up a new session in another month."

"I'll think about it. But I really doubt it. I have my hands full at the *Casa de Menores*."

"That I believe. See you at the party?"

"More than likely."

Mercedes left and Vachio picked up a newspaper and read while he ate his *empanada*. Soon another customer arrived. He was a man in his mid-to-late-20s, darkly handsome, with a trim athletic build and broad shoulders. He wore a black shirt, open at the collar to reveal a gold chain and a dangling cross, tan slacks, expensive leather shoes, and mirror sunglasses. The man nodded to Vachio's greeting and buried his nose in the morning paper.

A few minutes later Alfonso came out and asked Vachio, "How wuz chor coffee, meester?"

"Fine. Can I have a little more?"

"Yes, meester.... At once. I get for chu." Alfonso smiled. "How was that?" he asked in Spanish.

"Pretty good. I understood you."

Alfonso grinned and returned to the kitchen to finish cutting his vegetables for the lunch soup. Vachio noticed the other customer grinning at him.

"He's practicing his English," Vachio said to him in Spanish.

"Yeah, I know. He wants to practice with me, too," said the man in perfect American English. "But I don't have the patience. I get too frustrated trying to explain things to him."

"Where are you from, man?"

"I'm Colombian. But I grew up in Queens, New York. Jackson Heights. How about you?"

"San Francisco."

"Oh yeah? I went there for my honeymoon. Nice little city. Real pretty. Yeah, real pretty. My old lady loved it."

"That's nice."

The man stood up and stuck out his hand. "My name is Jaime DeLeon. But since you're American, you can call me Jimmy."

Vachio introduced himself and the men chatted. Once started talking, Jimmy went on and on, his voice a machine gun staccato. "So it's like this. I'm here because my old man died and left me part of a candy factory he has here in town. But my half-brother and his side of the family want to screw me out of the inheritance. And I say that ain't gonna happen. No one does Jimmy DeLeon like that. Not even family."

"So what do you have to do?"

"Well, the will states that me and my older brother split things 50-50. And it's fine with me if he wants to buy me out. But he offered me way below market value. So I came here to look things over and assume my share of the partnership." Jimmy laughed. "We'll see how long my bro likes having me around before he pays what it's really worth."

"I take it you two don't get along."

"You take it wrong. Up until now we've always gotten along well. I mean, when we've been around each other. But his aunts and uncles are putting him up to this. They never liked my mother or me or my little sister. They want everything to go to the children of his first wife. But the old man didn't see it that way. I was his favorite son and my mom was his favorite wife. I'm not gonna let them play us that way. It's bad enough how they treated my mom..." Jimmy stopped. "Hey, you don't wanna hear all this, do you? Maybe you have to go somewhere?"

"No, I don't mind. I'm in no rush."

"Thanks, man. I need to blow off some steam. You're a good guy to talk to. Here, I'll pay for your snack."

Vachio laughed and waved off his money. Jimmy called Alfonso and paid both bills, ignoring Vachio's protest.

"Now, where was I..."

"You were talking about your mom and how bad they treated her."

"Oh, right... Well, the thing is, most of my father's family and his first wife's family were all from around here in Santander. They all knew each other and there were a lot of interrelationships between the families. So after the death of my half-brother's mother, my father took up with my mother. He was over 40 and she was only 18. That was one problem for them. The other big problem was that she was from Cali..."

"So what?"

"Right. You say so what, I say so what. But these people are really tribal, man. From the day my mother came to live in Bucaramanga with my father, they gave her hell. They kept insinuating that she had married my dad only for his money and social position and all that. And how was she supposed to raise a stepson who was only six years younger than her and a bunch of other crap like that." Jimmy took a deep breath. "Anyway, after three years of this my mom had enough. I was two-years-old and she didn't want me to grow up in the middle of all that back-biting. So she convinced my father to move to New York. My father already had business interests there and one of my mother's sisters lived there so it seemed a natural move. My father agreed and we went. He took my younger sister along, she gets along great with my mom, and we left my brother here to stay in school and live with an aunt and uncle since he was already 15 and never took to my mother. My father spent the next 25 years going back and forth between Colombia and New York. But now he's gone. And he left us one hell of a mess to unravel because of his different business interests."

"So how are things going?"

"Not bad, really. But when there's money involved..." Jimmy shrugged, smiled ruefully, and spread his palms in the air. "It brings out the worst in a lot of people. You know what I mean?"

"Yeah, I've seen it before.... So how long have you been here?"

"Two months."

"Do you like it?"

"Ah, it's all right. But I miss New York. It's too slow for me here. And when it comes to business, these *Santandereanos* are too cautious and conservative for my blood. But it's all right. My mother has moved back to Cali. So I go to see her regularly. And that's a city I like. It's a moving happening place. And I've noticed some very interesting business possibilities there.... Have you been to Cali?"

"Yeah, I was there for a short vacation before I came here."

"How'd you like it? Great, eh. *Mucho* party time."

"Yeah, it was party time. But to tell you the truth, it wasn't really my style."

"How's that?"

"I don't know. It was cool. But maybe a little too flashy for my taste. It kind of reminded me of the Los Angeles glitz scene. Lots of people acting hip and wearing gold chains with the silver cocaine spoons on 'em."

Jimmy laughed. "Yeah, but lots of fine ladies wearing almost nothing, too. And lots of salsa to get them shaking."

"No doubt about that."

"So what else you want out of life, man?"

Now Vachio laughed. "More than that."

Jimmy glanced at his watch. "I have to shove off now. My wife is coming in from the States today and I have to get her at the airport." Jimmy chortled. "I have a hot reception planned for her. We haven't been together for two months. She should be nice and horny."

"Why didn't she come sooner?"

"She's been keeping an eye on our discotheque in Queens. It's a great place. Strictly first class. We don't allow any low lifes or bums. But I'm not always sure how far I can trust the manager when I'm not around so she was keeping an eye on things."

"Huh."

"So will I see you here again?" asked Jimmy. "I'm here at least three times a day. This is my second office."

"Yeah, I'll probably see you here. I'll be coming into town at least once a week. Maybe more."

"All right, then. Later." Jimmy shook hands and walked down the street to a nearby taxi stand.

Vachio hung around the café a while longer, helping Alfonso with his tortured English. Then he took a leisurely walk up Calle 36 and long the Avenida de las Americas. It was a gorgeous day, hot, but with enough cloud cover and breeze to keep the weather pleasant. Most of the homes in this district were fairly new, trim stucco jobs. They were Spanish-style, painted in white and soft pastels, with red-tile roofs and wrought-iron grillwork, shaded and adorned by luxuriant tropical trees and bushes. The streets were clean and fairly well-maintained. Shiny new Renaults abounded. It was a pleasant and prosperous neighborhood. Vachio's fellow strollers looked relaxed and without apprehension. This sure ain't Bogotá, thought Vachio, turning around to retrace his steps to his bus stop. I might just get to like this place.

8

Vachio deposited the projector and the movie on Pacho's desk in the early afternoon.

"Very good, Vachio," Pacho said, patting Vachio on the back. "Is the movie any good? I might want to see it myself."

"It's about wild animals of North America."

"Oh. Well, the kids should like it. And it's educational as well."

"I hope so."

Gustavo came out of his office and looked over the projector and the movie.

"When can I show the movie?" Vachio asked.

"Whenever you want," said Gustavo.

"How about tonight?"

"Make it tomorrow."

"All right. But where?"

Gustavo scratched his head. "We like to show movies in the chapel but with the number of boys we have now that is impossible."

"How about in shifts?" suggested Vachio.

"That's a possibility. But it's hard to coordinate."

"He can show them in the patio, Don Gustavo. We've done it before. You just project the film against the white wall near the side exit. It's not great. But it works pretty well."

"Yes, that would work. And it makes security easy," said Gustavo. He turned to Vachio. "What do you think of that?"

Vachio shrugged. "Whatever works is fine with me."

Vachio walked out of the office satisfied with the way things were going for him. It was time to push his good luck. Vachio entered the interior patio and strolled around the perimeter of the empty play yard. All the boys were in classes or shop. He went over to his recreation room and unlocked the door. The mess looked even worse than the first time he had seen it. Maestro Ordoñez still hadn't touched it. Vachio made his decision and locked the door.

Vachio went to the wood shop to get Barranca. He would have preferred Rolo to help him with the recreation room but for some reason he had wanted nothing to do with the job. With deep misgivings, Vachio had settled on Barranca out of the interested candidates.

"Hi, Maestro McCorney?" said Vachio, entering the cool wood shop. It smelled pleasantly of the wood shavings that littered the floor and unpleasantly of glues and varnishes.

"Vachio! How goes it?" said McCorney in a pleased tone of voice. He was a short wiry young man with dirty blonde hair and a pleasant manner. His real last name was McCormick, from his Scottish immigrant grandfather, but over the years in Garrotero the Hispanicized pronunciation of the surname had evolved into McCorney. Everyone, even his best friends, called him McCorney instead of by his first name, Edwin.

"What can I do for you?" McCorney asked.

"Can you let Barranca out of class today? I need him to help me clean out the recreation room."

"Of course."

Barranca let out a yelp and came over to stand by Vachio. "I'll do a good job, Profé," said Barranca, putting his arm on Vachio's shoulder. "But it's a big job. I can use some help. Let me use Felipe there to give us a hand."

Vachio looked at McCorney. "It's all right with me if it's all right with you."

"Of course, Vachio. Take whoever you need."

"Thanks."

Vachio and the two boys left the woodshop and headed across the yard to the recreation room.

"We'll need a broom and dust pan," said Barranca to Vachio.

"Yes. Go ahead and get one."

"Go get a broom and dust pan from the guards," Barranca ordered

Felipe.

Felipe was a little guy. One of Barranca's gang of younger boys. "Right away," he said, and sprinted over to the guards up on the terrace.

Vachio opened up the recreation room and said to Barranca, "This is what we're going to do. We're going to take everything out of the room and pile it up over here." Vachio pointed to a spot of ground just beyond the tile walkway. "Then we're going to sweep out the room and clean the floor with a mop and water. Got it?"

"Yes, my *Jefe*."

"All right, forget that *Jefe* crap. Let's just do it."

"*A la orden*." Barranca saluted Vachio in military fashion and entered the room. They opened up the big double doors and started to carry stuff out and pile it in the dirt. A few minutes later Felipe came over with the broom and dust pan. Barranca snatched the broom from his hands and began to sweep with a fury, kicking up a cloud of dust and bat shit.

"Hey, stop that until we get everything out of the room," said Vachio. "You're making me sick."

"Ay, Profé, it's only a little dust."

"Cut it."

Vachio stepped outside to rub his stinging eyes and sneeze out some dust. He had just recovered enough to reenter the room when he spotted Maestro Ordoñez hurrying toward him.

"Vachio. What are you doing here?" he asked, his eyes on the pile of junk.

"We're cleaning up the recreation room so that we can use it."

"But Vachio, I told you I would take care of this for you."

"Yes, you told me that....last week."

"I've been very busy, Vachio. But I will certainly take care of it this week."

"Get back to work," Vachio said to Barranca, who had stopped to listen to the conversation. Then he turned back to Ordoñez. "I realize how busy you must be, man. That's why we're handling this ourselves. It's no problem. We don't mind doing it."

Ordoñez flushed. "But you can't leave these things out in the patio. The kids will trash everything. Especially the desks. I need to find a place for them before they are moved."

Vachio considered this for a moment. "All right. We'll keep the desks in the room. But everything else, and most of it is pure junk, has to go. I need this room now." Ordoñez started to protest but Vachio cut him short. "I have permission from Don Gustavo to do this. You can talk to him about it."

"I will." Ordoñez turned and headed for the terrace.

Vachio grinned, then he and the boys finished emptying out the room. By the time Ordoñez returned with Gustavo, Felipe was dumping water on the floor and Barranca was mopping it out of the room. Gustavo, with a slight smile tugging at his lips, inspected the room and nodded to Vachio in approval. Then outside by the pile of junk he turned to Ordoñez and said, "Maestro Ordoñez, I want these things cleared out of the yard before the boys finish classes."

"But Don Gustavo, where am I supposed to put them?"

"Ordoñez, you are in charge of facilities. Who would know better than you?"

"But I can't..."

"I don't want to hear about this. Take care of it."

"But the desks..."

"The desks can stay until he finds a place for them," offered Vachio. "We'll place them on one side of the room."

"Very well," said Gustavo. "Now, if you gentlemen will excuse me, I have other matters to attend to." Gustavo turned and left. Ordoñez grumbled under his breath and quickly assembled a crew of boys to help him move the things. It took him all of 15 minutes to accomplish. Vachio had his recreation room. Now all he needed was some equipment.

On Tuesday, Vachio inaugurated his weekly night at the movies. He passed the word during the day, inviting anyone who wanted to come, and was pleased that a handful of shop Maestros and off-duty guards accepted his invitation. "Sure, I'll come," said McCorney. "I'll come a lot if you get good movies. The cinema here in town shows lots of cheap trash. We have to go all the way to Bucaramanga to see anything decent." The boys, after gently razzing Vachio for not getting a *Pistolero* or Karate Kid kind of movie, showed their appreciation by behaving well during the recreation period.

At 7 p.m. everyone, including Pacho and his wife and three children, assembled under the awning on the west side of the patio and the projector was set up on the ping pong table. After a few trial runs and snafus, and plenty of unsolicited advice from Pacho and one of the guards, Vachio managed to project a fairly good picture against the wall adjacent to the cafeteria gate. Vachio then designated Rolo as his technical assistant, much to Barranca's chagrin, and turned the operation of the projector over to him.

The movie, despite a few glitches where the film was spliced together and broke, went over well. The boys lust for violent action was satisfied by scenes of wolves tearing apart elk and by wolverines and badgers catching and eating their prey. Everyone enjoyed the spectacular scenic panoramas of the northern lands and laughed over the strange habits and curious appearances of some of the animals. Afterwards, to Vachio's satisfaction, the boys sat still for another half hour and asked questions and discussed the film. When it was all over and the boys were beginning to scatter, Vachio called out to them, "Now, don't you think that was better than some tired old Gunslinger movie or

Karate trash?"

"No!" shouted more than a few. "It was boring. We want movies about *Pistoleros* and Brucie Lee Karate. You hear?"

Vachio laughed. "You guys loved this film."

"It was better than nothing," said Amarocho in a serious aside. "But don't make this a steady diet."

"Don't listen to him, Vachio," said Little Abel. "I thought this picture was great."

Vachio shrugged and thought to himself. You can't please all of the people all of the time. But it went well.

By Wednesday morning, Vachio's confidence was buoyed enough to take on the formidable Doña Berta. He waylaid Cabrera and talked him into signing the requisition form for the art supplies he needed by telling him that a written schedule of events for the patio would help keep the boys under control. Then he went to Gustavo's office and popped in on him before Julia could stop him. Gustavo looked up in irritation from his paper work.

"Vachio! What is it?"

"I won't take any of your time. I just want to know one thing." Vachio held up the requisition. "Cabrera signed this so everything is in order. I just want to know that if Doña Berta gives me a problem with this again, you'll back me up."

"You have what she asked for. Why would she give you a problem?"

"I don't know. But I feel she might.... Will you back me?"

"Yes, Vachio, I'll back you up. But take care of this now. I'm leaving for Bucaramanga within the hour."

"I'll do it this minute."

Vachio went to the supply room and found Doña Berta at her desk. "Good morning, Berta," said Vachio in a formal tone of voice.

"Good morning," said Doña Berta, her manner cool and guarded. "What can I do for you?"

Vachio placed the requisition before her. "Here are the signatures you asked for. I'd like you to fill my order now."

Doña Berta picked up the requisition slip and examined it as though she were reading the fine print in a legal contract. "Everything seems in order," she finally said.

"Yes, it is. Signed and countersigned."

"Yes, but...there is a little problem..."

Vachio waited, anger starting to well inside of him.

"...We're short on the specific materials you are ordering. You'll have to wait until we get more in stock."

"What do you mean, short? The shelves are filled with what I asked for."

"To you it might seem so. But I'm in charge of maintaining stock for the entire *Casa de Menores*. And school classes take priority. But, of course, I'll keep your requisition on file."

Vachio took the requisition from her desk. "I'll keep this requisition. I wouldn't want an accident to occur."

Doña Berta rose from her desk. "What are you implying by that remark?"

"Don't worry about it. We'll resolve this right now."

Vachio left the supply room and went straight to Gustavo's office. "She refused me again," said Vachio.

Gustavo sighed and rose from behind his desk. "You know, Vachio, sometimes I think I'm Director of an insane asylum and not a correctional institution. How do we expect the boys to cooperate with the program when we can't get the staff to do it?"

"I don't know."

"Let's go."

Gustavo double-timed it to the supply room, Vachio on his heels, and greeted Doña Berta with a benign smile.

"Don Gustavo!" Doña Berta rose as he approached her desk.

"My Dear Berta," said Gustavo in a low voice. "You will take this requisition and fill it for Vachio here. I don't have time for any more of this nonsense."

"But Don Gustavo, we're short of those supplies."

"Berta!" Gustavo's voice rose tight and hard. "You will fill this requisition. And—you will fill any other reasonable requisitions Vachio makes from now on without any problems. Am I understood?"

"But Don Gustavo, the teachers..."

"Berta! I don't have time for this. You will do as I say. If you are running out of certain things, than you send me a requisition and we will get you more." Gustavo walked over to the shelves and started assembling some of the items Vachio had requested. Then he placed them on Berta's desk. "Do we understand each other?"

"Yes, Don Gustavo," she said, lowering her eyes.

"Good. I expect my staff to cooperate with each other. I don't want to go through something like this again."

"No, Don Gustavo."

Gustavo smiled and said, "I hope your mother is in good health. Say hello to her for me." Then he left the room.

Berta filled Vachio's order at a snail's pace. When Vachio tried to speed things along by helping her, she snapped at him, "This is my job. You wait. I'll make sure the count is exact."

Vachio started to say something but thought better of it. Vachio knew he had won this battle with Berta but the war was far from ended. He had only deepened her resentment of him. But I have the supplies, he thought. Things are finally moving along.

That night there was an electrical blackout in Garrotero, a frequent occurrence for lack of power capacity. Vachio and Raimundo went out to the front stoop to take advantage of the light from a single electric bulb from a bakery across the street that had its own generator. Vachio sipped on a beer and felt mellow. He was quietly celebrating the small victories he had achieved on the job that week.

"You know," he said to Raimundo, "I think I might just have turned the corner on this job."

Raimundo looked away toward the blackness of the plaza and remained silent.

"Did you hear me?"

"Yes, man, I heard you. I just don't want to say anything about it and spoil your mood."

9

Shortly after Vachio stepped into the patio Thursday afternoon for the recreation period, he was surrounded by Leal and his gang of younger boys. Without provocation they started to rag on Vachio. When Vachio tried to respond, he was drowned out by a chorus of *gamin* invective. Vachio was shaken by this sudden and concerted verbal assault. He shook his head in bewilderment and tried to walk away to the other side of the patio, figuring they would soon grow bored with this game. But Leal and his crew followed right on Vachio's heels, jabbering at him the whole time. Vachio kept walking, the insults poured against his back, "Dumb *gringo*. Imbecile. Idiot! *Pingo*!" and many others he couldn't understand, the boys growing bolder and cruder as they noted Vachio's confusion.

Vachio turned at bay on the edge of the micro-soccer field and faced his tormentors. "What the hell is going on here?" he yelled at them.

The boys stepped back a pace at the sound of his voice but Leal rallied them by saying, "All he can do is yell. He's nothing." The boys crowded closer to Vachio and continued to taunt him.

Torres and Galindo, as though on cue, and many of the boys gathered around to watch the fun. The two guards grinned and exchanged comments, waiting to see what Vachio would do. Vachio saw he could expect no help in this direction. He had to do something. He focused on Leal, the leader of this rat pack. Vachio pointed his finger at Leal and said, "Don't get personal with me, man. You are looking for a big problem."

"Really? What are you going to do? Put me in jail?" Leal roared with laughter and the others joined in.

For a moment Vachio was at a complete loss. The insults hit him from all sides. In his confusion he glanced at the two guards. Torres quickly stepped through the crowd of boys and offered Vachio his *garrote*. "Here. Take this and use it. It's the only way to deal with these animals." Torres smiled and thrust the *garrote* into Vachio's right hand.

Silence descended on the rat pack. For a fleeting moment Vachio fingered the smooth, well worn wood. He had an impulse to crash this club against the side of Leal's smirking face. Then he shook his head and tossed it back to Torres. "I didn't come here to use this shit. I'm not going to do it."

"Suit yourself," said Torres, shrugging. "But if you don't use it, you won't last here." Torres thumped the *garrote* against his hard palm. "This is all they understand."

"We'll see."

Torres smiled and looked at Galindo. They walked away to watch from the terrace, leaving Vachio to fend for himself. Leal and his boys immediately closed around Vachio, laughing and capering, thrusting hands near his face, bumping him. Vachio felt the panic of claustrophobia. He was engulfed by shaved heads and jeering faces. The boys started to tug at his arms and pinch his skin. Vachio looked around him. Some of the boys beyond the circle of Leal's gang were watching with detached grinning faces, others were shaking their heads in pity. He knew their thoughts. This *gringo* counselor is a pathetic fool.

This look of pity shook Vachio from his confusion. He pushed through the circle of small boys and went to the soccer field. He picked up the tough leather micro ball and waited for Leal to approach him. Then he threw it at him, hard.

"Hey!" gasped Leal, the ball bouncing off his chest. "What the..."

Vachio didn't give him a chance to continue. "All right, big mouth. You think you're bad because you can talk trash. Let's play a little ball. Let's see how bad you are. Come on, we'll play your game. Soccer!"

Leal stared at Vachio, anger and confusion intermingling on his face. His hand rubbed his stinging chest. The other boys fell silent.

"What about it? You're wasting my time," said Vachio. He turned and walked to the center of the soccer field.

"Yeah, what about it?" piped up Rolo. "Nothing but sissy talk from you, boy." Now most of the boys, including his own gang, laughed at Leal.

Leal reddened and his jaw clamped tight. He picked up the soccer ball lying at his feet and yelled, "I'll show you what!" He threw the ball in the general direction of Vachio. Vachio laughed and stopped the ball with his foot. Then he passed it to another boy who had joined him on the field.

"Let's play!" yelled Amarocho.

The older boys took the field and picked sides, placing Vachio and Leal on opposing teams. Everyone understood what this was about. Vachio was left to guard Leal.

The game began and Leal did his best to humiliate Vachio. He kept up a steady flow of trash talk and tried to dribble the ball between Vachio's legs. After a few misfires, Leal succeeded, and Vachio was razzed by the players and spectators crowding the sidelines. Then the ball went out of bounds off of one of Vachio's teammates.

"All right, man. You got me that time," Vachio said to the laughing Leal as he prepared to throw the ball in bounds. "But that's a clown act. Play real soccer."

"I'll do it again," laughed Leal.

"I'll be waiting for you."

Seconds later the ball was slid over to Leal and he went into his dribbling act again. This time Vachio crowded him and blocked his attempt to slide the ball between his legs. The ball spurted over to one of Vachio's teammates and he took it down the short field for a goal.

"Leal, you clown! Start playing soccer," Amarocho screamed at him. Leal muttered under his breath and took his position for the kick-off.

Vachio's teammates came up to him and slapped his palm, congratulating him on a good play. They taunted Leal for a clown and laughed at his muttered curses. The spectators quieted down and stopped hassling Vachio. A few of them turned their barbs on Leal. Vachio grinned as he stood across from Leal. This was even better than he had hoped for.

But now Leal was simmering. When play resumed, he slashed at Vachio's legs and came in with his elbows up as they contested the ball. Vachio warded him off with relative ease, he was much bigger and stronger than this kid, but the supposedly accidental elbows and kicks still stung. Vachio warned Leal with his eyes more than once. Leal continued his dirty play, and some of his teammates were emboldened to do the same. Vachio began to steam. Then came the clincher. As Vachio ran up the sideline without the ball, his eyes on a teammate in the center of the field, Leal crashed into him from the side, digging an elbow into his ribs and trying to trip Vachio down with an extended leg. Vachio staggered forward but managed to keep his feet. Then he ran back to confront Leal, white hot anger burning inside. "You went too far that time, asshole. You try to hurt me you better watch out. I warn you."

"It was an accident," smirked Leal, retreating to the other end of the field. "What's your problem?"

In a rage Vachio kicked the ball all the way to the basketball court. All the boys stopped and stared at him. They had never seen him like this. Vachio was oblivious to their looks. He stood on the sideline, bare-chested and drenched in sweat, his breath coming in quick gasps, his eyes stalking Leal. A few raindrops spattered against his burning face from the sultry threatening sky. Vachio looked up and tried to calm down. "I've got to keep cool," he muttered to himself. "He's only a stupid kid."

Vachio walked toward his own goal, as far from Leal as possible, while a boy went to retrieve the ball. He could feel a welt developing where Leal's bony elbow had dug into his rib. "The little bastard!" he muttered. The first fat raindrops, prelude to an afternoon downpour, kicked up dust on the dirt field. A fall on this field caused horrible strawberries on the skin. Leal had intentionally tried to trip him, to maliciously injure him. Thunder rolled from the bosom of the eastern mountains, jangling his nerves even more. The ball was back in play and Vachio, his eyes slitted, watched Leal scramble after it on the other end of the field.

The rain fell harder and a brisk wind whipped swirling chalky dust into the air. A wild melee in front of the opposing goal resulted in a save by the goalie and a long throw-out to Leal. He dribbled by one of Vachio's teammates at midfield and came free with a full head of steam. Vachio shifted over to meet him, the wind roaring in his ears. Leal saw Vachio coming and shouted something. Through a curtain of swirling dust and steady rain, Vachio saw Leal's face as a grotesque taunting mask. Vachio accelerated right before impact, anger driving him, and drove his foot against the ball and followed through with his entire body. It was like an explosion. Leal was sent tumbling to the left, the ball spun crazily to the right, and Vachio continued on toward the opposing goal. One of his teammates recovered the ball and passed it to Vachio. He took the ball on his foot and headed in a straight line for the goal. The lone defender took one look at his face and stepped aside. Vachio rammed the ball past the goalie at point blank range. Then he shook his head to clear away the fog and headed back upfield. The players stood staring at him in shock.

Leal lay writhing on the field, holding his left leg, tearfully cursing Vachio and complaining that he had been fouled. Everyone, including his own teammates, ignored him. Vachio finally went over and asked him, "Are you all right?"

"What do you care? You did it on purpose."

"Not really. I could have done worse if I was trying."

"Go to hell, man!" Leal spat off to the side.

"You went too far. Next time you better think first."

Leal struggled to his feet. "I'll remember. I'll definitely remember."

Vachio shrugged and walked to midfield to resume the game. Leal limped around near the sideline and continued to complain that Vachio had fouled him.

"It wasn't even a foul," said Rolo. "It's a goal for us. Now, if you can't play anymore, get your ass off the field. Do your teammates a favor. You suck anyway."

"What? You want something with me, you triple son-of-a bitch!" Leal screeched.

Rolo took a step toward him, his face disdainful. "Do I want something with you, *sapo*? Anytime, anyplace, any way you like. I'm here at you service to give you a beating. *Sapo*!" He hissed the final name.

Leal looked at Rolo's steady eyes, snarled something under his breath, and limped off the field.

Rolo snickered. "Fucking *sapo*. Come on, let's play."

Leal was replaced and the game continued. But within minutes, the sky opened up completely, pelting the players with beebee-sized hail, and sending crackling lightning bolts too close to the patio for comfort. The players raced for cover under the awnings and settled down along the benches to wait out the storm.

Vachio paced alone under the awning toward a far corner of the patio, still upset and wired from the incident with Leal. He paused near the dormitory and stood for a few moments, deep in thought, watching the hail spatter against the patio dirt. As he stood there, several boys walked past and nodded respectfully to him. A handful quietly patted his arm or back and continued on their way. In their eyes, Vachio had done exactly the right thing to Leal. If anything, he had shown restraint compared to other functionaries. Vachio understood this, but it still left him troubled. True, he had to do something about Leal. It was essential for him to establish and maintain his physical integrity. He had avoided the use of the dreaded *garrote* to get his message across.... But Vachio wasn't convinced he had acted properly. Moreover, his violent response was completely genuine and spontaneous. He had exploded, lost control. He could have seriously injured the kid. Nothing Leal had done that day warranted that. Vachio sat on the bench and watched dully as lightning bolts crackled against the green eastern mountains.

Soon a group of younger boys came over to spin their tops near Vachio. They laughed and chatted as they played. Looking at them, Vachio realized all over again that these were just children locked up in this nut house. What had occurred between him and Leal was nothing special. Similar incidents, or much worse, occurred in the patio or in the dormitory more than once a day. Vachio shook his head and thought, Hell, at least I can leave this place whenever I want. But these kids... Vachio looked up at the dark clouds and brooded.

"Ey, Vachio!"

Vachio turned and saw Rolo before him.

"What's up with you?" said Rolo, sitting next to him on the bench.

"Ah, nothing." Then Vachio thought of something. "Actually, I was wondering why Leal acted the way he did. Do you know anything about it?"

"Who knows," said Rolo, his eyes evasive. "He's been acting strange lately. Maybe he has a touch of fever."

"Come on, man! He's never acted that bad."

"What's the difference? You put him in his place. It's no big thing. He's just a lousy *sapo* anyway."

"Maybe. But what happened today seemed planned. Like he was

put up to it."

Rolo looked at the kids spinning the tops. They had come closer, one of them brushing against Vachio's leg.

"Hey, you guys! Beat it!" said Rolo to the boys.

The young boys stood their ground for a moment, muttering insults and protesting under their breaths, but when Rolo stood up and raised his hand they slunk off like a pack of jackals confronted by a lion.

"You didn't have to do that," Vachio said to Rolo, shaking his head.

"Do what?" Rolo was genuinely puzzled by Vachio's reaction.

"Scare them off that way. They weren't bothering us."

"I want to tell you something and I don't want them to hear it. They have big mouths."

"All right. What?"

"Between you and me, what happened today was no accident. Leal is the puppet of some of the guards. They put him up to it to get you to do something bad."

"But why?"

Rolo shrugged. "Because they want something they can hold over your head. Why else?"

"Which guards?"

Rolo stood up. "Hey, man, I can't tell you that. I'm no *sapo*. But I think you can figure it out easily enough."

"Galindo and his boys?"

A slow smile spread across Rolo's face. "See you later."

Rolo walked away and Vachio remained on the bench to think over the situation. At the end of the recreation period, Vachio ran across the patio through the steady rain to the terrace. Leal was sitting with his legs crossed near the exit gate at the feet of Torres. As soon as he saw Vachio, Leal glared at him and began rubbing his leg.

Vachio ignored him. "Let me out," he said to the turnkey Oliva.

Leal said something out of the side-of-his-mouth to Torres. Torres laughed and called to Vachio in a cordial voice, "Young Leal here tells me you don't mind playing rough."

Vachio stopped and looked at him. "If I have to. You already know that."

"He doesn't play rough, he plays dirty," snapped Leal.

Vachio took a step toward Leal and said in a low voice. "You only got from me what you were giving. Don't cry if you can't hang."

Leal started to say something else but Torres cut him off. "Correct, Vachio. Absolutely correct. Young Leal still has much to learn. I believe you gave him a valuable lesson."

Vachio shrugged.

"You know," Torres continued, "we got off to a bad start when you didn't bring us those Swedish magazines. But that's not important. I think maybe you and me think in similar ways. Maybe, after we get to know each other better, we'll be like brothers. Like I am with Jaime

Galindo and some of the other men here."

"Maybe. This is a strange world."

Leal snickered. But the irony of the remark was lost on Torres. Vachio slipped through the gate and out of the patio before Torres could think it over and feel offended.

Vachio went straight home. He was going to grab a beer, swing in the hammock, and think things over, but he was sidetracked by a guest in the house. She was sitting on the couch near the doorway, sipping a lemonade and chatting with Renata.

"Vachio, I want you to meet someone," said Renata. "This is the Doctora Gloria Cabrini. She's a physician."

"Glad to meet you," said Vachio, shaking her hand. She was in her late 20s or early 30s and was a tad overweight. She had a plain face with a hint of a mustache but it was illuminated by vivacious blue-green eyes. "Where do you work?"

"At the clinic right near the *Casa de Menores*," she said. "I work on the boys from there often."

"Yeah? How did you get that job?"

"I'm doing my one year rural service.... I'm about halfway through my sentence."

Vachio laughed. "Is it really so bad for you?"

"Ay, man. Bad? It's not bad. It's worse than I can possible describe."

"All right, wait a minute. Before you tell me anything more, let me go get a beer."

"We have fresh cold lemonade here, Vachio," said Renata.

"No, thanks. After work today, I need something a lot stronger than that." Vachio went to the kitchen and opened a cold beer, then he returned and sat facing Gloria. "Now tell me why it's so bad for you here?"

"Why? Well, because I'm from Bogotá, my parents are from Bogotá, and my grandparents were from Bogotá."

"So?"

"Son, can you imagine the torture for a pure bred *Bogotana* like myself to have to work in a rustic backwards place like this? I know I shouldn't say this, since I'm doing my civic duty and all that, but this place is hell for me. I'd rather work in a free clinic in Bogotá, or treating convicts there, than what I've experienced here."

"Come on, Doctora, I lived in Bogotá for three months. I wouldn't exactly call it a paradise."

Gloria straightened up in her seat, seemingly pleased by this challenge. "You're right. Bogotá is no paradise. But at least you can get good international food and fairly new release movies. Obviously, there is much more cultural activity and entertainment there."

"You always have Bucaramanga for a cultural outlet here."

Renata's snort was audible, and Gloria emitted a throaty chuckle.

"Bucaramanga! Son, I live in Bucaramanga. It's a big pueblo. And even if it comes to have one million inhabitants, it will still be a big pueblo. Although, I will say, it is an improvement over Garrotero. At least I can go out on a date there without everyone commenting on whether I'm about to get married or not, or if I'm a loose immoral woman."

"Ah, you just have a bad attitude," said Vachio.

"How long have you been here?"

"Two weeks. Three weeks if you count an earlier visit."

"Three weeks?" Gloria laughed. "Well, at least give yourself two months before you make any judgments." She winked at Renata.

"I'm not making any judgments. I'm just stating an opinion. You seem to have a bad attitude about things. Why do you sound so sour?"

This time Gloria flushed, and her voice turned hard. "Maybe you would understand a little better if you were a woman trying to treat machista country men. You wouldn't believe some of the things I've had to put up with here. Some of the men have even refused treatment from me because I'm a woman. I tell you, the ignorance and vulgarity of some of these people is appalling. And I won't even speak of the superstitions."

"Why not? It sounds interesting."

Gloria broke into laughter again. "All right, son, we'll talk again in a few months. And then we'll see if you still find everything so interesting."

"It's a deal. But for the moment, I'll only say one thing, right now where I'm working, I'm having as much trouble with some of the educated people as I am with some of the so called ignorant ones."

Gloria shrugged. "You're a newcomer here. It's hard for any outsider to come right in and be accepted. It certainly was, and still is on some levels, for me."

"Plus he's a *gringo*," chimed in Renata.

"Yes, he's a *gringo*. That carries all it's own weight here.... But it isn't a fatal disease. You can overcome that."

Vachio decided it was time to get another beer and by the time he returned to the living room, Doctora Gloria was expressing her thanks for a nice visit and preparing to leave. "Come by and visit me at the clinic some time," she said, shaking Vachio's hand. "I'll show you some of the things I have to put up with here."

"So what are you saying? Misery loves company."

"Something like that," she said, laughing. "But seriously, if you ever have a medical problem feel free to come by. We're a government subsidized clinic. Even for visiting *gringos*."

"Thanks. I'll remember that."

Gloria left and Vachio climbed into the hammock. He sipped his beer and enjoyed a cool afternoon breeze.

"So how did you like her?" Renata asked him.

"She seemed all right. Maybe a little snobby.... But she had a good laugh. A real laugh. I think she's probably a conscientious doctor."

"She has a good laugh so you think she's a conscientious doctor?" Renata laughed. "Vachio, you say some strange things some times."

"Why? What's so strange about that?"

"Ay, Vachio."

"Anyway, I wouldn't hesitate to go to her if I had a problem."

Renata shook her head and went to the bedroom to look after the baby. Vachio swayed in the hammock and thought. He had quite a few things to think about.

10

Sunday morning at breakfast, Raimundo chose to grill Vachio about his relation with Opala. Vachio chewed on a bread roll and washed it down with coffee, trying to ignore him.

"So you get up at five in the morning to go out on a hike with a woman who has a child and a husband gone away to Moscow for four years..."

"Yep," said Vachio, slurping more coffee.

Raimundo's booming laugh grated against Vachio's ears. "That is folkloric, son. She must be a real nature woman, eh?"

"A real trooper," said Vachio, refusing the bait.

"So? Have you screwed her yet?"

"Raimundo!" Renata interjected. Up until then she had listened avidly as Raimundo pumped Vachio for information, but this obscenity bugged her. It wouldn't have bugged her if Raimundo had used a more decent phrase such as "make love."

Vachio glanced briefly at the two of them, then over at Marta, the maid, sitting at the end of the table. She was giggling, almost in hysterics. She thought Don Raimundo was one of the funniest men alive.

"I'll say this one time," said Vachio. "It's none of your business. Now, can we change the subject?"

"Oh, touchy touchy," scoffed Raimundo. "Well, that tells us what we want to know. You didn't even touch her, eh?"

Vachio rose from his chair. "Think whatever you want. I'll leave it to your imagination."

Raimundo was surprised for a moment. He was used to Vachio coming back at him with retorts he could play off. "Come on., man. Don't be a baby. Sit down."

"No. I have something to do in Bucaramanga."

"Like what?"

"I'm going to meet the *gringo* colony there. My social life is expanding."

"Oh, well well. And where did you go to school, meester?"

"*Ciao*."

Vachio went to catch his bus. It was still way to early too go, he would have preferred to loaf around the breakfast table for another hour or so, but he was in no mood for Raimundo's heavy-handed humor. Raimundo was his pal but sometimes... No, he wasn't going to tell them anything about Opala. It would get blabbed all over town; Marta would see to that. And besides, his relationship with Opala was going nowhere. He had seen her twice since their little outing, and he was no more attracted to her now than he was then. On top of that, her sister Gertrude had made a play for him one night at her house when Opala stepped outside to talk to one of her political comrades. That's all he needed right now. A family love triangle to go along with all the bullshit at the *Casa de Menores*.

Vachio got off the bus near the Colombo-Americano and headed for the small café operated by Alfonso and Luisa to while away some time. Vachio was so immersed in thought he actually walked past the café and was well up the street before he was brought up short by a sharp voice. "Hey, man! Where you headed in such a hurry?"

Vachio looked up and turned around. It was Jimmy DeLeon. "Man, I don't know where I'm going? Anywhere. Somewhere."

"Then how about here?" said Jimmy, laughing. "You tell me your problems and I'll tell you mine."

"Yeah. Why not." Vachio took a seat at Jimmy's table and ordered a coffee and a pastry.

"So what's on your mind?" Jimmy asked.

"It's a long story."

"I've got time. I'm waiting for my old lady to show up. And since she went shopping, I don't expect her back anytime soon. You know what I mean?" Jimmy laughed at his own joke.

"All right, man, I'll tell you a little..." Vachio launched into his story, telling Jimmy about his problems at the *Casa de Menores*, starting with Gustavo's promises to him during his site visit, and ending with his confrontation with Leal at the guard's instigation.

At the end, Jimmy whistled and said, "Man, that's fucked up. You come down here with the best of intentions, volunteer your time and efforts, and they clown you that way.... If I were you, I wouldn't put up with that shit. I'd go somewhere where I'm appreciated."

"Don't think I haven't been considering that option."

"You know, man," said Jimmy, rubbing his chin, "I may have an option for you to consider."

"Oh?"

"Would you like another coffee? I think I'll have another."

"All right."

Jimmy ordered the coffee. Then when it came, he took a deep

drink as though it were beer, wiped his lips with his napkin, and said, "Do you like business?"

Vachio laughed. "It's never held any fascination for me. That's why I'm in social work."

"All right, let me rephrase that. Do you like money?"

"It's not to like or dislike. It's just something I know I need."

"Exactly. And since we all need it, isn't it better to have plenty of it so you can tell jerks like that Señor Director to go fuck himself?"

"Well, I wouldn't say he's a jerk. He means well."

"Yeah, yeah, whatever. But you get my point, don't you?"

"Sure. And if I didn't know better, I'd think you were leading up to some pyramid scheme."

Jimmy laughed. "Nah nah. None of that bullshit. I deal in straight business and hard commodities. Payment in hand for products delivered. And it's possible I could use someone like you for this new venture I'm thinking about."

"What makes you think that? You barely know me."

"I know you well enough for what I have in mind. Look, Gary, I own several businesses. I've hired a lot of people in my time. I'm used to making quick judgements. And they damn well better be good ones or I stand to lose money. Now in your case, from what you've told me about yourself and from what I see, I think you're *correcto*."

"How do you mean that?"

"I think you're *correcto*. A correct person.... You see, in Colombia, when someone does straight business with no bullshit, we say they are correct and worthy of confidence."

"You mean someone you can trust."

"No, there is a difference. For example, I can say that my family is *de confianza*, that I can trust them, but I wouldn't always say that they are *correcto*. In fact, in some cases, they would be even more likely to abuse my trust and take advantage of our relationship to get over on me in a business transaction. As my brother is trying to do right now. You understand?"

"Yeah, I think I do."

"Good. That's another thing I like about you. I can see you have a real feel for Spanish. You're going to be completely bilingual. And I need someone like that, too. And I also think you're too sharp a guy to be wasting your time at any *Casa de Menores*."

"Now hold on, man, don't jump to wrong conclusions. I don't feel like I'm wasting my time there. I may be pissed off about what's going on, but I'm not even close to ready to give up on what I'm trying to do."

"Yeah, I hear you. And I respect where you're coming from. What you want to do is admirable.... But just hear me out. Because if you come in with me, you may someday have the bread to run your own *Casa de Menores* any fucking way you see fit."

"Sure, I'll listen to anything. Go Ahead."

"All right, it's like this.... I think I told you before that I was looking over some business possibilities in Cali."

"Yeah, I remember."

"Well, I've got something solid cooking there right now. An export business between the west coast of Colombia and the west coast of the U.S. It's perfect for you, guy. That's your home turf. And I can use a good man like you to look after things when I can't be around."

"What kind of business?"

Jimmy smiled. "Tropical fish."

"Tropical fish?"

"Hell, yes! Tropical fish! There's bucks to be made."

Vachio shook his head incredulously. "Yeah, man, if you say so."

"I don't say so. I already know so. It's a very lucrative venture when you have the right connections." Jimmy was about to go on when he was interrupted by the arrival of a young woman.

"This is Roxanna, my wife," said Jimmy, moving over to give her room at the table.

"Pleased to meet you," said Vachio, shaking her ring-studded hand. Roxanna was a tall woman, flashily dressed, revealing to advantage an opulent figure. She was of mixed-race, close to a *mulata,* with regular features, light brown skin, green eyes, and a bright smile.

"Oh, you speak English. Good," she said.

Vachio smiled. "And what part of New York City are you from?"

Roxanna chuckled. "Is my accent that obvious?"

"Yeah. You must be proud of it."

"I'm from Washington Heights in Manhattan."

"She's really from the Dominican Republic," said Jimmy, placing his left hand on her hip and sitting her down. "She's a hot Dominicana. Right, babe?"

"I was born in the Dominican Republic. But my family moved to New York when I was two."

"So how do you like it here?" Vachio asked.

Roxanna frowned. "It's kind of conservative here. I'd rather be in New York but I can't convince Jimmy to come back home."

"Don't worry, babe, I'll be going back to New York soon. It's just that there are some business things here I can't pass up."

"Business things?" Roxanna curled her lips. "And what might her name be?"

"Come on, baby, you know you're the only one I love."

"I'm the only one he loves," said Roxanna, looking at Vachio, "but not the only one he sleeps with."

Vachio began to feel distinctly uncomfortable.

Jimmy smiled, but his voice turned from playful to ominous. "If you don't like our marriage arrangement—you know what you can do."

"That's fine," she said in Spanish. "I can share for now." Roxanna finished with a sly smile.

Looking at her, Vachio didn't get the impression she was the type to sit around by herself at home waiting for hubby if she wasn't being satisfied.

Roxanna ordered a coffee and the three of them chatted. She was quick and lively in her conversation. At one point, she reached across the table and framed Vachio's face with her hands.

"You know," she said, smoothing back Vachio's hair, "I could really do something for your look."

"What's wrong with my look?"

"Long hair doesn't suit you, honey. You would look cute with medium length hair. Not too short. Because then your ears would stick out. But medium length." Roxanna squinted her eyes and grinned. "Yeah, medium length."

"Ah, my hair is fine the way it is."

Roxanna laughed. "It could be much better. Anyway, what's with you? You one of these rebellious characters trying to make a statement?"

"Not really. I just don't pay that much attention to my hair."

"Then let me cut it for you. You'll like what you get."

"She can do what she says, Gary. Roxanna is a trained beautician. I even let her cut my hair. And I can afford the best."

"Well, maybe I would like to keep my hair shorter in this climate."

"Yeah, all right. What do you say, Jimmy? Let's invite him over to the apartment one evening.... I'll cook up a pan of lasagna, too."

"Sure, let's do it. But not for a couple of weeks, huh. Remember, I'm going to Cali to get that business set up."

"Yeah, in two weeks. *Está bien.* My sister is coming from New York to visit then, too. That's perfect. We'll have a hair-cutting party. Let's do it on a Friday night. What do you say?" She looked at Vachio.

"Sounds fine to me."

"Good. It's an appointment."

"Well, we better get going, babe," said Jimmy, rising from his chair. "We've got that thing at my brother's house today."

"Yeah, I almost forgot. And I wish you had." Roxanna took a pen out of her purse, wrote their address on a napkin, and gave it to Vachio. "Don't forget. In two weeks. Come around seven or eight."

"And think about what we were talking about earlier," said Jimmy. "I'll have more details for you when we meet again.... Remember, tropical fish. It can't miss."

"Yeah, tropical fish," muttered Vachio.

11

Monday morning, Vachio went to work writing a schedule of events to distribute to staff and, with the help of Barranca, started doing the posters with the names of the groups, group leaders, and planned activities for said groups during the recreation hour and at night.

Renata came up the stairs at mid-morning and saw Vachio hard at work on the floor of one of the spare upstairs rooms, his magic markers and poster boards at his side, and clucked approvingly. "Now you're getting down to the job, Vachio. This is what you needed to do at the very beginning. Now you are busy."

Vachio looked up and gave her a wry smile. "Yeah, I'm busy. Now let's see if they'll follow a written schedule any better than they follow verbal instructions. Otherwise this is a busy waste of time."

"Ay, Vachio, that's no way to think. You have to be more positive."

"All right, I'll be very, but very positive."

A few minutes later Raimundo came up and stood looking over his shoulder without saying a word. Vachio sighed and set down his green marker. "All right, start laughing."

"Laughing? Why would I do that? This is very good what you're doing."

"Yeah? Do you think the kids will follow the program now because it's on paper?"

Raimundo emitted a gurgling laugh. "Of course not. Don't be crazy. But the administrators will be very happy. They all have to do a lot of useless paperwork and nothing will please them more than to see you doing some as well.... You'll be one of the gang now, man. This should get them off your back for a while."

"Well, that's something anyway."

"No, really, what you're doing should help. Now come downstairs for a moment. I want you to meet a friend of ours who just arrived from Bogotá."

Vachio followed Raimundo downstairs and was introduced to Pablo Montero, a short, balding, bespectacled man with a ready laugh and an air of mischievous alertness. He was dressed sloppily, in dark slacks, leather sandals, and a white shirt, the shirttail out and flapping behind him. Pablo was a physicist at a university in Bogotá. He was originally from Barcelona and was a friend of the Gerstners from apartment parties in Bogotá.

"Let's have a little something to eat," said Renata, flushed with pleasure at the arrival of this guest. "Pablo can fill us in on all the gossip about our old friends."

"Surely," said Pablo, grinning amiably. "But there are very few of the old crew left."

The table was laden with scrambled eggs, thick slices of ham, bread and butter, jam, fresh fruit, and coffee. Pablo and the Gerstners sat down for a leisurely brunch, and talked about people Vachio didn't know. Vachio bolted his food. He needed to go check on Barranca.

"Well," said Vachio, rising from his seat and extending his hand to Pablo, "I have to go to work now. We can talk some more tonight."

"Where are you going in such a hurry?" asked Raimundo.

"Work."

"Work? You can go to work anytime. I was going to ask you if you could show Pablo around the town in a little while."

"I have things to do this morning," said Vachio, a slight edge to his voice. "But if Pablo wants to come to the *Casa de Menores* with me, I'll be happy to show him around. It's probably the biggest tourist attraction here anyway."

"I'm agreeable to anything," said Pablo. "I don't need anyone to put themselves out for me. I came here to relax."

"Now here's a reasonable man," said Vachio, looking at Raimundo.

"Pablo, you stay here with me," said Renata. "We have a lot to catch up on. I'll show you what there is to see in this town later."

"But Reina, you're pregnant. And this heat."

"Yogi!" Yogi was her pet name for Raimundo because his body reminded her of Yogi Bear. "I'm pregnant, not an invalid. A walk is very good for me."

"Yeah, Yogi, listen to your wife," said Vachio. Then he turned to Pablo. "It'll be more interesting for you to visit during the recreation time at four. That's when all the kids are out in the patio. And having a visitor is interesting for them, too."

"I look forward to it," said Pablo. "I see *gamines* in Bogotá all the time. It will be interesting to meet some of them in captivity."

"It is that. But be sure to come with empty pockets. Otherwise, they'll steal you blind."

Vachio excused himself and went to the *Casa de Menores*. He found Barranca in one of the empty classrooms, bent diligently over a poster board.

"Hi, Profé," he said. "Look! I've finished two of them. And I would have finished them all if they didn't keep moving me from place to place."

"Why aren't you working on the desk in the recreation room?"

Barranca shrugged. "I don't know, Profé. The guards won't let me."

"Won't let you? That's what that room is for."

"I don't know why. I wanted to work there."

"We'll see about this."

Vachio went out to the terrace and found Ramon on duty.

"Why can't Barranca work in the recreation room?" Vachio asked him.

"He can. If you're around to watch him."

"Look, this is the point, I'm not always going to be around to watch them. At times they are going to run the program and they need access to that room."

"Yes, yes, I understand. But it's too dangerous."

"Why?"

"Come on and I'll show you."

They went down to the recreation room and Ramon opened it up and pointed to the rafters. "You see that gap between the ceiling and the walls to let the air circulate?"

"Yes."

"And the desks?"

"Yes."

"Well, man, it's no trick for the boys to pile them one on top of the other and escape over the wall.... Unless they are under supervision."

Vachio sighed. Ramon was right. Those damn desks.

"I see what you mean. But Ordoñez was supposed to get these desks out of here."

"Ordoñez?" Ramon laughed. "He might get around to it by next year. And until then, we can't allow any boy, let alone a weasel like Barranca, unsupervised access to that room. It's our responsibility if there is an escape. You understand?"

"Yeah, yeah. I'll go talk to Gustavo."

Vachio found Gustavo outside of his office and explained the situation. Gustavo listened with an air of impatience, but agreed to go down into the patio and look.

"I doubt they could pile the desks up high enough to reach that space," said Gustavo, eyeing the ceiling. "And the opening isn't very large. I don't see a problem."

"I don't know," said Vachio. "But I think I could squeeze through there."

"I agree with Vachio," said Ramon. "That would be easy for any of the smaller boys."

Gustavo considered this for a moment. Then he shook his head and closed up the room. "I really don't have time for this. You'll just have to wait until Ordoñez gets those desks moved."

"Yeah, but...what about when I can't be here and the boys need access?"

Gustavo looked at Ramon. "Then the guards will have to keep an eye on the situation."

"With all respect Don Gustavo, that stretches us too thin. Especially at night."

"If we can just get those desks out of there it's no problem," said Vachio. "Let's talk to Ordoñez. I'll be happy to help him move the desks."

"Ordoñez is in the lot behind the cafeteria, Don Gustavo," added Ramon.

"All right. All right. Let's go," said Gustavo.

On the walk over to the lot, Gustavo mumbled under his breath about stupid little details and no one able to do a thing without him getting involved. Walking along beside him, Vachio felt as irritated as Gustavo. He didn't like bothering him over this stuff, either.

They found Ordoñez working with McCorney, welding a soccer post together. This time Ordoñez was prepared. He gave Gustavo five good reasons why he couldn't possibly move the desks out any time in the near future. "But don't worry, Don Gustavo. I will take care of it in time." Ordoñez smiled at Vachio.

"Yeah, don't worry," said McCorney to Vachio. "The kids can't escape by climbing those desks. Half of them are ready to fall apart anyway."

Gustavo turned and walked off. Vachio caught up to him.

"So what do I do?" Vachio asked him.

"You will supervise the boys in that room."

"And when I can't be around?"

"Then the guards will have to do it. It is their job to cooperate with you and the program."

"Yeah, but..."

"That's it," said Gustavo, waving his hand. "I don't have time for this." He turned and left Vachio standing in the patio.

Yeah, right, thought Vachio. The guards cooperate with me? Some of them don't cooperate with you. Ah, hell!

Vachio called Barranca and they posted the week's recreation schedule on the wall.

"Nothing to worry about, Profé," Barranca assured Vachio. "With me helping you out, the program is going to run smooth. You can count on me for anything."

"Show me, man. Don't tell me."

Barranca laughed. "Ay, Profé, you're a hard one. But you'll soon see."

That afternoon at the recreation period, Vachio assembled the group leaders and gave them their assignments.

"But we want to play soccer today," immediately complained Amorocho. "Not volley."

"You always want to play soccer," said Vachio. "But you can't every day. We have to rotate the groups so everyone gets a chance to play once in a while. Your group gets to play soccer on Wednesday."

"Wednesday? Only Wednesday?"

"You get to play every night if you want. What's the problem?"

"My group wants to play today."

"Well, you can't. Now get your ball from Barranca and get your group together."

Amarocho mumbled under his breath, his complaints echoed by several other group leaders unhappy with their assignments. Those who were pleased with their assignments mocked them.

"Go to shit!" the hot-tempered Amarocho barked at Pedro Caballero, the biggest mouth among the jeering boys.

"I'll stick you in your own, faggot!"

Vachio jumped between them. "Cut that stuff! You guys are supposed to be the leaders here. You act like bigger babies than Little Abel."

Amarocho and Caballero glowered at each other and muttered curses.

"That's right! Listen to Profé Vachio," chimed in Barranca, sitting as though he were some Oriental potentate behind the desk in front of the recreation room entrance, ready to dole out the basketball, volleyball, micro-soccer ball, and the ping pong equipment. "Show some maturity."

Amarocho and Caballero immediately forgot their dispute and turned on Barranca, burning his ears with curses.

"Shut up! All of you!" yelled Vachio. The boys quieted down, momentarily impressed by Vachio's anger. "I don't have time for this. There is a guest here who wants to see the yard and I need to get him and show him around. So I want you leaders to get your boys together, get out there, and show me what you can do."

"*Si, Duce. A la orden,*" said Mocho.

"Yeah, get going." Vachio walked away from them, deliberately turning away as though he had complete confidence in them. When he reached the terrace and turned back to look, he still saw them grouped around Barranca, arguing with him. Vachio shook his head and went to the kitchen where he had left Pedro Montero.

"Since you're a physicist, you might enjoy this experiment I'm trying today," Vachio said to Pedro on the way to the patio.

"What is it?"

"Seeing how the boys do trying to organize themselves."

"Do you expect success?"

"I don't know. But we can't do much worse than with me trying to do it alone."

Pedro laughed.

"Did you leave your wallet and other stuff at the house?" Vachio asked him.

"No. I thought you were joking."

"Joking? No, I wasn't joking. They'll pick you clean. Come on, give me your wallet."

Pedro handed over his wallet but he insisted on keeping his loose change and pens. "I'll do a little experiment myself. I don't think these kids can rob me. I do live in Bogotá after all."

"Whatever. I'll bet you a beer they clean your pockets."

"You're on."

They passed through the gate and Vachio saw the usual mayhem down in the patio. The only difference was that some of the kids were running amok on their peer group leaders instead of on Vachio.

"These plans always look so good on paper," Vachio said to Pedro. "Then you have reality."

"What do you mean? The kids look like they're having a good time to me."

"Yes, they're definitely having a good time. It's just not organized."

"Organized?" Pedro looked out over the crowded patio. "How can you organize so many in so small an area?"

Vachio laughed and patted Pedro on the back. "Hey, I think I like you."

They descended the steps and Vachio and Pedro were soon surrounded by a group of clamoring *gamines*, most of them the kids who were assigned to play nonexistent table games.

"Where did all these guys come from?" Pedro asked.

"They're supposed to play table games but we don't have enough. But this is good for today. You can be their table game."

Vachio helped Pedro get situated on a stone bench in the middle of the patio and said, "You can be my special guest speaker today, Pedro."

"Sure, I'm game. But what do I tell them?"

"Tell them all about how you worked hard, overcame obstacles, and became a physicist. Inspire them."

"Where are you going?" asked Pedro, his eyes betraying panic as the boys grew bolder and pressed around him.

"To help out the peer leaders. See you soon."

Vachio first went to the basketball court to check on Rolo. He was red-faced and cursing, still trying to get his group organized into teams.

Vachio laughed and clapped him on the shoulder. "Hey, now you know how I feel. Not so easy, is it?"

"These little jerks," Rolo muttered, and screamed at Bumbuco who had taken the ball and run off to the other end of the court to play alone. Vachio helped Rolo get the boys organized into teams and got them started playing. Then he moved on to the next group. After going around to five of the eight groups, Vachio realized he was wasting his time. As soon as he got one group up and going and moved to another, the group he had just finished organizing would dissolve into bickering confusion. It was like trying to put out a brushfire in a high wind; and it was evident that many of the boys considered frustrating Vachio and their own peer leaders a much better sport than any other game they were being offered. Within a half hour, realizing it was more fun to mess with authority than to represent it, five of the peer leaders wanted to resign. Vachio got them together and tried to pump them up. Inside he was cracking up at the looks of baffled irritation on their faces. He knew that was the face they had seen from him over the last weeks. Finally Vachio shrugged and turned them loose.

"You're on your own, guys. Do the best you can." Then he turned to go check on Pedro.

The boys around Pedro were snapping their hands with glee and laughing hysterically. Vachio smiled. Pedro was a hit. Vachio drew closer to get in on the joke.

"Say *azul*," said little Abel.

"A-thool," said Pedro, in his strong Spanish accent.

"A-thool! Did you hear that?" said Little Abel, cracking up. "He speaks funny Spanish."

"No, man, he speaks the mother Spanish. From Spain," said Vachio.

"It sounds funny," repeated Little Abel. The other boys agreed with him.

"I actually spoke *Catalán* first," added Pedro.

Vachio noticed several of the boys holding Pedro's pens and confiscated them. "Here," he said, handing them back to him. A look of surprise came over Pedro's face. "But how..."

The bell clanged for dinner assembly and the boys scattered. As Vachio and Pedro left the patio, Vachio said, "I hope they weren't too hard on you. They can get pretty stupid with their little games."

"No, on the contrary, I had a good time with them." Pedro chuckled. "It's not exactly like teaching a class at the university."

"No, I imagine not.... Did you check your pockets yet?"

Pedro rummaged through his pockets and found nothing. "I have no idea when or how they did it. You were right."

"You owe me a beer."

"Sure. With pleasure." Pedro shook his head. "I must say, I really admire the way you have with these boys."

"Admire me? Please, stop with the flowery compliments."

"No, truly. I think you strike a good balance with them. You are demanding that they do and think for themselves. And you talk to them as though they were responsible human beings. Not subhumans. That will serve them well in the future."

"Huh, I wish certain administrators shared your opinion. Then I might actually feel good about working here."

"Be patient. You haven't been here very long. They aren't used to the American way of doing things."

My way is not necessarily the American way. There are plenty of administrators in the United States who think just like the ones here. Believe me, I've worked with other big organizations in the States."

"Well, whatever the case, I like your style. I encourage you not to lose heart. You have something to offer these boys."

"Thanks."

Vachio was disappointed when Pedro Montero left Garrotero after only three days. Not that he blamed him. He was going to spend the remainder of his vacation on the tropical beaches of Cartagena.

12

Raimundo burst into the house Thursday evening with his eyes alight and a grin on his face. He approached Vachio, swaying gently in the hammock and listening to music, tired after chasing the kids around, and said in English, "Man, the shit is really going to hit the fan now." Raimundo guffawed. "Garrotero *folclórico*."

"What are you talking about?" asked Vachio drowsily. He already had two beers in him and Raimundo had roused him from a pleasant dream.

"Gustavo finally made his move. He's going after the bad guards."

Vachio sat up in the hammock and shook his head. "Say what?"

"Gustavo did it. This afternoon he did an interview over the radio and with the newspaper. He accused a faction of the guards of gross corruption and of carrying on homosexual relations with some of the kids."

"So? Is that a secret?"

Raimundo laughed. "Ay, man, sometimes I think you're dense. Of course it's no secret! But to say it publicly! Over the radio and in the newspapers!" Raimundo whistled. "That's like slapping those macho guards in the face. They have to do something in return."

"Yeah, well, when they do, let me know," said Vachio, slipping back down in the hammock. "Right now I want to finish my nap."

Raimundo shook his head and went to tell a more receptive audience, the maid Marta, all about the scandal.

But later that night, Vachio began to feel the urgency of the situation. Gustavo came over, drank two full beers, very unusual for him, and spoke to Raimundo as though he were making plans for war. His voice was exalted and betrayed some nervousness. "This time," Gustavo thundered, slapping the glass table top, "Bogotá cannot ignore the situation. With this public stink they have no choice but to send investigators. Finally we will get some action against these corrupt degenerates."

"Have the guards made a move yet?" Raimundo asked.

"My sources tell me that they are having an emergency meeting at Galindo's house right now."

Raimundo rubbed his hands together gleefully. "Sources? You mean spies, right Gustavo?"

"As you wish."

Raimundo looked at Vachio. "*Folklórico*. Very *folklórico*."

"Or maybe a tempest in a teapot," said Vachio in English.

The very next morning the guards made their move. Through their spokesperson, Jaime Galindo, Chief of the Guard's Union, they released a statement denying all charges made against them by the esteemed Señor Director. And furthermore, it wasn't the guards carrying on homosexual relations with the boys, but the very same Señor Director himself.

That night Gustavo came over to the house and railed against the guards for a good two hours. "Can you imagine the gall of those shameless degenerates. To accuse me of the very same filth they inflict on the poor boys. And yet, that cunning low-down Galindo has hit me where it hurts."

"No," said Raimundo. "He attacked you in a transparent obvious way. Who would believe you capable of being a child molester."

"Raimundo, I appreciate your support. But you know as well as I know that there are many ignorant people in this town who whisper that I'm a homosexual."

"Why would they think that?" asked Vachio.

"Because I'm 37 and I choose to remain a bachelor. Most of them can't understand that I've chosen to devote my life to these poor abandoned boys rather than raise a family of my own.... Anyway, I've disturbed your weekend enough with this problem," said Gustavo to Raimundo and Renata. "It's time for me to take leave. See you soon."

Raimundo started chortling as soon as Gustavo went out the door. "Man, is this *folklórico*, or what? Garrotero City."

"It's bizarre. No! Make that stupid," offered Vachio

"Why do you say that?"

"Who cares if Gustavo is gay or not. As long as he does his job in a professional manner, he's no different than a heterosexual male teacher working in a girls high school."

"Ay, Gary, don't be naive. Maybe that is so in Germany, or in the United States, but this is Garrotero."

"Naive, nothing! There are places in the United States that would react the same way to this issue as here. And despite what you say, probably in Germany as well. I don't think sexual preference is the issue here. It's child molestation and abuse of power."

"Of course, of course. Anyway, I don't think Gustavo is gay. I know for a fact that he goes to the prostitute bars here in town once in a while."

"Whatever. I don't care if he is or he isn't. That's his business. I'm just worried about what I'm supposed to say when these government investigators come around and start asking questions."

"It's really not your concern. You are a guest worker here. Don't get involved."

"Don't get involved? How can I not be involved? I'm here."

"Just steer clear of it. You don't know anything anyway."

Vachio laughed. "No, I don't know anything. Hell, on my site visit a couple of the guards and some of the boys sounded me out on what I thought about having sex with young boys."

"But have you seen anything?"

"No. They haven't done anything in front of me. Except for some punishments."

"Then you don't know anything. Leave it that way, Gary. Please leave it that way. You don't want to get mixed up in this mess."

"Well, we'll see. I may not have a choice."

On Sunday, everyone took a holiday from the scandal. The Germans went to the market, Vachio went to Bucaramanga to loaf and visit some of his new friends, and Gustavo stayed out of sight.

Monday morning, Vachio went to the *Casa de Menores* bright and early. He hung out by the front entrance with Pacho and chatted. Pacho was casual. Too casual. He didn't mention "The Situation." Then, just as Gustavo emerged from a phone conference in his office and came to the front door of the reception area, Jaime Galindo and Torres showed up. Torres slowed his step and for a moment his eyes locked with Gustavo's. Pure hatred radiated from both of them.

"How goes it, Señor Director?" said Galindo, gently nudging Torres along.

"How goes it with you?" countered Gustavo.

"Fine."

They continued on and went to the patio to talk to the guard on duty. Gustavo, acting distant and preoccupied, called Pacho into his office for a private conference. Vachio whistled to himself and went to talk to Maria Elena in her office. Maria Elena was polite and evasive. Her idea was to ignore "The Situation" and it might disappear. She also advised Vachio not to get involved.

It was a hot cloudy muggy day. Vachio roamed the corridors and the two patios, snooped around the kitchen, and visited the workshops, trying to get a feel for which way the wind was blowing. The professors and administrators were tense, inordinately quiet and polite. The guards lurked along the terrace, holding whispered conferences throughout the day. The boys were sullen, snapping at each other more than usual and with added venom.

During the recreation hour, to blow off some steam, Vachio decided to play basketball with the older boys. After about 10 minutes of play, while standing still looking to make a pass, he suddenly felt a wave of dizziness wash over him.

"Time out," he called, after regaining his equilibrium. He suddenly felt drained, shaky, his pulse hammering in his ears. It scared him. "Take my place," he told Mocho.

"Man, you don't look so good," said Mocho, eyeing Vachio and coming up close. "You've gone pale. What's wrong?"

"I don't know. Maybe the heat. I need to sit down for a moment."

"The heat? It isn't that hot."

Vachio sat on the stone bench in the middle of the patio. His torso sagged forward and his head fell into his hands. Two of the younger boys came over and sat on either side of him, rubbing his back with comforting hands and chirping sympathetically. A breeze kicked up and seemed to knife through his body. Vachio was convulsed by shivers. What's wrong with me? he thought. He had felt a little out-of-sorts and lethargic since lunch, but he had attributed this to nervousness over "The Situation." Now he knew it was something else.

The skies opened up and a late afternoon downpour commenced. Vachio breathed a sigh of relief. The recreation period was finished. He could leave. The rain revived him a bit and he made it home and slid immediately into the patio hammock. Gusts of cool, moisture laden air, whipped off the mountain peaks, buffeted him in the hammock. Vachio knew he should go up to his bedroom and get under the sheets but the cool air felt good. Vachio reached up and touched his cheek. It was burning. He covered himself with the gray blanket he used for a pillow, folded the edges of the hammock into a cocoon, and fell into a torpor.

Vachio revived to the sound of Raimundo's booming voice. It was dark now and everyone was seated in the dining room . Vachio rolled out of the hammock, came shakily to his feet, and went to join them.

"Hey, sleepy head," called Raimundo, munching on a sausage. "We thought you were going to miss dinner."

"I don't feel very hungry," said Vachio, the bright overhead light hurting his eyes. He flopped onto a chair.

"And what's the cause of this miracle?" asked Renata.

"I'm not feeling right."

"You don't look right," commented Marta, folding towels at the portable ironing board nearby.

"Have a beer. That'll fix you right up," said Raimundo. "We're expecting Gustavo shortly."

"Eat something," added Renata.

Vachio sipped at the beer thirstily. It tasted foul and sour to him. He picked listlessly at Renata's excellent potato salad and forced down some bread and butter. The food had no taste. He had no desire to eat. Something is wrong with me, he thought.

Gustavo arrived before dinner ended. He was bursting with energy and his freckle-spotted hands waggled in the air as he talked. "I got the word from Bogotá this afternoon. Two special government investigators are arriving on the morning plane. Now, at last, these disgusting individuals will have to face up to their crimes." Gustavo went on and on, waxing jubilant as he described possible punishments for Galindo and his crew.

Vachio tried to follow the conversation, but the words were a jumble in his groggy mind, the faces at the table bulbous and shifting, as though they were underwater. He pulled himself together and asked Gustavo,

“So, what’s going to happen tomorrow?”

“Tomorrow all classes and shops are suspended but the attendance of all personnel is mandatory. The investigators have full authority to interview anyone they please.”

“What about me?”

“What about you? You’ve only been here a month. I don’t know what you would have to say. But if the investigators interview you, answer their questions honestly.”

“All right.” Vachio stood up. “Excuse me, but I don’t feel too well. I’m going to bed.”

“What’s wrong?” asked Gustavo.

“I don’t know. Maybe it’s something I ate. See you tomorrow.”

The next morning, after a night of tossing and turning, Vachio dragged himself off to the *Casa de Menores*. Now, in addition to his fever and lack of appetite, Vachio’s muscles had begun to ache and the sun stabbed at his eyes like a dagger. I’m not getting any better, he thought. What the hell is this?

Vachio entered the outer patio and took a seat on the bench under the shade of a potted Arica palm. He propped himself against the wall and looked around, watching the goings-on in a semi-delirious haze. Most of the staff of the *Casa de Menores* was assembled in and around the patio. They stood or sat in tight groups, speaking in low voices, nervous laughter bursting out in spasms. They looked as skittish and high-strung as young colts. For the first time since his arrival, Vachio was completely ignored. He was grateful for this.

At regular intervals, a pair of boys were brought up from the lower patio and taken into Emilio Montoya’s office for interrogation by one of the government investigators. Another young man, slim and earnest, wearing a white *guayabera* and olive drab slacks, strolled purposefully about the patio and talked to the *professores* and the *maestros*. Pacho hovered near his elbow, his face anxious and eager to please, offering suggestions.

After a while McCorney came over and sat beside Vachio. He puffed nervously on a *Piel Roja* cigarette and held tightly to the bench with his right hand. “Have they interviewed you yet?”

“No,” said Vachio.

“Maybe they won’t. He’s conducting random interviews.”

“Whatever.”

McCorney crushed out the spent cigarette with his heel and went to talk to Don Miguel on the other side of the patio. Seconds later Jaime Galindo took McCorney’s place. Vachio glanced at him. Galindo’s eyes followed the investigator. “What are you going to tell the investigator?” Galindo asked Vachio.

“I’ll tell him what I’ve seen.”

“You haven’t seen anything!” Galindo’s face was before Vachio’s eyes. It was tight and worried, the usual oily tone gone from his voice.

"Leave me alone," Vachio answered. "I'll say what I will."

Galindo started to say something else, then he took a good look at Vachio's wan perspiring face and left.

A few minutes later the investigator came abreast of Vachio, Pacho at his shoulder, and looked directly at him. Vachio raised his head and looked at him. Pacho gestured toward Vachio, then said something in a low voice to the investigator. The investigator nodded slightly and passed on to interview someone else. Vachio was disappointed and relieved at the same time.

A short time later, Maria Elena, on her way to the kitchen, paused to say hello. "How are you?"

"Not so good," admitted Vachio.

Maria Elena stooped down and eyed his face. "You don't look good. Actually, you look pretty bad."

"Probably not as bad as I feel."

"You better let the nurse examine you."

"Is she here?"

"No. She's at the clinic. You better go right now."

"Yes. I'll go. But what about the investigation?"

"Oh, don't worry about that. It really doesn't concern you that much."

If Vachio had felt better, he would have argued that point with her; instead, he nodded and teetered to his feet. He felt much worse than he had even an hour before.

"Will you be all right?" she asked, steadying him with her hand.

"Yes. I can make it there alone."

Vachio made the block-and-a-half walk to the clinic in a stumbling haze. Fortunately, the Doctora Gloria was standing in front of the building having a smoke when Vachio arrived. She took one look at his face and emitted a low whistle. "Ay, now you come to visit, with the face of a puppy with distemper." She tossed her cigarette in the street and told Vachio to stick out his tongue. "Uh huh. We're having a run of this," she said after a quick look.

"What is it?"

"Dengue, *mijo*. Bad luck."

"Are you sure? I mean, you haven't even examined me."

Gloria laughed, but her eyes were sympathetic. "Has to be. With those yellowish eyes of yours. I seem to recall them being greenish when I met you the first time.... But if it will make you feel better, tell me your symptoms."

"I feel dizzy and weak. I don't have an appetite. And my muscles ache..."

"Do your bones ache?"

"No."

"They will. This thing hasn't hit you with its full force yet.... No, there is no doubt. You have dengue."

"What can I do for it?"

"Go to bed right now. Get plenty of rest. Drink as much fluid as you can to keep from dehydrating. And try to force down some food to keep your strength up.... That's about it. Unless you want some sleeping pills or some pain pills."

"No, I don't like pills."

Gloria shook her head. "I don't envy what's in store for you. I hope you have a high pain threshold."

"How long will it last?"

Gloria shrugged. "It varies with the individual. From five days to two weeks. Most of my patients have it about a week."

"Can it be fatal?"

"For children and old weak people it can." Gloria patted him on the shoulder. "But you should be all right. You're young and strong. Go home and go to bed. Don't even think about working for a week. And if there is any complication, send for me."

"All right, thanks, Doctora."

"Forget it. That's what I'm here for. Now go right home and get to bed."

13

As the Doctora Gloria had predicted, Vachio's condition worsened. Sitting at the dinner table that night, one arm twined around the back of his chair for support, Vachio felt pulses of pain from inside his bones. It was terrible, like nothing he had ever experienced, as though mice were nibbling away at him from inside out. He tried to describe the pain to Raimundo, Renata, and Marta, but his thinking was fuzzy and disoriented, his tongue a swollen rope in his mouth. Renata and Marta treated him sympathetically, but their concern sounded clinical and perfunctory to Vachio. Raimundo, on the other hand, seemed offended by Vachio's condition and tried to jolly him out of it by peppering him with good-natured jibes. Vachio's only response was a dull stare. He was defenseless. None of them had ever had dengue before. Vachio wondered if he had contracted it that day at the beautiful grotto with Opala. He had received a number of mosquito bites there.

Abruptly Vachio rose from the table. "See you guys later," he slurred. "Don't bother me for anything. I'm going to bed."

"Bah, you make it sound as though you were dying," scoffed Raimundo.

A flash of anger shot through Vachio. He marshaled some strength and said, "Right now I feel as though I don't care one way or another. Understand? Now lay off."

"But Gustavo is coming over to tell us about the investigation in a little while."

"Fine. You tell me about it later. *Ciao*."

Vachio wobbled up the steps to his room on the second floor and collapsed on the bed. He couldn't believe how weak he felt. All he wanted was to get away from other people and suffer alone. At that moment, the crisis at the *Casa de Menores* was a bizarre joke. A nothing. The only thing that mattered was this throbbing toothache emanating from the marrow of his bones.

With the shutters closed, Vachio's room was dark as a tomb, a cavern with high beamed ceilings and plaster walls, smelling faintly of old wood and creosote and fine yellow dust. The only furnishings were the bed, his seaman's chest which doubled as a night stand and a closet, a straight-back chair to lay his clothes on, and a bare mattress in one corner of the room for guests. Vachio had no interest in sprucing up this room. It was for sleeping in at night. He spent most of his time at home in the open patio downstairs, even taking most of his *siestas* in the hammock there. But now, for the first time, this room felt like a welcome place of refuge.

Vachio lay on his back and stared at nothing, bathed in sweat, trying to lay as still as possible. The slightest movement sent shivers of pain through his bones and muscles. Vaguely he heard the sounds of children playing in the street below and the voices and laughter of his friends filtering up from the kitchen. These familiar sounds made him feel lonelier. No one could accompany him on this trip. Mentally he girded himself and reviewed his preparations for the long night ahead. He had a pitcher of water within reach, a dry towel next to him on the bed, and a wet cloth to put over his forehead. He was set. There was nothing else to do but surrender and try to float with the pain and fever until it ran its course. "Sleep, man. Sleep," he murmured.

But sleep came hard that night, in fitful interludes, interrupted by fever and the roar and rattle of Copetran buses along the main street. Vachio began to understand dementia that night. He had vivid hallucinatory dreams, and he was unable to separate dreams from delirium. He kept thinking about what Fredy had told him. "This house is full of spooks and evil spirits. Twenty-two men and 11 horses were massacred here in 1899 during the Palo Negro Civil Conflict." That night, asleep or awake, unable to distinguish, Vachio saw the massacre. The rush of an unruly mob against the fortified house, torches flaring in the night; the shooting, garroting, and stabbing to death of the men; and the ultimate madness, the beheading of the horses, their heads displayed on pikes from the second floor balconies. It was all so vivid. The smell of gunpowder and blood, the screams of angry frightened men, the whinny of horses, and the silence of death. Vachio even saw himself amidst the tumult, swinging in his hammock, yelling at the frightened men, "*Liberal Conservador, la misma mierda*."

The crowing of the roosters and the barking of dogs just before dawn put an end to Vachio's nightmare. Then the gray light of morning insinuated through the creases in the door. Vachio sat up, his muscles and bones screeching at him. His shirt was soaked through with perspiration. He took it off and toweled himself off. Then he put on a fresh one and ducked back under the sheets. He slept peacefully for a few hours.

Around mid-morning Vachio struggled out of bed, dressed, and went downstairs to eat something. He held onto the railing as he descended the stairs. Walking made him dizzy. He felt as limp as a washed out rag. He made it to the sofa by the stereo and collapsed there. The cement floor of the patio glared into his eyes.

"How do you feel this morning?" asked Marta, coming close to him as she swept dust from one end of the patio to the other.

"How do I look?"

"Half dead."

"That's how I feel."

"That's too bad.... Do you want to eat something?"

"I don't know if I can. But I suppose I should try."

"I'll make you something."

"Really?"

"Really. What do you want?"

Vachio considered briefly. Marta had a very limited repertoire. "A soft boiled egg and two slices of toast.... And some juice."

"All right. Coming right up." Marta padded off to the kitchen, her bare callused feet slapping against the concrete. Vachio was surprised and touched. Marta rarely did anything for him without a tip of some kind. She was more of a social project and teenage daughter for the Germans than a maid. She didn't know how to cook, and did as little cleaning as possible. Her main jobs were to wash clothes and dishes, help take care of the baby, and lend her raucous laugh to the corniest of Don Raimundo's jokes. Much of the time Vachio saw her chewing on candy, gossiping with teenage friends, and reading Condorito comic books and True Love magazines. In return for this she received room and board, a competitive salary, tips from Vachio for walking next door to buy beer, and a paid education.

Marta brought Vachio his food on a T.V. tray. The egg was overdone, the toast slightly burned, and there were seeds in the juice. It didn't matter. Food didn't appeal to Vachio in his condition. He thanked Marta and forced most of the food and juice down. Then he collapsed sideways on the couch and lay there like a zombie until Renata came in to take charge of little Sylvia.

"Hi, Vachio! Are you feeling any better?"

"No," said Vachio, struggling upright."

"I saw the Doctora Gloria. She says you have a bad case of dengue."

"Yeah, that's what I told you last night. What did you think? That I was faking?"

"Well, no, but we thought you might be overreacting a little from depression at the situation in the *Casa de Menores*."

"Overreacting? Me?... Please."

"Well, sorry. Can I get you something to eat?"

"No, thanks. Marta already gave me some breakfast."

"Marta?" Renata wrinkled her nose.

"It wasn't so bad. Food has no taste to me right now."

Renata laughed. "All right. But let me know if you need anything."

"Yeah, thanks. For now I just need to sleep."

"Go ahead, then."

Vachio stayed on the couch for a while longer but the increasingly bright light soon drove him back to his bedroom. He spent the remainder of the day there, falling in and out of feverish dozes.

Shortly after nightfall, Raimundo tapped on the door and came in. "How do you feel?" he asked, his bulky body silhouetted against the light from the patio.

"About the same," said Vachio, raising up on an elbow, his voice thick and drowsy, even the soft reflected light hurting his eyes.

"Well, we're going out for a while to eat. All of us. Even Marta."

"All right."

"Will you be all right? Do you need anything?"

"I'll be fine. I don't intend to move from this bed."

"Is it that bad?" This time Raimundo's voice was solicitous rather than doubtful.

"It's the worst thing I've ever felt. Truthfully."

"All right, man. Get some rest."

Shortly after Vachio heard the big door slam shut below as the family left the house, the sounds of a commotion came from the side street in front of Gustavo's house. Vachio heard drunken shouts and a metallic bang. Then he heard a woman shouting, a sudden silence, and the low buzz of a crowd. Vachio sat up in bed but felt too weak to get up and open the shutters to see what was going on. Ah, probably nothing, he thought. Drunken shouts and loud voices were fairly common on that street; there were several *cantinas* nearby. Vachio settled back into his misery and thought no more about it.

Sometime later Vachio was roused by loud pounding on the front door. He lay still for a time, listening, wondering why no one answered the door. Then he remembered that no one was home. He crawled off the bed and dazedly descended the staircase and staggered to the outer door. He swung it open and Gustavo was revealed in the murky light, his eyes blazing, his face red and furious.

"Where is Raimundo?" he demanded, stepping past Vachio without waiting for an answer and hurrying through the corridor and into the patio. "Raimundo! Raimundo!" Gustavo called.

Vachio followed behind him and, weak from his efforts, grabbed onto one of the pillars near the door for support. Gustavo wandered on toward the kitchen before turning back. Vachio stared at Gustavo as he approached, wondering what the hell had gotten into him. Then he saw the gun swinging loosely in his right hand.

"Where is the German?" Gustavo asked, shaking the gun.

"They went out to eat. But what's going on here? What are you doing with that gun?"

"What am I doing with this gun?" yelled Gustavo, his nostrils flaring. "I'll tell you what I'm doing with this gun.... I'm going to kill me a son-of-a-bitch!"

"Whoa, whoa," said Vachio, a wave of vertigo hitting him. "Calm yourself. Tell me what's going on."

"I need to find Raimundo."

Vachio made it to the lounge chair and sat down. Gustavo paced before him, tight-lipped, a demented look in his eyes, muttering, "I'm going to kill that son-of-a-bitch."

"Can you put that gun down," said Vachio, shading his eyes from the light. "It makes me nervous."

Gustavo stopped pacing and looked at him. "Don't worry. I know how to handle it. I used to be in the army."

"That's what worries me."

Gustavo sat on the couch near Vachio and set the gun on the coffee table.

"Now tell me what's going on."

"That son-of-a-bitch came to my house with a machete. To my house...and called me out. Called me *chorizo* son-of-a-bitch and slashed my door with the machete..."

"Who?"

"One of the guards. Torres.... He'll pay for it."

Vachio was having trouble following Gustavo's description. "But how..."

"I wasn't there when he came. I was a few blocks away. My sister was at home. After he hit the door she called him a coward for threatening a woman and he left. And now I'm going to find him and make him pay for this insult."

Vachio rubbed his eyes with both hands. The room was spinning and bleary. "Why do you want Raimundo?"

"I need a witness for when I find that Torres. I need a friend to back me up."

"Well, he should be back at any time," said Vachio, thinking to stall Gustavo and let him cool down. "Calm yourself. We'll sit here and wait for him."

For a long moment Gustavo stared silently at his gun. Then he scooped it up and came abruptly to his feet. "I can't wait. I have to go out and find him. Where did they go?"

"I have no idea. Maybe Bucaramanga."

Without another word Gustavo banged out of the house.

"Shit!" muttered Vachio. "Torres. Who else?"

Vachio shook his head and rose from the lounge chair. His body screamed at him in pain, his brain was foggy. The hell with this, he thought. I'm going back to bed. Let them settle their own vendettas.

Vachio slipped back into bed, Gustavo's visit already taking on the character of a surrealistic dream. But when Raimundo returned to the house, Vachio called him up to the bedroom.

"Gustavo was here looking for you. He had a gun. He wants to kill the guard Torres."

"What? What? What thing? You're delirious."

"No, man, he was here. I'm sure he was here. You have to talk him out of it."

"Where is he?"

"I don't know. He went to look for you." To reinforce the urgency of his words, Vachio rose from the bed and walked out to the balcony. Raimundo's face was pale and anxious.

"Are you sure about this?" Raimundo asked.

"I'm sure about what Gustavo told me. Torres went to his home with a machete."

"Shit! This is too *folklórico*.... I better find him."

"Yeah, man, or the shit may really hit the fan."

Raimundo went downstairs and had a brief conversation with Renata. Vachio hung onto the balcony railing and watched until he disappeared through the door.

14

Vachio crawled out of bed as soon as he heard Raimundo's voice booming from the dining alcove the next morning.

"Well, well, well," said Raimundo, his voice loud and jovial. "How is the patient this morning?"

"Slightly better," said Vachio, sitting at the table. "What happened last night?"

"Gustavo shot four guards," said Renata.

"Ha, ha," said Vachio. "Right. Come on, what happened?"

"Fortunately—nothing. Just some harmless macho posturing to add to the folklore of the pueblo," said Raimundo.

"How's that?"

"Well, after I talked to you last night, I found Gustavo at the plaza talking to a crowd of men and waving his gun around. He gestured and threatened against Torres and Galindo, called them sons of bitches and dirty degenerates, and made a big public spectacle. He showed Garrotero he was ready to go to war to defend his honor. Then me and a few of his other friends talked him into going back to his house for a drink. We told him that if Torres really wanted something with him, he would know where to find him. So we got him home and things settled down."

"What about Torres?"

"From what I hear, his brother got a hold of him and kept him dead drunk at a bar on the outskirts of town where Gustavo wasn't likely to find him. Torres' brother works for DAS. He knows it would be bad news for his brother to tangle with the Señor Director of the *Casa de Menores* regardless of the outcome. Incredible, eh! *Folclórissimo*." Raimundo burst into gleeful laughter.

"I'm relieved nothing happened. Because when I saw Gustavo, he really did look ready to shoot someone."

"Ah, don't exaggerate the thing. The both of them got to make their threats and prove their machismo. Nothing happened except for a little excitement. This is how these things usually go here."

"I saw Gustavo last night. I saw his eyes. If he had run into Torres at the time I saw him, something would have happened."

"Ah, it was nothing."

"Yeah, whatever you say, man. But I've seen people who looked like that before. And I've seen them do some nasty things."

"Well, nothing happened."

"For now."

"Do you want some breakfast?" Renata asked Vachio.

"Yeah, I'll try some black coffee and juice. And some bread."

Vachio drank the coffee and ate some bread with orange marmalade. Everything still tasted insipid to him; the ache in his bones and muscles still made every movement hurt; but his fever had cooled, and he was enjoying windows of increased lucidity.The worst symptoms of the dengue were subsiding.

The next three days saw Vachio's condition steadily improve. He still spent most of his time in bed, but he was now able to sit up and read between naps. He began to take interest in the future again and the sounds of the children playing in the street below frustrated him. He was itching to get up and back out into the world.

Raimundo kept him informed of the continuing soap opera at the *Casa de Menores*. Torres was away on leave. The investigators had finished their interviews and returned to Bogotá to "make a study of the matter." Gustavo kept a low profile around town and stayed away from Raimundo's house for a while. The *Casa de Menores* ran on automatic pilot.

By Sunday evening, Vachio was able to eat a complete meal for the first time in a week. He still felt weak and shaky, a residual soreness remained in his bones and muscles, but his head was clear and his temperature normal. Monday he ate a good breakfast and lunch and by late afternoon, at the height of the day's heat and humidity, he was able to take a cool shower and feel pleasure in it. After his shower, he stepped on the scale wearing only soccer shorts and was shocked at the result. He had lost twelve pounds. "Madre!"

"What's wrong?" asked Marta, pushing dust around the patio.

"I've lost a lot of weight. I haven't been this skinny in about five years."

Marta stopped sweeping and eyed Vachio's torso. "It's done you good. You were starting to get a beer gut."

"Yeah, I suppose I was." Vachio patted his stomach. "But I wouldn't recommend to anyone to lose weight by catching dengue. Not even you."

Marta swung the broom at Vachio's calves. "Bug off, Vachio. I liked you better when you were sick."

"Maybe I wouldn't have got sick if you had kept my room clean."

"Don Raimundo says I don't have to clean your room unless you pay me extra."

"I already pay rent. That should include getting my room cleaned. What kind of maid are you anyway?"

"I'm not your maid. You want your room cleaned, you pay me extra."

"Ah, I can clean my own room."

"As you like." Marta resumed her walk across the patio, hurling dust into the air with looping sweeps of the broom. Vachio shook his head and laughed. He hadn't liked Marta very much at the beginning, but she had become like a pesky younger sister to him.

That night Gustavo came to the house for the first time since the incident with Torres. He sat at the table and picked listlessly at the treats set before him by Renata. Vachio had never seen him so subdued.

"I'm feeling much better now," Vachio told Gustavo. "I'm going to work tomorrow."

"There is no reason to hurry back. Take some more time if you need it."

"No. I'm ready. I need to get back. I was going crazy sitting around here today."

"Fine. We'll be glad to have you back."

Gustavo turned from Vachio and started playing with Sylvia, shaking a rattle at her and making cooing noises. Raimundo emerged from the bedroom, fresh from a shower, and came right to the point. "So what's the word on the government investigation of the *Casa de Menores*?"

Gustavo handed the rattle to Syvia and gave a rueful shrug. "It's hopeless. I received the word from my sources in Bogotá today. They are going to whitewash the whole thing and advise me to proceed as though nothing occurred."

"Don't tell me that!" said Raimundo.

"That's the way it is. They don't want any scandal or the problem of taking on the guard's union. It's not worth their trouble. The welfare of the boys isn't worth their trouble."

"Idiots!" hissed Raimundo.

Gustavo turned to Vachio. "You see how it is here. You see the handicaps I have to work under."

"Is this the final word?" Vachio asked

"No, not yet. The official word won't come for another month. The official verdict has to be produced and notarized. Then I will be commended for my diligence, praised for my conscience, and told that insufficient evidence was produced against the guards."

"But can't you appeal?"

"I could. But my sources tell me that would be a waste of time. The higher-ups in Bogotá want this matter to disappear. That's the final word."

"It's a shame," said Raimundo.

"Yes, a rotten shame. It's the kind of thing that makes me seriously consider resigning my position and moving into the private sector."

"Ah, Gustavo, don't talk that way," said Renata. "You've done so much for those boys. No one could do more."

"Thank you for your words of support, Doña Renata. And I certainly have no intention of resigning at this time."

Suddenly Gustavo smiled and his voice regained its normal effervescence. "I still have *La Obra* to push forward. And when that job is completed, there will be another opportunity to cleanse the *Casa de Menores* of its trash. You hear me?"

"That's it!" affirmed Raimundo.

"*Eso!*" said Renata.

Vachio stared off into space, pensive. No one asked his opinion and he didn't offer one. Gustavo left the house in a much better mood.

The next day Vachio went to the *Casa de Menores* and summoned Barranca at lunch time. "So how did things go while I was away?"

"Pretty well, Profé. You know you can count on me to take care of business..."

"Yes, I know. Were there any problems?"

"Well, just the same one as before. The guards won't give me a key for the recreation room. And sometimes they don't feel like opening up the room and giving us the equipment." Barranca shrugged. "You know how that goes, the guys have nothing better to do than screw around and get into trouble."

"So Ordoñez hasn't taken the desks out of the room yet?"

"No."

Vachio grunted. Here we go again, he thought. But now isn't the time to push this.

"Well, I'm back now. I'll get the room open."

"That's fine, Profé. But what if you get sick again? Or you go away to Bogotá or somewhere? It will always be the same. You have to do something about this."

"We'll worry about it later. *Manaña por la tarde*."

"Ay, Profé! Don't you start with that."

"What else am I supposed to do? That's what everyone tells me. Hell, man, I feel like I came back from the grave. Why should I worry about that nonsense?"

"Because we expect better from you, Profé."

"Go eat your lunch."

Vachio went to the administrator's table, sat next to Cabrera and asked him, "How did things go while I was away?"

"Were you away?" Cabrera asked, slurping his soup. "I didn't notice."

"Good. That means the program is working. It should run the same whether I'm there or not."

Emilio Montoya laughed.

Cabrera looked at Vachio and cracked a rare smile. "Seriously, I had my mind on more important matters."

"I can imagine." Vachio left it at that. He had returned to work with a different attitude. Once his mind had cleared and he recovered from the worst effects of the dengue, Vachio had spent long hours thinking over his situation in the *Casa de Menores*. He realized it was useless to get so frustrated and rant and rave over things. The situation was absurd. Here were the administrators, demanding that he gain the guard's cooperation to run a program, and the Director of the prison and one of the guards almost kill each other in a personal duel. Hell, these guys were not only playing games with the *gringo* volunteer, they were playing just as many games with each other. He would do his own thing and let the bullshit roll off his back. Maybe stoicism and endurance would turn the tide in his favor.

Armed with this new attitude of equanimity, and the continuing preoccupation of the administrators and guards over "The Situation," Vachio decided to start a new project. He went out to the *Casa de Menores* farm and asked Maestro Felipe for a small piece of land and permission to plant a vegetable garden. After hearing Vachio out, Maestro Felipe set down his hoe, mopped at his brow with his bandana, and frowned. "No offense, Vachio, but I don't have time to take care of a vegetable garden. I've got too much to do as it is."

"No, no, no. This is my project. I'll take care of it."

"What do you know about these things?"

"Well, my father is a gardener. My grandparents were farmers in Europe, and when they came to the United States, even though they lived in a city, they maintained a vegetable garden and fruit trees in the yard. They even had rabbits and chickens. And when I was a boy, I used to watch them work and help out a little."

"How does that qualify you to do a vegetable garden."

"Well... I've had my fingers in the soil. It's in my blood."

Maestro Felipe chuckled at this response, but he remained skeptical.

"Look! I already have the seeds." Vachio showed Maestro Felipe his Peace Corps issue packets of carrots, radishes, lettuce, and spinach seeds. "See. I'm serious."

"Having seeds is nothing. You have to know what to do with them."

"Of course. Of course.... Look, Felipe, no bullshit. All I need from you is a little piece of land; that you show me how to set up the garden; tell me how often to water and fertilize; and let me have one of the boys as a helper."

"I can't spare Geraldo, Vachio. He's my right hand."

"You keep Geraldo. Any one of the boys will do. Or Gustavo can send another from the *Casa de Menores*."

"There is no room for another."

"How about Medellín?"

For the first time Vachio saw a spark of interest in Felipe's eyes. Medellín was the bane of his existence; the brain-damaged street kid was a nuisance to him. "Medellín won't be much of a help. He is a poor brute animal."

"That's fine. I don't need a rocket scientist. Just someone to handle a shovel, pull weeds, and water the ground."

Maestro Felipe laughed. "All right, Vachio. If you're truly serious, come back here tomorrow around ten and I'll get you started."

Vachio returned at ten the next day and found three of the boys already cutting a section of the grass near the house for the vegetable garden. Maestro Felipe came up to Vachio and said in a gruff voice, "We have a little extra time today. I can get you started with the harder things like cutting the grass, plowing it under, and setting up the rows. Then you and Medellín are on your own."

"I appreciate it, Felipe."

"It's nothing." Felipe excused himself and set to work. Vachio grabbed a shovel and pitched in. Everything, including planting the seeds, was accomplished in one week. Vachio was very happy. Going to the farm was a great psychological boon for him. He jogged there in the morning to stay in shape, enjoying the cool shade under the trees, and was able to think and reflect at ease. On the farm, everyone sharing in the work, he could talk to the boys without all the distractions and power games of the patio. But most of all, he was gratified by the help Maestro Felipe lent him. The taciturn gruff man had promised nothing, but had delivered far more help than Vachio could ever have expected. It gave Vachio hope for better things at the *Casa de Menores*.

Gustavo came out to the farm on Friday morning to talk to Maestro Felipe and to look over Vachio's new project. The idea of Vachio growing vegetables seemed to amuse him. "You could probably get more done for the recreation program if you hung around the patio in the morning and put this kind of effort there."

Vachio, shirt off, sweat dribbling down his chest, thrust his hoe into the soft soil and said, "About all I was accomplishing hanging around the *Casa de Menores* in the mornings was a coffee addiction."

Gustavo chuckled. "You know, some of an administrators best work can be accomplished during a *tinto* break. Don't underestimate that."

No, I believe you. But I personally wasn't getting anything done.... At least working here I can produce a few fresh vegetables for the table at the *Casa de Menores*. And it gives Medellín something positive to do. But if you have some problems with this..."

"No, it's fine, Vachio. If this pleases you, you have my support. I just can't get used to the idea of a man with a college degree grubbing around in the dirt like a worm. You should leave this to the boys."

Vachio grimaced. "This kind of work doesn't hurt anyone. In fact, it makes me feel good." Vachio slammed the hoe into the ground. "I get rid of a lot of frustrations this way."

"Very well," said Gustavo, grinning. "If it makes you feel good. Do it. We want you to feel content here."

15

Friday night Vachio went to keep his appointment, delayed by a week because of his illness, with Jimmy DeLeon and Roxanna. This change of plan worked out well for Vachio. On Saturday, Vachio and the three Peace Corps Volunteers stationed around Bucaramanga were scheduled to go to Cúcuta for a regional meeting of their union, per diem and travel expenses on *Cuerpo de Paseo* Colombia. Vachio had arranged to sleep over at the volunteers' apartment, and in the morning they would all pile into a *colectivo* taxi and head for the border with Venuzuela.

Jimmy DeLeon lived in a new condo complex on La Avenida de las Americas in the upscale Cabecera District. He greeted Vachio at the front door with a warm smile and handshake, salsa music blasting from his ultra-modern stereo system, and immediately offered Vachio a Scotch and Soda. Vachio was about halfway through his drink, sitting alone on a plush white couch, Jimmy out of the room handling a phone call, when Roxanna came out of the bedroom and whistled, "Ay, man, what happened to you? You've lost weight and your hair is even worse than it was before."

"Hey, thanks. You're looking great yourself."

"No, but...come on, what happened?"

"I had dengue fever."

"Ouch! *Poerecito.*" Roxanna came close, took a patch of Vachio's hair, and ran some strands through practiced fingers. "What happened to your hair? It's all dried out and frizzed."

"I've been working on the prison farm. The sun did me in."

"You a farmer? Come on, you're kidding me, *chico.*"

"No way. I'm out there shoveling manure and eating dirt."

"Well, this will be a challenge. But I think I can fix you up."

"We'll see."

"All right. If you're ready, come into my office."

Vachio followed Roxanna into the kitchen and she told him to take a seat. She wrapped a large towel around his neck and draped it over his chest.

"You're not going to use all that stuff on me are you?" Vachio asked, looking at the kitchen table which was crowded with barber instruments and cans of hair sprays and jells.

"Of course not, *chico.* For you all I need are my best pair of scissors, a brush, and a comb. That is, unless you want me to spray your hair in place."

"No thanks."

"I didn't think so. But anyway, like I told you, this is a hair-cutting party. Later on I'm gonna do my sister and Jaimes' cousin. I need all my stuff and then some for them."

"Hey, the lasagna smells good," said Vachio, inhaling deeply.

"If you're hungry, we'll eat right after I do you."

"Whatever you say."

Roxanna went to work, snipping and combing the worst of the knots and tangles in Vachio's hair. When she reduced the mop to a manageable level, she brought out a flask of some strange milky-looking substance and said, "All right, *chico*. Sit back, close your eyes, and relax. Your hair is so bad I need to give it a protein bath."

"What the hell is that stuff you're gonna put on me?"

"Nothing bad. It's a mix of egg white, some animal placenta, and scent."

"Sounds scary."

"Relax, *chico*. Relax."

Vachio eased back in the chair and closed his eyes. He felt a cold sticky sensation on his scalp as Roxanna poured on the conditioner and spread it around. Then he felt nothing but warm pleasurable tingles, radiating from the crown of his head all the way to the tips of his toes as Roxanna massaged his scalp with strong skillful fingers. Within seconds, Vachio felt as though he were floating submerged in a warm pool.

He was returned to the surface by the entrance of Jimmy and two women. "Hey, man," said Jimmy, "I want you to meet two fine ladies. This is Jovana, Roxie's sister. And this one is my cousin Victoria. Or as she's better known, La Rica Vicky."

Vachio stuck his hand out from under the towel and shook hands.

"Does he speak Spanish?" Vicky asked Roxanna, as though Vachio weren't sitting there listening.

"Yes, he does. We have to be careful about what we say around him," said Roxanna, laughing.

"You mean to say, if I were to say, *Papacito rico*...he would understand that?"

"Of course I would," said Vachio in Spanish. "And you can say that to me as much as you want."

The three women started laughing and snapping their hands in the air. Jimmy winked at Vachio and left the room to continue his phone conversation. Vicky took a seat near the stove just to the side of Vachio. Jovana, who ran a hair salon in Manhattan, immediately started giving Roxanna advice on what to do with Vachio's hair. As the two sisters fussed over his hair, Vachio's eyes kept drifting to La Rica Vicky. Her eyes didn't waver at all. She stared right back whenever he made contact and her smile was full and friendly. Vachio let his eyes drift down the length of her. She was a *morenita*, moorish in appearance, with curly dark hair and light skin. Her figure was petite and full-bodied. But Vachio's gaze kept returning to her eyes. She has those kind of big dark intense eyes you can get lost in, he thought. And she's all around hot...

"There," said Roxanna, giving Vachio's neck a final dusting of talcum powder and handing him a mirror. "You almost look human now."

Vachio took a quick look. "Looks fine. You're a pro."

"Thanks."

"You're looking good now, *chico*," she said, and chased Vachio out of the kitchen so she could assemble dinner.

Vachio went into the living room and Jimmy, finally off the phone, handed him another drink. "That was one of my people in Cali," he said. "I'm really beginning to put things together on that business deal I told you about. Do you remember?"

"Sure. The thing about the tropical fish."

"Yes. Exactly. Did you think over what I said to you about it?"

"Jimmy, no offense, but I'm not too interested in business. I'm a social worker, man. At least at this point in time."

"That's cool. I hear you. I don't take this personally. I wouldn't want anybody working for me who wasn't fully committed to the business.... So anyway, how are things going for you at that prison?"

"It got kind of wild these last few weeks..." Vachio gave Jimmy a quick rundown on the scandal and near fight between Gustavo and the guards, and his bad bout with dengue fever. "...But things settled down this week. Everyone's attention was distracted from me and it's been helpful to go out and work on that farm. You know, like therapeutic."

"Yeah, I hear you. Back to nature and all that. Be another Thoreau or something, huh." Jimmy laughed. "You look surprised that I've read Thoreau. You shouldn't be. I thought of majoring in English at Long Island University. Then I dropped out after two years."

"Why'd you drop out?"

"I knew I could run my business things without what they were teaching there. Besides, I was more interested in chasing tail and partying than in being a serious student back then.... I don't know. I might go back someday when money is no issue. I enjoyed my time in college. Brief as it was..."

The conversation was interrupted by the arrival of the food. A big pan of lasagna, a tossed green salad, a pile of garlic bread, and red wine to wash it down. During dinner, Vicky sat next to Vachio and they became acquainted. Vicky was from Barranquilla but she was studying at the Industrial University of Santander and was living with an aunt in Bucaramanga. She was a *Turca*, that is, a Colombian of Arab descent. Her grandparents, of Lebanese and Syrian extraction, had come to Colombia at the turn of the century while those countries were still under the Ottoman Empire. As a consequence, they had Turkish passports, and the other Colombians still referred to their children and grandchildren as Turks. As Vachio and Vicky talked, he could see Roxanna and Jovana giving each other knowing looks.

Shortly after dinner, as soon as everything was cleaned up, Vicky gave a big yawn and said, "I need to go home and study for a test tomorrow. Will someone accompany me?"

"Where do you live?" Vachio asked quickly.

"Not far from here. A few blocks up La 33 and over on La 42."

"I'm going to my friend's on the Quebrada Seca. That's on my way."

"It's fine with me." Vicky looked at Jovana.

"Go ahead, youngsters. Go ahead."

"Yeah, man, go ahead," said Jimmy. "It'll save me the trip."

Vachio thought he heard conspiratorial laughter as they went out the door. Outside, in the warm tropic air, Vicky slipped her arm onto Vachio's as soon as they started up the street, and she did it with such nonchalance and ease it seemed like the most natural thing in the world to him.

"Would you like to stop and have a drink or something before you go home?" Vachio asked her.

"All right. But not here. There are too many gossipy people that might see us. I know a quieter place on a side street."

Vachio laughed. "I'm glad you want to. But I thought you had to study for a test?"

"I don't Have to study for this test. I can do it tomorrow morning."

"You think you're pretty smart, eh?"

"Smart enough, *pelado*. Smart enough."

They turned off the Avenida de las Americas and went to a chicken joint with an outside pavilion. Vachio ordered a couple of cold beers and they sat talking, their knees touching under the table, Vicky leaning toward him and patting his arm as they talked. Vachio began to feel lightheaded and effervescent. Vicky was intoxicating him. Before they knew it, two hours had elapsed.

"I better get you home, eh?"

"I suppose."

They walked the few short blocks to her aunt's house, a tidy but modest house with a wealth of plants along the front, and paused at the front gate.

"When will we see each other again?" Vicky asked.

"When do you want to?"

"When can we?"

"How about next Saturday. I'll be away this weekend."

"All right.... Aren't you going to kiss me?"

Vachio inclined his head and started to give her a light kiss on the lips. Vicky pressed forward and the kiss lingered and lingered.

When Vachio fell asleep that night his last thought was, La Rica Vicky.

The next morning bright and early, Vachio and three other Peace Corps volunteers went to the San Andrecito bazaar to commandeer a taxi. After about 15 minutes of negotiating and being passed from one driver to another, they found their man. Forest, a long tall drink of water from Texas, Hugh, a long tall drink of water from Arizona, Kenny, a medium-sized guy from Massachusetts, and Vachio, managed to squeeze into a brand new black Renault coupe.

The driver was short and trimly-built, with a laconic manner and a reposed face. His appearance belied his driving. He was a maniac. Calmly puffing on Marlboro cigarettes, his face impassive, playing soothing romantic music on the radio, the driver skidded around sharp mountain curves on two wheels, played chicken with massive big rigs, and raced his car up to 140 kilometers an hour on valley straightaways. Vachio felt as though he were in a movie with a fast action motion camera. The scenery shot past. Up the mountain away from the plateau of Bucaramanga, leaving steaming banana plants and lush ferns behind, they came to a stretch of trees and scrubby sub-tropical bush. Passing the town of Berlin, they soon hit the central spine of the *cordillera*. They raced over rolling green hillocks, sheep and cattle grazing peacefully on the lush grass under cloudy skies, the towering cold peaks of the *paramo* looming over them. Once again, as on other occasions in different parts of this large country, Vachio was struck by the raw natural beauty of Colombia. This is a landscape artists' paradise, he thought.

Crammed into the back seat, thrown from side to side by the motion of the vehicle, the volunteers passed the time talking about their relationships with women. Forrest went on and on about his girlfriend. She was hot, looking something like Sophia Loren, and had a temperament to match. They had a very tempestuous relationship that often resulted in fights and break-ups, and after awhile, in passionate reconciliations. Kenny was engaged to a woman from Bucaramanga and apparently wanted a traditional hands-off relationship until they were married, and Forest was constantly giving him a hard time over this. After one of Forest's digs, Hugh laughed and said, "I'm no fool. I'll never get married in Colombia and deal with all that bullshit."

"What if you meet the woman of your dreams?" Vachio asked.

"No way, man. Bucaramanga is famous for male volunteers marrying the local women. But I won't be one of them. Never."

"Never say never," said Kenny, who was fond of cliche sayings.

"Anderson, you're as good as married so don't even tell me anything. You're just like all those guys from the early 70s here."

"What happened in the early 70s?" Vachio asked.

"Man, it was unbelievable. Out of 40 male Peace Corps volunteers, 39 married women from Bucaramanga. It's a statistical fact." Hugh loved to quote figures like these. He was an accountant.

Vachio kept relatively quiet and listened as the other three went back and forth. He was thinking about the La Rica Vicky, but he didn't tell them anything about her.

They stopped for a break and a quick bite to eat in Pamplona, the first town in Norte de Santander. It was an attractive town, set in a small valley surrounded by beautiful mountains, with cobbled streets and colonial buildings and a cool bracing climate. Vachio would have liked to stay a little longer and look over some of the *ruana* shops, a specialty of Pamplona, but the cabbie gave them only 20 minutes and then the wild ride continued.

Down the *cordillera* they raced, the climate growing increasingly hot and dry, past coffee plantations, past stands of cedar, past the town of Chinacota, and finally to the baking plains and the city of Cúcuta, gateway to Venezuela. By the time the volunteers got out of the cramped cab, they were all stiff and sore and were spitting out dust from the road. They took only a few minutes to rest before piling into another cab and going to the volunteer house across town.

The volunteers in Cúcuta were an interesting crew. Forest referred to them as the "Kooks from Cúcuta." There were four of them, Harry Wegler, better known as Sherlock Schroom for his hobby of going out into the countryside to track down, gather, and freeze dry quantities of magic mushrooms; Jersey Marion, a 30-something politically sophisticated volunteer who had just been offered an office position in Bogotá, Paco Morales, an easygoing good-natured Mexican-American from

Chicago, and Dana, who Vachio already knew from their night together on New Year's Eve in Bogotá.

It was awkward with Dana at first. She was sending Vachio strong signals that she wanted to pick up where they had left off on New Year's. Vachio wasn't sure how to handle this situation. He was quiet and distant with her, but when the other volunteers dispersed for a while and they were left alone in the house, she confronted him. "You've found somebody, haven't you?"

"I don't know for sure. But I can't get her out of my mind."

Dana was silent for a moment. "You know, I have someone here..."

"But you're not stuck on him?"

"He's kind of immature. But he excites me. The sex is great."

Vachio gave her a wry look. "I'm not even going to ask you the next question. Forget it."

Dana laughed. "What the hell. You're only young and in *Cuerpo de Paseo* once."

"Yep. *Eso.*"

It turned into a pleasant weekend. The Kooks from Cúcuta were very hospitable. Late Saturday afternoon, they took a trip to San Antonio across the border in Venezuela just so the volunteers from Bucaramanga could say they had been there. The exchange rate was not favorable for someone making Colombian pesos. The visit was short, just long enough to drink a few Polar beers and stare at another monument to Bolívar. Then they returned to Cúcuta for an impromptu party with Colombian friends. Vachio spent much of the evening sampling and learning about magic mushrooms from Sherlock Shroom.

The next morning, eight volunteers piled into two taxis and took a ride to a resort in the foothills for their official meeting. They sat in a circle on a grassy field, surrounded by towering peaks, and dispatched their official business in about one hour. Marion, the regional volunteer representative, told them the latest gossip and rumors from his visit to Bogotá, read a letter of welcome from the new director and assistant director of Peace Corps Colombia, gave them his thoughts on these two worthies, and then presided over the election of his successor, Forrest, who ran unopposed. That was that.

The volunteers spent the rest of the day drinking beer, playing catch with the football and frisbee, and generally just relaxing and socializing. Vachio returned to Garrotero that evening with his batteries recharged, ready for another round at the *Casa de Menores*.

16

Monday night Gustavo came over to chat and to deliver a message to Vachio. "We have an official from the SENA office in Bogotá coming to inspect the *Casa de Menores* on Wednesday."

"Yes," said Vachio.

"I want everything in tip top shape and running smooth.... Including the recreation hour."

"I'll tell the boys. But I don't know how much difference it will make in their behavior."

"It better make a difference. You must impress on them the importance of this visit. It is a certification inspection."

"All right, I'll impress it on them."

Gustavo gave Vachio a sharp look. "I'm not sure you realize how important this is. We can't have those boys running wild like they usually do."

"I'll do my best. But it sure would help if I could get some recreation equipment."

Gustavo reddened. He started to say something more, but thought better of it and changed the subject. A short while later he got up and left.

Raimundo returned from seeing him off and said to Vachio, "Man, Gustavo is pissed at you. Why did you act so casual when he told you about the inspection?"

"Because that's the way I feel about it. The program will run the same. If it doesn't work when there is no inspection, why should it be any different when there is?"

"You know, man, this Zen attitude you're taking does not suit you. Why don't you quit playing these stupid games?"

"What games? I'll do what I'm supposed to do. But I can't guarantee any result.... No more than Gustavo can guarantee me what he promised."

"That's not the same."

"It's exactly the same. I still have no equipment. And I still have an office with old desks taking up half the room. So, I'm sorry, but excuse me if I don't get too concerned about one day of inspection. In fact, I would prefer that the inspector see what things are really like. Then we might get some action."

"Man, you mean to say, you don't care if the inspector thinks your program is a joke."

"What's he going to do? Fire me?" Vachio laughed. "I don't work for him. And if they want to complain to Peace Corps, well, my supervisor would be happy to transfer me somewhere else. Somewhere nice like Cali. Or Cartagena maybe."

"Bah! You just want to go to Cali for the women."

"No. I'm fine. I told my supervisor I want to stay here on my report.... But I'm not sweating over any bullshit anymore. I'm going to do my thing and we'll see how it goes. I don't know what else I can do."

"You can cooperate."

"Cooperate? Cooperation is a two way street."

"You are the stranger here. You have to prove yourself."

Vachio shook his head. "Man, I don't get it. When I ranted and raved and complained, you told me to be casual and play things cool. And now when I'm doing that, you want me to do something else. What's up?"

"You know what's up. You're not an idiot. Play the game, man."

Vachio laughed. "Which game? Gustavo's game? Cabrera's game? The guards' game? How about the boys' game? Come on, tell me. Which one?"

Raimundo shook his head and went to get his guitar.

"The only game I can play is my own game, man." Vachio yelled after him. "And if they don't let me be myself, then this game will be over for me. And you can tell your friend Gustavo that."

The next day, before Vachio could tell the boys to be on their best behavior for the inspection, the recreation period was pre-empted and both Don Gustavo and Emilio Montoya addressed the boys on the subject. The remainder of the day and night was spent cleaning and polishing the inner patio and the dormitory.

On Wednesday, Vachio worked at the farm for the entire morning and didn't arrive at the *Casa de Menores* until just before two. The inspector, a Señor Salgado, a slim dapper man with a neat goatee, was introduced to Vachio by Pacho at about three.

"I'm really looking forward to seeing your reaction program in action," said Señor Salgado. "The Señor Director has told me wonderful things about it. And I think it is tremendous for a man such as yourself, with so many fantastic opportunities in your own country, to volunteer your services to us."

"Really?" said Vachio, trying to discern irony in his voice.

"Absolutely. I'm a firm believer in a strong recreation program for these boys. And in this respect, we lag far behind the United States. Your expertise is needed and appreciated."

"Well, thank you. I can only hope it lives up to your expectations. But..."

"I believe it's time for a *tinto* break," said Pacho hurriedly. "Follow me, Doctor."

They retired to the cafeteria, along with Emilio Montoya, to have a *tinto* and a slice of jellied guava.

At four o' clock, Vachio was left alone with Señor Salgado and they went to the interior patio just after four. As they passed through the gate, Vachio half-smiled, hearing the roar and shouts of the boys, expecting to see the usual mayhem down in the yard. He stopped at the top of the steps and rubbed his eyes in disbelief. A furious and orderly basketball game was in progress, ditto with micro-soccer, volleyball, and ping pong. Barranca was behind the table in front of the recreation room, distributing fragments of table games to an orderly line of younger boys. The peer leaders were on the job and running their units. Even Jaime Galindo was down in the yard supervising the soccer game. Vachio couldn't help it. He burst into laughter.

"This is marvelous," said Señor Salgado, turning to Vachio with shining eyes. "Marvelous."

"It's pretty incredible."

They descended the steps to the patio floor and before they had gone very far, Rolo raced up to them and said, "Profé Vachio, good afternoon. I have Group A in position and ready to begin play. Do you have any instructions for me?"

Vachio reached over and put his hand on Rolo's forehead. "Are you feeling all right? Since when do you call me Profé?"

Rolo's eyes rolled in confusion and he fidgeted in place. "Stop joking, Profé. Do you have any instructions?"

"No, you're doing fine. Carry on."

"Yes, Profé. Thank you." Rolo raced off to his group.

"Very, but very impressive," said Señor Salgado. "It's amazing to me how you have managed to secure the cooperation of these *gamines*."

"No one is more amazed than me."

"No! You are too modest."

Vachio sighed and decided to keep his mouth shut. He wondered what Gustavo had threatened the boys with to secure this level of cooperation.

Vachio escorted Señor Salgado around the patio from play station to play station and explained the mechanics of the program. It was the same story at each site—the boys played with order and energy, and all of them addressed Vachio as Profé.

At the end of the recreation period, Señor Salgado turned to Vachio, shook his hand firmly, and said, "Señor Vachio, I congratulate you. I have seen recreation programs at many different government institutions, but I don't believe I have ever seen a better one. This is a model program. I congratulate you. Truly."

Vachio mumbled his thanks and Señor Salgado was taken in tow by Gustavo and led from the patio. Vachio stood in the middle of the basketball court and shook his head incredulously. "This is really too much," he muttered. "What a joke."

Vachio went home, grabbed a cold beer from the frig, turned on the music and emitted low chuckles as he swung in the hammock.

"What's so funny?" Renata asked. She was sitting on the sofa, feeding Sylvia.

"Nothing is funny. I'm just a little giddy."

"Why?"

"Haven't you heard? I have a model recreation program."

"What?" Renata giggled. "Are you all right? Are you sure your dengue hasn't come back?"

"No. I'm fine. Really." Vachio told her about the inspection.

"Well, you have Gustavo to thank for that," she commented at the end.

"Thank him? For what? For leaving a phony impression of what's really going on?"

"He made you look good."

"Yeah, but so what? I know the whole damn thing was just a show. And nothing will ever really get changed like this."

"Ay, Vachio! Don't act so pure."

"Pure, nothing! You don't understand what I'm getting at."

"All right, tell me. What are you getting at?"

"They don't need me here. Today showed just how well they can do a recreation program if they want. The damn thing went off like clockwork. Like it's drawn up on paper."

"But you set up the program, Vachio."

"Big deal. I got it out of a book. Anyone could have done it. And now they can do it. They proved it. They don't need me. My job is finished here. I think I'll ask for a transfer to Cali."

"You're talking foolishly, Vachio. Think about what you're saying..."

Vachio peered at Renata over the edge of the hammock. She looked unsettled. She flushed and turned her head to burp the baby. Though Renata and Raimundo only discussed money and their business in German, Vachio suspected that the plastic factory was having its ups and downs. Renata was the accountant for both the factory and the household. Her pregnancy was showing now. It suddenly occurred to Vachio that, aside from the friendship that was growing between them, the rent money he paid was becoming very important to their growing family.

"Well, I was only thinking out loud," said Vachio laughing. "I'm not looking to leave here."

"I would hope not. Your work is far from finished."

Sure, thought Vachio. If it was ever needed at all.

That night Vachio went to the patio to show a movie Raimundo had brought from the German Embassy in Bogotá. It was a history of the World Cup Soccer Championships. The boys received it with tremendous enthusiasm and applauded long and loud at the end of the showing.

"Now this is the kind of show we want, Vachio," yelled Amaraocho, giving him the thumbs up sign. "Things like this. Not those propaganda films you've been bringing."

"Well, behave more like you did today and I'll see what I can do."

The boys soon scattered and Vachio was left alone with Rolo as he rewound the film and put the projector in its case.

"Tell me, man, and tell me the truth," Vachio said to him. "Were you guys threatened to act as well as you did today in front of the inspector?"

"Threatened?" Rolo laughed. "No, we weren't threatened. It was just strongly suggested to us not to do anything to embarrass any of the functionaries."

"So it didn't mean anything."

Rolo glanced at Vachio and quickly dropped his eyes. "No, Vachio, it meant something. You have to understand. We mess with you and cause trouble and do all these crazy things around you because we like you. Believe me, we could do much worse to someone else. But in front of the inspector...man, we would have behaved even if Gustavo hadn't warned us."

The next day at the recreation hour, it was business as usual. Only Barranca called him Profé, and the boys ran wild in the patio. Vachio could only shake his head. Friday afternoon, Vachio arrived for the recreation hour about 15 minutes late. Galindo let him into the patio and asked, "Vachio! Where have you been?"

"I was in Bucaramanga. Trying to get a basketball game arranged between us and the Bienestar Familiar Boy's Center.... And the bus left late.."

"Well, you have a guest looking for you."

"Who?"

"A young woman." Galindo leered. "She's not bad, either."

"What are you talking about, man?"

"Down there. Look." Galindo pointed to the bench in the middle of the patio and Vachio saw a woman, dressed in black jeans and a white shirt, surrounded by a group of boys. Vachio smiled. It was La Rica Vicky.

Little Abel raced up to the terrace steps calling, "Vachio! Vachio! Your friend is here for you."

Vachio came down the steps and little Abel tugged at his arm to hurry him along. "Vachio! Is that your *novia*?"

Vachio laughed. "I don't know. Maybe."

"She's nice. And pretty, too. She should be your *novia*."

"All right. Thanks for the advice, old man."

Vachio approached the group slowly, watching how Vicky handled herself with the boys. She was totally at her ease, laughing and joking with them as though she had known them for months. Vachio was impressed. This is no spoiled daughter of *mami* and *papi*, he thought.

"Hello," said Vachio, coming through the ring of boys. "To what do I owe the honor of this visit."

Vicky smiled on Vachio and her dark eyes glittered. "I wanted to see where you work.... I hope you don't mind."

"Of course not. Don't be crazy."

As if given a secret signal, the group of boys around Vicky faded back to give the couple space to talk.

"I was thinking. This might be a good place for me to do a report for my sociology class," said Vicky.

"That's for sure. And you could expand it to do one of street kids in general."

"That's a good idea."

"All right, come with me. I'll give you the tour."

As Vachio ushered Vicky around the patio, some of the boys grinned at him behind her back and gave him the thumbs up sign. Vachio kept his face impassive but he felt a curious pride in their approval. A little later, Cabrera came into the patio and was taken aback when Vachio introduced Vicky to him.

"A pleasure to meet you," said Vicky, extending her hand to Cabrera. "Gary has told me something of your work here."

Cabrera soon excused himself and walked off with a flustered look on his face.

"He didn't seem so bad," Vicky commented to Vachio. "Nothing at all like you said."

"I never meant to imply to you that he's a bad person. My problem with him is no longer personal. It's a matter of philosophy and how we view the world. I understand that now. And I think he does, too."

"Then you have made progress here."

"In certain respects."

"Gary, I was talking to those boys before you arrived. I don't think you realize how much they do esteem you. In their eyes, you have accomplished something here. They say you never lie to them."

Vachio, though he felt gratified by these words, shrugged. The boys had strange ways of showing their esteem for him.

The recreation period ended and Vachio invited Vicky over to the house for something to drink. Marta opened the door and stared at Vicky wide-eyed for a moment. Then she recovered and said to Vachio, "You'll have to keep it quiet. The baby and Doña Renata are taking a nap right now."

"Sure. We'll be quiet."

Vachio told Vicky to take a seat on the couch next to the stereo and he went to the kitchen to get a beer for himself and a soda for her. By the time he returned, Marta was talking to Vicky, trying to find out some things about her.

"Don't you have some ironing or something to do?" Vachio asked Marta, after she lingered on without getting the hint to leave.

"Well, yes, I should do some work now.... It was nice to meet you," she said to Vicky.

Vachio grunted and put a record on the stereo at low volume. As the sky turned blue-black, and the first stars appeared, they embraced and kissed. When the record ended, Vachio put on an album of old romantic Spanish ballads sung by Trini Lopez. Then they moved to the hammock, to take advantage of a cool breeze, and swing along to their embraces, kisses, and caresses. For a second it struck Vachio that this whole scene must be kind of corny. But he didn't care. It felt right.

That's how Raimundo found them when he arrived from work. He came up to the hammock and Vachio introduced him to Vicky. Raimundo shook her hand, said hello, and quickly excused himself to leave them alone. "I'm dead tired," he said on his way to his bedroom. "I need a *siesta*."

"Yeah, man, have a good one," Vachio said.

Then the record ended and the house fell silent.

"Where do you sleep?" Vicky asked.

"Upstairs in the end bedroom."

"Aren't you going to show me your room?"

"Yes. Right now if you want."

"It's time. Don't you think?"

17

The next couple of weeks were good for Vachio, maybe two of the best weeks of his life. His affair with Vicky burned with a low steady warming flame. It wasn't a love of passionate explosions and overriding compulsion, of which neither was temperamentally suited, but one of almost intuitive discovery and mutual accommodations. Both of them found ways to meet, at odd hours, in odd places, in between work and school. They met at cafés in Bucaramanga, at country road stops outside of Garrotero, and at the volunteer house in Bucaramanga. They met to go out and eat, to take walks, to make love, or just to talk and be with each other. Many of their meetings were clandestine, to throw Vicky's conservative aunt and the gossip mongers of Garrotero off the scent, and this added to the spice for both of them. They made love one early afternoon at the volunteer house when everyone was gone to work, at a gorgeous country glade under a tumbling waterfall, and at a rustic colonial hotel in a small town on the road to Barrancabermeja. La Rica Vicky thought of several of these spots, and Vachio found her an enthusiastic and imaginative lover indeed. She dreamed of places for them to go, and after they went out and found them, it remained for them to laugh and compare the dream to the reality.

Vicky was Colombian to the bone. Barranquillera to the bone. She had spark, wit, a ribald sense of humor, and loved to dance *Vallenatos*. But sometimes, after making love and hearing one of her dreams, Vachio would look deep into the dark pools of her eyes and imagine them at a desert oasis or in the plush private harem of some pasha. In public, Vicky was reserved and undemonstrative with Vachio, but in private, she stroked and petted him, trimmed his nails and cleaned the cuticles, even brought him little goodies such as *dolmas* and *baklava* that she prepared herself. Vachio had never been pampered by a woman like that before. He had to admit—it felt great. Vachio found some of his most buried and secretive yearnings fulfilled in this relationship, and it colored the way he looked at the world.

Things were about the same for him at work. There was still no recreation equipment, the desks were still piled up in his office, and he still received occasional admonitions from Cabrera to get the kids under military control, but Vachio cut back on his snappy retorts and went about his business. As Gustavo said, his attention fully turned to *La Obra* once again after his failure to get rid of the bad guards, "All of this will seem like a bad dream once we move into our wonderful new *Casa de Menores*. One year at the latest, friend Vachio. One year at the latest. Just keep on plugging the way you are." Vachio would nod his head and go along with Gustavo's enthusiasm. What does it matter if it's true or not, Vachio thought. It's something to live for. And life ain't bad right now.

It was after another glowing update from Gustavo, about imminent and more than sufficient funding for *La Obra*, that Vachio left the *Casa de Menores* one morning to go check on his sprouting vegetable garden at the farm. He was about halfway there, whistling as he thought of his date with La Rica Vicky for later that evening, when a cement-mixer truck rumbled up from a side road behind him. Cussing under his breath, Vachio was forced to step into a roadside ditch to let the truck pass. He covered his eyes and nose to protect them from the dust and waited. To his surprise, the truck stopped right next to him and the driver rolled down the window and said, "Come on in. I'll give you a lift down the road."

Vachio looked up warily. The man was dark and burly, wearing a gray felt hat and a candy cane striped T-shirt. He looked familiar, but Vachio couldn't remember from where. Still, he walked around to the passenger side of the truck and hoisted himself into the cab. The driver immediately jammed the stick into gear and they started with a lurch.

"So how are things going for you at the minors' prison?" the man asked abruptly.

Vachio turned sideways and stared at him. "I'm sorry. But where do we know each other from?"

"I'm William," he said, laughing good naturedly. "Remember? The foreman from the famous *La Obra*."

"Oh yeah! Of course! Now I remember.... How are you?"

"I'm fine. Especially now that I found a new job building chicken and hog pens for this guy out in the valley here."

"How long will it last?"

"A few months."

"Then what? Back to *La Obra*?"

William guffawed. "*La Obra*? That's at a standstill. And has been since just after New Years."

"I know. But Gustavo said that he expects it to get back started any time now."

"Sure, of course he does. But pardon me if I don't hold my breath waiting around for it to happen. I have a wife and three children to feed and they could starve by then."

"You saying that you don't think it's going to get started again? Gustavo's been telling me that they're going to finish it this year no matter what."

"Well, who knows," said William, shrugging his massive shoulders. "If it were only up to Don Gustavo, I might believe it. But it's not only up to him. So..."

"So it may never get done?"

"No, I'm not saying it will never get done. But it's a government project. That says it all."

"What do you mean?"

"Look, man, I've worked in the construction trade since I'm 14 years old. I've worked on jobs for the government, for private firms, for private individuals, and even in Venezuela. And in my experience, there is no more unreliable employer than the Colombian government. Especially when it's anything coming out of Bogotá to another part of the country. These jobs almost always get delayed. And in some cases, they don't get finished at all and are abandoned, leaving the workers to scramble around as best they can. I mean, for men like me, you don't take anything on faith. You stay light on your feet and don't count on anything but the paycheck in your hand.... And that's just the way it is here. It's a son-of-a-bitch, man."

"You mean a triple son-of-a-bitch."

"Yeah, brother, that's right," said William, laughing. "You learn quick. You know what I mean."

"Well, I don't exactly know. But I'm beginning to have a pretty fair idea.... Anyway, I get off at this bend in the road here."

William turned the corner and ground the truck to a stop in front of the lower gate.

"Thanks for the ride," said Vachio. "And for the information. You've confirmed something I suspected."

"For nothing, bro. For nothing. Good luck."

A day later, Vachio received a call at the *Casa de Menores* from

Fortuna in Bogotá. "I can't talk long, Gary.... Ay, this connection is terrible..." She paused as the static garbled her voice. "But there are some changes here with the new administration we need to talk about.... And some new volunteers in Bucaramanga I need to see...static, static...So I'm coming to see you this Thursday.... See you then. Bye."

The line clicked and Vachio returned the phone to Gustavo. "So, Doña Fortuna is going to visit us and look over the program. This is good news. She is a wonderful lady. I have the utmost respect for her."

"Yes. She is a fine person."

"We must prepare a warm welcome for her."

On Thursday, Fortuna arrived by taxi at around 2:00 in the afternoon and before Vachio could get her out to the farm so they could talk alone, Gustavo brought her into his office for a private conference. Then he assembled some of the usual administrators, Maria Elena, Emilio Montoya, Pacho, and they went to the cafeteria for a snack. Gustavo went on an on about *La Obra*, describing its progress in glowing terms and harping on how much it was going to facilitate Vachio's job. With great effort, Vachio kept his mouth shut and let Gustavo talk.

Right before the recreation period, Emilio Montoya slipped away, and at 4:00, Vachio was left to show Fortuna his program. They went into the patio and the show of order and efficiency performed for Señor Salgado was repeated for Fortuna. The peer leaders were on their jobs, the different cells were functioning, and the guard Ramon was supervising a group of kids.

"Gary, I can't believe this," said Fortuna. "This is wonderful."

Vachio laughed. "This is not how it normally is. You're being given a very distorted view of things. The normal recreation period is chaos and mayhem."

"I think you're being a little hard on yourself, Gary. Gustavo has told me that despite some problems, that you are doing good work here."

"That could be. But the recreation period is not usually like this. This is all for your benefit."

"Profé, how are you?" said Amarocho, pausing from the volleyball game he was supervising to salute Vachio. "Señora, my compliments."

Fortuna smiled. "It's obvious these kids appreciate you, Gary."

"What I'm saying was just proved by what that kid said. Amarocho is usually one of the biggest pop-offs in here.... And he's one of the better kids in general."

"You're being modest. Say what you will."

Vachio laughed. "I wish I were. And when have you ever known me to be so modest?"

"I've known you to be confident about what you can do. And that's something I've always liked about you. I consider it one of your best assets."

"Some people would call it something else."

Fortuna was quiet for a moment as they walked over to the micro-soccer field. Then she said, "Gary, remember that time in Bogotá when I took the *Gamin* Group out to eat at that restaurant near the lift to Monserrat?"

"Of course. We had only been in-country a few days."

"And remember, I told everyone there that the specialty of the house was French Onion soup with cheese bread?"

Vachio laughed. "Sure, I remember. And I looked at the menu and ordered Cream of Asparagus."

"Right. But all the other volunteers ordered the French Onion as I suggested. And remember the reaction they had toward you?"

"Yeah. A couple of them thought I was showing off or trying to be different because I ordered something else. That was ignorant of them. I ordered the Cream of Asparagus because it's one of my favorite soups and because I don't particularly like French Onion.... It wouldn't have bothered me if any one of them had ordered something different. I don't even know why they tripped."

"Because they didn't want to be responsible for their own decision. But you took the chance. And how was the Cream of Asparagus soup at that place?"

"It was very good. One of the best I've had anywhere."

Fortuna smiled. "That's when I knew you would be a good volunteer, Gary. You weren't afraid to make your own decision and it was good for you. So all I can tell you now is continue to trust your own judgement. I have confidence in you. If this place is not working out, we'll find a place for you that will. I've heard what Don Gustavo has to say about the situation here. Now I want to hear what you have to say about it."

"Well, I know these guys have more pressing problems than to worry about the feelings of a Peace Corps Volunteer. And I'm not expecting any special treatment or even want any. But I did expect to be treated as an adult and not as some sort of mascot..."

Fortuna chuckled.

"What you said about the restaurant is right on the money for my situation here. When I came for my site visit, Gustavo handed me this menu and said here you have all these different options for your recreation program. Pick and choose what will be best. But, I'm telling you, the French Onion is the best option. So I look at the menu and make my choice. Then Gustavo says, very well my friend, you've had your say. But since I'm paying for the meal, I insist you order the French Onion. Anyway, we're all out of everything else." Vachio shook his head. "Now, I could go along with the French Onion if I knew that was all there was available. The problem is, I don't believe it. And I'm not being allowed to do my work and utilize my abilities as I know I can."

"But Gustavo says with the new *Casa de Menores* all of that will change."

"Fortuna, I've asked around outside of the *Casa de Menores*. I've talked to the foreman of the construction project. The new *Casa de Menores* may never happen in my time here. And maybe not even after my time. And besides, I can't live for some future *Casa de Menores* utopia. I have kids to do something with right now. And there are things that we can do. But every little damn thing I try to do becomes this big involved hassle. For example, the other day, I try to arrange a basketball game between my team of older kids here and an institute in Bucaramanga. Now, when I approached Gustavo with the idea, he said, 'Of course. We can arrange a game for outside of the *Casa de Menores*. That's no problem' Fine, so I arrange the game, within the time frame they gave me. But then, when I tell them the date and time, they say, Well, we need the truck for something else that day. And we can't afford to bring another guard for security. And we can't do this, and we can't do that, and we can't...Huh! Finally you just throw your hands up and say, The hell with it! And I go back and ask the director of the other institution to bring his kids here. But he's not happy about that. He wanted a home and home series which will probably not happen now.... You see, that kind of stuff has nothing to do with money or facilities. It has to do with bullshit institutional inertia. And it's just a great big waste of everyone's time."

Hearing this, Fortuna looked upset. "If things are that bad, Gary, then maybe we should transfer you."

"Yeah, but, I balance that stuff with working with the boys. Sometimes it's so good, it makes putting up with all that other crap worthwhile. And my living situation here is good. I like the people I'm staying with, and I like living here in general. So...who's to say it would be better anywhere else?"

"Perhaps we can set you up with something else to do here."

"I'd listen to whatever you might have. Especially a side job because I don't really have enough to do here. But I want to stick it out here at the *Casa de Menores* a while longer and see what happens."

"All right, Gary. I may just have something for you."

The recreation period ended and Fortuna consulted her watch. "Do we have time to go out to that farm you told me about and look at the vegetable garden?"

"Not really. It gets dark here very fast.... How about early tomorrow morning?"

"Tomorrow I need to be at Coldeportes in Bucaramanga at 11:00 to visit the two new volunteers at their site. And I need to get to Bucaramanga now and get a room. I came here straight from the airport."

"You don't have to stay at a hotel. We have plenty of room for you where I live.... The place used to be a hotel."

"I wouldn't want to impose on your housemates."

Vachio laughed. "It's no imposition. It's a pleasure for us to have guests. Please. I already told them you might stay."

"Well..."

"At least stay for dinner. Renata is preparing something special tonight.... You can always get a cab later if you want."

"All right, Gary. It sounds nice."

Vachio brought Fortuna to his house and as Raimundo and Renata were still at work, they sat at the dining room table and drank lemonade and talked while they waited for them. Fortuna had spent the afternoon listening to Vachio's problems, now Vachio spent the early evening listening to her difficulties with the new administration in Bogotá:

"You know that I had a wonderful working relationship with Rolando, Gary. He allowed me to implement the *Gamin* Program and was one of my biggest backers. But now, with Gabriel, it's a whole different story. He is not a fan of our *Gamin* Program. We've had arguments over it in our staff meetings and he is adamant about not allowing any new volunteers into the program.... Therefore, it has to die. And they want to change the entire role of the program coordinators. Instead of having coordinators by profession—social worker, business, health, etc.—they want to make us regional coordinators in charge of groups of volunteers in zones..."

As Fortuna continued, Vachio noting how obviously upset she was, he couldn't help wondering how these changes would affect him. He was already fairly well-informed of the situation in Bogotá. He had talked to the two new volunteers, Peter and Emily, a married couple working in Special Education, shortly after their arrival in Bucaramanga. They had gone through training with the new regime, and Peter had told Vachio that the new director, Gabriel Kino, and the assistant director, Hank Estevez, were both professional political operatives who had no previous background in Peace Corps. They had accepted these Peace Corps posts while waiting for something more in their line of interest, preferably in Washington, D.C. But Peter had also said that the two of them struck him as competent and professional and motivated to do a good job. At a get-together at the director's house, Gabriel Kino had let his hair down and did some shooters of tequila with Peter and a couple of other volunteers out in the garden. Then he confided that Peace Corps Colombia was on the rocks and that he was essentially a caretaker. His instructions were to streamline and pare down the operation to the point where a program termination could be quickly achieved, and that Peter's group would more than likely be the last. "It's all pretty shaky," Peter had told Vachio. "It's not likely we'll finish out two years here."

"So will you still be my supervisor?" Vachio asked Fortuna.

"For now. But if they break us up into regions, you may get someone else. And the way things are going back in the office, I'm seriously considering resigning my position."

"I sure hope you don't do that. I've heard about some of your problems with the new guys, but I've never heard a volunteer say a bad thing about you. And I personally couldn't imagine having a better supervisor than you. And I'm not the only volunteer who feels that way."

"Thank you, Gary. I appreciate that. But I've been here almost five years. And even though I love Colombia and I've had a wonderful experience here, I think there just comes a time when you have to move on to new challenges. My time has arrived, I think.... But I need to get the twins situated before I leave. So more than likely, I'll stay on until at least the end of this year and perhaps longer."

"Well, I guess you have to do what's best.... So, how are the other guys doing? Sean and Nancy? Jerry and Pam? What's up with them?"

"Overall, it's all pretty positive for them. There have been some problems. We had to pull Nancy from her job site and switch her to a hospital in Cali because we never could work out a compromise with the priest. But she's doing well now. I saw them just last week.... And Pam is doing well with Padre Javier in the *Gamin* City in Bogotá. And Bill is coming along well at his job site after some initial problems."

"Good."

"I don't have to tell you too much about them because you're going to have the chance to see some of them yourself in a couple of weeks."

"What do you mean?"

Fortuna smiled and reached into her bag. She pulled out a plane ticket and handed it to Vachio. "Did you forget about the conference in Cartagena? You can talk to them there."

"All right! I did forget. Cartagena on Peace Corps."

"You're going to love Cartagena, Gary. It's a fabulous city. One of the most beautiful places in Colombia."

"I'm looking forward to it."

Fortuna talked about Cartagena until they were interrupted by the arrival of Raimundo and Renata. Raimundo was loaded down with groceries from a trip to the supermarket in Bucaramanga and was in a jovial mood. He immediately brought out a bottle of wine and snacks to start the evening off. Renata went to cook the chicken, already well-marinated, and prepare the salad and some other dishes. Gustavo showed up for dinner about an hour later and the four of them passed a very pleasant evening. Fortuna hit it off well with Raimundo and Renata, and Gustavo's respect and admiration for her was obvious. No one mentioned work.

Near the end of the evening, Fortuna turned to Vachio and said in English, "I can see why you want to stay around here. Your friends are very nice and you have a good situation.... Don't worry, we'll work something out."

18

The next morning, bright and early,a middle-aged nun showed up at the house and asked for Doña Fortuna. Marta asked her to wait by the front door and went to the dining room table where Fortuna and Vachio were finishing up breakfast.

"Gary, this is a surprise I have for you," said Fortuna. "That woman over there is Sister Magdalena. And she wants to talk to you about writing a proposal for a Peace Corps Partnership Program.... Are you interested?"

"Maybe. What's it about?"

"It's about building a training center and retreat for poor children. It may be just what you're looking for. But I'll let her tell you about it."

The three of them sat by the couch near the front door and Sister Magdalena gave Vachio her pitch. "We already have the land for the training center. The plans are drawn up and ready to go. And we have seed money to get started from a West German institution. But this isn't nearly enough..." Magdalena stopped and looked at Fortuna.

"This is where you can help, Gary. A partnership program in Ecuador with the money already raised fell through. It's just sitting there, waiting for someone to come up with a new proposal.... Do you think you can do it?"

"Sure. I can write a proposal. But what else is involved?"

"Well, if the donors accept your proposal, you would be responsible for disbursement of the funds and for writing a monthly progress report to keep donors informed of the progress of the work."

"I could do that..."

"Señor Vachio," interrupted Magdalena, "if you want to do more, we have plenty of work for you. In fact, we requested a full time Peace Corps volunteer but were turned down. Now, Doña Fortuna has told me about your situation in the prison, and if you're not content there, we would be happy to have you come and work with us."

"Well, I don't know about that. But I 'd definitely like to look into this partnership project."

"Señor Vachio, we do very valuable work with poor and needy children. Not to demean anyone of good will and good intentions, but government institutions, such as where you are working, often do more to harm young children than to help them. They are training centers for vice and advanced criminal techniques. What my organization is about, Youth for Action, is not only to provide practical training for unskilled young men and women of poor means, but also to instill in them good Christian values and a sound moral base. And in alliance with our adult membership, many of whom are successful businessmen, we have a network that provides jobs and opportunities after the young person's initial training and spiritual orientation is complete..."

Listening to Sister Magdalena, Vachio thought, This woman is a match for Gustavo when it comes to talking.

"Well, Sister Magdalena, I'm definitely interested in writing this proposal for you guys. We need to set up a meeting so you can show me all your facts and figures and the job site and whatever else might help to secure this funding."

"Certainly. At your earliest convenience. How about tomorrow?"

"Tomorrow? Well, yeah, I suppose. Where? And when?"

"At my office in Bucaramanga. I have all the pertinent information there. And after that, we can come here to Garrotero to look at the site. It's just outside of town here. Near where they are building the new *Casa de Menores*.... How does 10:00 sound?"

"That's fine."

"Or we could take a quick look at the site now if you like."

"Uh, can't do that right now. I need to show Doña Fortuna the *Casa de Menores* farm."

"That's fine. The site is within walking distance of there."

Vachio's head was spinning. He needed time to think. "Not today, sister. I want my full attention on this matter when we do it. I have some other things on my mind today."

"Well...as you say."

"We better get going," Vachio said to Fortuna. "Don Gustavo is waiting for us."

They left the house and Sister Magdalena followed them to the *Casa de Menores*, talking the whole way. "We need someone to help us do fundraisers. We're planning a bikeathon, and picnic-dances, and..."

She didn't stop until they came to the entrance to the *Casa de Menores* and Gustavo said, "Well, Mother Superior Magdalena, to what do we owe the pleasure of this visit?"

"The usual, Don Gustavo. Doing the work of our Lord in my own humble way."

Vachio looked at them in surprise. Neither one seemed very thrilled to see the other. Sister Magdalena soon excused herself to catch a bus back to Bucaramanga and her parting words to Vachio were, "Don't forget. Tomorrow at 10:00. We have a lot to talk about."

Gustavo left Vachio and Fortuna alone for a few moments to issue some orders to Pacho.

"So what did you think of Sister Magdalena?" Fortuna asked him.

"Man, I don't know. My head is still spinning.... But I'll say one thing, she seems like a hustler. I don't think she'll sit around and wait for manna from heaven. She'll go right out and shake it out of people."

"Does that bother you?"

"No. You do what you have to do. I just wish the people in the

Casa de Menores thought more like that. I've suggested a fundraidser to buy recreational equipment and all I hear from them is, That's provided for in the budget. And I'm like, yeah, in what budget year?"

"I think you definitely should listen to what she has to offer, Gary?"

"I will."

"But I mean everything. Not just about the partnership project."

"I will."

"Good. And we can talk things over in Cartagena."

"Yeah, Cartagena. That should be nice."

The next morning, Vachio went to his meeting with Sister Magdalena. Her office in the convent was situated in the heart of old Bucaramanga. She was only a few blocks from the governor's offices, the old central plaza, and, of course, the famous House of Bolívar. It was a poor, deteriorating barrio, with big families living in small apartments and crumbling old houses, and street vendors everywhere selling everything from magic love potions to bars of soap.

Sister Magdalena served Vachio a *café con leche* and a slice of jellied guava and asked him questions about himself and his family. Then she got down to business and subjected Vachio to an intense sale's pitch. "You really should consider coming to work for my organization, Action For Youth. You could accomplish much more working with us than with the *Casa de Menores*.... That place is a training school, that's certain. A training school for vice and criminal behavior..."

"Sister, please. If you go on that way, I'm going to leave. Let's just stick to the business at hand. I've had my share of dealings with the Catholic Church and I wouldn't say that they are always models of truth and virtue."

Sister Magdalena looked shocked for a moment. But she quickly recovered her poise and assurance and said, "When dealing with human beings, my son, you always have to take into account human frailties and weaknesses. Only the Lord can help us to overcome these."

"Yes, well, there are a number of people at the *Casa de Menores* who have told me in other words essentially what you just said. And they consider themselves good and decent people trying to do the right thing. All right.... So let's stick to your project proposal. That's what I'm here for."

Sister Magdalena eyed Vachio as though debating whether to throw him out of the convent. Then she smiled and brought out the plans for the construction, the project declaration of intent, and a very detailed budget proposal. Vachio read through all the material and asked a few questions. When he was finished, he looked at Magdalena and said, "I think I can help you with this. But, you can't just talk to the donors about spiritual regeneration of poor children and all that. You need to show them a serious social problem, like *gaminismo*, and emphasize some concrete remedies—like education, job training, and job placement. That's what they want to hear about. That's your hook. They want to believe that they are making a difference in the day-to-day lives of poor children."

"Yes, definitely. This will be a youth capacitation center. We will offer practical job training and placement."

"I hope so."

"I swear it. But, of course, we will never abandon our true mission which is spiritual healing and growth through the Lord."

"O.K., that's fine. But if I write this proposal, I have to emphasize the more worldly benefits of it."

Sister Magdalena smiled. "You sound like you know what you're doing."

"I've written project proposals for nonprofit organizations I've worked for in the past."

"Were they effective?"

"Very effective. I was a good fundraiser. But for this to work, I'll need copies of all your paper work, a personal letter from you to the donors, and as many photos as you have of the site and of your group. I can get the rest of the stuff, background and photos on *gamines*, from Peace Corps."

"You'll have them by tomorrow?"

"All right, then. Let's get together tomorrow and you can give me the paper work."

"All right. I have other things to do this morning."

"Now, Sister, if this works and we receive the money, I expect certain considerations in return."

"Such as?"

"Such as hiring boys from the *Casa de Menores* to work on the construction of the center."

"That's fine. In fact, it's a good idea."

"And I maintain control of the disbursement of the funds."

"Well...I don't know. The money..."

"That's required, Sister. By the terms of the partnership program."

"But I have a say in where the money goes?"

"Of course. The biggest say. As long as the money goes exclusively toward construction of the center. I will only release the money when I'm positive of that."

"Very well. Agreed."

Vachio left the meeting with the feeling that Sister Magdalena was prepared to move mountains to make this project a reality. I can get things done with this woman, thought Vachio. Without all the bullshit I get at the *Casa de Menores*.

As Vachio walked along the busy Calle 36 toward the city center, checking out the street action as he went, he heard his voice called by a young boy selling popsicles. He did a double-take. It was Chino, a boy released from the *Casa de Menores* just the week before.

"Vachio! How are you, man?" Chino was a small boy of about 12, with a big wide grin splitting his dark face, his straight black hair covered by a checkered beret.

"I'm all right. How about you?"

"Not so bad. Just selling these popsicles."

"I thought you were going home to Valledupar. What are you doing here still?"

Chino looked uncomfortable. "Ah, you know. I guess I just like it here better."

"Yeah, but who are you staying with? Isn't your family there?"

"Yeah, but...I should get going, Vachio. It's good to see you. Tell everyone at the *Casa de Menores* that I miss them."

"Wait up, man. Don't go yet. Where are you staying?"

"Vachio. You know. I'm a *gamin*. See you around."

Chino took off and Vachio watched him go to the corner and talk to an old man who was dispensing popsicles from a portable ice box. That's who he's probably staying with, thought Vachio. And that guy has him working like a little slave. And who knows what else.... So this is where some of them go after the *Casa de Menores*. Vachio shook his head and walked off.

The next day, Sister Magdalena showed up on time and with all the information and photos Vachio had asked her to bring. After surveying the site, a large plot of semi-cleared land wedged in among the sugar cane, with only a caretaker's shack and a pile of new bricks in a corner of the field, Vachio committed to write the proposal.

The next two weeks sped by for Vachio. He was busy working on the proposal, taking care of his regular duties at the *Casa de Menores*, seeing La Rica Vicky, and looking forward with eager anticipation to his trip to Cartagena. Things were going well. Nothing had changed at the *Casa de Menores*, but the situation was tolerable. What the hell. It's a job, thought Vachio.

Vachio and some of the volunteers from Bucaramanga were scheduled to leave for Cartagena late Sunday morning. That Saturday night, Vachio went to the patio and opened up the recreation room for Barranca.

"I'm not going to hang around here tonight," Vachio told Barranca. "We have a guest from Bogatá at the house."

"Not to worry, Profé," said Barranca with his most ingratiating smile. "You know things are in good hands with me. Forget about everything. Have a good time with your guest."

Vachio ascended to the terrace and stopped to talk to the duty guards, Ramon and Julian. "I won't be around here tonight. But I'll come back in a few hours to make sure the equipment is put away."

"And?" said Ramon, not even looking up from his card game with Julian. "Hit me, *pingo*.... Ay, shit! A lousy deuce."

"The recreation room is open. Barranca is in there."

"So?"
"Just letting you guys know."
"All right, you let us know," said Ramon, rising from his stool to let Vachio out of the patio. "See you later."
Vachio returned home without giving it another thought. Over the last few weeks, this procedure had become routine. Vachio would leave Barranca in charge of the recreation room, and the guards would go down into the patio every 15 minutes or so to make sure nothing funny was going on inside the room.
At the house, Renata was preparing a wonderful meal in honor of their guest—cracker snacks, raw vegetables, pimiento olives, potato salad, candied yams, and a haunch of smoked ham with hot mustard on the side. Vachio's mouth started watering.
"So where are these guys?" Vachio asked Renata. "I thought his plane came in around noon?"
"It came a little late. But Raimundo took him out to Girón and to a few other sites."
A few minutes later, Raimundo and their guest arrived. Vachio had already heard quite a bit about him. He was a painter, originally from Port-au-Prince, Haiti, and was working as an art instructor in Bogotá. One of his original paintings, the shadowy stick man stevedore hauling a pastel blue bale against a bright yellow backdrop, was the featured decoration in the living room.
"Gary! I want you to meet our good friend," said Raimundo. "Raoul Codis. Better known as the black Gauguin."
"Don't listen to Raimun," said Raoul. "I'm nothing like Guaguin. I do tropical surrealist motifs, but of Caribbean black people. Therefore, I'm the black Raoul Codis."
Vachio laughed at the chastened look on Raimundo's face. Raoul was certainly an impressive figure. He was about 30, soft-spoken, articulate in three languages, and was sleek and handsome in the Sidney Poitier mold. He had also brought a bottle of cognac to share.
Over dinner, he proved to be an interesting and intelligent companion. He spoke with passion of his artistic endeavors and told Vachio about his days as a student in New Orleans.
"I understand you're going to Cartagena tomorrow," Raoul said to Vachio.
"Yes. And I'm very excited about it. Cartagena is the city in Colombia that I've always heard the most about. You know, because the gold of the Spanish Empire went through there and it was always getting attacked by pirates like Francis Drake, and Morgan, and Jean LaFitte. It has a lot of history."
Raoul chuckled. "I share your enthusiasm about that city. I spent six months there painting street scenes."
"How did you like it?"
"I loved it. I'd be there right now if I hadn't been offered such a

good position in Bogotá. For me, it was a special, almost holy place."

"Why?"

"Because Cartagena was one of the principal ports of entry for black slaves in Latin America. And there is a tremendous Afro-Hispano cultural and artistic tradition there. For my field of interest, it was like making a pilgrimage to Mecca or Jerusalem.... And man, I just love the architecture in that city.The only comparable place I've been to would be New Orleans. And that's not the same. Cartagena is unique because it's a much older city than New Orleans."

"Where's a good place to go?"

"Go to the old town near the Castillo de San Felipe and just walk around. You still have cobbled streets, old colonial Moorish-Spanish architecture, and lots of ornate metal grillwork and balconies. The metal work especially fascinated me. They have these old lampposts with fancy curlicue designs, and because of the hot humid climate and the sea air, the metal is pocked and sometimes attains a verdigris patina that is incredible. I loved to paint those lampposts, catching the different shades of color and the cast of the shadows caused by the hot sunlight at different times of the day."

Before Vachio was even aware of the passage of time, two hours had elapsed and they were almost finished with the cognac.

"Oh, man," said Vachio, rising from his chair. "I need to get back to the prison for a while before lights out."

"For what, man? You don't have to work tonight," said Raimundo.

"To show face, what else? But I'll only be gone a few minutes."

Vachio returned to the patio and was admitted by Julian. Ramon was already down in the yard making his final rounds before assembly and confinement to the dormitory. Vachio started down the steps and headed for the recreation room. Ramon was standing by the door. For some reason it was closed and locked.

"Where the hell is Barranca?" Ramon shouted to the boys standing in the vicinity.

The boys shrugged and walked away from him. Immediately Ramon started cursing and pounding on the massive green doors with his right fist. When he noticed Vachio, he said, "Hurry up, man. Open the door. Something is wrong here." Then he turned and yelled toward the terrace, "Julian! Ring the bell for assembly. Now!"

Vachio got out the key and fumbled with the lock, a sick feeling in the pit of his stomach.

"Hurry up, man. This smells bad to me," said Ramon.

Vachio opened the door and flicked on the light switch.

"Ay, shit!" hissed Ramon. "This is our asses."

Vachio whistled under his breath. The old desks were piled one on top of the other in the far left hand corner of the room, reaching almost to the top of the wall. There, a rope made of knotted pillow cases dangled from the corner support beam. An escape had occurred.

The boys were assembled and a head count was taken. Ten boys were missing. The off duty guards were summoned from the sleeping quarters and a search party was organized. Ramon thrust a flashlight into Vachio's hand and said, "You come with me. We're going to search the cane fields out along the road to Bucaramanga."

Vachio started to protest. Why should I help these guys look for escaped kids? That's their job, he thought. They sure as hell don't help me with mine. Then he looked at Ramon's taut worried face. Ah, what the hell. It'll be an experience.

"Let's go," said Vachio.

Ramon and Vachio walked up the inclined road at the edge of town. Ramon muttered and cussed as they walked. As duty chief, the escape was primarily his responsibility. He admitted to Vachio that, absorbed in his card game, he had failed to check the recreation room for more than an hour, giving the kids ample time to effect a clean escape and gain a good head start.

"Ah, don't worry about it," said Vachio. "Where can they go?"

"That's not the point! An escape happened on my turn. Don Gustavo can have my job for this."

"Well, maybe we'll find them."

Ramon muttered a string of curses in reply and urged Vachio to hurry. Vachio decided to keep quiet for a while. They passed the propane gas depot, the Christmas tree-like chain of lights strung outside the road house, and soon came to the service road entering the cane field. They plunged into the swaying rows of tall cane, the flashlights casting feeble pools of light in the inky blackness. Hordes of insects buzzed around their heads and the ground was mushy and sucked at their shoes. A horrible stench of rotten eggs came from decomposing sugar cane stalks left in the irrigation ditches.

Vachio moved slowly and carefully forward, his feet sinking into the muck, cursing under his breath. He flashed his light into gaps between the cane and half-heartedly looked for any sign of the boys. This search is a waste of time, he thought. The boys could hide anywhere in these miles of fields out here.... More than likely they're out on the road trying to make it to the city. Anyway, where can they go? They're *gamines*. There is no there for them out there.

Vachio stopped and looked at the weird shadows cast by the rustling stalks of cane on the service road. The moon was half-obscured by a vagrant cloud. An eerie feeling suddenly came over Vachio and he shivered involuntarily. A shadow had seemed to jump at him from between the rows of cane.

"Let's go back," said Ramon, returning from a foray between the rows. "This is a waste of time."

"Well, at least we tried."

"Yes. We had to do something. Don Gustavo will appreciate my diligence and effort."

Vachio grunted. He returned with Ramon to the *Casa de Menores* and quickly said good night. There was nothing he could do.

19

Before the flight to Cartagena departed, there was a swirl and confusion as Colombian women tried to stick carry-on things, mostly gifts for relatives and friends, into every available nook and cranny of the plane. Watching their bustle, flutter, and laughter, Hugh, who was sitting next to Vachio, exclaimed, "Aren't these women great, Vachio!"

"Which women?"

"The ones here. Isn't it great the way they go on and on about bringing every last one of their little nieces and nephews some kind of gift after a trip?"

"I guess. If you say so..."

"I love it. It's like where I work, at the Chamber of Commerce, whenever I come back from a trip to Bogotá or anywhere, all the secretaries say to me, 'Hugh! How was your trip.... What did you bring me?' And they smile and give me a hug. Even if all I give them is a piece of candy or any other stupid little thing."

"I thought you told me that you hated that," said Vachio, giving Hugh an odd look.

"No way. They're so cute about it."

"Are you feeling all right, man? Are you sure you don't have dengue or something?"

Hugh had his attention on a family group of women, a sappy smile on his long face as he watched them and listened to their happy chatter.

Vachio looked at him and chuckled to himself. When he had first met him, Hugh knew to the day and hour his moment of termination from Peace Corps and was looking forward to it with great pleasure. Of all the Peace Corps volunteers Vachio knew, Hugh was the one who most made fun of the Colombian way of doing things. But now, with the time only a few months away, he had been struck by a panic attack. Hugh had tried to get a contract extension and went into a depression when it was denied. He had waited too long.

"So what are you planning to do when you get back to the States?" Vachio asked him as the plane took to the air.

"I'm not going home right away. My sister and a friend are coming to meet me and we're going to take a trip all the way around South America."

"How long?"

"Six months.... Nine months.... A year. However long the money holds out."

"Cool. I like that plan."

"Yeah, man." Hugh let out a big sigh. "I'm not in any big rush to get back home and take up a career as a corporate clone."

"Who says you have to?"

"I'm an accountant, Vachio. What else can I do?"

"You're only limited to what your imagination can dream up, man."

"Yeah, I know. That's how you think. That's why I like talking to you about these things. But I wasn't raised that way. I was raised to be a good responsible citizen and take care of business."

"Hold up, man. I consider myself very responsible.... I only take on responsibilities I intend to fulfill. That's responsible. Doing stuff you hate out of some misguided sense of duty and making everyone around you miserable is the worst kind of irresponsible to me."

Hugh laughed. "See what I mean. You always have a different take on things. That's what I like about you. But most people don't think that way.... Especially my parents."

"My parents don't think that way, either. So what?"

"You say so what. But it's not that simple."

"I don't say anything is simple. If you want to live an alternative lifestyle—you just have to go for it. But don't expect any support from people who are afraid to make the jump. You ain't gonna get it.... Anyway, who says being a corporate clone is so bad. You'll get your car every three years, cable T.V. so you can O.D. on sports, and your three weeks of paid vacation. What's so bad about that?"

"I don't think that sounds so good anymore. We've been spoiled here."

"Speak for yourself, man. I work in a prison, not the Bucaramanga Chamber of Commerce. But whatever..."

After arrival in Cartagena, the volunteers from Santander piled into a taxi and went out to the Boca Grande District near one of the nice beaches. Forest had been in Cartagena only the weekend before, attending a *Cuerpo de Paseo* party at Janie and Big Bob's place that had drawn volunteers from all parts of Colombia, and he knew of a reasonably priced pensión in this very expensive city. The Peace Corps per diem allowance for volunteers didn't come close to covering basic daily costs unless expenses were pooled. Five volunteers shared one large room.

As soon as they were settled in, Vachio announced, "Well, I'm going to the beach right now. This is the longest time in my life I've been living without the smell of the ocean."

"You're gonna go now, man," said Forest. "We were going to look up Janie and Big Bob and see what's on the agenda for tonight.... Anyway, it's too damn hot right now."

"I don't care. I'm going to the beach. I'll see you guys later. I've been waiting months for this."

Vachio changed into shorts, a T-shirt, and sandals, grabbed a towel, and walked the two blocks to the Caribbean past expensive resort hotels and restaurants. Boca Grande beach was wide and clean, with shimmering white sand, and statuesque black women selling mangos and cold beer out of plastic ice buckets. It was early afternoon and the heat and humidity were intense enough to bubble your skin. Vachio had most of the beach to himself.

Vachio bought a mango and a beer, rented a white tent to keep the sun off, and relaxed. After a while he went in the water. It was blood warm and buoyant. He swam out a ways and lay on his back, feeling his body massaged by gentle swells. It was a delicious feeling. Vachio hadn't realized just how much he missed the ocean until that moment. Then his thoughts turned to La Rica Vicky. She was from the coast as well. It would be nice to share this with her, thought Vachio.... Damn, I must be stuck on that girl.

Vachio stayed in the water a good half hour before returning to the beach. As he was toweling off, he saw Forest approaching from the sea wall and waved to him.

"Hey, man, didn't take you long to get here," said Vachio. "I thought it was too hot for the beach right now?"

Forest laid out his beach towel and unslung his long lean body. "Yeah, but in a little while the hard bodies will be showing up and I wanted a good spot to watch from."

"Where are the others?" asked Vachio.

"In a nice cool bar having an ice cold beer."

"So what's up with Janie and Big Bob?"

"Ah, nothin' man. They're still burned out from the party last week-end.... And I don't blame 'em. You know, living here in Cartagena, they get guests all the time. That gets old after a while."

"Ah, poor babies. I guess that's just the price you pay for living in paradise.... At least that's what Big Bob told me when I was in Bogotá for language training."

"They do have a great house. Right near the beach, too.... I wouldn't mind living here."

"What? Don't tell me you're tired of Bucaramanga."

"Ah, the Buc's all right. We like it just fine. It ain't the most exciting place in the world, but we don't get bugged by Peace Corps supervisors all the time like they do in the real nice places like here and Cali."

Vachio laughed "You mean like Peter says, huh...the Salt Lake City of Colombia. Nice place to live. But who wants to go there on vacation."

"Man, I wouldn't say that. But the Buc's all right. We like it fine just the way it is."

"And then you have Garrotero," said Vachio, laying back on his towel with a sigh.

Forest laughed. "Yeah, you can watch the donkeys take dumps on the street there."

"Or see plastered campesinos get into machete fights at the market, or watch street dogs chew each other up on La Quarta, or have a big prison break at the *Casa de Menores* like we did last night," said Vachio, shielding his eyes from the sun.

"Not my idea of entertainment, guy. I'll take our six theaters and nice bars and discos over that."

"Yeah, but it's *folclórico* in Garrotero City. We invent our own entertainment."

"If you say so. It sounds boring to me."

Vachio smiled and closed his eyes. The weekend before, Forest and Peter and Emily had come to Cartagena for Janie and Big Bob's party, attended by about 40 Peace Corps volunteers from the length and breadth of Colombia. From what Vachio had heard, the party had raged on all night, featured a couple of near fights, and ended up with a group of volunteers skinny dipping in the ocean at daybreak and getting busted by the Cartagena police. "It was a fucking great party!" said Peter. "Totally out of control. And you missed it." Vachio had laughed. He knew what these parties were like. People got wasted and competitive, one volunteer trying to outdo the other in their level of outrageousness, and things got sloppy at the end. Vachio wasn't sorry he had missed it. He had gone with La Rica Vicky to a colonial town in the mountains called Zapatoca. They had stayed at a funky old hotel, made love over and over, and hiked around in the cool fresh mountain air and gazed at incredible panoramic vistas. Whatever turns you on, Vachio thought.

That night, the Santander crew went to a casino in one of the fancy hotels for a while, and then hit a funky old tourist sailors' bar in old Cartagena recommended by Janie and Big Bob. The place was run by an Englishman and featured a live parrot who cussed in English and Spanish, beer and rum from all over the world, fish nets hanging from the ceilings, pirate statues, and battered old stools and sea chest tables. The place was jammed, mostly with foreign tourists and Cartagena prostitutes, and blasted the latest reggae from Jamaica.

"Damn! This place is a gold mine," said Peter. "I wouldn't mind getting up a business like this when I'm done with Peace Corps.... What do you think, Vachio? Do you want to be my partner in a *gringo* bar? We'll get Hughie in on it, too."

Vachio laughed. "I think it's a good idea, man.... For you. I've got other ideas."

Later that evening, Vachio met a veteran volunteer in Cartagena named Conrad and his girlfriend Luisa. They sat at a sea chest next to a peg-legged wooden pirate and after a few stout ales, Conrad told Vachio what was bugging him. "Man, I just don't know what to do. I'm supposed to terminate in a few months but I'll be damned if I'm ready to go home. I mean, I'm ready. More than ready. But Luisa and

I are in love and we're going to be married."

"Yeah. What's the problem?"

"Man, the problem is, I'm from College Station, Texas. Aggieville. And I'm afraid if I take Luisa back there, she is gonna be treated like just another spic."

"You know that for sure?" Vachio looked at Luisa. She had a dark complexion with a smattering of freckles, regular features, straight black hair, dark eyes, and a sleek athletic figure. She was cute. Racially, she was a mixture of European, Indian, and black blood.

"Let me put it this way, man, my mother and father came here to visit a few months ago to meet Luisa and her family. While they were here, they were all smiles and sweet as sugar. Luisa's parents thought they were so gracious. Then, two weeks ago, I get a letter from my mother saying, "Conrad, dear, Luisa is pretty and smart and very nice. But hadn't you better consider the social consequences of bringing her home to Texas..."

"Uugh!" exclaimed Vachio.

"Damn right! Man, I was so pissed.... Here's Luisa, smart, educated, from a good family, and I have to worry about social consequences.... Hell, I can stay here. The Marine Institute wants to hire me when I finish with Peace Corps. And Luisa's family is behind us 100 percent. But..."

"You miss home."

"Yeah, I miss home. And I don't see any goddamn reason why my wife can't be welcome there. Hell, man, you're from San Francisco. Isn't it a lot more tolerant there about that sort of thing?"

"There are lots of interracial and intercultural couples. But you still have to deal with bullshit there, too.... But probably not nearly as intense as what you're talking about."

Conrad put his arm around Luisa's shoulder and hugged her. "Maybe we should go to San Francisco, honey baby."

"We can stay here, love. My family will help us get started."

Conrad looked at Vachio and said in English, "With all the white Colombian women here, I had to fall in love with a *morenita.*"

Vachio shrugged. "That's the way it goes."

The next morning the conference began. It was a two day affair, with seminars and volunteer presentations lasting from 10 a.m. to 2:30 p.m. with time out for lunch. Then everyone could hit the beach or whatever. Wednesday was a national holiday and the volunteers had the option to stay over and enjoy the city. The real purpose of the conference was to meet the new director and assistant director in a more informal setting, and to give some stressed-out volunteers a vacation.

Vachio had lunch with Fortuna and they talked over the Partnership Project. She had brought photos and articles about *gaminismo* for Vachio to use in his statement of problem material, and Vachio turned over what he had already written concerning the budget, site, and purpose of the center.

Fortuna was pleased. "You jumped on this in a hurry," she said.

"Sure. I have the time. And it's easy to do things when there's cooperation.... That Sister Magdalena is kind of a pain-in-the-butt. You know, real pushy. But she does what she says she will."

"Have you thought over working with her as your primary job here."

"Yes. But I think I'll stick with the *Casa de Menores* for the time being."

After the meeting, Vachio returned to the pensión with Forest to pick up their beach stuff. Forest tried to open the door but it was chained from the inside. Forest rapped on the door and rattled the chain. Then Hugh came to the door, a towel wrapped around his waist, and said, "Can you guys just give me about 10 minutes. I have a girl in there with me.... A real nice girl."

"Ah, man, you're cutting into my beach time, Hugh," said Forest. "At least toss us our things."

"Just give me 10 minutes. Ten minutes."

Forest and Vachio smiled at the look on his face. "Come on. Let's leave the guy in peace," said Vachio.

"You can have 15 minutes," said Forest.

Vachio and Forest went to a fruit juice bar to wait. They ordered guava softies and sat under a fan to stay cool.

"Hugh cracks me up, boy," said Forest. "Did you see the look on his face when we showed up.... Man, I thought he was about to faint."

"He did look pretty nervous," said Vachio. "But good for him. He got a girl for himself. I heard her in there."

"Yeah, but he cracks me up."

About 20 minutes later they went back to the pensión, just in time to see Hugh furtively hustling a woman away from the building.

"Man, he cracks me up," said Forest.

Vachio and Forest grabbed their things and walked straight to the municipal beach near old Cartagena. It was jammed with locals and was a welter of noise, sound, and squalling children. Boom boxes blasted *Cumbias* and *Vallenatos*, whole families picnicked in the sand, a big soccer game was being played in the middle of everything, little boys whacked pebbles with sticks in imitation of their favorite baseball players, and more than a few young men were sparring with professional intensity.

"Some of these kids want to be the next Kid Pambele," said Vachio, mentioning the name of a world champion Colombian boxer.

"Yeah, he's from here."

Vachio looked around at the scene and chuckled. The two *gringos* were beginning to draw stares and funny looks. This reminds me of the public swimming pools in my neighborhood, thought Vachio.

"Come on, man. Let's get on to the Boca Grande Beach," said

Forest. "I want to see the hard bodies."

"I see plenty of hard bodies around here."

"You know what I mean," said Forest, already headed up the beach.

They walked about a half mile up the beach, in the shadow of the big tourist hotels, and found a small group of Peace Corps volunteers already hanging out. They bought beer and mangos and compared notes on people around Colombia.

"So did you here what happened to Carlos?" Janie asked Vachio.

"No. What?"

"He turned out to be a Moonie. And he left his job in Villavicencio and started cruising around Colombia."

"You're kidding?"

"No. He did it. He came here and stayed with us for a while."

"So what happened to him?"

"Braniff Award. They sent him home. Now he's selling ceiling insulation in Los Angeles."

"Damn! Big Carlos a Moonie. I don't believe it." Carlos Gamoboa had been Vachio's roommate at the Hotel Tundama during their first three days in-country. He was a friendly bear of a man, with curly black hair and a beard,who gave everyone hugs at the slightest provocation. "Man, after that news, I gotta get in the water and cool down."

Vachio waded into the surf and joined Forest out near the break line. Forest was standing with his head toward the beach, bouncing up and down on his toes, scanning for incoming hard bodies.

"Whooee, you see that one. She's an eight," said Forest. Then he nudged Vachio in the ribs. "Hey, look who's coming. It's Hank Estevez."

"How is he? I've never really talked to him."

"He ain't a bad old boy. I talked to him a lot the last time I was in Bogotá. He's from New York."

Hank Estevez was the Assistant Director of Peace Corps Colombia. Of Puerto Rican descent, he was short and stocky, probably a little bull at one time, but his body was beginning to turn roly poly.

"Hey, Hank! I hope ya'll can swim if you're gonna come out here with us," said Forest, throwing his arms over his head.

Hank looked up and gave Forest a dirty look. Then he started dog-paddling toward them.

"He don't look too happy about that remark," Vachio said.

"Ah, he's got a sense of humor."

Hank introduced himself to Vachio and then set his sights on Forest. "So, I meant to ask you the last time we talked, why did you join Peace Corps? I mean, no offense, but most Peace Corps volunteers I've known joined up because they didn't have much going for them back in the States."

Forest emitted a weak laugh and said, "Ah, man, you know, I joined up to get some foreign experience on my resume."

"Yeah, foreign experience. All right." Hank turned to Vachio. "How about you?"

"I don't know how you can even ask that question. Look at us, we're here in the Caribbean on this beautiful beach, in this beautiful city, sucking down beers, and you're asking me why I joined Peace Corps.... How much would this cost me if I came here on vacation? This is the life, man."

Hank chuckled. "That's a good answer."

"What about you, Hank? You're in the Peace Corps. So what didn't you have going for you back home?" asked Forest.

"I'll admit to you guys, I'd rather be working in Washington where the action is. This job was an appointment for my work on Carter's election campaign. I look at it as a positive detour in the road. But our situations aren't comparable. You guys are volunteers. I make $40,000 a year. That's a lot of money in Colombia. And then the perks—a free home, car, servants, and an expense account."

"Yeah, well, I expect to have that some day," said Forest. "Like I said, I'm just getting my foreign service experience." Then Forest laughed and swam away.

Hank looked after him with a half-smile on his face. Then he turned to Vachio and asked, "What's your job here?"

"I work in a *Casa de Menores* in Santander."

"Oh, you're the guy who does that."

"What's that mean? Am I famous or something?"

"No, but we've had discussions concerning your post. Frankly, we're not too happy about having a volunteer work in a prison right now. We'd prefer to get you out of there."

"It's not really a prison. It's more like a reform school."

"No. We think it's more like a prison."

"It's not that bad. Really."

"Look, don't be concerned about us finding something else for you to do. We have other jobs available."

"I'm not concerned about that. I just don't think it's that bad."

"We don't like the situation." Hank was shaking his head and slapping at the water.

"Look, Hank, you come from the Bronx, right?"

"Yes..."

"Well, when you were a kid, did you have to deal with other kids trying to steal your lunch money and that kind of thing?"

"Yes, I did. But what's your point?"

"I grew up in that kind of a neighborhood, too. And between you and me, because I know you understand, the *Casa de Menores* is no worse than that. And I'd say not as bad. I can deal with the danger part. It's other things that are more of a problem..."

Hank looked thoughtful. "All right. I still don't like the idea. But you can stay there—for now."

20

Vachio returned to Garrotero Wednesday night, feeling refreshed and ready to go. Then the next morning, at breakfast, a boy from the *Casa de Menores* came with a summons from Don Gustavo for a private meeting as soon as possible.

"What's this all about?" Vachio asked, looking at Raimundo across the breakfast table.

"I'm not sure," said Raimundo, picking at his soft boiled egg. "But I've heard that a few of the guards and administrators are blaming you for the escape Saturday night."

"What? How do they figure that?"

Raimundo shrugged. "I don't know. I'm just telling you what I heard."

"That's bullshit!"

Vachio finished off his breakfast and headed straight for Gustavo's office. He was angry and spoiling for a fight, but he determined to keep his temper under control and hear Gustavo out before he said anything.

"Vachio, good morning," said Gustavo. "How was your trip to Cartagena?"

"It was great."

"Good. I'm glad to hear that..."

"How did things go around here? Were the escaped boys found?"

"Seven of them were picked up the same night of the escape. They all boarded a bus going to Bucaramanga together. I merely alerted the police and they were picked up at the terminal as they got off. Another was caught the next day trying to hitch a ride on the main highway." Gustavo smiled. "The boys were very easy to spot. What with their patched clothes and short haircuts. They still reek of being *gamines*."

"And the other two? Who are they?"

"Barranca and Felipe.... And we're pretty sure they've gone to Barrancabermeja to seek help from Barranca's mother. We have a man down there waiting for them." Gustavo smiled. "The boys are very predictable at times."

Vachio nodded, wondering when Gustavo would get to the point. Boys ran away from the *Casa de Menores* fairly often, usually singly or in pairs, and were generally recaptured in a short time. Of course, this mass escape right under the noses of the guards was another story. It was downright humiliating.

"Vachio, I've called you in here to answer a complaint. Several of the guards have blamed you for the escape and now I want to hear your version of what happened."

"What can I say? It's a joke. I'm not responsible for security."

"Yes, that's true. But the guards claimed you opened up the recreation room and left Barranca alone in there."

"That's right. Barranca is in charge of the recreation room when I'm not in the patio."

"Don't you think it's negligent to leave him alone without supervision?"

"No. That's his job.... As the recreation plan calls for."

"But Vachio, to leave a boy like Barranca in charge?"

"What about it? He's been in charge for a while and I never heard any complaint or objection until now.... Anyway, he's not the first trustee to run since I've been here when given the chance."

Gustavo looked thoughtful. "So you are saying the guards are at fault for this escape."

"Well..."

"Were all the guards on duty making their normal rounds?"

"I can't say. I was out of the patio for two hours after I opened up the recreation room."

"What were they doing when you left?"

"Playing cards."

"So they were negligent?"

Vachio shrugged. "You know as well as I do that they often play cards to pass the time and the boys don't usually escape."

"Vachio, we're going around and around. Someone was at fault for this. If not the guards, then you must at least accept some responsibility for this escape."

"No! I don't!" Vachio felt his temper flare. "My job is not security. That's the guards' job."

"Vachio, up to a point, security is the responsibility of every employee of this establishment."

"Well, sure, if I see a boy escaping over the wall I'll do what I can to stop him. But it's not my job to make rounds."

"Then what you're saying is that the guards are at fault for not making their rounds."

"No, I don't know. But I do know...ah, forget it."

"Go on."

"I told you a long time ago that those desks and the opening up near the roof was a problem. That's how the boys escaped. One of the smaller ones climbed up a pile of desks and rigged up a rope for the others.... They could never have done that if those desks were removed as I requested."

Gustavo's face turned red. "So what are you saying? That I'm at fault?"

"I'm saying that there is plenty of fault to go around," said Vachio, struggling to keep his voice calm. "If I had stayed in the patio Saturday night and kept an eye on the recreation room—there would have been no escape that night. If the guards had kept a closer eye on things—there would have been no escape that night. But if Ordoñez had removed those desks—there could never have been an escape."

"So as you see it, Ordoñez is accountable."

Vachio shrugged. "I suppose he is in a way. But if I've learned anything in my time here, it's that things only seem to get done when you really want them to get done. You're at the top and no one makes a move without your say so. And this attitude extends through the whole hierarchy."

Gustavo turned pale and his hands pressed against his desk top. "This is how it has to be. Otherwise it would be chaos here."

"Maybe so. But in the case of my program, I have to be able to delegate responsibility to some of the boys. I mean, look, I was gone in Cartagena for three work days for a conference, and next week I'll be in Bogotá for a week of language training. Obviously, I need someone to run the recreation room when I'm gone. And if the recreation room is not secure, then there will be no recreation room and few activities when I'm not around. That's just logical. And what's going on around here does not allow me to implement my program."

"According to certain members of our staff, you have no discernible program."

"I would be happy to answer my critics—to their faces. But since I've been here, even though I'm supposed to be a department head, I haven't even been invited to a staff meeting. What's up with that?"

Gustavo shifted uncomfortably in his chair. "I don't think it would be wise to have you at a staff meeting as yet."

"Then when? A month before I leave?"

"Vachio, please, be patient. There is still resistance to your presence here from certain ignorant staffers. But most of us support your efforts and you are making progress."

"Be patient! I've been here almost five months. Damn near a quarter of my contract time. And I still don't have a viable recreation room, any equipment, or the privilege of being treated like a legitimate staff member. I'm nothing but a mascot to you guys. And I don't like it. You're wasting me here."

"Vachio, you're overreacting."

"No, I'm not overreacting. I want to go to a staff meeting and face my critics. If they're going to criticize me behind my back, they should be able to do it to my face. And I should be able to voice what I think as well. You need to treat me as though I am really part of this operation."

"It's not a good idea."

"Then maybe it's not a good idea for me to continue at the *Casa de Menores*."

"Don't talk foolishly."

"Gustavo, I haven't said anything to you before this, but Peace Corps is not too happy about my continuing here. In Cartagena, I spoke to the assistant director, and he wanted to pull me out of here."

"But why?"

"Because they think it's too dangerous."

"That's absurd."

"Is it? I never told anyone in Peace Corps about what happened between you and Torres. Believe me, if I had, they would have yanked me out of here the next day. I can assure you of that.... I kept my mouth shut because I want to continue here. But I see no point in continuing here if things are like this. I'm not going to be anybody's whipping boy or scapegoat. You understand?"

"What would you do?"

"I've already been offered a full-time position by that Sister Magdalena. Or I could be transferred almost anywhere else in Colombia. Fortuna and the assistant director have both made that clear."

"But you have a contract with us. You can't just walk away from it."

"That's not correct. You have a contract with Peace Corps to supply a volunteer. I have a contract with Peace Corps to work at some job. The two do not necessarily go together."

Gustavo drummed his fingers on the table top. "You're a little upset right now. We'll speak of this later after I conduct a full investigation of the escape."

"What is there to investigate? We already know what happened. That's not going to change.... But I want to defend myself before my accusers. I demand to go to the next staff meeting."

Gustavo sighed. "Very well, Vachio. I don't like this at all. But if you insist..."

"I insist."

"The next staff meeting is in three weeks."

"I'll be there."

Vachio had never felt more depressed about his job at the *Casa de Menores* than he did that night. He talked over the situation with Raimundo and even he was sympathetic this time.

"There's no doubt, Gary, they do look on you as some sort of mascot. But didn't you tell me that so far as Peace Corps is concerned...as long as they like you, that's good enough."

"Yes, I told you that. That's how the top administrators feel. We're essentially here for the public relations—to show Colombians that Americans are good people. But that's not good enough for me. And I won't be scapegoated for their screw ups. I'll take responsibility for my mistakes. Let them take responsibility for theirs."

Raimundo laughed. "Yeah, but in some cases, if they screw up, it can mean their job. But what can they do to you?"

"That's not my problem. And if I wasn't here, they couldn't use that excuse."

"Well, it's like the saying goes, the shit rolls down hill. And you're at the bottom, son."

"That's what they think..."

"You know, man,if you really want a real job, you could resign from Peace Corps and I could use you in the factory."

"Get serious. Doing what?"

"I am serious. You could work in dispatch and a few other things.... We'll keep you busy."

Vachio shook his head. "No thanks. The truth is, I can't stand the noise or the smell of that burnt plastic at your factory.... And besides, I didn't come here for that. I'm a social worker. I'd rather go over and work full-time for that nun."

"The nun?" Raimundo's voice was scornful. "What does she have to offer society? Pie in the sky? All she does is take people's money in the name of God."

"You don't even know her, man."

"Gustavo knows her. She used to come to the *Casa de Menores* and bother him for handouts..."

Vachio laughed. If Gustavo is bad-mouthing her, he thought. He must consider her a real threat.

"...She'll just put you to work building monuments to God and herself. How is that going to help with the *gamin* problem?"

"Well, I'm not totally sure about her yet. But I would have some real authority with her to get some programs of my own together. She already agreed that once the construction begins, we can use boys from the *Casa de Menores* to work."

"Big deal. How many jobs would that be?"

"Whatever. It's better than nothing. And I'm sick of playing the clown at the *Casa de Menores*." Vachio looked at Raimundo, knowing almost everything he said would be relayed to Gustavo. "I'm not going to talk about this stuff anymore. But if certain things don't change at the *Casa de Menores*..."

"What?"

"When the time comes, if it comes, I won't warn them again. I'll just make my move."

A day later, Barranca and Felipe were brought back to the *Casa de Menores*. When Barranca saw Vachio in the cafeteria, he asked permission to speak to him and they sat at a side table. Barranca dropped his eyes and mumbled, "Sorry, Profé, I couldn't stand it here any longer. I just had to escape and go see my mother."

"Whatever, man. You did what you thought you had to.... But you know I can't trust you anymore."

"You mean, when I get off restriction, I can't run the recreation room anymore?"

"You must be kidding to even ask. Of course you can't. I got in trouble over this, too. I've already put Geronimo in charge.... That is, whenever the recreation room is reopened."

"I didn't mean to let you down, Profé. I had to see my mother."

"You did what you thought you had to do. Now you have to suffer the consequences."

On Friday morning, Montoya asked Vachio to go down to the patio with him and they found Ordoñez removing the desks from the recreation room. Additionally, McCorney and Vega, another teacher, were installing steel bars across the length of the air passage."

"Now you'll have a secure recreation room and office," said Montoya.

Vachio shook his head and said, "For months I asked to have those desks removed and they did nothing. And now, it's overkill.... What a system."

"Well, at least they're finally doing something. And this is a permanent solution."

"Yes. But we have a saying in English for this. A day late and a dollar short.... And I still need recreation equipment."

On Saturday, Vachio met La Rica Vicky for lunch at their favorite Antioqueño restaurant. She was excited and bubbling over with news. "Gary, can you believe it. My visa to the United States has been approved. I'm going to visit my grandmother in Washington, D.C. and enroll in a special summer course at American University."

For a moment Vachio was stunned. "When are you going to leave?"

"Not for two months. But I'm so excited. I've waited for more than a year to have my visa approved. And now it's happened."

"Congratulations," said Vachio, staring at the table.

Vicky was so excited she barely noticed his disappointment.

"How long will you be gone?"

"At least six months. Maybe longer if I can get approval to study longer."

"So what about us?"

Vicky leaned across the table and kissed Vachio on the lips. "We'll be in touch, of course. I wouldn't change you for anybody."

"Long distance love doesn't work too well."

"It does if the sentiment is strong enough.... Gary, we'll be writing all the time."

"Yeah. Well, at least no one can say you're hanging out with me to try to get a visa."

Vicky laughed and she changed the subject. But this was a hard blow for Vachio. He wasn't at all sure he wanted to marry Vicky, but he had come to count on her as his confidante and friend as well as his lover. But what could he say? This was something she really wanted. Just as he wanted to adventure travel, alone, as he had told her on more than one occasion.

The next week, Vachio returned home after the recreation period and he found Tomás Barbosa, Arnulfo, and the rest of the crew sitting at the dining room table in excited conversation with Raimundo and Renata.

"Vachio! Did you hear what happened?" Raimundo asked.

"No. What?"

"The American Ambassador and 12 other ambassadors were kidnapped by M19 at a party at the Brazilian Ambassador's residence."

"What? What?"

Raimundo and Tomás gave Vachio a rundown. Masked and heavily armed *guerrilleros* had stormed the residence and taken all diplomatic personnel hostage inside the residence. Now they were holed up inside with their captives, issuing proclamations and negotiating with the government.

As Vachio listened, he felt his heart flutter. This might be the death blow to Peace Corps Colombia if the Ambassador is killed or injured, he thought. And aside from that, he's a nice guy. What a bitch!

"What an unbelievable plan! What execution!" said Tomás, his eyes alight. "This was a masterstroke.... And they even have women involved in this. Can you imagine—women!"

Yeah, I can imagine, thought Vachio. It doesn't take much imagination.

"Vachio, you don't look so well," said Arnulfo.

"I'm not. This might be the event that knocks me out of Colombia. This is real bad news. I have to get to Bucaramanga and see if the office called any of the volunteers there."

"What for? You can't do anything about it. And you're going to Bogotá next week anyway," said Raimundo.

"It doesn't matter. I need to find out what I can."

"It's got nothing to do with you, man. It's a diplomatic kidnapping. They probably just want money," said Raimundo.

"Whatever. I'll see you guys later."

Vachio hopped on the bus and went to Bucaramanga. He found Hugh and Forest at the volunteer house, discussing the situation.

"So what have you heard?" Vachio asked.

"Not much," said Forest. "I called Bogotá and talked to Hank. He said to just sit tight and wait. There's nothing we can do."

21

By the time Vachio reached Bogotá the next week, the hostage crisis had settled into a stalemate. The M19 revolutionaries were an educated, media savvy group and were doing nothing rash. The Acronym, M19, stood for March 19. On that date, in 1970, after a 20-year period of officially alternating the presidency between the *Liberales* and *Conservadores* parties, an open presidential election was held. Rojas Pinilla, a former military dictator of Colombia who held power during some of the worst of *La Violencia* and brought a measure of stability to the situation, ran as an independent, left-leaning populist. According to a number of independent observers, not to mention his loyal followers, he won the election and had it stolen from him by the traditional parties. On that day, and from that rationale, M19 was born and had steadily grown. They were essentially urban revolutionaries noted for spectacular, headline-grabbing robberies and kidnappings. The takeover at the Brazilian Ambassador's residence was their greatest coup and gave them their most attention and leverage to date. What they wanted from the Colombian government was an acknowledgement that the election of 1970 was rigged, a more open political process, money, and a plane to Cuba.

In Bogotá, Vachio had a brief chat with the Peace Corps Director, Gabriel Kino. "We're not going to get too worked up over this situation," he told Vachio. "The leaders of M19 aren't fools. They know that if they kill the hostages, or even harm them, they're dead meat. Our greatest concern is that the Colombian government will become impatient, storm the place, and cause a blood bath."

"And if that occurs?"

"Then Peace Corps is almost certainly out of here.... But don't worry about it. We'll be able to place you guys in another country."

"But I like it here."

Gabriel laughed. "Don't worry. From all reports, the hostages are being well-treated. These guys are reasonable. They want money and media attention."

Vachio thought over what Gabriel had told him and found it reasonable. Why worry about it, he thought. I can't do anything about it anyway.

In-service language training was a breeze for Vachio. He wasn't sandbagging his knowledge of Spanish anymore and he had improved rapidly in the English-free environment of Garrotero. Vachio and his two teachers, both from Medellín, had a good time joking around during the daily four hours of classes. The rest of the time Vachio had to himself. He finished off the project proposal for Sister Magdalena and turned the material over to Fortuna to copy and send out to the donors. He visited with friends and caught up on the doings of the volunteers from his group. He went out to good restaurants and enjoyed some of the other nice things Bogotá offered. It was a vacation.

One day, late in the week, he ran into Julie Christiansen at the Peace Corps office. For one of the few times in Vachio's acquaintance with her she was alone, and she looked distraught. They walked out the front door together and looked at each other.

"Which way are you going?" Vachio asked.
"Toward Chapinero."
"I'm going that way."
Julie looked at him for a moment. They had never been on the best of terms. "Let's go."
They started along and to Vachio's surprise, Julie suggested they stop and have a coffee when they came to a café.
"Sure. I'm through with business for the day," Vachio said.
"I'm not. But I have a few minutes."
After they took seats and ordered their coffee, Vachio asked her, "What business are you up to?"
"I'm getting my papers in order for termination."
"Termination. Why?"
"Because I just can't get comfortable here. I'm tired of the harassment I get on the streets and now with what happened to the Ambassador, I just feel it's getting too dangerous. I don't feel safe here."
"Well, danger is a relative thing. I mean, where I grew up in the States it wasn't exactly safe."
"Don't start with that! You're not a woman. You don't know what it's like here for me."
"No, I don't. But I know what I perceive. And I don't perceive Colombia as so personally dangerous. From what I've seen here, people mess with you if they have some reason. Sometimes in the States, it was just pure random violence."
"Marin was never like that. I never felt there like I do here. I could walk around freely in Marin."
"Well, let's not get into that. Me and you grew up in different places and it wasn't the same. I can only tell you what I experienced."
Julie sipped her coffee.
"Are you sure you want to terminate?" Vachio asked.
"I'm sure. It's not just the danger here.... Peace Corps just can't find a job for me that gives me any feeling of satisfaction."
"Join the crowd."
"What? Not you, too. I've heard about what you're doing from Dorrie. You have that job in the prison and you're working on a Peace Corps Partnership program.... You are doing things here."
"Maybe. But you're talking about satisfaction. And I don't feel so good about what I'm doing in the prison right now.... Truthfully, I'm not even sure why the Colombians want me there except maybe as some kind of pet."
Julie smiled. "But they like you?"
"Some of them do. Some of them don't. And it's hard to know how to take things at times." Vachio took a sip of his coffee. "For example, a few weeks ago, we took some of the boys out to this unfinished swimming pool at the new *Casa de Menores* they're building..." Vachio

paused to make sure he had Julie's attention. "...So there was me, the social worker, the psychologist, about 40 boys wearing only shorts to keep them from running away, three guards, and the two pet dogs. We get to the swimming pool and the water is dirty and full of green algae scum and other crap. There's water running into the pool from a creek coming off a cow pasture. Man, I look at that water and I say to the social worker and the psychologist, 'You can't let them go in there. It's filthy. They'll get sick.' They look at each other and agree. But no one says anything to the guards. Meanwhile, even the kids are leery about jumping into the water and they're all just standing around and waiting. Finally one of the guards says, 'Hey, let's throw the *gringo* in to test the water.' The guards all get a laugh out of that and I say, 'You'll end up in there before I do, brother.' Then he laughs like he was only joking, but he was only half-joking, and he says, 'Throw the two dogs in. If they're all right after a few minutes it should be fine.'"

"No way. You're making this up."

"No, I'm not. They threw the dogs in and they paddled around for a while. So that same guard says, 'It's all right. Go for it. Get in there.' The kids still hesitated, but finally a few crazy ones jumped in and eventually almost all of them. I couldn't believe it. I look at the social worker and I say, 'I can't believe this.' And she says, 'But they'll be disappointed if they can't swim after coming all the way out here.' So I look at the psychologist and I say, 'Would you let your kids swim in that?' And he says, 'Absolutely not. But my kids aren't *gamines*. These guys have swum in even worse.' I just shook my head after that."

"So did they get sick?"

"Yeah, quite a few of them came down with colds. But since none of them died it wasn't considered a big deal.... But I will say, the director of the prison was not too happy when he heard about what happened. To his credit."

Julie was shaking her head incredulously.

"Throw the *gringo* in. I'll never forget that one," said Vachio. "Ah, what memories."

Julie quickly finished her coffee and got up to leave.

"Well, the best of luck," said Vachio, rising from his chair and shaking her hand. "Whatever you decide to do, I hope it works out for the best."

"What about you?"

"Oh, I'm here for the duration...however long that is."

"Even after what you just told me?"

"Oh, I've been lucky. The good has outweighed the bad here for me. And I've learned to think of incidents like that as folkloric. But who knows? The way things are going with Peace Corps, none of us may be here long. Are you going back to Marin?"

"Yes. I'm going back to school."

"Well, maybe we'll meet again there."

"Who knows," said Julie. "Bye." She walked off, her long blonde hair swinging behind her.

Vachio sat down and ordered another coffee. Then a faraway look came into his eyes. Julie was one of the first persons he had met in Peace Corps. During orientation, on arrival at the Holiday Inn in Miami's Little Havana, Vachio was assigned a room from a master list by a Cuban clerk and issued his key. On opening the door to his room, he was staggered. Two attractive young women, one wearing a revealing nightie and the other a white bathrobe, stood facing him from the middle of the room. Before Vachio could recover from this initial surprise, he heard a shriek from the bathroom just inside the doorway. He turned to see a butt-naked elderly woman toweling off after a shower. She screeched louder when Vachio looked at her and slammed the door shut.

"What are you doing in our room?" asked the woman in the translucent nightie. She was a willowy blonde with a striking figure and seemed more surprised than irritated by Vachio's arrival.

"I believe this is my room, also," said Vachio, holding up his key to show them the room number.

"It looks like it is," said the woman in the bathrobe. She was pretty, also. Another tall blonde with green eyes, a golden tan, and the body of a swimmer.

"Well, I guess that makes us roommates. Glad to meet you. My name is Gary Vachio."

"My name is Nancy," said the one in the bathrobe.

"Julie," said the other, appraising Vachio.

Vachio looked beyond the women and saw only two king-size beds. Two beds for four people. Julie and Nancy were thinking the same thing. They looked at each other.

"So who's going to sleep with him?" asked Julie.

"I guess I can," said Nancy. "You don't snore do you?"

"Not that I know of," said Vachio.

"Well, I can sleep with him if you don't really want to," said Julie.

"Hey, I'm easy. Whatever you decide is fine with me," said Vachio. He smiled and shook his head. For a moment he thought he had died and gone to heaven. Two bookend blondes arguing over who was going to sleep with him. "Man!" he exclaimed. "I heard that Peace Corps was kind of liberal, but I never expected anything like this."

"Excuse me," said a voice from behind Vachio, abruptly shattering his fantasy. "There's been a mistake. The room clerk gave you the wrong key."

Vachio turned and saw an apple-cheeked young woman, freckled and wholesome looking, with a friendly smile and a conservative appearance. A Christian Scientist as it turned out.

"My name is Michelle," she said. "Glad to meet you." Then she relieved Vachio of his key. "You're upstairs a floor."

Vachio swallowed his disappointment and turned back to Julie and Nancy. "Well, I knew it was too good to be true. But I guess I'll be seeing you guys around. Bye."

He left to meet his three male roommates, the vision of Julie and her sexy nightie swimming in his head. Then, that evening, after a long day of orientation sessions, a series of painful shots for tropical diseases, and meeting a slew of new people, Vachio spotted Julie and Nancy sitting in a quiet corner at the hotel bar. Vachio, feeling as friendly and frisky as a puppy dog, slid through a boisterous group of Argentine officers on shore leave from a merchant ship and made it over to their table.

"Hi, roomies. Mind if I join you?" he said.

Nancy smiled and immediately started to slide her chair over to give him room. Julie stared at the table and poked with her straw at a foamy Strawberry Margarita. Then she looked up and gave Vachio an irritated look. "To tell you the truth, I would mind. We're having a private conversation here. Women things. And we've already been bothered by a bunch of guys in here already."

Vachio froze. He could feel his knees shake and the blood rush into his face. What's her problem? he thought. Then he recovered and cold anger rushed through him. Who is she to compare me to a bunch of drunken Argentine sailors on shore leave?

"Hey, why don't you lighten up? I didn't come over here to bother you. I came over to get acquainted.... We are going to be together for a while."

"But you are bothering US," said Julie, staring into her drink. "Why don't you just go away."

Vachio glanced at Nancy. She looked as shocked by Julie's attitude as Vachio.

"Am I bothering you?" he asked Nancy.

"Well, we were having a personal conversation, but..."

"You don't have to explain anything to him," said Julie.

"I don't mind if you sit down," said Nancy, giving Julie a quick look.

"Thank you." Vachio pulled up a chair and sat down. Julie stared morosely at her drink. A charged silence fell over the table. Normally Vachio would have shoved off, but Julie had gotten under his skin, trying to push both him and Nancy around.

"So where are you from?" Vachio asked Nancy.

"I'm from Arizona. Tempe."

"Oh, yeah. Near Phoenix."

"That's right. And where are you from?"

"San Francisco."

Julie raised her head and looked at Vachio with a flicker of interest. Vachio noticed and asked her, "How about you?"

"California," she murmured.

"Oh, a home girl. What part?"
"Do you mind?"
"What part?"
"Tiburon."
"Oh! I see. Mahvelous Marin. That explains a lot."
"What does that mean?"
"Nothing necessarily. But let's just say, I've been there."
"Good for you. And what part of San Francisco are you from?"
"The Mission District."
"Oh! I see. That explains a lot, too."

Nancy was totally lost. "Did you guys grow up near each other or something?"

"Yeah, pretty close," said Vachio. "Tiburon is just across the bay from San Francisco."

"Oh! Then you two should have a lot in common."

Vachio laughed. "Well, we should." Then he looked at Julie. "But in some ways, we come from different planets. Right, Julie?"

"Whatever you say," she answered, stirring her drink. "Frankly, you're boring me."

Vachio stood up and said to Julie. "Well, I'll be getting out of you hair now. But maybe some day we can have a personal conversation. You know, about Bay Area things."

"You're obnoxious."

"I'm obnoxious?... *Adios Señoritas*."

"*Adios*," said Nancy, repressing a grin. Julie looked up and gave Vachio a brief glare.

Damn! What's with her Vachio had thought, walking to the other end of the bar that night. She's got an attitude.... But that didn't give her the right to ruin my chances to get to know Nancy. Ah, maybe the pressure of leaving home is already getting to her.

For the remainder of orientation, Vachio and Julie maintained a truce, and even spoke amiably to each other at social functions. Vachio had to admit, he was attracted to her. But whenever he tried to swing their conversations to a more personal level, Julie slipped away like a phantom. They were like a pair of magnets, strongly attracted and then repelled when their fields contacted. Several times during group sessions, and they always seemed to end up in the same group, they clashed. But Vachio no longer took it personally. In fact, he enjoyed butting heads with her. It was stimulating and revved up the group as a whole.

And now she's leaving, thought Vachio. I guess I'm not too surprised. She wants the world to conform to some standard of her own that doesn't exist.... It's too bad she's leaving, though.

22

Back in Garrotero, life went on with its traditional rhythms. A country fair was held on the outskirts of town, complete with a temporary bullfight arena, and on the culminating weekend of the festivities, a goodly portion of the townspeople got plastered on sweet red wine and watched *novilleros* fight bulls of debatable quality in almost farcical but real and bloody combat. Block parties with *Vallenato* and Cumbia bands were held in strategic sectors of town and the central plaza and the two main entrances to Garrotero were festooned with bunting and banners. People were drinking and dancing in the streets, fireworks exploded around the clock, and even a machete fight or two occurred between drunken cane cutters. Raimundo held an open house party that weekend, with his band of old men playing in the patio, and neighbors and friends wandering in and out from early morning Saturday until almost midnight on Sunday.

Vachio spent much of the weekend with La Rica Vicky, wandering from one block party to another, going on amusement rides at the fairgrounds, and stealing up to his room now and again to make love. It was a bittersweet time for them. La Rica Vicky had bought her plane ticket to Washington and was officially enrolled in classes starting in July. Both of them realized their days together were numbered and at least in Vachio's case, he didn't know if they would ever see each other again once she left. Vicky seemed to take it for granted that they were already engaged forever.

On Monday evening, after the festivities had died down and most of the town was recovering from hangovers, Vachio was up on the second floor working on a new schedule for the boys when he heard strident shouts from the main street below. He went to the balcony and looked toward the plaza. A young man, wielding a machete, was screaming curses and slashing at doors as he worked his way up the street toward Raimundo's house. Vachio saw several open doors hastily slammed shut and a large crowd, keeping a prudent distance, forming behind the crazy man.

"What's going on?" Arnulfo yelled to Vachio from his office at street level.

"Man, there's some crazy guy with a machete coming."

"What?"

"Close your door. There's a crazy guy."

Arnulfo looked up the street at the approaching man and for just an instant he froze.

"Close the door!" yelled Vachio.

Arnulfo slammed the double doors shut and banged the security bar in place.

A few seconds later the man vaulted onto the curb and slashed the door with his machete. Then he hopped back onto the street and charged an approaching car. The car slowed down but the demented man and the vehicle still met with solid impact. The machete flew out of the man's hand and he fell flat on his back, unconscious, spittle dribbling out of his mouth. The buzzing crowd pressed forward and two policemen emerged from their midst and took charge of the situation, It was quickly determined that the man wasn't seriously injured, nor was anyone hurt by him despite his manic sword play. He was wrapped up and carted off to the clinic for observation.

A short while later, after the crowd wandered off, Vachio came out to talk to Arnulfo. He stood in front of his office, sipping some horrible homemade pineapple wine Raimundo had given him, his dark face almost pale.

"Man, I can't believe it. That was Benito. He would have attacked me if I hadn't jumped inside," said Arnulfo, his voice shaky.

"You know him, then?" said Vachio.

"Know him? We went to school together for years. I would even call him my friend."

"What happened?"

"He just went crazy.... Crazy, man. He just lost it."

"Anybody suspect why?"

'His friends say that his *novia* ran off with one of the out-of-town *novilleros* in for the fair. And that he's been drinking *guarapo* and *aguardiente* without stop since yesterday afternoon.... Man, he just went crazy. I can't believe it. Benito was always calm and quiet."

"Huh, those are the worst ones when they blow."

"I can't believe it."

Vachio patted Arnulfo on the back and went back inside.

"Just another quiet evening in Garrotero City," said Raimundo, handing Vachio a glass of the pineapple wine.

Vachio took a sip, grimaced, and poured the rest of it into a potted palm. "This batch is even worse than your first one. It's only good for plant food."

"That's your nerves talking, Gary. This is much better than my first batch."

"I don't think so, man. If I drink this crap, I'm liable to go off like that poor guy did tonight.... I'll take a beer."

A few weeks later, Gustavo came to the house on Sunday evening for a quick visit. He sat down, drank a beer, and got to the point. "Vachio, I know I said you could attend tomorrow's staff meeting but..."

Vachio stared at him. Nothing had changed in the *Casa de Menores*. The official recreation period was still preempted whenever an assembly was required, the basketball with the bulging bladder had finally given out, leaving the boys to play hoops with the volleyball which was quickly wearing it out, and the construction of the new *Casa de Menores* was still on hold.

"...I really don't think it's a good idea. Don't take this wrong, but I know your temperament. And I don't believe anything positive will be accomplished."

"Maybe not. But it will make me feel better to air my feelings."

Gustavo shook his head. "It may make everyone feel worse."

"So what you're saying is that they are talking behind my back at the meetings. And I don't even have the right to speak up for myself."

"Vachio..."

Vachio stared off into space.

Gustavo sighed. "All right, Vachio. I know this is a mistake. But come to the meeting."

The next day Vachio took his seat at the round table with all the other department heads. There was an air of tension, and Doña Berta and Cabrera looked especially uncomfortable. The meeting started off with announcements from Gustavo, and then Julia read the minutes from the previous meeting and Vachio heard for the first time the details of how he was blamed for the mass escape of the boys. When Julia finished, Gustavo asked, "Any comments?"

"I have a few," said Vachio.

"The floor recognizes, Señor Vachio," said Gustavo.

"Those accusations are nonsense. All of you in here know it. It's not my job to handle security. And I don't appreciate being blamed for things I didn't cause. I'll take the blame for my own mistakes, but not for anyone else.... That's all I have to say."

"Well, you have plenty to take blame for," said Doña Berta.

Vachio turned and looked at her. "That is true. But that escape wasn't one of those things.... So why don't you say what you really mean?"

"You have no manner, Vachio. Since you arrived here, you've gone around demanding things as though you were something special."

"That's not so. I've only asked for things that were originally promised to me.... And, to clarify that, I've only asked for things for the boys, not for myself."

Doña Berta started spluttering. Vachio could see Gustavo out of the corner of his eye, an amused grin on his face.

"Now what I want to know is why from day one you've given me a problem?" said Vachio to Berta.

"I've never given you a problem. Don't think you're so important."

"Really? Well, if that's the case, you just don't want to do your job. Because the only thing I've ever asked you to do was give me materials to use for the boys.... And that is your job, isn't it?"

"Don't you tell me what my job is! Just because you're from the

United States you think you know so much."

"Ah, thank you. Now we're getting to the heart of the matter. Now the truth comes out. Resentment..."

Doña Berta turned pale and slumped down in her seat.

"To put things in a clearer light," continued Vachio, "I don't think I know so much because I come from the United States. I acted the same way there..."

Emilio Montoya tittered.

"...But let me ask everyone in this room one question. Have I ever told any one of you how to do your jobs?"

No one answered.

"No, I haven't. I'm not guilty of that.... So what I want to know, considering that you've never had a recreation director here, is what makes you guys think you know better than I how to do my job? I may be young, but I've been doing this kind of work for a while."

Cabrera cleared his throat. "Vachio, this is the principle problem we have with you. We all think you're a good person and you're doing what you think best for these children. But this isn't the United States, this is Colombia. Things aren't the same here. And frankly, some of your methods are disruptive to the overall functioning of the school..."

The others nodded their heads.

"Disruptive? How so?" asked Vachio.

"Vachio," said Maria Elena, "I don't know what it is about you, but the boys get too excited and unruly when you're around. And maybe you're comfortable with them this way, but we're not. That is the disruption Professor Cabrera is referring to. We don't want them treating us with...what's the word? Familiarity. Yes, the familiarity with which you seem to want them to treat you."

"The truth is, Vachio, the boys don't treat you with proper respect," said Cabrera. "And sometimes this attitude carries over to us."

"Well, I'm not sure that we agree on the same definition for respect," said Vachio. "I want the boys to treat me with confidence. I want them to feel that I'm their friend, not just another functionary throwing rules at them."

"But Vachio, we've all seen it," said Cabrera. "The boys treat you with too much familiarity and take advantage of you. They joke with you and even insult you at times. And you do nothing.... That is a lack of respect."

Vachio felt himself about to lose his temper. He counted to three, gathered his thoughts, and said, "Maestro Cabrera, it's true that to my face the boys sometimes get upset and insult me. This I won't deny. And I don't like it. But they're honestly talking to me and we have a chance to get things out into the open and deal with them. Whereas in your case, and in the case of several others of you in here, the boys address you as Profé and Doctor to your face, but behind your back, they're calling you son-of-a-bitch and even worse." Vachio heard several people gasp. "In my mind that is not respect. That is called fear. And fear creates resentment and simply drives people to do things in secret."

The room was dead quiet. Then finally, Cabrera, his face beet red, burst out, "But you have no recreation program, Vachio. You have no program."

"I still have no equipment. But ask the boys if we have a program. I think that they might have a different idea than yours."

"Vachio, with all due respect," said Maria Elena, "this is another problem we have with you.... You seem to have an answer for everything. No one can tell you anything."

Vachio was stung by this criticism from Maria Elena. He gave her a hurt look. Of all the administrators, he had expected her to have the most understanding of his position. "Maria Elena, if there is one thing I'm certain of, it's that I don't know everything. But I am looking for answers. And perhaps I'm looking for answers outside of what would be considered the normal and accustomed way of doing things. You see, you guys have a system here. And you're doing things according to that system. But are you positive it's the best way or the only way to do things?"

"We have a proven record here, Vachio," said Cabrera.

"A proven record of what? Every time I go to Bucaramanga below the Carrera 15, I see graduates from our school here living right back on the streets. And none of you can deny this is so."

Suddenly Gustavo stood up and said in a voice that brooked no argument, "Vachio, I know what you're getting at. And I respect your position. But there is no problem with the system. The problem is with the people within the system—using it, abusing it, and prostituting its noble goals and aims for their own purposes. Our system here is as close to perfect as you will find..."

"But..."

"It's time to move on to other business," said Gustavo.

For the rest of the meeting, the administrators avoided Vachio's eyes. Well, at least I gave them something to think about, he thought. But it doesn't make a damn bit of difference.

As soon as the meeting was over, Vachio blew out of the *Casa de Menores* and caught a bus to Bucaramanga. He didn't want to talk to Raimundo about this. He wanted to get away and think.

He jumped off the bus near the Colombo-Americano and headed for Alfonso's Café. Jimmy DeLeon and Roxanna were there drinking beer. Vachio sat down at their table and emitted a long sigh.

"What's wrong with you, *chico*?" Roxanna asked Vachio.

"Ah, man, that damn *Casa de Menores*. I'm tired of their shit."

"What happened now?" Jimmy asked, signaling Alfonso to bring a round of beers.

Vachio gave them a quick rundown on the meeting, including the details of the mass escape, and by the time he was finished, both Jimmy and Roxanna were frowning with indignation.

"Man, that is a bunch of bullshit. They don't give you any equipment but they say you don't have a program," said Jimmy.

"I mean, really," said Roxanna. "You can't even make lemonade without lemons. What do they expect from you?"

"I don't know. I think they want me to just shut-up and take it."

"You know, man," said Jimmy, "I'm a Colombian, but sometimes I get bent out of shape the way they do things here. You know what happened to me and Roxie last night?"

"What?"

"We were eating at this fish place up on 33rd.... You know it, La Gran Marinera? The place with the thatched bamboo huts and all that?"

"Yeah, I know it."

"Well, anyway, that's our favorite restaurant. We go there about twice a week.... Right, Roxie?"

Roxanna nodded.

"So we're there last night, at our favorite table, and there's almost no one else in there. Then suddenly this group of about 10 people come in and the manager comes over and tells us that we have to move."

"Why?"

"Yeah, that's what I ask. And the guy tells me because the governor and the mayor are here and we're at their favorite table. So I say, 'So what? There's plenty of other good tables here. And this is our favorite table, too.' But the guy just shakes his head and says, 'No, you have to move. It's the governor of Santander and the mayor of Bucaramanga and they want this table.' So I'm like, tough shit. And these guys start acting like they're gonna get physical or something. So I'm ready to throw some blows but Roxie calmed me down and we just walked out of there without paying. And I'll tell you, man, I'll never go back there again. They're a bunch of low-life punks. Man, shit like that would never happen in New York."

"Well, I don't know about that," said Vachio. "I mean, if the governor and mayor of New York came and wanted your table, they'd probably ask you to move."

"Yeah, but these guys weren't asking—they were ordering," said Roxanna. "And we spend a lot of money there. *Chico,* in New York, our money is as good as anyone else's."

Vachio shrugged. "Yeah, in New York they would probably have given you the meal free or a bottle of something or other to smooth things over."

"Not these guys," snapped Jimmy. "They weren't giving nothing away. They just ordered us to move. That's how these honchos act here. Like they're better than everyone else and you have to bow down to them. Fuck that!"

Vachio drank his beer.

"You know, Gary," said Jimmy, his voice calm now, "you're almost like family now. And I don't like that game they're running on you at that *Casa de Menores*.... I have an idea."

"What?"

"I'm going to donate six boxes of candy to you so that you buy equipment for those poor kids."

Vachio laughed. "Why don't you just donate the money?"

"No, man, no cash. This is extra candy we usually just distribute to the workers. But it has a wholesale value of over $3,000 pesos."

"Three thousand pesos. I can buy quite a few things with that."

"Good. Do you have anyone to sell it to?"

"I could probably sell it to Don Ramon. The guy who owns the store next to my house."

"All right, man, I'll leave that up to you. Come by the factory tomorrow and we'll work out the details."

"All right. I'll do it.... I don't know if the director of the prison will like it. But I don't care anymore."

23

The next morning, Vachio met Jimmy at the candy factory. It was a huge three story building, and aside from candy, one entire floor was devoted to the manufacture of infants' clothing. Jimmy showed Vachio around, introduced him to a score of workers, and then invited him up to his office for a *tinto* and to hand over the six boxes of hard candy.

"There's only one problem," said Vachio, looking at the large boxes stacked in two rows on the office floor. "How do I get these things moved to Garrotero?"

"In a cab," said Jimmy.

"Yeah but, cabs are expensive from here to there."

"Come on, guy. You have to do something."

"I am. I'll be selling the candy, buying the recreation equipment, and getting it all to the prison."

Jimmy considered this. "All right, what the hell. If I'm gonna do this, I might as well do it right. How about if I bring the candy over tonight?"

"That's fine. And I'll have a dinner ready for you and Roxanna at my house."

"Done."

That night Jimmy lived up to his word. He arrived in Garrotero at around six and said, "The Candy Man is here."

Vachio, who had already made arrangements to sell the candy to

Don Ramon for 10 percent less than normal wholesale price, unloaded the boxes of candy right into his store. Then in front of Jimmy, Don Ramon handed Vachio a wad of bills totaling $3,000 pesos. How easy this is compared to trying to get money out of the *Casa de Menores*, thought Vachio. Boy, are they going to be surprised when I show up tomorrow with a box of recreation equipment.

Vachio introduced Jimmy and Roxanna to Raimundo and Renata and they sat down to beers, cold cuts, bread and salad. Vachio noticed Raimundo looking askance at Jimmy's black silk shirt, tan slacks, and expensive shoes. Roxanna was wearing a red jump suit and was decked out with enough gold to open a small jewelry store. Conversation was a little strained. Jimmy kept talking about his high tech Disco in Queens and Vachio could see Raimundo's eyes roll. Mercifully, Jimmy pleaded another engagement that night and they soon left. Outside, Jimmy said to Vachio, "Man, I don't know how you live in this town. It smells like donkey shit here."

"I barely smell it anymore."

Jimmy laughed. "All right, then. I'll see you around in civilization. Let me know what happens with the equipment."

Back in the house, Raimundo said to Vachio, "Is that guy really related to Vicky?"

"Yeah. They're cousins on her father's side.... But she told me that they're not that close."

"I guess not.... That guy is a little flashy, isn't he? Or did he watch too many gangster movies when he was a kid?"

Vachio laughed. "Nah, he's all right. He grew up in New York. He's got that street style, that's all."

"Yeah? Well, I'd be careful about getting involved with that guy. There's something about him..."

"All right, I don't want to hear it right now. The man just donated $3,000 pesos to the recreation program.... And anyway, we don't really hang out. I mostly talk to him at this café in Bucaramanga. That's all."

"So why is he giving you this money?"

"Because I told him how screwed up things are at the *Casa de Menores* and he wanted to help."

"All right, Gary. I hope you know what you're doing."

"I'm going to buy some recreation equipment now," said Vachio, waving the wad of bills. "Finally. And don't tell Gustavo or anyone else. I want this to be a complete surprise."

The next day, Vachio went to the San Andrecito Bazaar in Bucaramanga and bargained for a basketball, a volleyball, two micro soccer balls, a new ping pong paddle set, and some other odds and ends. With the money left over, he hired a taxi and brought his haul to Garrotero.

That afternoon, at the recreation period, Vachio strolled into the patio with his bag of new toys, finally fulfilling his build-up as a *gringo* Santa Claus. Vachio dumped the new equipment onto the patio basketball court and stood by with a grin as the boys went crazy. For minutes they passed the brand new balls from hand to hand, fondling them, bouncing them, and spinning them. Then Rolo let out a shout, "*Bravo* for Vachio! *Bravo*!"

The rest of the boys joined in and before Vachio could stop them, a group of older kids picked him up on their shoulders and paraded him around the perimeter of the patio while the others shouted and waved their arms. Vachio glanced up to the terrace and saw Jaime Galindo watching them, his face a glowering mask.

Cabrera came into the patio after the demonstration by the boys and shook Vachio's hand. "Congratulations.... Now where did you get these things from?"

"A Colombian friend donated the money for them. You have him to thank."

"Yes. And we have you to thank. You arranged this."

Cabrera left the patio and went to tell the other administrators the news. One by one, with the notable exceptions of Gustavo and Doña Berta, they came down into the patio to congratulate and thank Vachio. He went home that night glowing with satisfaction.

Then the next morning, Vachio received a summons from Don Gustavo to appear at his office immediately.

"Way to go on that equipment," said Pacho, as Vachio appeared in the outer office. Julia smiled her approbation as well.

"Thank you," said Vachio.

"Go right in. Don Gustavo is waiting for you," she said.

Vachio went in and waited as Don Gustavo, without even acknowledging his presence, stared down at some papers on his desk. Finally, Gustavo raised his head and said in a cold lifeless voice, "I congratulate you on your coup."

Vachio felt a chill.

"Vachio, I hope you didn't spend your own money on this."

"No, I didn't. The money was donated by a Colombian friend."

"I see..." Gustavo drummed his fingers on the desk. "Just today, some money became available for the recreation program as I always said it would. We're going to Bucaramanga in a few minutes to buy whatever you need."

"But why? I already have what I need for now. Save the money for later."

"I said we're going to Bucaramanga to buy whatever you need," continued Gustavo in that same dead voice.

"Well, if you insist. We can use some more table games."

"Wait for me in the outer office. I'll be with you in a few minutes."

Vachio, shaking his head, sat outside with Pacho and Julia. Gustavo is pissed off about this, thought Vachio. What's with him?

On the ride to Bucaramanga, Gustavo barely said two words. Vachio also maintained silence. He was both amused and irritated by Gustavo's attitude. They went directly to a sporting goods shop in downtown Bucaramanga and Vachio broke the silence after looking at the prices. "This place is expensive. I bought my stuff way cheaper at San Andrecito."

"We have an account here, Vachio. This is where the *Casa de Menores* does its business for recreation equipment. We pay with a voucher."

"All right."

Gustavo ordered a basketball.

"But I already bought a basketball," said Vachio.

"We can always use another. There are two baskets, aren't there?"

"Yes." Vachio decided to keep his mouth shut. It was obvious Gustavo was going to do whatever he wanted and all he wanted to hear from Vachio was mindless agreement.

"How about table games? We need table games, right?" asked Gustavo.

"Right. Pick them out. You know better than I what these kids like."

"And boxing gloves. We can always use boxing gloves."

"Whatever you say. The more the better."

Gustavo finished his shopping and they raced back to the *Casa de Menores*. After lunch, Gustavo, with Vachio by his side, went down into the patio and showed off the new games and balls. The boys exchanged a few odd looks, even the most veteran among them had never seen such a wealth of materials for their use, but the younger boys were especially happy to receive the new table games.

That night, Vachio told Raimundo about Gustavo's odd behavior.

"Odd? There's nothing odd about it, man. You made Gustavo look bad by bringing in that equipment. You made him lose face."

"Oh, I see. But it was all right for me to look bad all these months without any equipment."

"Better you than him, son. He's the Señor Director."

"That's bullshit. If I were in his place, I would be happy to receive a donation like that—from anyone. And let me ask you, how many times has he said, 'I'm sacrificing my life for the boys.' And then he gives me this attitude when someone does something for the boys. Come on, man. You know that's bullshit. The only people in the *Casa de Menores* who don't seem happy about what I did are him and Jaime Galindo." Vachio laughed. "Hey, maybe this will bring those two together."

Raimundo looked thoughtful for a moment. "Well, it does smack of a jealousy thing.... But what the hell! You have your equipment. More equipment than you ever dreamed of. Take advantage of it. Don't get bogged down in their stuff."

"Easier said than done, man. Easier said than done."

A few days later, Vachio received a special delivery mail gram from Fortuna in Bogotá. It stated that not only had the funding for Sister Magdalena's project come through, but that an additional 1,500 dollars had been pledged from other donors, bringing the total to over $4,000 U.S. When Vachio gave Sister Magdalena this news, she could barely conceal her excitement. "Vachio, do you know what this means? With this money we can begin the construction this year."

"Well, I don't know. But it might be better to wait until the New Year."

"Why?"

"Because these things are like avalanches. Once you get funding from one source, it's easier to get funding from others. Why not send my proposal to other organizations, along with the information about the donors you already have, and see what happens.... Just concentrate on the fundraising until the end of this year. Then you might have enough money to start and finish the project without any stoppages. That's always the most economical and efficient way."

Sister Magdalena considered this for a moment. "That's good advice. And now I have some for you. Why don't you come and work for us full-time now. We're gearing up to put on a bikeathon and we need someone with your energy and knowledge to coordinate it."

"I'm sorry, sister. I can't make that commitment. But I'll help out where I can."

"You're still not ready to leave that horrible prison."

"No. I'm still not ready."

Sister Magdalena smiled and folded her hands on her lap. "Very well, my son. But remember, whenever you want, you have a place here with us. And on your terms."

The following Tuesday, at the recreation period, Vachio was told that one of the micro footballs he bought had been kicked over the wall the night before and lost. That same afternoon, the new volleyball suffered the same fate.

"What the hell is going on here?" Vachio asked Oliva.

"You know how destructive these kids are, Vachio."

"Yeah, destructive. They wear things out fast. But to lose two new balls in two days. Something weird is going on?"

Oliva shrugged. "I wouldn't know."

On Friday, while Vachio was organizing a basketball game among the younger boys, Leal came onto the court and stole the ball. He started dribbling in mad circles and capering like a young chimp.

"Come on, clown, give up the ball," said Vachio. "I'm not in the mood for this today."

"Who cares what mood you're in. I feel like playing basketball," said Leal.

"Give up the ball, man."

"Come and get it," said Leal, and dribbled to the other end of the court. Then he came back and dribbled just beyond Vachio's reach. Vachio stood with his hands on his hips, staring at him. This little fool is going too far, he thought. I'm not playing with him today.

"Come on, Vachio. Let's see you get the ball from me."

"Listen, man, give up the ball right now.... Or this time I send you to one of the guards."

"Yeah, right. I'm scared." Leal dribbled the ball in a circle around Vachio.

"Last chance..." Vachio had never sent a boy to the guards for punishment.

Leal laughed and slapped one of the younger boys who tried to get the ball away from him.

"All right, that's it.... Maestro Oliva!"

"At your order," said Oliva, rising from his chair.

"I want this Leal punished. He's disrupting my program."

Oliva grinned and beckoned to Leal with his *garrote*.

Suddenly Leal's face went deathly pale. "But no, Profé, please...." Leal dropped the ball.

"Come, Leal. Don't make me wait or it will go even harder on you," yelled Oliva.

Leal trotted away and up the steps to the terrace. Oliva made him turn and hold onto the balcony with his hands, exposing his bare back. Then Oliva gave him three whips with the knotted cords at the end of the *garrote*. Vachio was shocked. He thought Oliva would make him do push ups or something like that. He never imagined he would whip him.

After the punishment, Leal ran back down into the patio, tears streaming down his cheeks, a few drops of blood oozing from mottled purple welts on his upper back and shoulders.

"You son-of-a-bitch!" he screamed at Vachio. "I'll get you for this."

"Hey, man, I never thought he would whip you. Sorry about that.... But you deserved a punishment. It's time you learned not to screw up everyone else because you want to do something."

"The hell with you, you bastard!"

Vachio's face turned hard. "Watch it, man!"

"You watch it!" Leal turned and ran to a pile of broken concrete slabs laying on the side of the carpentry shop. He picked up a big chunk and ran back toward Vachio, holding it in both hands over his head. "Now, you son-of-a-bitch! Now, let's see."

Vachio faced him. Leal was about 15 feet away, holding the chunk of concrete in a throwing position. "Put it down, man. You're only going to get in worse trouble."

"I'll put it through your head."

"All right, then. Throw it! Come on!" said Vachio, using the reverse psychology he had seen in innumerable movies.

Leal reared back and heaved the concrete straight at Vachio's face. Vachio ducked and it passed harmlessly overhead. In the next instant, Leal ran and Vachio chased after him. Vachio had only one thought—to grab this kid and thrash the living daylights out of him. He was completely consumed by the white hot rage of self-preservation. His actual well-being had been threatened.

Vachio caught Leal by the micro-soccer court and flung him to the ground. Then, before he could do anything else, Rolo and several other of the older boys grabbed hold of him and wouldn't let go. Leal got up and ran to the protection of the dormitory.

"All right. I'm all right now," said Vachio, shaking free of the boys.

"Damn, Vachio. You looked ready to kill that *sapo*," said Rolo. Are you sure you're all right?"

"Yeah, I'm sure. Leave me alone." Vachio shook free of them and headed for the terrace. He had to get away. At the gate, Ramon, who had witnessed everything without intervening, smiled at Vachio and said, "That's the way you have to be here. Now you are like one of us."

Vachio felt his stomach turn. "Let me out."

"Of course, Profé. Of course." Ramon gave Vachio the thumbs up sign.

Vachio walked out of the *Casa de Menores* and straight to the farm. He sat down with Maestro Felipe and they drank cup after cup of *guarapo* and Vachio poured out his heart to him.

"I think I have to get out, Felipe. I don't like what this place is doing to me."

"Lucky you that you can get out," said Felipe. "I would have left this place long ago if I had a better alternative."

"And I would have left months ago if it weren't for the kids. But..."

Felipe poured Vachio another cup of *guarapo*. "You have to do what's best for you in this instance, Vachio. If you're filled with anger and bitterness, you'll be of no practical use to these boys."

"Well, I've been thinking.... Maybe I can go to work for that nun as my official job, and work for the *Casa de Menores* as an extra thing. You know, show them movies and play basketball and stuff with them.... But I've had enough of the bullshit. I'm about convinced that government institutions aren't the way to go in the rehabilitation of kids. It's time to make a move."

"Let's hope it's the right one," said Felipe, tipping his cup toward Vachio.

Walking home that night in a driving rain storm, Vachio sobered up and decided to put his decision on hold. He kept his thoughts to himself and went about his regular business.

Then, in the middle of the next week, while Vachio was taking a siesta at home, one of the trustees from the *Casa de Menores* appeared at the house with a message from Oliva. "You better come quick, Vachio. One of the kids stuck a knife in the brand new basketball and ruined it."

"What?"

"I don't know anything else. It happened during shop."

Vachio put on his shoes and went right over. Oliva let him through the gate and showed Vachio the basketball. It was not only punctured, but had been ripped diagonally in two long cross cuts. Vachio shook his head in disgust. The ball was beyond repair.

"Who did it?" he asked Oliva.

"It was Little Alonso."

"Alonso?" Vachio was surprised. Of all the boys in the patio, Alonso would have been one of the last suspects. He was generally a good-natured cooperative boy.

"Do you want him punished?" Oliva asked.

"No. But I do want to talk to him. Right now."

"I'll send for him. He's in the metal shop."

As Alonso made the long walk across the yard from the metal shop at the back of the patio, Vachio took the wasted basketball in his hand and went to meet him. Alonso saw Vachio coming and ducked his head in shame. They met near the bench in the middle of the yard and Vachio, trying to suppress the anger in his voice, held the ball before Alonso's eyes and asked, "Why?"

"I'm sorry, Vachio.... I didn't mean to. It's just that...during wood shop, I got angry at one of the other boys and I had a knife and...you know, instead of stabbing him.... I was so angry I went outside and saw the basketball and I stabbed it.... That's what happened, Vachio. I swear it."

"You stabbed the ball? Kid, you not only stabbed the ball, you tore it down both seams.... This ball can't be fixed. If you had only stabbed it, it could be patched." Vachio took Alonso by both shoulders and made him raise his head. "I want you to tell me who put you up to this."

"No one, Vachio, I swear it.... I just got mad at the other kid and I had to do something to release my anger. I swear to you that's what happened."

"I don't believe you, man. Not the way this ball was damaged.... Tell me the truth."

"Vachio, that's the truth. I swear it.... Please."

Vachio stared at the boy for a moment and shook his head. He's lying, thought Vachio. I know it. But he's scared stiff to tell me the truth. "All right, Alonso. Go back to class."

Alonso looked up nervously. "Will I be punished?"

"Not by me. But I'm sure you will be."

Alonso walked away and Vachio fired the flattened ball against one of the backboards and left it lying on the ground. That does it, he thought. That ball wasn't even supposed to be outside in the yard at that time. And almost all the equipment I bought has been lost or damaged in two weeks. Nothing Gustavo bought has been touched. Only a fool could believe this is a coincidence. *Se á acabó*. That ends it for me.

24

Vachio never directly blamed Gustavo for the destruction of the recreation equipment but he did blame him for the attitude toward the recreation program as a whole. As the Señor Director, he set the tone—and through his actions the tone had always remained ambivalent unless he was spurred to action by a crisis. Vachio had seen enough. Without saying a word to anyone, he met with Sister Magdalena and told her that as soon as they had the operating capital from the donations, she could count on a fulltime Peace Corps volunteer.

Two weeks later, Vachio received the word from Fortuna that the money had arrived. In the mail gram she wrote.... You might consider coming to Bogotá to pick up the check and cash it into pesos at the American Embassy. The exchange rate is much more favorable than at the Banco de Colombia and it will give you added money for the project.... Vachio considered this excellent advice. They stood to gain almost $400 dollars extra in the exchange. He told Sister Magdalena about it and she agreed at once.

"Only, if it's all right with you, I'd like to wait two weeks before I go. There are things I need to take care of here first, and if I go by bus to save money, it's at least a three day trip."

"Whatever you think best," said Sister Magdalena, delighted by the unexpected monetary windfall coming her way. "I trust your judgement."

Vachio wanted to put this trip off so he could meet La Rica Vicky in Bogotá. She was flying out of Bogotá to Washington, D.C. at that time and had secretly arranged a stopover so that she and Vachio could spend one more night together alone. At the moment they were separated. Vicky was spending two weeks with her family in Barranquilla prior to heading for the States, leaving Vachio feeling even more isolated in his time of decision.

The next two weeks passed in slow motion for Vachio. He worked his usual shift at the *Casa de Menores*, but he also spent most of his mornings working on the plans for the bikeathon for Sister Magdalena. He was quiet about his activities, and Raimundo was too preoccupied with his wife's advancing pregnancy and his own problems to notice anything unusual in Vachio's behavior. Vachio told Raimundo nothing.

He knew Raimundo would only try to talk him out of his decision and the time for that was past.

One day before he was scheduled to leave for Bogotá, Vachio walked into Gustavo's office and said, "I need to talk to you."

"I'm pretty busy right now, Vachio," said Gustavo. "Can't it wait?"

"No, it can't. But I won't take up much of your time."

"Very well, Vachio. Go ahead."

"I'm leaving for Bogotá tomorrow to pick up a check for Sister Magdalena."

"Yes."

"This check means that from here on out we have the means to begin the construction of her youth center..."

Gustavo looked apprehensive now.

"...It also means I am severing my official working relationship with the *Casa de Menores*. From now on, I'd be willing to continue to show movies and participate in activities with the boys, but you no longer have any official say over my activities here. It's up to you to decide if I may do this. I want to continue working with the boys in at least this limited capacity.... That's all."

"One moment, Vachio," said Gustavo. He got out from behind his desk and told Julia to hold all his calls and allow no visitors. Then he closed the door, sat down at his desk, and said, "Vachio, I want you to think this over before you make such a rash decision."

"I've been thinking this over since our last meeting. If you'll remember, I said that if things didn't change I wouldn't remain at the *Casa de Menores*. Well, as far as I can see, nothing has changed. It's time to move on for me. You guys don't need me here. You're perfectly capable of running your own recreation program."

"Vachio, don't be hasty. It may not seem so to you, but you have made progress here. I can see that progress. And with the inauguration of the new *Casa de Menores*..."

"Please, don't talk to me about the new *Casa de Menores*. The work is stopped. And you're no closer to finishing than when I was here on my site visit. Even if you had a big crew working around the clock, you would never finish by the new year."

"But Vachio, we will finish. And that's when we'll need you the most. Everything will be on a much larger scale."

"Gustavo, with all due respect, I sincerely doubt I'll still be in Colombia by the time *La Obra* is finished.... Even if I still were working with the *Casa de Menores*."

Gustavo assumed a hurt look. "Vachio, I'm surprised. You're talking like a defeatist."

"No, I'm talking like a realist. I've done my own investigation.... And aside from that, the new *Casa de Menores* was never the issue for me. It was what I could do with what I had. I've done what I said I would do; you have an organized recreation program in place. Now it's up to you guys to run it with Colombians."

"Vachio, we're far from being able to do that."

"Not at all. You've already demonstrated that you can do it. First, when the inspector from Bogotá came; and second, when Fortuna visited me. On both occasions the recreation program ran perfectly. And all I did was walk around and watch. You don't need me here. All you need is the will to put the effort into a program. I'm nothing more than decoration. The sister has much more for me to do. And she's willing to give me real responsibility—not just a title."

"You're giving up on us..." Gustavo refused to give in without a fight. He harangued Vachio for more than an hour, using guilt and every other ploy in his arsenal. Vachio sat unmoved through it all. The time for talk was long past. Vachio's decision was made.

Finally Vachio rose and extended his hand. "I hope you allow me to come here and show movies and do what I always wanted—just be a friend to these kids.... And now I have to go. I'm catching a night bus to Bogotá."

Gustavo limply shook Vachio's hand. "I will keep the door open for you if you change your mind."

"That's not going to happen. I'm already committed to my course. And you know, I'm sorry about how things have come out, but I'm not sorry that I came here to work.... I'll see you around."

On the 10 hour bus ride to Bogotá that night, swaying in the back seat as they swung along hairpin bends on the mountain road, Vachio thought of the boys. They were the ones who had made his decision difficult. Outside of them, he felt no attachment to the *Casa de Menores*. Well, if Gustavo lets me, I'll still do some things with them, thought Vachio. But it sure won't be the same. They'll probably think I'm a traitor.

On arrival in Bogotá, Vachio went straight to the Peace Corps office and picked up the check. Then he went to the fortress-like American Embassy in lower Chapinero and had it cashed into pesos. That was that. Then it was on to the airport to meet Vicky.

It was a strange last night they spent together. Vicky was cheerful and upbeat, almost giddy, as she bubbled over with her plans to travel around the United States in between her studies. Vachio was subdued and pensive. They ate dinner at the Refugio Alpino and over coffee, Vicky said, "I'll write every week. I'm going to tell you everything that happens to me."

"Oh, yeah? Will you tell me about the new men you meet and go out with?"

"I will if you tell me about the women you meet."

"I won't."

Suddenly Vicky giggled. "I'm going to miss that sense of humor."

Who says I'm joking? thought Vachio.

At the pensión, they stayed awake all night, talking and making love. Vachio forgot his doubts for the moment and it was like their first night together, as though they were discovering each other all over again. At the first light of gray dawn, Vicky clung to Vachio and said, "Hold me tight. I won't let you go—ever."

Vachio was silent, staring at the darkness over her shoulder.

At the airport, watching Vicky pass through the checkpoint, Vachio wondered if he would ever see her again.

Vachio returned to Bucaramanga with the money for the project and immediately prepared an addendum for the proposal. Sister Magdalena duly sent the material out to the other international aid organizations and the results were rapid and beyond all expectations. The German organization that had pledged the initial seed money doubled their contribution. A Dutch aid organization matched their funding level. Operation Care chipped in with a pledge of building materials. The snow ball was rolling.

On the home front, the bikeathon was a smashing success, and a follow-up barbecue/dance surpassed expectations. The money poured in from both foreign and local sources. By November, Sister Magdalena had more than enough funding to complete the initial phase of the construction. Vachio spent the rest of the month doing background checks on contractors to see who would be awarded the contract to begin construction on January 15th. Even Vachio was stunned by the success of their various ventures. For Sister Magdalena, it was a simple matter of faith. "God wants this, friend Vachio. We owe it all to Him."

"But why on this and not the new *Casa de Menores*?" Vachio answered. "Don't those kids deserve a better chance than what they were born with?"

"The sad truth is, Vachio, people have very little faith in our government entities. And from what you've seen, can you blame them?"

"I suppose not. That's why I'm working with you."

Gustavo's *La Obra* was still paralyzed, the funding held up in the capital while studies were made to examine the expediency of giving such a wonderful and modern institution to the housing of *gamines*. Vachio knew that he was right about the new *Casa de Menores* not getting finished while he was in Colombia, but it gave him no satisfaction.

Vachio kept in close contact with the *Casa de Menores*, continuing to show movies when he could get them, and going into the patio to play sports and visit with the boys, but the attitude toward him had changed completely. Most of the administrators had taken Vachio's desertion as a personal affront and treated him with cool politeness. The boys also were more reserved. They no longer teased Vachio. The intimacy and intensity of their relationship was gone. Vachio was hurt by this more than by any other consequence of his decision to leave the *Casa de Menores*. But he felt no regret at leaving. Almost every time he went to see Sister Magdalena at the convent in Bucaramanga, he saw former *Casa de Menores* kids working the streets. Occasionally he heard of one who was killed. It was a vicious revolving door, and Vachio saw no hope for these kids caught up in the machinery of the system. There has to be a better way, he thought. Maybe the sister's way is better. But then again, maybe it isn't. Who knows what she'll do once she has her center.

But while Vachio was still ambivalent about what he was doing with Sister Magdalena, Peace Corps was ecstatic. He was involved in a high profile project that would show concrete results. Vachio was written up in a Peace Corps magazine and praised for his work by the top Peace Corps Colombia brass. Ah, what the hell, he thought. It's good publicity. But I sure wish I knew what it's all about.

Right before Vachio was to go to Cali to attend a special education conference, and from there to Bogotá to catch a plane to the Amazon for his vacation, he and the other Peace Corps volunteers received shocking news. Julie Christiansen, who had terminated from Peace Corps because she felt Colombia was too dangerous, was murdered on Mount Tamalpais in Marin County by a serial killer who haunted hiking trails.

25

"Glad you could come," said Jimmy DeLeon. "Have a seat."

A bottle of good Scotch, mineral water, and a silver ice bucket sat on the table. Vachio took a seat and looked around. The restaurant was dark and smoky, decorated with paintings of rural scenes in Antioquia and with wood signs engraved with homely sayings from the same region.

Jimmy poured Vachio a healthy glass of Scotch and Soda and asked, "Well, how are you getting along in Cali this time?"

"Pretty well. Just taking in the sights and loafing around."

"Where are you staying?"

Vachio mentioned the name of a three-dollar-a-day pensión on the edge of downtown.

Jimmy shook his head. "Never heard of it."

"It's a dump. But I have to be careful with my money.... And anyway, I'll be moving to the Aristí Hotel tomorrow for the conference. That's on Peace Corps. It's supposed to be a three-star hotel."

Jimmy shook his head. "Man, you should be staying in better places than that. You've been raising lots of money for other people. When do you get your cut of the pie?"

"Like the nun says, '*Dios se lo pague*,' the Lord will pay me."

Jimmy laughed. "That's not a very reliable source."

Vachio shrugged. "Money couldn't buy the experiences I've had here. And now I'm going to the Amazon like I've wanted since I don't know when.... I guess I don't feel too underprivileged."

"Ay, man, you are a case. You crack me up sometimes. But I think you must have a little masochist in you."

"I don't know why you say that. I usually get what I need."

"Yeah, but you could get whatever you want. And in total comfort."

"I know. By going into business with you.... Tropical fish, right?"

"Well, I've gone a little beyond tropical fish," said Jimmy, lighting up a cigarette. "We're handling more lucrative merchandise now..."

Vachio waited.

"What do you hear from my cousin Vicky?" asked Jimmy, suddenly switching gears.

"According to her letters, she's doing fine. She's going out to California on her vacation."

"Really? How is she going to afford that?"

"She lined up a bunch of people to stay with—including my family."

Jimmy laughed. "That Vicky is a go-getter. She doesn't wait for things to come to her."

"No. That's for sure."

"So, are you guys going to get married?"

"Who knows."

"She's a great girl, man. And you guys make a good couple. Anyone can see that.... And she's been well-raised. She knows when to look the other way when she should. She won't give you trouble after you're married."

"How's Roxanna?"

"She's back in New York looking for a new manager for the discoteque. We had to get rid of the other guy. He wasn't correct.... Are you hungry?"

"Yeah, I haven't eaten since breakfast." Vachio glanced at the menu. "How's the *bandeja paisa*?"

"It's great here, man. This is a *paisa* restaurant."

Vachio ordered the *bandeja paisa*. It was his favorite typical Colombian dish, consisting of beans, rice, sweet banana, *chicharón*, slices of avocado, and a piece of grilled steak.

During dinner, Jimmy talked about the new sailboat he was going to buy when he returned to New York. "I'm going to get a 70-footer, man. It's going to be great. The kind of boat you can live on if you want."

"Business is good, eh?" said Vachio, chewing his steak.

"It's not good, man—it's great. In fact, it's so good, I'm thinking of buying a new house farther out on Long Island."

"That's nice."

Jimmy poured Vachio another stiff drink. "You know, you could have all these things, too."

"You said the word, man.... Things. They are just things."

"Still on the social worker trip, eh? Well, that's all right. If you come to work for me, you will have money to do whatever you want.... Build a hospital, a reform school, whatever you want. Doesn't that pique your interest?"

"I don't know. Right now not much is making sense to me."

Jimmy smiled. "That's my point. With enough money, you create your own world. Spend it anyway you want."

Vachio yawned. "You're talking about selling cocaine, aren't you? Let's get to the point."

Jimmy grinned and filled Vachio's glass again. "You're right. But I'm not asking you to sell cocaine. You would be part of my management team. I want your eyes and ears and brain. I have other people to handle the menial labor..."

"Jimmy, before I left San Francisco, when I told people I was going to Colombia, I had at least half-a-dozen people ask me to get involved in some kind of cocaine dealing. And you know, some of them had very respectable high-paying jobs. I wondered what made them want to risk what they had worked so hard for just to get a little more money. And now I have to ask you the same question. Why? How much money do you need?"

"All I can get, man. I want all I can get. That's what makes this fucked-up world go 'round.... You know that. Don't try to play the saint. Hell, you could be a modern Robin Hood if that's what turns you on. I don't care. You've seen how things work here. Can you honestly tell me that the government does anything for people?"

"There are other ways to do things."

"Yes. And one of them is this way. And it can be very effective."

Vachio sipped his drink and stared over Jimmy's head. Maybe Jimmy is right, he thought. Man, I'm getting drunk.

"I have to go to the bathroom," said Vachio, rising from his seat. "Where is it?"

"Around the corner there," said Jimmy, pointing past the nearest building support pillar.

Vachio took his time, Jimmy's words running through his mind. By the time he returned to the table, Jimmy was at the bar discussing something with a short stocky man with a large beer gut. The man wore a red silk disco shirt with poker hands imprinted on it. Vachio sat down and finished his drink while he waited for Jimmy.

Suddenly the conversation between Jimmy and the man turned loud and heated. "Listen, you triple son-of-a-bitch, I want my money now!" yelled Jimmy.

"Or what, son-of-a-bitch?"

"You know what. No one screws me and gets away with it."

The man got off the bar stool and assumed a fighting stance.

Jimmy jumped off his stool and pulled a gun. He pointed the gun at the man's head and the other patrons along the bar dove for cover. Then Jimmy thought better of it and slammed the gun down on the bar counter. "Take care of this gun for me," Jimmy said to the bartender. "Don't give it to me even if I ask. I don't want to kill this son-of-a-bitch yet."

The short stocky man tried to grapple but Jimmy warded him off with his left elbow and connected with several solid rights to the head. The man went down next to the bar and Jimmy gave him a well-aimed kick to the head and several more to the ribs. Just like that, in a matter of seconds, it was over. The man lay on his back, stunned, a trickle of blood coming from his mouth and nose. Jimmy recovered his gun from the bartender and gave him some money to cover the cost of the glasses that had broken as the other patrons scrambled away from the bar. Both the bartender and Jimmy were almost casual in their actions, as though this were a normal occurrence. Vachio couldn't believe it.

Jimmy sat at the bar while a couple of men splashed water on the fallen man and wiped off the blood with a bar towel. Then they brought him to his feet and Jimmy said, "You better bring me my money, son-of-a-bitch. You have one day."

"I'll bring you something, man. You can be sure of that.... I'll see you around."

"I'll be waiting," said Jimmy, patting the gun under his shirt.

The man left the bar and Vachio got up to leave. He stopped at the bar and said to Jimmy, "Is this what it's all about, man? You kill him or he kills you? Is this your great business?"

Jimmy shrugged. "That was nothing, man. He's a cheap punk. You get things like this one in a while.... There are risks in any business. You want the money, you got to have the guts to do what it takes to get it and to keep it. That's the way it is."

"You're looking for El Dorado, man. It's the road to ruin."

"What the hell are you talking about, man? Are you crazy?"

"No, I'm not crazy. I just know there has to be a better way..."